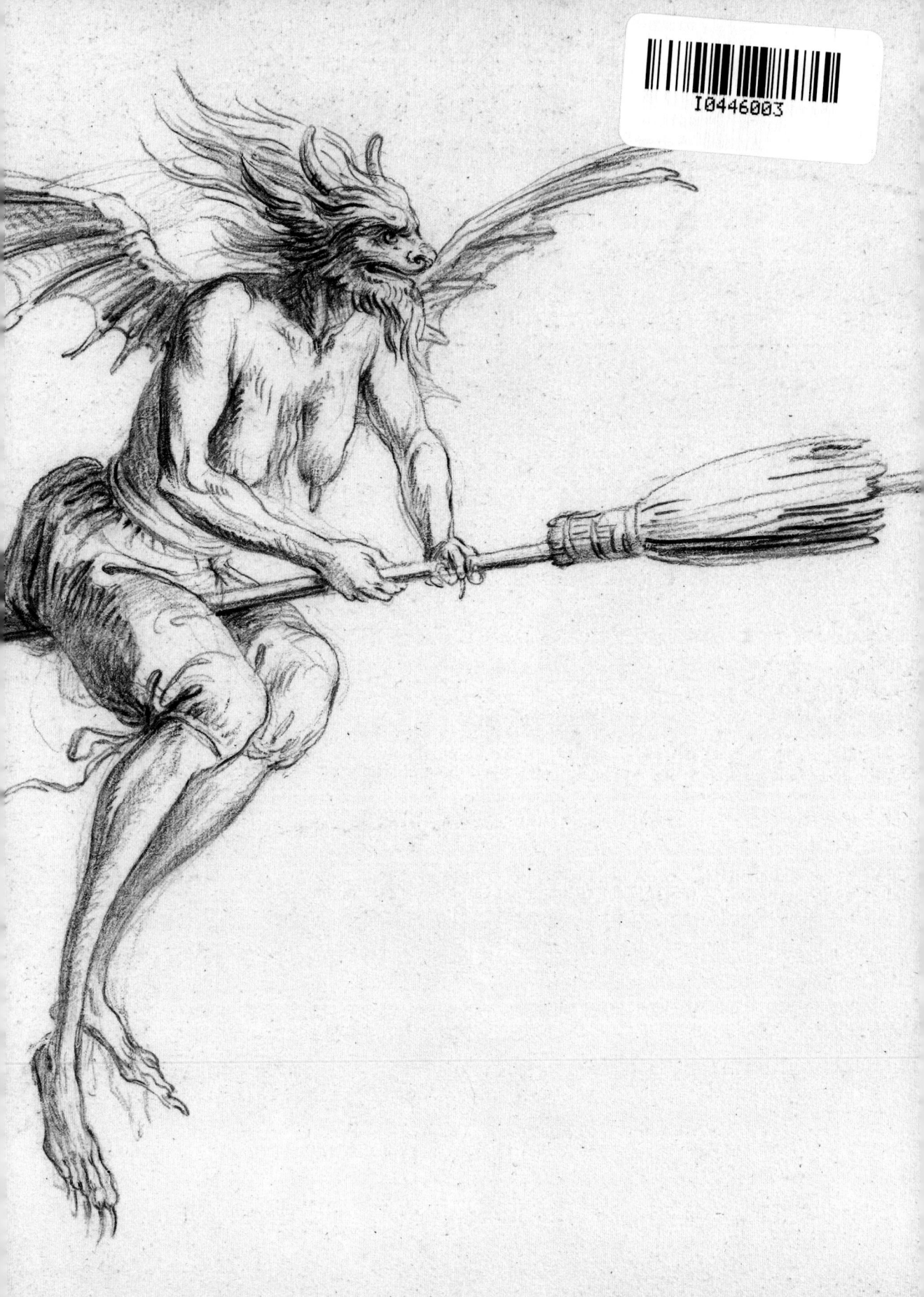

Pandemonium

A VISUAL HISTORY OF DEMONOLOGY

Pandemonium

A VISUAL HISTORY OF DEMONOLOGY

Ed Simon

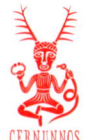

CERNUNNOS

TABLE OF CONTENTS

Toward a Demonic Poetics

If I exorcise my devils,
Well my angels may leave too.
—TOM WAITS, "Please Call Me, Baby" (1974)

I am not the author of *The Necronomicon*. For a brief and disturbing portion of time one evening several years ago, however, I questioned whether I might be. Invented by the American master of weird fiction H.P. Lovecraft, and first mentioned in his short story "The Hound" published in 1924, *The Necronomicon* is an ancient grimoire—effectively a magic book—compiled in the eighth century by a "half-crazed Arab" named Abdul Alhazred, with a complex reception history that sees it variously translated into Greek, Latin, and English, condemned by the Inquisition in the fourteenth century and the Puritans in the seventeenth, and generally flickering at the margins of human knowledge. While Lovecraft is ambiguous on the exact contents of *The Necronomicon*, it's generally implied that they concern the worship of entities known as the "Elder Gods," ancient creatures of seemingly infinite dimension and immortal longevity who exist beyond good and evil. They are, what most traditional believers might think of them as, effectively demons. In his posthumously published 1938 fragment "History of *The Necronomicon*," Lovecraft describes the volume as having been "rigidly suppressed by the authorities of most countries, and by all branches of organized ecclesiasticism. Reading leads to terrible consequences." So, you will see then why it was so unsettling to briefly question whether it was actually I who was the author, editor, and redactor of the infernal volume.

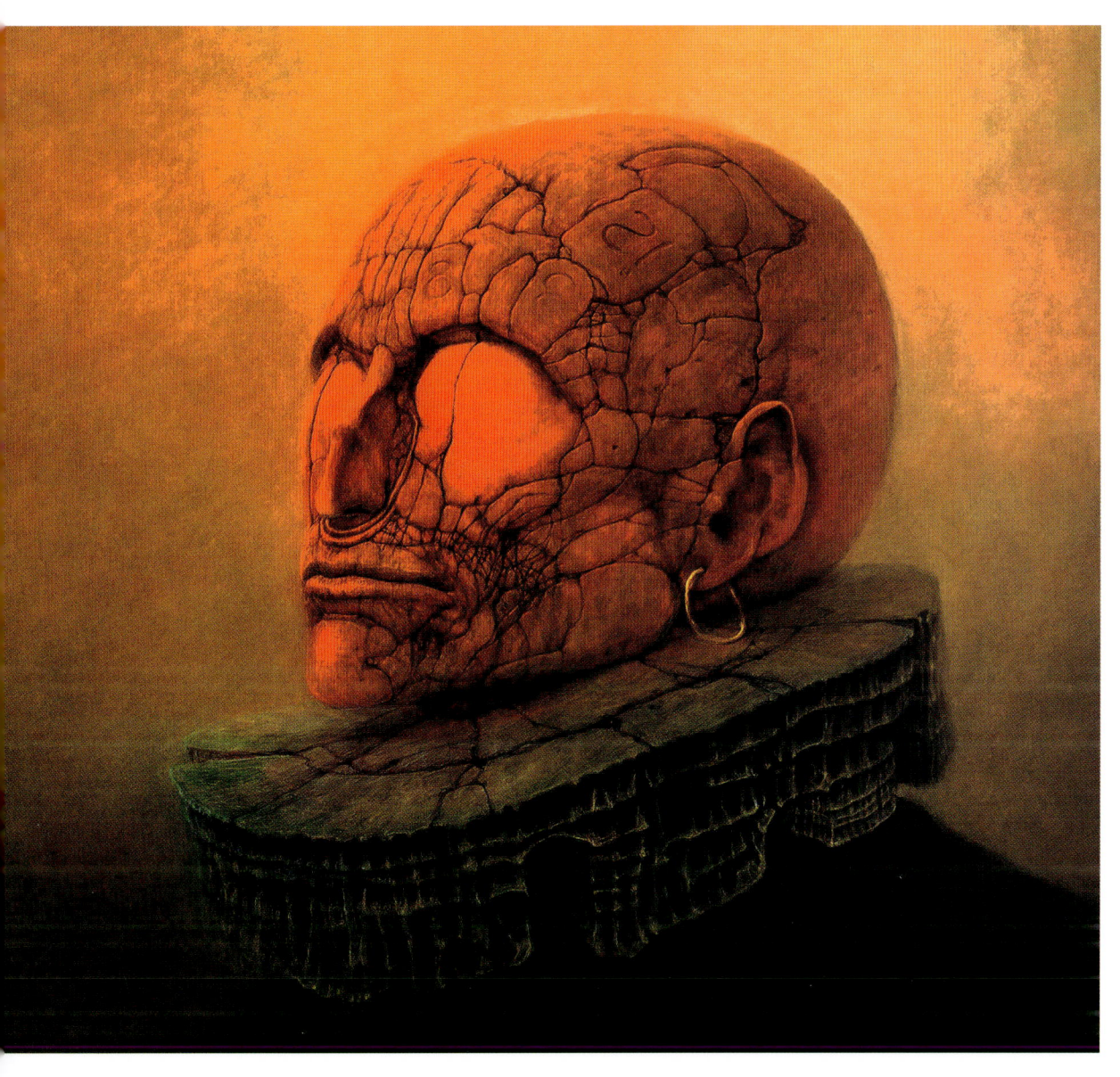

ABOVE

The demonic figure in Polish artist Zdzisław Beksiński's untitled 1984 painting, held by the Historical Museum in Sanok, Poland, wears a ruffled Renaissance collar and stares out from eyeless sockets. He is an eternal creature who exists where past, present, and future all collapse into a hellish singularity.

That *The Necronomicon* doesn't actually exist, that it never existed and was only born from the fevered nightmares of Lovecraft, is no impediment to such a fear as I felt—in fact, the book's nonexistence was paradoxically the cause of my anxiety. As with so many of our contemporary fabulisms, my paroxysm of terror was facilitated by modern technology, for the reason that I came to (briefly) fear that I had somehow broken beyond the bounds of time and space and authored *The Necronomicon* was because of a certain website named after a tropical rainforest. It was a little more than a decade ago when, bleary-eyed and under-caffeinated, I decided to see if there were any listings for *The Necronomicon* on said website. Despite the fictionality of the grimoire, any number of editions have been published that claimed to be the "real" *Necronomicon*, based on some ancient Babylonian or Assyrian text. On the off chance that such a claim wasn't mere grift, I thought it prudent to grab my own copy of one of these editions (as one does). And so I typed "*The Necronomicon*" into the search window. For a second, when I saw my own name, I thought that I had accidentally signed into my personal account, only to discover that the listed author of *The Necronomicon* was "Ed Simon." Sweaty-palmed and with racing heart, I checked to see if this was some sort of algorithmic error, if I was accidentally listed as the author of *Pride and Prejudice* and *Moby Dick* as well, perhaps some wayward bit of code that reinscribed customers' names over those of the women and men who rightfully wrote those books. But no, I was completely signed out of my own account, and there on my screen, for anyone looking to purchase a copy of *The Necronomicon*, my own name was listed as the author of what's supposedly the evilest book ever written.

As it turns out, of course, I wasn't the author of that particular edition of *The Necronomicon*. Several incarnations of Lovecraft's imagined book have been published; in 1973, the science-fiction writer L. Sprague de Camp wrote the introduction to a limited-edition book with that title, which was inscribed in an undecipherable fictional language and released by an obscure press; George Hay penned a hoax version of *The Necronomicon* in 1978; and the Canadian occultist Donald Tyson compiled his own version in 2004, borrowing copiously from Lovecraft's writing for the book. The so-called *Simon Necronomicon* is by far the most popular book with that title, having sold eight hundred thousand copies, even though it bears little resemblance to the supposed contents of the grimoire as enumerated by Lovecraft, and seems to largely draw upon ancient Sumerian mythology (its press's claim that it was "potentially, the most dangerous Black Book known to the Western world" undoubtedly helped to move product as well).

Written as though it were a translation of a collection of genuine Mesopotamian incantations and conjurations, the *Simon Necronomicon* is situated within a frame tale wherein it's claimed that the grimoire was an ancient text known to Lovecraft, and that following the spells within the text (some of which demand human sacrifice) has the power to "unleash dangerous forces." As to the identity of the editor, there have been various hypotheses as to who this pseudonymous "Simon" is, none of whom are me. And, it should be noted, that despite the author being frequently listed at several sites as "Ed Simon," the given name there seems to stand not for "Edward," but rather "Editor," though this hasn't stopped several gothic-inclined adolescent fans of the edition to make the same mistake that I did, and occasionally send me emails thanking me for editing the translation.

I share this anecdote with you not as a parable that gives a clear-cut lesson about demonology, but because I wish to convey a bit of what I fell for in that strange instant in which I genuinely wondered whether or not that cursed book with my name on the cover was actually somehow written by me. Think of it as the cracked numinous, the uncanny sense wherein, according to all those accurate clichés that describe fear, our skin crawls and our hair stands on end. If *The Necronomicon* is supposed to be a book that reveals the horror which exists deep within reality, the actual terrifying nature of existence that we veil behind our hypocritical pieties and our jaundiced optimism, then for a few minutes I felt like I was seeing that nature laid bare, as if I could approach the demonic singularity that radiates out such malignance through every crevice of our damned lives. As an aesthetic experience, there is something of the sublime in those instants of cosmic horror, and while I'm too cheery to think that that emotion is the final word on existence, I'm also enough of a realist to know that there is something of the demonic within the core of our universe, and occasionally you're unfortunate enough to glance at it and see its warped smile and red eyes looking back at you from the depthless blackness of the abyss.

When I reveal that I'm writing a book about demonology, I'm invariably asked if I believe that demons are actually real. "*Of course, I don't think that demons are actually real,*" is the expected response and the one that I give. "*I'm a modern, secular, educated, liberal, agnostic man. I don't believe in demons and devils, goblins and ghouls, imps, vampires, werewolves, ghosts, or poltergeists either.*" Yet whenever giving the doxology of all of that which we're not to have faith in, I'm mentally keeping my fingers crossed, because so much of that question depends on the definitions of the words "believe," "demons," "actually," and "real." Since the Enlightenment, Western intelligentsia have been the inheritors to a rather anemic model of knowledge known as the correspondence theory of truth, whereby the validity of a statement is ascertained simply by whether or not it matches empirical reality. If I say, "The dog is in the yard," that statement is either true or false depending on whether or not said dog is in said yard. Easy enough, but then what of statements like "A thing of beauty is a joy forever," "I think that I shall never see/a poem as lovely as a tree," or "I wondered lonely as a cloud?"

A fundamentalist adherence to the correspondence theory of truth, trumpeted by logical positivists and other philosophical heretics, would consign John Keats, Joyce Kilmer, and William Wordsworth into a bin marked "meaningless" (even though I think we can all ascertain that there is meaning, even if it's the "slant" truth that Emily Dickinson writes about). And so, you can imagine what is made of statements about divinity and diabology (though theology has, in my estimation, always just been a branch of poetics anyhow). That the correspondence theory of truth doesn't even match its own exacting prescriptions to what is legitimate or not is a bit of self-referential absurdity best passed over; concluding that as a model it's clearly ineffectual in describing whole swaths of human experience is sufficient enough. You can see my difficulty with the question of whether or not I "actually" believe in demons—I reject the entire

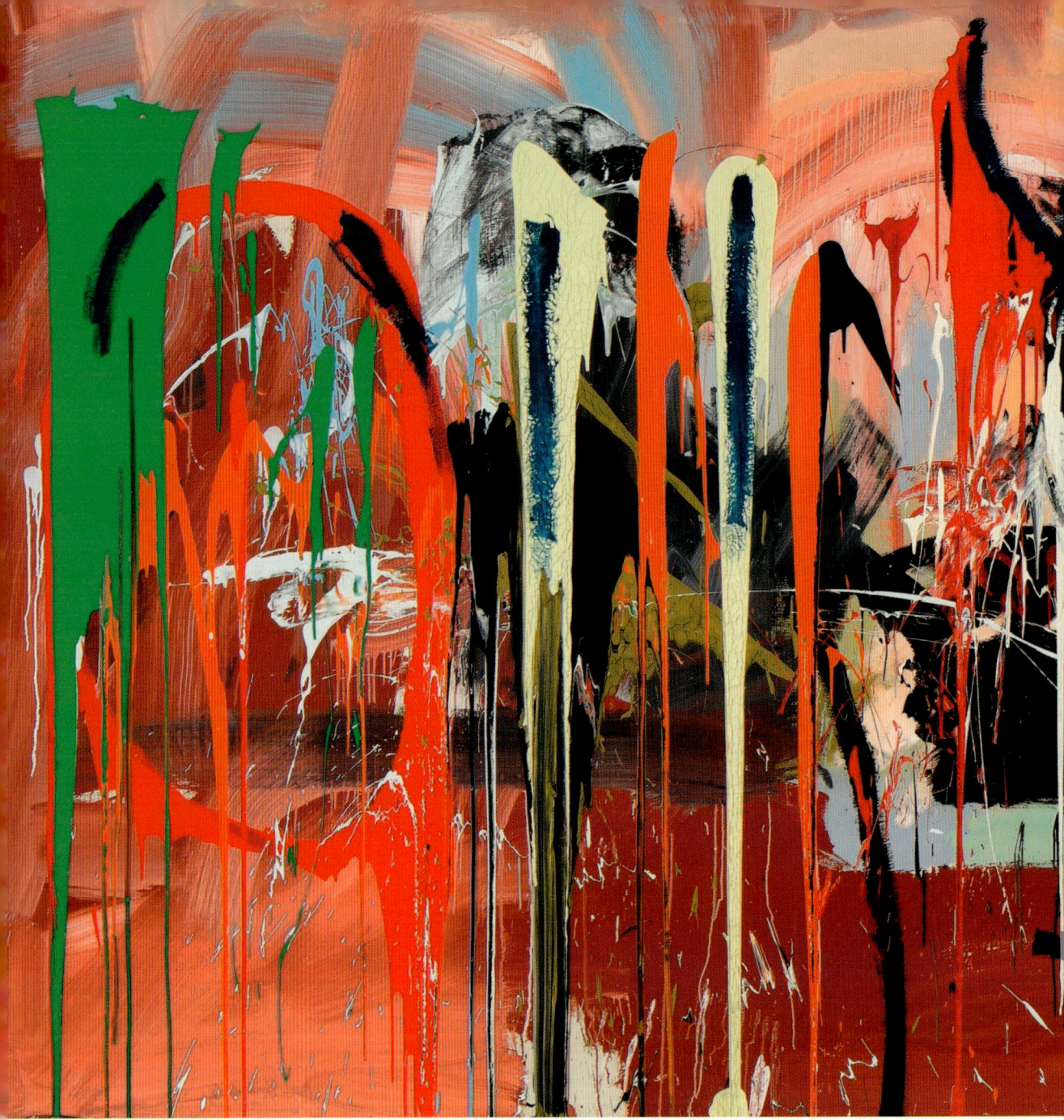

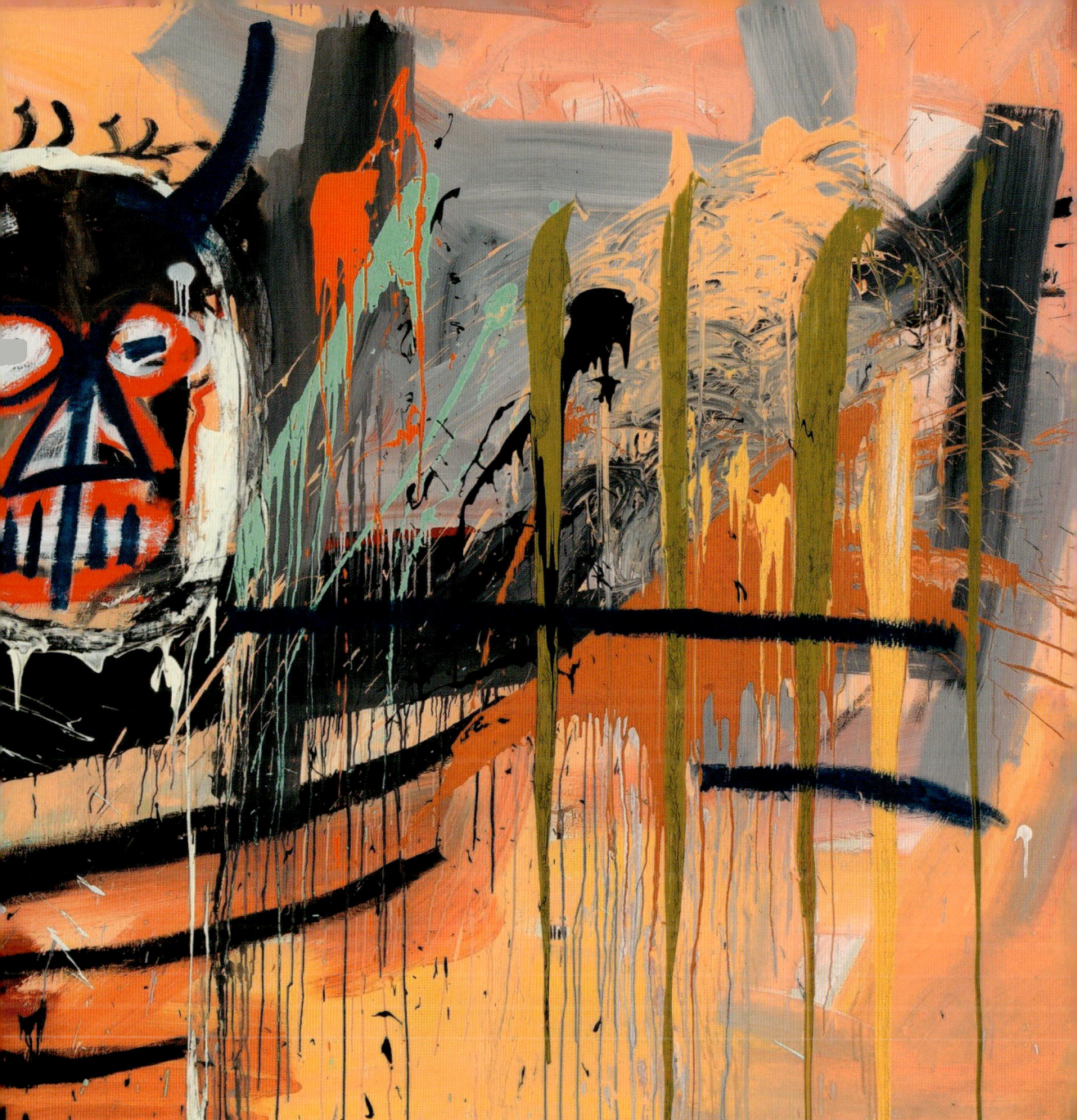

Untitled (Devil) *by Jean-Michel Basquiat, 1982.*

epistemological attitude in which the query is posed. If the question is asked in the spirit of ascertaining whether or not demons exist as tangibly as a dog in the yard, then obviously the answer is in the negative, and yet in those moments of sublime terror when approaching the core of the cracked numinous, I can't help but know what I felt. That warped smile and those red eyes might not be staring back at me from the yard, but they're staring back from *somewhere*.

Of the approaches that the modern person has in considering demonology, there's obviously blunt literalism, equally blunt denialism, and then a sort of vast middle that reduces demons to "metaphors" or "symbols." Concerning those who think of demons as being as "real" as the dog in the yard, little can be said. Such fundamentalism is its own capitulation to the exigencies of modernity; it's as positivist as anyone adhering to the correspondence theory of the truth, it merely chooses to ascent toward that which anyone can see is an absurdity. Those who adhere to this contention may think that they're taking part in a venerable spiritual tradition, but they hold to the same epistemological framework as any rationalist or skeptic, they just choose to believe in something demonstrably wrong. Denialists are a different species, to harp on the non-existence of demons is to miss the point in the same way as the literalists but toward a different direction. Smugly emphasizing that demons aren't real seems about the same as arguing that "Truth is beauty, beauty is truth" is an absurdity because it can't be reduced to symbolic logic; those who expel poetry in favor of the syllogism live a shallow existence. Most obnoxious of this type are those who reject anything that to them has the taint of the spiritual, the divine, the transcendent about it, consigning millennia of human experience and expression into the trash can because it doesn't conform to a model of truth that has only existed for a few dozen generations.

Most appealing is perhaps those who maintain that demons are potent and powerful explanatory symbols, that they are deeply significant metaphors. Such a position has the benefit of being partially true, of course. *Demons are powerful metaphors.* In Lucifer we have a symbol of unbridled pride, in Azazel the intermixing of good and evil, in Moloch the horrors of rapacious consumption. And of course, from a literal perspective, one need not believe that there is a bat-winged entity in the bowels of the earth, or that goat- and bull-headed deities stalk our nighttime. Yet there is something finally unsatisfying in reducing the demonic to the mere metaphorical. I do not say that with any self-satisfaction, for metaphor is the grand medium of language, the atoms of our thoughts and emotions, wherein no true human expression can take place without that blessed word "like." When considering the demonic, however, the metaphorical model offers what's ultimately an incomplete understanding of something that is realer than real, which exists in a dark poetry that is uttered beyond the realm of mere words. Demonic names are performative, they're incantatory, they're ritualistic, and even though they don't correspond to "actual" things in the "real" world, they very much gesture toward that aforementioned dark *something*.

Between the correspondence theory of truth and the metaphorical theory of truth, I propose a third option—that our demonology conforms to some type of reality, but an ineffable one, a hidden one, an inexpressible one that can neither be measured nor understood but that is somehow closer to us than the atoms of our very breath. In such a schema it is held that the postulates of demonology are always poetic, that they are not to be verified or disproven, and that the signifier and signified of the word "demon" is forever deferred. Holding that words like "demonic" or "satanic" are metaphorical terms for evil, that they carry within them all the overloaded cultural connotations that they imply, is an obvious truism—but they're more than metaphors as well. What is the reality to which they refer, endlessly contingent and always shifting, filtered through centuries and a multitude of cultures and faiths? I have no idea, having never seen behind the veil.

That is the nature of the numinous; it's forever beyond my simple comprehension, or of anyone else's perceptions as well, for that matter. In *Pandemonium*, there is an emphasis on the importance of demonic names—Azazel, Mephistopheles, Lucifer, Baphomet, Moloch, and so on—because being able to a give proper name to something is crucial to controlling it, an inviolate principle of demonology. Don't mistake my personal argument as being that these names refer to things in quite the same way that the word "car" simply corresponds to that which is parked in front of my house. The truths that they convey are something far more elemental, charged, and indefinable. The German Lutheran theologian Paul Tillich wrote in his 1951 *Systematic Theology* that "God does not exist. He is being itself beyond essence and existence. Therefore, to argue that God exists is to deny him." Insomuch as the demonic is within the realm of the sacred, where that word connotes not goodness so much as those things that are other from our profane reality, I think that paradoxically something like this is true for demons as well.

What's offered then is a theory of demonology as filtered through something that I call "demonic poetics." As a neologism, it is meant to refer to the parsing of how humans have interacted with this numinous reality, this demonic *something*, throughout history. "Poetics" because there is an understanding that literary language is relative, allegorical, symbolic, metaphorical, and that it gestures toward the transcendent; "demonic" for obvious reasons. When presenting a history of demonology, what is necessarily being explicated is humanity's understanding of the subject rather than the reality itself, for the simple reason that the latter is impossible to approach rationally. "The truth is difficult to get at; it is dynamic rather than static; and it exists in the tension between the knower and that which is known," writes Jeffrey Burton Russell in *Mephistopheles: The Devil in the Modern World*. "We cannot ever grasp ultimate truth, but we can point toward that truth by engaging ourselves, by thinking clearly, and by not muddling categories."

Chief among the categorical mistakes people make is to assume that a scientific truth is the same across all domains of experience, an error that is the heresy of positivism. That's not to reject science at all—far from it, for as Russell makes clear, the empirical method is the "most impressive and dramatic system in human experience," but that has led some to erroneously assume it's the only system, and to thus reject truths that in poetry and faith would be nonsensical in science (and it is within the former that demons live). Russell, whose knowledge and reasoning have indelibly marked *Pandemonium*, sought a phenomenological approach to understanding absolute evil, wherein the subject of the satanic and the demonic can't be approached the same way that we discuss a chemical reaction or genetic sequencing, but rather by examining the experience of people as they've been impacted by that ineffable *something* hidden beyond the sensory realm. His attitude is such that though it is "true that the Devil cannot exist in a scientific sense . . . he can [still] exist in a theological sense, in a mythological sense, in a psychological sense, and in a historical sense; and these approaches are, like science, capable of fixing a course on truth."

What's clear, obviously, is that many people in the past did literally believe in demons, and that they were as tangible and visceral as a hammer and a chair. But because the largest swath of human history also coincided with the experience of a charged and enchanted reality, there was also always the perspective that demons (and all other sacred things) had an elevated, transcendent, realer-than-real constitution to them as well. Because ours is an era rendered anemic by the tyranny of positivism, where disenchantment reduces everything to the ontological status of a hammer or a chair, we've tended to disbelieve in things that can't be measured and weighed. Russell and I agree that that is a philosophical mistake. I see no reason why my not believing in imps scampering through the darkness of my basement means that I must reject the existence of demons crawling through the blackness of my soul. To that end, I would pose several principles that motivate this work (see opposite page).

Pandemonium will largely be an exegesis of these principles, though they in large part emerged through the actual writing of the book itself. As a set of axioms, or arguments, or theses, they are not necessarily self-evident, which is of course part of the reason why I have systematized them. There is a sense in which *Pandemonium*'s chapters have been organized according to this schema, such as in analyzing a given demon who is representative of an era's zeitgeist, the focus on close readings of literary works, and the emphasis on the variability of individual demons' symbolic import, as with Lucifer's evolution from being the embodiment of evil and rebellion to being understood as a Romantic hero. It's taken as a motivating given that there is this intangible *something,* an ineffable sacred for which language is inadequate, so that our discourse must always be constructed (though no less significant for it).

Throughout this book, you may discover that true to its subtitle, *Pandemonium* is more a history of demonology than it is of individual demons. Certainly, all that you would expect is here in terms of demonic hierarchies, ancient grimoires with their incantations, and the conjurers who garnered a reputation for working in the occult arts. There will be ample consideration given to otherworldly entities with names like Ba'al and Mammon, but more than an encyclopedic listing of such creatures (for there are other volumes which do that) this is the first comprehensive popular history of demonology as a discipline of study. That means that the focus is on how people—from Cornelius Agrippa to John Dee, Aleister Crowley to Anton LeVey—have imagined the demonic, and the resultant work that they produced in that regard.

Furthermore, *Pandemonium* doesn't limit itself to figures normally categorized as occultists, as I also provide an analysis of how the demonic influenced the work of ostensibly mainstream philosophers like René Descartes, Friedrich

The Principles of Demonic Poetics

1.

Whether demons exist or not, peoples' experience
of them absolutely exists.

2.

The demonic is a network of metaphors, symbols, and
images that define the diabolical; they shift and interact
with each other in different ways across the centuries.

3.

As symbols, demons can mean variable and often
contradictory things.

4.

There is no clear distinction between categories
of the aesthetic and the occult, and demonic poetics
is an interpretive frame that understands the literary
and the magical as fundamentally the same thing.

5.

Some demons are always more symbolically ascendant
in a given epoch.

6.

Demons exist at the crux of the transcendent,
the numinous, the sublime; they are by definition evil,
but they are also by definition an aspect of the sacred.
There is a something at the core of being that
encompasses both the divine and the diabolical,
but our language to describe it is always contingent.

7.

A history of demonology is by necessity
a history of the world.

Nietzsche, and Hannah Arendt (among others). The hermetic tradition, so often marginalized by mainstream academe, has exerted a greater influence than has been supposed, and the glittering sheen of the demonic can be espied within the cannon far more than is given credit.

Though I'm (technically) an academic, *Pandemonium* is not a traditional scholarly volume, though it is an interpretive and a critical one, and I've certainly relied on the invaluable research of historians, theologians, philosophers, and literary theorists. I make no claims to this being a comprehensive study, though it is wide-ranging. Undoubtedly *Pandemonium* reflects my biases, interests, blind spots, and prejudices, so for that I beg a certain indulgence and understanding. More important than any individual analyses, any particular close reading, any recounting of a particular figure, event, or text, what's most crucial is the basic argument of *Pandemonium*—that because Satan is the prince of this world, any history of demonology is de facto also a history of the world. Demonic poetics is always an expression of the ineffable, where our words are ever variable, so that demons provide invaluable imaginative metaphors for each epoch to uniquely understand itself in relation to not just evil, but reality more generally. In the details there is certainly much to quibble about, but to the detriment of my academic career, I've always held that it's more important to be interesting than completely correct, and while I hope that I'm both, the bulk of desire is that I'm at least the first.

A final personal anecdote, though perhaps it's more of a parable, if slightly askew. More than a decade ago, when I briefly lived in that grubby industrial metropolis of Glasgow, I used to sometimes take the train to Edinburgh to spend the day. While both cities shared a certain Scottish melancholy, Edinburgh was the far more gothically atmospheric, a town of narrow, crooked cobblestone streets lurching up the side of a steep mountain, a cloistered medieval place that wore its history as thick as the dark clouds that would move across the Midlothian lowlands. True to its general demeanor, Edinburgh had a number of ghost-haunting tours that you see in any city with a history that's long, bloody, or preferably both. These are the sorts of sojourns through moody seaside dock districts and drafty old manors where hard-up drama students wear period costume and speak in affected old-fashioned diction. Not being particularly better than anyone else who chooses to part with a few quid in that endeavor, I ventured to take part in Edinburgh's manifestation of that venerable and corny tradition.

The particular tour that I went on were through the South Bridge Vaults, a honeycombed network of subterranean rooms accessible from street level through a number of heavily padlocked doors, which in the eighteenth century housed a massive destitute population displaced by the Georgian revitalization of the area across the valley from Edinburgh's original Old Town. Within this chthonic realm of the forgotten there was a community of the impoverished and the criminal, an entire hidden kingdom underneath the footsteps of respectable Edinburgh crossing the South Bridge. Taverns, distilleries, slums, and brothels all lined the vaults; it's long been legend that the notorious serial killers William Burke and William Hare, who supplied fresh corpses to the anatomy students at Edinburgh University, would commence their hunt within the district. This was an area for rogues, libertines, rakes, and swindlers, an unhappy and cursed place. Bricked up and forgotten for two centuries, the vaults had been rediscovered accidentally by a Scottish rugby star in the 1980s, and quite predictably they became a star feature for the city's fanny-pack-wearing tourists.

When I toured in a damp and cold Scotland of 2007, the Edinburgh Vaults delivered on their promise of providing an appropriately unnerving experience. All were composed of tightly packed, crumbling tan bricks, which give each one of the subterranean vaults the appearance of a large oven. An enthused guide led us through the network of claustrophobic rooms, our path illuminated by electric lights in iron cages meant to look as if they were lit by gas. We were entertained by our chaperon (again, predictably, a drama student) with a combination of historical accounts, grotesque stories, and naturally, reports of supernatural occurrences. One room, identically to all the rest, had been the site of a massive conflagration in the eighteenth century whereby a hundred people were literally baked to death, leaving the city authorities unable to tell where one person's body part ended and another's began, the whole bevy of humans reduced to a burnt, quivering mass of flesh. In another, we were told of how Burke and Hare would kidnap women and men, stab them, bundle them up, and then deliver them to the medical school where they'd be carved apart for educational purposes. And then, finally, there was the most terrifying room of all.

Otherwise nondescript, and supposedly of no historical import, this particular vault had been chosen as the site for a neo-pagan group's worship services. Altars and chairs had been set up, and the members would gather once a week like any other religious community, but they encountered a problem. Every single week they'd discover that though the vault was locked, all of their ritual objects were scattered about, the chairs knocked over, the pages ripped out of their books. Finally, the leader of this particular community, a druid who had some knowledge of the ancient hauntings that bedeviled this land, volunteered to spend the night to see what force, whether human or spectral, took to vandalizing their grove. Our guide, with theatrical flourish, reported that in the morning, the shaking druid, a man familiar with the exigencies of the supernatural, refused to give detail on what he'd witnessed during the night, but he demanded that his group's place of worship be moved out of that vault immediately. As a final offering, he assembled a number of rocks and arranged them in a circle with a diameter about the height of a strapping man, performing a ritual to forever imprison that which had been haunting the vault into the cairn. Whatever had happened to the druid that night, whatever he'd experienced, he took great care to make sure that this powerful force, this absolute evil, would be constrained by this magic, incapacitated lest somebody should disrupt its prison.

Our guide was good. She made a showy routine out of the circle, emphasizing that though she was too cautious to ever step across its boundaries herself, Great Britain was a free country, and certainly any one of the people on the tour would be welcome to enter into the supposed spirit's domain if that was their decision. On our tour was a young man who couldn't have been much more than nineteen or twenty, who embraced the aesthetic of the vaguely disreputable British chav subculture. Think oversize Burberry jacket, backward ball cap, gold chains, and expensive tennis shoes. He was with two pretty women, and perhaps in an effort to seem fearless, he jumped into the center of the cairn, aped a few obscene gestures, loudly laughed, and gave his audience a profane closing V-sign. After his performance, the group continued on its way, but something seemed wrong with the young gentleman. Where once he was loud, now he was quiet; where before he was vulgar, now he seemed cowed; where once he was a braggadocio, now he was a frightened boy. After around half an hour had passed, our fearless explorer into whatever abyss was in that circle started to cry, breaking down in front of the women whom he had once clearly hoped to take home, and he was all but nonverbal when asked by the guide what was wrong. The group had to stop as an ambulance was called, and a security guard arrived to take the young man up to streel level.

Now, I've no idea what happened there. Perhaps, despite all the initial swagger, he was the psychosomatic sort, impressionable and easily made anxious. Or, maybe he was an actor employed by the tour group to give a bit of eerie verisimilitude to the proceedings. Finally, maybe he met whatever exists within that infinite kingdom of the impossible; perhaps he went deep within that abyss and came out the other side changed, different. If the demonic is a *something* that exists at the core of the invisible, a land beyond words or description, language or normal vision, then demonology has always provided a safer means in approaching that realm. Demonology is built with the stones which capture that force within, each pebble a name that humans have chosen to try and make sense of something which is fundamentally senseless. All of you now reading are standing on the outer side of those rocks, looking into the pure negation that is contained by that cairn. Take it as prudent advice that it's best never to cross that threshold. Are demons real? I'm not going to step into that circle. Would you?

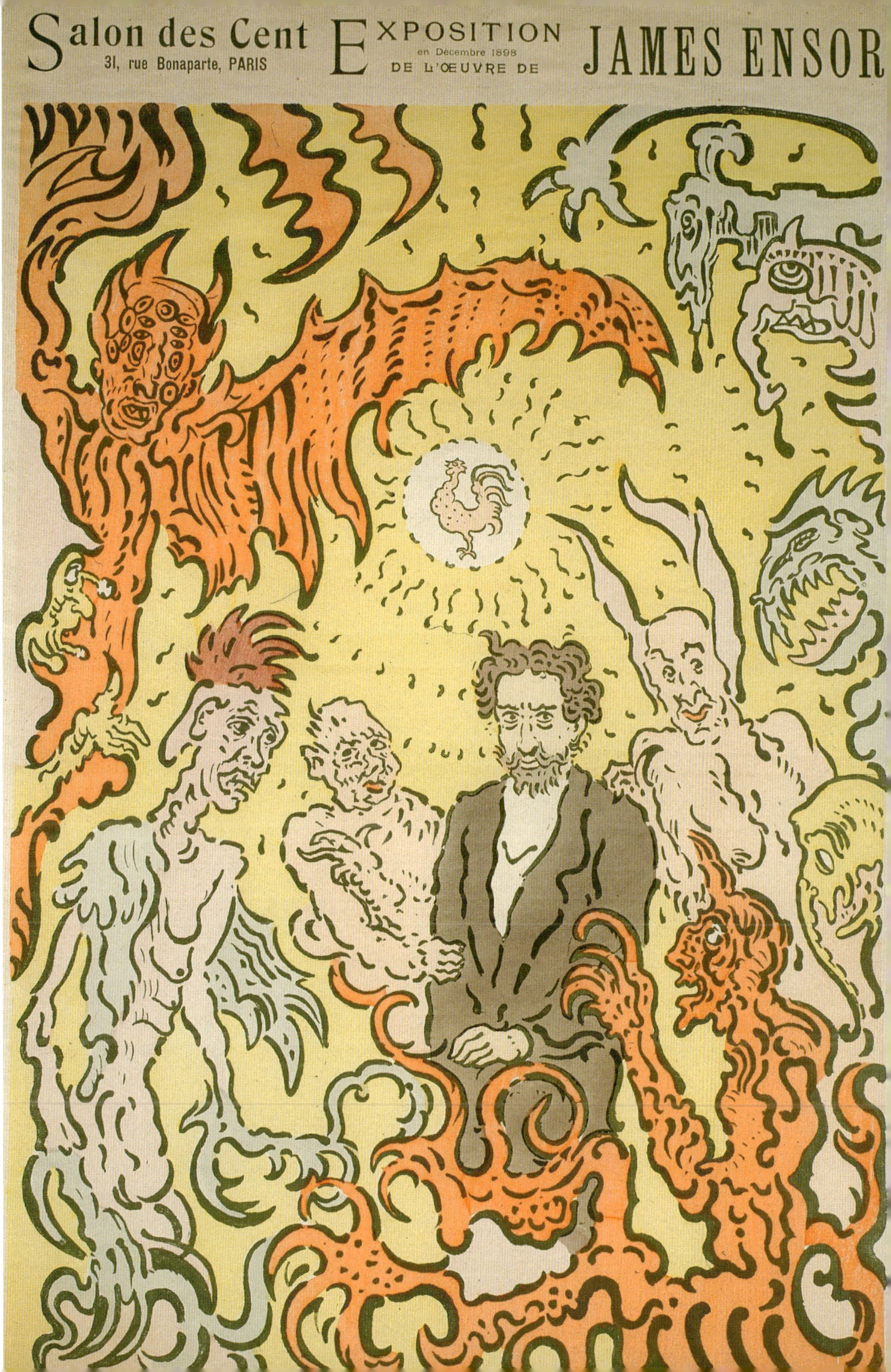
Salon des Cent
31, rue Bonaparte, PARIS
EXPOSITION
en Décembre 1898
DE L'ŒUVRE DE
JAMES ENSOR

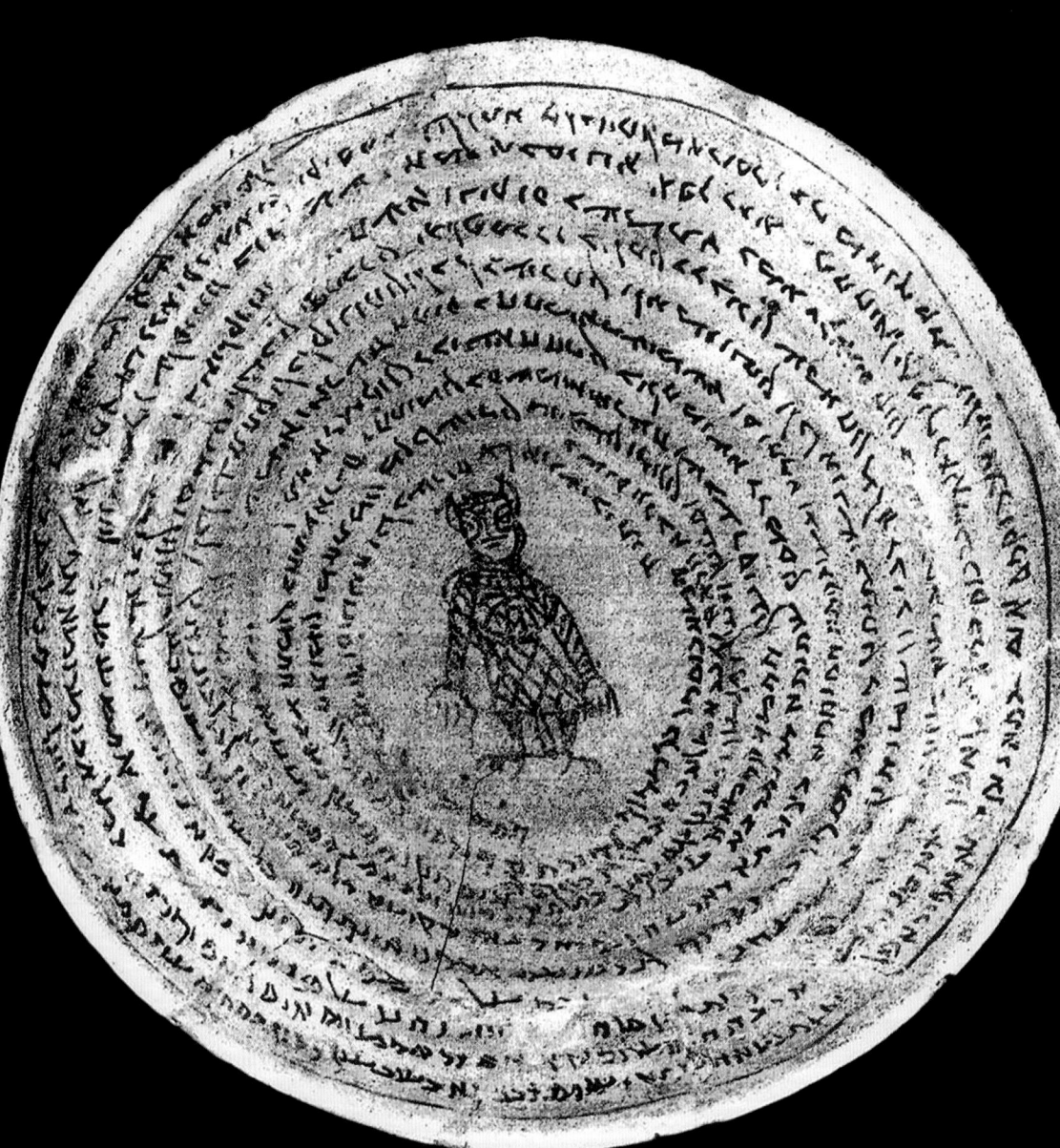

CHAPTER ONE

We Are Legion

Demons from Scripture and Antiquity, c. 500 BCE–800 CE

I form the light, and create darkness: I make peace, and create evil:
I the LORD do all these things.

—Isaiah 45:7

And Azazel taught men to make swords, and knives, and shields,
and breastplates, and made known to them the metals of the earth
and the art of working them . . . And there arose much godlessness,
and they committed fornication, and they were led astray,
and became corrupt in all their ways.

—1 Enoch 8:1

ON ANCIENT DEMONS

Dedicated to Near Eastern antiquities, Berlin's Voderasiatisches Museum exhibits among other treasures the opal-colored splendor of the massive Ishtar Gate that once opened onto Babylon, as well as the front wall of the temple to the goddess Inanna, which marked the center of the ancient city of Uruk. In a less traversed part of the museum, however, there are more modest objects to be contrasted with the splendors of Babylon and Persepolis that line the main galleries. Of ultimately unknown provenance, but undoubtedly dug out of the ground in either Iraq or Iran alongside similar artifacts, a number of rough-hewn, earthenware pots or bowls are on display. Made of the red clay found in the Mesopotamian deserts, or from the thick mud that cakes the banks of the Tigris and Euphrates, they are known as incantation bowls.

While there are variations, incantation bowls are similar in size (not much larger than the sort of pot you might root a houseplant in) and almost all of them are decorated with finely lettered text, sometimes in Syriac or Persian, occasionally in Arabic or Hebrew, but mostly in Aramaic, spiraling in from the lip of the ceramic to its center. Oftentimes they have an illustration of an individual figure at the nadir of the pot, almost always amateurishly (if charmingly) rendered, depicting a monstrous, inhuman, alien creature. To pick up such an artifact, to feel the roughness of the unglazed clay in your hand, the sleight weight of the jagged and primitive thing, is to touch something made by a believer in demons. The purpose of the bowl was to tame those secret things that so disrupt our world. Such an object is proof of the past's foreignness, a shard from a tradition impassably distant from modern civilization. What's most important to remember about an incantation bowl is that its function was estimably practical—to use a magical formula to trap, bind, and imprison a demonic spirit, thus preventing the propagation of its evil (for a time). Ultimately, the incantation bowl was a tool.

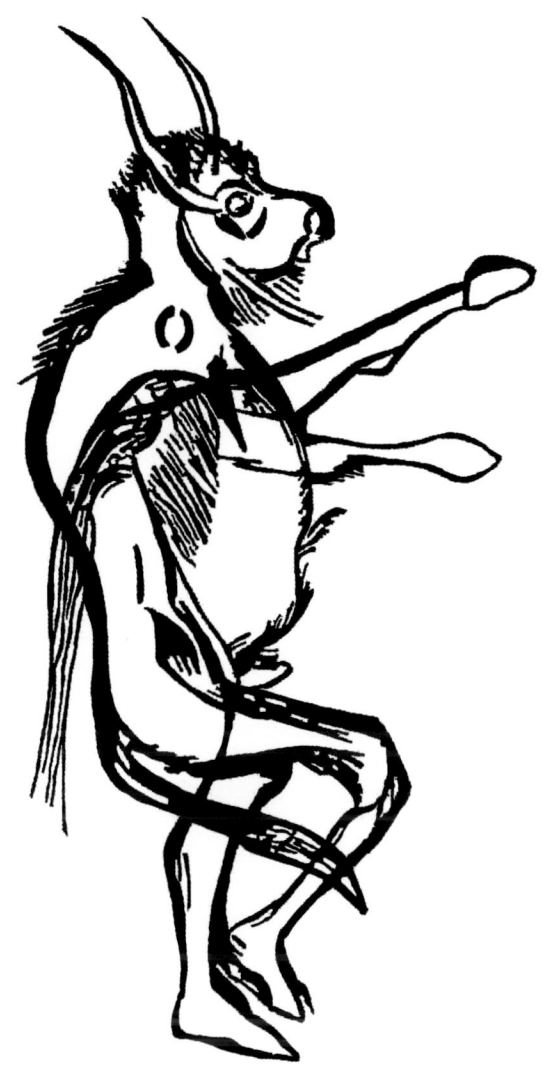

Discovered in 1914, the cave paintings at Trois-Frères, France, present a menagerie of chimerical forms rendered during the Upper Paleolithic period, some fifteen thousand years ago. Among the oldest representational images to ever be found, scholars have long argued that they provide a visceral, if mysterious, entry into prehistoric religion. This drawing, made by archeologist and Jesuit priest Henri Breuil, depicts one such ancient painting, of perhaps a shaman wearing animal skins, or of some sort of goat- or bull-headed deity. Historian Margaret Murray claimed in her 1921 The Witch-Cult in Western Europe *that it was the earliest depiction of what she termed the "Horned God," a being worshiped throughout European history whom the later Church conflated with Satan. Despite once having widespread academic endorsement, Murray's hypothesis has long fell into disfavor, even while the goat god of Trois-Frères conjures some sort of elemental, archetypal, caprine figure who flits through history.*

These are not great art pieces—they do not reflect a high degree of aesthetic sophistication, but in their roughness they emphasize how visceral and real demons were to the people who made them. The purpose of such a tool wasn't mere abstraction, but rather to help personify the often seemingly random pain, tribulation, suffering, and misfortune of an often cruel and capricious existence. They exist because for the people who made them they were just as needed as a knife or thimble. Jeffrey Burton Russell writes in *The Devil: Perceptions of Evil from Antiquity to Primitive Christianity* that for all of the unusual names we have had for demons—Belial and Baal, Mammon and Moloch—the psychological need humans have for them is simpler, for they are ultimately the "menacing spirits of the thunderstorm or the lonely grove, avenging ghosts of the dead, bringers of disease, and violent spirits who possess the soul." What can't be forgotten as concerns demons, despite the wide variety of strange names and still stranger visages that we associate with them, are that they fundamentally express a basic truth—life is frequently defined by pain. Life is often marked by evil.

Incantation bowls speak to the real fear that women and men had of demons, for whether or not those beings were "real," those ancient lives were demon haunted. A few thousand incantation bowls have been found on excavations across Iraq and Iran, Jordan and Israel; housed in places such as the Schøyen Collection in London and Oslo, the Israel Antiquities Authority in Jerusalem, and in the private collections of the wealthy. The religious context of the incantation bowls is complicated; the demons named are often indigenous to Sumerian and Babylonian religion, the imagery used is variously Zoroastrian, Christian, or Mandaean (a gnostic sect that still exists). Of the extant bowls, the vast majority are Jewish in origin, reflecting a thriving culture of theurgy from the sixth to eighth centuries, especially among the descendants of the Jews who were exiled to Babylon after the destruction of the Temple in the sixth century before the Common Era, but who still made the banks of the Tigris and Euphrates their home a millennium later.

"Despite the prohibition against practicing in magic and the sages' ambivalent attitude toward it, magic features prominently in ancient Jewish scholarly writings," writes historian Naama Vilozny in her contribution to *The Archeology and Material Culture of the Babylonian Talmud*, in which she provides a thorough survey of known incantation bowls. Dating from around the sixth century, not long after the compilation of the Babylonian Talmud—the extensive collection of biblical commentary that marks Jewish practice and life—the incantation bowls are evidence of cultural syncretism, of the ways in which beliefs that don't seem immediately congruent with strict monotheism can find a home within orthodoxy. Demons provide a potent vocabulary of wickedness. In the Voderasiatisches Museum, one example is a bowl featuring a bestial figure bedecked in the uniform of a Persian soldier (the armor looking almost like reptilian scales), clawed feet and hands poking out from his body, and on top of his black-eyed visage there curve two horns. The creature's name is Ashmedai, and to those of ancient Babylon who molded this artifact he was feared as the king of demons.

The British Museum has a similar incantation bowl also meant to ward off Ashmedai (whose Aramaic name derives from Persian, but is often Latinized to Asmodeus). Inscribed on that particular artifact, in the same Aramaic that the Talmud is written in and the same Aramaic spoken by Christ, the Creator writes, "I did not know the name and I did not know the magical practices and identity of Ashmedai, king of demons." Like all incantation bowls, it worked as an amulet, a bit of good magic to bind and expel those demons that bedevil our earthly existence. "Bound . . . removed, you are sealed and you are countersealed," the craftsmen wrote on the lip at some point between the fifth and the eighth century after the Common Era. "I extend over you . . . great ones . . . of iron and chains . . . And I enclose you and seal you with the great seal of the princes, of Gabriel and Michael and Raphael," the archangels who act as a divine check on all of the subjects of hell.

Here by the rivers of Babylon some nameless artisan sat down and wept for whatever evil had ruined his fortune, or harmed his family, or corrupted his life. Whatever had compelled him to make the object, buried upside down in the earth, the better to trap and constrain the demon named therein, he knew the identity of the creature that tormented him. And by being able to put a name to this being—Ashmedai—he was able to claim some degree of sovereignty over the evil that otherwise controls this world. Ashmedai was not the only demon featured on artifacts from the period. The fallen angel Samael, the Light Bearer, is sometimes depicted and the infant-killing succubus Lilith was a perennial favorite, the later always pictured with tangled hair and her labia spread wide. Other demons were similarly grotesque, sharing clawed appendages and wild hair, shackles binding their hands and feet as when they were first cast out of paradise, the better to prevent them from tormenting people.

As iconoclastic as Jewish practice historically is, the prohibition on images could be ignored in the production of these popular artifacts, the engagement with such superstition sometimes recognized as necessary to do battle against those infernal things that stalk the earth. After all, demons "are more numerous than we are and they surround us like the ridge round a field," says Rabbi Huna in the Talmud. "Every one among us has a thousand on his left hand and ten thousand on his right hand." Demons speak to the ruptures of existence, the feeling that things are disordered, wicked, debased. Writing in the third century after the Common Era, around the same time as the compilation of the Talmud, the Greek Neoplatonic philosopher Porphyry noted that demons "are not clothed in a solid body . . . nor do they all have a single shape. They take many forms . . . [and] administer large parts of the regions beneath the moon . . . [being] responsible for the sufferings which happen round the earth, such as plagues, crop failures, earthquakes and droughts." Parallel to Rabbi Huna's conclusions concerning the demonic population, Porphyry writes that they "find their natural place in the air and on the earth and thus exist cheek-by-jowl, as it were, with human beings."

Every culture, every faith, every people has a conception of the supernatural, or the numinous, and so, when it comes to personified representations of evil, there is also no exception. Russell writes that "a legion of lesser spirits who personify specific evil . . . can be found in most societies. These spirits of extreme heat and cold, barrenness, disease or storms are sometimes considered ghosts, sometimes gods" and sometimes creatures more infernal. Demons, devils, spirits, and specters populate the mythologies of the world, and ancient Judaism drew upon a rich repository of Near Eastern faith in conceiving of what that personified evil might look like, with Ashmedai's goat-like appearance possibly

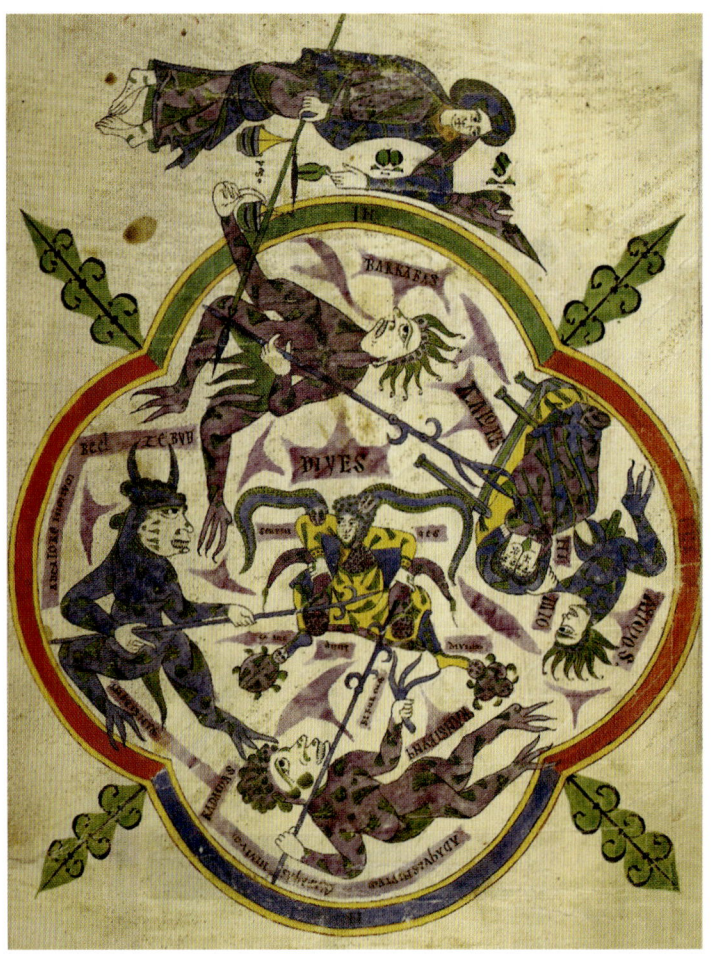

deriving from Sumerian, Assyrian, Babylonian, or even Greek precedents. P.G. Maxwell-Stuart explains in *Satan: A Biography* that "contained in these early Middle Eastern religions there were indeed notions, which would later flow into Judaism and thence into Christianity, thereby providing an ambience for the rise of Satan, and indirectly sow seeds from which his character could grow." One of these lieutenants of the Prince of Evil was the aforementioned Ashmedai, who makes an appearance in the biblical Book of Kings, the apocryphal Book of Tobit (which is only canonical to Orthodox Christians and Roman Catholics), and the compendium of religious disputation that is the Jewish Talmud.

Ashmedai is a convenient case study in how demons were understood in Jewish antiquity, and throughout the Mediterranean basin, where a fruitful hybridization of traditions from across the Near East would have an influence on Western demonology, drawing from Mesopotamian, Persian, Egyptian, and Canaanite mythologies. Anthropologist Gerald Messadie writes in *A History of the Devil* that the prototypical Mesopotamian "had a frightening image of his gods, perhaps the most frightening in any religion." He goes on to describe how their deities were a panoply of "half-human monsters with animal heads: lions, panther, dog, sheep, ram, bird and snake," such as the winged and dog-faced god of the southwestern wind known as Pazuzu, "a demon with four wings, a bat's head, and a scorpion's tale" or the succubus Lilith, the "she-devil of childbirth fever, a female nightmare generally depicted suckling a dog with one breast and a pig with the other."

Ashmedai draws from Persian sources rather than from Babylonian ones, his name etymologically similar to that of the god of evil in Zoroastrianism, the figure possibly borrowed by the Jews during their years of exile in Babylon centuries before the Common Era (while also leaving behind the diaspora communities that would one day manufacture incantations bowls). Traces of figures like Ashmedai and Lilith flit like shadows through respectable scripture, for it's from such pagan origins that Jewish demonology, developing uncomfortably in tandem with the faith's strict monotheism, appropriated a cast of devilish characters.

For the vast majority of classical pagans, including the Canaanites, Sumerians, and Babylonians from whom so many demonic names were borrowed, nature was neither good nor evil. Malignant spirits were certainly real, and to be feared and controlled if possible, but they were not representatives of any cosmically absolute evil, for such an evil didn't exist. When Jewish monotheism posited that ours was a world governed by one Creator, the problem of evil—known by theologians as theodicy—became much more pronounced. How could the supposed existence of one all-powerful and all-good God be reconciled with the brutal reality of our evil world? Earlier biblical texts, such as that of the prophet Isaiah, render God fully responsible for evil, so that every failed crop, every famine, every plague, and the death of every innocent child is finally His fault. While still a totally orthodox understanding of the Lord, there is a certain natural resistance to its otherwise logically unassailable conclusion. In embracing the coteries of minor demons who exist in pagan religions, there is a devaluing of God's awesome omniscience; in God's awesome omniscience there is the uncomfortable realization that He must be the author of evil as much as good.

There was to be a solution of sorts, at least psychologically, in the Zoroastrian religion of the Persians who liberated the Jews from Babylonian captivity in the sixth century before the Common Era. Messadie writes that for the Zoroastrians, the "God of Good . . . constructed the world on the principle of equilibrium, and the Adversary is one of its two terms." A dualistic faith that was the first to posit the existence of not just malignant trickster spirits but of absolute supernatural evil, Zoroastrians held (and still hold, as there are small communities of them around the world) that existence was cosmically balanced between two gods of equal power—Ahura Mazda, who was the benevolent creator of the world, and his nemesis Ahriman, who is the primogeniture of all evil. In the latter there are intimations of Satan, and indeed Jewish texts written after their interaction with Zoroastrianism began to evidence the development of a nascent theology of the devil, and thus of demonology as well.

To the Jews, and then especially the early Christians, evil could find its impetus, inspiration, and ultimate source from Satan. Russell explains that "Dualism radically . . . [freed] God from responsibility for evil . . . assigning it instead to an independent and hostile spirit . . . Insisting on monotheism, they left the God with at least partial responsibility for evil; tending to dualism, they shifted much of the blame onto the Devil." Though technically a creation of God, ascribing evil's presence by recourse to Satan helped in some way to offset the uncomfortable reality that the Lord must be the final cause of all misfortune that exists in the world. By the fifth century the Christian theologian Pseudo-Dionysius the Areopagite could write that demons "cannot be evil since they owe their origin to God. The Good is the creator and preserver of good things. If they are called evil, it is not in respect of their being, since they owe their origin to the Good."

The narrative of how first Judaism and then Christianity and Islam incorporated a pantheon of supernatural beings into a rigidly monotheistic perspective is a history of how religion is able to alter itself during its interactions with other cultures, but also of faith's genius in adapting because of theological utility. By the time of the ecclesiastical First Council of Braga in 561, the Church would conclude, "Whoever denies that the Devil was originally a good angel created by God, contending instead that he arose from the chaos and the darkness and has no creator, but is himself the principle and the substance of evil . . . Let him be anathema." Scriptural and prophetic writing from the period before the Jews' exile in Babylon was already clear—God was He who rendered both good and evil, a being who dwelled in the light and crouched in the darkness, because as Russell makes clear, "the concept of the origin of evil was very much in flux."

OPPOSITE PAGE

Cast in bronze, and a little over fifteen centimeters (six inches) tall, this Assyrian statue of the demon Pazuzu, which now makes its home in Paris's Louvre Museum, was crafted sometime in the early first millennium before the Common Era. An anatomical panoply of the avian and the canine, the reptilian and the insectoid, Pazuzu commanded howling wind, which was associated with the plague. "I am Pazuzu," an inscription reads, "king of the evil spirits of the air which issues violently from mountains, causing much havoc."

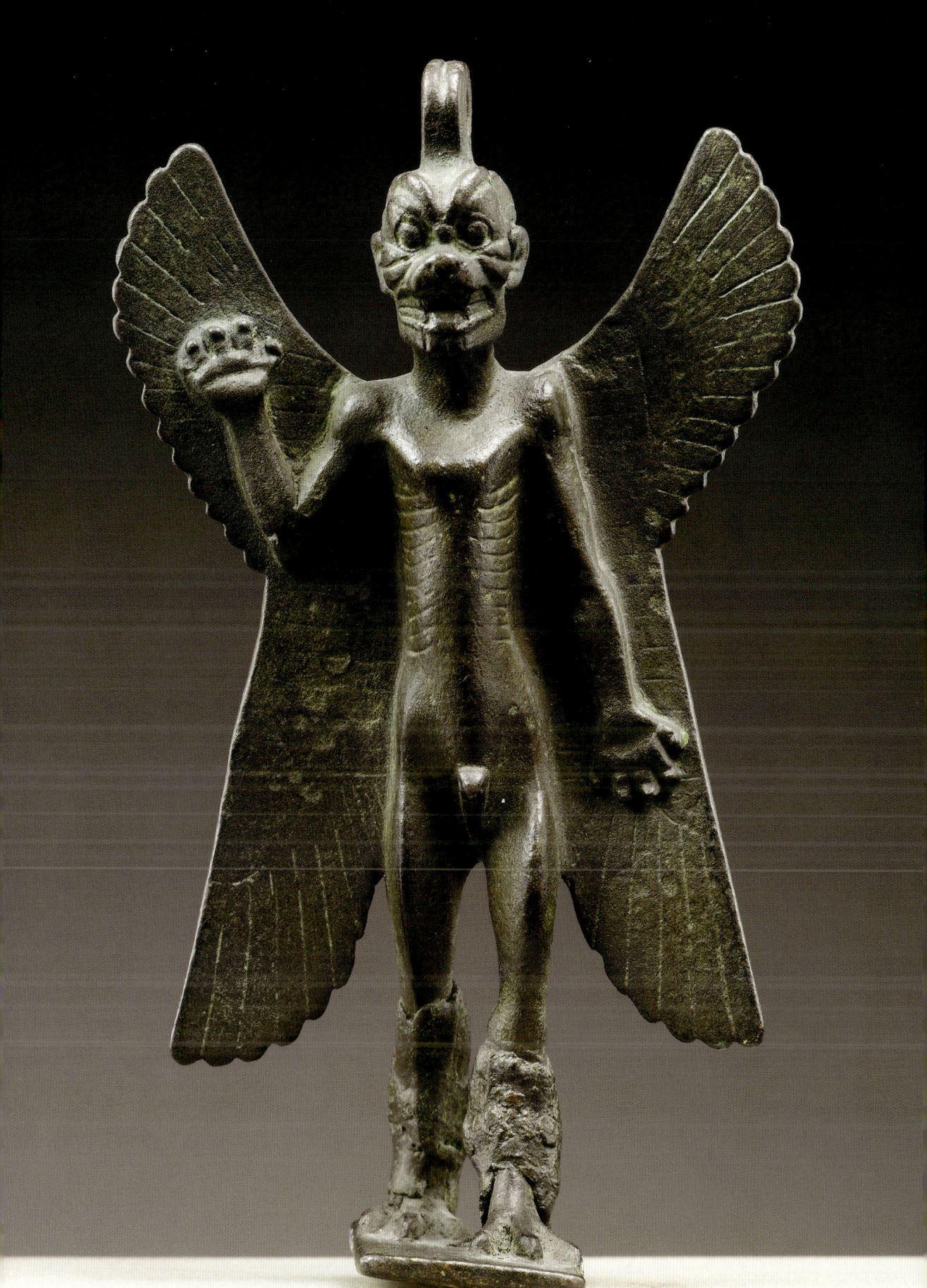

In the centuries after the Jews returned to their homeland and rebuilt the Temple, Persian beliefs about an absolute malignancy of almost equivalent power to God were enumerated in apocryphal writings, which would have a profound effect on later monotheism by supplying a narrative of how evil was introduced into our world. "The use of symbolic language, cosmic battles, end-time predictions, the combat between good and evil, and the emphasis on evil's hold over the present age are all the hallmarks of this literary genre," write T.J. Wray and Gregory Mobley in *The Birth of Satan: Tracing the Devil's Biblical Roots.* A whole host of extrabiblical texts were written in the centuries both before and after the advent of the Common Era, but it was the apocryphal Book of Enoch that would introduce into the Western lexicon an invaluable demonological narrative—that of the rebel angels' fall.

"The whole earth has been corrupted through the works that were taught by Azazel: to him ascribe all sin," writes the anonymous scribe of Enoch. Only considered canonical by Ethiopian Jews and Christians, and all but lost to European readers until the seventeenth century (when poet John Milton would read it), the Book of Enoch would still have a profound influence on mystical Judaism and early Christianity, for as Wray and Mabley note, it "would become foundational in the history of diabology," providing a compendium of demonic names, including such personages as Bezaliel, Kokabiel, and Gadreel. If earlier biblical literature was reticent to ascribe that much power to a being other than God, then the author of Enoch had no issues in identifying the universal dark principle in the fallen angel Azazel, who in later writings would be reconfigured as Lucifer. The author of the book is associated with the mysterious figure of the seventh generation mentioned in Genesis, he who "walked with God: and he was no more; for God took him," for Enochian literature promised to reveal certain celestial secrets from a human who'd been elevated to the level of archangel.

Written anywhere between three centuries before the Common Era to a century after, the Book of Enoch expands on passages from Genesis, embellishing certain cryptic asides into an extensive new narrative. Central to the story of how evil was introduced into the world was a subsection of Enoch with the cryptic title of "Book of the Watchers." In those passages the author elucidates the exact ways in which a group of angels came to earth in the antediluvian era, seduced human women, and sired a race of monstrous and gigantic beings known as the Nephilim (such an account is also in Genesis), while imparting to humanity certain teachings ranging from metallurgy to cosmetics, astronomy to divination.

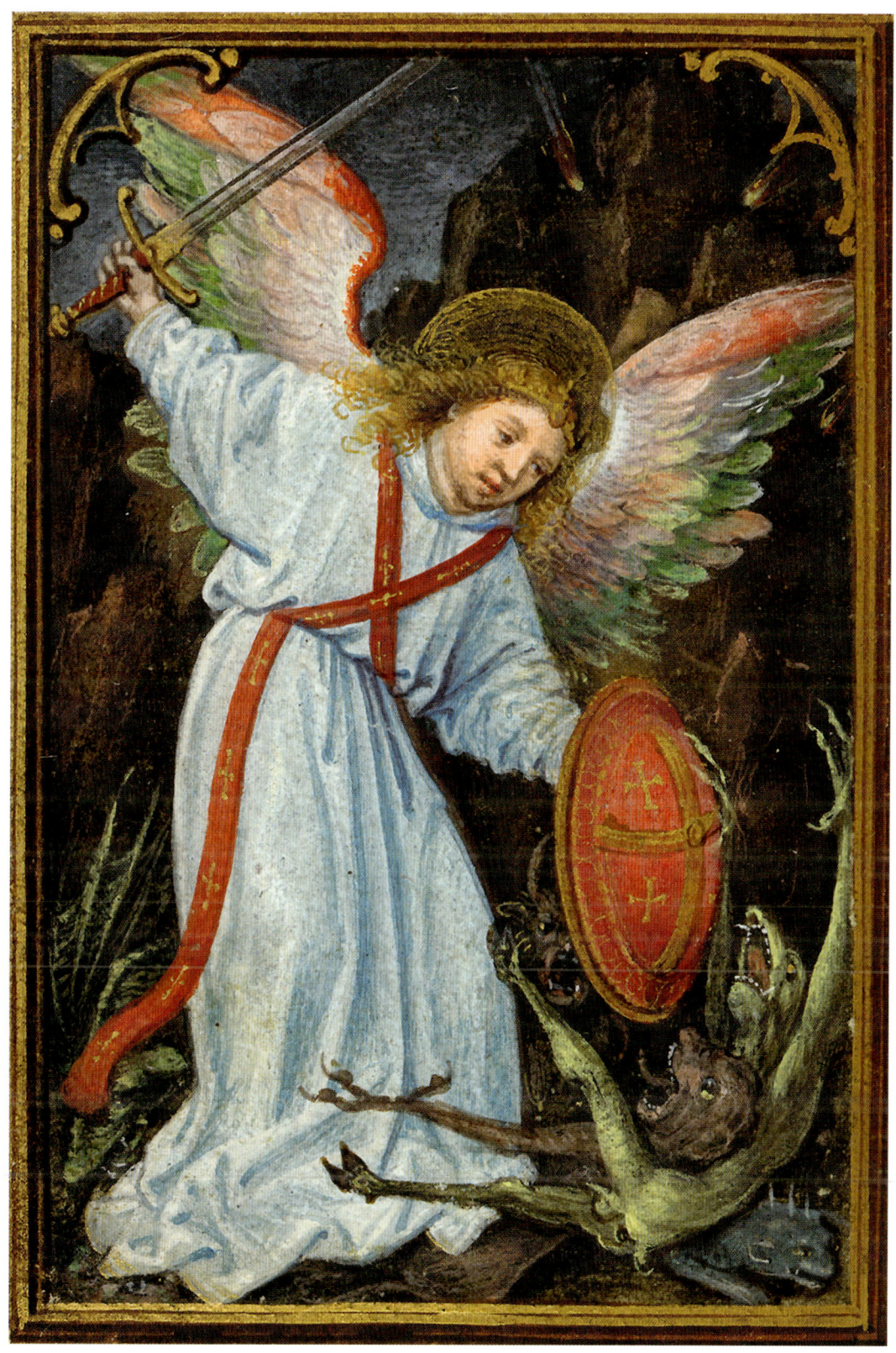

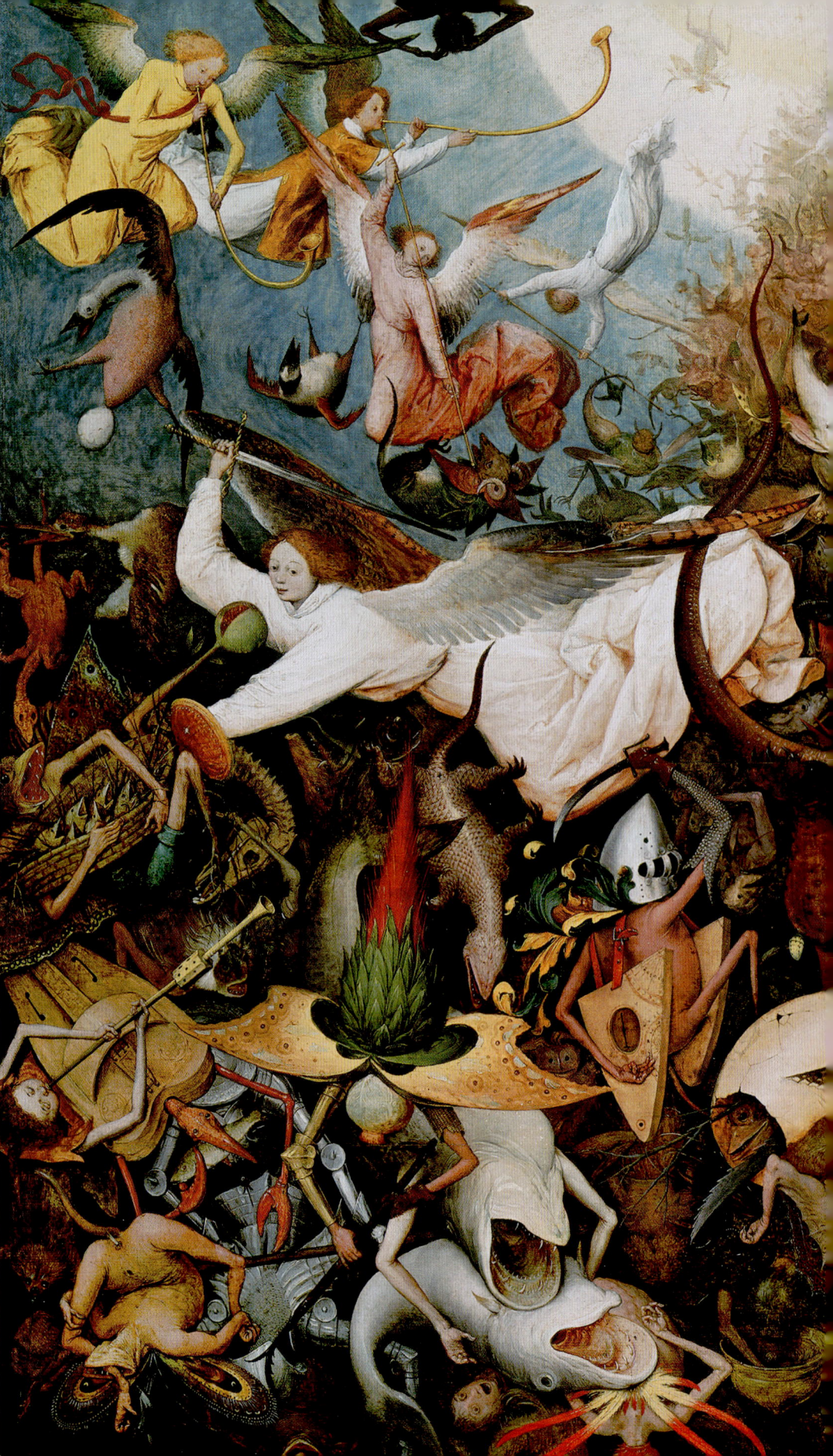

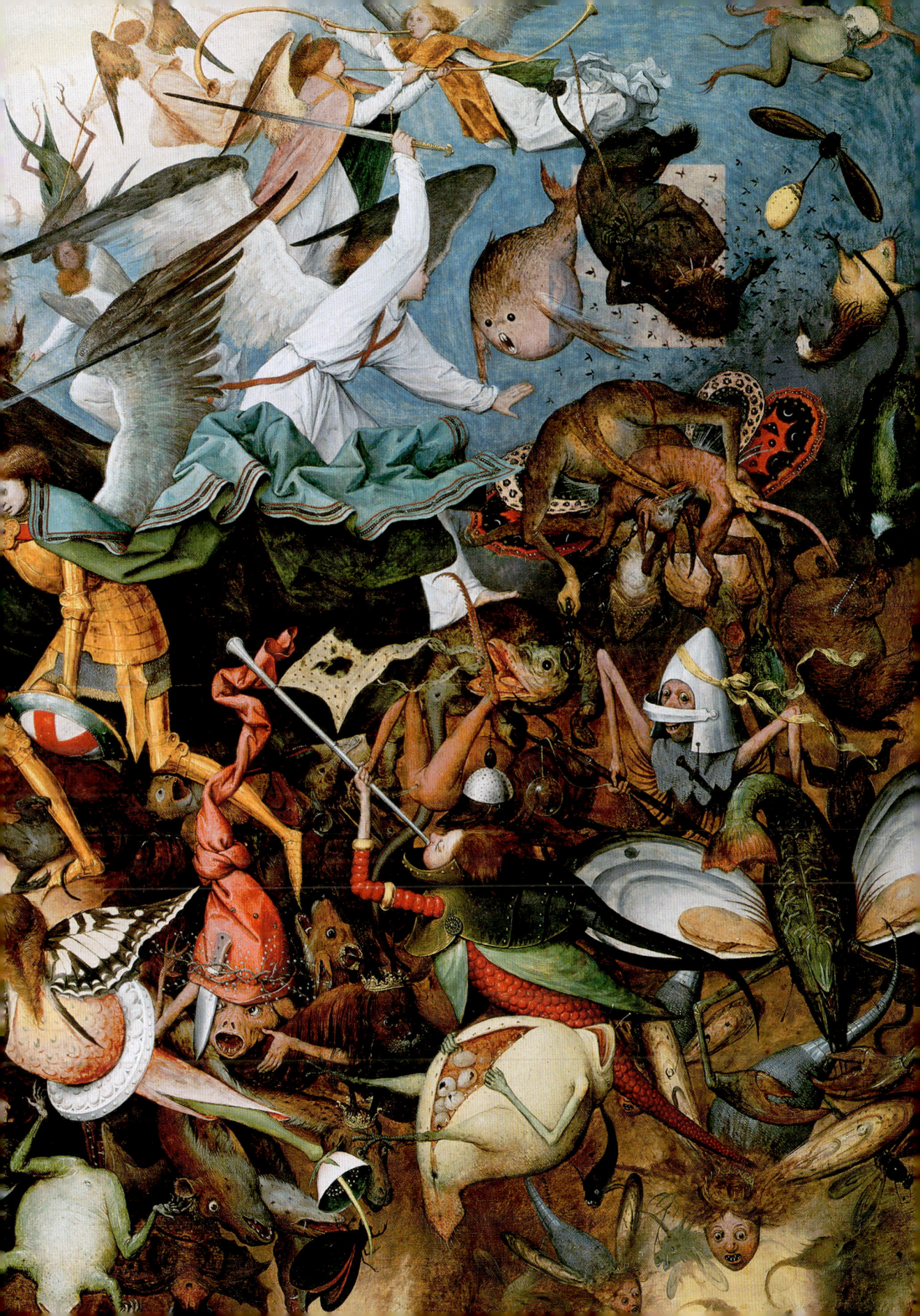

Chief among the leaders of the angels, or Watchers, were Azazel and Samyaza, both of whom are arguably models for Lucifer in the Book of Revelation. In the Book of Enoch, God would ultimately command the archangel Michael, the same being who in more canonical accounts is responsible for casting Lucifer out of heaven, to take Azazel, Samyaza, and the other Watchers and to "bind them fast for seventy generations in the valleys of the earth, till the day of their judgment and of their consummation, till the judgment that is for ever and ever is consummated. In those days they shall be led off to the abyss of fire."

The Book of Enoch bears some similarity to the far more famous Book of Revelation, most likely written a few centuries later, during the second century of the Common Era. Enoch notably places the Fall of the angels long after the events of Revelation; John of Patmos, the author of the more recent book, envisions the cosmic rebellion as having happened before the creation of earth, the expulsion of a third of the angels into hell acting as prelude for the serpent's temptation of Adam and Eve, and thus the ultimate fall of humanity. "And there was war in heaven," John of Patmos wrote. "Michael and his angels fought against the dragon; and the dragon fought and his angels, And prevailed not; neither was their place found any more in heaven. And the great dragon was cast out, that old serpent, called the Devil, and Satan, which deceiveth the whole world: he was cast out into the earth, and his angels were cast out with him."

From Revelation, and apocryphal precedents like Enoch, the Abrahamic traditions would gather an infernal vocabulary, a damned lexicon whereby evil could be discussed in personified forms. "The subject of cosmic war serves primarily to interpret human relationships—especially all-too-human conflict—in supernatural form," writes Elaine Pagels in *The Origin of Satan*. The demons became powerful metaphors for discussing a multitude of evils, but the nature of the fallen angels also provided an allegory, that if not literally factual, then is deeply true as regards the exigencies of human violence. Everything that marks our fractured world was settled during that epic war over heaven, a conflagration that happened before time even existed. Like a crack running down through reality itself, the insurrection of the rebel angels against God's sovereignty is supposed to explain the malignancy of our existence, the warped nature of our being. The fetid decomposition of a corpse left in the woods, maggots and mayflies crawling out of the sockets were once had been eyes—due to the Fall. The horror of starvation, drum-tight bellies stretched across jagged ribs, and the nightmare of pandemic, with corpses jumbled into anonymous mass graves—due to the Fall. The atrocity of war, limbs hacked off by machete and bullets to the head, women and children raped, bodies immolated in ovens—all due to the Fall.

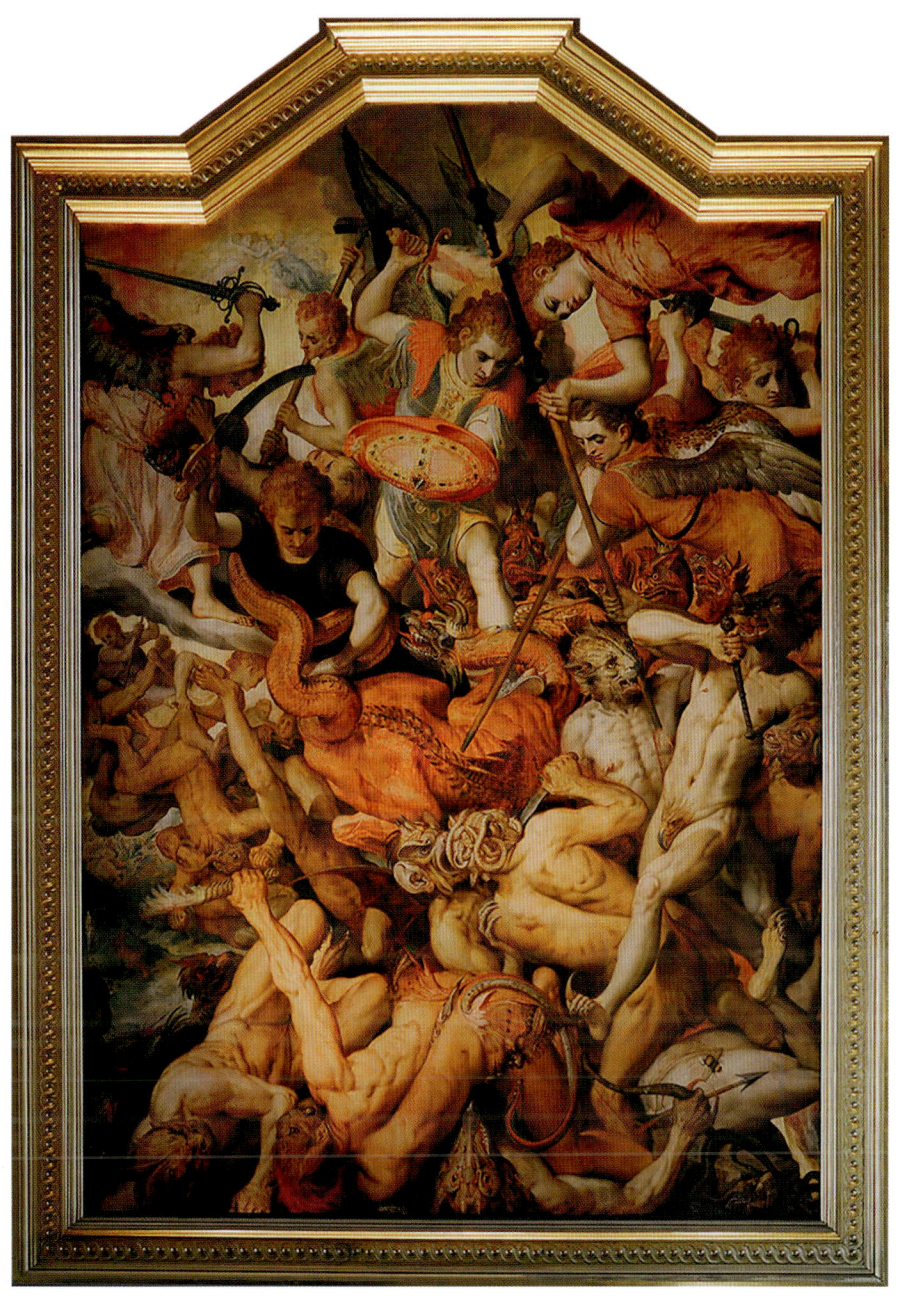

Sixteenth-century Flemish painter Frans Floris's central panel from his triptych The Fall of the Rebel Angels, *housed at the Royal Museum of Fine Art in Antwerp, Belgium, depicts a menagerie of canine, equine, feline, and caprine demons. This detail shows one pig-headed demon with a beautifully Apollonian physique, but with his penis replaced by the beak of a fearsome eagle. For all of the variability in their depiction, it is the monstrous otherness of demons that so often marks them out as debased and fallen.*

Before the temptation of the first couple in Eden, both scripture and apocrypha tell us that there was a greater battle in heaven, when the archangel Lucifer amassed a third of the angels against the Lord. They were, of course, cast out and into perdition, but the legacy of that event was disunion, disorder, discordance. As a result, life is marked by chaos, fracture, violence, irregularity, pain, conflict, famine, brutality, disease, suffering, death, and evil. Lucifer's compatriots had once been angels, but after their failed revolution their domain was a different kingdom. Deep within the bowls of the earth, in that realm of sulfur and bitumen, they'd now serve not as celestial beings, but rule as demons. The implications of this Fall, and the arguably more famous one inaugurated by Adam and Eve's temptation by the serpent, are argued about across religions and denomination, by theologians and sectarians. For some the temptation was a felix culpa, a "fortunate Fall" that allowed for human agency in our own affairs.

For others it was the ultimate metaphysical explanation for wickedness, cruelty, and death. Nor should it be said that story of the temptation in Eden is necessarily unique to Judaism and Christianity, or that only these religious traditions saw in the past a possibility of perfection squandered by the pride of imperfect and ultimately fallen beings. Classical paganism traditionally allowed for a past golden age, in which injustices were unknown, inequities were nonexistent, and pain, suffering, and illness weren't even imaginable. Nor was the idea of that divine conflict that finally made the temptation possible totally sui generis to Christianity. The war in heaven, as first explicated in the Book of Revelation, convincingly shares some thematic similarities to the battle between the gods and Titans in Greek myth, for example. Yet the cosmic definitiveness of Adam and Eve's temptation and fall from grace, as first alluded to in Judaism, and then elaborated on by Christianity (especially in the Latin West with St. Augustine's conception of original sin), elevated the mere squabbles among the pagan pantheon into an epic that supposedly marks reality down to every second and particle of existence.

The war in heaven shouldn't be understood as a prosaic hypothesis to explain the physical world, but as deeper poetry that sings (or shrieks) of that which is transcendent. Maxwell-Stuart writes that the "borderline between metaphorical and literal was easily blurred" so that a "kind of unease permeates this type of literature as the reader becomes increasingly aware, if only at a subliminal level, that neither a literal nor a metaphorical reading of the text is satisfactory, and that the words on the pages are like fingers grasping for sunlight." Books like Enoch and Revelation are not reporting, but prophecy; not theory, but liturgy; not testimony, but something deeper, elemental, and in a language that can't quite be translated for our lowly comprehension. Not fact, but truth. Heaven's war isn't exactly allegory either, though certainly there's an element of that. If you were to ask the early Church Fathers whether the events described in Revelation actually happened, they would be incredulous that such a basic question had been posed. But its veracity was less important than what the story meant, and that the Fall's implications, its perversions, its effect occur every day. The importance of the Fall was that it never ended, and rather, that it is a process, phenomenon, and principle not just some event. Less than history, or certainly science, the war in heaven should be understood as literature and theology, philosophy and psychology, because the Fall of the angels didn't happen—it's always happening.

THE AGE OF AZAZEL

T hough Jabal Munttar is only a little under ten miles outside of Jerusalem, its location deep within the arid and dusty heights of the unforgiving Judean desert give the mountain the appearance of being on an alien terrain. Nothing but the stubbiest of plants grow from the sands. Sunbaked and brown weeds tentatively push out through the reddish clay of the desert, piles of rock and stone are scattered across the earth, intermixed with the crumbled remains of Corinthian columns that once marked Roman temples and of toppled masonry from a Byzantine monastery. This is, in some ways, the original howling wilderness, an inchoate, unforgiving, chaotic, undifferentiated space of negation, a metaphor as much as a place. Stretching from the Negev where Satan once tempted Christ down to the saline pool of the Dead Sea, the extremity of the desert served as an inspiration for those who envisioned our most enduring language of eternal perdition.

The desert, Jeffrey Burton Russell explains in *Satan: The Early Christian Tradition*, "took on a dual meaning . . . a place of refuge from the temptations of society, but it was also a place where temptations came directly from the Devil." First Judaism and then Christianity were faiths that emerged from the scorching sands of the Judean desert, and it has indelibly marked their sense of both the sacred and the damned. Here, at Jabal Munttar, there is a representative entry into the role that demons have played in the imagination and fears of the ancients, for this was the location where the High Priest of Jerusalem's Temple was mandated by God to make a sacrifice on the Day of Atonement, not to the Lord (though by His command), but rather to placate the dangerous prince of this world who was known as Azazel.

We've already encountered this particular demon in his role as the leader of rebellion in the Book of Enoch, but as with his fellow fallen angels, with their variable and reoccurring names, he spectrally flits in and out of our vision like a shadow. Over the centuries demonologists have argued how many of the different names associated with individual demons—Ashmedai, Azazel, Belial, Beelzebub—refer to discrete beings, or rather to permeable manifestations of the ever mercurial chief adversary whose title is Satan. As appropriated from the pagan Canaanite faiths from whence Azazel's name is derived, the demon was very much his own person, a lieutenant in the infernal horde with an integral role in the balance of the cosmos. With the exception of the incantation bowls, demons are rarely depicted in either Jewish or Christian sources before the fifth century, but the iconography of Azazel has often associated him with the creature whose death is given as an offering. When Azazel is depicted, it is with the horns and beard of the goat, that beast that whether because of its association with the Yom Kippur ritual, or because of its undeniably unnatural and uncanny appearance, is frequently represented with an almost archetypally demonic pallor.

Azazel's Hebrew name betrays the residual element of polytheism that marks both Judaism and Christianity, for its suffix -el is also a Semitic word that's most often translated as "Lord," and evidence that the demon, alongside other demons like Bael and Samael, as well as archangels such as Michael and Gabriel, is most accurately viewed as a sort of "son" of God, if not originally a god himself. The Canaanites worshiped a mountain deity whose name was El, the plural of which is Elohim, to which Alexander Waugh has written in *God* has "caused no end of embarrassment in Jewish and Christian circles since it occurs over 1500 times in the first 15 books of the Bible . . . in which only *one* god is *supposed* to exist." Both the singular and plural would come to be conflated with another Middle Eastern deity called Yahweh, both of whom would become interchangeable with the supposed one true God, but for those who lived in what would be ancient Judea, the name El is "omnipresent throughout the history of most Middle Eastern religions; it is Babylonian, Phoenician, Aramaic, Canaanite, Arabic, and Hebrew," as Waugh writes.

Rabbis and the Church Fathers dealt with the grammatical embarrassment of that scandalous plural by maintaining that the word didn't imply what it would seem to: as a solution the Jews argued that "Elohim" signified the singular God's multifaceted splendor, the Christians claimed that it was an indication of the Holy Trinity. More likely, it would seem to be a trace of that pagan past when the supreme god El did have many children, including beings that would come to be regarded as archangels like Michael, and that fallen lot which includes Azazel. That still intimate connection between God and His demon can be seen in the unusual sacrifice offered by the High Priest at Jabal Munttar, when every Yom Kippur a "kid goat is to be offered to Azazel, who is, if not the Devil himself, is at least one of his lieutenants. That kid, the now-familiar scapegoat, is to be caste, alive, off a cliff," as Messadie writes.

This ritual was one in which the high priest, descendant of Aaron, the brother of Moses, would offer a kid to the Lord and a second goat to Azazel while in the desert outside of Jerusalem, onto which the sins of the people had been transposed, as signified by two pieces of red cloth affixed to the horns of the unfortunate animal. Such a strange act of piety shouldn't be misinterpreted, for it was neither genuflection nor worship offered to Azazel, so much as the demand from the God who was worshiped that the darker forces that help maintain our universe must also be acknowledged. For humanity owed a debt to Azazel, and God made sure that his son was able to collect what was his.

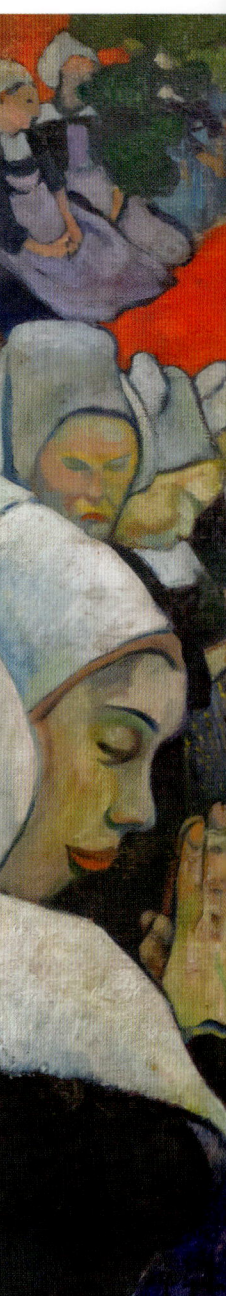

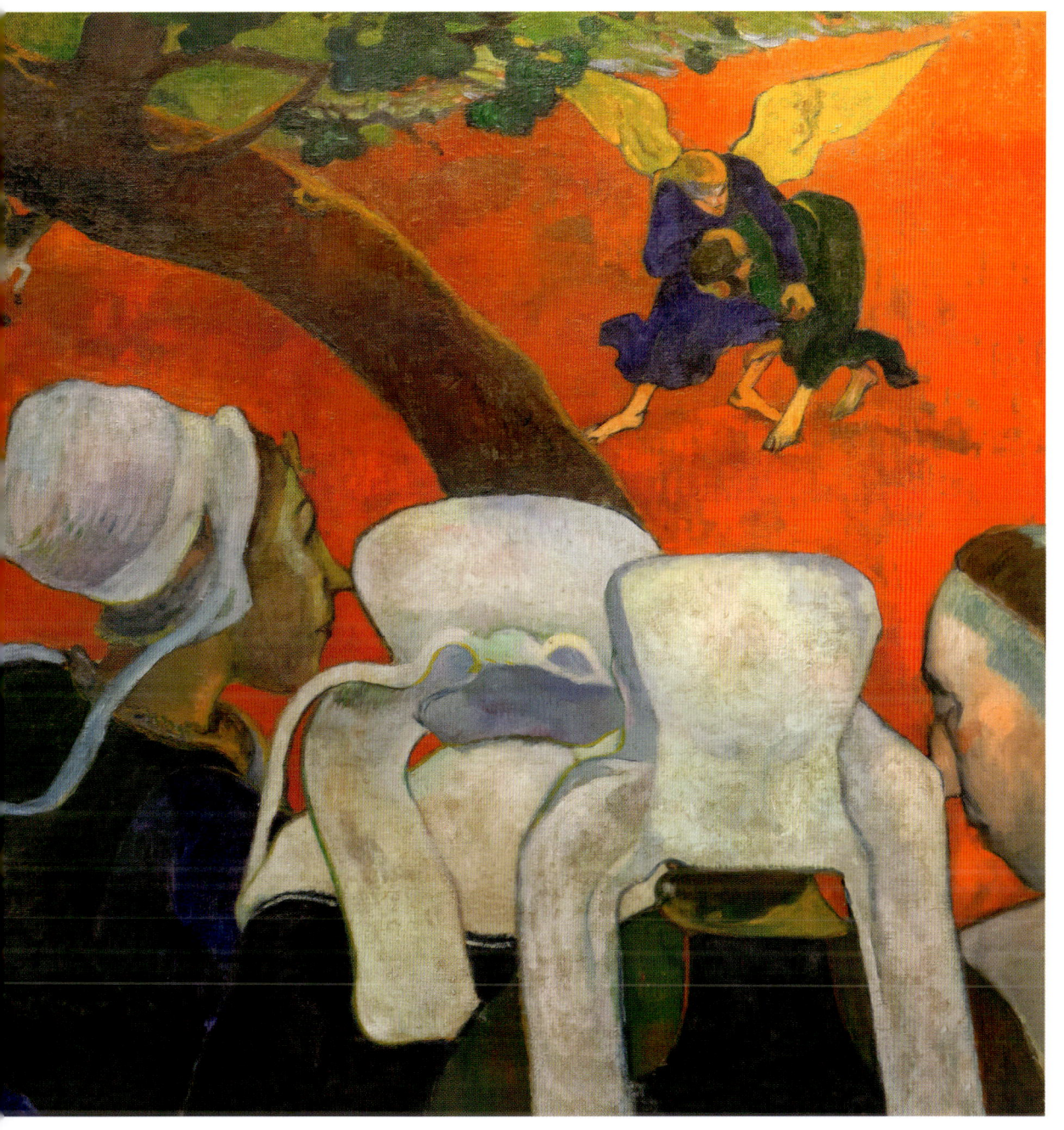

Nineteenth-century French impressionist painter Paul Gauguin's Vision after the Sermon, *held at the Scottish National Museum in Edinburgh, presents a group of contemporary peasant women in an ecstatic reverie watching the moment in Genesis when the patriarch Jacob wrestles with a mysterious angel throughout the night. While the identity of the angel is often interpreted to be God, a countertradition also identifies the being with Azazel.*

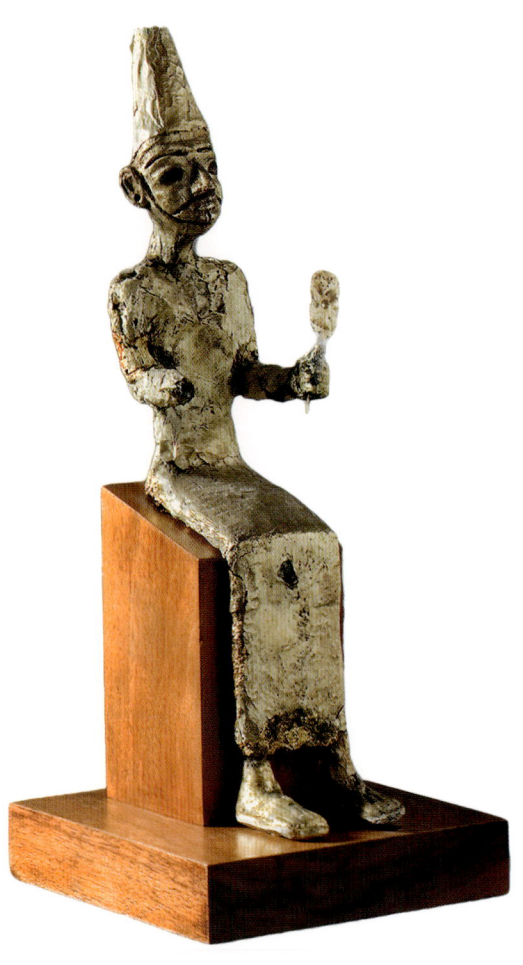

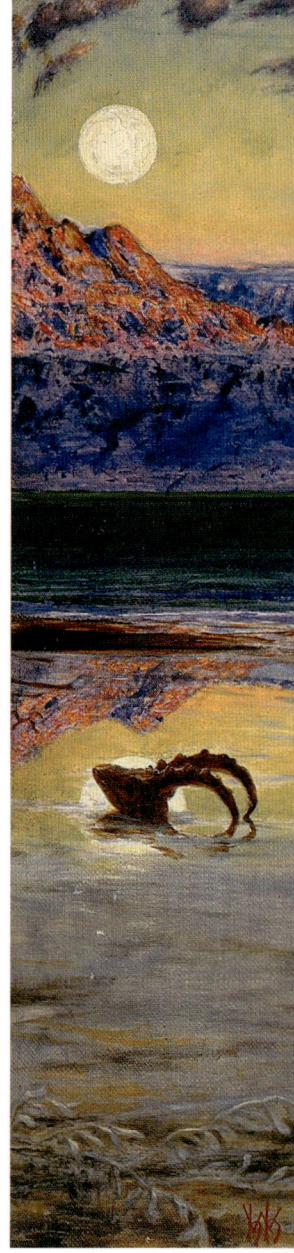

ABOVE

This small votive figurine housed at the University of Chicago's Oriental Institute, discovered at Megiddo in Israel (a city associated with the biblical war of Armageddon in Revelation), depicts the ancient Canaanite deity El. A mountain deity, El would later be conflated with Yahweh, the two merged together and becoming the one true God of ancient Judaism and Christianity. Often translated as "Lord," El's progeny are seen in the multitude of both angels and demons whose names contain his, from Raphael, Gabriel, and Michael, to Azazel.

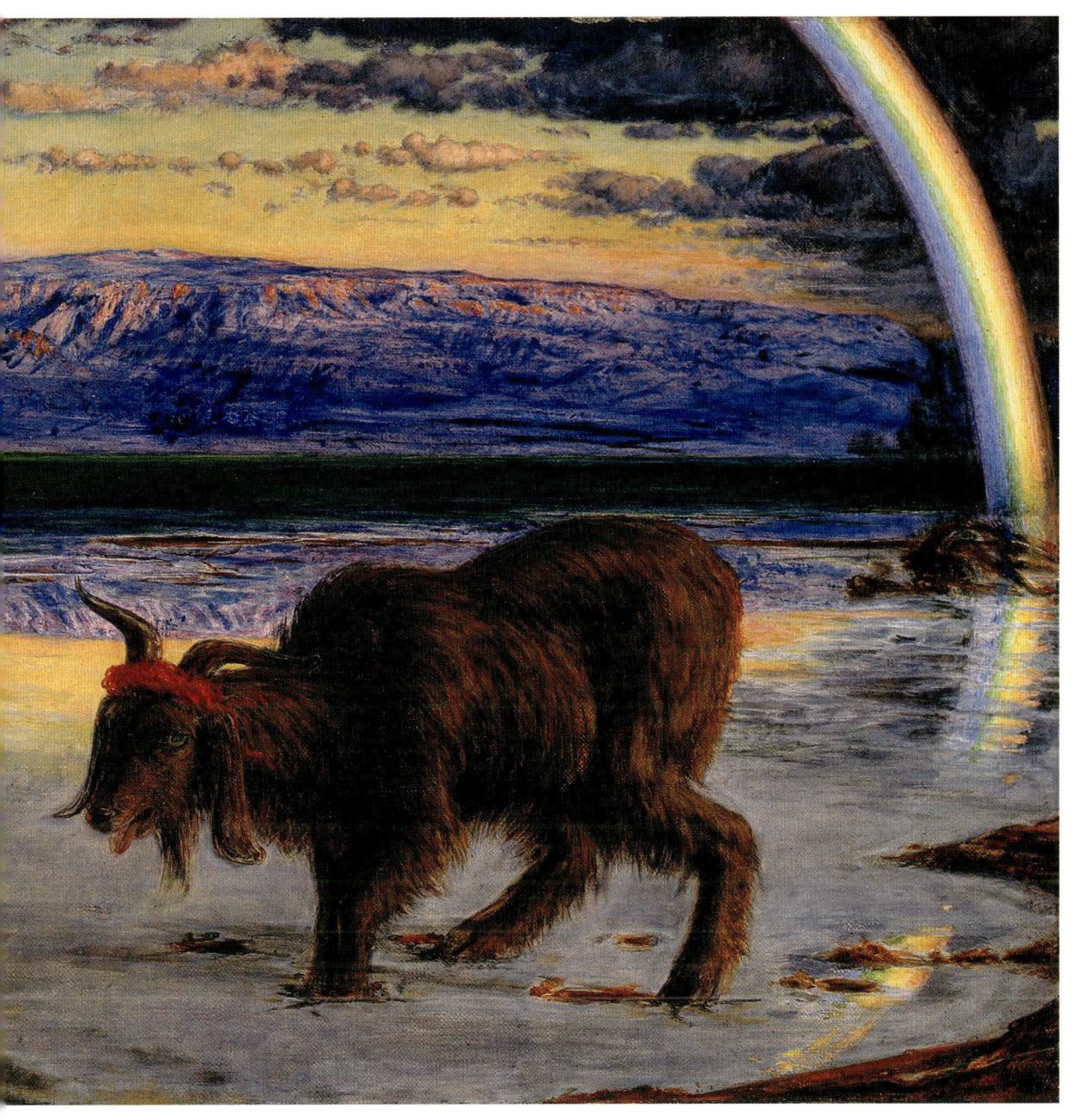

ABOVE
Nineteenth-century English artist William Holman Hunt depicts the unfortunate sacrifice in his hallucinogenic painting The Scapegoat, *housed at the Manchester Gallery of Art.*

The biblical Book of Leviticus details how all of the members of the priestly line, descendants of Aaron who are to perform the sacred rituals of the Temple, are to cast lots for the selection of two young goats to be sacrificed on Yom Kippur. One is reserved for the Lord, but the other is to be taken to Jabal Munttar, where the scribe says that the priest "shall lay both his hands on the head of the live goat, and confess over it all the iniquities of the people of Israel, and all their transgressions, all their sins, putting them on the head of the goat, and sending it away into the wilderness . . . The goat shall bear on itself all their iniquities to a barren region," for there shall Azazel claim his bounty. Such a practice, what the twentieth-century French philosopher René Girard called the "scapegoat mechanism," of transposing sin onto an innocent creature whose blood sacrifice secures an undeserved redemption, is enduring and widespread across religions.

A variation of it is the central precept of Christianity, whereby the scapegoat offered to Azazel is replaced by Jesus Christ, whose life was given as a ransom payment to Satan. Not the only theological theory of atonement in Christianity, the ransom theory, as with the earlier Yom Kippur ritual of the scapegoat, has disturbing implications that in contemporary, secular, bourgeois faith are often repressed. God's demand of a sacrifice to Azazel shows the inextricably close connections between the divine and demons; It is a statement of how the sacred and the profane are often equivalent, and how an experience of the diaboli-cal remains an experience of the numinous. Girard argued that the scapegoat mechanism, the presentation of an innocent life as sacrifice for a community's iniquity, marks civilization itself. "Scapegoat effects," writes Girard in his classic study *Violence and the Sacred*, "are more deeply rooted in the human condition than we are willing to admit."

Girard judged not the scapegoat mechanism; he saw it as a necessary aspect of containing the power of violence that always seethes just beneath the respect-able surface of a society, where the blood sacrifice acts as both a valve on the volatility of humans, and as a means of acquiring an atonement that none of us actually deserves. In antiquity the necessary scandal of the scapegoat was more obvious, the sense that the Devil must be given his due was clearer. As much as Satan and all of his compatriots were a way to square the existence of evil with that of an omnibenevolent Creator, there still existed a deep piety that under-stood God and the Devil to be connected in their transcendence, connected in a manner that mere humans with their unbridgeable distance from things eter-nal never could be.

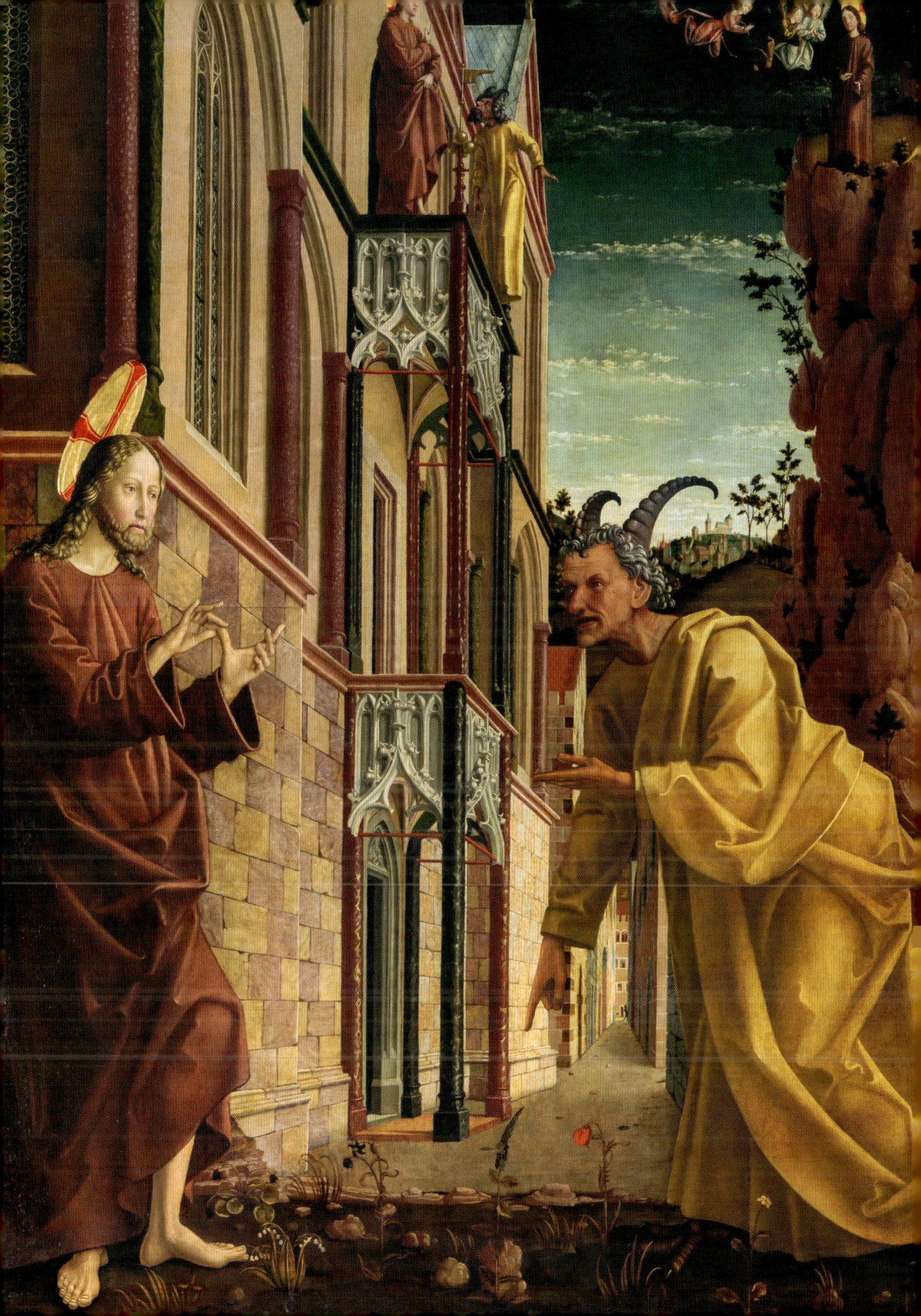

Azazel is a monster of the desert. He stalks the Judean wilderness, but he also stalks the void in our experience, the desert of what it means to be a compromised and fallen human. What the scapegoat ritual confesses is that we must acknowledge that darkness within all of us lest we be consumed by it; God's command to offer sacrifice to Azazel is precisely a reminder that true reverence must be genuflected before the total complexity of what it means to be alive. The Devil, you see, is owed his due. One interpretation of the biblical Book of Job, the greatest consideration of theodicy ever written, which was penned sometime after the exile in Babylon, was that it dramatizes the effects of not offering Azazel that full measure of devotion that the demon is owed.

It was that book that first referred to *Ha-Shaitan*, "the Adversary" in Hebrew, with the singular article—the Satan. This being, who answers God that he has been "roving about in the earth and . . . walking about in it," as part of a wager convinces God that he must torture the righteous Job so as to extract a condemnation of the Lord. "Have you not put a hedge around him and his household and everything he has?" asks Satan. "You have blessed the work of his hands, so that his flocks and herds are spread throughout the land. But now stretch out your hand and strike everything he has, and he will surely curse you to your face." The conventional interpretation is that Satan's test of Job's will is a commentary on the purity of true worship, of trusting in the Lord even as fortunes fall. A different interpretation could have it that Job actually deserved to be punished, because in his piety he'd refused to acknowledge those dark things of the earth, and that in allowing for the man's torture, God was merely giving to Azazel that which he deserved. Far from being a lesson about the capriciousness of the Lord, Job's example proves that it's possible to be too good.

Respect and deference offered to a fallen angel like Azazel was a precise acknowledgement that he once had been of heaven, perfect in a manner that mere humans never could be. It was also a tacit admission that in a universe controlled by the singular king of heaven, evil must find its ultimate origin in God. Pagels writes that "this greatest and most dangerous enemy did not originate, as one might expect, as an outsider, an alien, or a stranger. Satan is not the distant enemy but the intimate enemy—one's trusted colleague, close associate, brother," true both in heaven and on earth. If antiquity was the age of Azazel, it was in this strange respect that understood God and the Devil to be much closer to each other than either is to us, that the drama of redemption takes place far from the machinations of mere men and that a sacrifice offered to Satan is as good as one offered to the Lord. There is a wisdom in understanding that this world belongs to the demons, and conducting yourself accordingly.

DEMONS IN SCRIPTURE
AND APOCRYPHA

Simultaneously ineffable and strikingly physical, demons fall between the realms of the sacred and the profane. They're indescribable in the depths of their evil and their metaphysical significance, but estimably visceral in how we imagine them to appear. Unlike God, a similarly distant eternal being, there is a commonly agreed upon understanding of what demons look like. Demonic fallenness lends itself to a consensus on their appearance that in contemporary culture isn't necessarily extended to the Lord, for whom any description would seem to fall short. In some ways this is an inversion of matters in scripture, where angels like the seraphim and cherubim are graphically (and terrifyingly) described, whereas concerning demons, a reticence of detail can only underscore how disturbingly alien they are.

Literary scholar Timothy K. Beal argues in his study *Religion and Its Monsters* that "Monsters are in the world but not of the world. They are paradoxical personifications of *otherness within sameness*." When it comes to the demonic mode, the operative sentiment is one of sublimity. As a result, there are few visual depictions of demons proper before the fifth century, with the exceptions of pagan gods who were later recategorized by early Christians as actually being fallen angels. Biblical and apocryphal literature fills some of this void, with books like Revelation psychedelically describing the presence of things hellish, yet the Hebrew scriptures tend to contain a deficit of adjectives as concerns demons. Consider Satan's first appearance in the Book of Job, wherein the reader is giving no details on what he looks like, making him all the more terrifying.

Still, demonic imagery has a certain consistency to it, as it grows out of Near Eastern mythologies. Demons are configured as bestial and animalistic, otherworldly and uncanny, chimerical and mercurial. A visual language often accompanies our imaginings of demons; they are associated with animals like goats, bats, cats, dogs, reptiles, and insects, often monstrously recombining the attributes of several different creatures. The mixture of the human and the animal only serves to underscore their sheer alterity and their liminal status between the transcendent and material worlds. Of course it has to be emphasized that part of this iconography comes from the appropriation and subversion of various pagan gods that Jews and Christians would incorporate into their demonology, so that the majority of entries in a reference such as the exhaustive *Dictionary of Deities and Demons in the Bible* are drawn from the polytheistic faiths that the authors of the Bible were familiar with, figures drawn from Babylon, Assyria, Canaan, Egypt, and so on.

Beal explains that the Bible stitched "together a new monster from old skins … for a new cosmic, political, [and] always theological crisis," that crisis namely being the engagement of monotheism with an often belligerent wider culture, so that figures from Asherah to Ziminiar find their place in both canonical scripture and apocryphal writing not as gods but as demons. Because so many of these gods are bestial themselves—think of Moloch's bull head or of Anubis's jackal face—demons themselves are necessarily animalistic. Furthermore, the beasts that are associated with demons are animals of a particular class; the predatory, the pestilent, the parasitic. They are associated with the animals that threaten us, that endanger us. Their appearance, even if unspoken in scripture, but rather mediated through folklore and tradition, draws from pagan antecedents, but also speaks to deeper, universal, archetypal fears. Within scriptural writing, hobbled together from a diversity of conflicting traditions and accounts, a cavalcade of demons haunts us, reference and allusion to them within the pages of the canon evidencing the ways in which they flit about as strange vagrants of the sacred order.

The demon Lilith finds her origins in Mesopotamian mythology that placed such succubae as inhabitants of the realm of the dead. Alluded to in the biblical book of Isaiah as a "lamia" (a type of cannibalistic creature from Greek folklore), Lilith is most fully explored in rabbinical literature such as the Talmud and the apocryphal Alphabet of Ben Sira. *In those accounts, Lilith is configured as the first wife of Adam, partially as a way to reconcile chronological contradictions in the Book of Genesis. According to these narrative, Lilith refused to submit to her husband through prescribed missionary intercourse, and so she was transformed into a night demon (the King James Bible translates this as a "screech owl"). Traditionally understood as preying on the newly born, the beautiful woman with bestial bird feet shows the ways in which sexuality and the demonic have been conflated for centuries. This bas relief housed at the British Museum and believed to have been crafted somewhere in Iraq during the second millennium before the Common Era gives a sense of Lilith's fusion of eroticism and horror.*

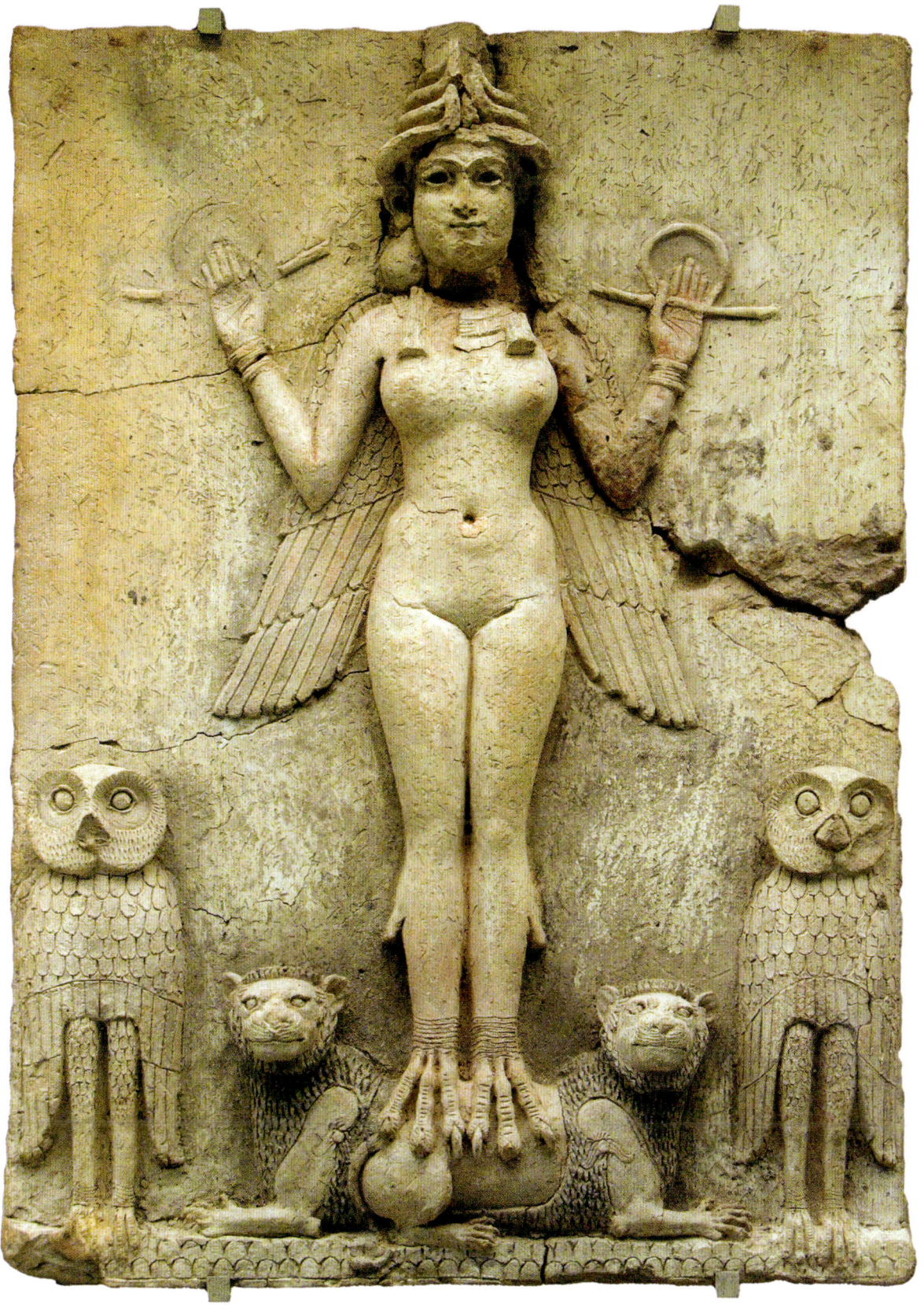

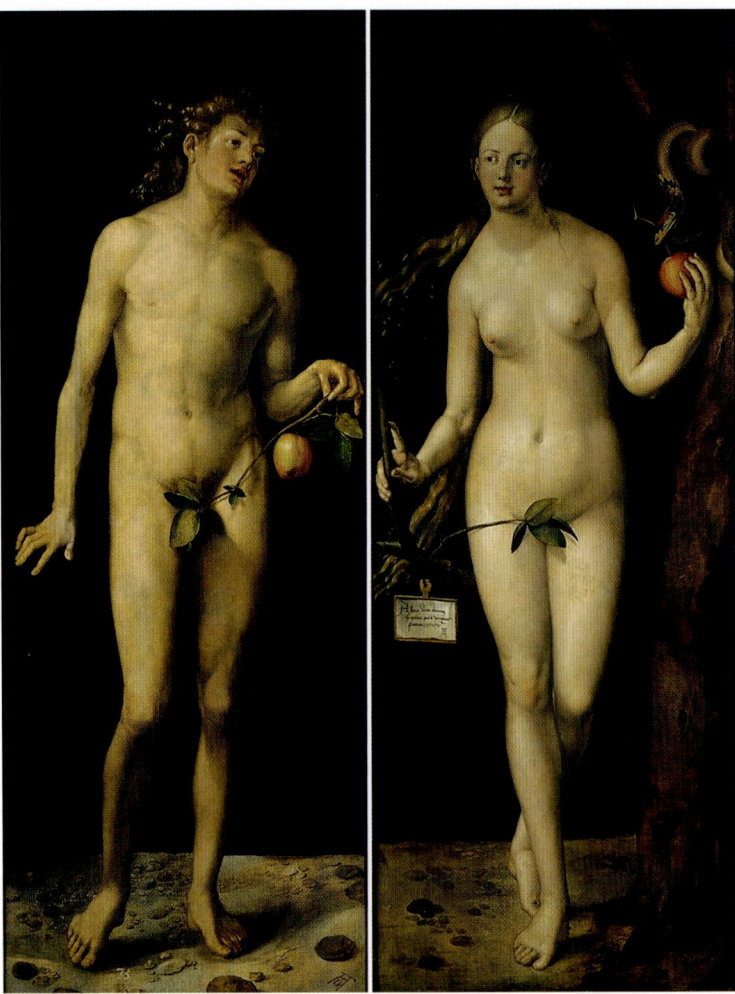

Few figures in the Hebrew scriptures are as enigmatic as Genesis's serpent. The slithering, serpentine creature convinces the first couple to eat from the Tree of Knowledge of Good and Evil, condemning humanity to our miserable fallen state. Yet for all of the associations that the serpent has with Satan, the text itself never says as much. A perennially popular subject for artists (in part because it afforded the opportunity to paint the female nude), the sixteenth-century German painter and engraver Albrecht Dürer's Adam and Eve, *housed in the Prado Museum in Madrid, Spain, frames his subjects in an eternal and undifferentiated darkness, relegating the responsible snake to a corner of his canvas, the focus clearly on the humans.*

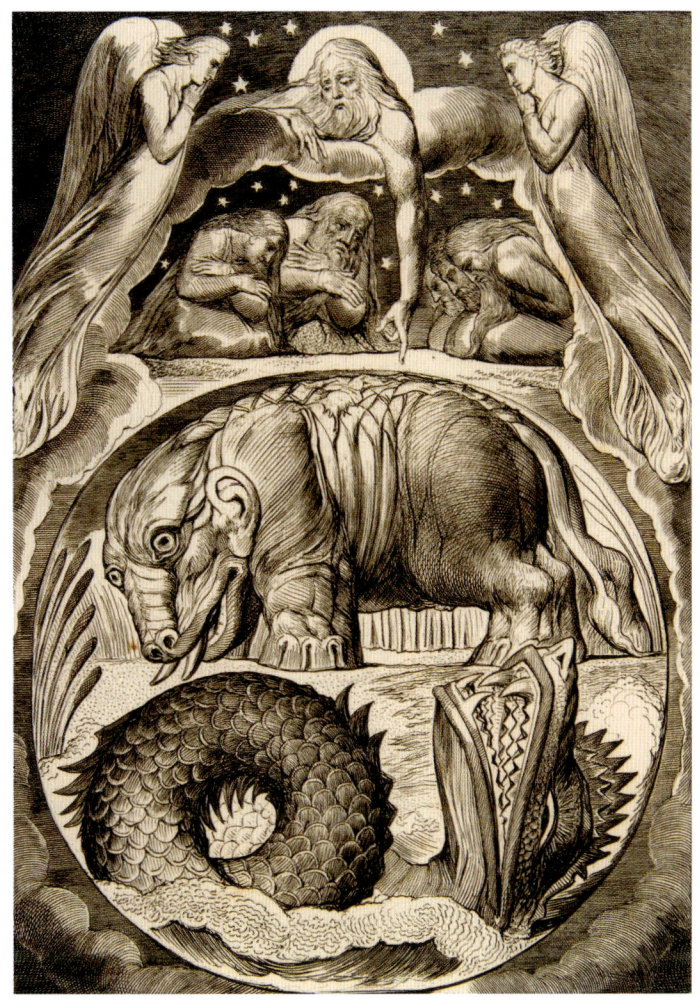

ABOVE

Both Leviathan and Behemoth, the mysterious, monstrous, and massive crea-
tures mentioned in Job, Isaiah, and the Psalms, are not demons proper, but
they are reveal traces of the strange pagan milieu in which monotheism devel-
oped. With shades of the chaos gods from which creation emerges according
to several different mythological systems, the hulking Behemoth and the sea
serpent Leviathan indicate both God's power and the multiplicities of creation.
"Behold, Behemoth, which I made as I made you," says God from the whirlwind
in Job, answering the sufferings of His servant with a display of cosmic magnifi-
cence. Effectively God's companions, or his pets, Leviathan and Behemoth, are,
like the demons, essentially value-neutral. Expressions of sublimity as much as
anything else. Asma writes that these "giant beasts of earth and water . . . serve
as evidence of God's power and strength; they act as living billboards for God's
sublime creativity and awe-inspiring authority." In the eighteenth-century poet
and lithographer William Blake's imagination, Leviathan is presented as a
reptilian sea creature, while Behemoth evokes an elephant or a rhinoceros—
bestial creatures reflecting the awesomeness of God.

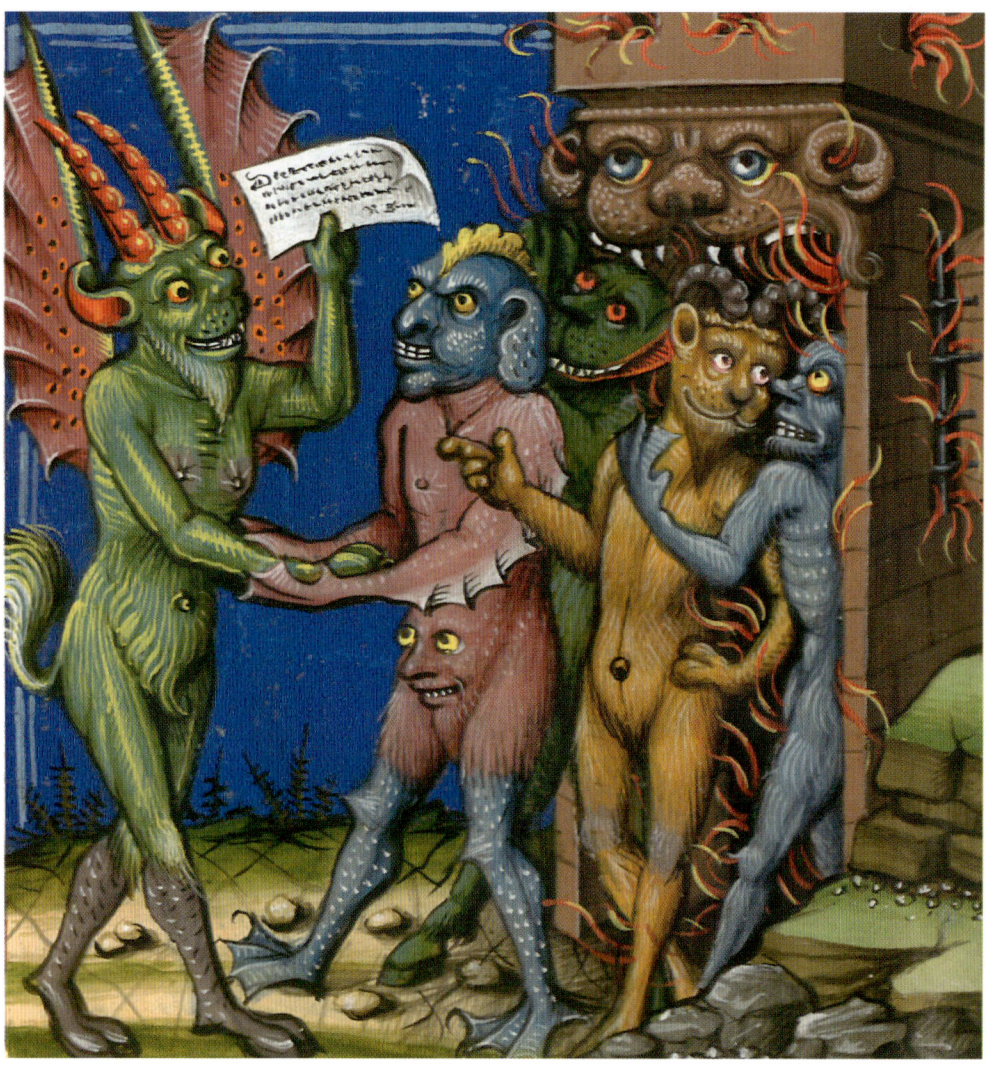

ABOVE

Some twenty-seven times the demon Belial, a mysterious figure whose name translates variously to "worthless" or "yokeless," is mentioned in the Bible. This wasn't a commentary on Belial's self-esteem so much as it was on his ability to negate all meaning; he was a creature whose purpose was to drain creation itself of purpose. In the apocryphal War of the Sons of Light against the Sons of Darkness *found in Qumran among the other Dead Sea Scrolls, it is written that Belial was created "for the pit, angel of enmity; in darkness in his domain, his counsel is to bring about wickedness and guilt. All the spirits of his lot are angels of destruction, they walk in the laws of darkness; toward it goes their only desire." This fifteenth-century illustration of Belial (on the far left) is from an edition of the fourteenth-century Italian canon lawyer Jacobus de Teramo's* Consolatio peccatorum, seu Processus Luciferi contra Jesum Christum. *In that work Lucifer sues Jesus Christ for the latter's harrowing of hell, and Belial acts as the Devil's attorney.*

THE GREAT GOD PAN IS DEAD

In the center of that universal city of Rome sits a great temple to all the gods, a building commissioned by the Emperor Trajan and then constructed by the Emperor Hadrian—the perfectly proportioned domed, porticoed, and columned Pantheon. Long regarded by architectural historians as an almost perfect building, this triumph of classical design is renowned for its massive dome topped by an oculus, its intricately patterned marble floors, and the engineering marvel of the concrete that held the structure in place. Built in the second century, the Pantheon was dedicated to the deities of the Roman pantheon—stately (if jealous) Jupiter and stormy Neptune, wise Athena and beautiful Apollo. The senator Cassius Dio noted in his *Roman History* that the Pantheon "received among the images which decorated it the statues of many gods, including Mars and Venus," though he hypothesizes that the name is just as apt simply "because of its vaulted roof" that makes it "resemble the heavens."

If it stood for four centuries in honor of the pagan gods, by the seventh century it was dedicated to the worship of just one—the incarnate Son of God who'd been executed by the Romans themselves. Antiquity's eclipse is in many ways the story of Europe's depaganization, as the multitude of polytheistic sects that practiced from Sicily to the Hebrides, Gibraltar to the Black Sea, were replaced by Christianity. Temples dedicated to the old gods were often rapidly transformed into churches, while aspects of those faiths were sometimes appropriated by the proselytes of the new religion, eager to make converts. There was, of course, the additional question of how to interpret all of those old gods, to which the keenest minds of the early Church had an ingenious solution—those deities were indeed real, but were simply demons deceiving credulous people into worshiping them.

The second-century Christian convert Justin Martyr writes in his *First Apology* that he once "worshiped Dionysus the son of Semele, and Apollo the son of Leto, who in their passion for human beings did things which it is shameful even to mention; who worshiped Persephone and Aphrodite . . . or Asklepius, or some other of those who are called gods." Martyr looked back with shame on his genuflection before these "spiritual forces of evil in heavenly places," explaining that when it comes to the pantheon he now "despises them, even at the cost of death . . . We pity those who believe such things, for which know that the demons are responsible." Suddenly the old gods of Greece and Rome were the demons of Christianity, and not just in the Mediterranean. As the Gospel message spread throughout the known world, the gods of the Near East and Central Asia, of the Norse and the Celts, were similarly recategorized as demons rather than deities. Maxwell-Stuart explains that there was a "common tendency of early Christians to identify the numerous pantheons of deities worshiped by their pagan ancestors and contemporaries as no more than demons posing as gods and goddesses," so Saint Clement could remark in his exhortation to the Greeks called *Protrepticus* that "the gods of all the nations are images of demons."

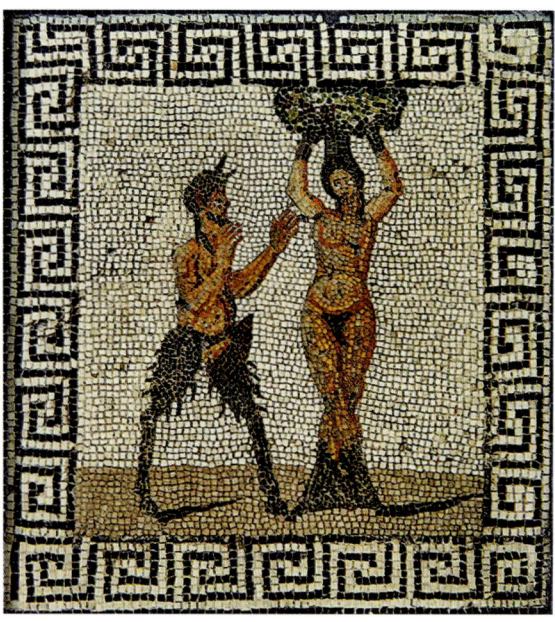

There are enough other antecedents that it seems unlikely that Pan's physiognomy alone supplied the template for Western demons, and yet the virile, lusty, chthonic Greek satyr has enough of the Satanic in him that it seems impossible he didn't remind Christians of the Devil. Arguably an example of the trickster archetype, the demigod Pan was associated with sexuality and nature, and it's in that fallen realm that the Church Fathers saw reflections of the fallen angels. The Roman historian Plutarch records that during the reign of Tiberius, the sea echoed with the declaration "The great god Pan is dead"; an announcement that later Christian apologists saw as a declaration of Christ's birth and the eclipse of everything pagan and demonic. This tile mosaic from Roman Pompei, now housed in the National Archeological Museum of Naples, Italy, shows a horned, goat-legged satyr with a prodigious erection approaching a nymph.

Squat, ugly, snub-nosed Bes is an uncharacteristic Egyptian god, having none of the literally animalistic qualities with which we associate the rest of their pantheon. Yet like Pan, he may have had an outsized influence on the visual vocabulary of demonology. Among his worshipers, the deity was a representative of the good who was invoked by believers for protection, but as with other pagan gods he was reduced to the demonic by Christian interpreters. In part, it was precisely Bes's connection to sexuality that (as with Pan) justified his designation as a demon. This amulet was made several centuries before the Common Era, and is now housed in the Louvre.

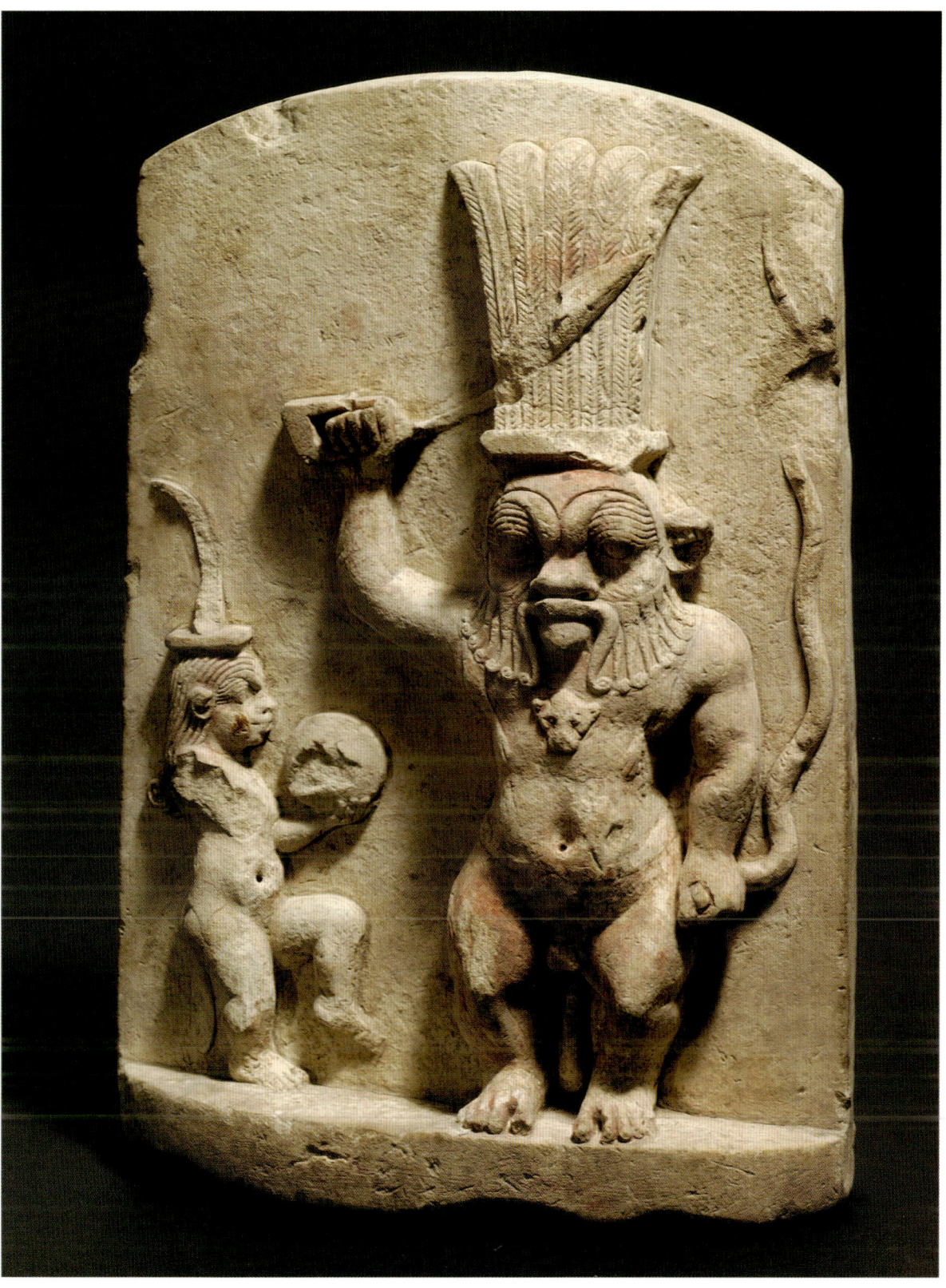

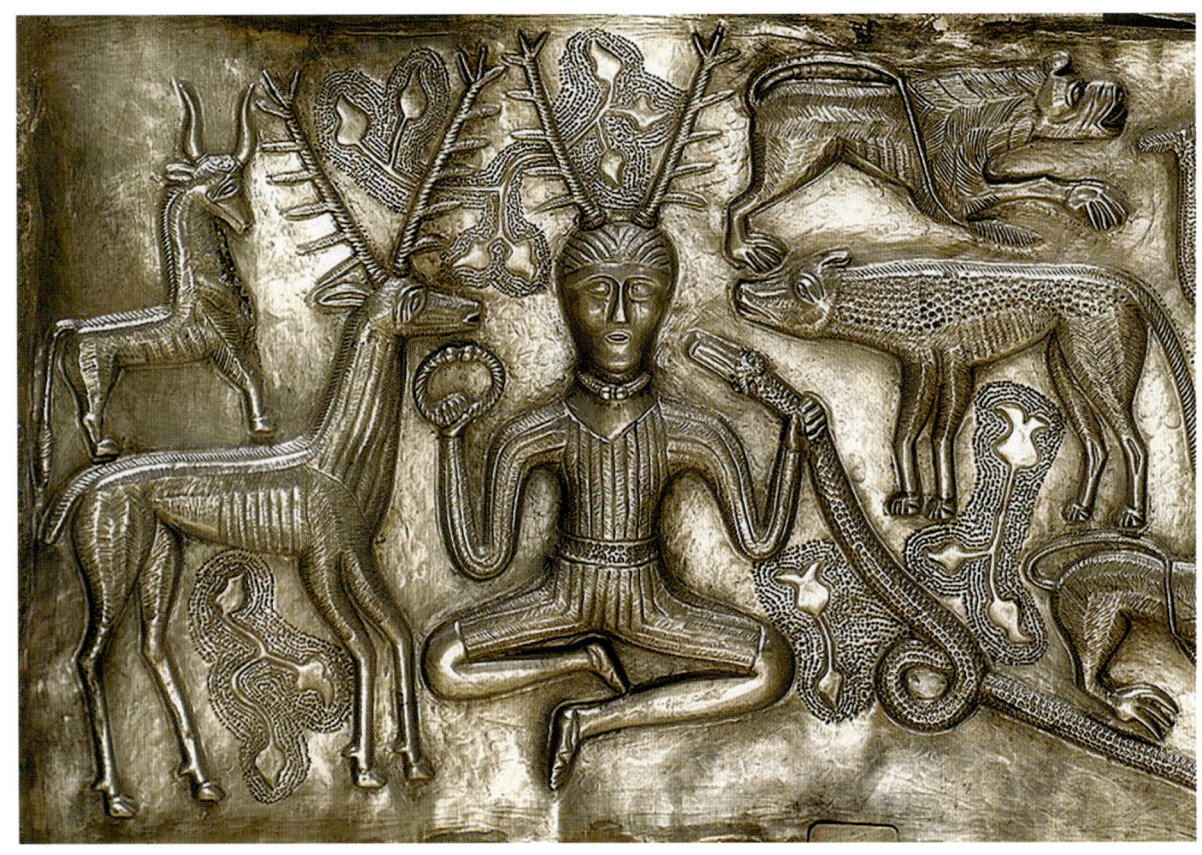

Cernunnos figures, antlered shamanistic priests, are common in the art of Celtic-speaking antiquity. They are found throughout Gaulish Europe, such as this example rendered on the Gundestrup Cauldron and displayed at the National Museum of Denmark. The significance of this image, of which there are around fifty examples dating from the earliest years of the Common Era, remain obscure; yet for those who hold to Margaret Murray's hypothesis concerning the "horned god," Cernunnos is regarded as the template for the archaic European pan-deity who was latter interpreted by the Christians as a demon, using that as pretext to persecute his worshipers who were subsequently labeled as witches.

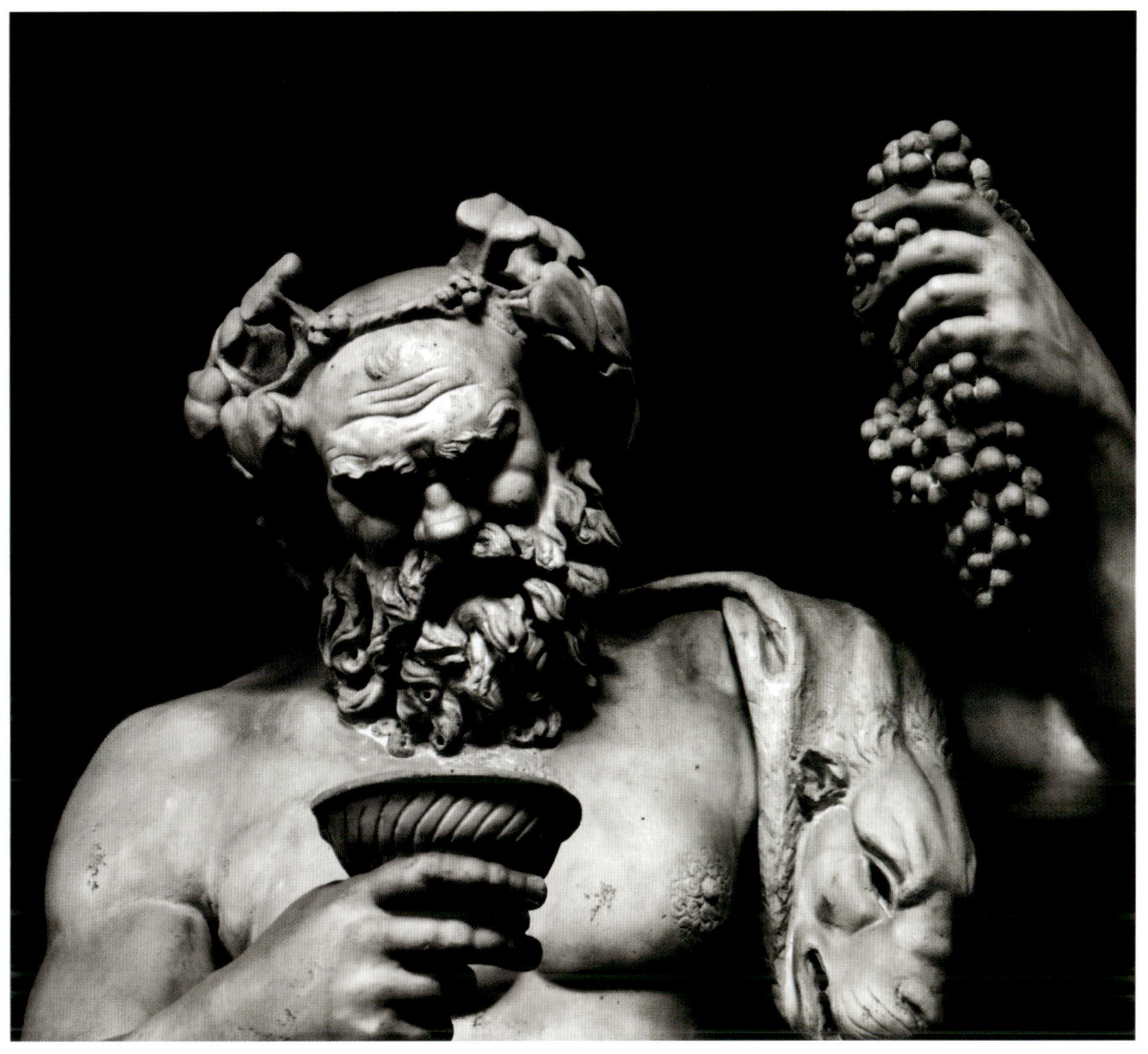

CONVERSION OF THE DEMONS

Upon the basalt steps at the south transept of Rome's Santa Francesca Romana there are a pair of indentations that according to legend were left by the kneeling legs of the saints Peter and Paul when through prayer they undertook a night battle against the formidable sorcerer Simon Magus. The rock is smoothed and worn down, as if the apostles were warm knives cutting into cold butter, for the ferocity of that struggle two centuries ago was apparently so intense that it had converted basalt into lava once again. In several different accounts, Peter and Paul engaged Simon in spiritual battle at the behest of the cruel Emperor Nero, who saw in the magician a messiah more potent than Christ, a wizard with the ability to float and fly through the air. Writing in his *Catechetical Lectures*, the fourth-century theologian Cyril of Jerusalem claimed that "Simon promised to rise aloft to heaven, and came riding in a daemon's chariot on the air; but the servants of God fell on their knees." It was only through the intensity of their dual prayers, calling upon the Christian God to defeat Simon, that the levitating necromancer was brought back down to earth. "They launched the weapon of their concord in prayer against Magus," writes Cyril, "and struck him down to the earth." And so here at the site where Peter and Paul prayed, where one day Santa Francesca Romana would stand, Simon Magus crashed into a Roman street just as Lucifer had once been cast from heaven.

This church, site of the mythic battle between Christ's disciples and a heretical magician, is a stone and concrete reminder of the narrative contained in, among other sources, the apocryphal Acts of Peter and Paul. Written sometime in the fourth or fifth century after the Common Era, this pseudo-scripture recounts the mission of Peter and Paul as they traveled to Rome, and their encounters against the Samaritan wizard. "All pious men abhorred Simon the magician," writes the author of the acts, "and proclaimed him impious." There is a substantial literature about the mage, who with theurgy and incantation was able to summon demons to his command, and was given the power to soothsay and levitate, who traipsed through the Roman sunset on a chariot pulled by devils. Traditionally understood as being the founder of the heretical sect of gnosticism, Church Fathers like Justin Martyr, Irenaeus, and Hippolytus make reference to Simon; the historian Josephus tells his account, and a preponderance of apocryphal scripture with titles like the *Acts of Peter* and *Recognitions and Homilies* explicate the diabolical ministry of the sorcerer. Even the canonical Book of Acts makes reference to the heretic and blasphemer, its author (traditionally identified with the gospel writer Luke) describes a certain Simon who "used sorcery, and bewitched the people of Samaria."

Because of his associations with gnosticism, a variant of early Christianity that claimed that the earth was the creation not of God but of a demonic interloper known as a demiurge (who himself went by several different names), Simon Magus was long a convenient cipher for heresy among the orthodox. He has been identified as the precursor for the Faust legend, and he lent his name to the sin of "simony," the selling of church offices that so enraged medieval and Reformation critics of clericalism. The later etymology comes from the Book of Acts itself, in which Simon offers payment to Peter, asking the apostle to impart upon him the power of the Holy Spirit, the better by which to work his magic. According to the Book of Matthew, abjuring the spirit is the one unpardonable sin, but Simon's attempt to bribe God speaks to an uncomfortable relationship between religion and magic. After all, though he was a Samaritan (a group related to the Jews, though with different scripture and rituals), and though he worked magic we'd associate with a pagan wizard, Simon Magus was himself a Christian. "Simon himself believed also," writes Luke, "and when he was baptized, he continued . . . and wondered, beholding the miracles and signs which were done."

To observe that religion is related to magic is neither to denigrate the former nor to elevate the later, but rather to simply acknowledge the transcendent import of both. After all, it can be hard to tell the difference between an incantation and a miracle. Simon's desire to use the Holy Spirit as just another aspect of his magic is the ultimate example of taking the Lord's name in vain, but the very idea that the manipulation of letters and words in this way can affect things is itself a variant of magical thinking. It's the same reason why Jacob's angelic interlocutor in the Book of Genesis (sometimes understood to be Azazel) is reticent to give his name upon his loss of their wrestling match, for to be able to call on the devils for your own purposes implies that you may also be capable of calling upon God as well. Simon's example also tells us something about the nature of faith in the ancient world, for as a Christian he presumably believes the good news of the gospels, he understands the claims of scripture to be metaphysically true, and yet that doesn't render any ethical transformation. Lucifer, it could be said, couldn't help but be a believer, for who among us has actually stood in the presence of the Lord?

Despite the platitudes of liberal Christianity that interpret Christ as a great moral exemplar and the early Church as simply a means of explicating those ethical axioms, the ministry of Jesus and his followers was enmeshed in a supernatural, transcendental, apocalyptic, and magical worldview. Nor can contemporary conservative Christians quite comprehend how deeply strange the context of the early Church was, whereby a magician like Simon Magus could master both the demons and angels to his command. Messadie writes that the "whole of Jesus' public ministry in fact revolved around foiling Satan, Beelzebub, Azazel, or whatever other name the Devil went by," with Russell concurring that "demonology is central, not peripheral, to the teaching of the New Testament." While apocryphal works like the Acts of Peter and Paul may seem abundantly unnerving to contemporary readers, that's mostly an issue of familiarity, for the New Testament itself is deeply strange and disturbing in its accounts of demonic possession and exorcism. From the temptation of Christ in the desert by Satan (also variously recorded in extrabiblical accounts as Azazel of Samael) to the depiction of seven exorcisms performed by Jesus, the New Testament is as demon haunted as any text from antiquity.

Each of the three synoptic gospels recount variations on how Christ interceded in the sufferings of the demonically possessed. The story of the Gerasene demoniac, whom the Messiah performs a successful exorcism on, exists in variations across the first three gospels, but it's the version in the Book of Mark that is the most recounted, not least of all because of its unsettling language. In that account, Christ asks the demon that is possessing his victim what his name is, the better to use the power of magic words to cast out and bind the being. "My name is Legion, for we are many," comes the uncanny and eerie response. Christ expels the collection of demons into a herd of treyf swine passing through the area, who then fall off a cliff into the sea. An arresting scene, this moment when Christ learns the identity of the specter tormenting this otherwise nameless man, for in that transition from the singular to the plural there is a sense of the enormity of that which is being faced. This collection of demons self-designating as a Legion, the term used by the Roman armies then occupying Judea, collapses the authority of Satan with that of the temporal powers that oppress us. Within this man are warring impulses, creatures in conflict, a cacophony of voices diabolical, for in the name Legion there is a whole phalanx holding a soul enraptured.

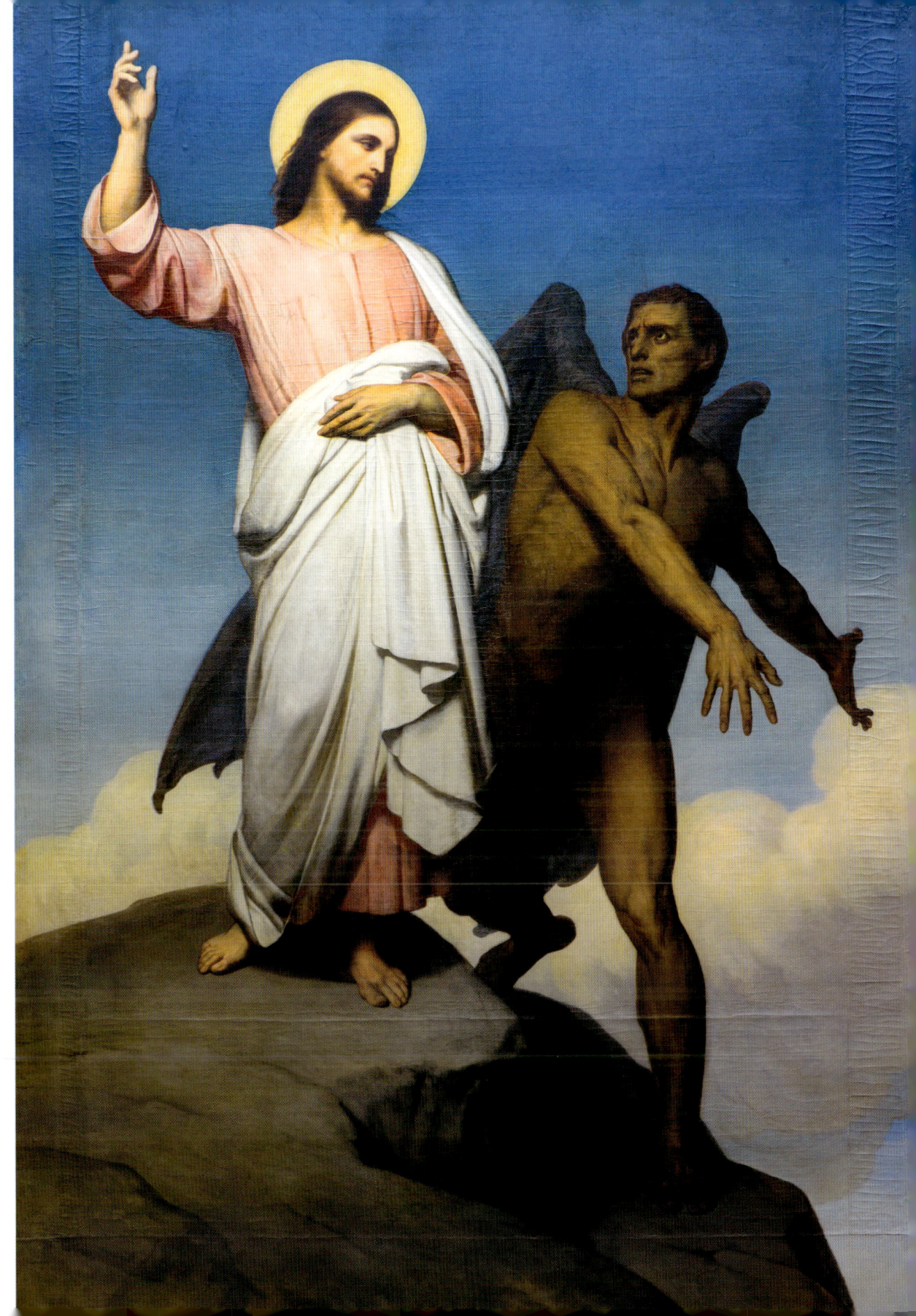

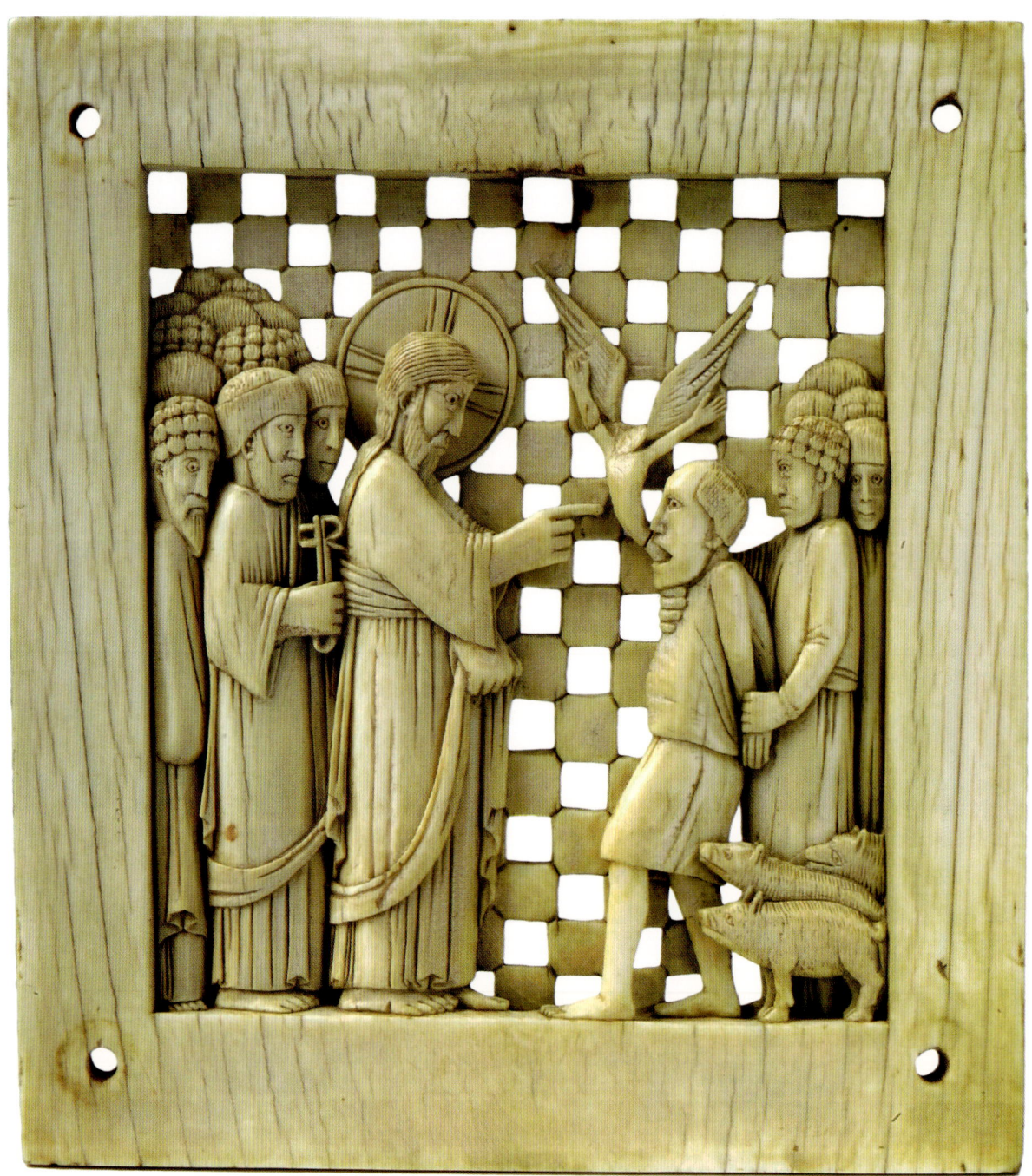

This tenth-century German ivory from the Magdeburg Antependium, held by the Hessisches Landesmuseum in Darmstadt, provides a pictorial history of Christ's miracles, including this scene from Mark of the Gerasene demoniac's exorcism. The unfortunate man regurgitates a small, man-shaped demon, appearing as a winged homunculus. The emergence of the creature from the mouth could indicate a conflation of wrong-speech, in the form of heresy and blasphemy, with possession.

"The exorcism of demons is no quirk in the gospels, no strange and irrelevant accretion introduced from contemporary superstition. It is central to the war against Satan and therefore an integral part of the gospel's meaning," writes Russell. As with Judaism before it, and in large part sharing a similar system of categorization, Christianity developed a complex demonology so as to understand the conduits through which absolute evil infects us. If anything, the early Church zestfully obsessed over the legion of demons that it inherited from earlier traditions, seeing in our fallen world a conspiracy of evil beings who threatened to tempt and torture them at every turn. Representative is the celebrated example of the third- and fourth-century Desert Father Saint Anthony the Great. In the Egyptian wilderness, Anthony was instrumental in the development of early Christian monasticism, seeing in the isolation and severity of the desert the possibility of the soul's purification. Supposedly Anthony was originally a swineherd, perhaps a reference to the demon Legion's untimely end, but it was in becoming a monk that he'd indelibly mark Western religion for the next two millennia.

If the desert was a site for spiritual contemplation, then it also was where the quiet was such that their inner psychological legion could find itself unleashed upon the uneasy novice, as it so famously was in Anthony's case. According to accounts from the fourth-century bishop Athanasius of Alexandria, the unfortunate monk found himself tormented by demons while holding vigil in the Egyptian desert. He encountered "a creature of mingled shape, half-horse and half-man" as well as "a maniken with hooked snout, horned forehead, and extremities like goat's feet." These beings tortured the monk, making him imagine that he'd been buffeted through the air and dropped on his head, that they'd broken his bones and burnt him with red hot pokers. The medieval compendium of hagiographies known as *The Golden Legend* says that Anthony's demons "came in the form of diverse beasts wild and savage, of whom that one howled, another sniffled, and another cried, and another brayed and assailed" the saint "with the horns, the others with their teeth, and the others with their paws."

Anthony would be saved from his tribulations by the intercession of Christ, but it wouldn't be his last encounter with the demonic. When reading legends about his travails in the desert, it's hard not to wonder how much of Anthony's suffering is rendered in a metaphoric language, used to describe his psychological pain, his own inner legion. In that sense, there is something surprisingly modern about the story, the way in which the demons have been relocated from the sandy soil where they can be trapped by magic bowls and rather placed within the suffering mind itself. There is as much of the Freudian id in Anthony as there is the demonic Ashmedai. Anthony's story marks the eclipse of the ancient approach to demonology and a harbinger of the medieval, which is in part why his temptation and torture was such a favored subject for artists in the coming centuries, depicted by masters from Michelangelo to Hieronymus Bosch. For all of the psychological richness of the depictions of Anthony, that tradition also took part in an emerging medieval affectation that concealed an ugly aspect of demonic poetics, a rhetoric that projected fears, and paranoia, and anxieties onto the marginalized, and marked them for persecution. Pagels writes that visions like Anthony's "have been incorporated into Christian tradition and

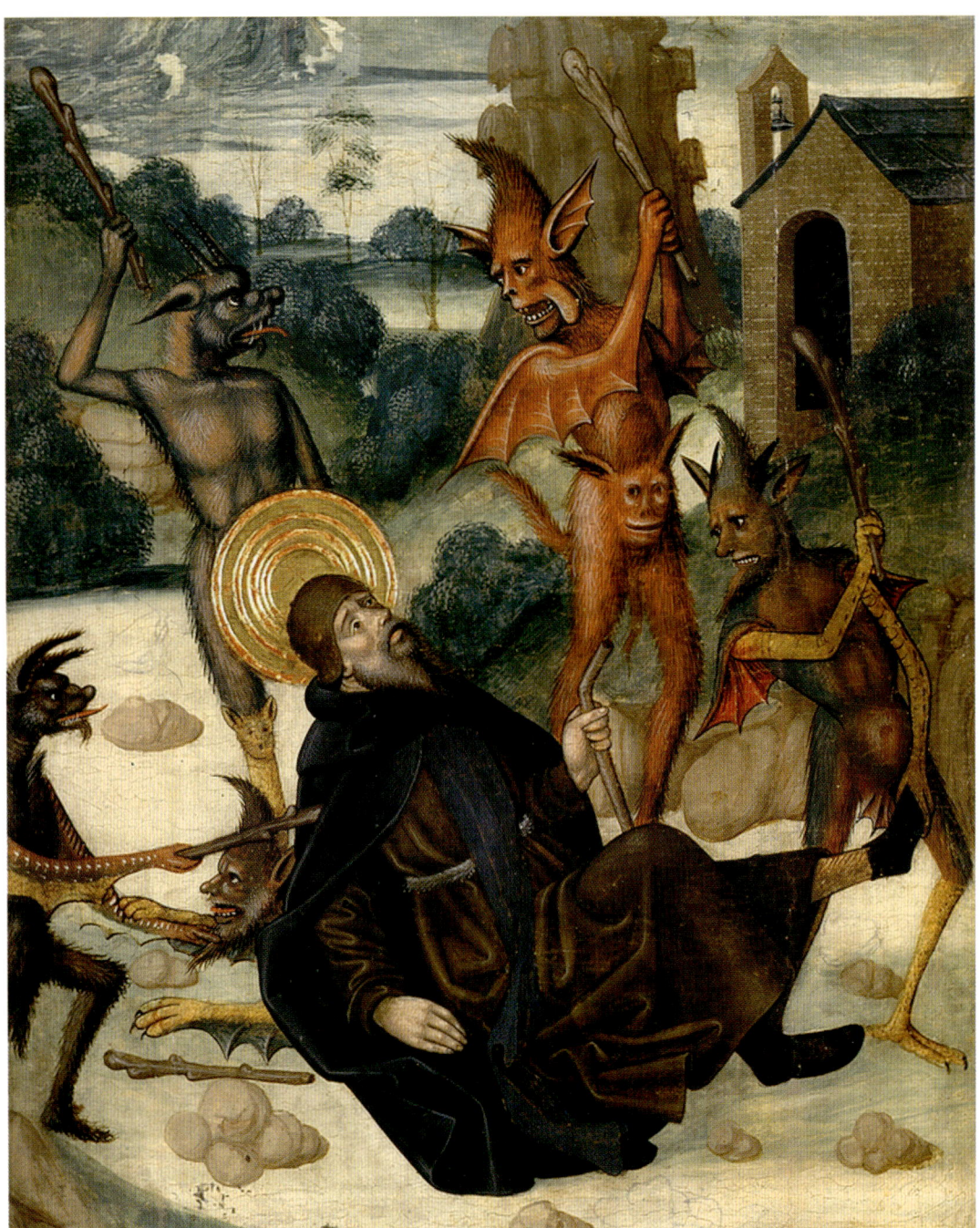

A perennially popular theme in medieval and Renaissance art, Saint Anthony's torture at the hands of a group of exotic demons delivered to its audience prurient violence. In this fifteenth-century painting housed in Madrid's Prado Museum and made by the Spanish artist Juan de la Abadia el Viejo, a scrum of devils kick, punch, and slap the monk.

have served, among other things, to conform for Christians their own identification with God and to demonize their opponents—first other Jews, then pagans, and later dissident Christians called heretics."

Examine Bosch's copious artistic explorations of Anthony's demonic encounters that were produced in a series of paintings in the sixteenth century. His demons are as bestial as can be expected, creatures with canine, feline, and avian faces, grasping claws and sharpened teeth, tugging, ripping, and pulling at the brown robes of the desert monk. Yet a curious detail in his painting *The Temptation of St. Anthony* is a dwarfish figure whose whole body is encompassed by a conical cap that looks like a funnel; in that same painting another demon, with a face that appears as if a cross between a cat and an insect, coal black eyes staring out from a reddish, whiskered face and framed by massive, papery fly wings, wears the same hat as the little man, while he whispers in the ears of a rat dressed like a cleric. Meanwhile some sort of bird creature on skates dons the same cap. What could be explained by recourse to the surrealism with which Bosch is so often associated with is better understood through the context of his time period. The headgear that these assorted demons sport are the conical hats that many Christian princes compelled Jews to wear, so as to differentiate themselves from the wider European community. Bosch's anti-Semitic intent is clear, and sadly not remarkable for both the medieval and Renaissance periods. In his understanding, the demons that assaulted Anthony weren't just marked as otherworldly—they were marked as Jews. And so this vocabulary of demonization, which has such utility in explaining evil and sorrow, became itself a source of evil and sorrow as Christians used it to justify the violent persecution of Jews and other minorities.

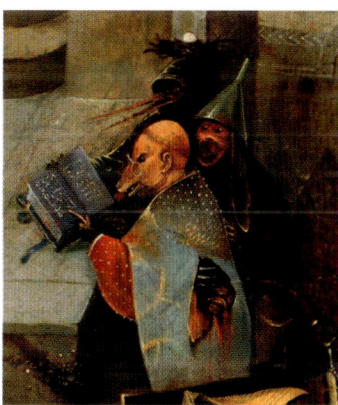

A detail from the fifteenth-century Flemish painter Hieronymus Bosch's The Temptation of St. Anthony, *held at the National Museum of Art in Lisbon, Portugal.*

The greatest trick the Devil ever pulled was convincing people that they were persecuting him while they gleefully murdered the innocent. No rhetoric of demonization, no demonic poetics, is ever value-neutral, and the ethics of its deployment must be cautionary. When we hear the tale of Peter and Paul fighting Simon, there is an element of the epic mode, but we must be wary as well. The exact same idiom of demonization that Bosch deployed is threaded throughout the history of Christianity, even within the heart of Christendom. For three hundred years, from the sixteenth century until Napoleon's invasion of Rome during the nineteenth, the city's Jews would be virtual prisoners inside of their ghetto, within eyeshot of Santa Francesca Romana. There they were persecuted, oppressed, and condemned in a manner that not even Anthony could imagine. Such suffering was made possible, in part, by the conflation of the Jews with a legendary Samaritan magician, and other matters similarly demonic. It speaks to a devilish presence that's very real, but ironically engaged by those whom believe themselves to be the most pious, the partisans of a one true Church. Beyond the walls where Santa Francesca Romana would one day stand was the soil upon which Simon Magus supposedly crashed, the same site that by legend it's said that in the sixteenth century the Jewish ghetto would be constructed. And so the Devil would use the new faith to torture the old, same as it's ever been.

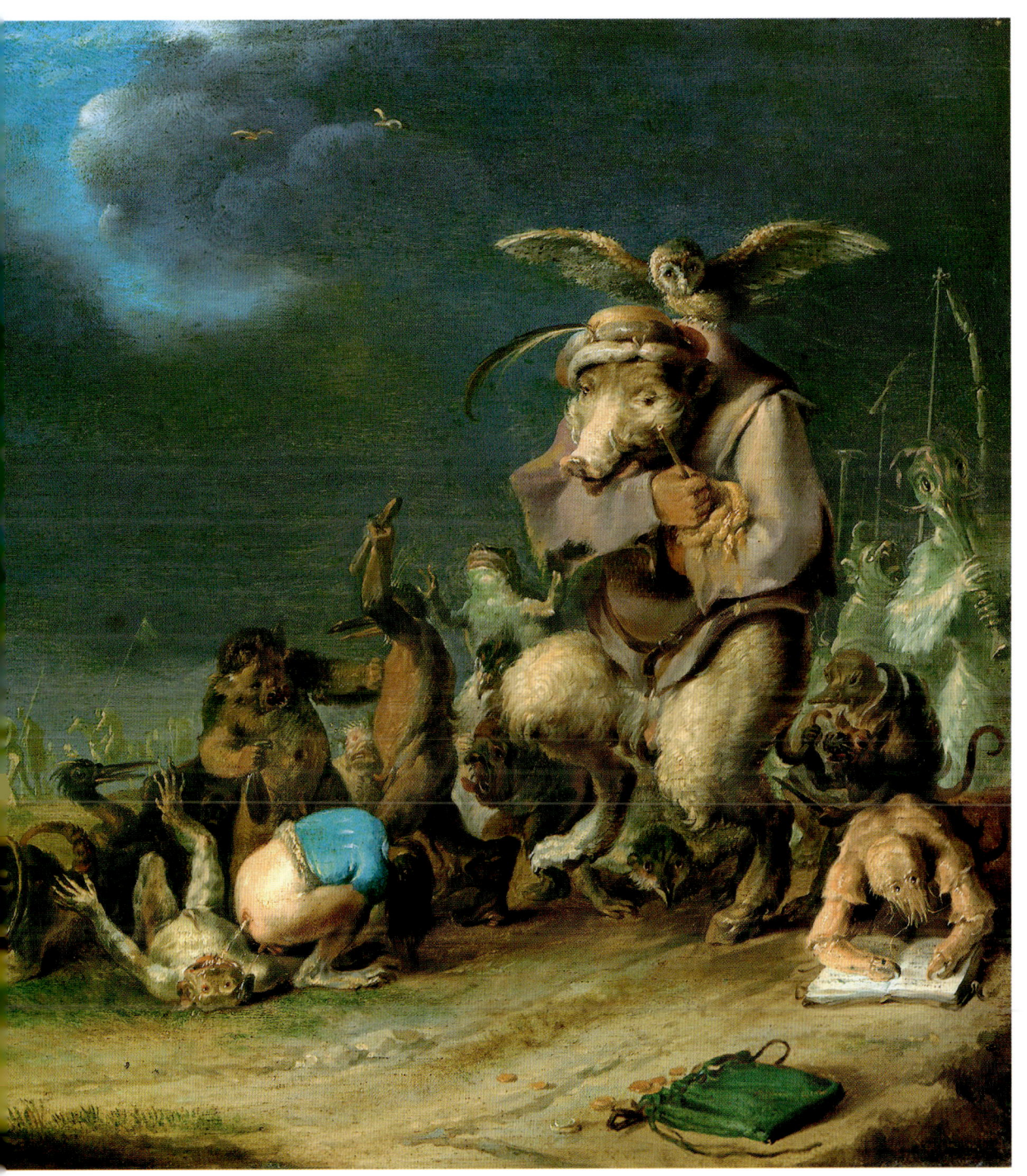

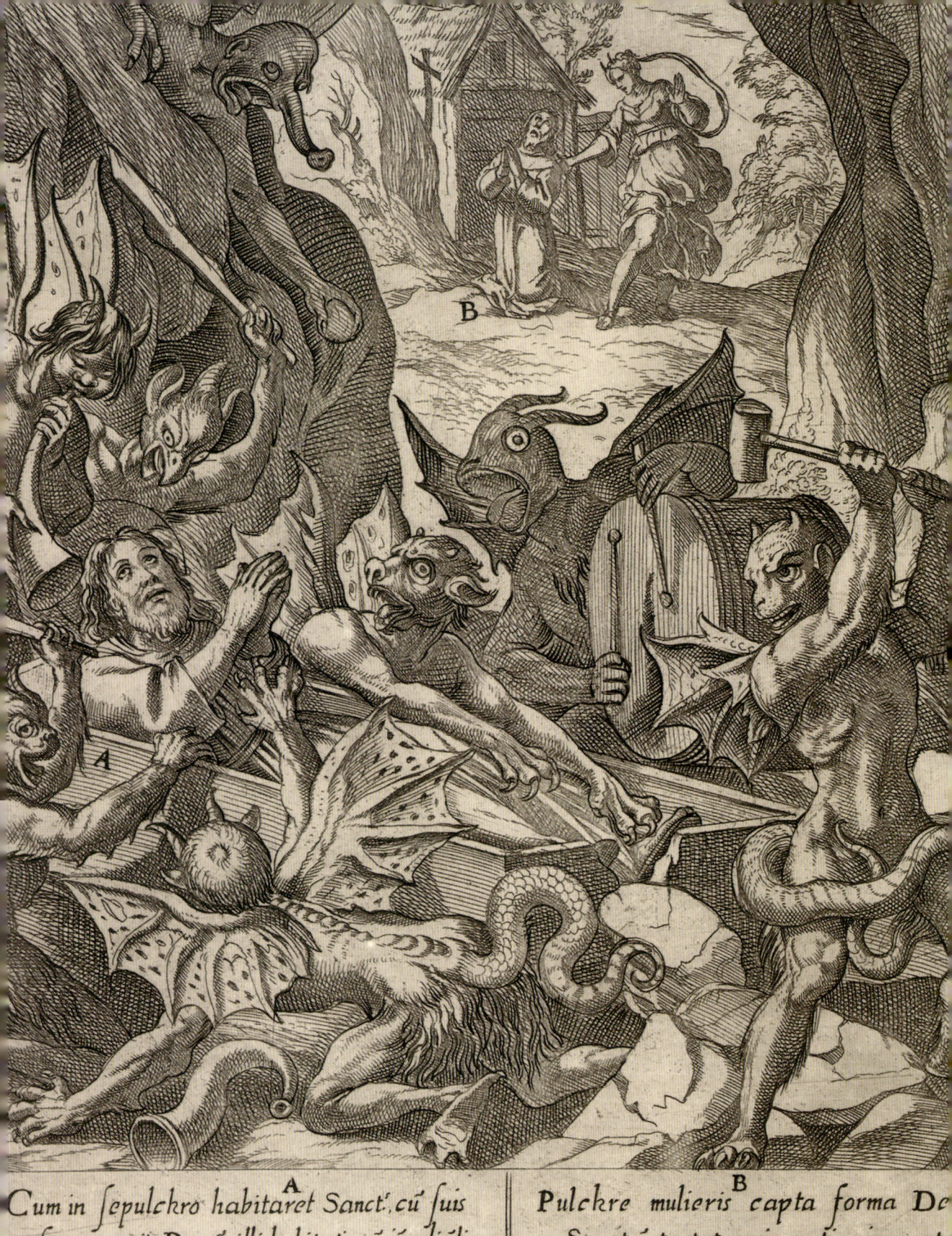

A

Cum in sepulchro habitaret Sanct. cú suis
socys uenit Demó illi habitatióe ipedié̃di
causa cúq̃ maximis clamorib, lacerauere ac uerb.ʳᵉ
Il Sᵗᵒ habitando in uⁿ sepulcro, uenne il Demonio

B

Pulckre mulieris capta forma Dᵒ
Sanctú tentat qui continuis orati
tentatióe reÿcit
Il Demonio in forma di bella donna te

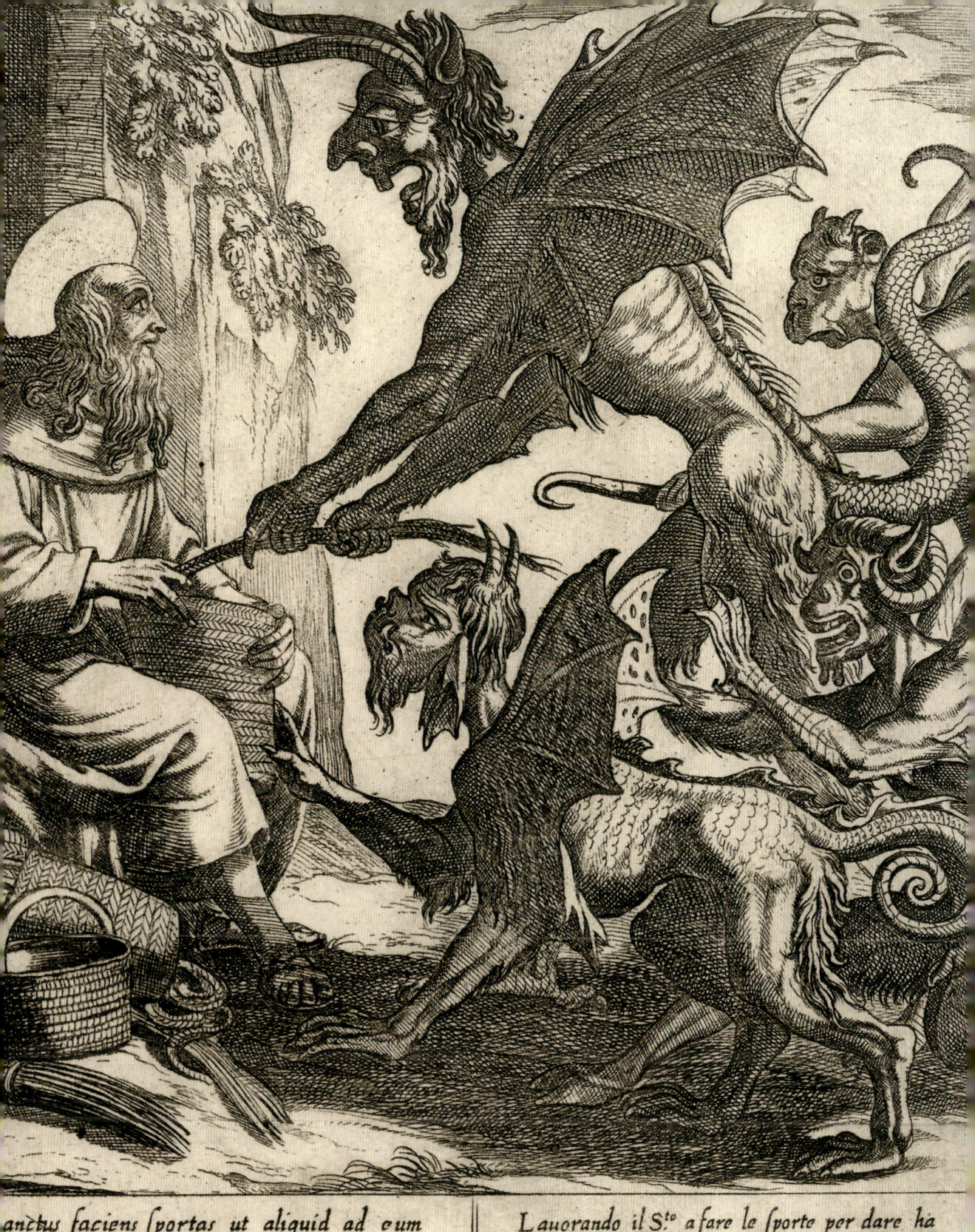

anctus faciens ſportas ut aliquid ad eum
deferentibus daret maxima uidit animal ei
treciam furans et ſtatim ſe ſigno Crucis
muniit dicens Chriſti ſum famulus ſi ad me
ipſe ſe miſit fugere nolo et ſtatim cum

Lauorando il Sᵗᵒ a fare le ſporte per dare hà
quelli che li dauaõ qualche preſente uidde una
gran beſtia che li toglieua la treccia é ſi
fece ſubito il ſegno della croce in fronte
dicendoli io ſon ſeruo di Chriſto ſe ti ha

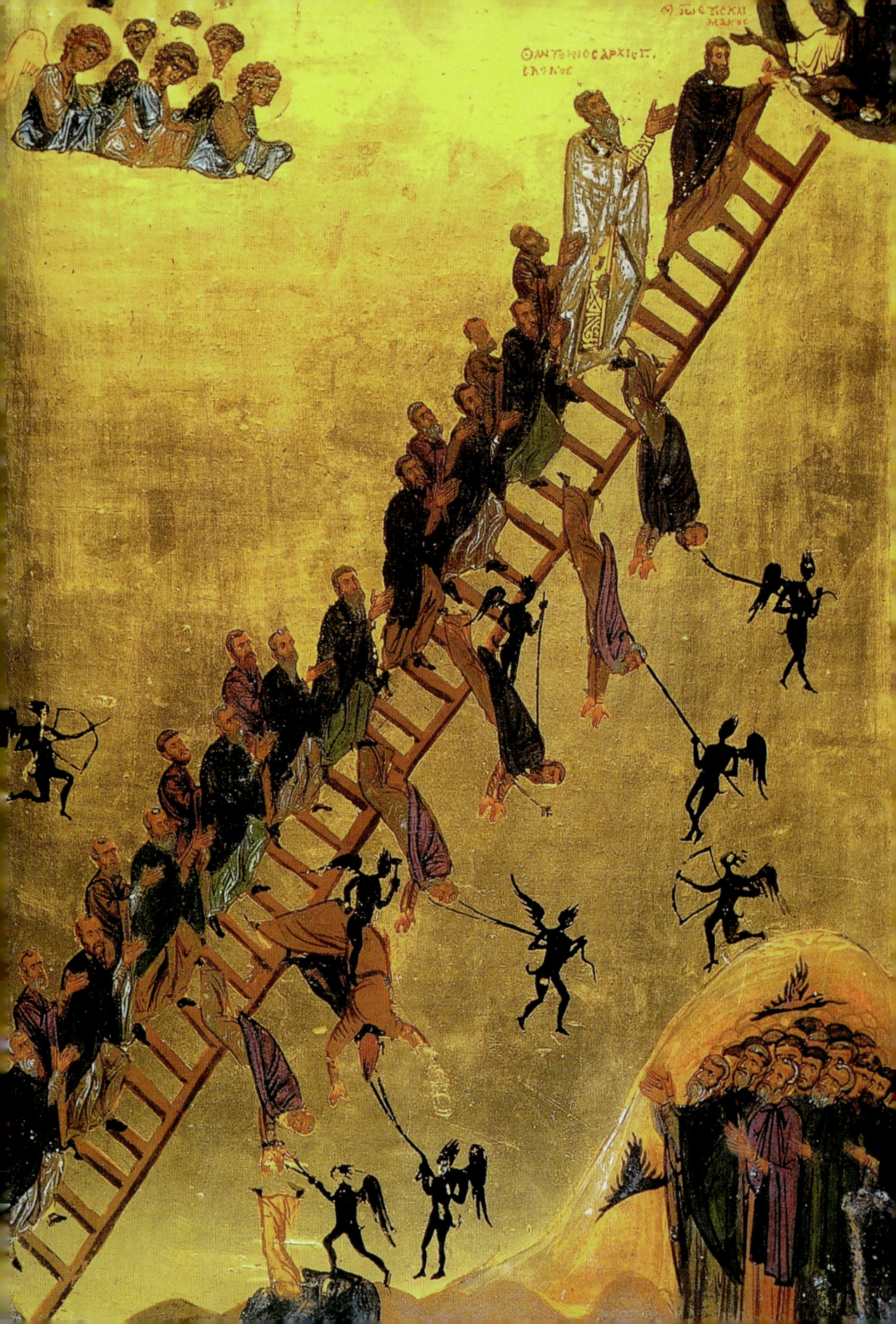

CHAPTER TWO

Deliver Us from Evil

Medieval Demonology, c. 800–1500

"The Banners of the King of Hell Advance
Closer to us," my master said; "so look
Straight ahead and see if you can spot them."

—DANTE ALIGHIERI, *The Divine Comedy* (1308–21)

May the Holy Cross be my light
May the dragon never be my guide
Begone Satan
Never tempt me with your vanities
What you offer me is evil/drink the poison yourself.

—Benedictine formula for exorcism,
manuscript held at Metten Abbey in Bavaria (1415)

ON MEDIEVAL DEMONS

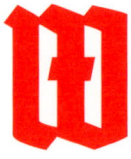here the Bosporus's wine-dark waters link Asia to Europe in the resplendent capital of Constantinople—the city's skyline dominated by the massive blue dome of the cathedral named Hagia Sophia, whose interior is decorated with glimmering, golden mosaics reverentially depicting the angels who had once fought the war in heaven—the greatest thinker of the eleventh century was the monk Michael Psellos. Conversant with both the inner workings of both the Byzantine emperor and the Orthodox patriarch, Psellos was historian and political adviser, theologian and rhetorician, known by his colleagues at the University of Constantinople as the Chief of the Philosophers in those decades when schism would permanently tear asunder the Latin West and the Greek East. Despite his sober academic interests, particularly his dedication to the writing commentary on Plato, Psellos was drawn to more esoteric subjects as well.

Judith Herrin writes in *Byzantium: The Surprising Life of a Medieval Empire* that Psellos "claimed that he could practice theurgy, the art of summoning ancient spirits . . . [that] he wrote a treatise on alchemy, the transformation of normal metals into gold, and practiced astrology." According to Herrin, Psellos studied such disciplines despite their being "strictly forbidden by the Byzantine Church." He was living at the Olympus monastery, constructed upon the graveyard of those pagan deities who were now understood to be fallen angels, when the Greek Orthodox and Roman Catholic Churches finalized their disunion in 1054, and it is around that time that he penned one of his most useful books— *On the Operation of Demons.*

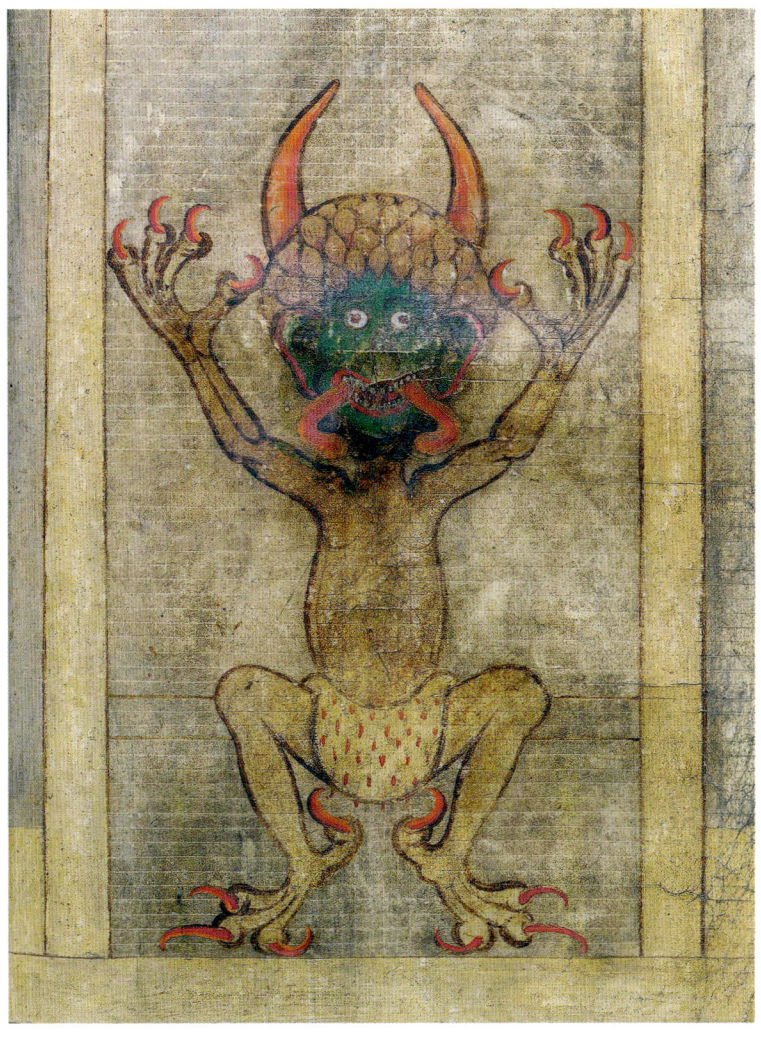

Attributed to a thirteenth-century Benedictine monk known as Herman the Recluse, the Gigas Codex ("Giant Book" in English) is the largest extant medieval manuscript in existence, measuring more than two feet wide by three feet long (approximately sixty by ninety centimeters). Produced in the Bohemian monastery at Podlažice, the Gigas Codex contains, among other books, an almost complete Latin Vulgate, Flavius Josephus's Antiquities of the Jews, *and Isidore of Seville's encyclopedic* Etymologiae. *Intended to be a repository of all human knowledge, the Gigas Codex is currently stored at the National Library in Stockholm; it was taken from the monastery by Swedish troops in 1648 during the Thirty Years' War. Due to its size, intricacy, and beauty, the Gigas Codex has generated an assortment of legends, none more popular that the claim that its provenance can be traced to Lucifer. According to the most popular tale, Herman was punished with immurement by his fellow monks for violating his vows. If he could produce a work of scribal brilliance, he would be freed from the walls of his prison, so he prayed to the Devil to accomplish this task. The page that depicts a fearsome, horned, reptilian demon is thus interpreted as the Prince of Lie's signature. Writing generally about magic books, scholar Richard Kieckheffer notes in* Forbidden Rites: A Necromancer's Manual of the Fifteenth Century *that there was a "notion that demons could infest a book," and that such a volume was "itself a magical object, treasured and closely guarded by its possessors."*

Psellos's treatise was written as a theological diatribe, aimed against the Persian religion of Manicheanism, a type of post-Christian neo-Zoroastrianism that incorporated both the teachings of Christ and of the Buddha, and that had once been practiced from Guangzhou to Gibraltar. The single greatest intellectual competitor to Christianity in the years between that religion's birth and the rise of Islam (indeed Saint Augustine had been a believer in his youth), Manicheanism borrowed from Zoroastrianism a dualistic understanding of reality, seeing good and evil as separate and equally powerful principles. *On the Operation of Demons*, written in the form of a Platonic dialogue, explicates the nature of evil's agents as a way of proffering an argument about how misfortune propagates in the world. More crucially it was arguably the first of a genre—the taxonomic guide to individual demons.

On the Operation of Demons wasn't the first listing of demons: after all, similar litanies had been offered in the Enochian literature, and a first-millennium pseudographical text known as the Testament of Solomon provided similar gloss that was especially influential in the Middle Ages. Nor was he the first thinker to consider demonology, as Church Fathers in both the East and West had interrogated the topic. *On the Operation of Demons* was different in that Psellos offered a systematized classification of his topic, bringing a scholastic and rationalist rigor to a discipline long mired in the inky blackness of magic and ineffability. Even more notably, in a tradition whereby texts had origins of unknown provenance, and where works were often attributed to illustrious names that had no role in their composition, this was a book that by contrast had a clear and identifiable author.

There had been previous compendiums of demonic names, some going back centuries before Psellos. One of the most influential examples to focus specifically on the demonic hierarchy was the Jewish apocryphal text the Testament of Solomon, portions of which were written in the earliest century of the first millennium, but which wouldn't be redacted into a single document until well into the Middle Ages, subsequently having a powerful influence on occultism and demonology as it developed into the present day. Attributed to the biblical Solomon, the testament details how the Judean king was able to use a magical ring to compel hell's minions to use their magic in the construction of Jerusalem's Temple. Variations on the legend exist in other texts as well, but the central conceit of the Testament of Solomon is disturbing in its implications—that demons can be commandeered through magic, even enlisted against their will into a mission of holiness. Where the Testament of Solomon bears similarity with Psellos's *On the Operation of Demons* is in the fixation on demonic names, for it's in knowing what words devils ascribe to themselves that a necromancer is able to control them. "For there are principalities, authorities, world-rulers, and we demons fly about in the air," one of the infernal crew informs Solomon, "and we hear the voices of the heavenly beings, and we survey all the powers." Thirty-six demons, including Asmodeus (or Ashmedai), Ornias, Beelzebub, Obyzouth, and Abezethibou are enumerated and described; they are monstrous and reptilian, deformed and bestial; one is described as if a dragon, another has no head, but a multitude of innumerable arms.

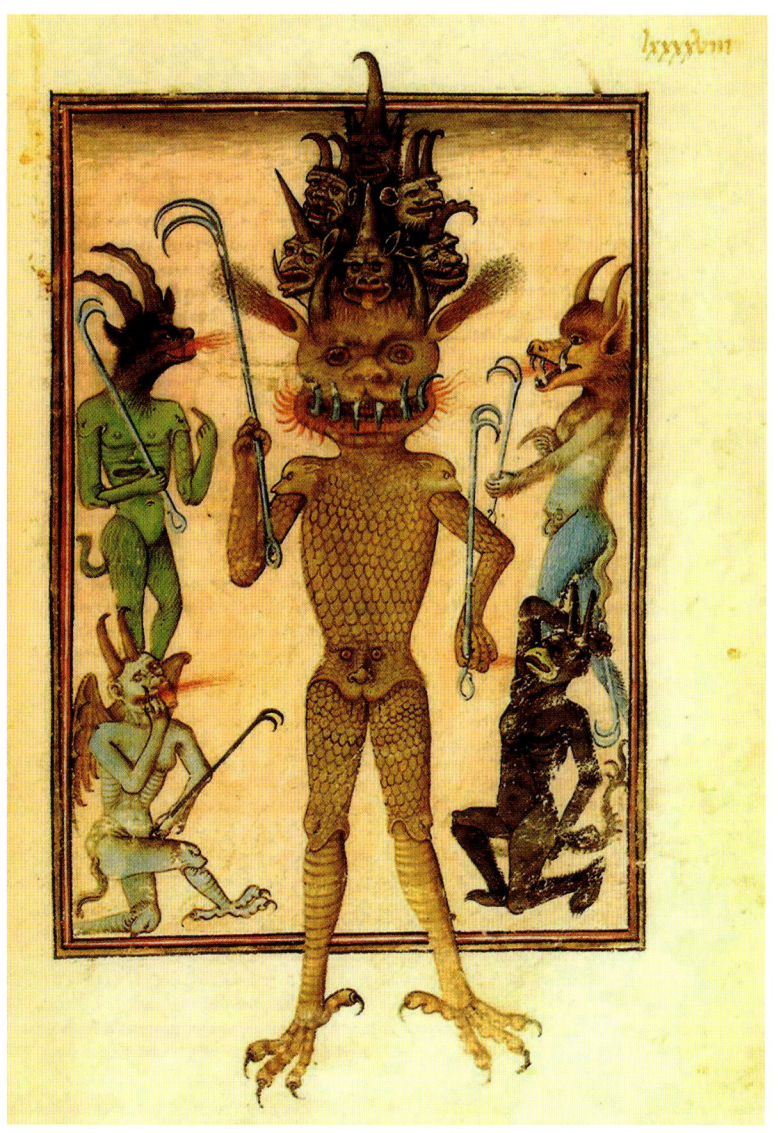

ABOVE

A picture from the fifteenth-century French book Livre de la Vigne Nostre Seigneur *showing Satan in Hell, depicting a horned being either wearing a crown of the living heads of his demons, or those creatures re actually growing from his body. Much of demonology precisely involves parsing the difference between Satan, the Great Adversary, and his various priests, officers, functionaries, and bureaucrats. While Satan has been close to universally associated with Lucifer since the Book of Revelation, disagreements between demonologists are often about the nature of the differences between him and those other demons, and whether those sundry beings—Baal and Beelzebub, Ashmedai and Samael—are separate consciousnesses, or rather manifestations of the single Satan, growing as if tumors from his pate.*

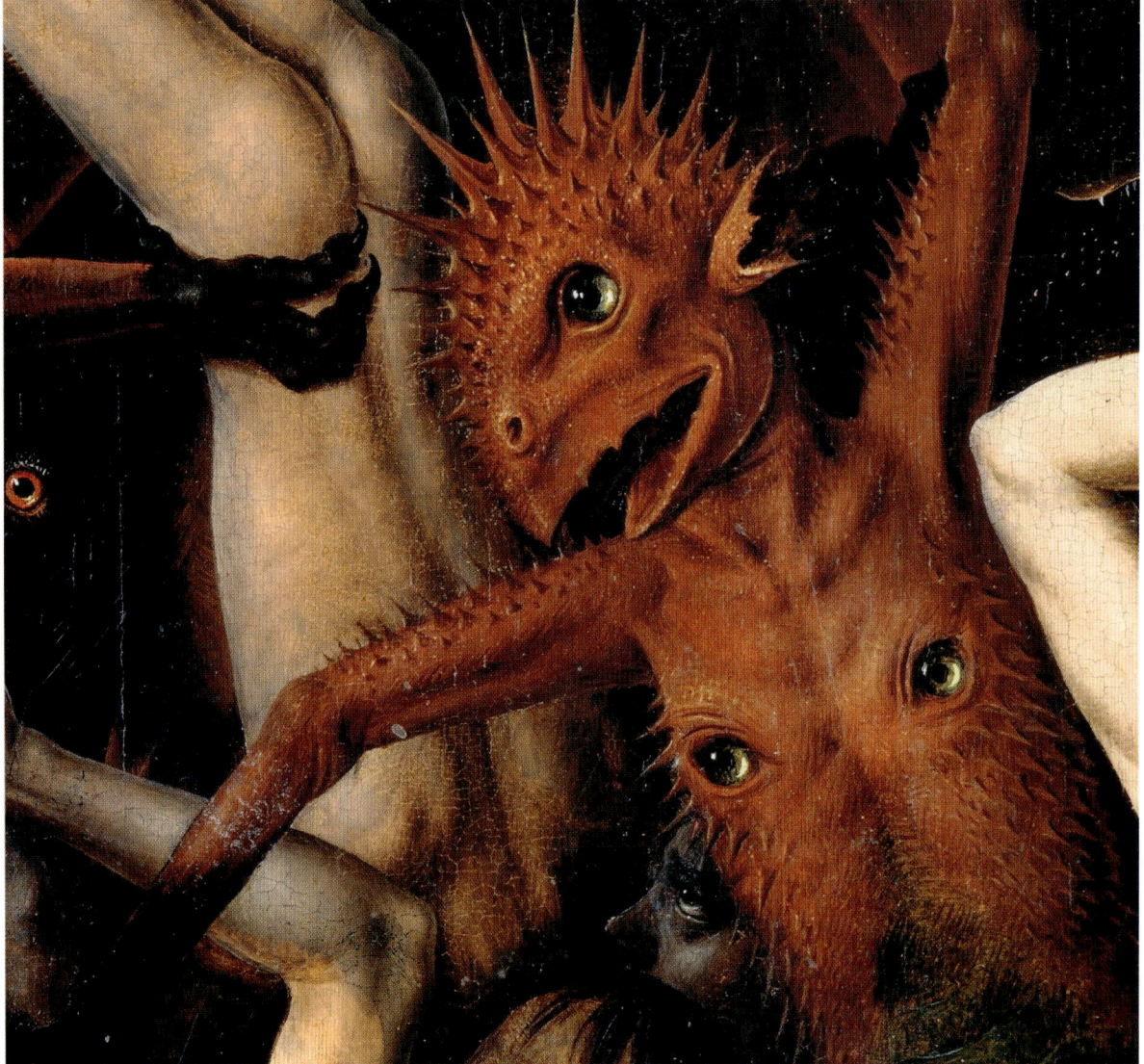

Medieval demonology was bedeviled by a paradox that marked the discipline from its ancient origins until today—the reality that such entities are both reflective of familiar human sin while also being profoundly foreign and other. While theologians during the Middle Ages believed that reason was capable of categorizing, classifying, and helping us to comprehend demons, it ironically didn't subdue them of any of their shocking difference. Fifteenth-century Netherlandish painter Dirk Bouts depicts such an otherworldly being in this detail from The Fall of the Damned, *painted in 1470 and originally intended to be part of a triptych; now housed in France at the Palais des Beaux-Arts de Lille. As depicted by Bouts, this demon is a composite of recognizable shapes, animals, and features, but when recombined, the being is of a terrifying, alien countenance.*

Although a fascination with demonic names, and their use in incantation, conjuring, and necromancy didn't find its origin within the Testament of Solomon, that apocryphal scripture was arguably the first to apply a taxonomic methodology for the fallen angels. Richard Kieckheffer writes in *Forbidden Rites: A Necromancer's Manual of the Fifteenth Century* that "Theologians as well as necromancers believed that the demons held various ranks, in a kind of hierarchy that parodied that of God's heavenly court," and that this notion of there being a rigorous, detailed, specific "science" of demonology "became part of mainstream theological tradition." Psellos worked within a discipline that had been inaugurated by the nameless scribes of the Testament of Solomon, and that systematic analysis of demons as a subject not just worthy of study, but capable of definite answers, would have a venerable genealogy throughout the Middle Ages.

"And are there many descriptions of daemons?" asks one of the participants in Psellos's dialogue. "There are many, said he, and of every possible variety of figure and conformation, so that the air is full of them, both that above and that around us, the earth and the sea are full of them, and the lowest subterranean depths." A committed student of Plato, Psellos's condemnation of Manicheanism was in part meant to assure readers that demons had no final agency separate from that of the ultimate good of God, and so was in keeping with a medieval understanding in both the West and the East that in fact minimized the power of the fallen angels. Throughout *On the Operation of Demons* there is a conflation of Psellos's subject with the classical concept of the "daemon," which is a sort of motivating spirit or consciousness that is able to speak to the individual on behalf of the divine. In that way, Psellos is in keeping with the gambit that redefined pagan deities as infernal spirits.

Writing more generally about this tradition, Kieckheffer observes that there was "a tension between the early Christian notion of demons as fallen angels, whose status is determined by their free moral act of rebellion against God, and the Greco-Roman conception of *daemons* as spirits linked with the world of nature," a tension which Psellos explores but doesn't reconcile. His understanding is eccentric, and the taxonomy which Psellos devised seemed to draw not from precedent in either theology or myth, but rather from his own idiosyncratic invention. Influenced by explicitly pagan Neoplatonist philosophy, *On the Operation of Demons* divides demons into six different categories—the *leliouria* who occupy the space beyond the stars, the *aeria* who live in our atmosphere, the *chtonia* who dwell on the land, the *hydaia* who live within the water, the *hypochythonia* who live within the earth, and the lowest of devils, the *misophaes*, who inhabit hell beneath, and which Jeffrey Burton Russell describes in *Lucifer: The Devil in the Middle Ages* as beings "who hate the light and dwell blind and almost senseless."

He argues that "Psellos" bizarre schemes were inconsistent and crude. A combination of pagan philosophical ideas with popular demonological traditions, they were far too incongruent with Christian tradition to have a living or lasting effect." Despite that accusation (and ignoring Psellos's influence on Neoplatonists during the Italian Renaissance several centuries later), *On the Operation of Demons*' structure, model, and intent were to be repeated in demonological works throughout the Middle Ages. While the medieval period is sometimes

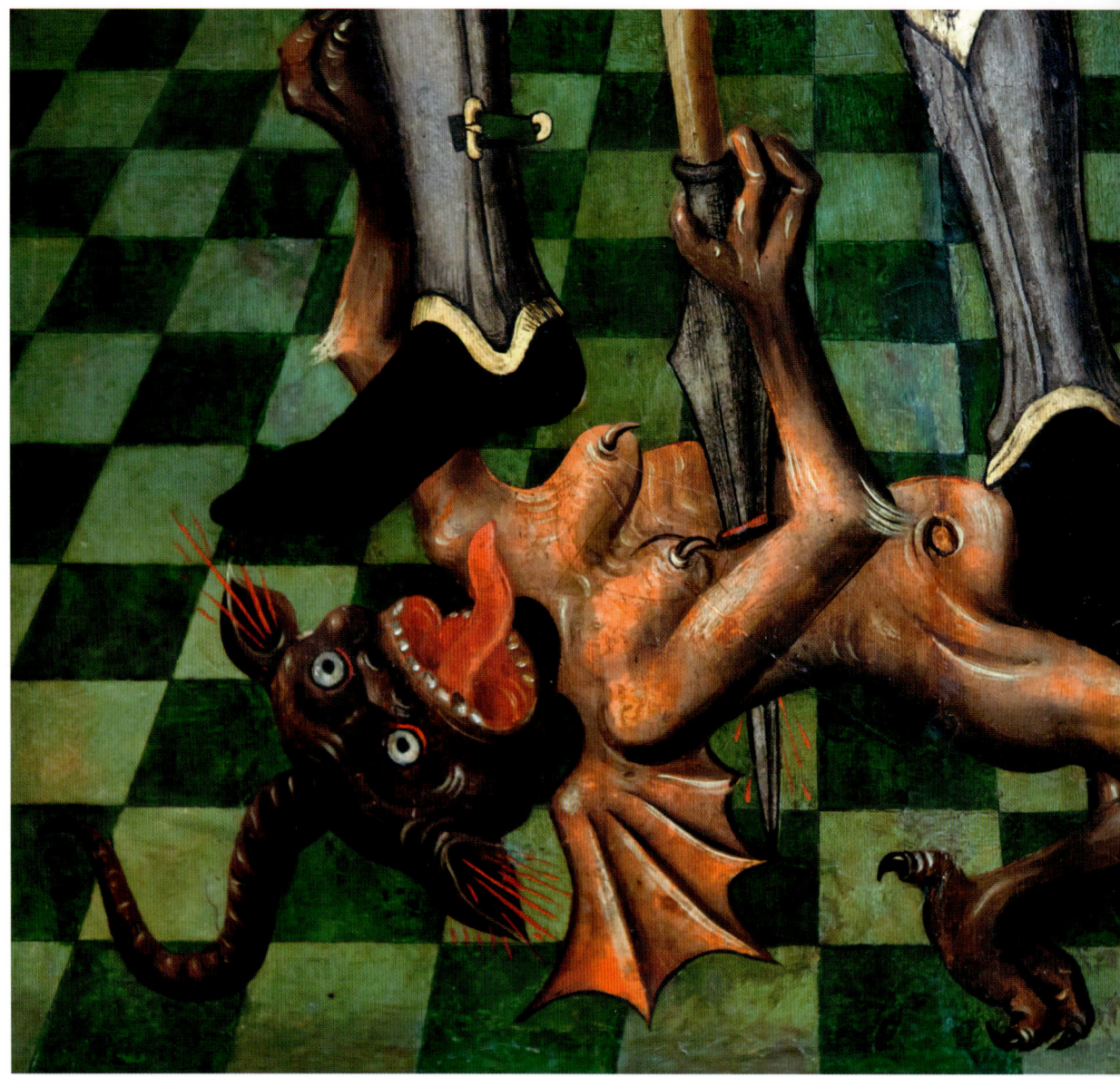

ABOVE

A detail from the fourteenth-century altarpiece of San Miguel, housed in the church of Nuestra Señora de la Asunción in Valladolid, Spain, and painted by an anonymous Master of Osma. Depicting the moment when the Archangel Michael has cast the dragon from paradise (that black slipper belongs to the angel, the contemporary checkerboard floor speaking to the eternal reoccurrence of the Fall). The Lucifer depicted by the Master of Osma shares some commonalities with other images, while adding unusual additions such as the feminine teats with claws emerging from the nipples. What these mix-and-match chimeras attest to is the demonic vocabulary developed in the Middle Ages, ever capable of novel combinations.

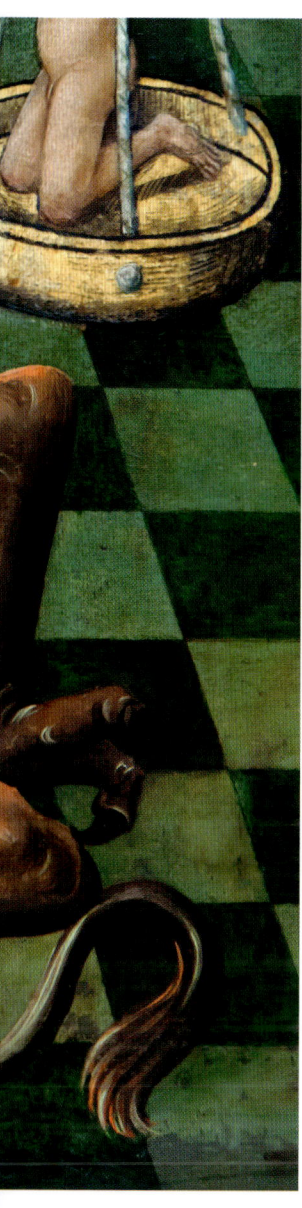

slurred as a millennium-long eclipse of antiquity until the renewal of the Renaissance, it was actually marked by an intellectual inquisitiveness that was precisely committed to explaining things by recourse to rational thought.

Intellectually, the Middle Ages were effectively a long debate between Plato and Aristotle, with Neoplatonism influencing the development of early Christianity in late antiquity, to be supplanted in the Catholic West by Scholastic Aristotelianism, which was in turn succeeded by Platonist humanism during the Renaissance. Throughout these intellectual convulsions, both Platonists like Psellos and Aristotelians like Thomas Aquinas provided demonic classification schema, and while differing on metaphysical issues regarding the corporeality of infernal spirits, or their ultimate origin, or their status within eternity, what these taxonomies share is a rationalist commitment to the idea that something definite and definable can be said about such supernatural entities. It reflected a shift in the Middle Ages, which, contrary to the stereotype of the age as marked by illogicality, actually enshrined reason as the paramount methodology of knowledge. If antiquity's perspective toward demons emphasized their fundamental realness, then the Middle Ages had a faith in their knowability.

Andrew McCall writes in *The Medieval Underground* that "Given the official belief in the reality of demons, it was only to be expected that, as God gradually came to be thought of as being more accessible to the ordinary Christian, so too would the Devil and his host of demons." This tendency is reflected in both the rigor that was brought to demonology, but also in the increasing detail that accompanied literary descriptions and artistic depictions of demons. Where ancient demons were left as inchoate and ambiguous (with the exception of the pagan gods later redefined as demons), medieval writers and artists were willing to put some flesh to the bone (or horns and scales as it were). From the sixth to the fifteenth centuries, representations of Satan and his minions took on a new physicality, a new tangibility, a new immediacy. While much of the accoutrement that we associate with the demonic—the caprine horns, the serpentine scales, the avian beaks—have their origins in antiquity, the full flowering of the idiomatic language of infernal description was a medieval innovation. From that network of rhetorical tropes, in metaphor, symbol, and connotation, came the language that we use to describe the demonic even today.

Ochre-faced devils, cloven-hooved imps, split-tailed demons, green-hued goblins, gaping hellmouths, ashen-faced gargoyles—all were rendered during the Middle Ages in stained-glass and stone, in patina and in words. Folklore and theology alike were enlisted in this collective cultural endeavor, the construction of a rich vocabulary of connotation and attribute, of character and hierarchy to personify agents of evil and chaos. Russell writes that "No picture of the Devil survives from before the sixth century; it is not known why." Again, excluding pagan demons and gods reclassified by Christians as such, the relative dearth of visual imaginings of the fallen angels was more than compensated during the ten centuries of the Middle Ages, when the hoofprints of devils walked across paintings and carvings, the stage and the page. Imaginative writers like Dante Alighieri crafted the literary language concerning demons, while scholastic theologians such as Thomas Aquinas provided the philosophical gloss.

The medieval demonic corpus, across theology and poetry, drama and prose, is too voluminous to supply more than the most superficial of overviews. For some writers and theologians, the demons were symbols of absolute evil; in other contexts (particularly on the stage), devils were figures of fun, at best comparable to tricksters, and in their most demeaning permutations they were represented as squawking, bumbling, farting fools whom Christ is always capable of overcoming. Yet what these various considerations of the infernal share is simultaneously a sense that some rational structure can be overlaid onto the subject, and that the very real presence of evil can be conveyed in a tangible manner. Representative of the medieval literary and spiritual approach to demonology is the twelfth-century Irish *Visio Tnugdali*, or *The Visions of Tundale*, written in Latin and translated into various European vernaculars over the ensuing centuries. Written in the Scots Monastery in Regensburg, Germany, by a Brother Marcus, The *Visions of Tundale* recounts the dreams of an Irish knight who has descended into hell, as Christ did after His Crucifixion, and from that harrowing comes back to the world of the living with an account of the demonic hordes that occupy that dark, ever-burning sulphureous and cacophonous fallen place.

With Brother Marcus's Irish-Gaelic original lost to posterity, his own Latin translation would provide the basis for the poem's popularity across the languages of Christendom. Drawing from an Irish literary genre of dream visions and fantastical travelogues known as *immram*, Brother Marcus's poem would have a profound effect on medieval demonological literature, especially through its influence on Dante in the thirteenth century. In its description of a demon that the knight encounters while in hell, a sense can be conveyed of just how detailed and exacting The *Visions of Tundale* could be in its demonic poetics, and by proxy how medieval literature and thought embraced complex world-building in its demonology:

For this beast was black as a crow, having the shape of a human body from head to toe except that it had a tail and many hands. Indeed, the horrible monster had thousands of hands, each one of which was a hundred cubits long and ten cubits thick. Each hand had twenty fingers, which were each a hundred palms long and ten palms wide, with fingernails longer than knights' lances, and toenails much the same. The beast also had a long, thick beak, and a long, sharp tail fitted with spikes to hurt the damned souls. This horrible being lay prone on an iron grate over burning coals fanned by a great throng of demons.

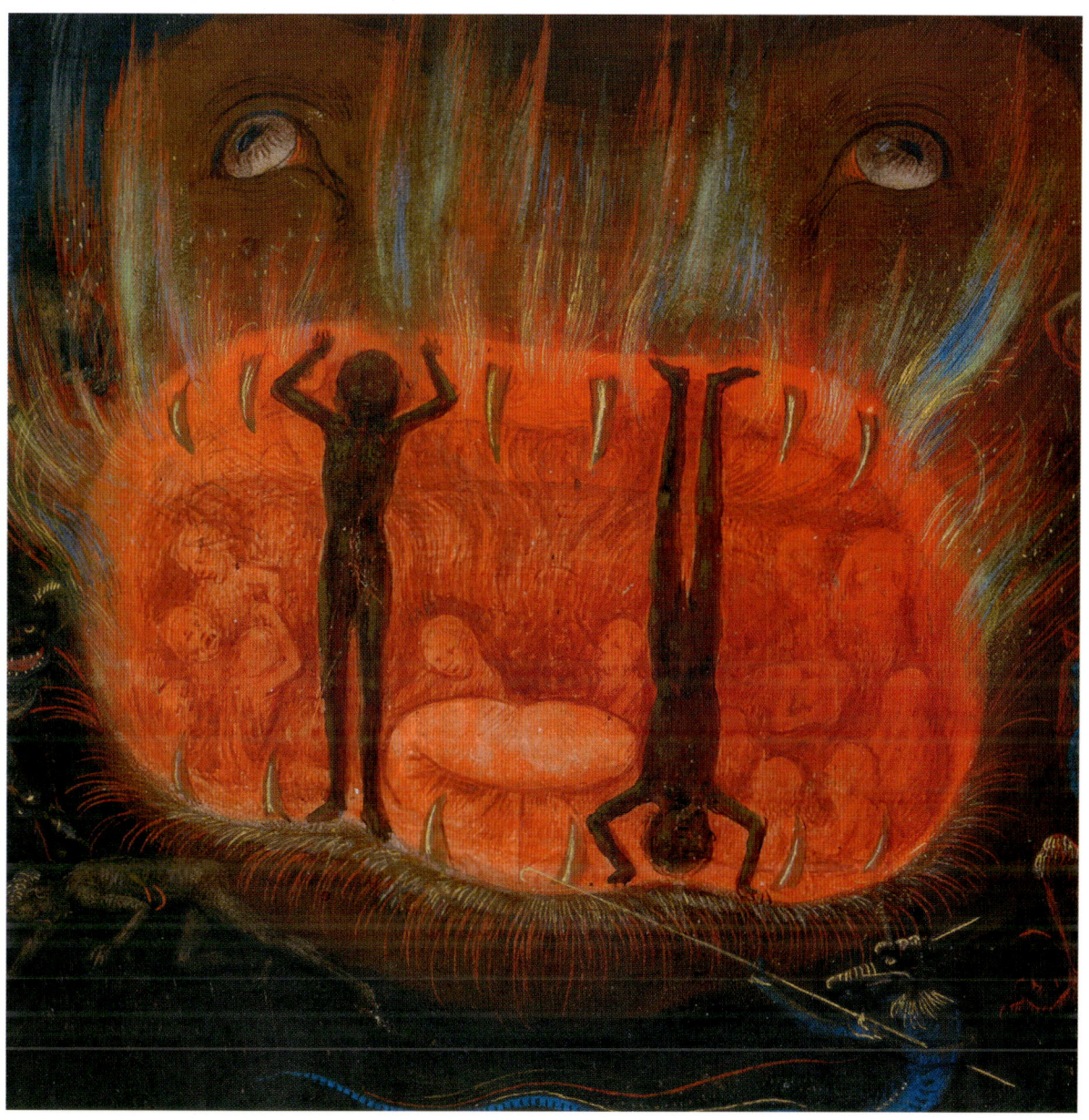

ABOVE

Illustration of a "hellmouth" from an edition of The Visions of Tundale *made by the fifteenth-century Burgundian artist Simon Marmion, now housed at the Getty Museum in Los Angeles. Hellmouths were a popular artistic trope in the period, a type of fissure or chasm in the earth that threatened to swallow humans whole, masticating them into the bowels of hell beneath. This metaphorical conflation of the bodily to the cosmic speaks to the ways in which the order of the universe was believed to be repeated across all levels; it also attests to the ways in which the grotesquerie of the physical could be overlaid onto the abstractions of the metaphysical.*

Because antiquity and the medieval world are, in many ways, a foreign country to our own understanding of things, the epistemological line between fact and fiction can be ambiguous. To ask in what sense The *Visions of Tundale* would be understood as "true" or not is to misapprehend the nature of truth in the time period. Brother Marcus did not claim to actually be his titular knight, or to necessarily have shared the same experiences with that character, and yet The *Visions of Tundale* also expressed more profound metaphysical truths that transcend the realm of mere affirmation. The historian Paul Veyne, writing in *Did the Greeks Believe in Their Myths?: An Essay on the Constitutive Imagination* makes an observation that's arguably equally accurate for the Middle Ages, that "truths are already products of the imagination and that the imagination has always governed. It is imagination that rules, not reality, reason, or the ongoing work of the negative."

In medieval debates about demonology—"Are these beings material or incorporeal? Are all of them the scions of the war in heaven, or do some have alternative origins?"—it must be remembered that they were not just figures of myth and literature, but of experience and encounter as well. For medieval thinkers, demons were potent metaphors and symbols, but they were also very much actual beings whose machinations affected individual lives. That's obvious in the guides to demonic names, from the Testament of Solomon to Psellos, and through other works that treated the subject soberly throughout these centuries. Consider the *Fortalitium Fidei* written by the fifteenth-century Spanish Dominican friar Alphonso de Spina.

Among other issues of Catholic apologetics, de Spina spends ample time providing description, taxonomy, and the hierarchy of demons, including digressions on incubi and succubae, the nature of familiars (infernal spirits who come in the form of animals), and the particulars of cambions (creatures produced in the sexual union of a demon and a human). For de Spina, demons weren't just metaphors, but facts; they weren't only allegories, but realities; they weren't merely symbols, but personalities capable of altering the world as surely as any woman or man can. When de Spina calculates that a total of exactly 133,306,668 demons were involved in Lucifer's rebellion, it may strike modern people as bizarre in its specificity, but what shouldn't be doubted is the earnestness of the friar's claim. There is a beauty in this kind of weirdness, this certainty about things infernal, things so fallen.

THE AGE OF LUCIFER, LEVIATHAN, AZAZEL, BELPHEGOR, MAMMON, BEELZEBUB, AND ASMODEUS

Sometime in the first few decades of the fifteenth century, most likely in the countryside around Norfolk, England, audiences experienced a theatrical innovation when they first watched drama in the round, in this case an anonymously written morality play titled *The Castle of Perseverance*. Stage drawings survive in the only extant manuscript of the anonymously written play, housed at the Folger Shakespeare Library in Washington, D.C., and those diagrams depict seating organized entirely around a round stage, differing from the hastily constructed wooden stages of the great medieval dramatic cycles held during Holy Week in places like York and Wakefield, while also prefiguring venues like the Rose and Globe theaters of the following centuries. Certainly a technological innovation in its own right, but also one, which, based on the plot of the play, would give its audience the opportunity to examine hell from a full 360-degree angle.

Viewers of *The Castle of Perseverance* would have largely unobstructed sight of the action in this allegorical morality play, as the title character Humanum Genus (which straightforwardly translates to "Mankind") is witness to a host of good and evil angels battling over his soul. In a demon-haunted age, where Satan's angels had a tangible reality to them, plays like *The Castle of Perseverance* would provide opportunity to espy devils with your own eyes, albeit in the form of men dressed up in red felt britches and hats, with black and green paint slathered onto their faces and horns strapped to their foreheads. The efficacy of such effects shouldn't be doubted, however, for as Russell writes, the Dark Prince "had broad popular appeal . . . owing to the plagues, famines, and wars that ravaged the fourteenth and early fifteenth centuries" and that "Nowhere did the Devil put in a more convincing appearance than in the mystery and miracle plays of the later Middle Ages."

Medieval drama provided the raw material in theme, language, and narrative that would be expanded by the great playwrights of the coming Elizabethan and Jacobean Ages, but the performances of this period differed in important ways from contemporary, secular theater. Harkening more toward the plays of ancient Greece, where theater was indistinguishable from religious ritual, the drama of the medieval period had a strong liturgical, if not sacramental, element. In mystery plays, such as those cycles held in York and Wakefield, audiences would see enactments of biblical stories from Genesis to Revelation, as performed by the workers who composed the guilds of the city. In miracle

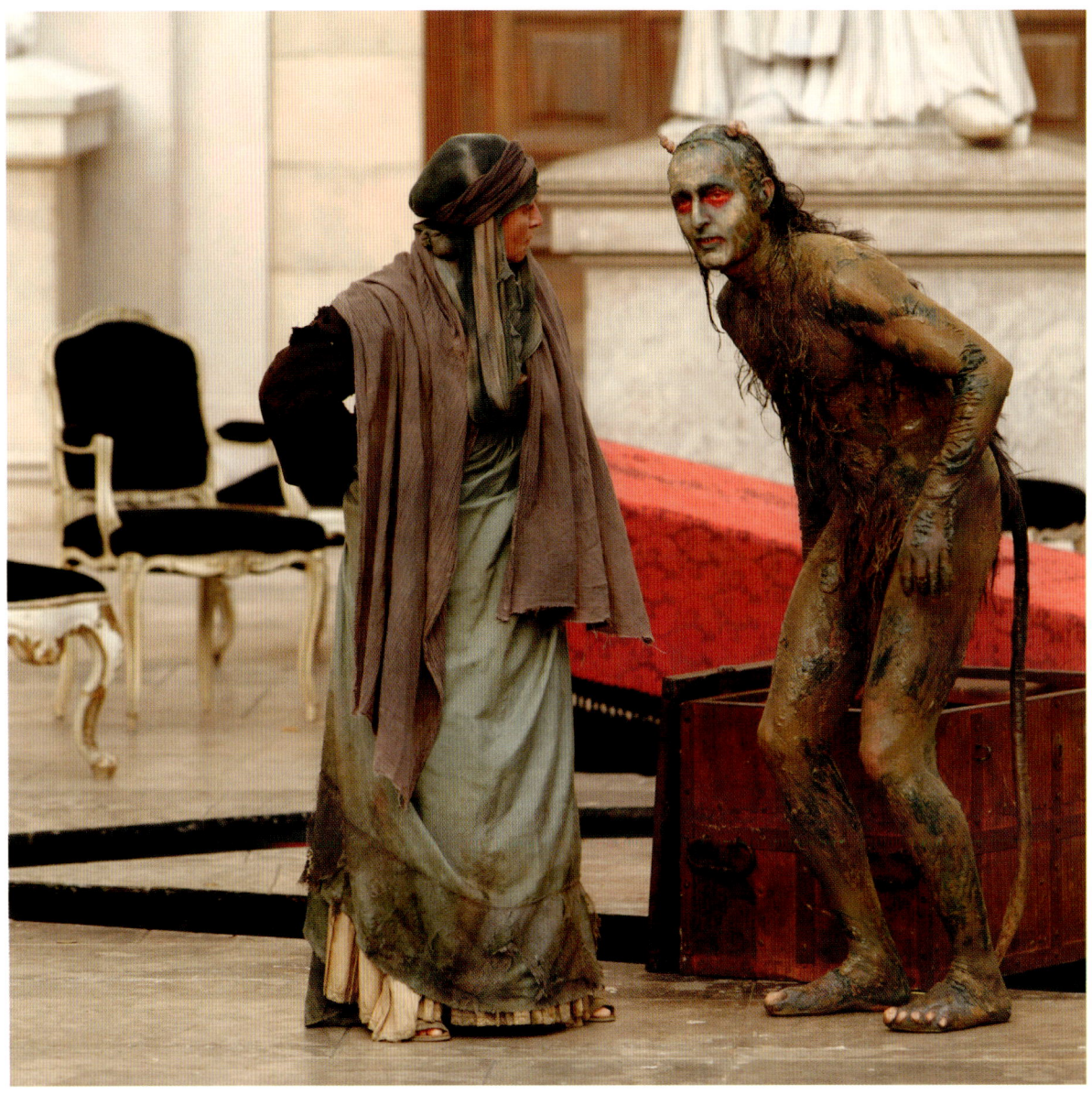

Actor Peter Jordan as the Devil in a 2009 production of Everyman, *with actress Elisabeth Rath as Good Works. In the Medieval theater, actors dressed as demons often appeared not unlike the* commedia dell'arte *players of the Italian Renaissance; there is something comic about theatrical devils, as indeed it was common to depict demons as objects of scorn, folly, and mockery. Darker implications also existed, however, as the incarnational theology of the period couldn't help but make audience members uneasy to "see" demons, especially as Medieval theater turned into that of the Renaissance, and conjurations might be uttered on the stage (with an attendant anxiety that such spells may prove successful).*

plays, hagiographical stories were presented in which saints' tales would be dramatically enacted. And in morality plays, the genre of medieval theater that is probably most staged in our own century, broad allegorical lessons would be dramatized, such as in the celebrated anonymous fifteenth-century plays *Everyman* and *The Castle of Perseverance*.

Despite the existence of a fourth genre of more secular medieval theater known as mumming plays, the preponderance of scripts from the time period engaged explicitly religious themes, and for audiences there wouldn't have been an easy distinction between seeing a play, or engaging in a sacred ritual. It was startling, disturbing, and immediate for audiences to suddenly see figures like God or Christ onstage, even if it was understood that these were men playing these characters. Something incarnational in that, for when a woman or man in the fifteenth century saw somebody dressed as a demon, there would have been a sense that this was a ritual that was more than just playacting; this performance was taking part in that numinous order of unseen realities. As John Harris writes in *Medieval Theater in Context*, "an element of danger often attached to the devils' performances, owing to the predilection of medieval audiences for seeing the 'father of lies,'" the stage providing view into a terrifying realm, even if it was a mirage of stage effects.

The Castle of Perseverance is written with all of the didacticism that marks morality plays; none of the characters are identifiable people (as a protagonist simply named "Mankind" would evidence), but rather broad types, whose sole function is to allegorically illuminate the nature of a conflicted soul. As the anonymous author notes, the purpose of the play is "To save you from sinning, / Forever from the beginning/Think on your last ending!" Yet when the play itself is understood as a representation of the divisions that exist within the human mind, *The Castle of Perseverance* can be experienced as a text of striking psychological intensity, where the representation of various angels and demons are experienced as a dramatization of the fractures that exist within the soul. Characters with names like "World," "Flesh," "Righteousness," "Truth," and "Death" toggle over the status of Mankind's salvation, variously tempting him in the direction of damnation or encouraging him toward repentance. Central to the travails of Mankind are the intercession of seven imps, each identified with the Seven Deadly Sins of medieval soteriology, and taking part in that venerable tradition that examines the human heart as enraptured to the claims of pride, lust, gluttony, envy, sloth, greed, and wrath. As one of the sins says, undoubtedly dressed in the costume of a demon, "Oh, Mankind, blessed might thou be! /I have loved thee dearly many a day, /And so, I know well, thou dost me."

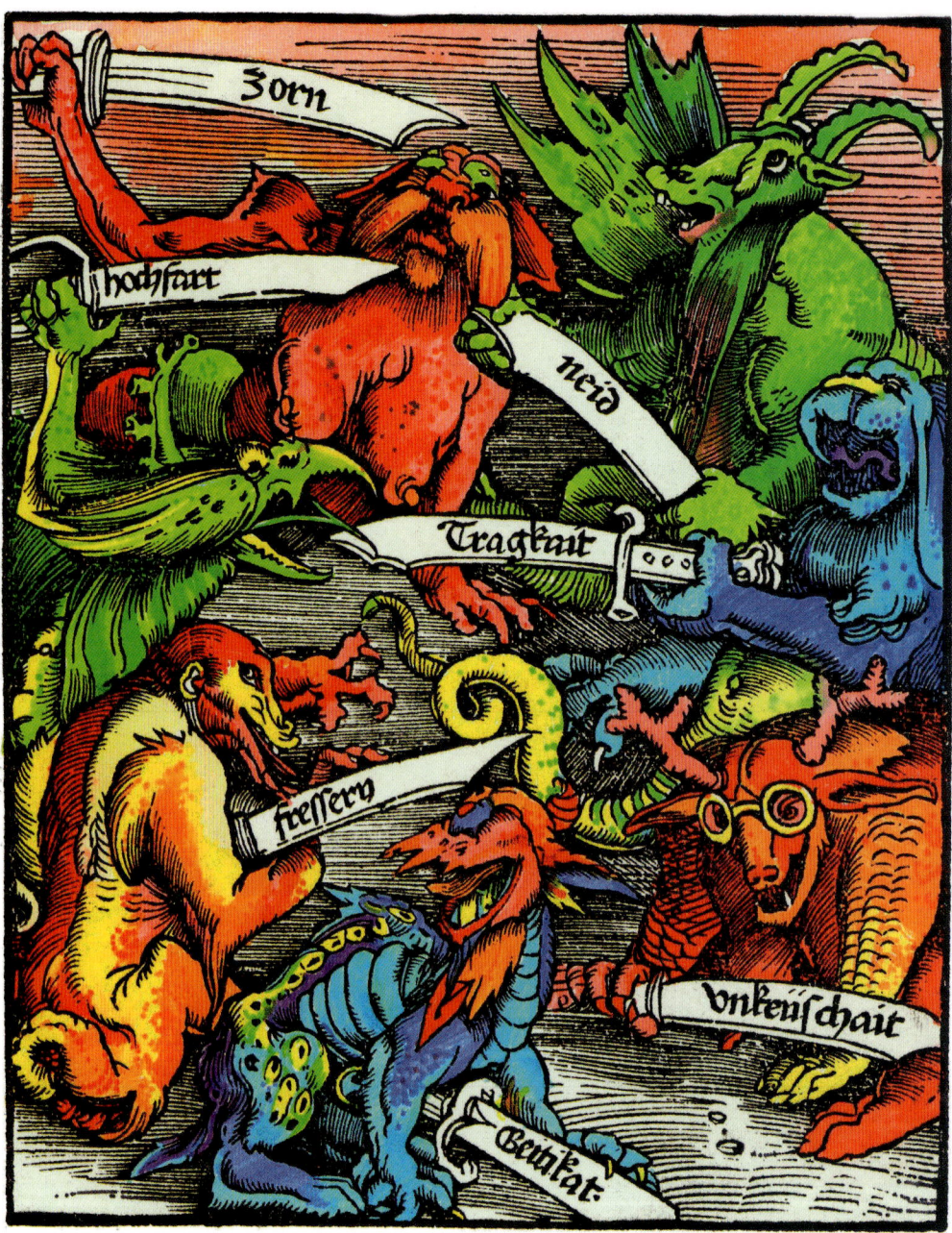

For all of the obviousness of its parable, *The Castle of Perseverance* expresses some fundamental psychological truths about humanity's death-obsessed attraction toward consumption, the endless desire for more, whether it be more acclaim, or wealth, or power. Christians from the time of Saint Augustine have called this predilection "original sin," and in the Middle Ages the most convenient model for discussing that universal attribute was that of the Seven Deadly Sins, whose demonic representations in plays like *The Castle of Perseverance* evidence their close connection to demonology. First attributed to the ascetic, anchorite, and desert father Evagrius Ponticus in the fourth century, the Seven Deadly Sins were not necessarily transgressions in and of themselves, but defects of character that if indulged without moderation could lead to trespasses.

Of variable listing, the conventional schema of the sins, including lust, gluttony, avarice, sloth, envy, wrath, and pride, are perversions of natural human inclinations, pushed to an extreme so that they ultimately violate the dignity of other people. Christian Schäfe explains in the collection *Vices in the Middle Ages* that according to theologians, the problem with the sins are that "they make the good that is the object of internal drives on which they set their hearts into an absolute, they take it to an extreme and elevate it over everything and everyone else—pride and envy, a self-assertion vis-à-vis others; avarice, the drive to self-preservation; lust, the sex drive; gluttony, the drive for sustenance." To eat food, to rest, to procreate, and so on are requirements for the continuation of life, but as Ponticus and theologians from Pope Gregory I to Saint Thomas Aquinas would argue, to countenance gluttony, sloth, or lust is to mire ourselves in evil, a libertinage that threatens the livelihoods of other women and men (it need not be asked why in an age when famine was common that gluttony, for example, should be so condemned).

There was great artistic import in exploring the Seven Deadly Sins, as *The Castle of Perseverance* demonstrates; the theme was explored in paintings from Hieronymus Bosch to Pieter Breughel the Elder, and this particular language of perdition was common throughout medieval literature. Geoffrey Chaucer has his parson preach on the subject in the late fourteenth-century classic *The Canterbury Tales*, explaining in his penitential sermon that the Seven Deadly Sins "all run about in the same pasture, so to speak, but manifest themselves in different forms." According to Chaucer's parson, they "are the chief sins because all other sins spring from them," even while "Each of these deadly sins has its own smaller branches and twigs." As can be seen in *The Castle of Perseverance*, a tradition had taken hold that associated each of these sinful attributes with a specific demon. Chaucer isn't as explicit, yet something of the Luciferian is preserved in his argument that "At the root of . . . [the sins] is pride, which is the root of all evil, and from this root grows the stems and branches of anger, envy, indolence, avarice . . . gluttony and lechery." The original rebellion in heaven was predicated on Lucifer's overweening pride, his inability to accept God's sovereignty in the creation of humanity, and so all other transgressions, whether in heaven, earth, or hell, stem from the sense that the individual self is preeminent over all other creatures.

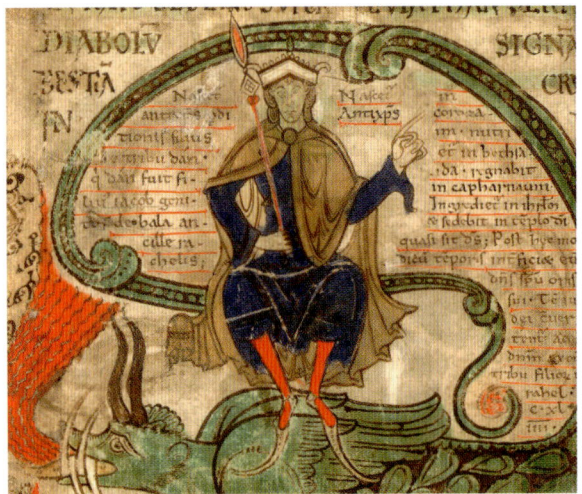
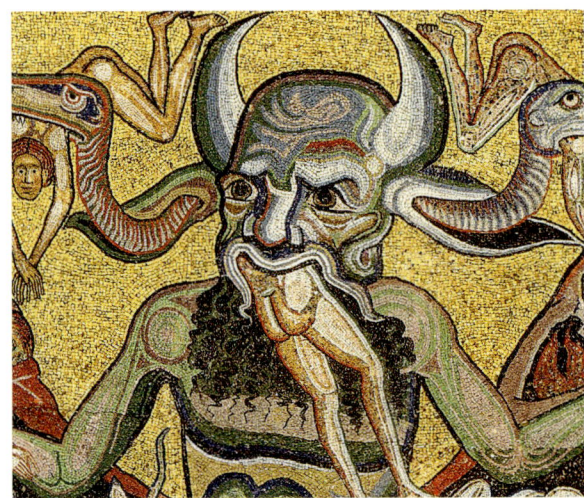
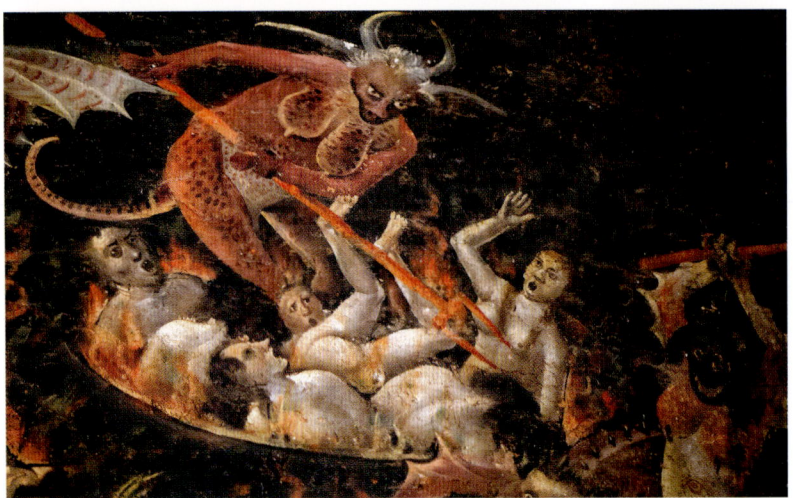
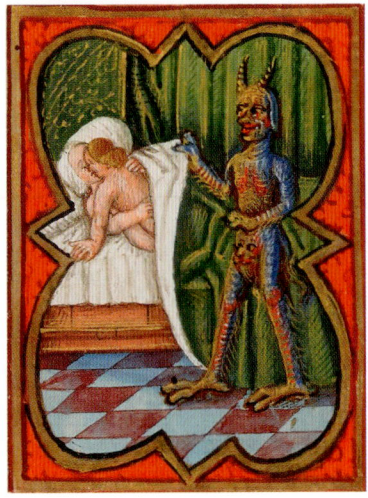

On the top left is a depiction of the Antichrist riding upon the back of the mighty sea serpent Leviathan, sometimes associated with the sin of envy, as imagined by an anonymous scribe compiling the twelfth-century Liber Floridus, a compendium of all knowledge; on the top right is a mosaic of Satan, associated with the sin of wrath, devouring a sinner in the lowest circle of hell. This later image was made sometime in the thirteenth through fourteenth centuries on the ceiling of the Florence Baptistry, and owes much to Eastern Orthodox aesthetics. The poet Dante was baptized here, and his description of a hungry Satan devouring the sinful, as if Chronos eating his sons, perhaps owes something to this mosaic. On the bottom left is a thirteenth-century mural from the Cathedral Basilica of Saint Cecelia in Albi, France, which depicts the punishments of the gluttonous when in hell; on the right is an illustration of lust from a fourteenth-century French Bibles moralisées held at the Bibliothèque nationale de France at Paris. The first image is a sterling example of the Middle Ages' reciprocal model of sin and punishment (as exemplified by The Divine Comedy) whereby the damned are punished by variations of their own sins, with a gluttonous man being force-fed by a demonic horde, one of whom is perhaps Beelzebub, the being associated with that particular sin. The fourth image would have illustrated a page of the "moralizing bibles" popular in Medieval Europe, with a demon espying a scene of unnatural copulation, this scene either depicting lesbian sex, or with a woman positioned on top of the man. Perhaps the demon in question is Asmodeus, who for all of his roles already discussed was also often associated with lust.

A book written not long after *The Canterbury Tales* is far less reticent to identify which sins are explicitly associated with which particular lieutenants of hell. Of the same tradition of demon-naming that Psellos practiced, as well as the genres of Enochian and Solomonic literatures from distant antiquity, the early fifteenth-century *The Lantern of Light* promised to enumerate devilish nomenclature, with the added innovation of explaining the role that these individual beings played in relationship to each of the Seven Deadly Sins. Frequently attributed to the theologian John Wycliffe, an Oxford-based proto-Protestant who is regarded as the founder of the heresy of Lollardy, *The Lantern of Light* still reflected a high-medieval worldview in the relationship of humans to sin and damnation. Whoever the author is, he lists the demons and which sins are their domains, noting that:

The first is Lucifer

that reigns in his malice over the children of pride.

The second is named Leviathan that lords over the envious.

The third devil is Azazel and wrath is his lordship.

The fourth is named Belphegor and sloth is his retinue.

The fifth devil is Mammon of those who are avarice

and he leads a sinful army of those that covet.

The sixth is named Beelzebub, that is the god of gluttons.

The seventh devil is Asmodeus. That is the leader of the lecherous.

Drawing from previous listings of demonic names, *The Lantern of Light*'s system of classification gives face and form to each one of these sins, so that, for example, Lucifer and Mammon are reaffirmed as lords of their respective vices, and other demons are established over their own sinful domains, such as Asmodeus's association with lust or Azazel's with wrath. The names are familiar, and sometimes their purposes are as well, but in the mind of *The Lantern of Light*'s author, these characters should be understood as the "cause" of these transgressions men and women commit every day.

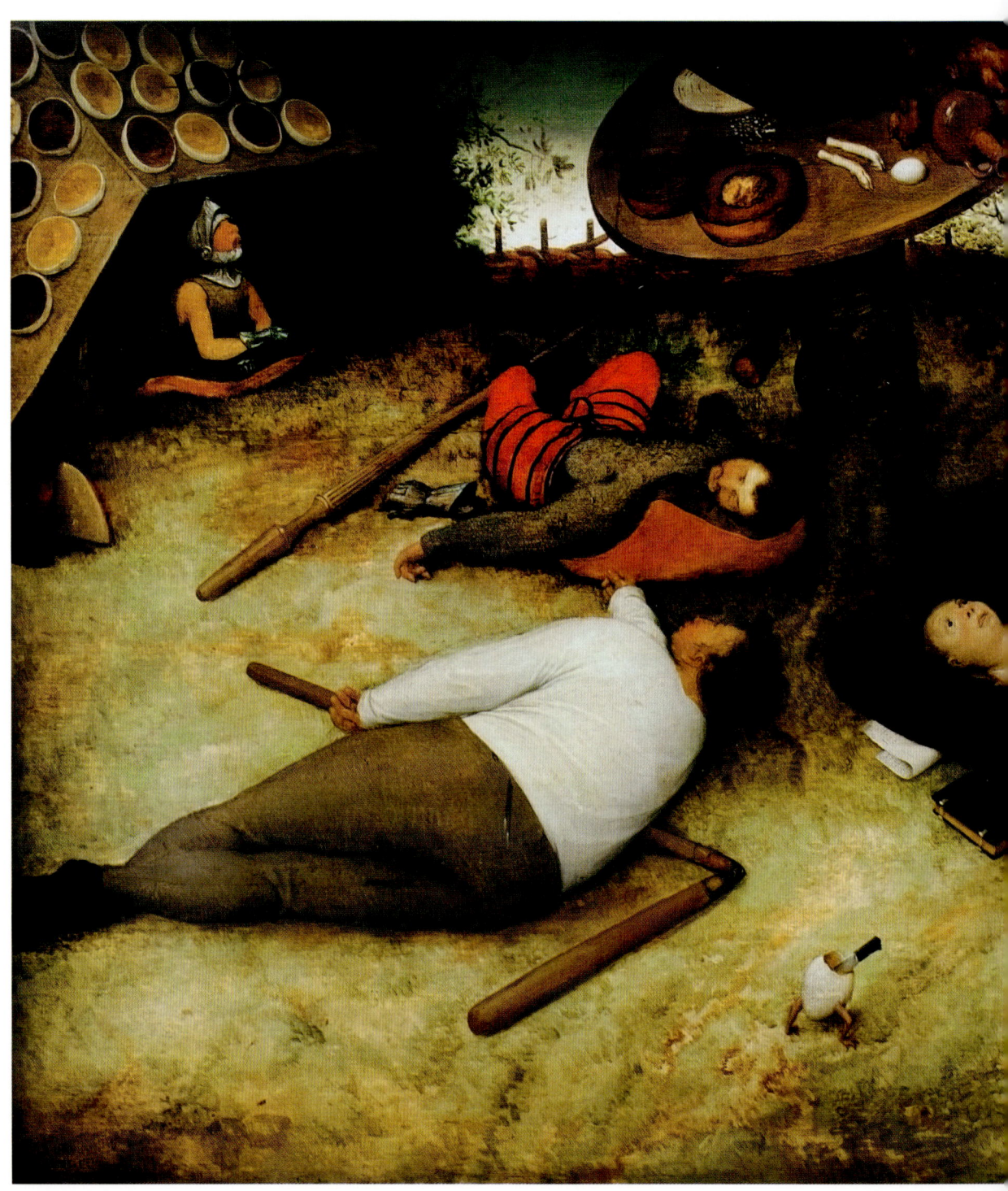

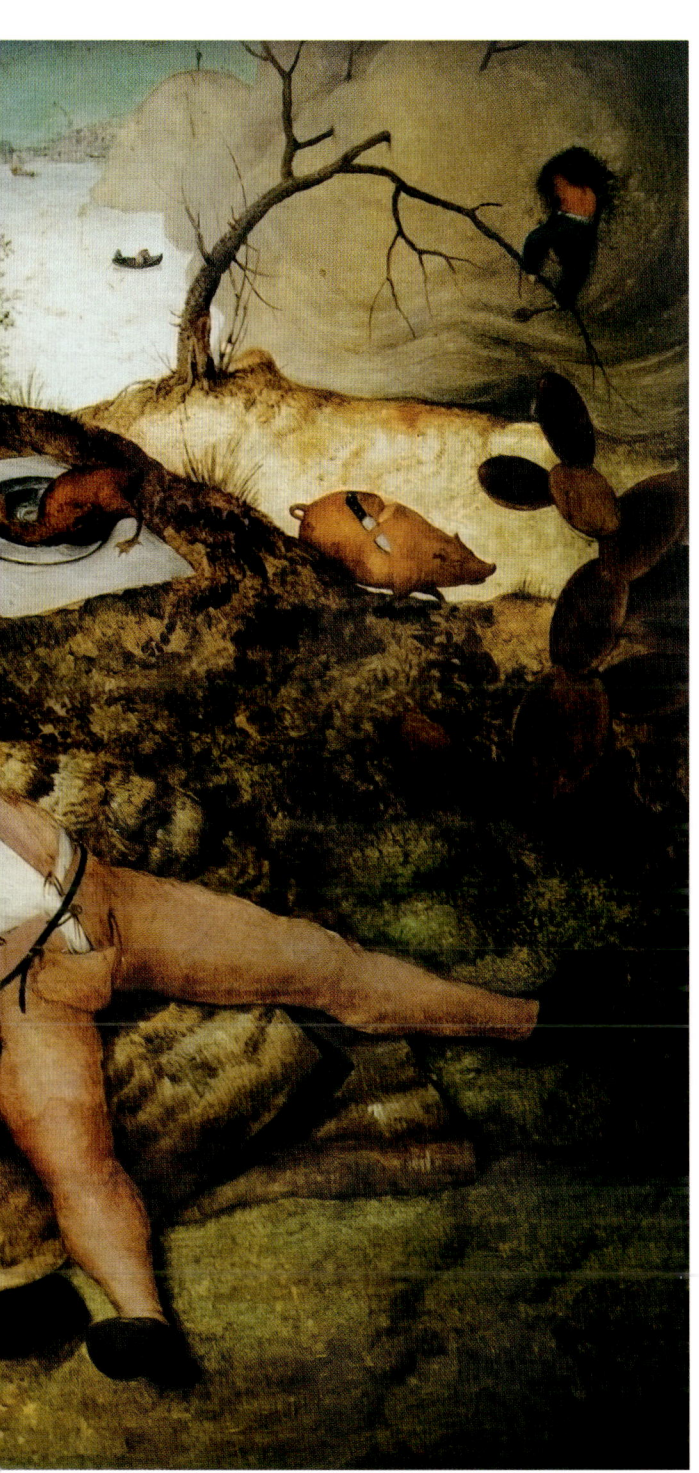

THIS SPREAD

Though the Netherlandish painter Pieter Brueghel the Elder lived firmly in the Renaissance and was strongly influenced by the Reformation, his themes were arguably still strongly medieval. The detail on the right is from his painting The Land of Cockaigne, *composed in 1567 and exhibited at the Alte Pinakothek in Munich. His theme is the legendary, paradisical, Edenic realm of Cockaigne, a mythic utopia where there are no cares, no work, and no scarcity. The indolent gentleman depicted therein presents a typical example of sloth, for which the demon Belphegor's influence was often blamed. On the right there is an illumination from the thirteenth-century French work* A Survey for the King, *intended as a moral guide concerning vice and virtue and now housed in the British Library. A trio of demons whisper into a cleric's ear as he stuffs church revenue into a sack, perhaps envoys of Mammon, who is traditionally regarded as the hellish sovereign of avarice.*

The Lantern of Light, even if authored by Wycliffe, evidences the thinking about sin that dominated medieval Catholicism, and by associating each one of the Seven Deadly Sins with an individual demon, it provided a potent vocabulary of perfidy with which to understand evil. If anything marked the reformations (both Catholic and Protestant) that would convulse Christendom in the sixteenth century, it was a turning away from Ponticus's system of understanding sin in favor of embracing the biblical Decalogue. Ethical philosophy reoriented itself away from the somewhat ambivalent example of the Seven Deadly Sins in favor of the clear-cut rules of the Ten Commandments. Where the Seven Deadly Sins allowed for some ambiguity—When does natural hunger become gluttony? When does the necessary attraction for one's spouse become lust?—the Decalogue is much more emphatic and absolutist in its prohibitions. The result is less an increase in moral certainty than it is a loss of the richly psychological negative capability that the Seven Deadly Sins allowed for, a strikingly sophisticated and almost novelistic sense of human complexity. An error in that the model of personified vice offered forth in *The Lantern of Light* is an acute and useful metaphorical system that can convey the realism of psychological experience in no less accurate a manner than does Sigmund Freud's tripartite division of the psyche into id, ego, and superego.

And what of the role of Wycliffe's demons in that—what use do they have for us today? How could those of us in this ostensibly secular modern age possibly see value in the seemingly superstitious oddities of *The Lantern of Light*? How could we ascribe that green-eyed envy that we feel when scrolling through social media and seeing the designer apartments or luxury cars of our friends and neighbors to something as arcane as Leviathan? If a car should cut us off in traffic, or if we fight about politics on some internet message board, who among us would blame Azazel for the white-hot intensity of pure rage that we feel? When endlessly scrolling through Twitter or Facebook, how could we blame Belphegor? Are the wealthy investment bankers and finance executives of Wall Street enraptured to something as esoteric as Mammon? When engorging ourselves at McDonald's, is Beelzebub to blame? When clicking through one more link of pornography, who would see Asmodeus as being responsible? And above all, does Lucifer in his overweening pride, his arrogance, his hubris, his sheer narcissism, mark us as perhaps more in need of medieval wisdom than we might first suppose?

The haughty imprimatur of proud defiance is apparent on his face even after his fall from heaven has transformed Lucifer—the Light Bearer, who was once God's most beloved—into this bestial creature. Pride has always been viewed as the most central of sins, the belief that you are owed more than those around you. It is the sin of inequality, and it was Lucifer's denial of God's creation of humanity that led to the war in heaven. This painting was the far left panel on a triptych, made by the Flemish painter Hans Memling in 1485, titled Earthly Vanity and Divine Salvation, *now housed at the Musée des Beaux-Arts de Strasbourg.*

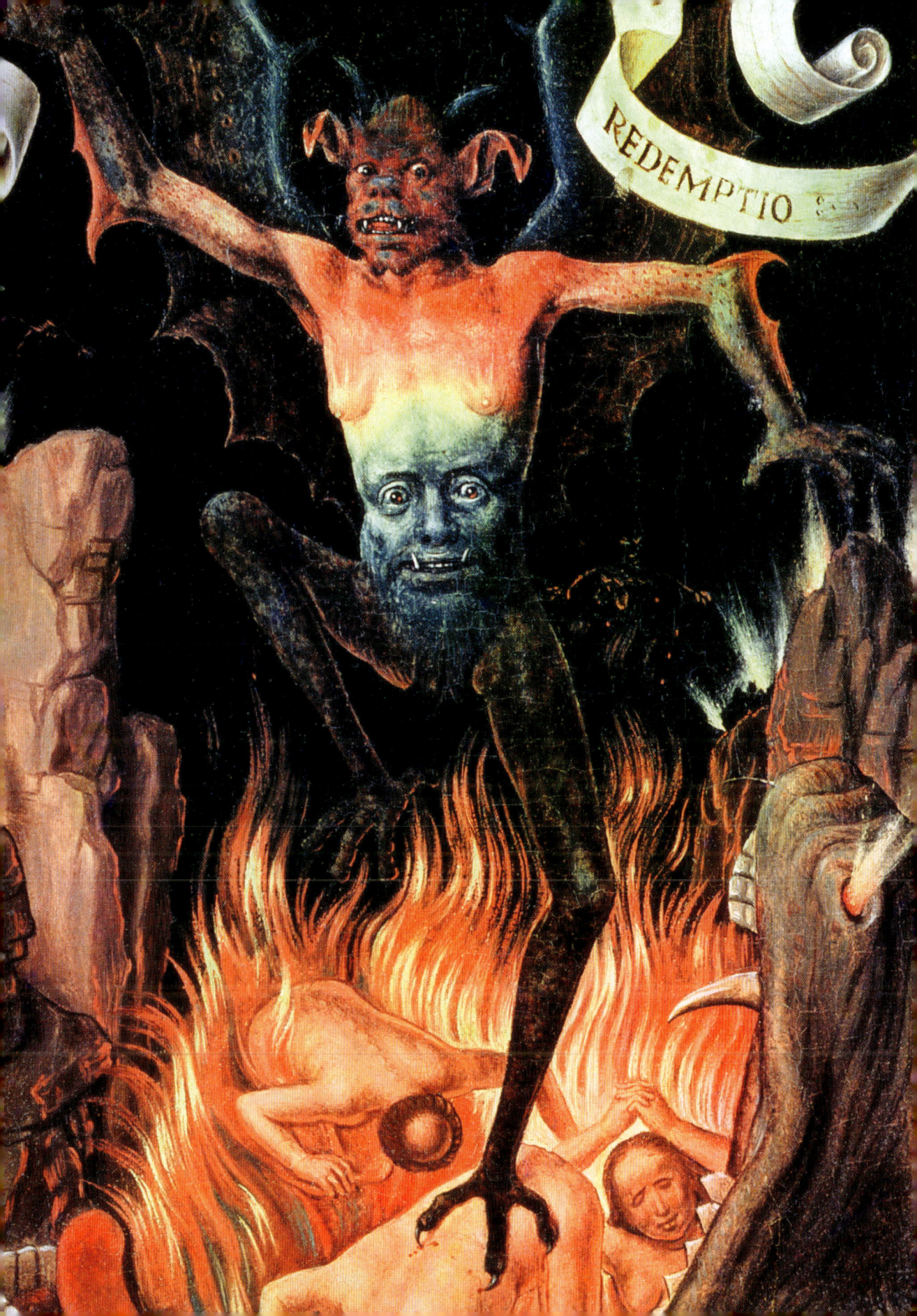

REDEMPTIO

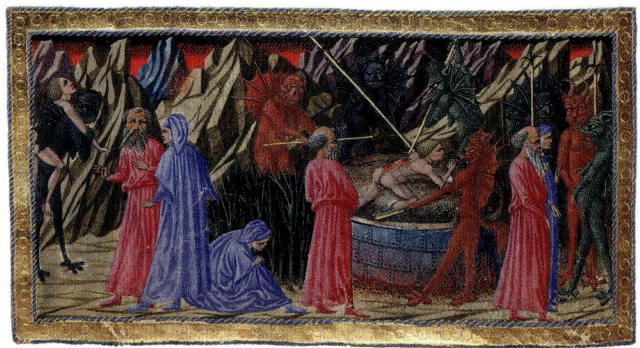

DANTE'S DEMONS

I n the syllabus of hell, few authors are more prominent than the thirteenth-century Florentine poet Dante Alighieri. His given name has become synonymous with perdition—the declaration affixed before hell's entrance in the *Inferno* section of his epic, *The Divine Comedy*, had been endlessly repurposed across culture as a diabolical idée fixe—"Abandon all hope ye who enter here." *The Divine Comedy* is the exemplar of medieval Italian literature, and arguably the greatest poetic work to be produced in the context of Catholicism, if not Christianity. Across its three sections, that number invoked throughout the epic's structure in homage to the Holy Trinity, Dante is first guided through the nine circles of hell by his hero, the classical pagan poet Virgil, followed by the author's subsequent voyages through purgatory and then Heaven.

Inferno is a work of complex world-building, with Dante drawing from scholastic theology, folk culture, and his own invention to posit a hell structured as a series of concentric circles, with the more abominable closer to Satan at the center of this subterranean cosmos, and with their punishments ingeniously appropriate to the nature of their sins. "Here sighs and lamentations and loud cries/where echoing across the starless air," Dante writes. "Strange utterances, horrible pronouncements,/accents of anger, words of suffering,/and voices shrill and faint, and beating hands—/all went to make a tumult that will whirl/forever through that turbid, timeless air,/like sand that eddies when a whirlwind swirls."

Conceivably the most effecting rhetoric of hell ever produced, Dante synthesized both past traditions as well as his own innovations, in which he appropriated the distinctive terza rima rhyme scheme that had been associated with the writings of the Albigensian heretics whom the Church had waged a crusade against in the previous century. When readers imagine hell, and its cursed citizens, it's more often Dante from whom they draw the images, rather than the Church Fathers, or Augustine, or Aquinas. From Dante's corpus would sprout flowers of inspiration in Western art and literature across the ensuing centuries, his descriptions rendered in art, his themes elaborated on in literature. Central to the *Inferno* are, as should be expected, the demons of perdition.

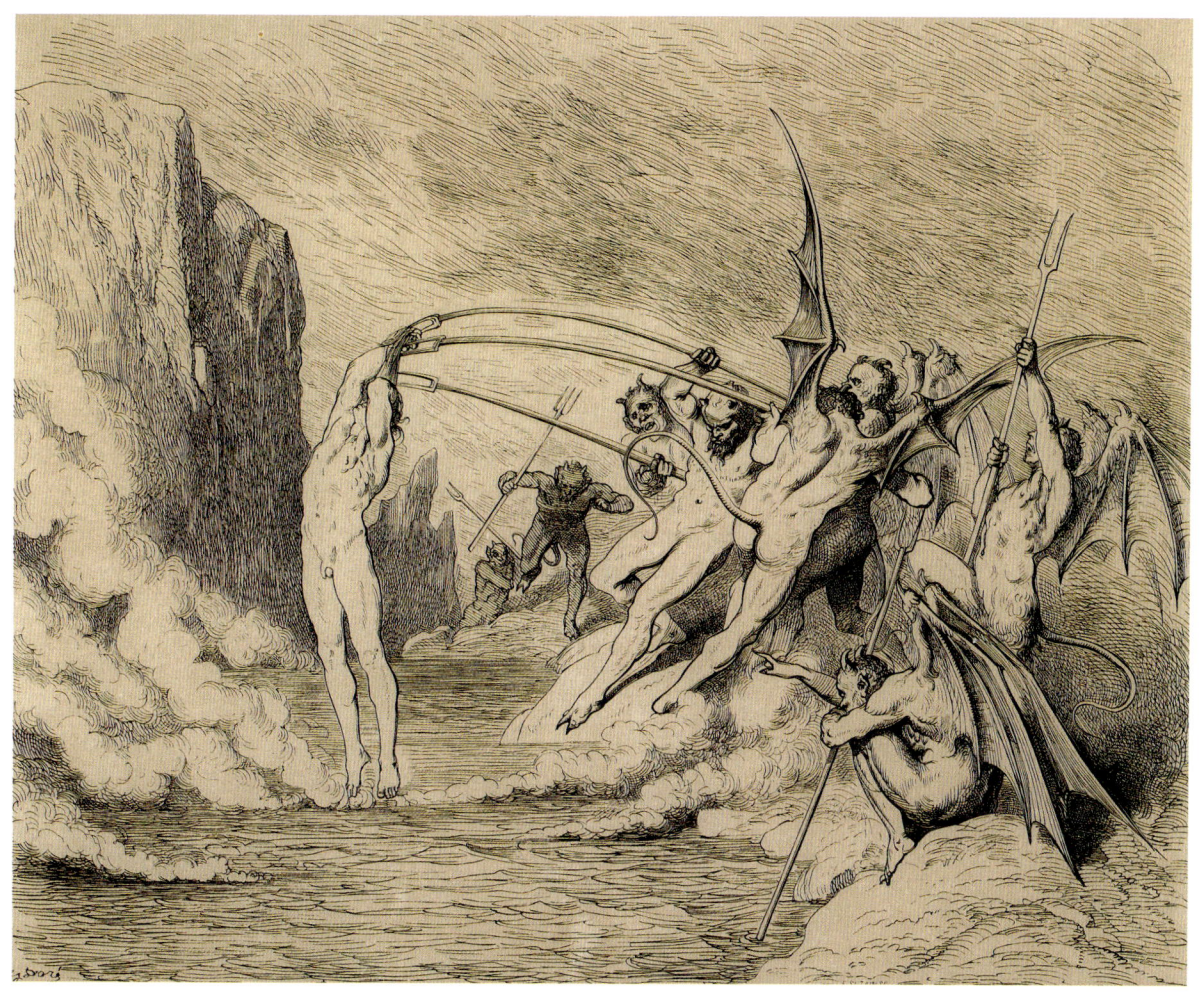

In a codex now housed in the British Library, the fifteenth-century Sienese painter Giovanni di Paolo imagines the scene in which Dante (in blue on the right) and Virgil (his partner in red) encounter the demons of Hell's eighth circle, known as the Malebranche (Italian for "Evil Claws)." Twelve of the Malebranche are named, given humorous titles such as "Red-Faced Terror," "Dog Scratcher," and simply "Goblin." Their task is the enviable job of forever pushing corrupt politicians into a cauldron of boiling tar. An estimably political writer, Dante had in mind some of his own adversaries who'd been involved in his forced exile from Florence, so that when he writes "They bent their hooks and shouted to each other:/And shall I give it to him on the rump?," he had some specific folks in mind. "And all of them replied, Yes, let him have it!"

The great French lithographer Gustave Doré, known for his interpretations of The Divine Comedy *and* Paradise Lost, *among others, in this 1890 sketch imagines the canto in which Dante and Virgil encounter the Malebranche.*

Yet Dante's rendering shouldn't be confused as simple moralizing, for in writing *The Divine Comedy* he was able to fully encompass the infernal with a psychological verisimilitude, so that critic Erich Auerbach would write in *Dante: Poet of the Secular World*, "Dante's rich imagery are not haphazard products of an irresponsible fantasy seeking to pile up horrors, but the work of a serious, inquiring mind." While the gothic has drawn from Dante for centuries, the poet was a serious ethicist as much as he was an exegete of horror. According to Auerbach, the Florentine "cast off the element of arbitrary fantasy" thus closer scrutiny "reveals that the poet carefully apportioned and defined . . . meanings, so that they require no commentary but rather help to elucidate the text." No cipher is needed to interpret the demons—they speak for themselves, because Dante's demons are not mere symbols, but actual persons, and in that they're infinitely more terrifying.

THIS SPREAD

Detail from the Italian painter Giovanni da Modena's 1410 fresco Last Judgement, *displayed at the Basilica di San Petronio in Bologna. The artist depicts Satan in the ninth circle of Hell, a freezing wasteland in which the three arch-traitors of Judas, Casius, and Brutus are forever devoured by this "Emperor of the kingdom dolorous."*

NEXT SPREAD

The fifteenth-century Florentine Renaissance master Sandro Botticelli imagines the subsection of hell's eighth circle in which seducers and flatterers are punished, where those who are guilty of excessive and strategic pandering are marched in single file for eternity by demons with whips, or forced to wade through rivers of human excrement.

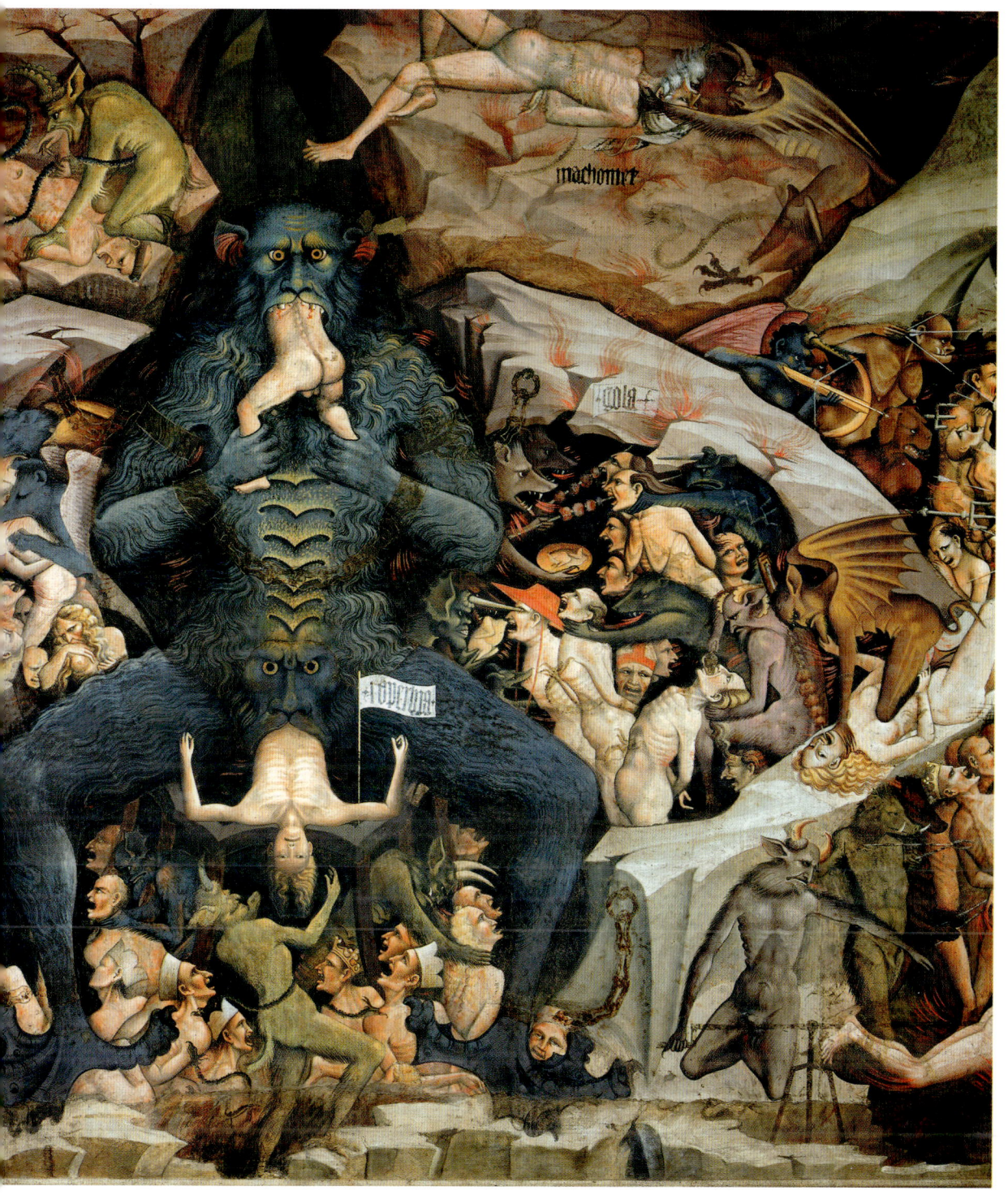

machomet

95

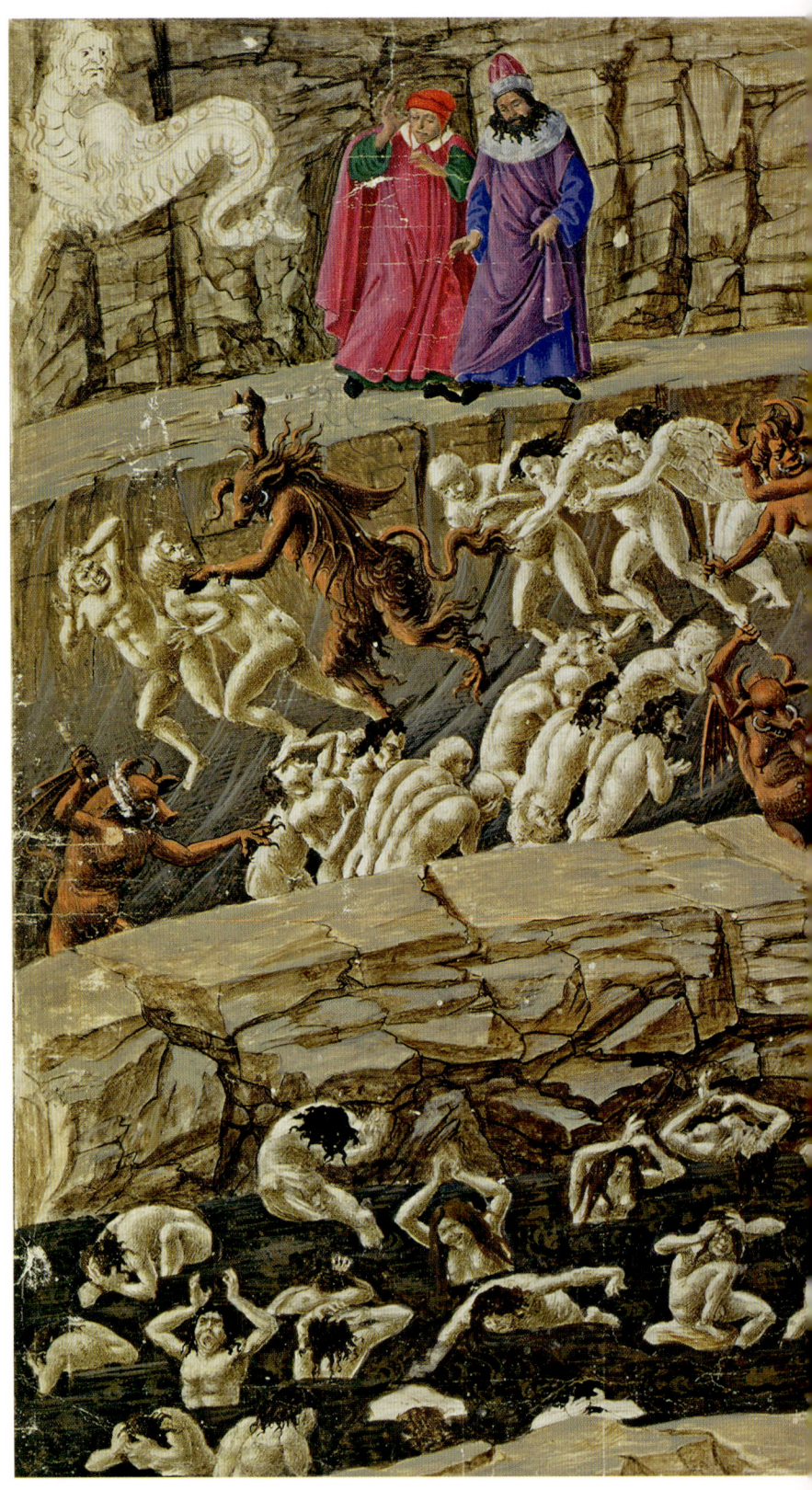

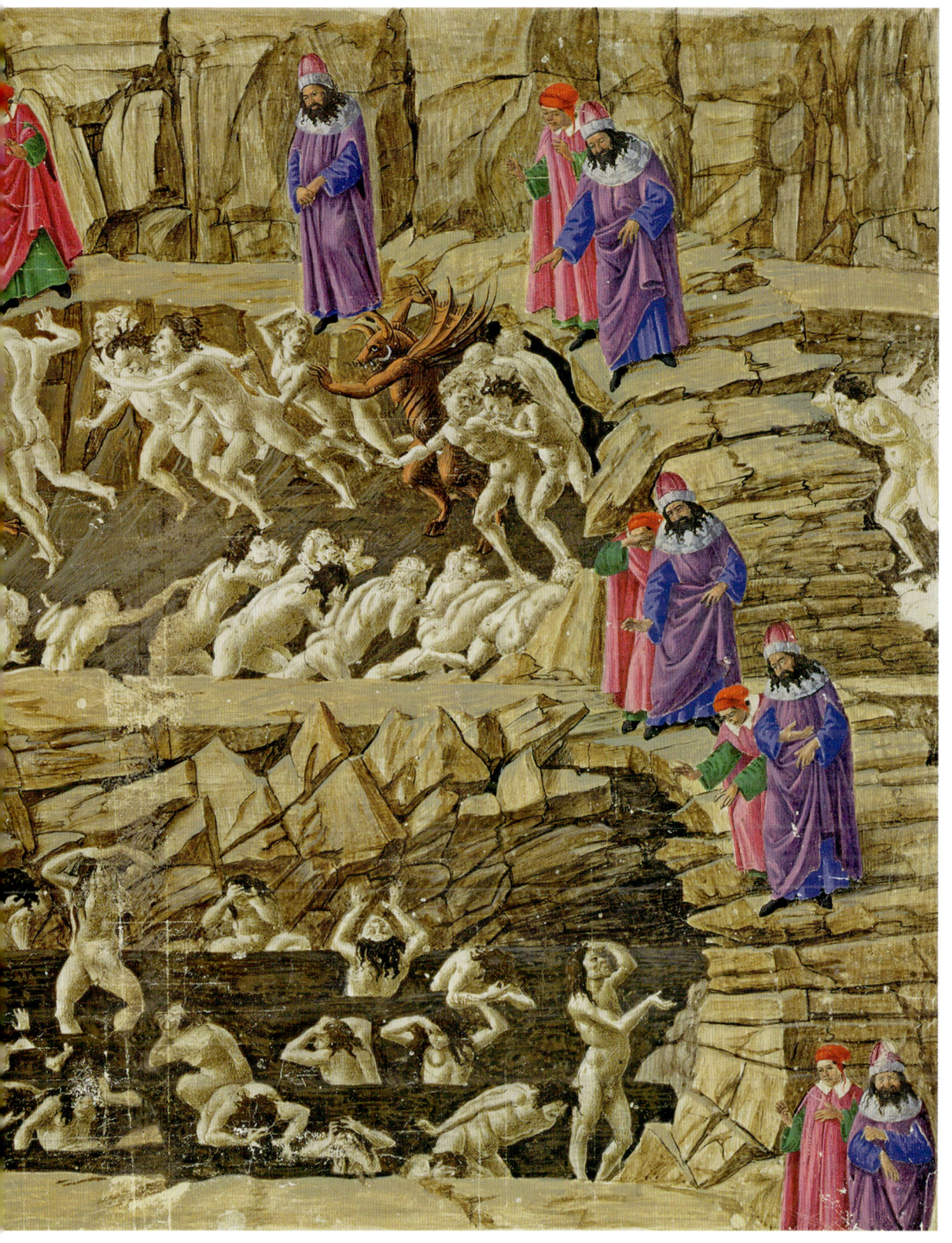

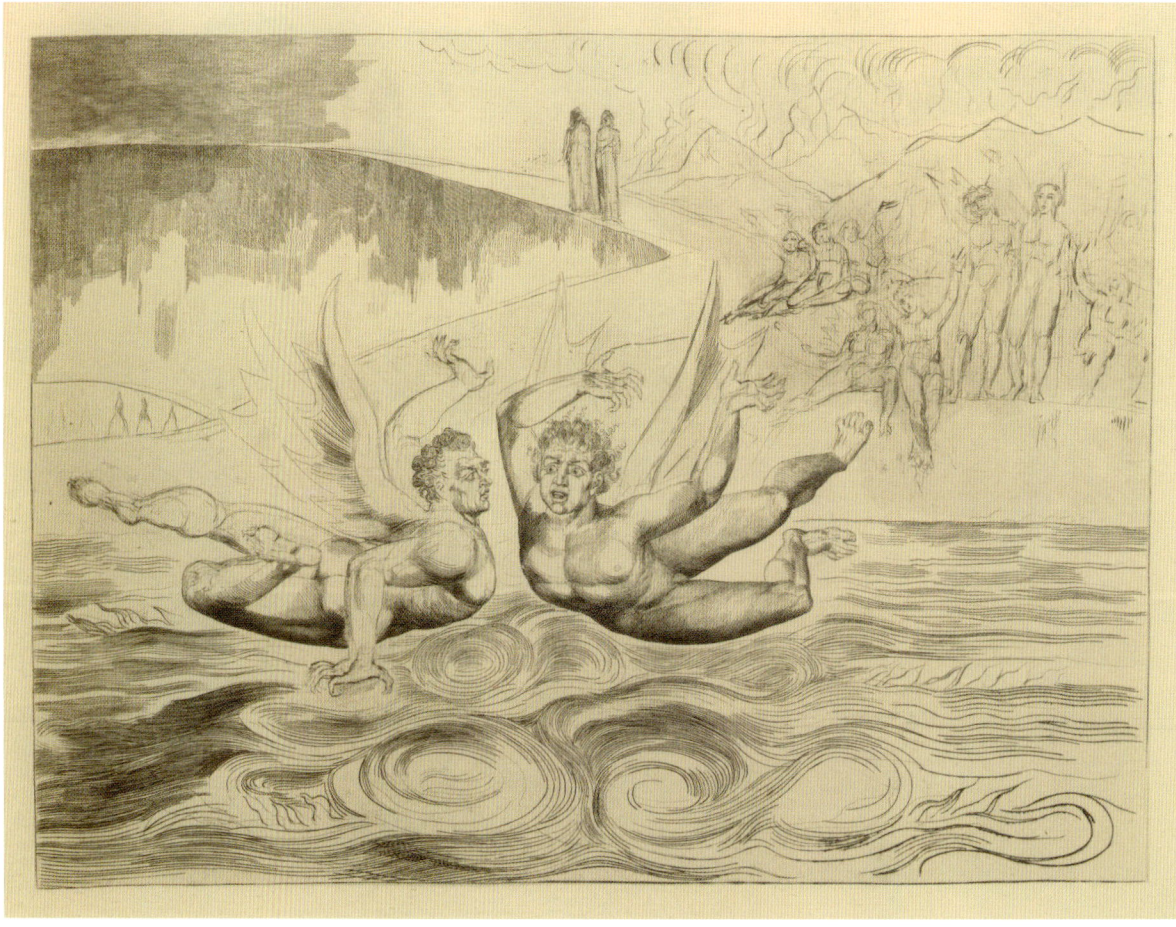

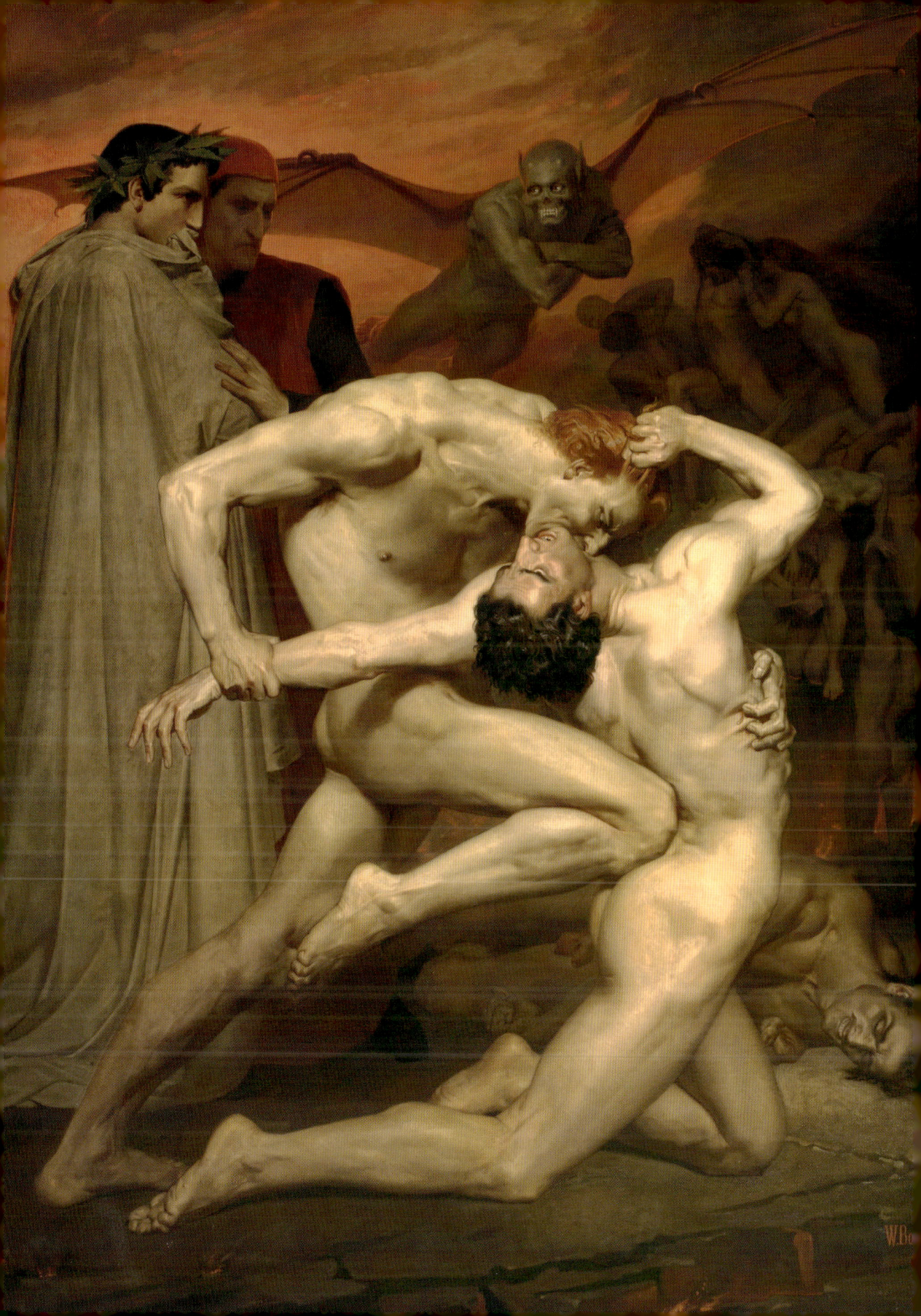

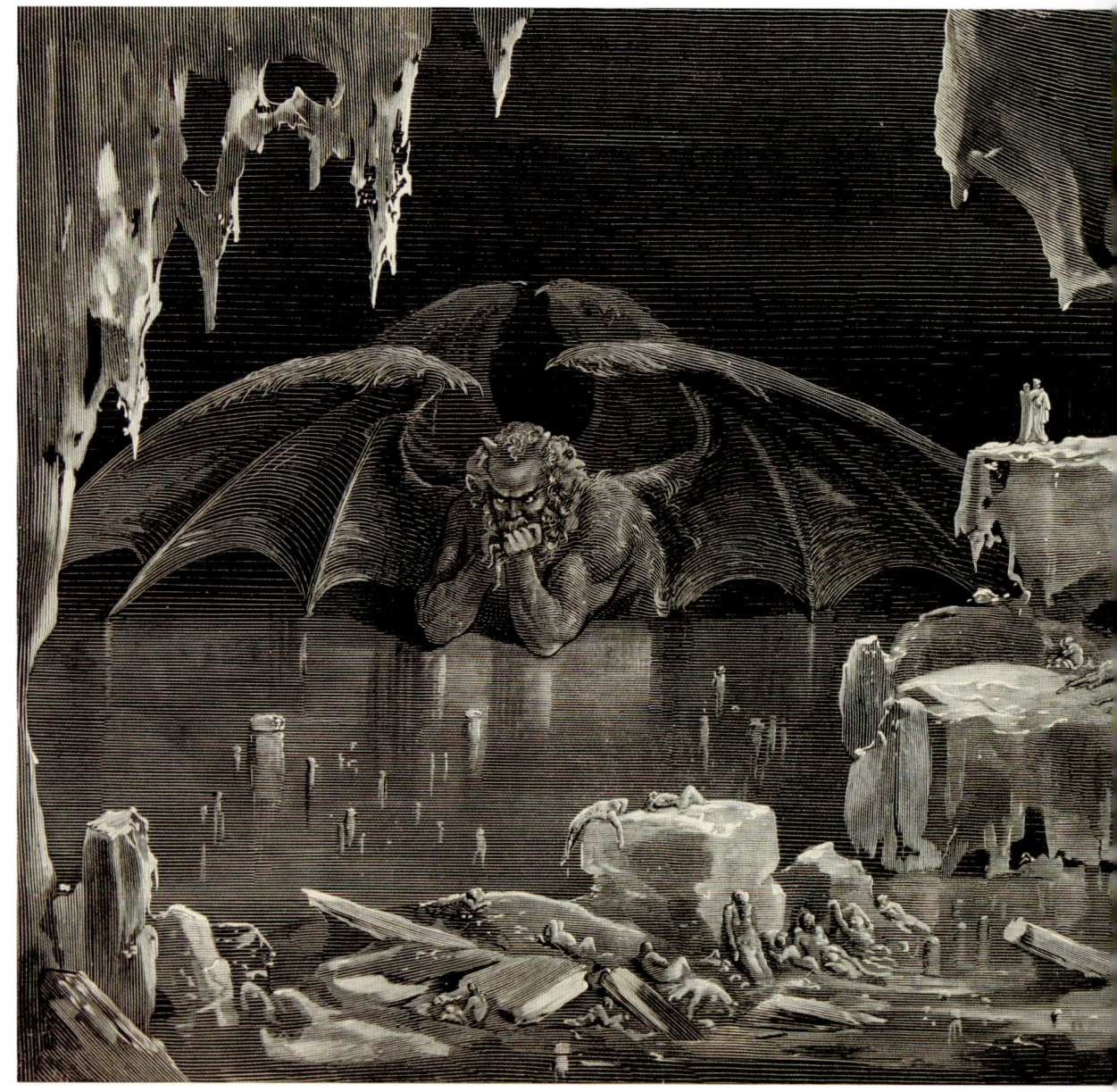

One of the consummate illustrators of the demonic, and of Dante in particular, the nineteenth-century French engraver, illustrator, and printmaker Gustave Doré presents Satan in the ninth circle from this 1857 edition of the poem. "He wept with all six eyes, and the tears fell over his three chins mingled with bloody foam," wrote Dante. "The teeth of each mouth held a sinner, kept as by a flax rake: thus he held three of them in agony." While Doré's Devil has some of the bestial characteristics with which he was often depicted in the Middle Ages, this post-Miltonic and post-Romantic Satan has more of the noble hero about him than Dante would have meant to imply.

THE ICONOGRAPHY OF EVIL

So expected and iconic is the typical demonic physiognomy—the cleft foot and horns, the forked tongue and tail—that it can obscure the inviolate axiom that all cultural phenomena have their own unique history. Nothing as mediated through the subjective experience of women and men doesn't have a cultural and social history contingent upon context, even phenomena that are transcendent or numinous. Maxwell-Stuart provides an overview of this demonic evolutionary ascent, so that "from the nineth century until the twelfth, the ruler of hell looks like a satyr or wild man in loincloth; from the twelfth to the fifteenth, he has horns and hoofs and a tail; and when he is shown with wings they are feathered, like those of an angel, until the fourteenth century when he is depicted with those of a bat." By the dawn of the early modern period, Maxwell-Stuart explains that fallen angels began to look more like unfallen ones, so that the descent of demons was made more explicit.

Whether or not we speak of demons as "real" in a metaphysical sense, or any other sense for that matter, the history of their representation is also a history of human culture attempting to comprehend the world, and in that regard all of the demonic regalia—the aforementioned cleft foot and horns, the forked tongue and tail—have a relative and contingent genealogy. Yet so archetypally powerful is the traditional visualization of a demon, it's hard not to think that there is something a bit more intrinsic to that form that gives it a universal sense of horror. After all, the grotesquerie that is associated with demons, and those medieval tableaus with fearsome horned creatures the color of earth, faces with split tongues emerging from where the genitals or anus should be, gaping and grinning hellmouths with rows of sharpened teeth, would seem to be terrifying regardless of the potential viewer's cultural origin.

Whether or not the standard uniform of the demonic is somehow implicit in the metaphysical order or not is a question for theologians, but from the perspective of art history the form of devils can be traced, as Maxwell-Stuart admirably accomplishes. While much of that which we associate with demons has its origins in antiquity, medieval artists supplied a powerful body of material from the ninth to the fifteenth centuries that gave texture to the concept, which supplied a nightmarish visual vocabulary that accomplished what only individual imaginations could do previously. Furthermore, medieval artists drew on a wide range of influences across European paganism, appropriating gods and folkloric figures into the appearance of demons. McCall explains that "chtonic fertility and hunting gods now became greater demons, the old Teutonic elves, hobgoblins and fairies were transformed into lesser demons, incubi and succubae." An important observation, since the demons of folk culture and art were not always the demons of theology and philosophy.

Where the scholastics would have formulated learned arguments about the demonic, the average Christian was free to construct more wide-ranging demonologies, so that the infernal horde would be joined by a vast array of attendant beings—strictly speaking, morally neutral creatures, though often associated with the malevolent—which included trolls, ogres, fairies, elves, goblins, gremlins, imps, leprechauns, the fey, brownies, and ghosts. That these were creatures related to demons was implicit in the popular imagination, even if religious justifications for belief in them was scant. The result was a rich and complex visual language of the wicked, which still provides the base for the demonological imagination.

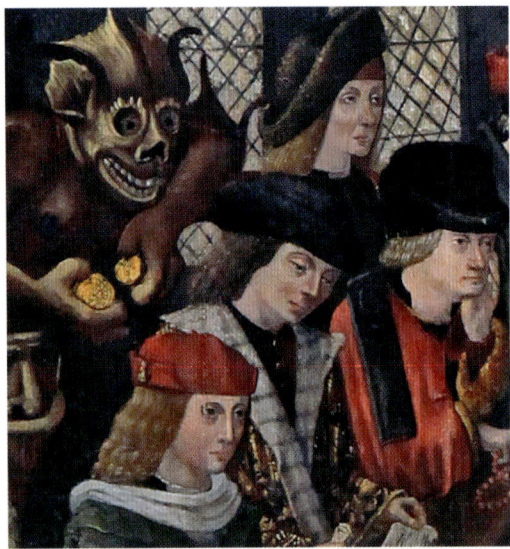

Detail from Jan van Brussel's 1475 panel The Dual Justice, *commissioned to hang in Maastricht's Council Chamber of Burgundy, now housed in the Bonnefanten Museum in Maastricht. The relatively little-known van Brussel imagines a grinning, simian demon clutching what appear to be gold coins behind a group of corrupt politicians and litigators.*

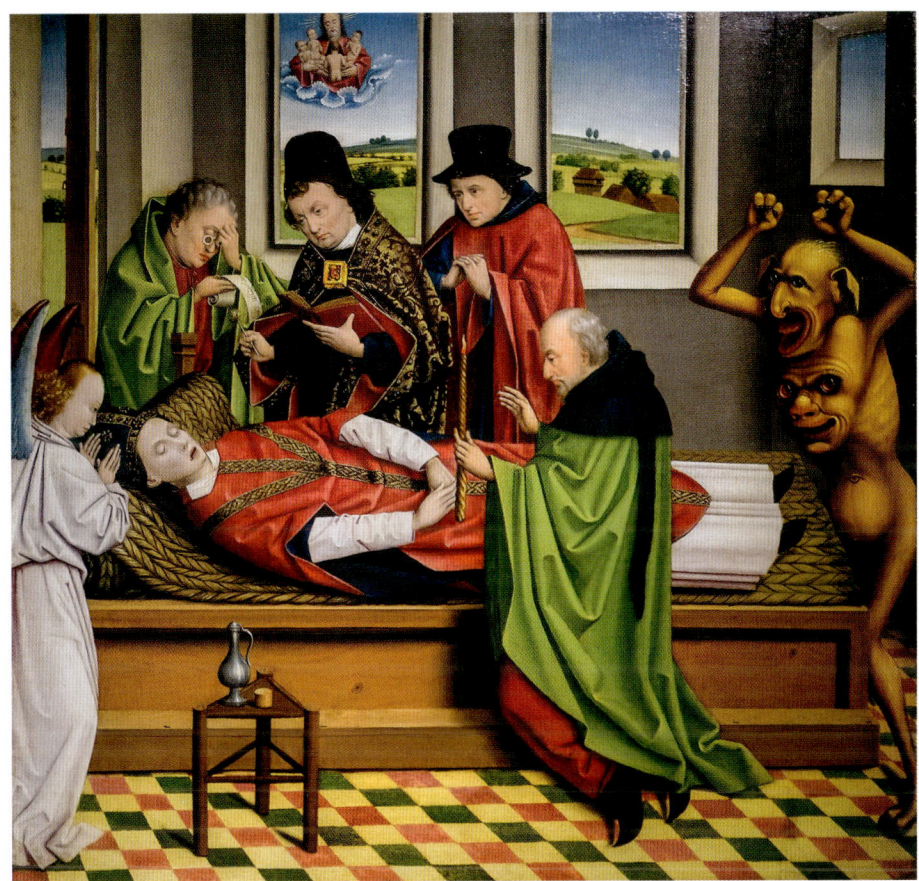

The Death of St. Martin of Tours, *painted by the late Gothic German master Derick Baegert in the late fifteenth-century, with the original held by the West-phalian State Museum of Art and Cultural History. Note the grinning, vacant, snub-nosed face leering out from the demon's stomach, a pithy visual encapsulation of our appetites' hunger for sin.*

Detail from Dirk Bouts's c. 1410 panel The Last Judgement, *showing a winged demon dropping an unrepentant sinner from a height during the apocalypse, the flinging down of the man ironically mirroring the descent of the fallen angels.*

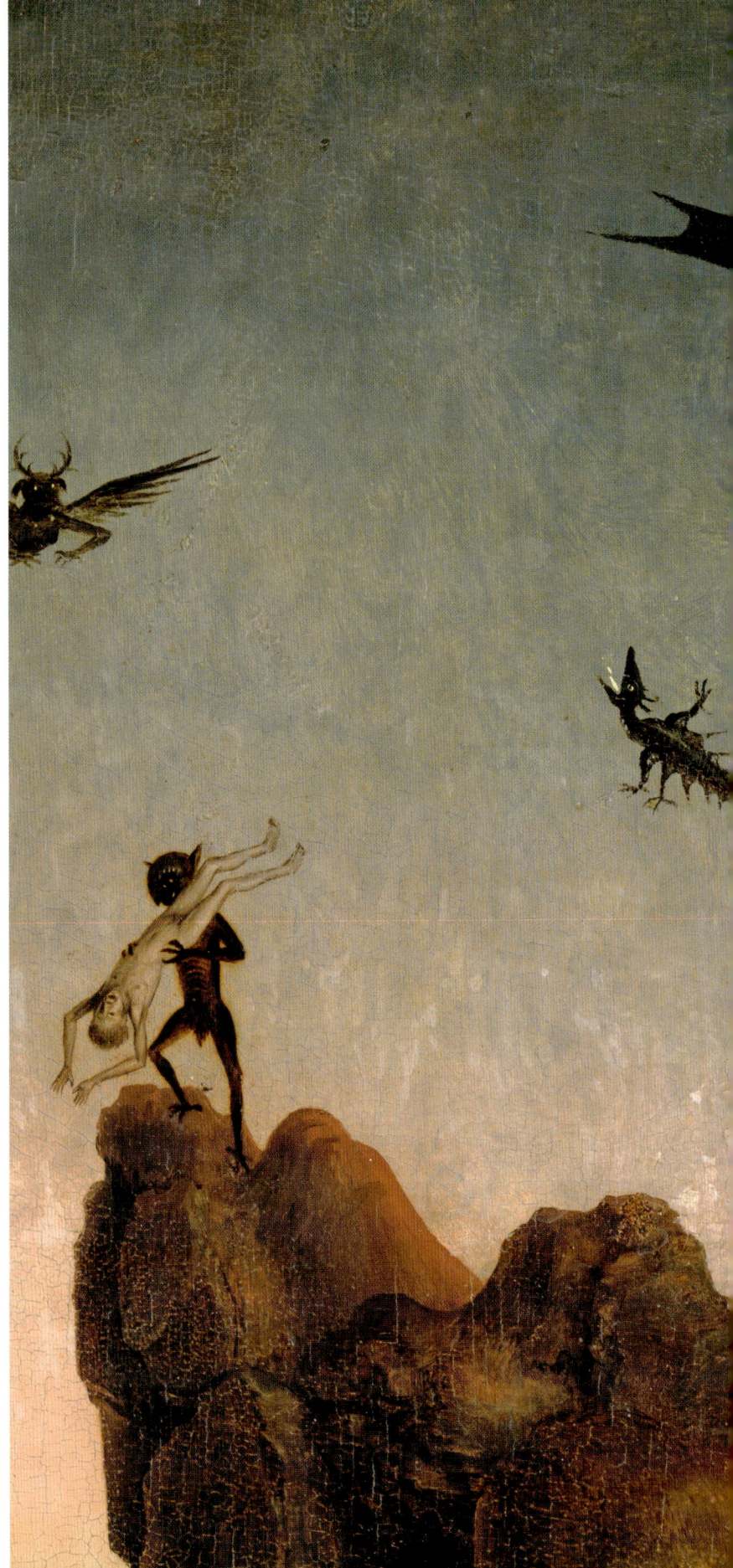

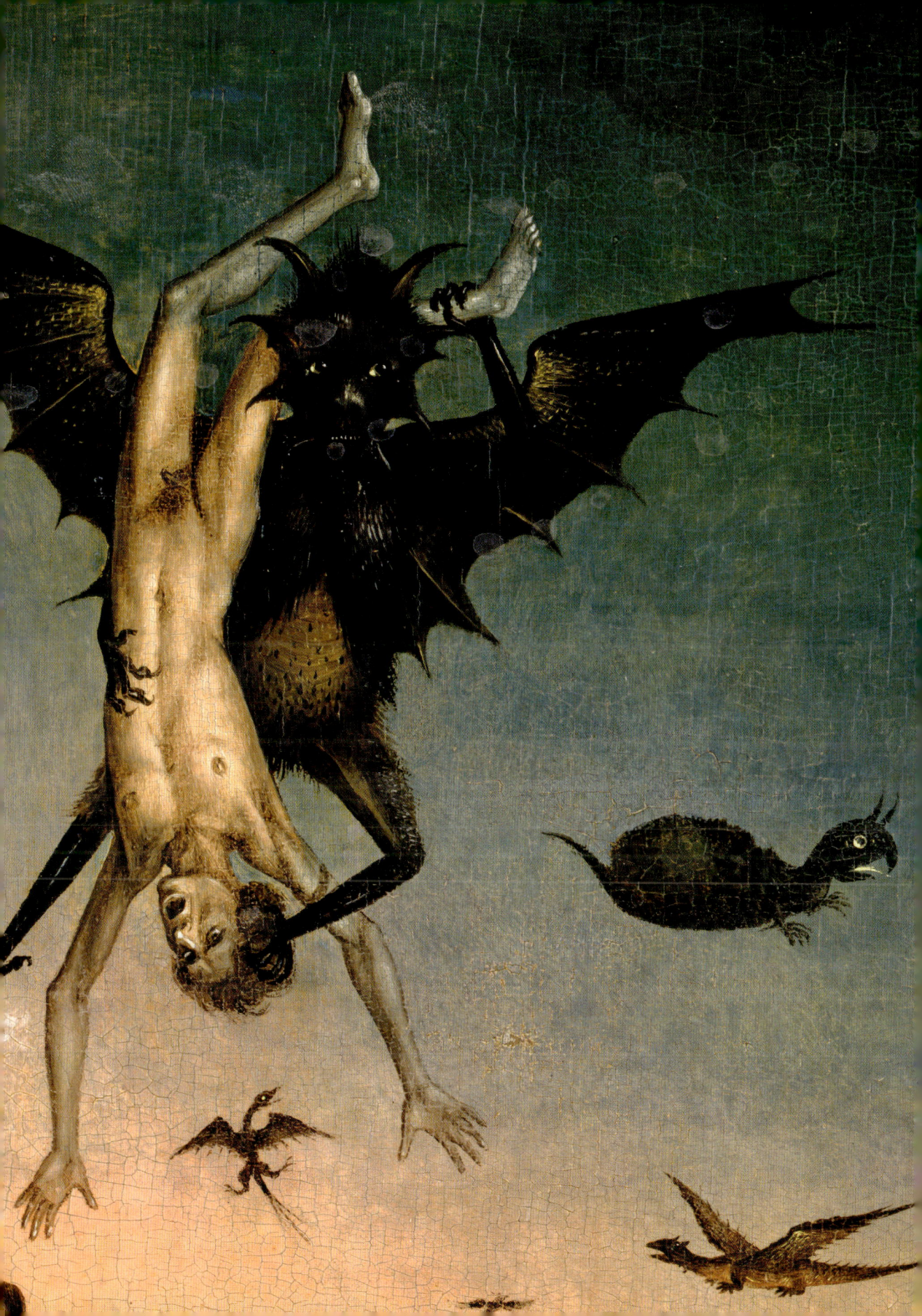

CONJURATION, EXORCISM, AND THE COMING OF THE WITCHES' SABBATH

On the eve of the first millennium's eclipse, when apocalyptic fervor burnt throughout Christendom, the French monk Rodulfus Glaber would be graced by a nocturnal visit from a demon at his bedside. "A mannikin-like being of terrible aspect appeared before me from the direction of the foot of the bed," writes Glaber in his *Historiarum*. The membrane between the world of the living and that of the dead, between salvation and damnation, was ever-permeable, and while medieval women and men were familiar with the illusions that daily bedevil all of us, be it dream —mirage, hallucination, or fantasy—Glaber knew the difference between a demon and a trick of the mind. With keen descriptive perception, Glaber apparently seared the creature's appearance into his memory, and recounts that:

As far as I could judge, he was of middling stature with a thin neck, skinny face, jet-black eyes, and a lined and wrinkled forehead. His nostrils were pinched and he had a wide mouth and blubbery lips. His goat-like beard covered a receding and pointed chin, while his ears were covered in hair and pointed. His hair was a disordered mop, and he had dog-like teeth. He had a pointed head, a swollen chest, a hunchback, and mobile haunches. Clad in dirty clothes, his whole body seemed to quiver with effort as he leaned forward, seized the head of the bed, gave it a mighty blow, and said, "You will not remain in this place." I woke in terror and, as happens when we are suddenly woken, such an apparition as I have described was still in front of me. He gnashed his teeth and said time after time, "You will not remain longer in this place."

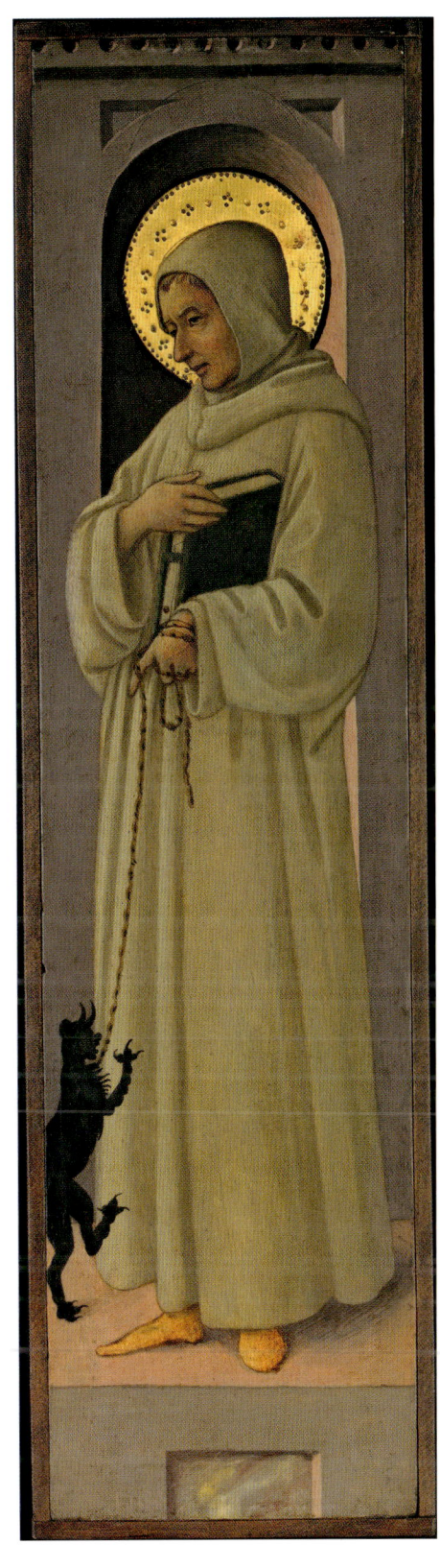

RIGHT

A fifteenth-century anonymous painting of the twelfth-century French saint Bernard of Clairvaux, based on drawings made by the Florentine artist Fra Filippo Lippi, now displayed at the Metropolitan Museum of Art in New York City. Bernard walks a small, and now harmless, demon on a leash.

All of the effects of the uncanny are evident in the *Historiarum*—the demon's twisted appearance (partially human but animalistic in its shape), the midnight violation of Glaber, the unsettling command from the devil itself. Glaber's narrative contains the ingredients of a classic ghost story, but it would be in error to see the passage as a creative experiment, for nothing in the *Historiarum* would indicate that the author didn't believe his experience was real. This sort of experience was not rare in the Middle Ages, and several different categories of demonic visitation could be identified. The monk's unwelcome nighttime visitor, sort of an inverse theophany, wasn't uncommon during these centuries, especially among the ascetic, the pious, and the holy, for whom such incidents marked them as particularly worthy of temptation from infernal forces.

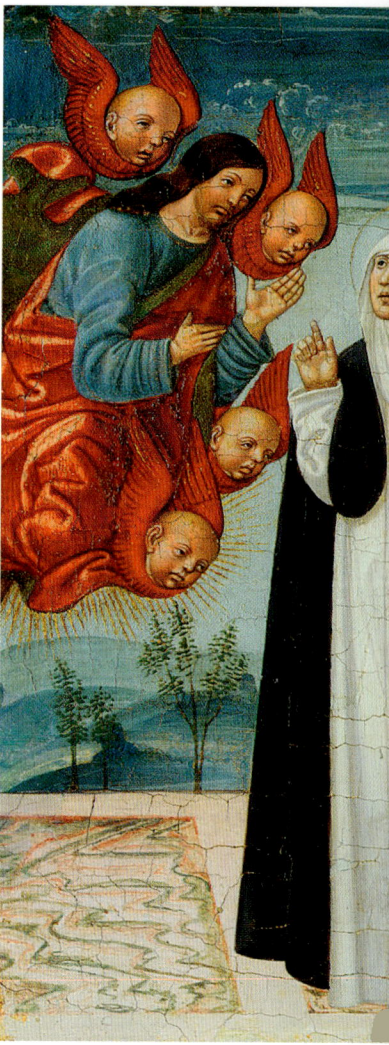

In addition to the sort of event that Glaber recounted, where a demon corporally manifests before the eyes of somebody, there can be added the twin categories of conjuration and exorcism. The latter refers to when an unwillingly possessed person must be expunged of the parasitic demon by the intercession of a cleric, while the former is the less common occurrence of a demon being purposefully summoned by a necromancer. Kieckheffer explains that it would be fallacious to see conjuration and exorcism as exact opposites. Rather they're both spiritual phenomena that are perpendicular to each other. He writes, "Both the exorcists and the conjurer were engaged in spiritual wrestling matches with the demons, and in both cases, they were keenly aware of the dangers," for as he explains, the "boundary between mainstream tradition and deviant usage is difficult to define with precision." An exorcist wants a demon to leave, while a conjurer wants them to appear, yet the rituals to achieve this are congruent with one another.

The exorcists "addressed demons with formal commands, whose power was derived chiefly from the sacred realities invoked in the formula of command," writes Kieckheffer, while the conjurer also "addressed demons with formal commands essentially identical to those of the exorcists, again powerful by virtue of appeal to sacred realities." Both medieval exorcists and conjurers had antecedents by way of example; the first in the form of Christ, and the second in figures like Simon Magus. In both circumstances—whether an exorcism or a conjuration—words and names were crucial, as language is the conduit on which sacred and infernal things can be controlled. Dialogue becomes the medium for the intersection of temporal existence with the demonic, as either priest or conjurer must enter into discourse with the Devil to make it do their bidding. As the monk Caesar of Heisterbach succinctly wrote in 1220, "Demons exist, they are many, they are evil and they infest people."

During the Middle Ages there was no shortage of demoniacs who were in need of an exorcist's assistance. "Essentially, the demoniacs were out of their minds," writes historian Sari Katajala-Peltomaa in *Demonic Possession and Lived Religion in Late Medieval Europe*. "They had fits and convulsions. They could tremble or lose the ability to use their senses . . . They rolled their eyes . . . and shrieked mindlessly. They could be violent . . . and some blasphemed God and the saints," she writes. Consider a nun named Sister Phillippucia, who in 1322 was targeted by a horde of demons, as the pious often were (some no doubt suffering under the obsessive dictates of scrupulosity). She writes of her own experience (in the third person)

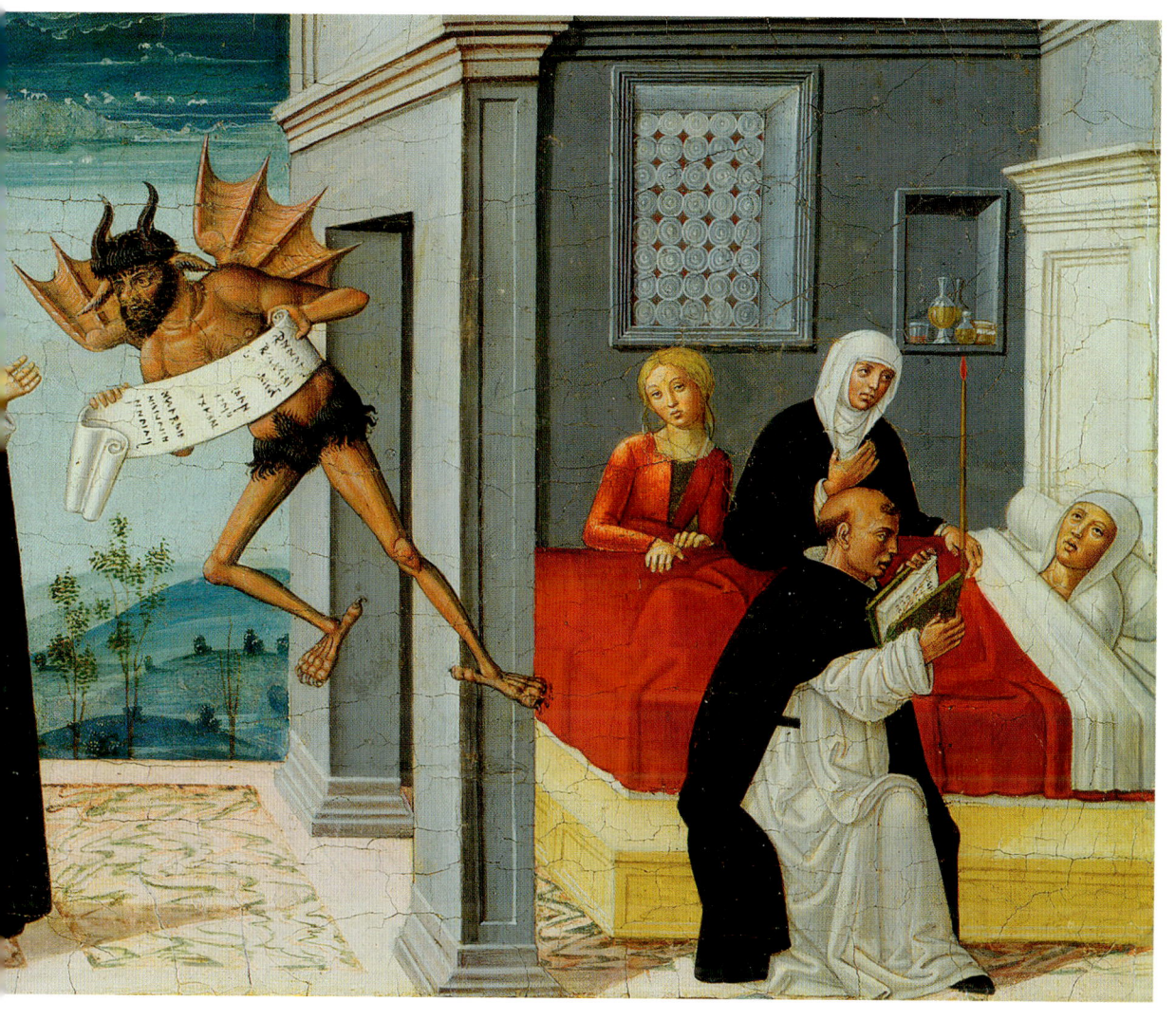

ABOVE

The fourteenth-century Italian Dominican lay nun St. Catherine of Sienna calls upon angelic cherubim to assist in the exorcism of her sister who signed a pact with a demon, as imagined a century later by Girolamo di Benvenuto. The piece is displayed at the Fogg Art Museum in Cambridge, Massachusetts.

that she was "invaded so forcefully that she used to roll her eyes back into her head, she twisted her mouth, danced in time, and would say many injurious and nasty things to the nuns of the monastery. Many visions appeared to her . . . images of various men of the foulest kind, and many beasts." Such cases weren't rare, as possession provided a common diagnosis for erratic, disturbing, and psychotic behavior. No doubt contemporary diagnosticians would evaluate these cases through the lens of psychiatric disease—schizophrenia, bipolar disorder, psychosis—and no doubt those might be in certain circumstances organically accurate evaluations. It would be a mistake, however, to thus interpret possession as being "not real," for whatever the metaphysical reality of the cause, the effect during this time period was as if the demons were real to those who believed in them.

Many hagiographies recount exorcisms of these unfortunate men and women, the expulsion of a demon from the body of a suffering penitent evidence of a cleric's saintliness. Almost as a matter of course the biographies of medieval saints will include an exorcism. There are celebrated accounts of rituals performed by saints and holy women and men such as Saint Benedict, Saint Malachy, Blessed William of Tours, Blessed David of Himmelrod, Saint Bernard of Clairvaux, the Blessed Hildegaard von Bingen, Saint Catherine of Sienna, and even Saint Francis. It may seem surprising that the last listed saint, so beloved and celebrated for his gentleness and his love of nature, should also have a reputation for effective spiritual warfare, and yet for Saint Francis the act of exorcism would be an act of charity and love, the release of suffering from those so afflicted by possession. In 1228, one of his hagiographers describes Saint Francis's relief of a woman who "moved by a brutal fury and deprived of all judgment, did horrible things and spoke sheer folly," while in 1263, Saint Bonaventure writes of his fellow monk that he had assuaged the suffering of a man who was "quite dashed down on the ground, and wallowed foaming, with his limbs drawn up, now stretched forth, now folded, now twisted, now become rigid and fixed."

If conjurers were not working toward the same goal as exorcists, then they shared the use of certain ritual incantations in their desire to compel demons to do their bidding. The extent to which magicians, alchemists, divinators, and necromancers attempted to conjure the appearance of demons during the Middle Ages is debatable. By the Renaissance of the sixteenth and seventeenth centuries, when the stereotype holds that medieval superstitions were in decline, occult and hermetic practices had ironically became common among scholars, in part because of the duel influence of a Neoplatonist revival, and counterintuitively a resurgent empiricism. The Middle Ages had its share of magicians, however, and the existence of manuscripts concerning demonic conjuration testifies to the existence of the practice, even if rare. Kieckheffer writes that "demonic magic . . . [is] the underside of the tapestry of late medieval ritual culture," and the inky traces of cloven footprints can be seen in magic books, or grimoires, written throughout the time period.

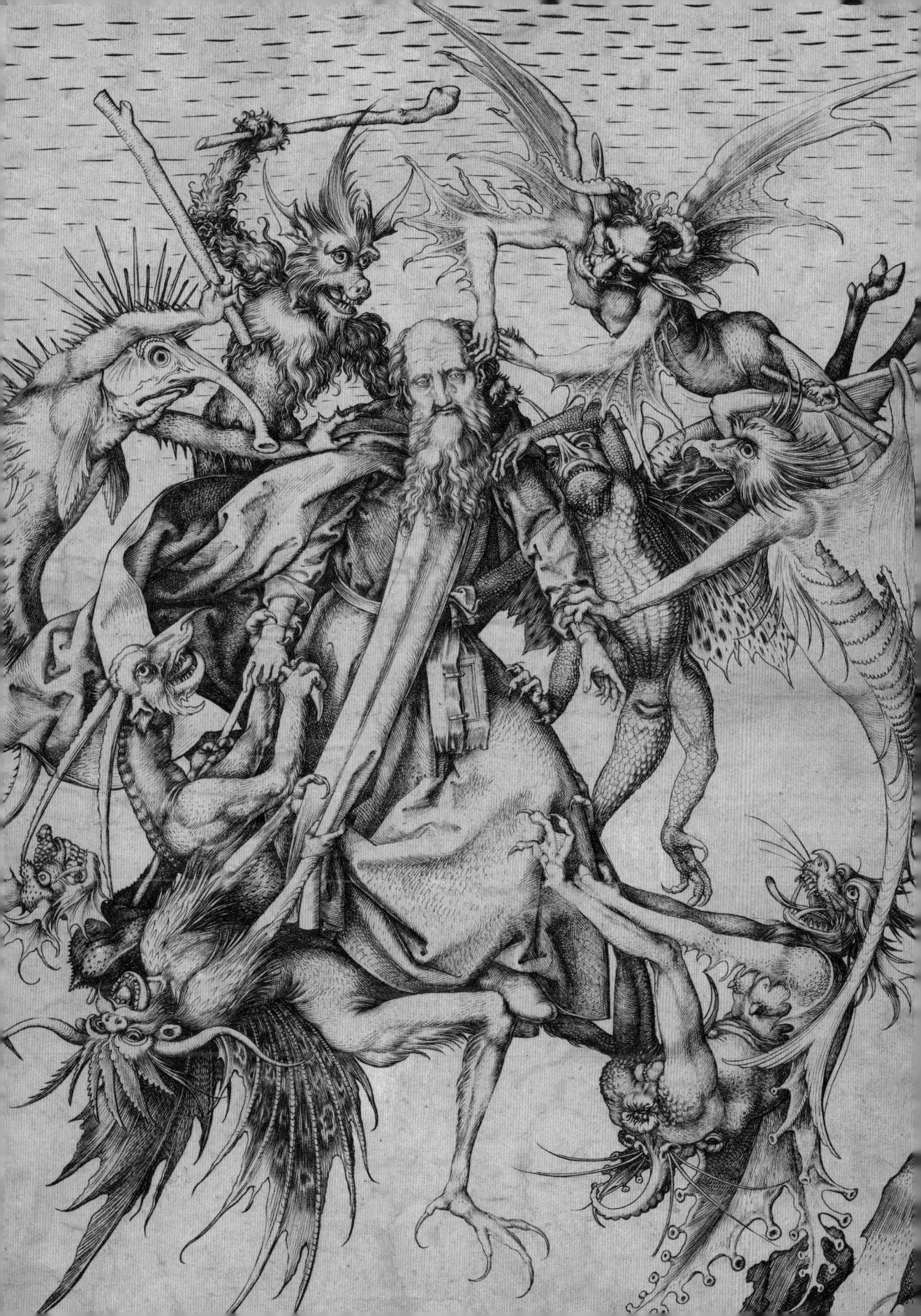

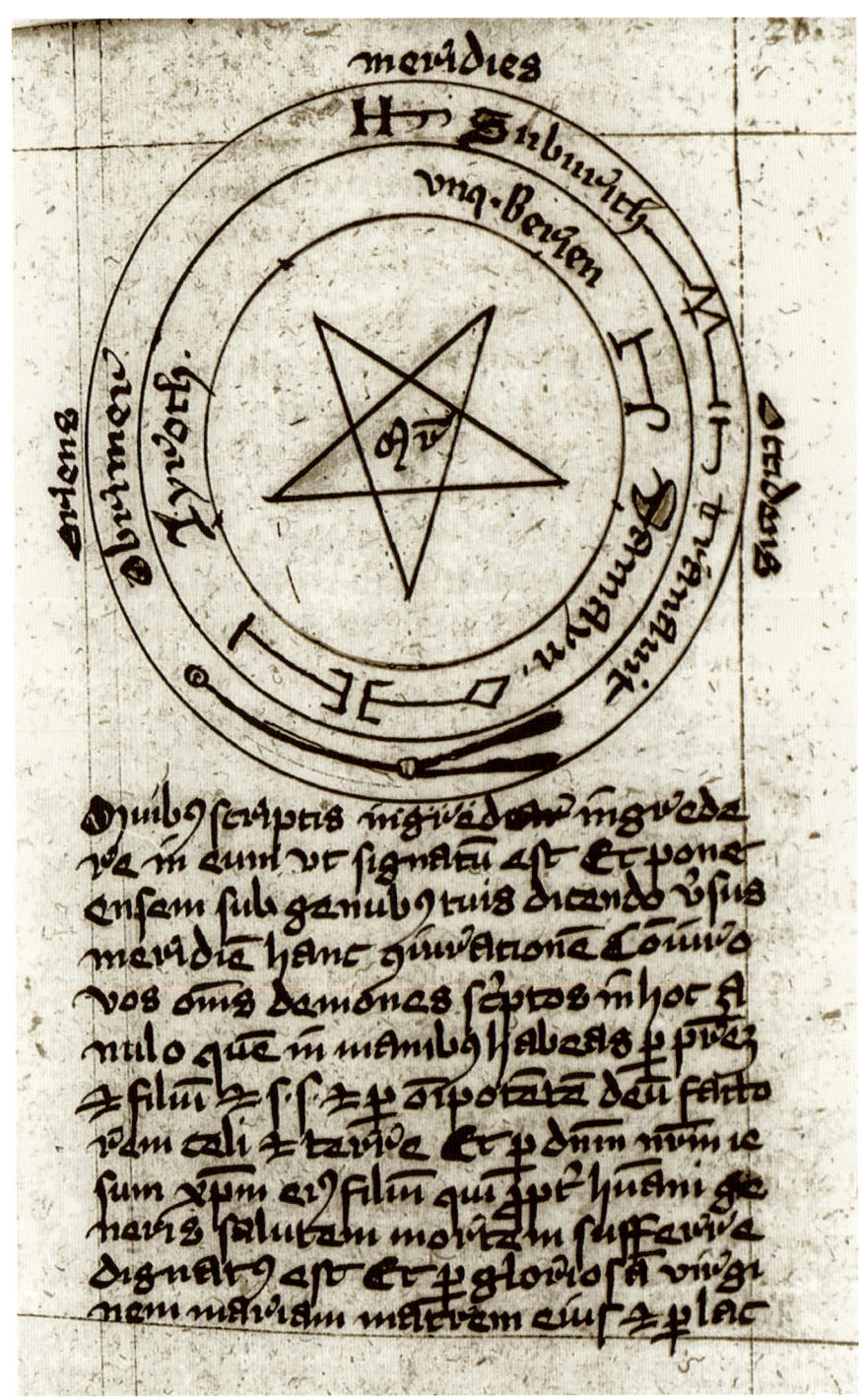

ABOVE

A handwritten page from the Munich Manual of Demonic Magic, *an anonymously written manuscript held in the Bavarian State Library. Note the pentagram in the center of the magic circle.*

Demonic conjuration in the Middle Ages was performed for all of the reasons anyone would undertake such an endeavor—for curiosity, for wealth, or for power. Theurgical incantation allowed for the magical initiate to claim control over the ineffable nature of reality, and as an exorcist compelled a demon to leave, so would a conjurer command them to appear and be controlled by the magician. Such rituals should be understood as distinct from general folk magic, the provenance of cunning women and men, who, though they'd often be accused of witchcraft in subsequent centuries, were understood as trading in a legitimate practice. By contrast, the conjurers of demons—with their focus on complex verbal formulas and the endless litany of demonic names—had a scholarly (and infernal) patina lacking in the more pragmatic magic of the lower classes. An example of the sort of formulaic language seen in these grimoires—strangely methodical, exacting, and precise—is in the anonymous fifteenth-century manuscript known as the *Munich Manual of Demonic Magic*, housed in the Bavarian State Library:

Here follows another experiment for invoking spirits so that a man can make a fine and well fortified castle appear, or for summoning countless legions of armed men, which can be easily done... with bare feet and head, kneeling, read this while facing west: 'O usyr, Salaul, Silitor, Demor Zanno, Syrtroy, Risbel, Cutroy, Lytay, Onor, Moloy, Pumotor, Tami, Oor and Ym, squire spirits, whose unction it is to bear arms and deceive human senses wherever you wish, I, so-and-so, conjure and exorcize and invoke you... that, indissolubly bound to my power, you should come to me without delay, in a form that will not frighten me, subject and prepared to do and reveal for me all that I wish, and to do this willingly, by all things that are in heaven and earth.

Etymologically, it's hard to say what the origin of these demonic names are—pantomime of Hebrew, Aramaic, or Latin, perhaps from some more inscrutable origin. Regardless, the *Munich Manual of Demonic Magic* underscores just how much of demonology, through antiquity and into the Middle Ages, was an issue of language; an issue of the permutation of letters and words, where incantation was often an issue of being able to properly name something.

Despite the aura of precision that such grimoires imply, the question of what's demonic was far more ambiguous in the Middle Ages than might first be assumed. That the task and vocation of the exorcist and conjurer were so similar should already be evidence of this, but the demons themselves could be far more ambivalent, for in the realm of the sacred and the damned there is a holiness regardless, one that departs from the mundanity of everyday reality. Who is to say whether a possession is angelic or demonic? Witness the example of Christina Mirabilis, a twelfth-century Belgian woman who was reputed to be able to survive within burning furnaces, to have the ability to walk along the floor of frozen rivers, and to have endured being accidentally crushed by a mill wheel, with no injury. Christina claimed to have visited both hell and purgatory (like Christ), and she could describe those eternal torments in exacting detail, often delivered in a deep, growling voice as she would spasm and roll, moving with a distinctive herky-jerky motion.

During her funeral, she supposedly jerked upright and flew to the rafters of the church, saying that the stench of sin from all of the worshipers could no longer be abided. While alive she had a reputation for being a "sin eater," ingesting food given to her by a penitent, and feeling their mental torments and the physical pain of purgatorial suffering. In this way she took part in the same tradition as the scapegoat sacrificed by the Hebrew scriptures, or by Jesus Christ himself. Today she is considered among the Catholic "Blessed" (though not canonized), and yet as her hagiographer Thomas de Cantimpre noted, "Men thought that she was possessed by demons." Her tale presents us with a reflection on the ways in which faith allows us to approach the sublimity of darkness, the profundity of horror, and the fact that light always implies a shadow.

Had Christina Mirabilis been born a few centuries later, there is little doubt that frightened people would have wondered if this agonized saint had been in communion with demons. Quite possibly that Christina would have been burnt at the stake as a witch. For all that is pejorative about the designation "medieval," it obscures that the Middle Ages was in some ways more tolerant than subsequent centuries (though obviously not in all ways). For the first half of the period, which people long and erroneously called the Dark Ages, an era that is perhaps more accurately referred to as late antiquity, there were few executions for heresy (until the Albigensian Crusades of the twelfth century), and there were few

An anonymous fifteenth-century Flemish painting of a young witch having cast a love potion so as to compel the young man at the door into her bed chamber, the original held at the Staatliche Museum in Leipzig, Austria. For most of the Middle Ages, to believe in witchcraft was a heresy, for the idea that mere women and men could flout God's powers through magic was seen as blasphemous, yet ironically by the high Middle Ages and then into the Renaissance, when God's omnipotence was most fully emphasized, belief in witches (and the subsequent persecutions) became a matter of orthodoxy.

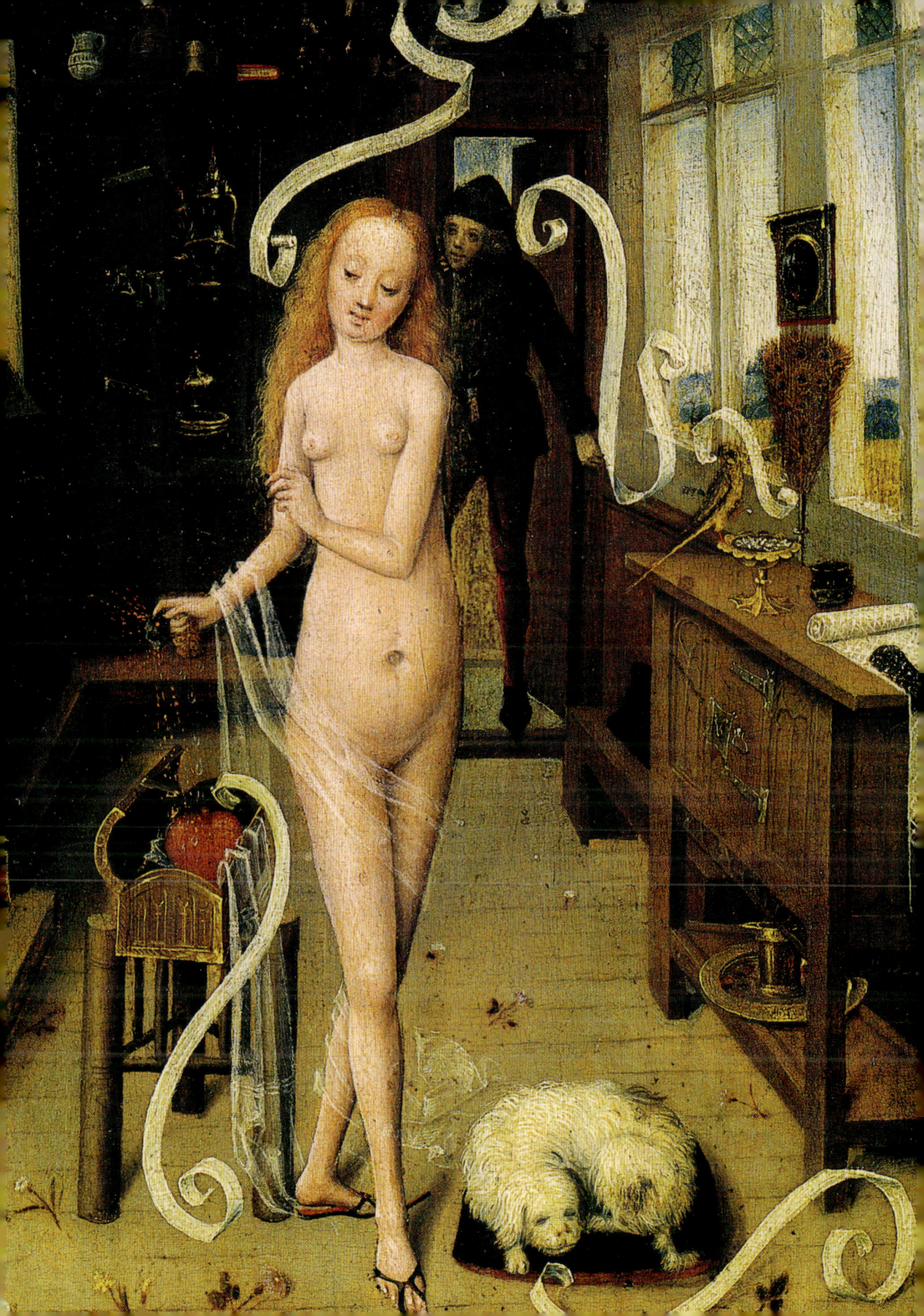

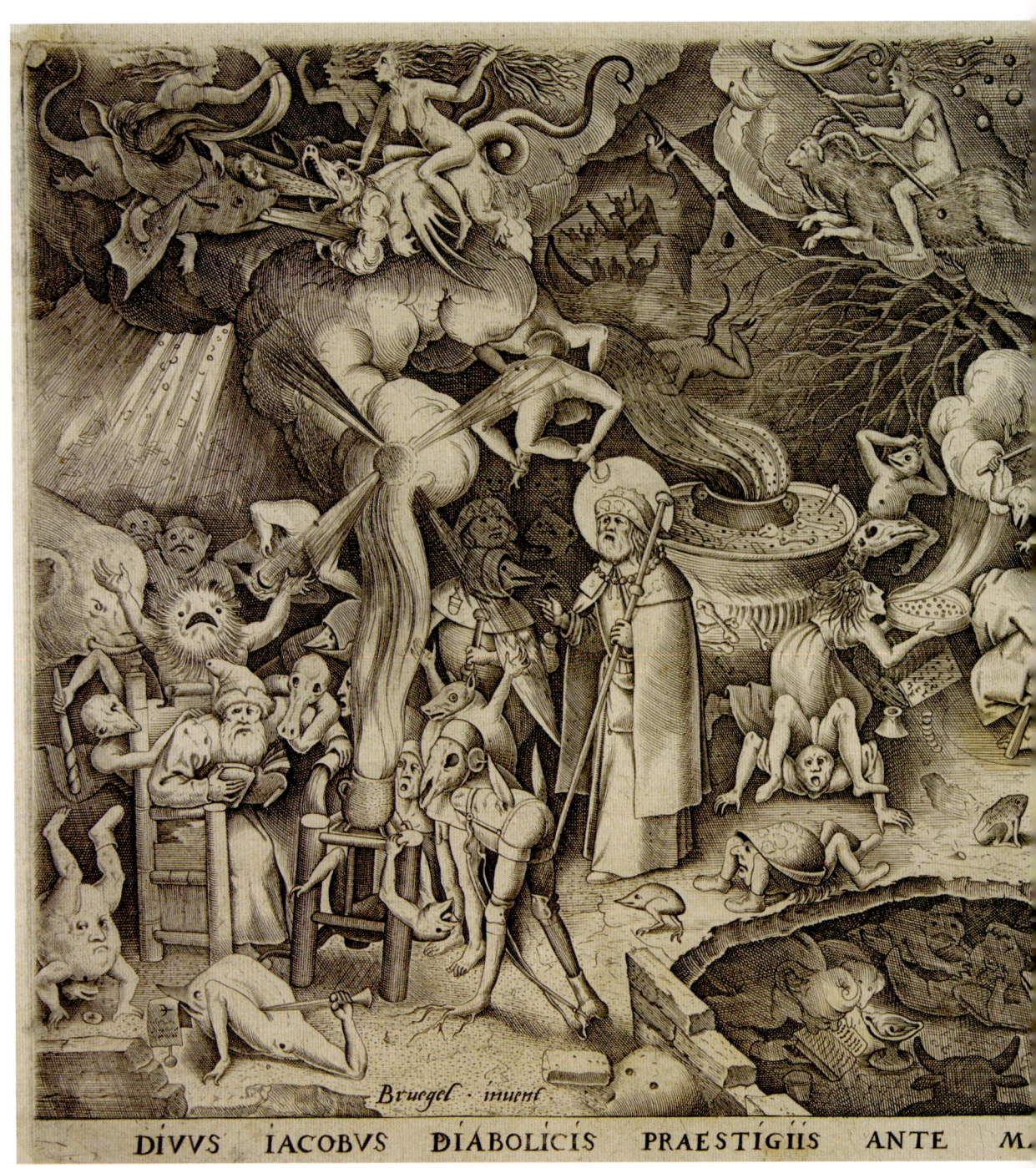

Bruegel · inuent

DIVVS IACOBVS DIABOLICIS PRAESTIGIIS ANTE M.

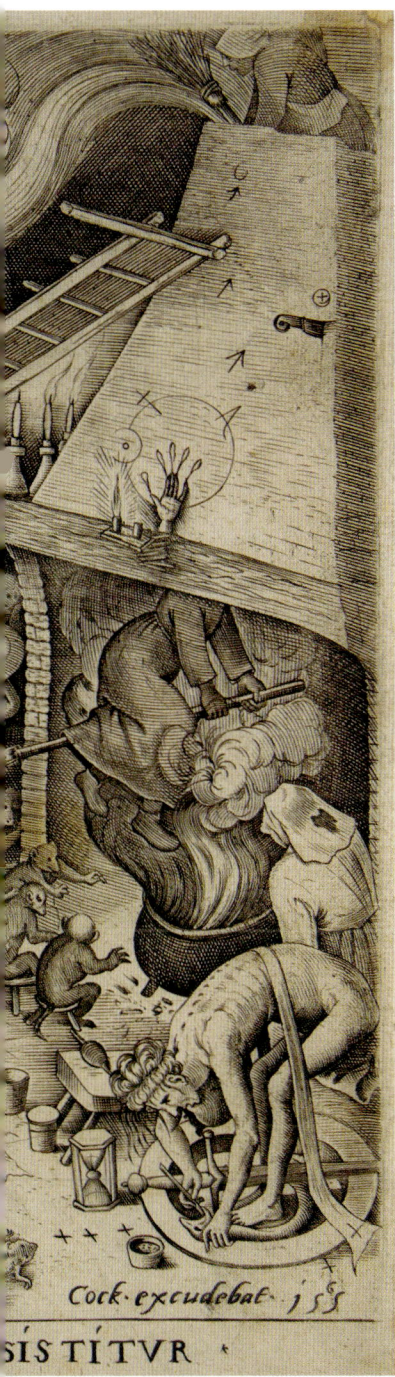

Cock· excudebat· 1565

SIS TITVR

persecutions against those who were considered witches. Indeed, that's one of the paradoxes of the coming modernity—that the true horror of punishment against "witches" (overwhelmingly women) came with those centuries that were regarded as exemplars of rebirth and resurgence.

Historians have argued about why the sixteenth and seventeenth centuries of the Renaissance, or early modern period as it's increasingly called, saw such a tremendous amount of violence against those who were accused of consorting with demons. That particular question will be explored in the next chapter, save noting that by the end of the Middle Ages it was already clear that a new oppression against those implicated in demonology was ascendant. It was in 1486—a year before the beginning of the Tudor dynasty, six years before Christopher Columbus's journey to the Americas, and thirty-one years before Martin Luther would nail his 95 Theses to the door of Wittenberg's cathedral—that a volume entitled *Malleus Maleficarum* would be printed. Written by a Dominican priest and inquisitor named Heinrich Kramer, *The Hammer of the Witches* (as its title translates) would provide guidance on the identification and punishment of those who supposedly entered into contract with demons. Its legacy would be thousands of dead.

THIS SPREAD

Pieter Brueghel the Elder's 1565 St. James and the Magician Hermogenes, *where the titular holy man disrupts a witches' Sabbath. Original at the Rijksmuseum in Amsterdam.*

NEXT SPREAD

In this detail from the fifteenth-century German painter Stefan Lochner's polyptych Last Judgment, *with the original held by the Wallraf-Richartz Museum in Cologne, demons and angels fight over the eternal fate of a man after he has been resurrected from the grave, following the millennial arrival of Christ. Though the eschatology of Revelation is firmly monotheistic, such narratives of dueling good and evil can't help but betray enduring Manichean inclinations. As the Medieval world transitioned into the early modern, apocalyptic enthusiasms would only grow, with the violence of the witch-hunts arguably an indication that people were increasingly fearful about the end of the world.*

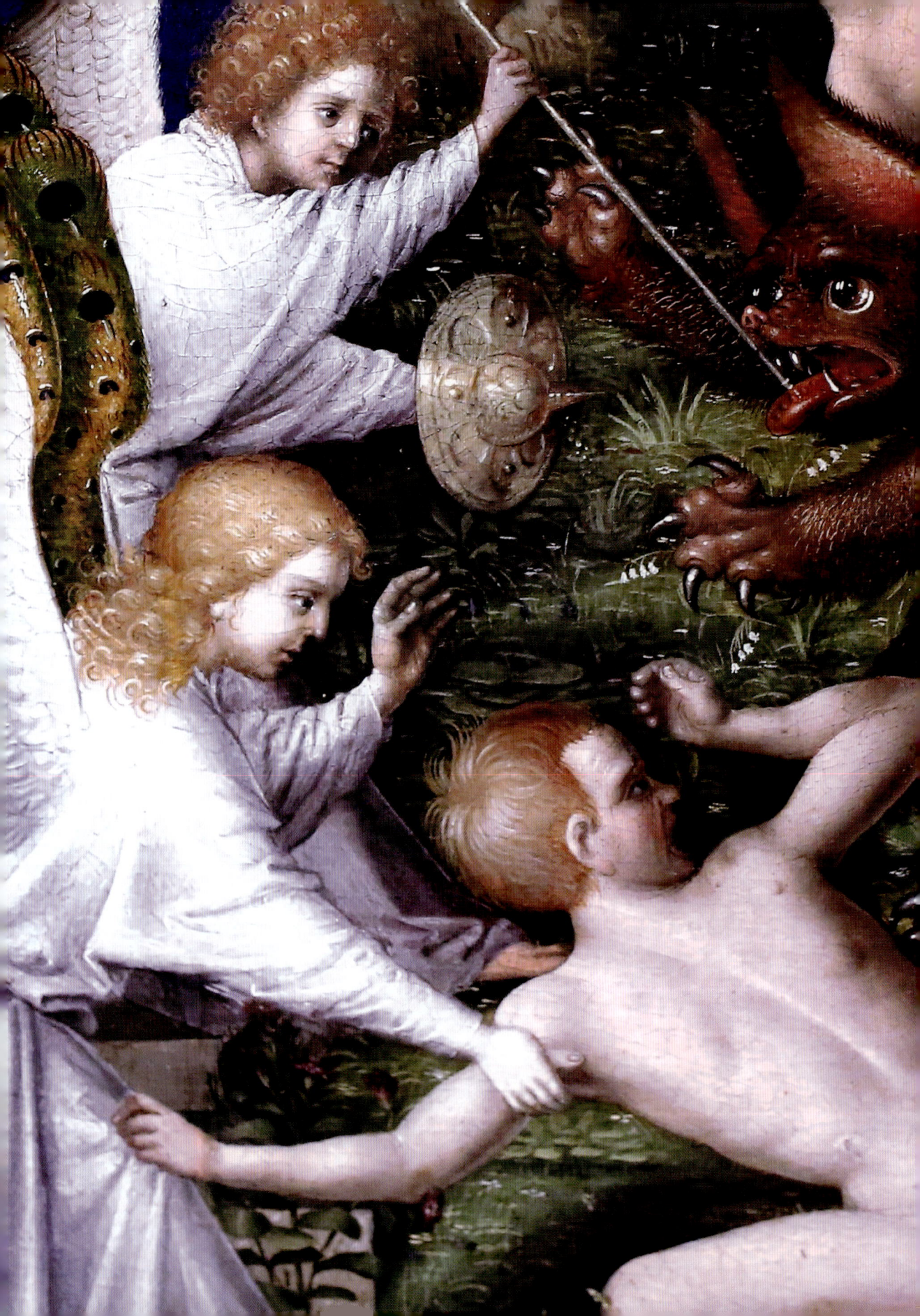

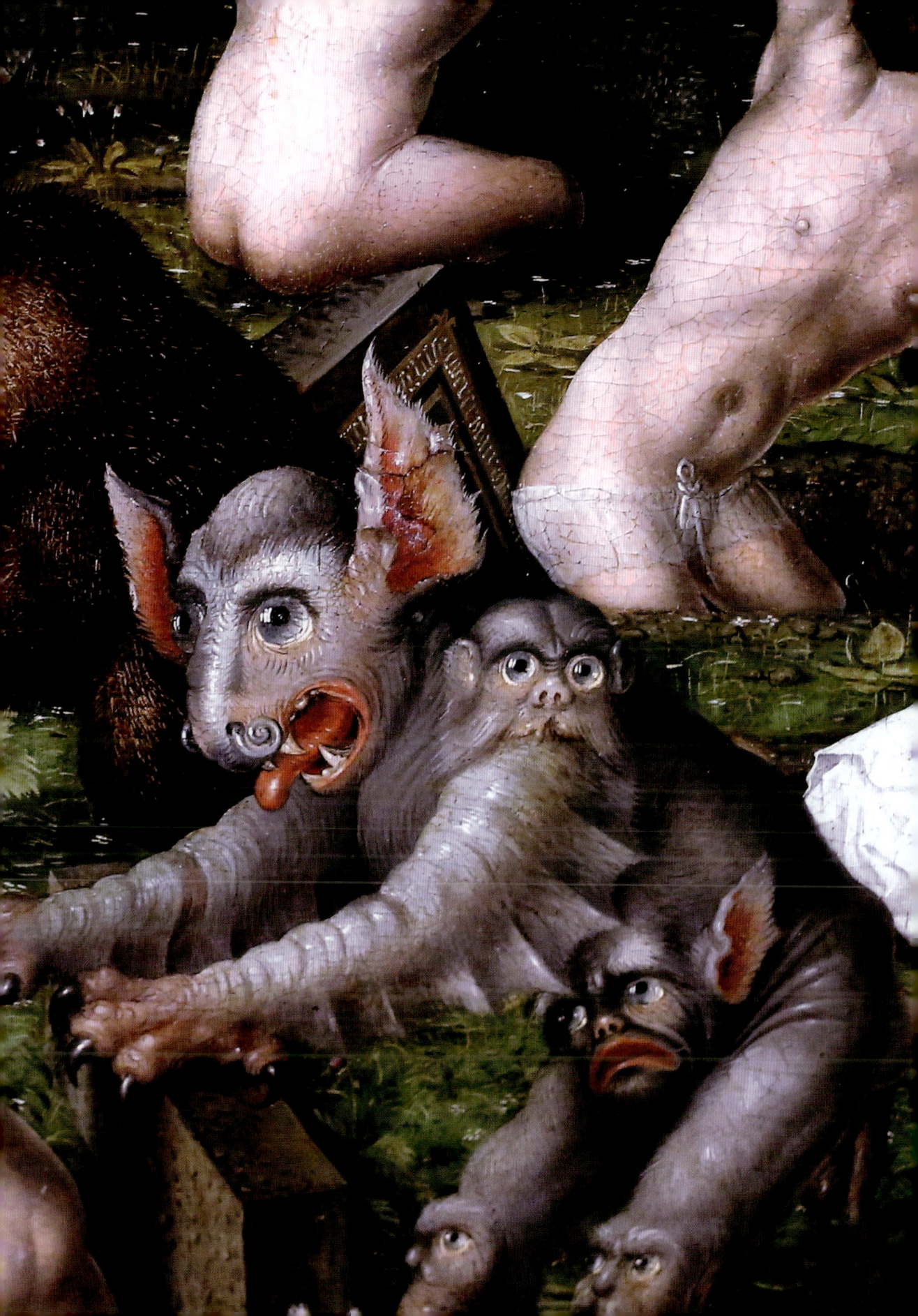

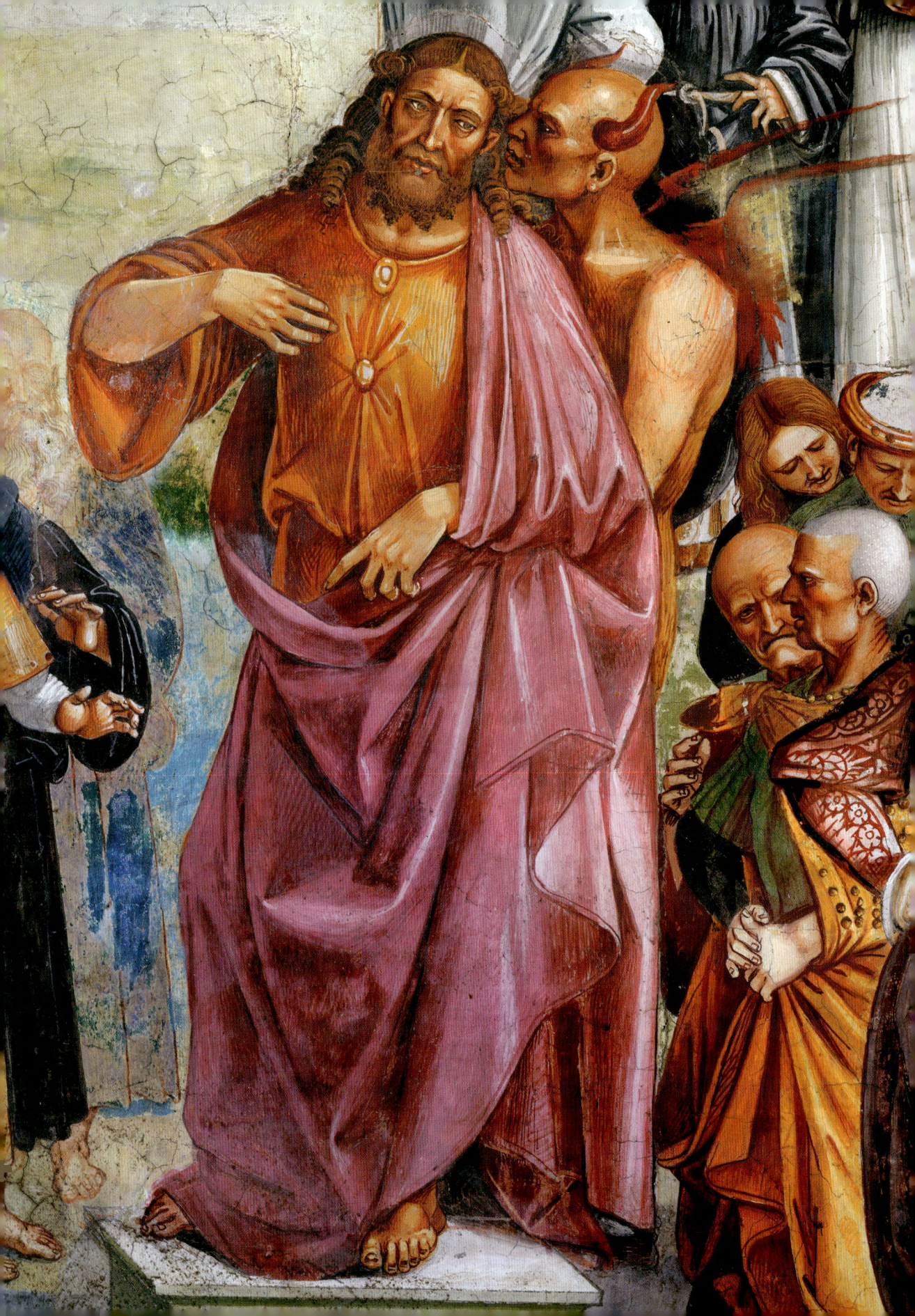

CHAPTER THREE

Why This Is Hell

Renaissance and Reformation Demonology, c. 1500–1650

Lamarton anoyr bulon madrisel traschon ebrasothea panthenon
nabrulges Camery itrasbier rubanthy nadres Camosy ormenu lan
ytules demy rabion hamorphyn.

—Demonic incantation
from Johannes Trithemius's *Stegonagraphia* (1499)

Hell hath no limits, nor is circumscrib'd
In one self place; but where we are is hell;
And where hell is, there must we ever be.

—CHRISTOPHER MARLOWE, *The Tragical History
of the Life and Death of Doctor Faustus* (1603)

ON RENAISSANCE
AND REFORMATION DEMONS

ing James I had been on the English throne for three years when in 1606 he saw a new production written by the playwright who was his predecessor's favorite. The setting would have been familiar—his native Scotland. The narrative thrust of the play may have been terrifying to a preternaturally anxious king—regicide. And some of the themes no doubt appealed to the new monarch—magic and witchcraft. Not only that, but James may have recognized some of the language, for one of the sources that William Shakespeare consulted in the composition of *Macbeth* was a work by the king himself, written in 1599 and titled *Daemonologie*.

Like the previous monarch, his distant cousin Queen Elizabeth I, James fancied himself a student of rare learning, conversant in the humanistic inquiry that had been popular on the continent for centuries. Unlike Elizabeth, he shared little of the latitudinarian disposition regarding religious settlement, having been born to the staunch (and executed) Catholic Mary, Queen of Scots, and raised among the austere Presbyterian reformers of Edinburgh, where he ruled as James VI for more than three decades before the union of the thrones. Intellectual inquiry combined with religious obsession lent itself to the penning of learned diatribes, polemics fitted in the dross of scholarship, with the most exemplary example his tract concerning the reality of witches and their intercourse (figurative and otherwise) with demons.

His birth city was the appropriate environment for somebody of James's sentiments; all winding cobblestone streets crawling their way up the mountain toward Edinburgh Castle, a midlands gloom hanging over the foggy, rainy, damp Scottish capital. The Reformation had been particularly severe in Scotland, where it was overseen by the zealous preacher and theologian John Knox, who'd spent years in John Calvin's theocratic Geneva. An attendant obsession with witches had also burnt through the country, which was paranoid and obsessed about occult plots threatening to blight crops or kill kings. Scotland was marked by a zealous persecution of those accused of witchcraft, with the number of people executed (most frequently burnt at the stake) in the thousands. England was comparatively less violent in this regard, and Shakespeare's audience would have been simultaneously fearful and intrigued by their new Scottish monarch, who fancied himself a witch hunter. As it was, James would introduce vociferous witch-hunting into English society, with Anne Llewellyn Barstow noting in *Witchcraze: A New History of the European Witch Hunts*, that in the "second week of King James I's first Parliament, the House of Lords passed a much stricter witchcraft law," whereby the death sentence could be rendered not just for having been a witch, but for the intention of being a witch, so that no crops need be blighted or pestilence actually spread for the auto-da-fé to be kindled.

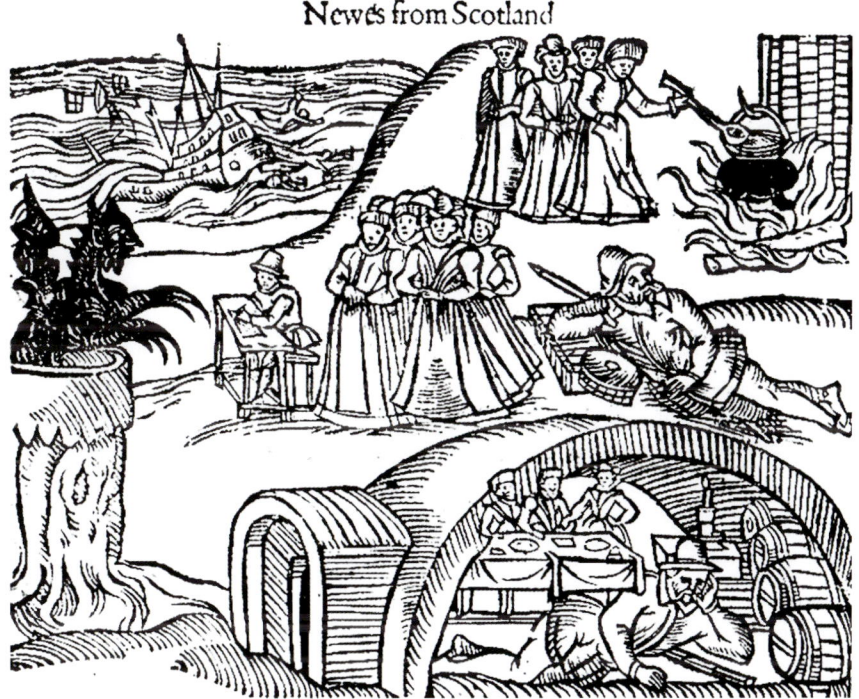

Newes from Scotland

A group of accused witches from the East Lothian region depicted in a 1591 pamphlet titled News from Scotland. *Many of the more than one hundred women and men who were accused of witchcraft in Scotland were ultimately executed in this region. In this engraving the witches gather before the Devil.*

"The fearful abounding at this time, in this country, of these detestable slaves of the Devil, the witches or enchanters, has moved me (beloved reader) to dispatch in post, this following treatise of mine," writes James in the introduction to *Daemonologie*, "to resolve the doubting both that such assaults of Satan are most certainly practiced and that the instrument thereof merits most severely to be punished." And punished they were, heartily and violently across Europe of the seventeenth century, with estimates of those murdered between fifty thousand and one hundred thousand people in the that century, though possibly many more (though an estimate that fully nine million people accused of witchcraft had been executed during these decades has long since been judged as grossly exaggerated). "Fair is foul, and foul is fair,/Hover through the fog and filthy air," as the Weird Sisters of *Macbeth* famously intone. For a group of Jacobean theatergoers, threatened by unseen specters and actual conspiracies such as that of the Gunpowder Plot foiled a year earlier, the paranoia, anxiety, and amoral relativism implied by the line must have resonated, for as Marjorie Garber writes in *Shakespeare After All*, the Weird Sisters are "the essence of ambiguity."

There is a profound irony that as much as the Renaissance is seen as the progressive flowering of learning and knowledge after the atrophied Middle Ages, and the Reformation as a casting off of religious superstition, it was precisely these centuries in which the bloodiest punishments were enacted against those who were called witches, when fear and belief in demons was most acute. "Nothing on this scale had ever been seen before, and it engulfed all ranks of society," writes Theodor K. Rabb in *The Last Days of the Renaissance and the March to Modernity*. He explains that such "otherworldly speculations" were the direct result of "desperate quests for reassurance amidst the upheavals and troubles of the age," because it was indirectly that which was most hopeful in both the Renaissance and the Reformation that exacerbated the bloodshed. Renaissance humanism placed mankind at the center of its understanding, while the Reformation defined God as the ultimate arbiter of all knowledge, but as different (and related) as humanism and Protestantism were from one another, they both in part served to fix certain eternal verities on a firm basis. They utterly failed in doing this, and the intellectual progeny of the era was a profound anxiety, with the victims of the witch persecutions martyrs to that desire "to resolve the doubting," as James put it. Both humanism and Protestantism were dual, sometimes parallel, and often conflicting methods and approaches to doing just that, but the ambivalence and ambiguity of the period was such that they arguably introduced profound doubts where they had not existed before.

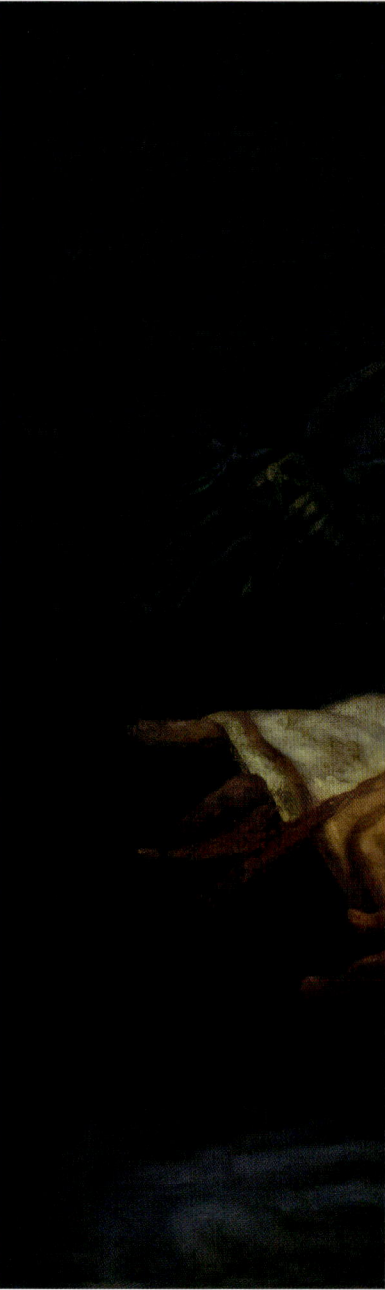

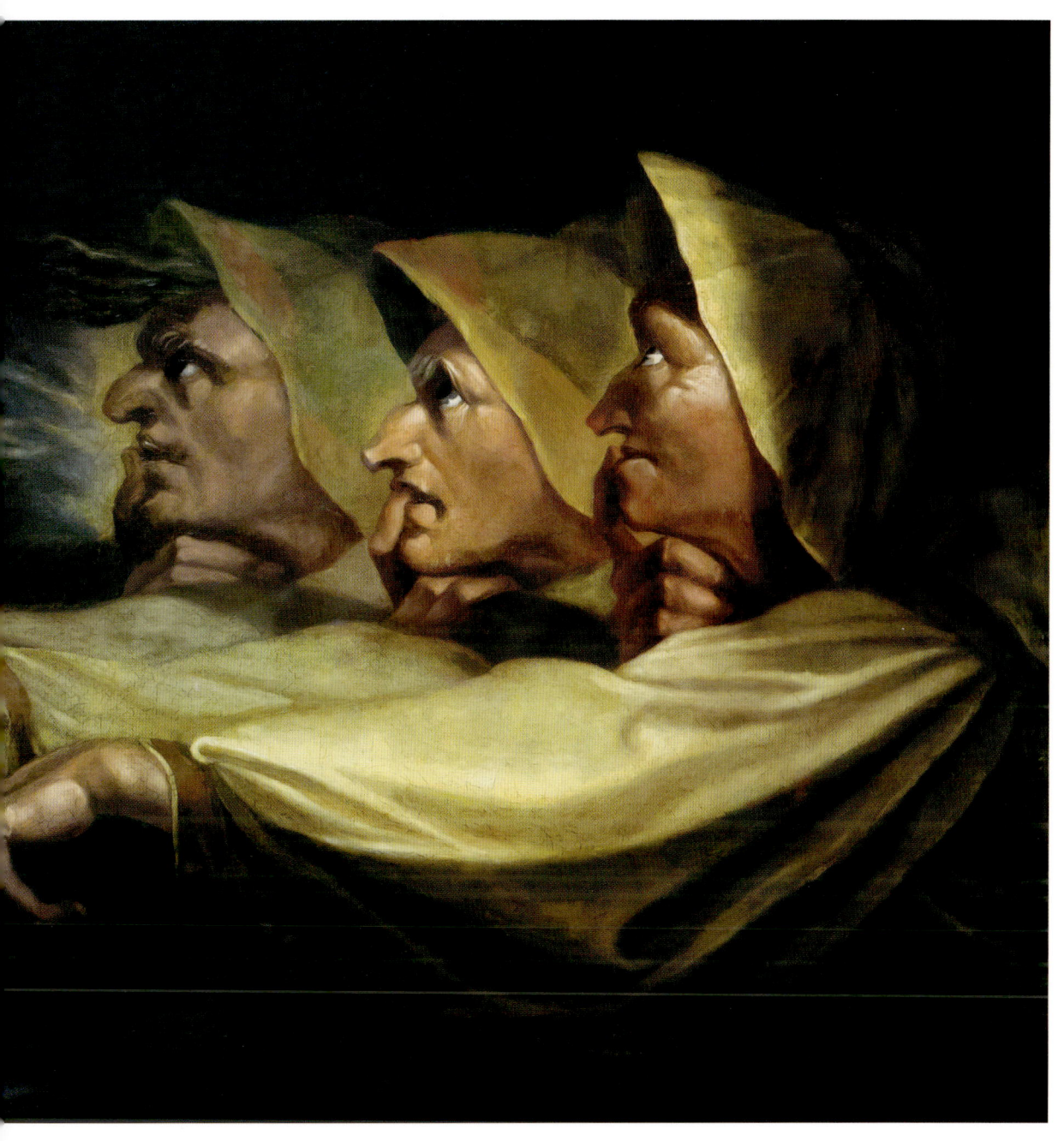

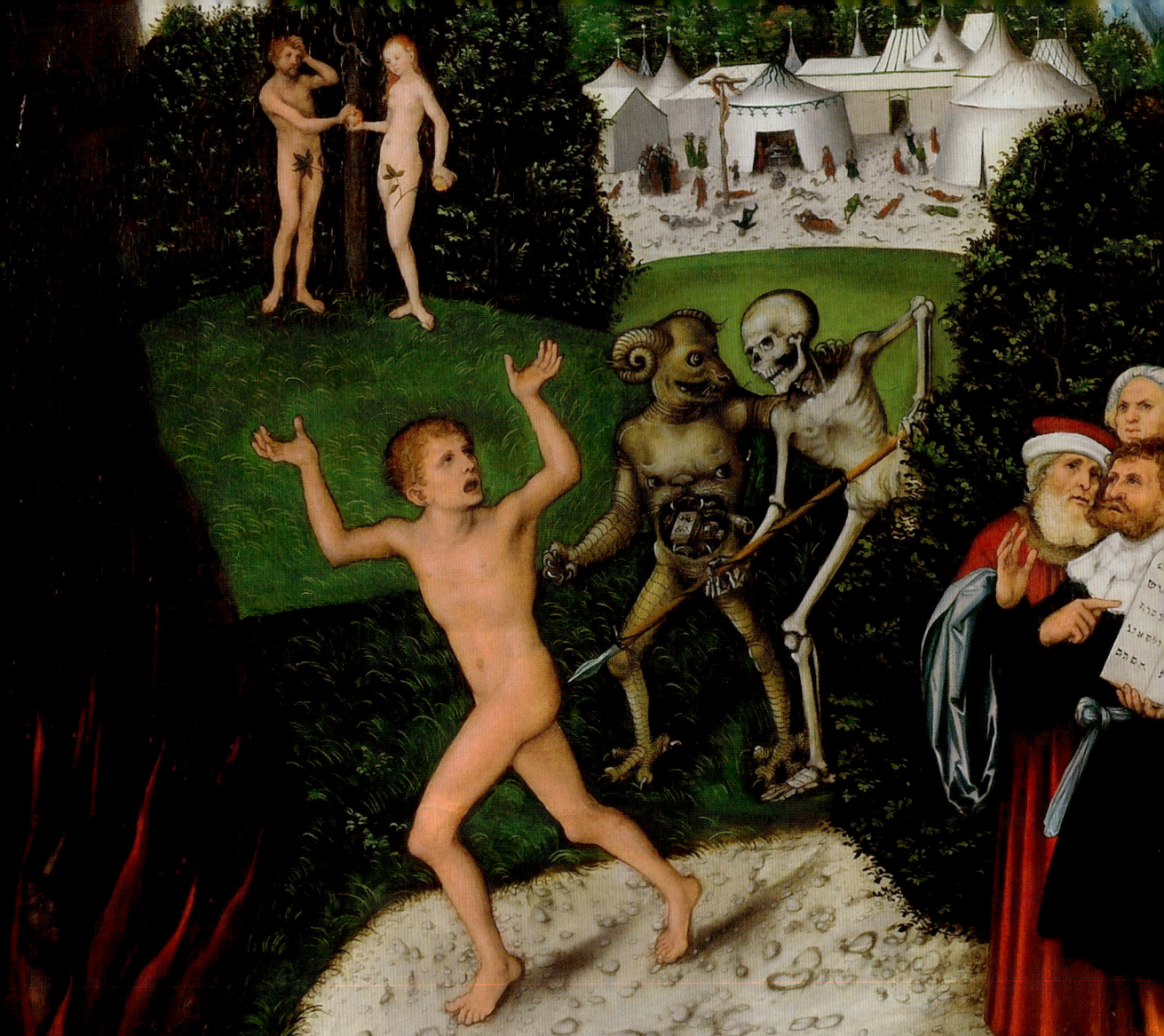

This detail from the German painter Lucas Cranach the Elder's Law and Gospel (1529), housed in the National Gallery Prague, Czech Republic, illustrates the theological principles that defined the Reformation. Arguably the most potent visual propagandist for Martin Luther's movement, Cranach both borrowed and invented his own pictorial vocabulary in the development of Merkbilder, a genre of didactic Lutheran art. Here a figure who believes that his good works alone will guarantee his salvation, as exemplified by the Hebrew patriarchs (including Moses holding the tablets of the Law), is surprised to find that his actions along can't merit heaven. The cackling green demon pushes the figure into the mouths of hell, evocative of medieval imagery but illustrating Protestant principles, only highlighting how much of the former Augustinian monk Luther's theology owed to the scholastic teachings that he both subverted and built upon.

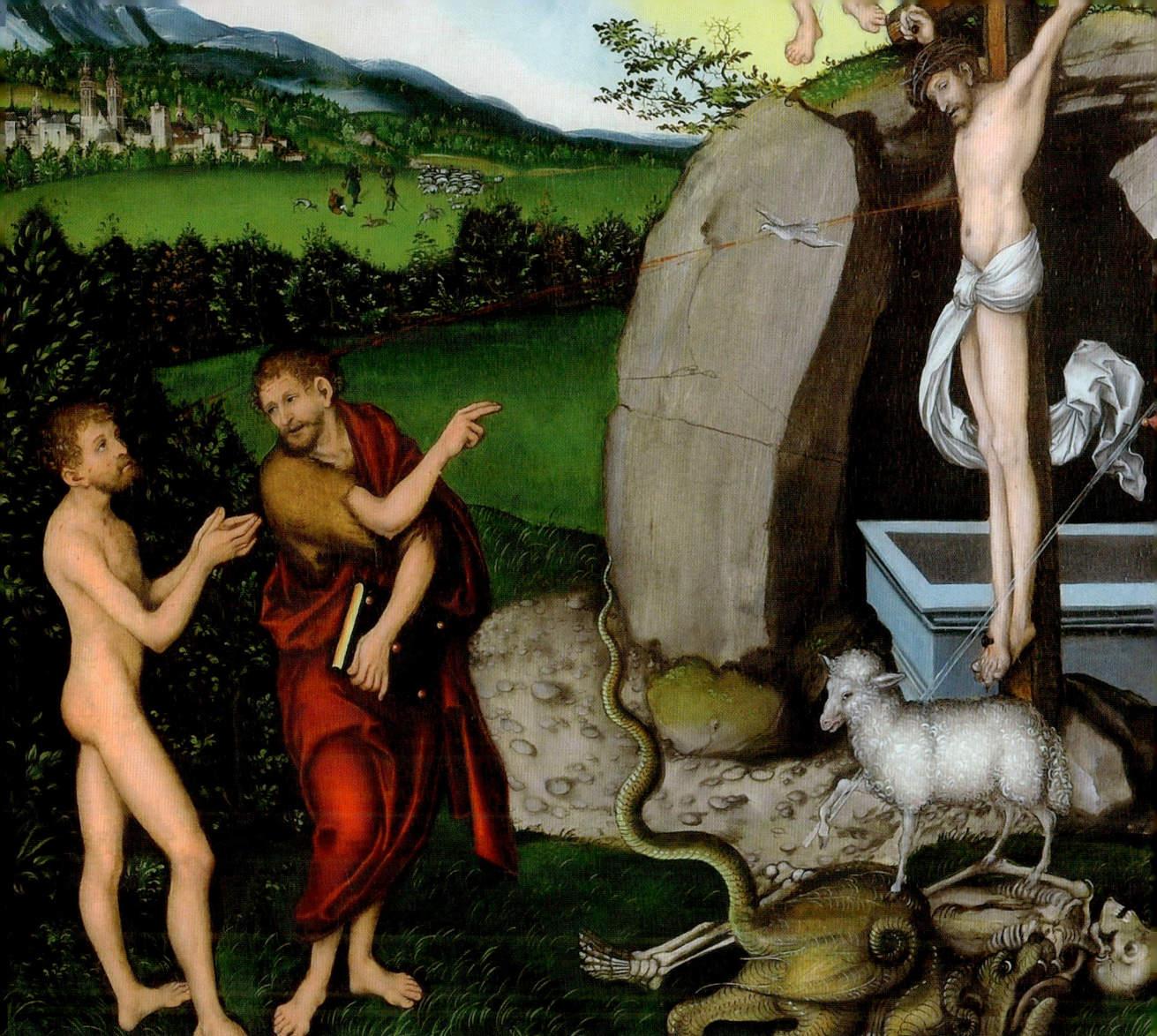

NEXT SPREAD

The German artist Albrecht Dürer's engraving Knight, Death and the Devil *(1513) was composed in a Europe on the verge of the Reformation's convulsions. A reflection on Psalm 23 with its famous invocation of "Though I walk through the valley of the shadow of death, I will fear no evil," Dürer presents an armor-clad knight in a desolate landscape stalked by a cadaverous grim reaper and a wild-eyed goatish devil, the later of whom harkens back to the tradition of the biblical scapegoat as sacrifice for the desert deity Azazel, while gesturing forward to the caprine countenance of the Baphomet. There is a bit of the memento mori tradition about the painting, whereby symbols like the hourglass would remind the print's owner of life's transience. Yet Dürer's iconography is also idiosyncratic and personal, making a full allegorical translation of the piece as in the older medieval style difficult.*

"But upon man, at the moment of his creation, God bestowed seeds pregnant with all possibilities, the germs of every form of life," spoke the Florentine humanist Giovanni Pico della Mirandola in his *Oration on the Dignity of Man*, delivered before the pope in 1486, the same year that the *Malleus Maleficarum* was printed. "Let a certain saving ambition invade our souls so that, impatient of mediocrity, we pant after the highest things and (since, if we will, we can) bend all our efforts to their attainment," he declared with effervescent optimism. Compare Pico della Mirandola to the reformer Calvin, who would write in the *Institutes of the Christian Religion* a generation later, in 1536, that "in the kingdom of God, we must look and listen only to his eternal truth, against which no series of years, no custom, no conspiracy can plead prescription." As diametrically opposed as these sentiments may seem (ignoring the complex relationship between humanism and Protestantism), they both emerge from an inclination that builds knowledge on a foundation of first principles, whether those axioms are reason and experience or faith and grace. A strange cost in that, however, the need to purchase such assurance both demonstrates and is the cause of a growing disenchantment. The witch hunts were made possible by a collective psychological insecurity.

As Jeffrey Burton Russell observes in *Mephistopheles: The Devil in the Modern World*, the Renaissance and Reformation "saw a vast increase in the Devil's powers [while they] also witnessed the beginnings of overt skepticism." If any mood marked the era, hovering in fog and filthy air, it was doubt, uncertainty, and anxiety. Fanaticism is never the mark of confidence—to the contrary. The immolation of so many hundreds of thousands of innocent people defined the violent birth pangs of the modern world as authorities attempted to exorcize uncertainty with the burning embers of the pyre. That melancholic sense of the sixteenth and seventeenth centuries, the cankered child of the initially optimistic Renaissance and Reformation, indelibly marked demonology.

As a discipline, demonology was concerned with two different human archetypes at this time—that of the witch and of the wizard. The former were mostly women who were accused of fraternizing with the Devil and his minions; the later were the educated scholars who consulted grimoires and plied their interests within a veritable golden age of necromantic obsessions. Rabb explains that esoterica, including demonology, "achieved a pervasiveness and power . . . that gave the culture as a whole a distinctive tinge," while Owen Davies argues in *Grimoires: A History of Magic Books* that the "real [occult] revolution has gone largely unremarked—the democratization of high magic." In part this enthusiasm for matters necromantic was initiated by the development of cheap print, so that occult practices and beliefs that had previously been the provenance of an elite coterie increasingly filtered through the wider culture. The European working class had long had their own set of beliefs, some of which had pre-Christian origins, such as the practice of healers like the cunning-folk, but when those practices were interpreted through the matrix of the new demonology the results were combustible.

Renaissance humanism, insomuch as it can be easily defined, was an intellectual movement of pedagogical reform more than an overreaching cultural shift. If anything marked the fourteenth- and fifteenth-century Italian Renaissance,

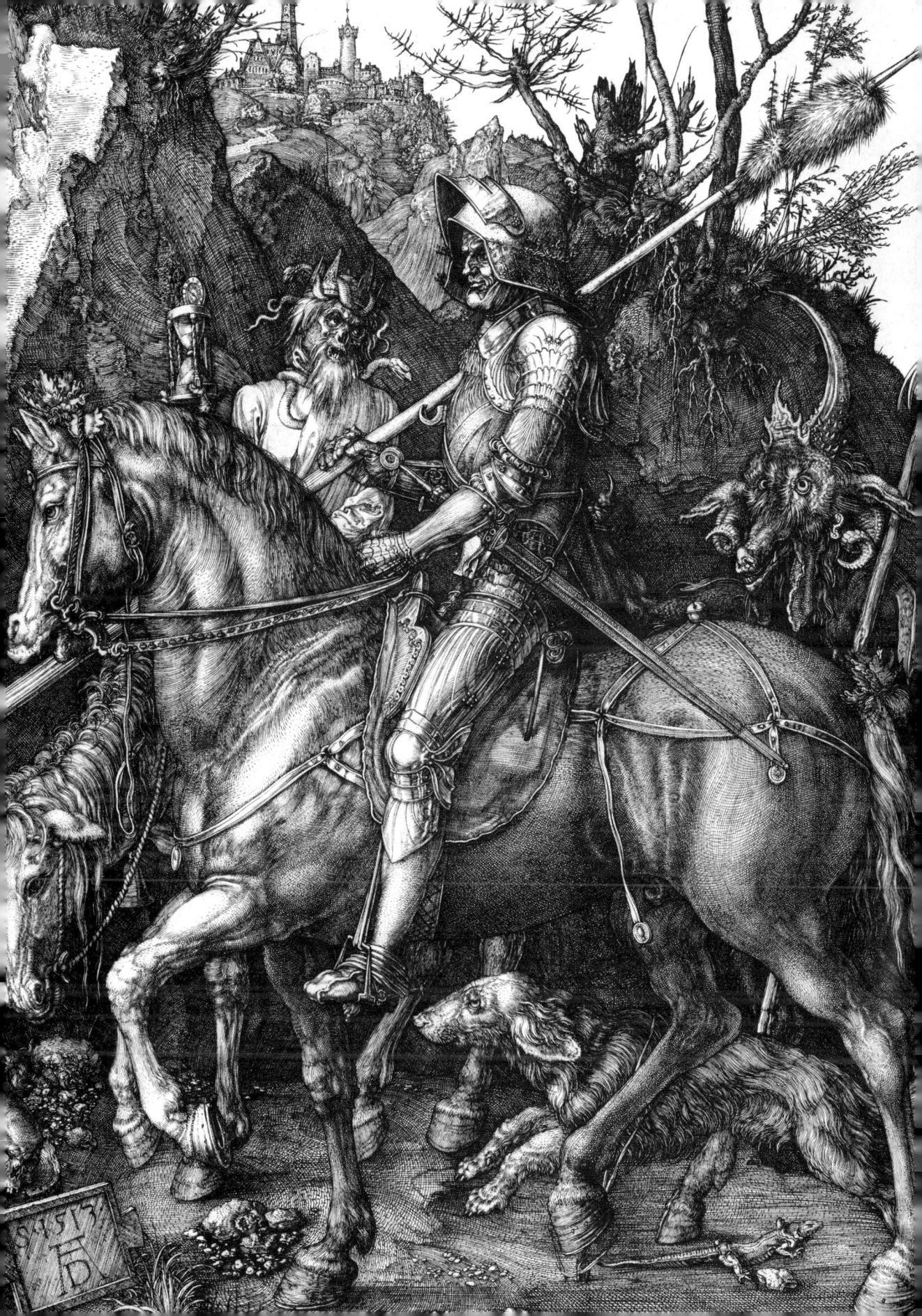

which acted as prelude to the spread of humanistic ideals throughout the entire European continent, it wasn't just a concern with objecting to the dogmatic dictates of faith, but rather to a specific reimagining of Plato's thought. Florentine Neoplatonists like Pico della Mirandola and Marsilio Ficino, in part influenced by past thinkers like Psellos, rejected the increasingly atrophied Aristotelianism of the medieval scholastics. Fifteenth-century Italy was awash in Orthodox Byzantine thinkers who were refuges from the Ottoman invasion of 1453, and they brought with them a Platonist ethos that would transform European universities. From Plato, figures like della Mirandola and Ficino borrowed a metaphysics that placed stock in ideas over matter, in forms over objects, in abstraction over the concrete, in the transcendent realm rather than experienced reality.

This Platonism was necessarily congruent with occultism more generally and demonology more specifically, for the contemplative, esoteric, and mystical nature of much of this philosophy was readymade for the obsession with words and formula that mark demonic poetics. When combined with an increased interest in the Jewish mystical tradition of kabbalah, which was embraced by first Catholic and then Protestant thinkers, the result was that the Renaissance became the most fruitful age for occult rumination.

This golden age of supernatural speculation was "At both ends … mysterious, both in where it came from and what became of it," writes Dame Frances Yates in her classic *The Occult Philosophy in the Elizabethan Age*. The sixteenth and seventeenth centuries weren't just populated "by tough sea-men, hard-headed politicians, and serious theologians," Yates writes, but also "spirits, good and bad, fairies, demons, witches, ghosts, conjurors." In trying to build a new world, the humanists had attacked the authority of scholastic philosophy while the evangelicals confronted the Roman Catholic Church, but in replacing the abolished order, new certainties were hard to find. The result was a desire to see meaning in coven and grimoire, whether what those things promised were real or not. No adherent was more associated with occultism as a philosophy, methodology, and tradition than was a sixteenth-century German scholar named Heinrich Cornelius Agrippa—also born the same year the *Malleus Maleficarum* would be printed.

With a boundless optimism reflecting the utopian promise of the humanists, Agrippa writes in *Three Books of Occult Philosophy* that "Man is a great miracle, an animal to be honored and adored; for he passes into the nature of God, whereby he becomes God." It was this precise variety of language which made Agrippa a potential heretic. That his optimism contained a core of darkness is integral to his perspective, for man "knows the rise of Demons, and he knows himself to have his original with, despising the part of his human nature in himself." In some ways *Three Books of Occult Philosophy* bridges the gap between necromancers and witches, providing (among other purposes) the scaffolding for the scholarly understanding of black magic and demonology during the Renaissance. Writing in *Europe's Inner Demons: The Demonization of Christians in Medieval Christendom*, Norman Cohn explains that while "It is generally believed that ritual magic … had nothing whatsoever to do with witchcraft," because of the differences between the universally male conjuror controlling demons and the largely female coven in bondage to them, a thorough reexamination of primary sources from the period, including grimoires and inquisitorial records, demonstrates a thematic similarity between the two figures. "One can observe how, over a period of generations," Cohn writes, "ritual magic and the struggle against ritual magic helped produce the fantastic stereotype of the witch."

Certainly such congruencies are visible in Agrippa's writing, not least of all because of his tolerant understanding of those who were punished for witch-craft, having once defended a woman who was accused of the crime. *Three Books of Occult Philosophy* solidified the common understanding of Agrippa, alongside the Swiss magician Paracelsus, as a kind of "Arch-magus," for he drew upon the teachings of Albertus Magnus and his teacher, the monk Johannes Trithemius (whose complex formula for demonic conjuration have more recently been discovered as cryptographic ciphers), and in return would influ-ence a host of occultists, including Elizabeth I's court astrologer John Dee, the German Hebraist Johann Reuchlin, the Italian philosopher Giordano Bruno (burnt at the stake in Rome's Campo de' Flori by the Inquisition), and even the German astronomer Johannes Keppler (whose own mother was charged for fraternizing with devils). Just as with Psellos or de Spiro, Agrippa pro-vides taxonomic detail for the Parliament of Hell, though some critics of the good physician thought that he may have been more diabolically self-inter-

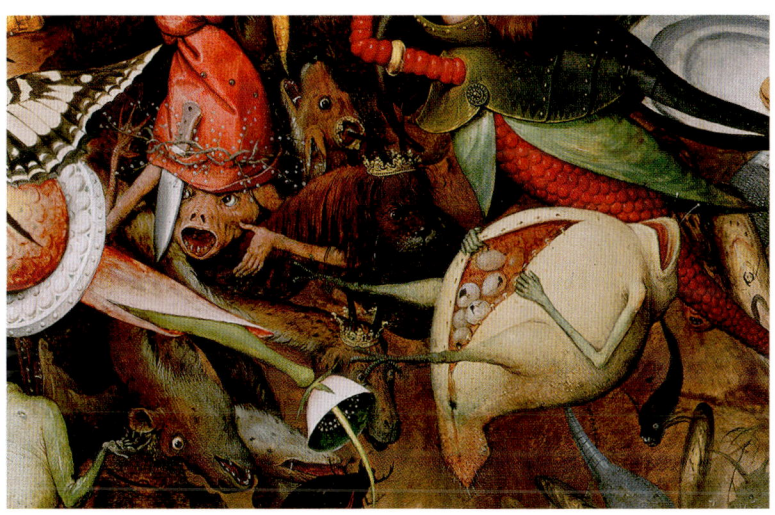

ested than he let on. Yates explains that Agrippa "figured prominently as a prince of black magicians and sorcerers" in contemporaneous accounts of his life. A witchy signifi-cance in the legend "of the black dog which was Agrippa's familiar spirit and which jumped into a river at his death... typical of Agrippa's image as the black conjuror of devils," as Yates writes. This was the context by which Christopher Marlowe, in his play *The Tragical History of the Life and Death of Doctor Faustus*, made Agrippa the mentor of Renaissance literature's greatest fictional repre-sentation of a conjuror.

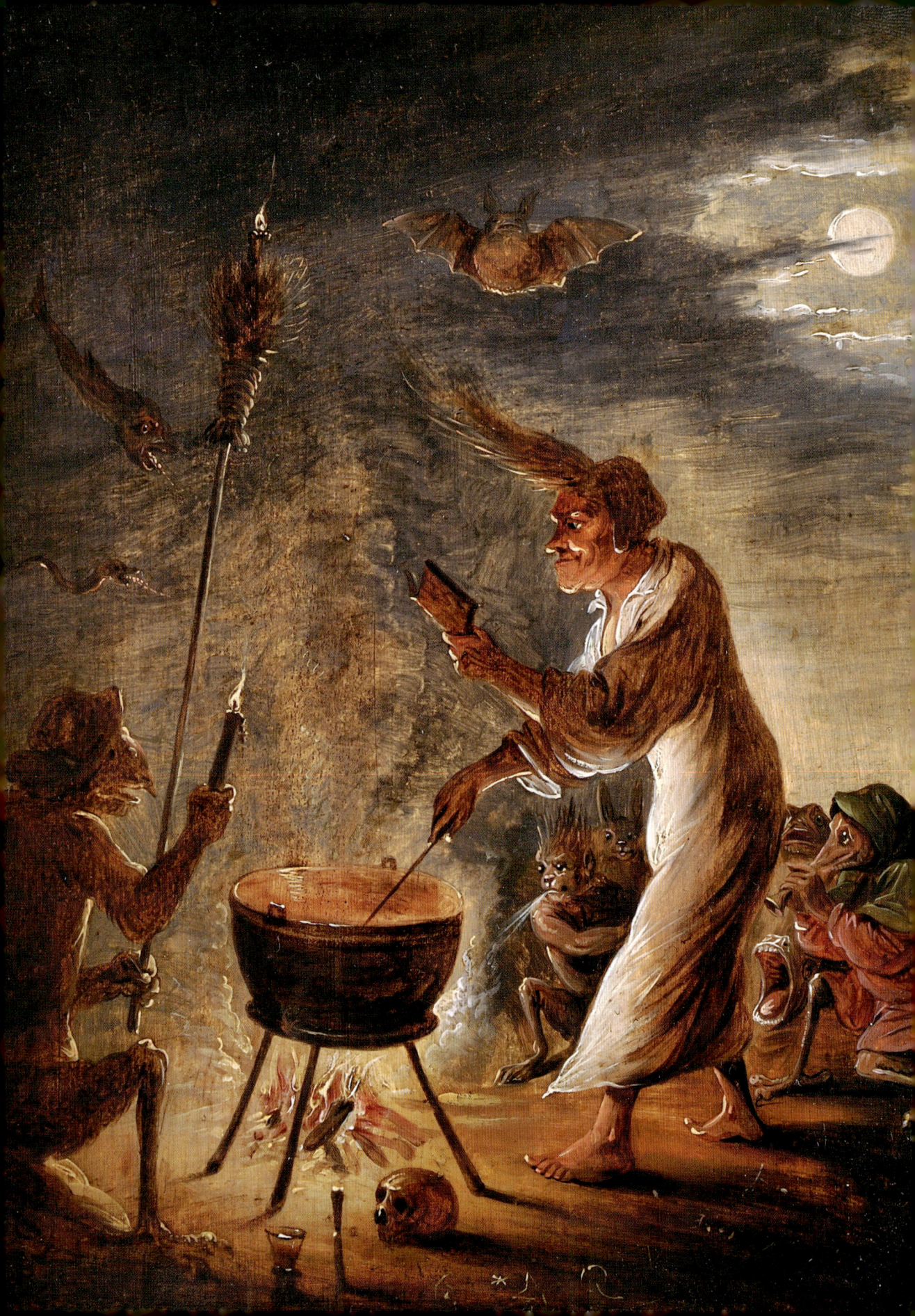

Despite both of their reputations for diabology, it's crucial to remember that neither Agrippa nor the previous medieval conjurors from whom he drew influence engaged demonology as a means to venerate infernal forces. To the contrary, Agrippa and his colleagues saw conjuration as its own form of reverence, by asking God to compel these demons to be servants toward a higher and sacred cause (as Solomon had once done). As Cohn claims, "conjuring up a demon was one long exercise in religious devotion," because the "demons are not to be worshipped but ... mastered and commanded; and this is to be done through the power of the God who created all spirits as well as all human beings."

The literary culture of the time, however, didn't present necromancers as so pure in intention, rather promoting the stereotype of the dark wizard that endures today, while the subsequent century would actually see the emergence of devilish devotion among occultists who did specifically spurn God, though Cohn reminds us that as concerns the Renaissance, "Nowhere, in the surviving books of magic, is there a hint of Satanism. Nowhere is it suggested that the magician should ally himself with the demonic hosts, or do evil to win the favor of the Prince of Evil." This was the legacy of Neoplatonic philosophy, but also the Hermetic corpus. That later discipline refers to a collection of texts dated to the third century but believed by Renaissance scholars to have been written much earlier, under the tutelage of a mysterious figures named Hermes Trismegistus, who was associated with the ancient Egyptian baboon-faced god Thoth—the inventor of writing. This collection was brought to Florence in the fifteenth century by a Byzantine refugee escaping the Ottoman invasion, and would be translated by Ficino with profound implications for philosophy and demonology. "Now magicians were conjuring demons by name," writes Cohn, "summoning them to manifest themselves in visible form, giving them precise instructions; and this implied a new and closer form of collaboration between particular human beings and particular demons."

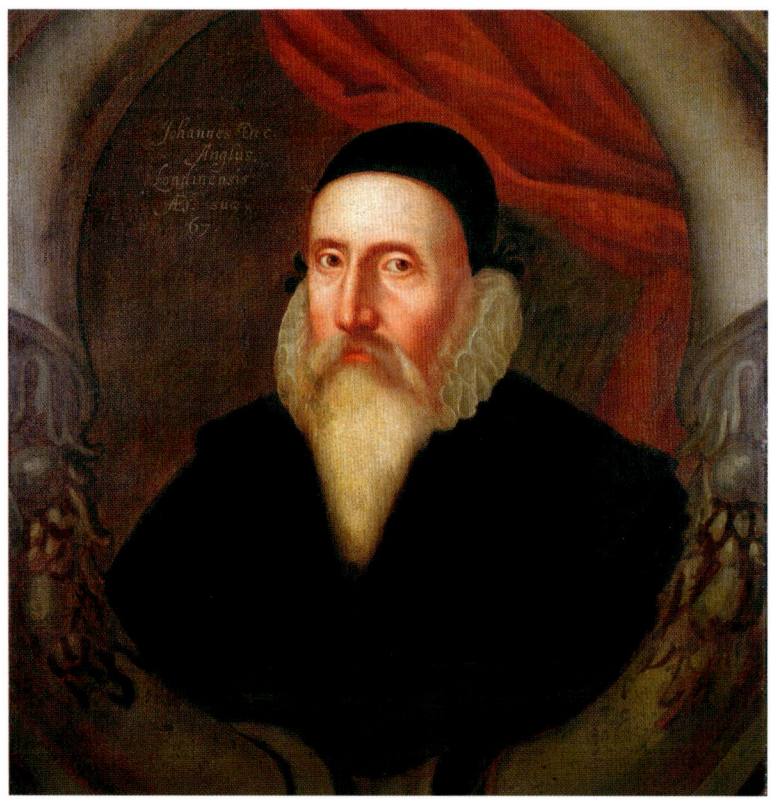

John Dee, the sixteenth-century English court astrologer under Elizabeth I, was an almost prototypical Renaissance magician. Famed for having the largest library on the British Isles, Dee wrote a variety of treatises about theurgy, and was conversant in occult learning. A conjuror himself, he and his associate Edward Kelley were involved in the discovery of a so-called Enochian language of angels, the tongue supposedly spoken by the biblical figure of Enoch before his assent to heaven. From the beard to the robes, Dee has the stereotypical visage of a wizard in this portrait by an anonymous artist, held by the National Maritime Museum in Greenwich, England.

The result was an increased perseveration on demonic names and hierarchies, even more so then in lists compiled in medieval manuscripts. Agrippa offered his own unique taxonomy, interpreting the subject through numeric scales of demons, which included the lowest category of novenary devils (among the nine listed are Merihem, the lord of pestilence, and Pytho who is sovereign of liars); quaternary devils that are associated with both the cardinal directions (Egyn of the north, Amaymon of the south, Oriens of the east, and Paymon of the west) and the elements (Samael for fire, Azazel for air, Azael for water, and Mahazael for earth); as well as ternary devils and binary devils, the last category of which includes only Behemoth and Leviathan. At the top of Agrippa's schema is the unitary devil, Lucifer, he who was responsible for introducing evil into the world due to his overweening pride. Providing such classifications was a popular pursuit, and examples include the German bishop Peter Binsfield's 1589 adaptation of Wycliffe's work from the previous century, King James I's aforementioned *Daemonologie*, which didn't list proper names but did categorize spirits into designations such as "Spectra" and "Fairies" (and included digressions on werewolves and vampires), and from the French Dominican inquisitor Sébastien Michaelis in 1612, *The Admirable History of the Possession and Conversion of a Penitent Woman*, which was based on his own experiences as an exorcist, and that contained several demonic names that have no antecedent. To these can be added anonymously penned demonological guides, including the sixteenth-century French *Book of Spirits* with entries on forty-six different infernal beings (including such novel creatures as Bulfas, Gazon, Furfur, Fenix, and Abugor). Even more influential was the "Ars Goetia" (meaning "Art of Sorcery") section of the Lemegeton, more popularly known as the *Lesser Keys of Solomon*.

Of unknown provenance, but believed to have been compiled partially from earlier material in either the sixteenth or seventeenth century, the "Ars Goetia" is perhaps the most significant demonological text to be written in a millennium. "Whatever the original source," notes Davies, and this "printed list of demons represented a valuable magical resource and circulated amongst learned spirit conjurers." The author (or authors) compiled a list of seventy-two demons, drawing from previous occultists including Agrippa, Trithemius, and others. Cohn explains that the form is marked by "descriptive lists of some scores of principal demons; detailing not only the forms in which each individual demon appears but also what offices he discharges and what powers he possesses."

As with Agrippa, the "Ars Goetia" claims that the demons are controlled by four lieutenants, each associated with a cardinal direction, and further divided into categories that in descending order include "Kings," "Dukes," "Princes," "Marquis," "Earls," "Knights," and "Presidents." Each one of the seventy-two demons is thoroughly defined, with an overview of their martial strengths and an associated mystical alchemical symbol given. For example, in respect to the categories listed above, the "Ars Goetia" identifies Baal as King of Hell, Amdusias as a duke, Vassago as a prince, Gamigin as a marquis, Furfur as an earl, Furcas as a knight, and Barbas as a president. Of the sixty-six additional demons that are described in the "Ars Goetia," there are a number of familiar characters, but as Cohn observes, "Other demons bear names that are quite unknown outside the ritual magic and Europe and were obviously invented *ad hoc*; but clearly they too are thought of as belonging to the same infernal hierarchy."

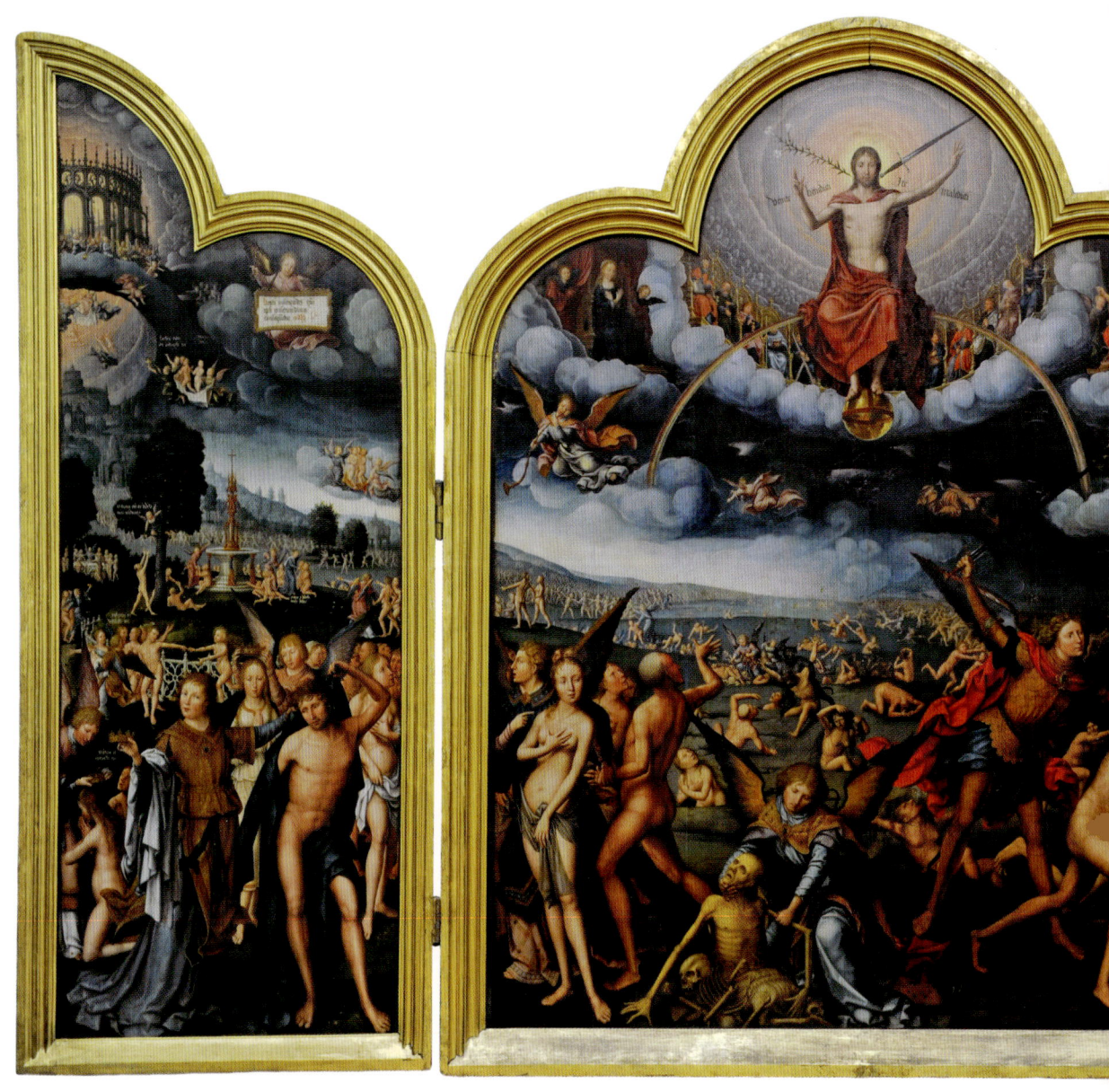

THIS SPREAD

The 1523 Triptych with the Last Judgment *by the French-speaking southern Netherlandish painter Jehan Bellegambe, now housed in the Gemäldegalerie in Berlin, Germany. A skeletal demon uses a funnel to pour coins into the mouth of a man, the pitcher which holds the lucre marked with the word "Avarice." The demon's connection to greed, and the punishment of those guilty of that sin, may help in identifying him as Mammon, most often associated with avarice. A connection between sins and other abstract qualities speaks to the manner in which demonic names were crucial in deriving a vocabulary of wickedness during this period, so that the personification of these attributes personalized intangible forces and attributes.*

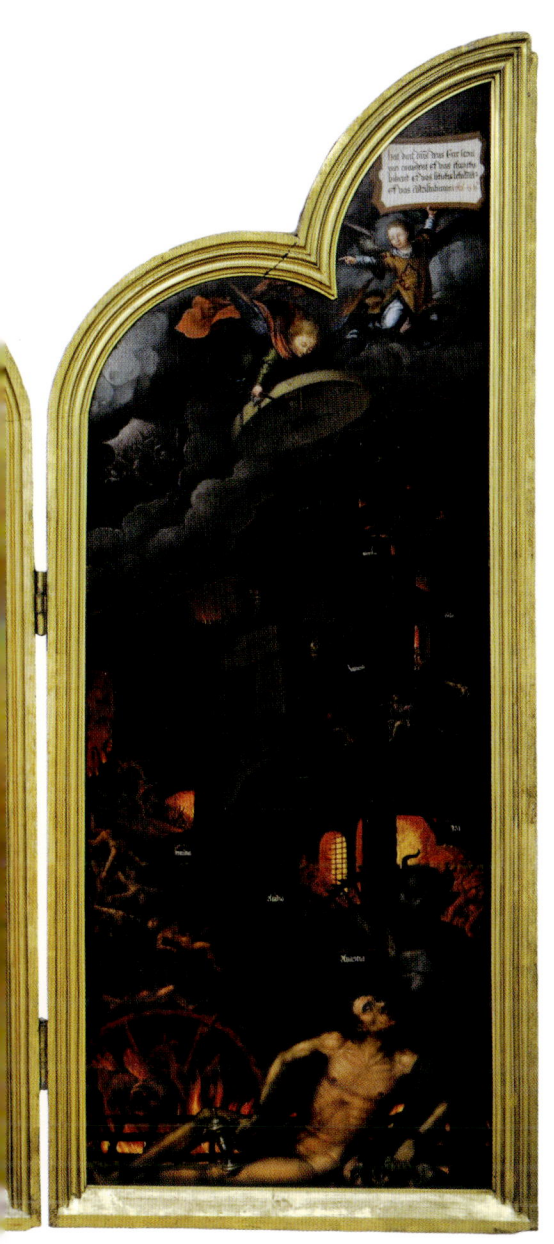

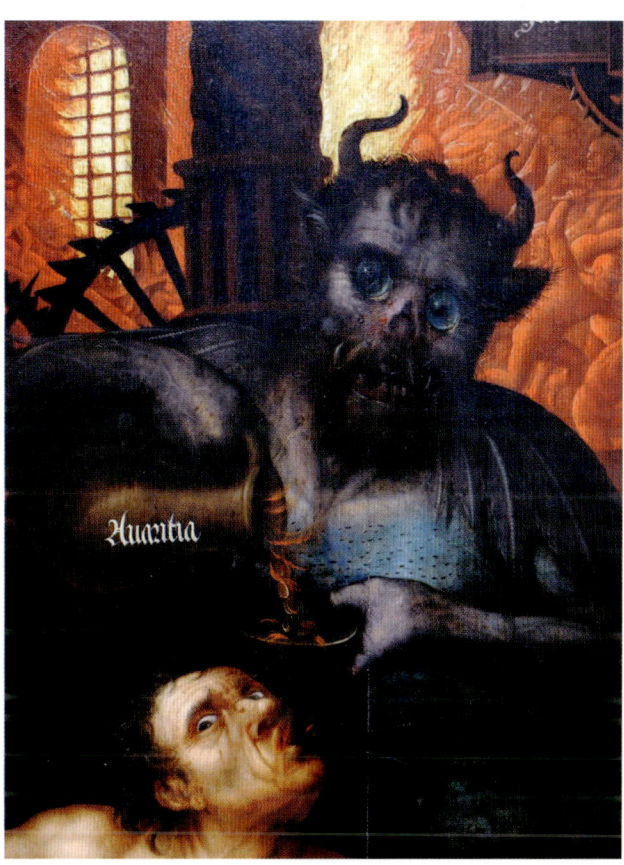

The earliest portions of the *Ars Goetia* can be traced to the thirteenth century, but the vast majority of material in the *Lesser Keys of Solomon* most likely derives from a sixteenth-century Dutch scholar and student of Agrippa's named Johann Weyer. Sharing a skeptical and relatively tolerant caste of mind with his teacher, Weyer's 1577 *Pseudomonarchia Daemonum*, or *The False Kingdom of the Demons*, was written to specifically refute the paranoia surrounding witchcraft, arguing that those persecuted were psychologically troubled unfortunates rather than being in league with the Devil. Despite such apparent rationalism, Weyer also provides not just demonic names, descriptions, and definitions, but also formula for conjuration, even while making clear that he holds mages to be defined by "oddness, deceptions, vanity, folly, fakery, madness, absence of mind, and obvious lies." Yet Weyer's skeptical disposition was neither secular nor materialist, atheistic or scientific, for his prose is evocative of the chimerical nature of Renaissance demonology, the surreal fusion of both definitiveness and otherworldliness, a certainty staked out in the midst of tumultuous epoch-defining doubt.

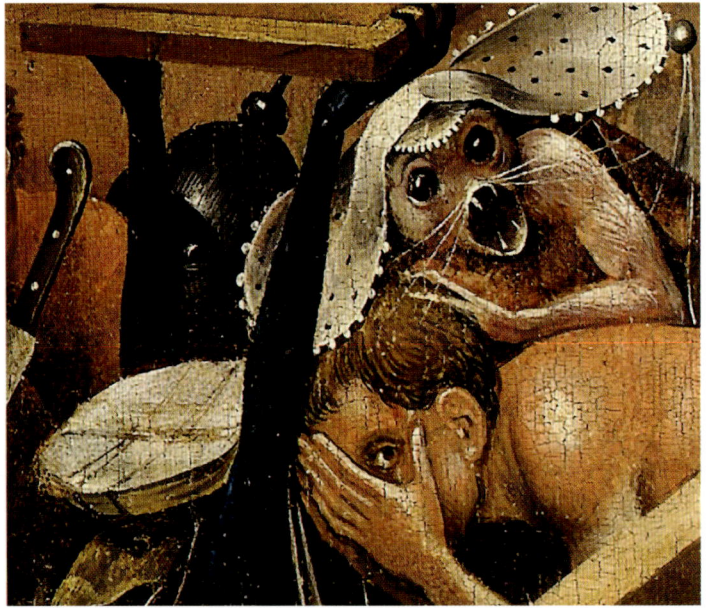

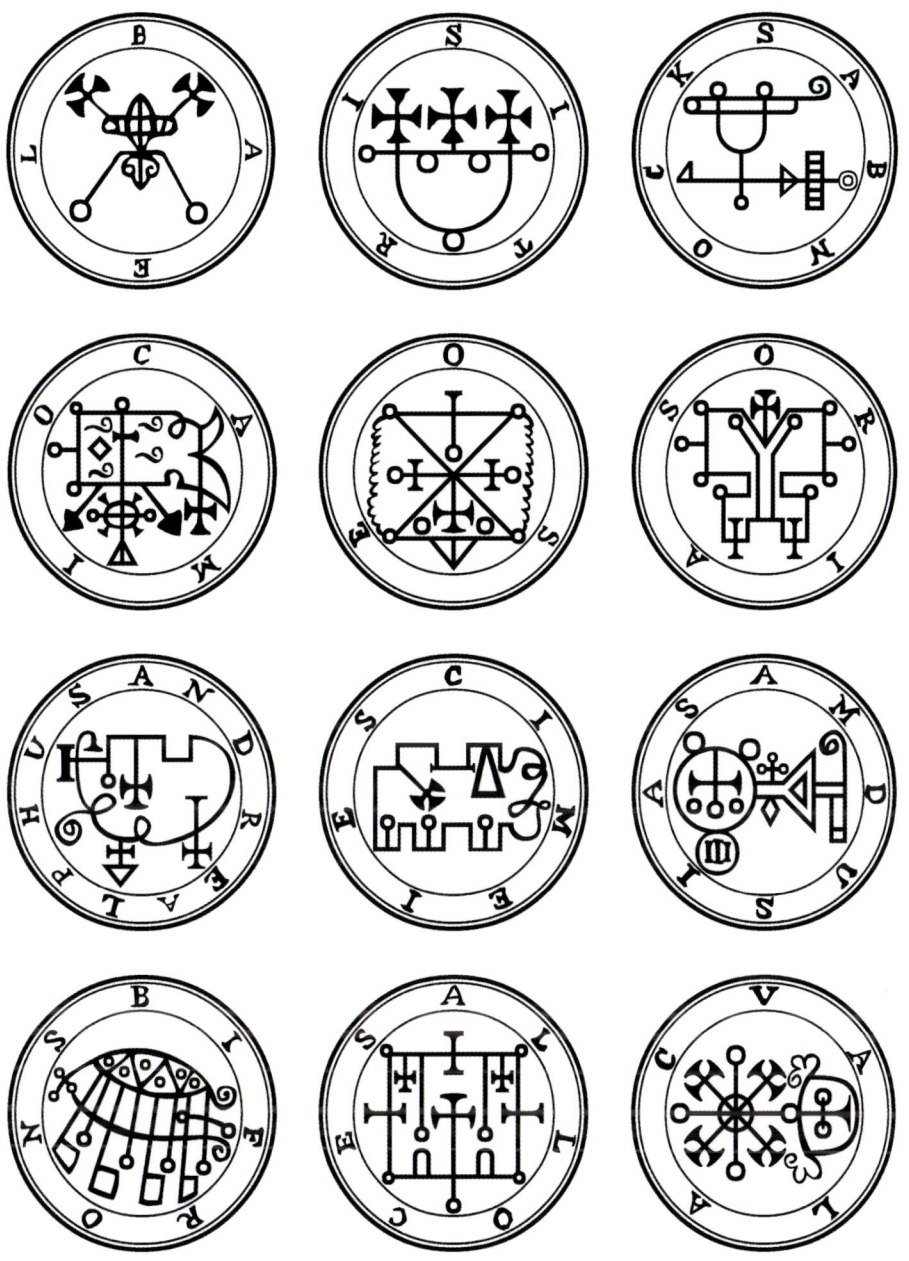

There are seventy-two symbols associated with each individual demon in the "Ars Goetia," as rendered in the twentieth century by famed English occultist Aleister Crowley in a 1904 edition of the Lesser Keys of Solomon. *Deriving from alchemical and kabbalistic sources, such strange symbols were instrumental to conjurors, both as an almost alphabetic shorthand, and in the task of actually summoning the demons for whom they were individually associated. Of the four examples above, starting at the upper left and moving clockwise, are the magical sigils for the demons Sitri, Amdusias, Andrealphus, and Bael.*

A translation was made into English less than a decade after *Pseudomonarchia Daemonum* was written, rendered by the English author Reginald Scot, who incorporated Weyer's list of demons into his 1584 volume *Discovery of Witchcraft*. Also written to dispel belief in witchcraft, Scott's book was the one that James I was specifically responding to in *Daemonologie*, but as with Weyer, the author still firmly believed that demons are real and can effect change in everyday life. Quoting Scot at length (while modernizing orthography and punctuation for better comprehension), the *Discovery of Witchcraft* enumerates a panoply of demons such as:

Purson, alias Curson, a great king, he comes forth like a man with a lion's face, carrying a most cruel viper, and riding on a bear, and before him go always trumpets, he knows hidden things, and can tell things present, past and to come: he bears treasure … he answers of all things earthly and secret, of the divinity and creation of the world, and brings forth the best familiars; and there obeys him two and twenty legions of devils, partly of the order of virtues and partly of the order of thrones.

Leraie, alias Oray, a great marquise, showing himself in the likeness of a gallant archer, carrying a bow and a quiver, he is author of all battles, he does putrefy all such wounds as are made with arrows by archers … and he has a regiment [of] over thirty legions.

Glasya Labolas, alias Caacrinolaas, or Cassimolar, is a great president, who comes forth like a dog, and has wings like a griffin, he gives the knowledge of arts, and is the captain of all murderers: he understands things present and to come, he gains the minds and love of friends and foes, he makes a man go invisible, and has the rule of six and thirty legions.

Berith is a great and a terrible duke, and has three names. Of some he is called Beall; of the Jews Berith, of black magicians Bolfry, he comes forth as a red soldier, with red clothing, and upon a horse of that color, and a crown on his head. He answers truly of things present, past and to come. He is compelled at a certain hour, through divine virtue, by a ring of magic. He is also a liar, he turns all metals into gold, he adorns a man with dignities, and confirms them, he speaks with a clear and a subtle voice.

Malphas is a great president, he is seen like a crow, but... speaks with a hoarse voice, he builds houses and high towers wonderfully, and quickly brings artificers together, he throws down also the enemies of edifications, he helps to good familiars, he receives sacrifices willingly, but he deceives all the sacrifices.

Shax, alias Scox, is a dark and a great marquise, like unto a stork, with a hoarse and subtle voice: he does marvelously take away the sight, hearing, and understanding of any man, at the commandment of the conjurer: he takes away money out of every king's house.

Focalor is a great duke coming forth as a man, with wings like a gryphon, he kills men, and drowns them in the waters, and overturns ships of war, commanding and ruling both winds and seas. And let the conjuror note, that if he bid him hurt no man, he willingly consent thereto.

It speaks to the gloaming nature of the Renaissance that a book written to dispel belief in one set of superstitions does so by fully engaging with another set. A Janus-headed age looking equally backwards and forwards. And while Weyer and Scot attempted the admirable goal of dissuading authorities of punishing the innocent for the imaginary crime of witchcraft (and the former was somewhat successful in this regard in his native Holland), this persevera-tion on diabolical power still couldn't help but make "witchcraft more fright-ening in a society already inclined to regard the world as a battlefield between God and the devil," as Julia Briggs writes in *This Stage-Play World: Texts and Contexts, 1580–1625.*

A cruel paradox of demonic poetics, and perhaps the essence of the diabolical itself, is that this chilling vocabulary of evil is more often than not successful in propagating malevolence rather than containing it. Certainly that's the case with the witch hunts that dominated early modern Europe, where a whole creative assortment of narrative elements—the idea of a coven, the Devil's pact, the witches' sabbat—lent themselves to the hideous punishment of innocent women and men. Davies explains that "the popular conception of the village witch was transformed into the greatest of satanic threats . . . through the theological reasoning of educated demonologists," so that there is a direct culpability on behalf of scholars for what transpired during the persecutions. The demonological imagination that lent itself to a terrifying collection of tropes that in a literary context might richly elucidate the human experience of evil was rather used precisely to propagate evil; hundreds of thousands of those on the margins sacrificed like scapegoats for a continent convulsing itself awake from the slumbers of its past.

Historiography produced over the past several generations has elucidated many details of the trials, facilitated by a careful and rigorous reading of the archival record concerning these powerless victims whom Scot described as "commonly old, lame, blear-eyed, pale, foul and full of wrinkles; poor, sullen, superstitious . . . lean and deformed, showing melancholy in their faces . . . doting, scolds, made, devilish." Trial documents, broadsheets, polemics, religious tracts, and theological treatises have all aided in helping scholars better understand how witch persecutions were enacted.

What must first be understood is that while the persecutions were encouraged by civil and ecclesiastical authorities, the impetus for them was born from the everyday hardships of life. "Often enough when misfortune struck," writes John Demos in *The Enemy Within: 2,000 Years of Witch-Hunting in the Western World*, "when the harvest failed, when hailstorms hit, when people or livestock mysteriously sickened—neighbors would turn on one another with accusations of dabbling in 'the black arts.'" Demos makes clear that witchcraft was a "favorite mode of *explanation* for painful and baffling experiences," for blighted crops, curdled milk, soured beer, unrequited love, broken friendships, and of course disease and death. While such pain marks human life since antiquity, during the sixteenth and seventeenth centuries it was often imparted to witchcraft. For elites, this became a convenient means of eliminating the traditional folk culture that was

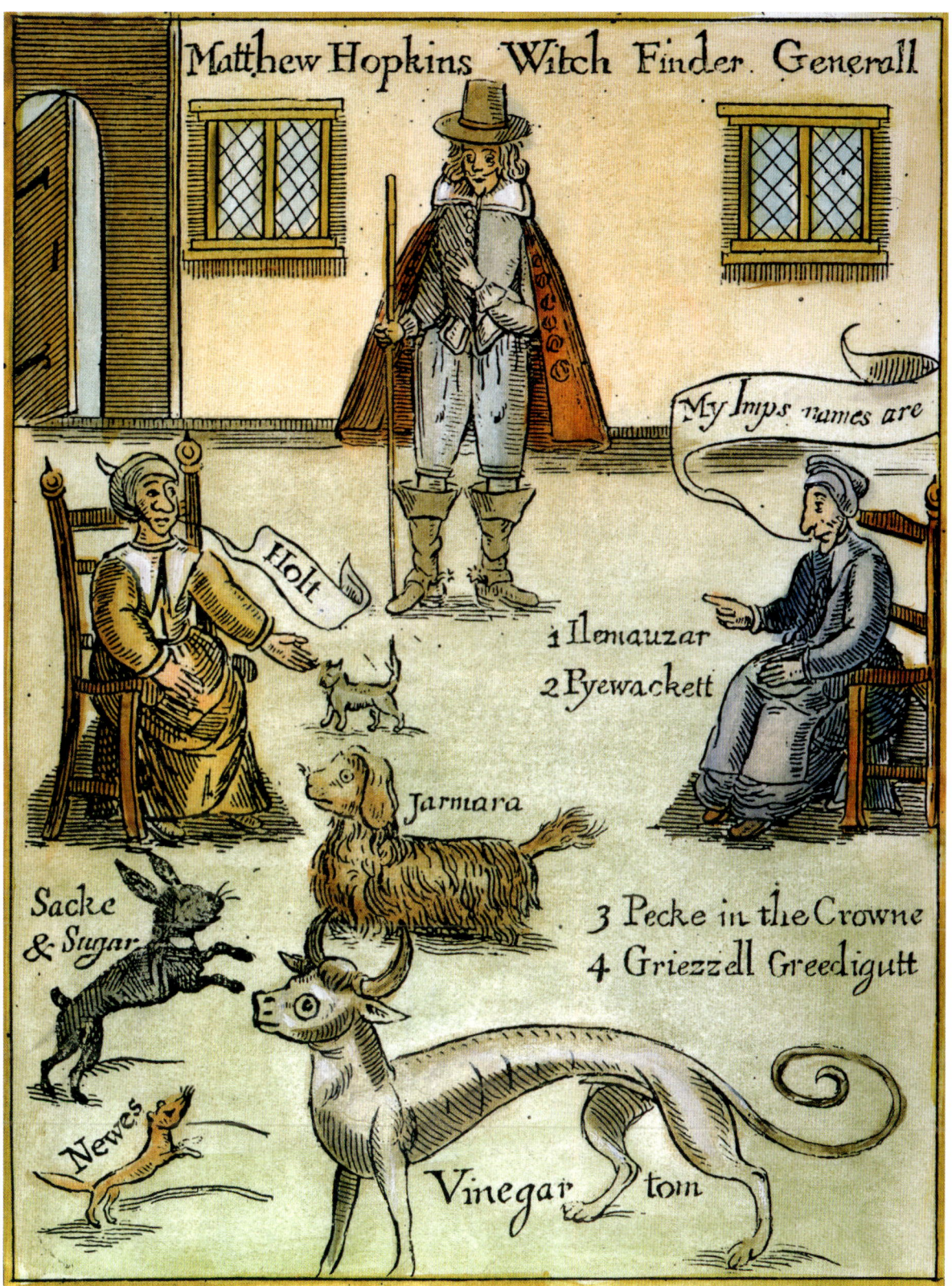

once widespread in pre-Christian Europe, while doing so under the state- and church-sanctioned seal of institutionalized misogyny, what Demos describes as "a fear, and a hatred, of women so generalized that it crosses virtually all boundaries." Four out of five of the people executed were women, so it's not unreasonable to see the witch trials as a "gynocide," as some feminist theorists have argued, a conscious and methodical persecution of a particular gender.

Such were the twitchy sentiments of the early modern period that the fifteenth-century French judge and demonologist Henri Boguet would write that witches "are everywhere, multiplying up the earth as worms in a garden," and estimating that Europe was home to no less than 1,800,000 women who'd entered into pacts with the Devil. Punishment became endemic, and as a result Europe is dotted with the graves of innocent witches—Marigje Arriens burnt for the crime of prophecy in 1591 in Schoonhoven, Holland; Allison Balfour, tortured, strangled, and then immolated upon the dark sands of Orkney, Scotland, in 1594; Merga Bien, one of two hundred people to be executed in Fulda, Germany, during the 1603 witch trials that convulsed that community; Sidonia von Borcke, the rare noblewoman to be punished, beheaded in the Duchy of Pomerania in 1620; Elizabeth Clarke, hung in 1645 in Essex—first of the victims of Matthew Hopkins, the notorious "Witch-Finder General" who traipsed the countryside during the convulsions of the English civil wars and was responsible for over a hundred deaths. And of course, across the Atlantic there are the twenty women and men hung at the town green of Salem, Massachusetts, in 1692, including Rebecca Nurse, John Proctor, and Giles and Martha Corey. While the most famous of witch trials, the tragedy of Salem isn't particularly marked by its severity, nor by its American location (for there had been other trials in the New World), but rather by being comparatively late in the course of the early modern witch trials. As enduring as the paranoia surrounding witchcraft had been, and as baroque as the explanations for its existence, equally mysterious is the sudden cessation of the persecutions.

It's sobering to realize that little more than a decade after the martyrs of Salem had been murdered, Ben Franklin—that veritable paragon of Enlightenment modernity—would be born less than twenty-five miles south of the notorious town. Indeed the physicist Isaac Newton, who by 1692 had already done the work that would revolutionize science, was fifty when John Proctor died upon the scaffold and Giles Corey was pressed to death. When Americans were hanging witches the mathematics that would one day make the moon landing possible had already been discovered. "How is it possible," asks historian Carlo Ginzburg in *Ecstasies: Deciphering the Witches' Sabbath*, "that a cultivated and advanced society . . . could unleash, contemporaneously with the so-called scientific revolution, a persecution based on a delirious notion of witchcraft?"

Hypotheses have been proffered since the eighteenth century about what drove Renaissance Europeans mad. If you ask a Catholic scholar they'll blame Protestantism, if you ask a Protestant historian they'll say Catholicism. Others have pointed to the seeming paradox Ginzburg noted, that in fact it was the propulsions of modernity that counterintuitively encouraged the persecutions, with historians like Keith Thomas in *Religion and the Decline of Magic* noting the concurrent rise of institutions like modern medicine at the same juncture as traditional healers were persecuted for witchcraft. Barstow writes that "Through healing, by both spells and potions, delivering babies, performing abortions, predicting the future, advising the lovelorn, cursing, removing curses, making peace between neighbors—the work of the village healer and her urban counterpart covered what we call magic as well as medicine," but with the rise of professions like medicine, the law, academe, and so on, the traditional arts were occluded by more contemporary roles. In this circumstance the punishment of the witches was the last gasp of antiquity, the final de-paganization before positivism, Puritanism, and privatization ushered in a disenchanted modern world.

The claim that the witch trials signaled the final eclipse of a pagan past has been put forward not without controversy, and it requires a bit of contextualization. Often identified with the early twentieth-century Egyptologist Margaret Murray, who in her 1921 *The Witch-Cult in Western Europe: A Study in Anthropology* claimed that covens were remnants of a continent-wide pre-Christian fertility cult that worshiped a horned god mistaken by Christians for the Devil, the hypothesis has waxed and waned over the decades, with most scholars today agreeing that such a thesis is grossly overstated. Ronald Hutton succinctly concludes in *The Witch: A History of Fear, from Ancient Times to the Present* that there is "no doubt that witchcraft was not a surviving pagan religion," and there is no reason to credibly contest that perspective in any literal sense.

Yet if we think of witchcraft as associated with "paganism" in a more figurative sense, there is a "kernel of truth" in Murray's claim, as Ginzburg notes in *The Night Battles: Witchcraft and Agrarian Cults in the Sixteenth and Seventeenth Centuries* (in which he traces the ways in which pre-Christian rituals were practiced unbeknownst by "witches"). A variety of healers like the Italian *striga* and *Friuli*, the Piedmontese *masca*, the German *vala*, and the English cunning-folk testify to the widespread endurance of beliefs outside of the official sanction of the Church, while both the Protestant and Catholic Reformations more strictly policed their differences, resulting in the persecutions. Such depaganization was required for the ultimate secularization of society, so the witch trials were a fiery and bloody dialect within faith itself. The result was our own cancerous modernity.

THE AGE OF MEPHISTOPHELES

The precocious twenty-three-year-old French philosopher René Descartes had his famous visions of November 10, 1619, during a fretful night in his drafty soldier's lodgings along the Danube River. He was stationed in Saxe-Wurtemberg during the bloody sectarian conflict of the Thirty Years' War, when he had that formative trio of dreams that would upend how he thought about philosophy, though he didn't impart those mirages to demonic intercession. Ultimately, he decided that these spectral hallucinations, which would inspire the birth of modern philosophy, had been sent through the intercession of the Virgin Mary, to whom he offered thanks four years later when he made a pilgrimage to the Basilica della Santa Casa in Loretto, Italy, where the faithful believe the Holy Family's Nazareth dwelling had been miraculously transported. An auspiciously surprising origin story for modern thought, since few figures are as associated with the radical skepticism and rationalism that marks secular thought as much as the Frenchman. "Descartes believed that nothing less than a complete overhaul of the principles of inquiry was required in order to establish confidence in the new ways of thinking," writes Anthony Gottlieb in *The Dream of Reason: A History of Philosophy from the Greeks to the Renaissance*, yet evidence of the numinous couldn't be expunged from his thought. Even though the philosopher's goal was nothing less than the dispelling of doubt, while building upon a firm foundation, an entirely new system of metaphysics and epistemology, his hyper-rationalist 1637 *Discourse on the Method* is in its own way demon-haunted.

No direct account of his dreams exists in his own words, though in 1691 his biographer Adrien Baillet writes that the philosopher had sensed, for several days before the visions that something external, or supernatural, "was exciting him in the enthusiasm with which he felt his brain heated . . . and human intelligence had no part in it." On that St. Martin's Day of 1619, there were actually three dreams Descartes had as he dozed by the fire. The first was, as Baillet records, a "representation of some ghosts which appeared to him, and which terrified him," these creatures having introduced a nightmare concerning Descartes's perambulations through regular life, with all of the uncanny déjà vu that marks those nocturnal terrors in which the normal seems disturbed, so that when he woke up he feared the vision was "the work of some evil genius who wanted to seduce him." The second dream concerned a clap of thunder accompanied by sparks of divine illumination, and the final revelation had the philosopher

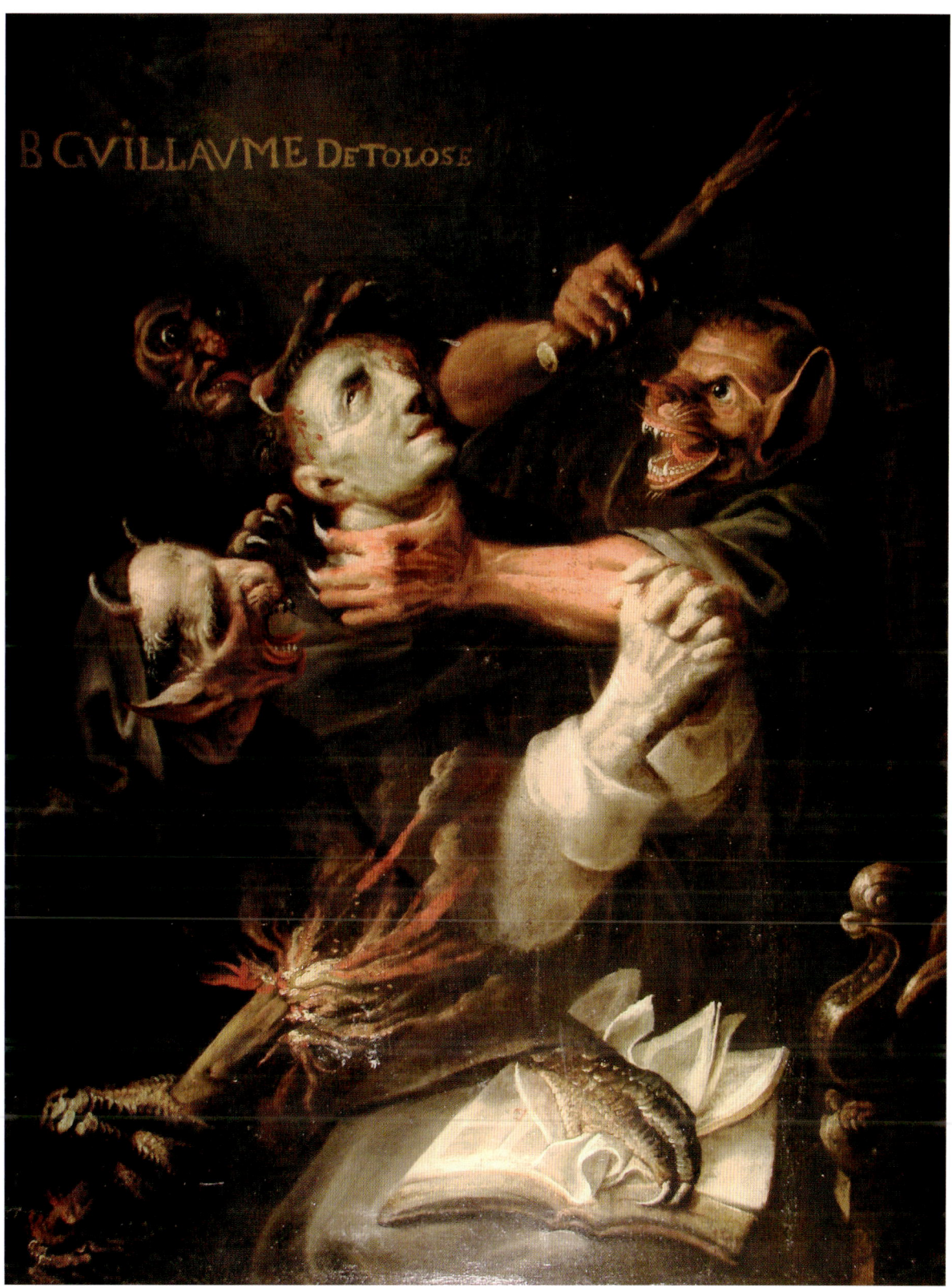

B GVILLAVME DE TOLOSE

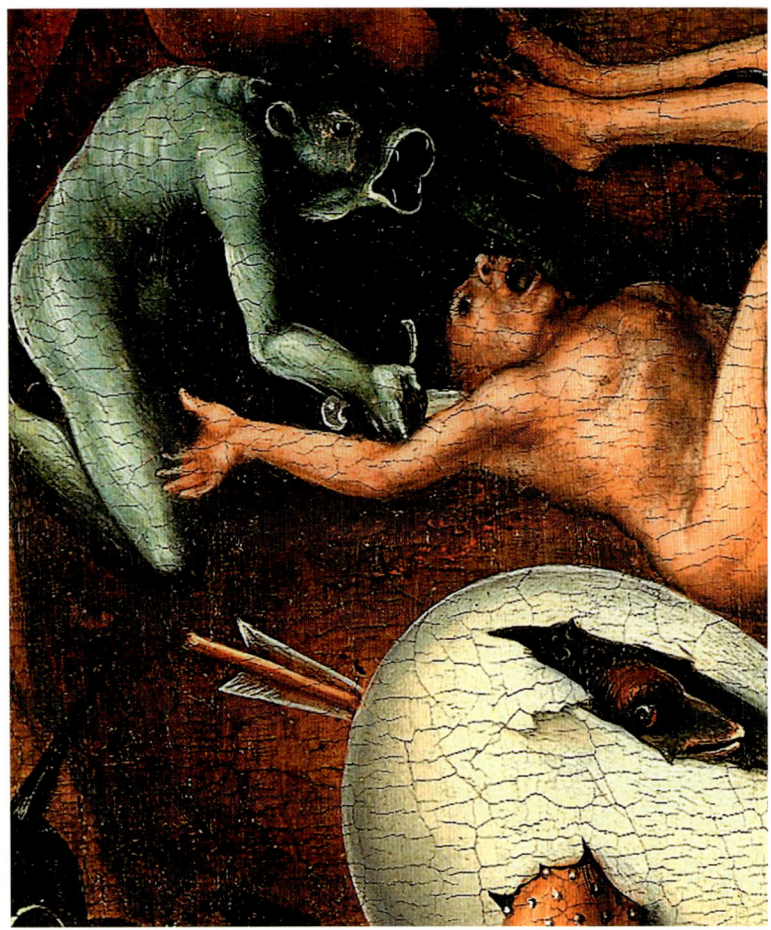

Detail from the French painter Ambroise Frédeau's 1657 painting The Blessed Guillaume de Toulouse Tormented by Demons, *depicting the medieval hero being tortured by, among others, a bat-like devil. The scene depicted by Frédeau would seem far removed from the rationality of his contemporary, the philosopher René Descartes. Yet there is more similarity than first might be assumed, as the torturous visions that Descartes encountered aren't dissimilar to the psychological nocturnal torments suffered by figures like the biblical patriarch Jacob and Saint Anthony.*

In a scene strongly reminiscent of Bosch, the German painter (and Lutheran propagandist) Lucas Cranach the Elder displays a shrieking amphibious demon garroting a suffering man in his 1525 triptych The Last Judgment. *A century later, and Descartes imagined nothing quit as visceral as this black-mouthed hell beast, and yet Bosh and Cranach's world shares a similar sense of the ways in which the subjective human mind is able to create elaborate chimeras of reality, the duplicity of illusion its own form of torture.*

coming upon an anthology of poetry, the book containing all of the metaphysical insight that Descartes required to dispel his fears about the potential evil genius who can impart into somebody's skull such unsettling emotions. Upon waking, Baillet writes, Descartes had the beginnings of his philosophical system, which so fully interrogated how one can tell the difference between illusion and reality, for "poets have written by enthusiasm and the power of imagination; there are in us seeds of knowledge, as in a flint, which philosophers draw out by reason, but poets strike them out by imagination, and they shine more."

The dreams that Descartes experienced over the course of that evening are a rough, figurative approximation of the rigorous, syllogistic logic that he applies in the *Discourse on Method*. Constructing his new system upon the ashes of medieval scholasticism (with its undue reverence to the authority of Aristotle) and Renaissance humanism (with its enshrinement of Plato), Descartes rather hoped to discover how certainty could be built from pure reason. If the sixteenth and seventeenth centuries were permeated by an all-encompassing doubt, then Descartes would embrace that doubt to methodological ends, hoping to find solid ground beneath the shifting sands of uncertainty that threatened to topple philosophy. His conclusions weren't necessarily radical—that logic can discern what's true, that God exists, and so on. Yet his way of arriving at these suppositions was revolutionary, for to do so Descartes momentarily embraced a radical skepticism that scraped away all that was assumed, and left the individual mind alone and without support before asking what exactly it is that we know.

To do this, Descartes embraced the idea of the demonic, inventing an omnipotent and malevolent specter for the purposes of a thought experiment whose role was to make us question everything before we could arrive at answers about anything. Writing in his 1641 *Meditations on First Philosophy*, Descartes envisions an evil demon, as with his first dream more than two decades before, who with the "utmost power and cunning has employed all his energies in order to deceive me." Like Christ harrowing hell, Descartes plumbs to the last circle of doubt, imagining that this demon is capable of making the "sky, the air, the earth, colors, shapes, sounds and all external things" so that they are "merely the delusions of dreams which [the demon]...has devised to ensnare my judgement." A nightmare where Descartes perhaps has not "hands or eyes, or flesh, or blood or senses, but as falsely believing that I have all these things." How is the individual to escape from this demonic delusion? How is any certainty to be proffered when our entire world could be an illusion imparted by an evil devil? The scholastic would offer the syllogisms of Aristotle, and the humanist the Platonist dialectic, but while both of those ancient philosophers traded in doubt and illusion themselves, Descartes entertains the possibility that all of those words of Plato and Aristotle, their dialogues and treatises, and indeed all of the authority of the Church and tradition, were chimeras. Perhaps all that existed was simply a figment of his own quivering, tortured mind, these illusory images of a nonexistent reality implanted by a sadistic demon into the philosopher's pineal gland.

The solution, Descartes argues, is that his own mind is only that which he can be certain of, but that this is solid enough to prove the entire universe. "Cogito Ergo Sum," the famous first postulate of the new Cartesian philosophy— "I think therefore I am." As with Euclid's geometry, Descartes tries to generate a whole system from his defined axioms; he was a bodiless mind, a disembodied soul, rotating in the void and constructing reality entirely from defined *a priori* principles. From the Cogito, this hard and undeniable fact of our own individual existence, Descartes builds outward, like a solitary man constructing his own castle, and the metaphysics that he unspools is one which remarkably holds to the status quo. As if awaking from that nightmare on St. Martin's Day, Descartes says that radical skepticism will lead us all to total certainty; that the rigorous application of logic can aid us in moving upward from the Cogito to tangible reality, so that we *know* there isn't such a demon, we *know* that God exists, we *know* that other people exist. Rather than basing these beliefs on custom, or common sense, or tradition, or authority, Descartes argues we can be certain of them because of pure rationality. The evil demon of Descartes's thought experiment, who threatened our belief in the sense of our lived experience, had finally undermined himself, exorcised by Descartes's logic. At least that's what the philosopher argued.

Because it's hard to be totally convinced by *Meditations on First Philosophy* and Discourse on Method, once the basilisk of Descartes's demon is introduced, it's impossible to fully expel him from the West's philosophical mind. Though Descartes's thinking certainly has its antecedents—Plato's cave for example, or the Taoist philosopher Lao-Tzu's gnomic parables—in its specificity his demon has had an enduring presence in our cultural nightmares. The philosophical thought-experiment known as the Brain in a Vat argument, attributed to James Cornman and Keith Lehrer in a 1968 paper, or the anxious plots of the Wachowski siblings in *The Matrix*, and the entire oeuvre of science fiction author Philip K. Dick speak to the nauseous paranoia that Descartes's evil demon can still move within us. Descartes never meant his thought experiment to be taken literally—his very point is that this imagined creature doesn't exist—and yet what demon haunts modernity more than this malignant specter?

If the Renaissance was defined by a deep doubt that Descartes unsuccessfully attempted to expel, then his demon is the truest exemplar of that age, and far from some remainder in a rationalist calculation, a momentary smudge on the ledger as the philosopher makes his argument. This devil is enduring. Contemporary scholars still rightly take Descartes seriously, where an Agrippa is regarded as an esoteric and eccentric remnant from an inaccessible past. But both were demon-haunted, albeit in different ways, and the being that Descartes conjures offers a new and modern punishment—relentless doubt, tricks of the eye and mind, the sense that the only real illusion is that we can know anything at all. Descartes, who was not a poet, never thought to name his demon, but if we had to refer to him in some way, we'd do worse than to christen this monstrous creature Mephistopheles.

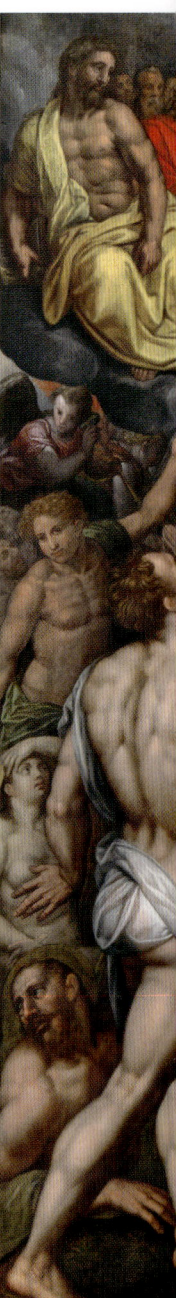

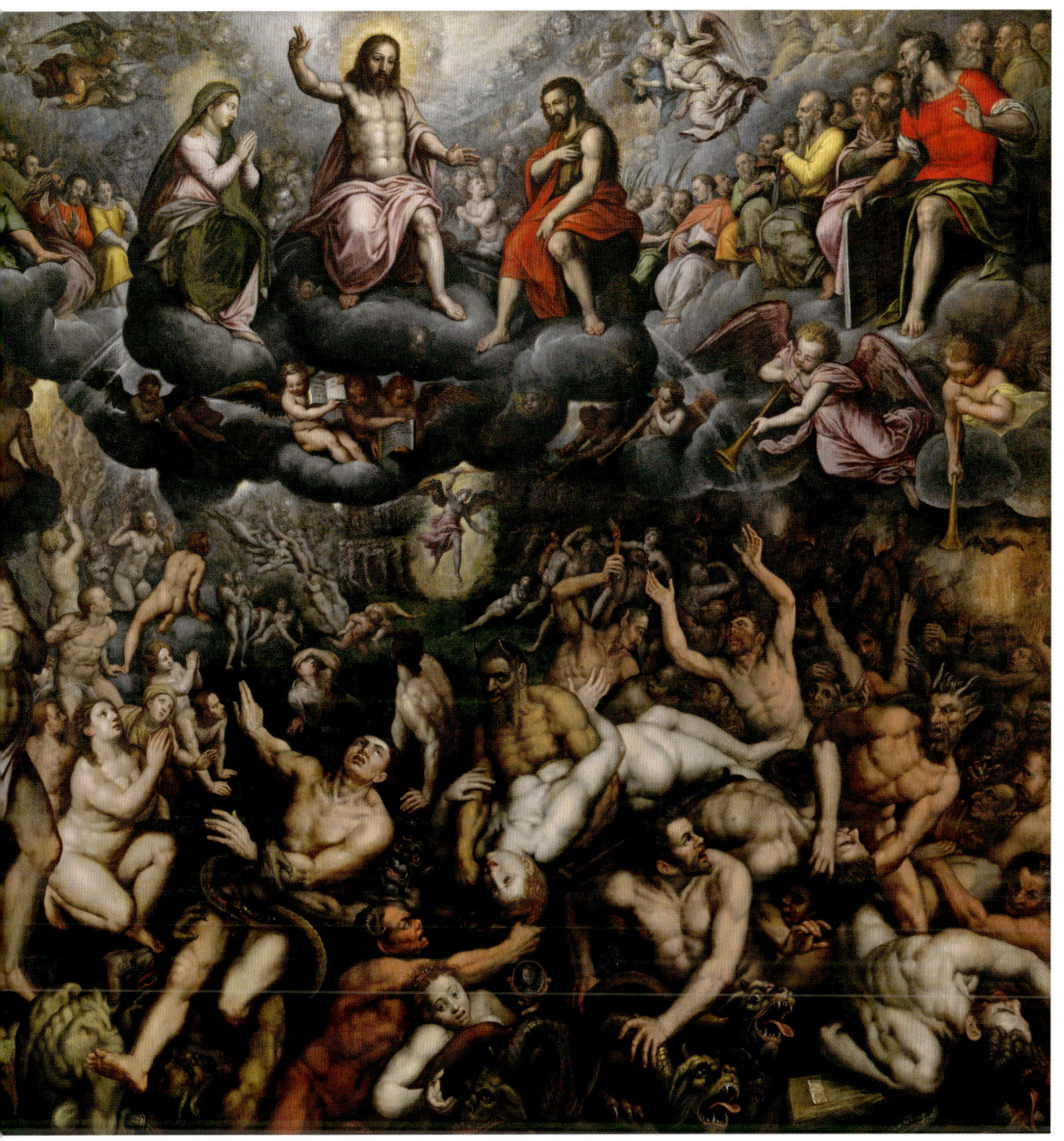

Flemish painter Raphael Coxie imagines the punishments of apocalypse in this detail from his 1589 Last Judgment, *commissioned by the aldermen of Ghent to hang in the guild house, and currently displayed in the Museum of Fine Arts in that same city. Owing much to* the apocalypticism of the period, Coxie's scene wouldn't seem to prefigure Cartesian philosophy in any literal sense, and yet Descartes's description of being buffeted by doubts is not unlike the torture that the damned suffer in the hellish non-space of perdition.*

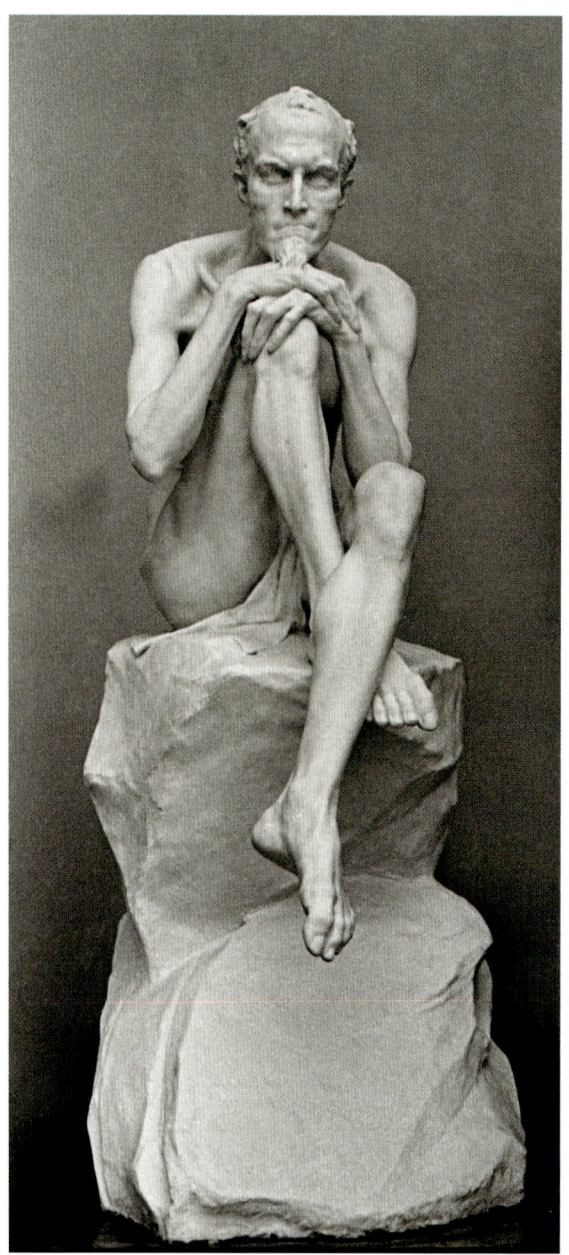

Russo-Lithuanian sculptor Marc Antokolsky envisions Mephistopheles as a thoroughly modern man in his 1884 piece held by the Hermitage Museum in St. Petersburg, Russia. Despite the name "Mephistopheles" being several centuries old by the time Antokolsky imagined him as a Romantic hero, those intimations of modernity were already present in the original legend.

Of unknown etymology, though perhaps meant to evoke Greek, Latin, or Hebrew (which gives the name an uneasy feeling of verisimilitude), Mephistopheles first appears in the late sixteenth-century genre of German *Faustbooks*, compendiums of lore concerning the ill-fated necromancer and his demonic intercessor. "That the name is a purely modern invention of uncertain origins makes it an elegant symbol of the modern Devil with his many novel and diverse forms," writes Russell. Mephistopheles, trading in doubt, illusion, and mirage, was in many ways not unlike Descartes's demon, and his function was the same—to demonstrate the ways in which uncertainty marked this age, this world turned upside down. While Renaissance occultism had no shortage of novel demons, idiosyncratic inventions of their authors' minds, only Mephistopheles has endured in the collective imagination. Having no precedent in scripture or myth, with a name first seen in print in the sixteenth century, it's hard not to have the uneasy sense that Mephistopheles's very novelty speaks to his reality, for it would be understandable to ask where else such a being could come from other than a hell closer than our very breaths, just visible beneath the surface of things.

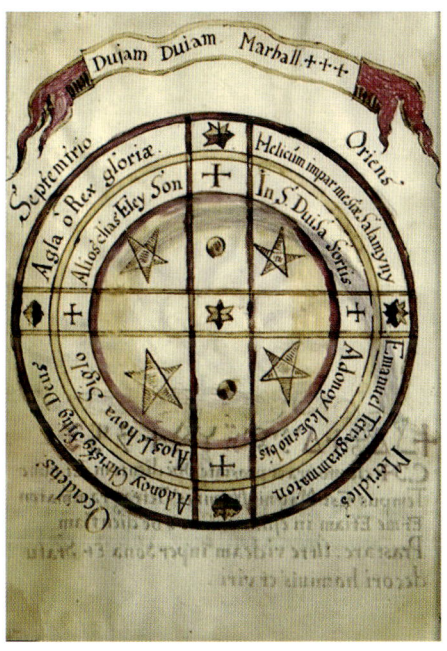
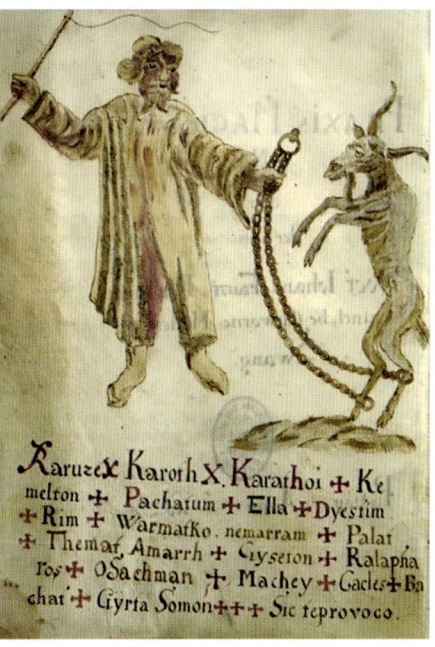

In Marlowe's play, the demon acts as counterpoint to Faust; where the latter is initially filled with enthusiasm about his new necromantic skills, the former is world-weary and tired, a being who knows the secrets of existence, but is drained of any sense of life. "Why this is hell, nor am I out of it," Mephistopheles tells Faust after being summoned to the world of the living. Unlike the bestial visages he wore in the medieval past, Mephistopheles is able to finally appear in the pleasing guise of a brown-robed Franciscan friar, as fully capable of effecting the senses and tricking the brain as the demon envisioned by Descartes. If the narrative of Faust, in its many permutations, is about anything, it's this— the ways in which the pursuit of knowledge can ironically lend itself to greater and greater uncertainties; that in trying to fix anything definite, understanding only dissipates like vapor from some ill-planned alchemical reaction.

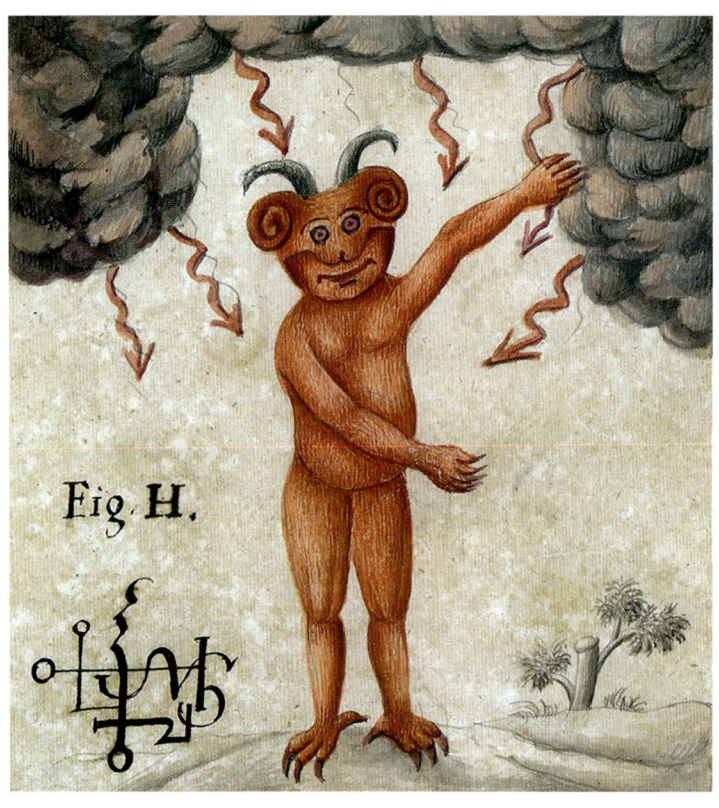
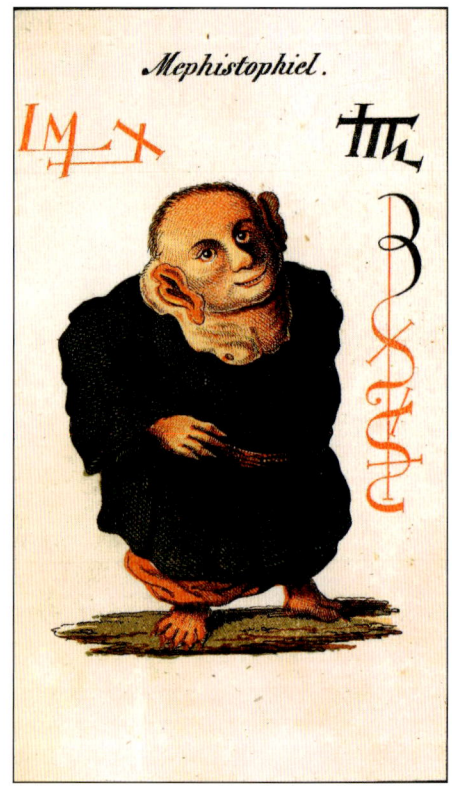

ABOVE

Illustration of a demon from Magia Naturalis et Innaturalis; or, Threefold Coercion of Hell, *a grimoire associated with Faust and printed in 1849, supposedly based on an earlier text from 1612. Note the alchemical symbol at the side, integral for summoning said demon. A depiction of Mephistopheles in his monk's robe is on the left.*

Based on a historical personage, the actual Faust has almost entirely receded into myth, a transformation that happened during his lifetime, in the first half of the sixteenth century. The historical Johann Georg Faust was a German scholar who became an itinerant occultist with a reputation for casting horoscopes and performing conjuration. A middling figure (to the degree that we're able to discern much about him at all), Faust at least had an uncanny talent for finding himself in significant historical junctures; he was associated with that black-hearted occult city of Prague when it was capital of the Holy Roman Empire and overseen by the wizardly King Rudolph II, who assembled a court devoted to astrology and kabbalah, divination and conjuration. Faust was also present for the horrific siege of Munster, when a combined force of Lutheran and Catholic soldiers overthrew a communist theocracy established by radical Anabaptists. And he'd ultimately expire in a house explosion sometimes around 1541, victim of his own miscalculated alchemical experiments. Compared to Agrippa and Trithemius, to Pico della Mirandola and Ficino, to Paracelsus and Albertus Magnus, the Faust of history was a nobody—and yet his name has become synonymous with black magic among the public in a manner that none of the others have.

"During his lifetime Faustus had acquired a black reputation, but it was nothing to the one he would acquire after death," writes Leo Ruickbie in *Faustus: The Life and Times of a Renaissance Magician*. "In death he became the blackest of black magicians." The term "Faustian bargain" is such that one needn't be familiar with the original narrative to understand the connotations of compromise, capitulation, and cunning that are associated with this trope, wherein somebody sells their soul in exchange for power, wealth, or knowledge. Faust wasn't the origin of the narrative theme concerning a pact with the Devil; the medieval nun Hroswitha had already depicted a diabolical pact in her story of Theophilus of Adana, penned in the tenth century, and that same century saw similar rumors about Pope Sylvester II having sold his soul to Satan. Yet only Faust has become so all-consumingly associated with that particular story about the levels to which an ambitious man is willing to go in pursuit of occult knowledge. First mentioned by Trithemius, authors connected Faust with diabology in tracts written as early as 1540, and his famed pact with the Devil was solidified as part of his myth by 1580, explored in a variety of works printed in central Europe throughout these decades.

The genre of *Faustbooks* functioned as equal parts sermonizing message against the dangers of Hermetic magic and prurient true-crime ghost story. Particularly popular among Lutheran reformers (Martin Luther's lieutenant, Philip Melanchthon, penned one), the *Faustbooks* served to warn readers about the inherent dangers in Renaissance learning. Russell writes that Faust's position as a scholar helped to consciously tie his desire to "obtain knowledge by his own efforts rather than to receive grace" to the "individualistic rebellion" that is the "original sin of humanity . . . and to pride."

The most popular and complete of Faustian chapbooks was the 1587 *History of Dr. Johann Faust*, printed by Johann Spiess, which went on to be the primary source material for Marlowe in the writing of his play two years later. "I suppose he looked up to Heaven, but his eyes discerned naught therein," Spiess (or whoever wrote the work) sympathetically writes of Faust's contrite last evening on earth. "They say that he dreamt of the Devil and of Hell." All of the elements that Marlowe would use in his play were already in the *History of Dr. Johann Faust*—the account of the alchemist rejecting religion and temporal learning, the invocation of Satan, the conjuration of the neologistically named Mephistopheles, the pact signed in blood, the acquired powers and subsequent exploits (including the ability to transport himself instantaneously, or to enjoy conjugal visits with demons disguised as the most beautiful of women), the failed attempt at contrition, and then finally Satan's retrieval of a soul to be tortured in hell. Even Spiess's version has some of the complexity and pathos inherent in its titular character's personality, a depiction that Marlowe appropriated when he removed Faust from the simple confines of morality play into something much more psychologically realized. If Marlowe was able to empathize with the good doctor, that's because he shared a bit of the Faustian disposition.

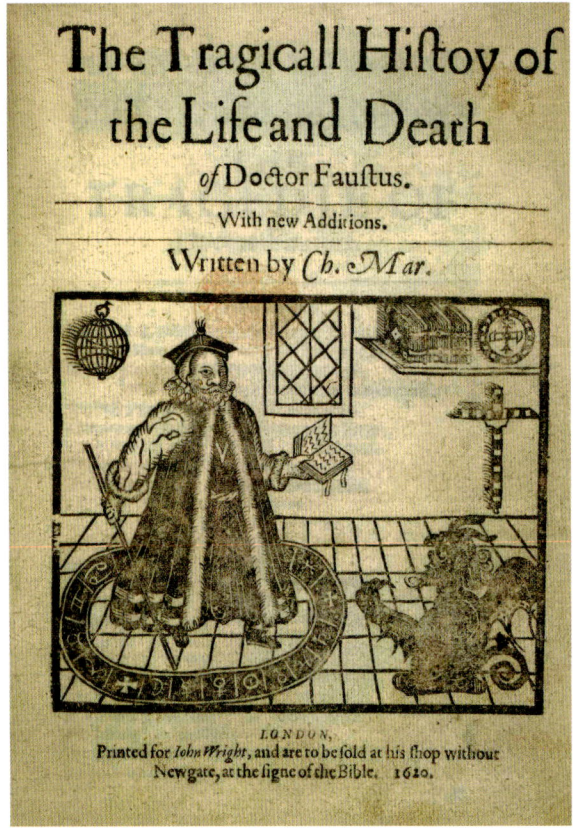

Frontispiece from a 1620 quarto of Marlowe's The Tragical History of the Life and Death of Dr. Faustus, *showing the necromancer within a magic circle at the moment he's conjured Mephistopheles, but before the demon has reappeared in the form of a monk. Marlowe's text exists in two different versions, a substantially shorter "A Text" and a later "B Text," which includes more comedic interludes, and with altered theological implications regarding Faust's agency. Differences between the texts are presumed to have resulted from stage adaptations that edited and revised the narrative and language over multiple performances.*

Notorious among the theatergoing public of late sixteenth-century London, Marlowe remains among the most influential playwrights and poets of the Elizabethan era, arguably only exceeded by Shakespeare. His life was dramatic, violent, and short, with the playwright having developed a contemporary notoriety for intemperance, sodomy, heresy, and blasphemy. Testimony attributed to an associate of his, and entered into record by the notorious state Privy Council (for whom it has long been assumed he worked as a spy on the Continent), claimed that Marlow had accused "Moses of being but a juggler" and "Christ was a bastard." Whether or not these freethinking sentiments can properly be assigned to the writer, critics saw a dangerous thread of atheism (or worse) in his plays. Author of only seven plays before his inglorious murder, supposedly over a tavern bill at the tender age of twenty-nine, Marlowe explored the new doubt in borderline sacrilegious works like *The Jew of Malta, Edward II*, and *Tamburlaine the Great, Part I* and *Part II*, but it was Doctor Faustus that would most fully embody the exigencies and contradictions of this supposed golden age. As Yates described the popular stage performances, the "diabolical apparatus used in the productions caused great excitement and terror. Shag-haired devils with squibs in their mouths ran roaring over the stage; drummers made thunder in the tiring-house; technicians made artificial lighting in the heavens. It was reported in the seventeenth century that there had been a visible apparition of the Devil on the stage in Queen Elizabeth's days during a performance."

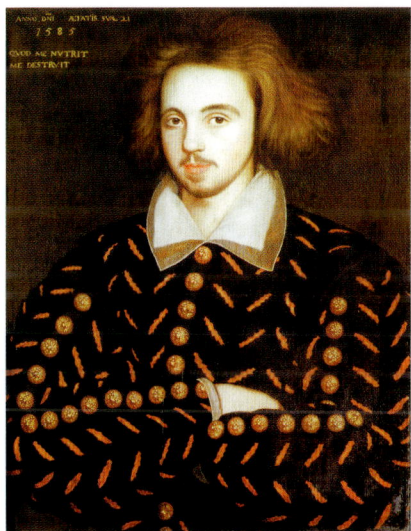

ABOVE

Anonymous portrait from 1585 believed to be of Marlowe, when he was a twenty-one-year-old student at Corpus Christi College, Cambridge. It is still displayed there.

So great was the infamy of *Faustus*, whereby the mock Latin incantations supposedly summoned an extra demon onto the stage during one of the performances (as reported by the anti-theatrical Puritan William Prynne), and Satan
himself appeared at the premier to ensure that he was accurately depicted, that
diabolical legends accumulated around Marlowe's biography. Rumor had it that
Marlowe had been a member of a secret coterie of distinguished intellectuals,
including the explorer Sir Walter Raleigh and the astronomer Thomas Harriot,
who were freethinking members of the "School of Night," a sort of atheistic
fraternity that resembled continental occult groups like the Rosicrucians, and
evoked later societies such as the Freemasons (it's sometimes thought that the
author's murder may have been related to either such a group or to his work on
behalf of the Privy Council). Evidence for the existence of a School of Night is
scant, but that Marlowe would be associated with such an organization—even
if a mere figment of the collective imagination—speaks to the way in which he
was so easily conflated with his most famous creation.

To speak of Marlowe as an "atheist"—or anybody else at this time in that way—
is an absurdity in the sixteenth century, for the intellectual framework of the era
precluded this as a fully fleshed-out theological possibility. And yet Marlowe was

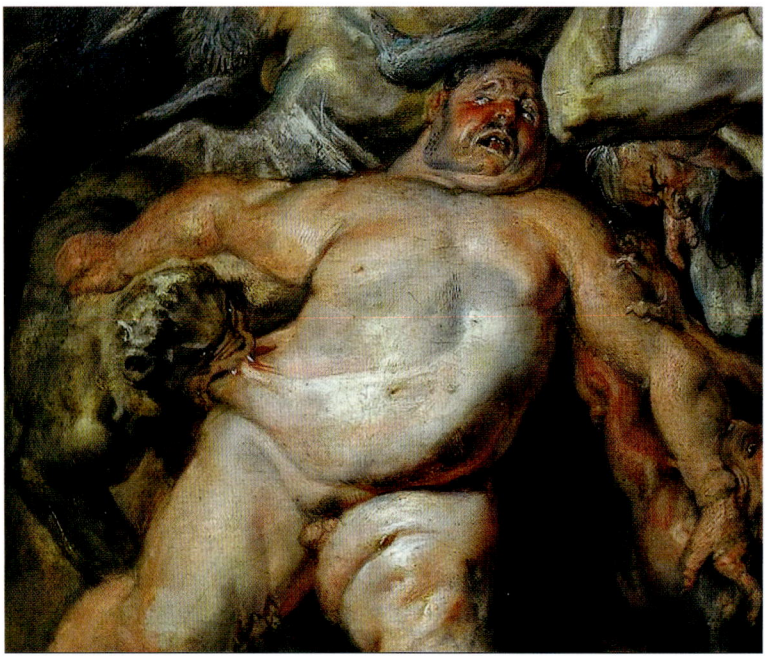

unequivocally a new type of thinker, a halfway point between the medieval and the modern, who embraced this anarchic new skepticism and saw something of libertinage in the possibilities of the infernal. David Riggs writes in *The World of Christopher Marlowe* that Marlowe's work "voiced the aspirations of blasphemers, sodomites, foreigners, unemployed scholars and the mutinous poor in Renaissance England," for whom there was perhaps a bit of sedition and freedom in the example of Faust and Mephistopheles. In thinking about the ways in which an artist can act as a weather vane for future culture shifts, consider the example of someone influenced by the playwright, a Cambridge student named Thomas Fineux who "learned all Marlowe by heart" and would "go out at midnight into a wood & fall down upon his knees & pray heartily that the devil would come & he would see him; for he did not believe that there was a devil … Marlowe made him an atheist."

As a work of representative poetics, Mephistopheles in some ways embodies the themes of the Renaissance, and of our subsequent human condition, more completely than the arid calculations of Descartes' thought-experiment ever could. Marlowe's source material used Mephistopheles in a manner that was almost identical to any punishing demon from previous centuries, but in *Doctor Faustus* this infernal being becomes a fully-fleshed character in his own right, a cipher

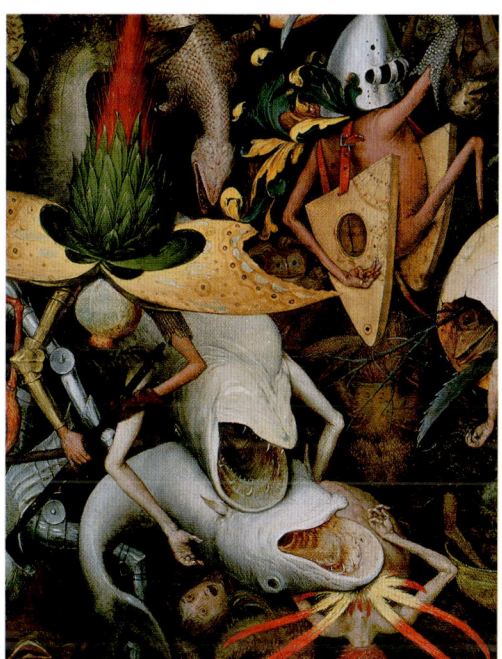

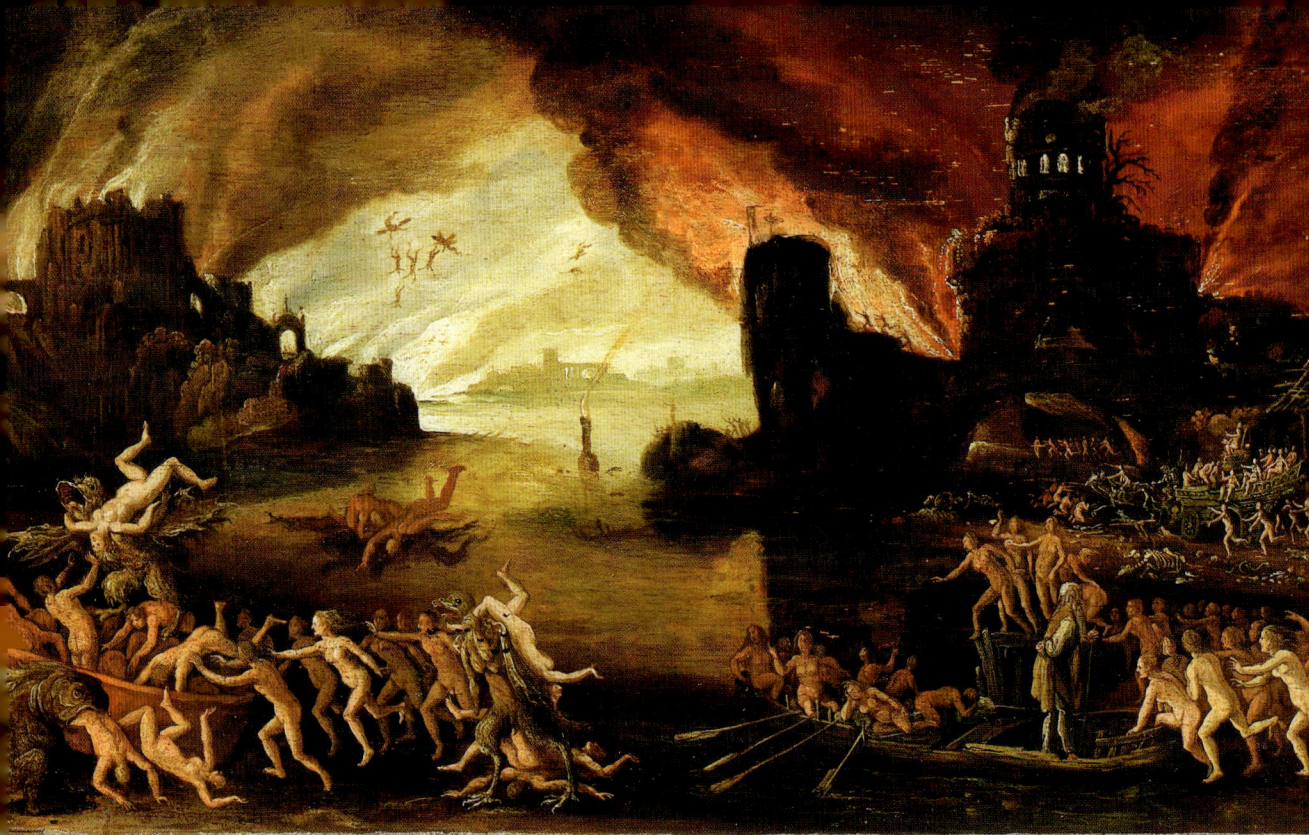

for the malleability of experience, the relativity of truth, and the omnipresent nature of all the illusion and trickery which plots our stage-play world. "Sweet Analytics, 'tis thou have ravisht me!" mockingly enthuses Faust, who goes on to reject all of the exigencies and equivocations of mere temporal learning, from medicine to theology. "Bid Economy farewell . . . Physic, farewell!" He continues:

> Philosophy is odious and obscure;
> Both law and physic are for petty wits;
> Divinity is basest of the three,
> Unpleasant, harsh, contemptible, and vile.

Such a crisis of epistemology mirrors Yates' observation about how Agrippa had surveyed "all human intellectual effort and decide[d] that all is empty, all man's learning is of no account, nothing can be certainly known about anything." A pact with the Devil can be rendered for all of the regular desires—power, esteem, wealth—but certainty is that which the new humanist most desires. Faust's motivations contain a fair amount of all those other rationales, but the scholar's anxieties are ultimately not dissimilar to that of Descartes's decades hence, for his prayer to Mephistopheles is to "Resolve me of all ambiguities." With mocking irony, trickery is threaded throughout the play, from Faust's demand after the demon's initial appearance to "return, and change thy shape;/Thou art too ugly

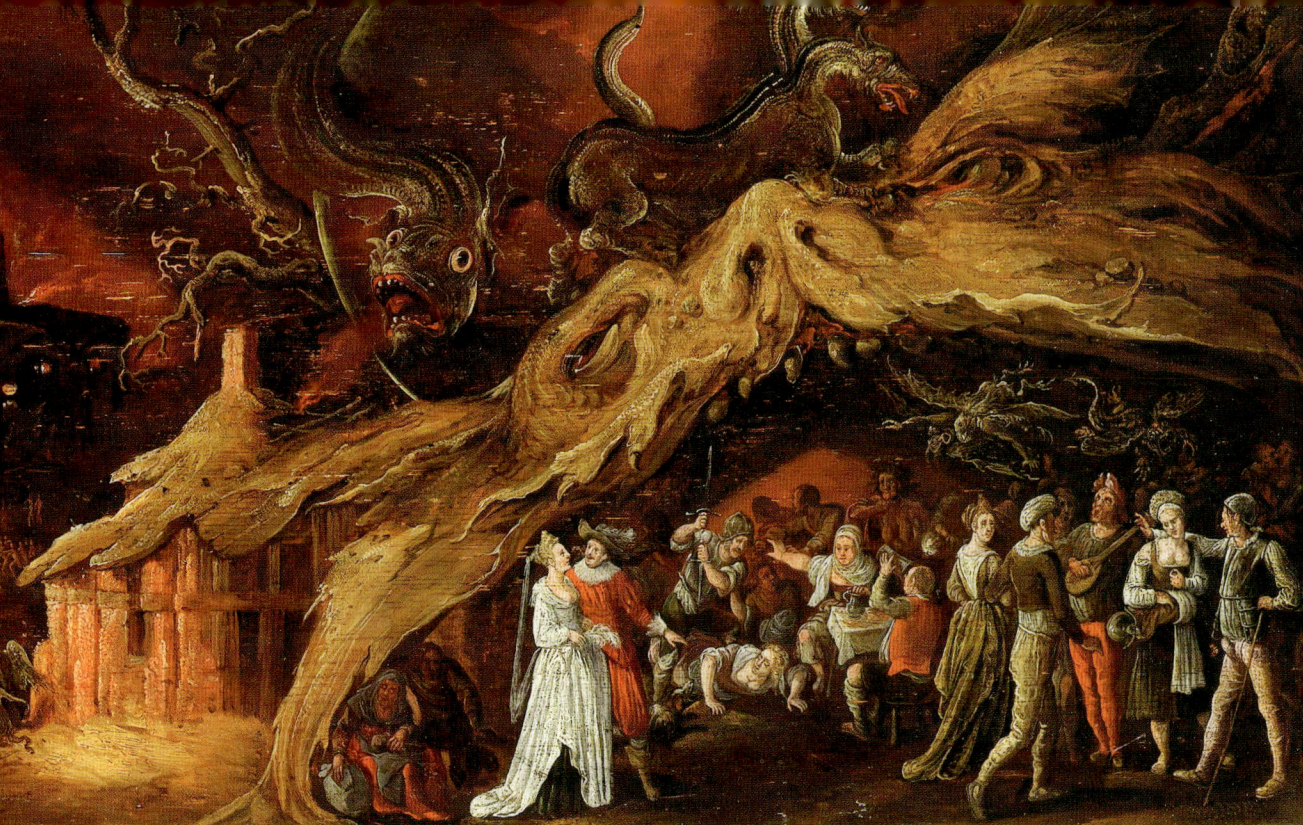

to attend on me," content to acknowledge the illusion of Mephistopheles monkish appearance as being preferable despite knowing it to be a fiction, to his erotic enthusiasms over the devil's conjuration of Helen of Troy whereby he asks "Was this the face that launched a thousand ships?" (it was not).

Doctor Faustus is many things, not least of which a satire on the cankered doubts of both Renaissance learning and Reformation piety. Repeatedly Mephistopheles scuttles Faust's desire to be resolved of ambiguity, letting the scholar be content to wallow in the momentary pleasures of sensuality, only to find himself inevitably condemned to his predestined hellish fate. There is a self-consuming quality to the potential of the period, liberty degenerating into libertinage, as the early

ABOVE

Detail from the Dutch painter Jacob Isaacszoon van Swanenburg's The Last Judgment and the Seven Deadly Sins, *painted sometime between 1600 and 1638, and housed in the Rijksmuseum in Amsterdam, Holland. Mentor to the young Rembrandt, van Swanenburg was known for his infernal subject matter, including paintings of Charon (the boatman of the River Styx) and of Christ's harrowing of hell. In this canvas he combines classical characters, such as the three-headed hound Cerberus, with the Christian theme of apocalypse. Note the wealthy burgers and aldermen who carouse and quaff their drinks in the bottom right-hand corner, seemingly unaware of the demonic haunted world in which they live—an apt illustration of the contradictions of the Renaissance, simultaneously light-filled and black, a veritable "darkness made visible" as John Milton would write.*

modern period prefigured the coming revolutionary secularism of the eighteenth century. "Marlowe embraced the skeptical and libertine ideas that lay embedded in his classical education," Riggs writes. "His drama and poetry show an unprecedented willingness to take those ideas…in earnest—as if the unspeakable crimes for which the only punishment was death and damnation were suitable choices." From the doctor's pact then arises the cruel individualism of modernity and our dark enduring night of solitary and imprisoning solipsism, which in his prescient nihilism Marlowe was able to comprehend four centuries ago. Faustus pushes the contradictions of the age to their extreme—an era of new learning permeated by growing skepticism, an epoch of evangelism in which atheism was becoming possible—and demonstrates how that dialect collapses into a monstrous simulacrum generated by Mephistopheles, that Lord of Doubt and Illusion, and who not even Descartes would be able to exorcise.

SEASON OF THE WITCH

"Go tell Mankind, that here are Devils and Witches," wrote the Boston Puritan divine Cotton Mather in a 1689 epistle, "and that tho those night-birds least appear where the Day-light of the Gospel comes, yet New-Engl. Has had Exemples of their existence and operation." Writing a few years before the events in Salem, Massachusetts, that would lead to three hundred individual accusations of witchcraft and almost twenty executions, Mather evidences the split that was beginning to happen in the conventional wisdom about witches. By the early eighteenth century, Mather had grown defensive about his role in touting the necessity of witch persecutions, and his own father Increase Mather expressed skepticism about the veracity of the Salem proceedings. Those trials were marked not by their particular violence, or paranoia even, but how relatively late in the seventeenth century they occurred. By the end of the seventeenth century, many authorities were much closer to Increase's position than they were Cotton's, as an eclipse on belief in witchcraft and the requirement in the biblical book of Exodus to "not suffer a witch to live" began to seem far less a literal injunction.

The sixteenth- and seventeenth-century explosion in fear over witchcraft and the subsequent decline marked the nadir of persecution against those accused of such sorcery, even while belief in witches can be traced back to antiquity. While there are precedents for shamanic healers and prophetesses in pre-Christian European religion, many of whom would be recategorized as witches by both Catholics and Protestants, there are scriptural examples of this archetype as well, such as the "witch of Endor" in the first Book of Samuel. Despite such antecedents, the theological position on even the existence of witchcraft has shifted over the centuries, with medieval thinkers largely viewing *belief in the existence* of witchcraft as heretical. By the early modern period, both Catholics and Protestants had reembraced the idea that nefarious black magic actually had an effect on the world, with the result being the massive persecutions that marked the period.

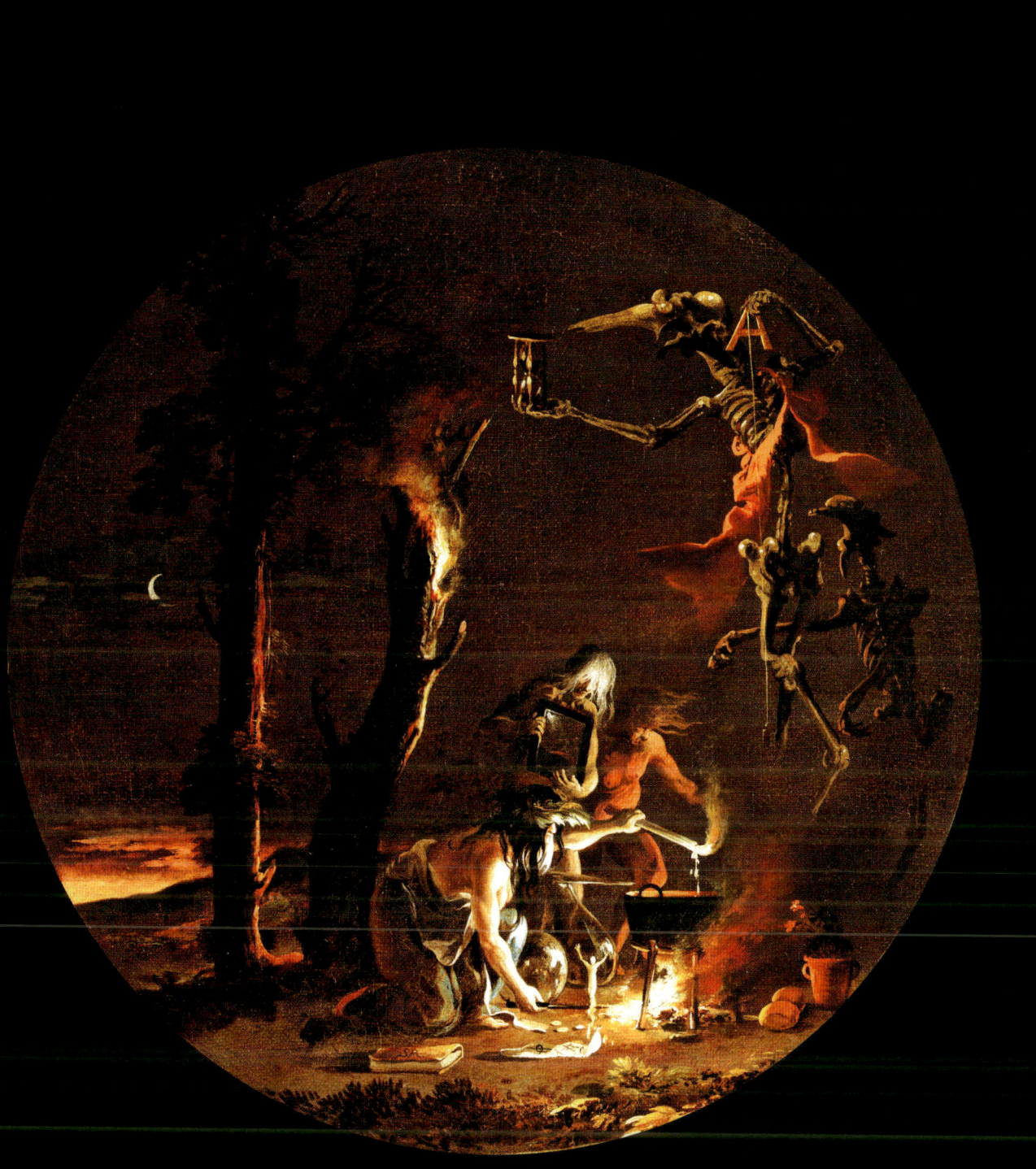

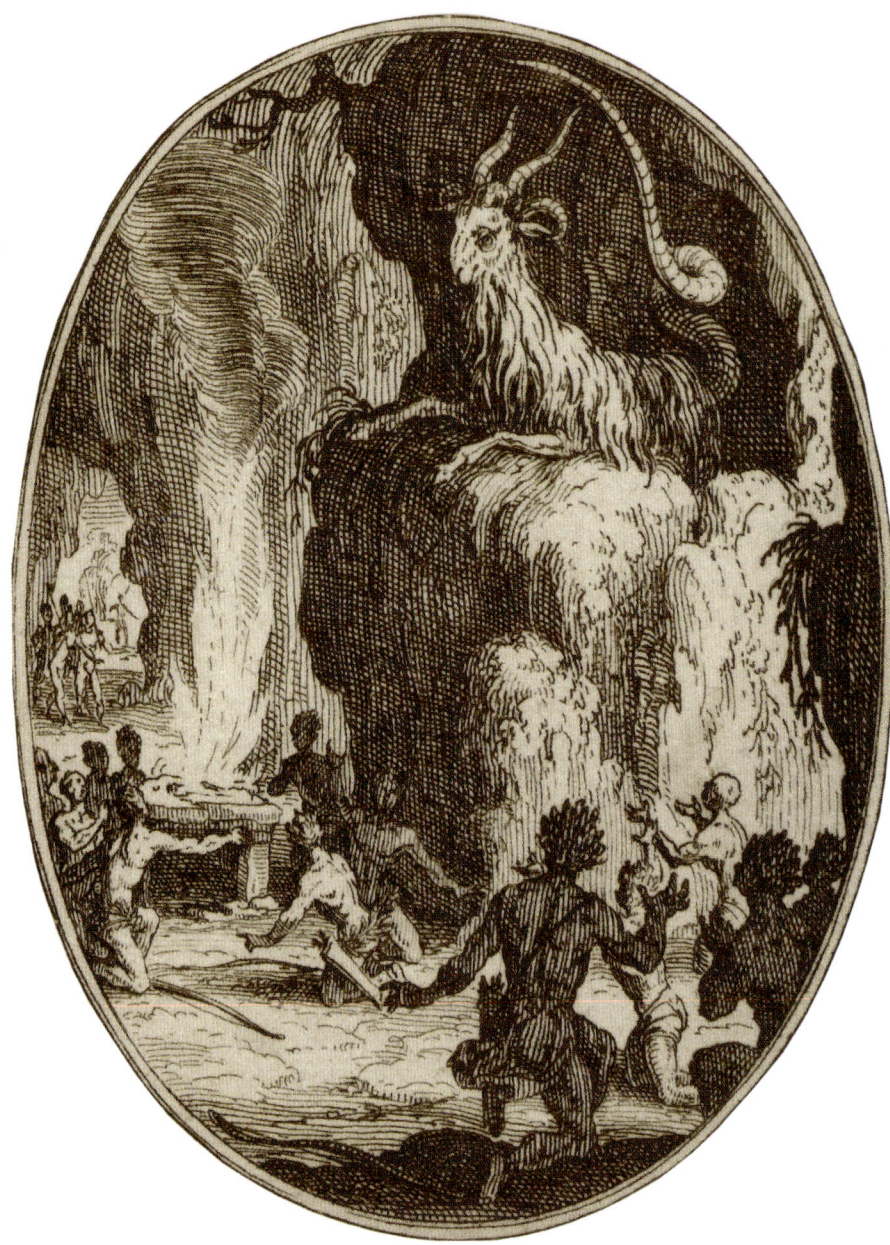

French lithographer Jacques Callot imagines a coven prostrating themselves before a goat-headed demon in his print The Cult of the Demon, *from the 1625 series* The Sacrifices, *with prints held by the Metropolitan Museum of Art in New York City and the National Gallery of Art in Washington, D.C, among other institutions. In Callot's rendering, the appearance of this caprine visage is real, with the women and men before it offering up their sacrifices to its indomitable evil. Such a Sabbath is where witches would have offered their services to the Devil by writing their names in blood on an infernal pact, a democratic version of the Faust legend open to anyone willing to sign over their mortal soul.*

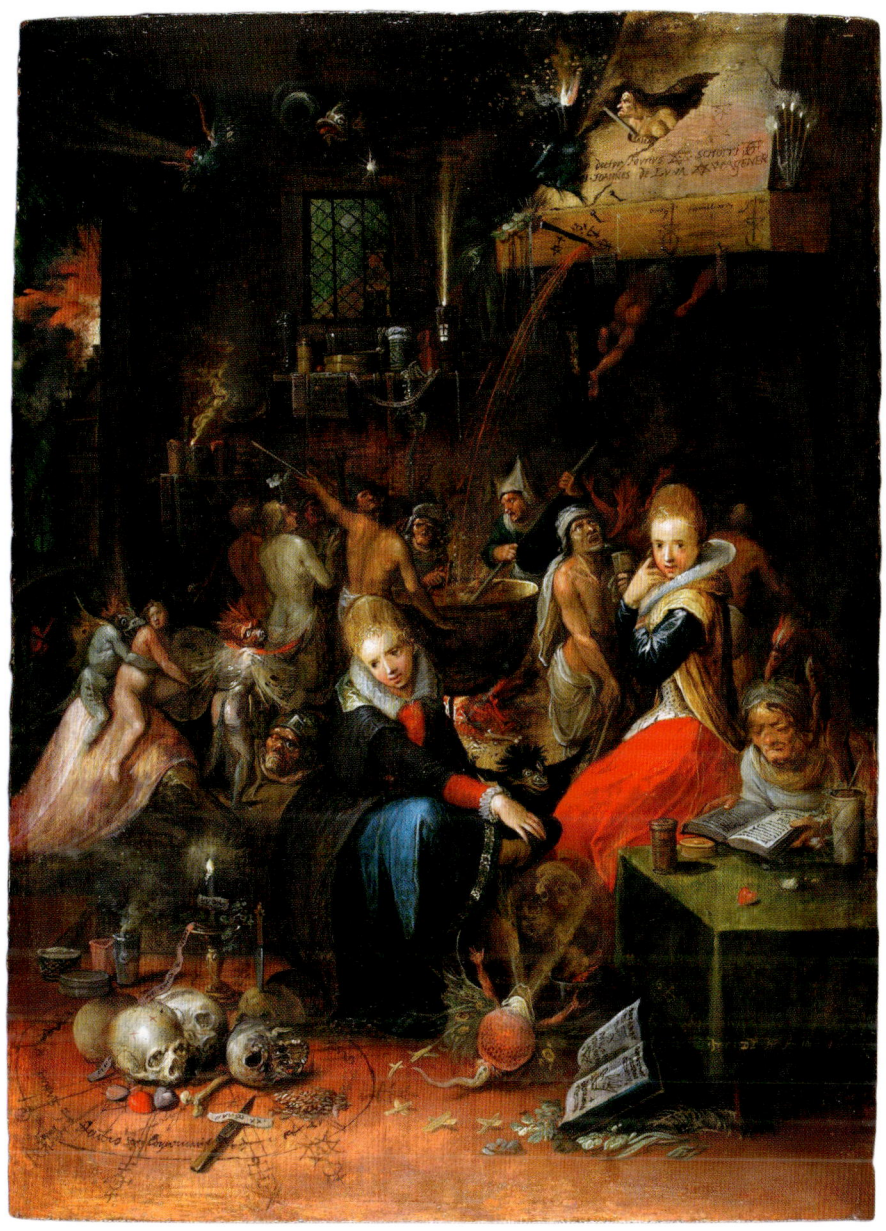

From these persecutions comes the standard representation of witches, particularly the narrative and visual qualities that we associate with them. Demos enumerates the process of how a witch entered into a coven as supposedly involving a "pledge of allegiance to the Devil, and a transfer of maleficent powers to the witch—sealed by a kiss (on the Devil's backside), by the affixing of a special 'mark' (on one or another significant part of the witch's own anatomy), or by sexual intercourse." From such dark imaginings grew some of the most potent aspects of the witch myth, in the form of a coven that regularly met at a "Sabbath." Ginzburg explains that it was during these centuries that not only the stereotype of witches meeting at night emerges, but also other mainstays such as their ability to fly astride poles or broom sticks and that they held "banquets, dancing, sexual orgies" in the presence of demons.

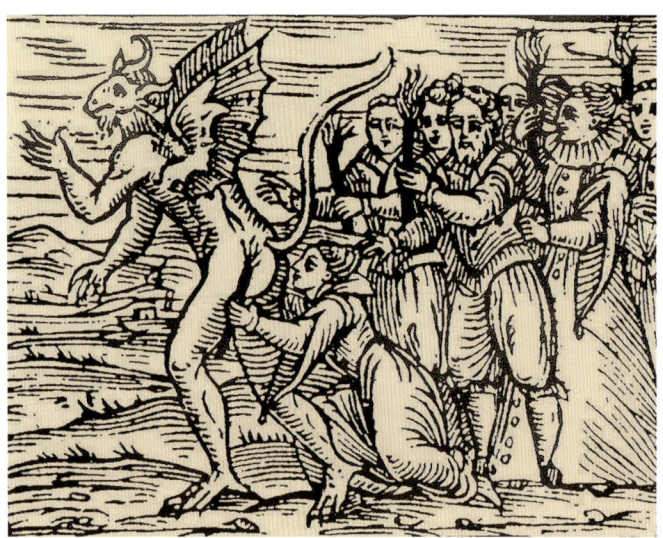 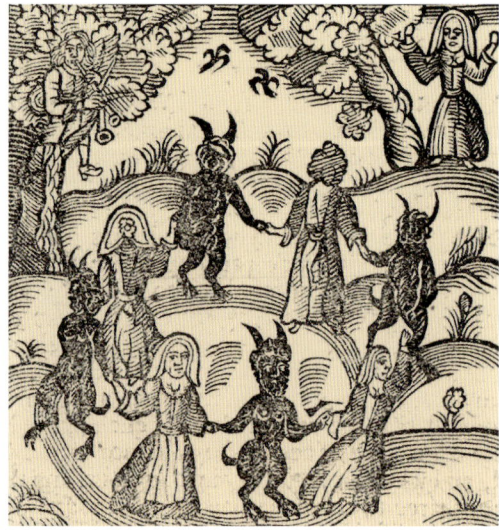

hundred thirty, whose image being here so liuely described, may saue vs further labour in discoursing of his maine and different parts and proportion.

OF THE NORVEGIAN
MONSTERS.

Hect. Boet.

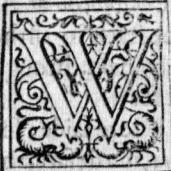

WHen as certaine Ambassadors were sent from *Iames* the fourth of that name king of *Scotland,* among whom was *Iames Ogill* that famous scholer of the Vniuersitie of *Abberdon,* they no sooner tooke shipping and hoysted sayle, but there sodainly arose such a tempestuous storme, that they were driuen to the coasts of *Norway* : and there going on shore, 10 they were very strangely affrighted, to see (as to them it appeared) certaine wild, monstrous-men, running on the tops of the mountaines. Afterward, they

Monsters lik Men

were told by the inhabitants that they were beasts (and not men) which did beare mortall hatred to mankind, although they could not abide the presence of a mans counte-

Hatred to mankind

nance, yet in darke nights, when the reuerent visage of humaine creatures are couered, they will come downe by troopes vpon the villages, and except the barking of dogges driue them backe they breake open dores, and enter houses, killing and deuouring who soeuer they find ; for their strength is so vnresistable and great, that they can pull vp by

The great strength of these beasts.

the rootes a tree of meane stature, and tearing the boughes from the bodye, with the stocke or stem thereof they fight one with another. Which when the Ambassad. heard, 20 they caused a sure watch to be kept all night, and withall made exceeding great fires, and when the light appeared, they tooke their farwell of those Monster-breeding-shores, recouering with ioy, the course which before they had lost by tempest.

Of the ÆGOPITHECVS.

Diuers shaps of apes.

The description of Pan.

Nicephorus Calisthius

VNder the *Equinoctiall* toward the East & south, there is a kind of Ape called *Ægopithecus,* an Ape like a Goate. For 30 there are Apes like Beares, called *Arctopitheci,* & some like Lyons, called *Leontopetheci,* and some like Dogs, called *Cynocephali,* as is before expressed ; and manye other which haue a mixt resemblance of other creatures in their members. Amongst the rest is there a beast called *PAN* ; who in 40 his head, face, horns, legs, and from the loynes downwarde resembleth a Goat, but in his belly, breast, and armes, an Ape ; such a one was sent by the king of *Indians* to Constantine, which being shut vp in a Caue or close place, by reason of 50 the wildnesse thereof, liued there but a season, & when it was dead and bowelled, they pouldred it with spices, and carried it to be seene at Constantinople : the which beast hauing beene seene of the auncient Græcians, were so amazed at the strangnesse thereof, that they receiued it for a god, as they did a Satyre and other strange beasts.

Of

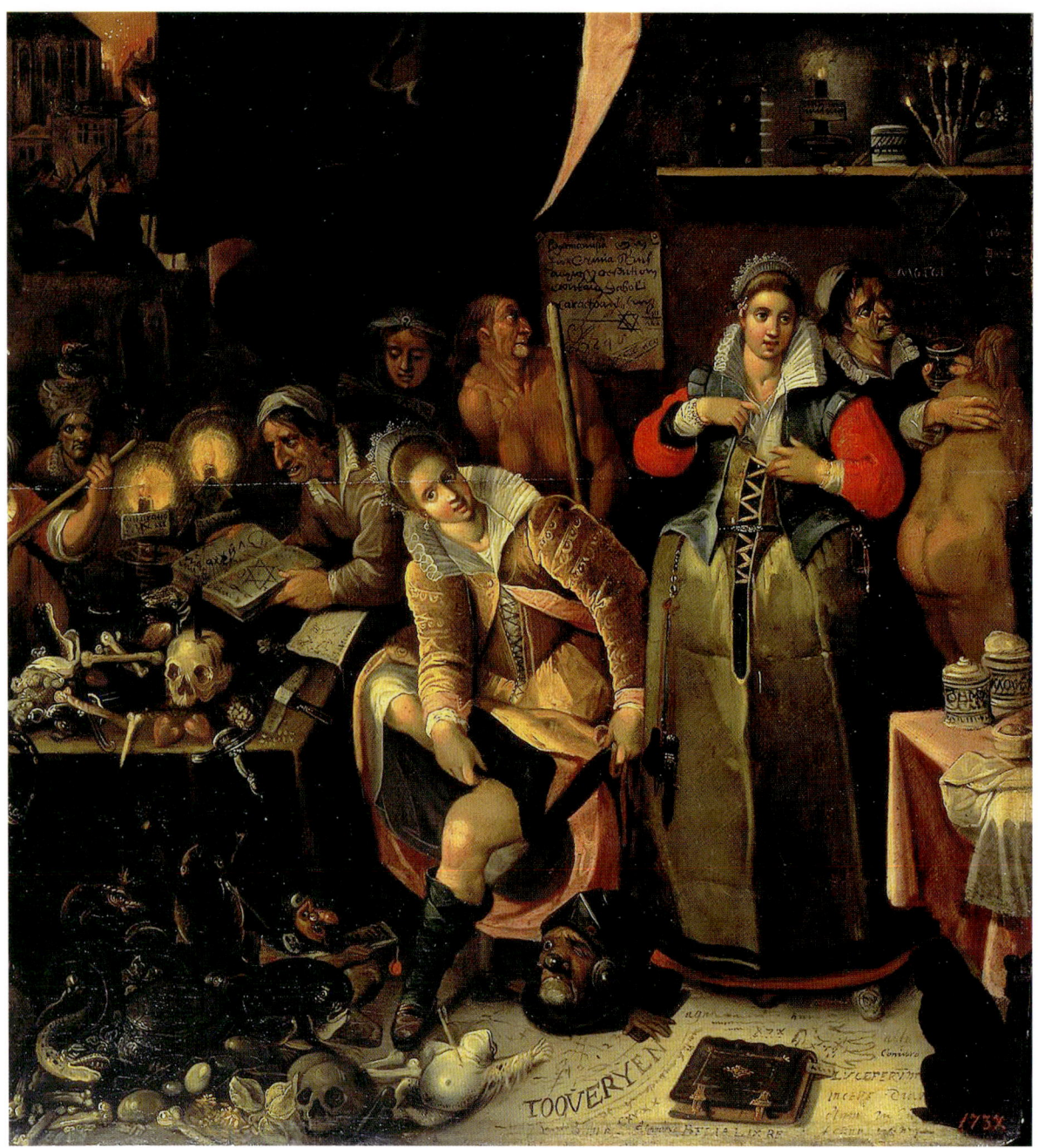

Detail from Frans Francken the Younger's 1606 Witches' Kitchen, *held in the Hermitage Museum, St. Petersburg. Again, the scene shows a much richer and lush dwelling than the vast majority of women punished for witchcraft would have been familiar with, even while it engages the tropes of the figure, from the dead frog at the foot of the aristocratic witch, no doubt intended for some noxious potion, to the nude, yet desexualized crones in the background.*

INTIMATIONS OF APOCALYPSE

The Reformation was a deeply eschatological age, as nervous Christians across the sectarian divide parsed political, religious, and natural events for indications of the end of days. This wasn't necessarily anything new; in fact, during the Middle Ages, especially around the turn of the first millennium, there were widespread and intense apocalyptic movements throughout Christendom. Yet the convulsions of the early modern period lent themselves to a particularly acute sense of apocalyptic despair and millennial fervor, as Christians anxiously understood current events through the lens of the Book of Revelation. During this period apocalyptic thought largely (though not entirely) became a Protestant phenomenon, as much of the medieval fervor around eschatology migrated into the new Reformation sects, with a representative official in Lord Protector Oliver Cromwell's Puritan Interregnum, which ruled England in the middle of the seventeenth century, writing that "Next unto our Lord and Savior Jesus Christ, there is nothing so necessary as the true and solid knowledge of the Antichrist."

Consequently, the authors of religious and theological tracts, treatises, polemics, and manifestoes spent considerable energy in trying to establish the identity of this enigmatic fellow, the figure whom Paul describes in the New Testament Book of Thessalonians as being one who "opposes and exalts himself above every so-called god or object of worship, so that he takes his seat in the temple of God, declaring himself to be God." The infernal corollary to the Son of God, the Antichrist was an evil figure of considerable charisma and power who would usher in the apocalypse—details of which depended considerably upon your theological perspective.

Christopher Hill writes in *Antichrist in Seventeenth-Century England* that the "charge of being a forerunner of Antichrist, or Antichrist himself, was part of the normal vocabulary of abuse of medieval politicians, freely used by popes and emperors from the eleventh century onwards." A venerable medieval tradition would conflate various popes with the figure of the Antichrist, though before the Reformation this was always an intra-Catholic issue. With the schisms of the sixteenth century, that tradition would migrate into Protestantism, with the pontiff a favored and frequent candidate for the position, though the Catholic Counter-Reformation was content to return the abuse, with Luther frequently configured as being the Antichrist. While not a "demon" per se, the tradition of divination and prophecy was necessarily connected to demonology, with Bruce McGinn arguing in *Antichrist: Two Thousand Years of the Human Fascination with Evil* that the figure can similarly "be seen as a projection, or perhaps better as a mirror, for conceptions and fears about ultimate human evil."

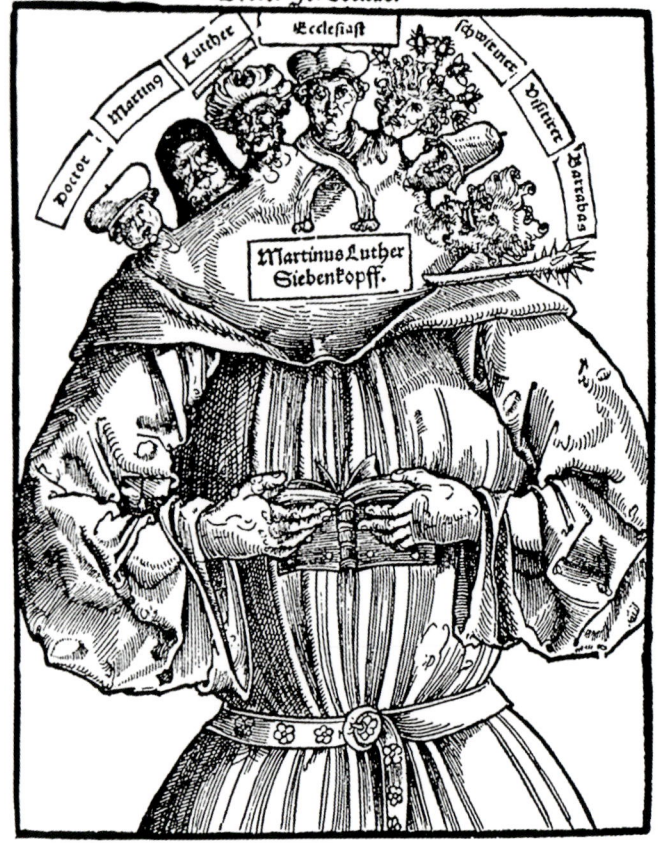

Sieben Köpffe Martini Luthers

Vom Hochwirdigen Sacrament des Altars / Durch
Doctor Jo. Cocleus.

Not to be outdone, Catholic polemicists responded to Protestant accusations in kind, such as in this frontispiece to the German pamphleteer Johannes Cochlaeus's 1529 diatribe The Seven-Headed Luther, *which imagines the father of the Reformation as having the same number of heads as the dragon of Revelation, each one symbolizing an aspect of the theologian's supposedly contradictory thought and personality.*

A contemporary drawing of the priest with his Van Dyke, his delicate curled mustache, and his wavy dark hair, doesn't do justice to his reputation as being charming, handsome, and sexually rapacious; Urbain Grandier was a well-educated scholar whom the nuns of the Ursuline convent in Loudun, France, would accuse of bewitching them into orgiastic ceremonies for Satan, possessed minions doing hell's bidding. There had been seasons of strange events among the sisters of the convent—convulsions and contortions among the nuns, meaningless, guttural, tongue-speaking glossolalia and foreign xenoglossy, and always the endless sexual dreams featuring Grandier performing all manner of perversion upon them. As part of his agreement with the devils, Grandier promised that after copulating with a nun, he would "make a slit below her heart . . . that this slit will pierce her shirt, bodice and cloth which will be bloody." With language ripe for a Freudian analysis, the contract stipulates that the bloody slit made by the priest upon the bodies of these women will be later accompanied with orifices made by the demons Gresil and Amand, an "opening in the same way, but a little smaller" for those creatures' carnal pleasure.

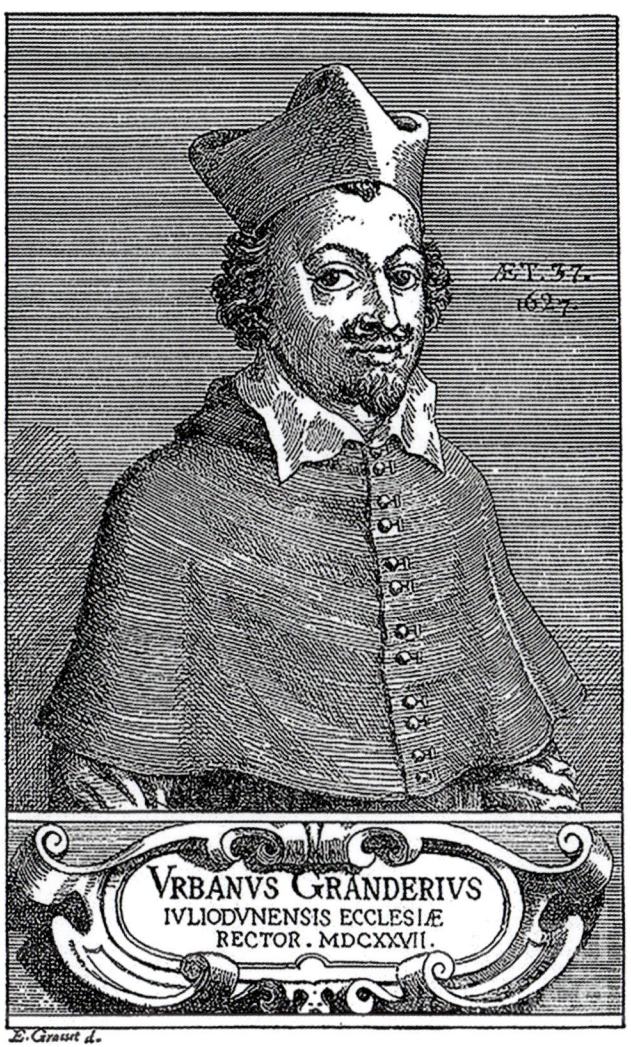

VRBANVS GRANDERIVS
IVLIODVNENSIS ECCLESIÆ
RECTOR . MDCXXVII.

E. Grasset d.

AN APPOINTMENT
WITH FATHER GRANDIER

egions of devils came to call upon Father Urbain Grandier one spring day in 1629, and if we're to believe his accusers, the priest respond with enthusiasm at the arrival of his demonic charge. According to the proceedings of his later trial, Grandier entered into a pact with such notables as Beelzebub, Leviathan, Astaroth, and of course Lucifer, on May 19 of that year. The contract written by these worthies promised Grandier the "love of women, the flower of virgins, the respect of monarchs, honors, lusts, and powers." All that was required for this was that once a year the priest will "trample the holy things of the church," desecrating the Eucharist under foot, and in return he would receive "twenty years happy on the earth of men," after which Grandier "will later join us to sin against God."

Central to his eventual prosecution was the testimony of the convent's Mother Superior, Sister Jeanne de Anges, who attested that Grandier had bewitched the nuns after throwing a demonically enchanted bouquet of roses over the convent's wall. Skeptics claimed that Jeanne de Anges was enraged after she was sexually rebuffed by the otherwise promiscuous priest, and that the possessions at the convent were an act of intricate revenge. Grandier attempted his own defense several times, to no avail; especially after the incident attracted the attention of Jesuit and Capuchin confessors who performed publicly attended mass exorcisms at the convent, including ones enacted by the celebrated mystic Jean-Joseph Surin, who would be haunted by evil spirits for decades afterwards. The spectacle of the public exorcisms drew thousands of Loudon locals, occasioning numerous conversions in a region that had been populated heavily by Huguenots. The clerics who put Grandier on trial in 1634 entered into evidence an actual, physical contract, a strange artifact of this supposed diabolical pact. The literary trope of a "deal with the Devil" is arguably as old as Genesis's temptation, yet for all of the supposed contracts between men and the Devil, Grandier's bill of sale is one of the few that a person can still touch.

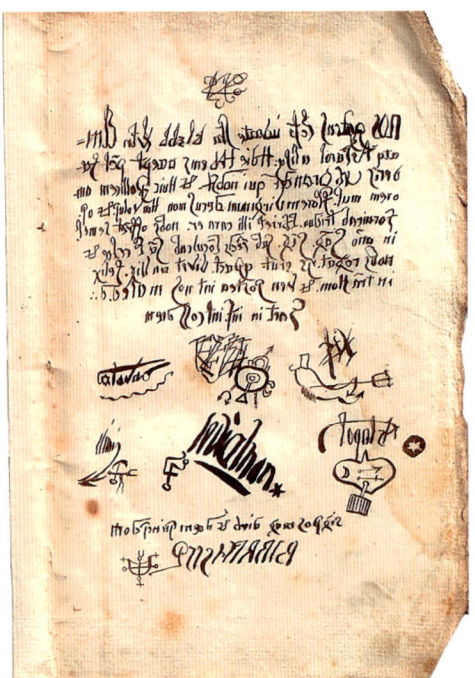

On frayed, yellowing paper, composed in backwards Latin and written in the abbreviated form known as secretary hand, is the aforementioned deal between the Jesuit and the host of demons, whereby Grandier gave hell the souls of his nuns in exchange for profane powers. Among the signatories are some of the most infamous of Renaissance demonology, with occult symbols standing in for luminaries such as Leviathan, Beelzebub, and Astaroth. Demonic names are crucial for both the necromancer and the exorcist alike, for it's in mastering their names that there can be mastery of the demons themselves. Such names on the parchment take a variety of Hermetic forms. One symbol is composed of a circle within a circle, with various curved lines sprouting off of the circumference; another cipher looks nothing so much like an abstracted reptilian creature with pitchfork. Hard to imagine the massive, chthonic sea creature of Leviathan or the insectoid, Lord of the Flies Beelzebub squeezing into Grandier's study lined with Montaigne and Rabelais so as to sign this contract, and yet its admission into the record was that which ensured the priest's demise. A longtime adversary of Grandier, a Father Mignon, claimed that the contract had been written by a priapic demon named Baalberith and was absconded from Lucifer's own library by another devil named Asmodeus. That the handwriting on the document resembled that of Jeanne de Anges was only noted decades later.

Grandier would ultimately be burnt alive in 1634. Nicholas Aubin, in his 1693 account of the incident, reports that a probe was "pushed back into the palm of his hand" by physicians searching for the telltale sign of the devil's mark, a "barbarous surgeon would make them see that the other parts of his body were very sensible," turning the "probe at the other end, which was very sharp pointed . . . [and] thrust it to the very bone." There is an unnerving symmetry to the accounts of Grandier's supposed mutilations of the Ursulines. Through all of these tribulations, the Jesuit never confessed to having signed the strange diabolical pact produced during his interrogation. For skeptics such steadfastness proved his innocence, for the faithful such was the power of those demons imparted to the priest even under the duress of torture.

What exactly transpired at Loudon has long been the subject of academic debate. Whether mass hysteria or a cynically calculated spectacle against a powerful priest is ambiguous. As regards the later hypothesis, it should be noted that Grandier was the author of a scurrilous satire against Cardinal Richelieu. Perhaps, as with any event from that foreign country that is the past, it's good to take to heart the advice given by the British novelist Aldous Huxley in his 1952 account *The Devils of Loudun*, when he cautioned that despite thinking "about events realistically, in terms of multiple causations . . . [as being] hard and emotionally unrewarding," the most honest way to approach a phenomenon from eras so distant spiritually and culturally from our own is to understand that explanations are more complicated than first might be surmised. Despite it being easier and "more agreeable to trace each effect to a single and, if possible, a personal cause," the reality of Loudun must always be multifaceted.

Was Grandier the victim of superstition, Machiavellian political maneuvering, personal animus? Did the Ursuline sisters believe themselves to be possessed? Were they coached? And how does metaphysical reality intercede in such circumstances? Loudun does not offer up her lessons so easily, but there is something to be said for viewing those seventeenth-century possessions as representative of the epoch's approach toward demonology. In Grandier's travails, we see a synthesis of two of the most frequent diabolical tropes—that of the mage, and of the witch. The priest harkens toward occultists with their goat-skinned grimoires, from legendary figures like Dr. Faust to actual magicians such as John Dee and Simon Forman. Yet in the contortions and screaming of the possessed nuns, Loudun must also be considered a brief in the history of early modern witch hysteria, a phenomenon that may have taken as many as one hundred thousand lives, the vast majority of whom were women.

In an additional sense the possessions at Loudun mark the midpoint of a transition that defined the contradictions of early modern diabology. Strung between the humanism of the Renaissance and the rationalism of the coming Enlightenment, it would be easy to assume that this would be a period that would see fear of Lucifer wane, of the dimming of that morning star. We find, as made abundantly clear by those murdered for the imaginary crime of being a witch, that the opposite is true. The new doubts and skepticisms inculcated by new science, new geography, new philosophy, and most of all new theology in the form of the Protestant Reformation and the Catholic Counter-Reformation paradoxically increased fears of the Devil. Medieval Christians understood how sacrament could hold Satan at bay, but with the Reformation there was a rejection of such means of spiritual warfare, and so a profound anxiety took hold.

In early modern Europe there was a loss of faith in the means of containing demons, but those demons could still howl. The result were events such as those at Loudun; Catholics just as privy to the new doubts as their Protestant cousins. Another result was an unprecedented literary flowering of demonic representations, for if medieval devils were squawking, farting, burping monsters equally held up for ridicule as for fear, then early modern devils were of an entirely more terrifying variety. This was the age that gave us Marlowe's great embodiment of modernity in *Dr. Faustus*'s Mephistopheles, as well as John Milton's immaculate Lucifer in *Paradise Lost*. The sixteenth and seventeenth centuries are best understood as a gloaming period, for this was an age that convulsed with the painful birth pangs of our modern world, when scores of women and men were pulled by the contradictions of faith and doubt that defined the era.

French Jesuit and philosopher Michel de Certeau explained this context in his 1970 study *The Possession at Loudun*, writing that those strange events should be seen as a "confrontation between science and religion, a debate on what is certain and what is uncertain, on reason, the supernatural, authority." Grandier, like many others, was a casualty of the era's contradictions. Had he lived only a century later, the priest would perhaps have been understood as simply a libertine, a rake worthy of a print by William Hogarth. As it was, Grandier rather found himself as kindling for a fire in Nouvelle-Aquitaine one summer day in August 1634.

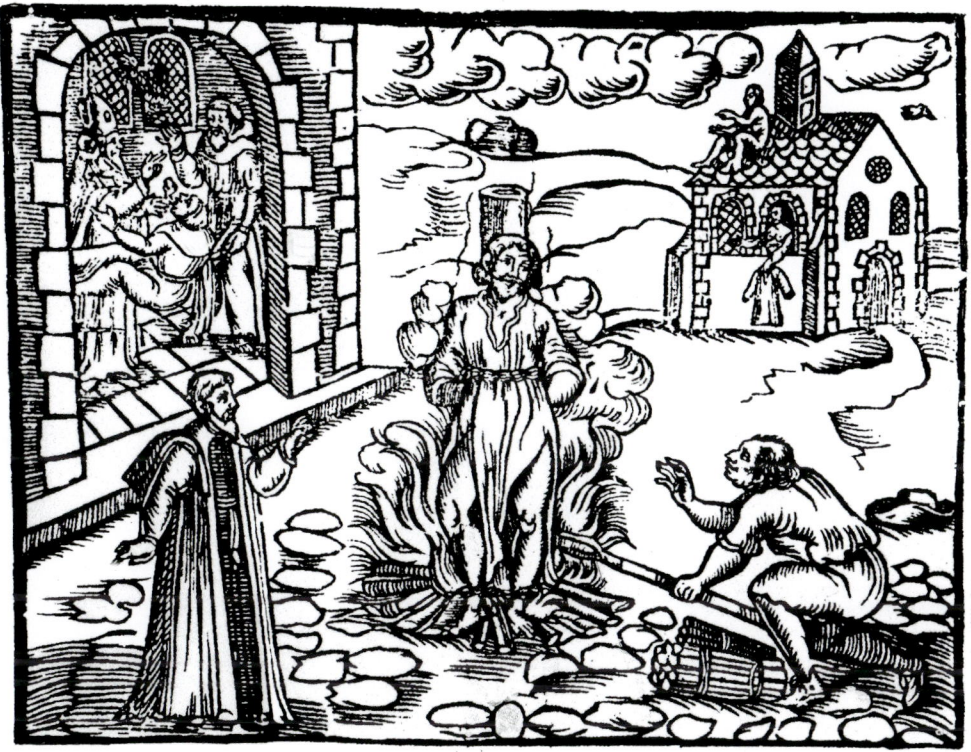

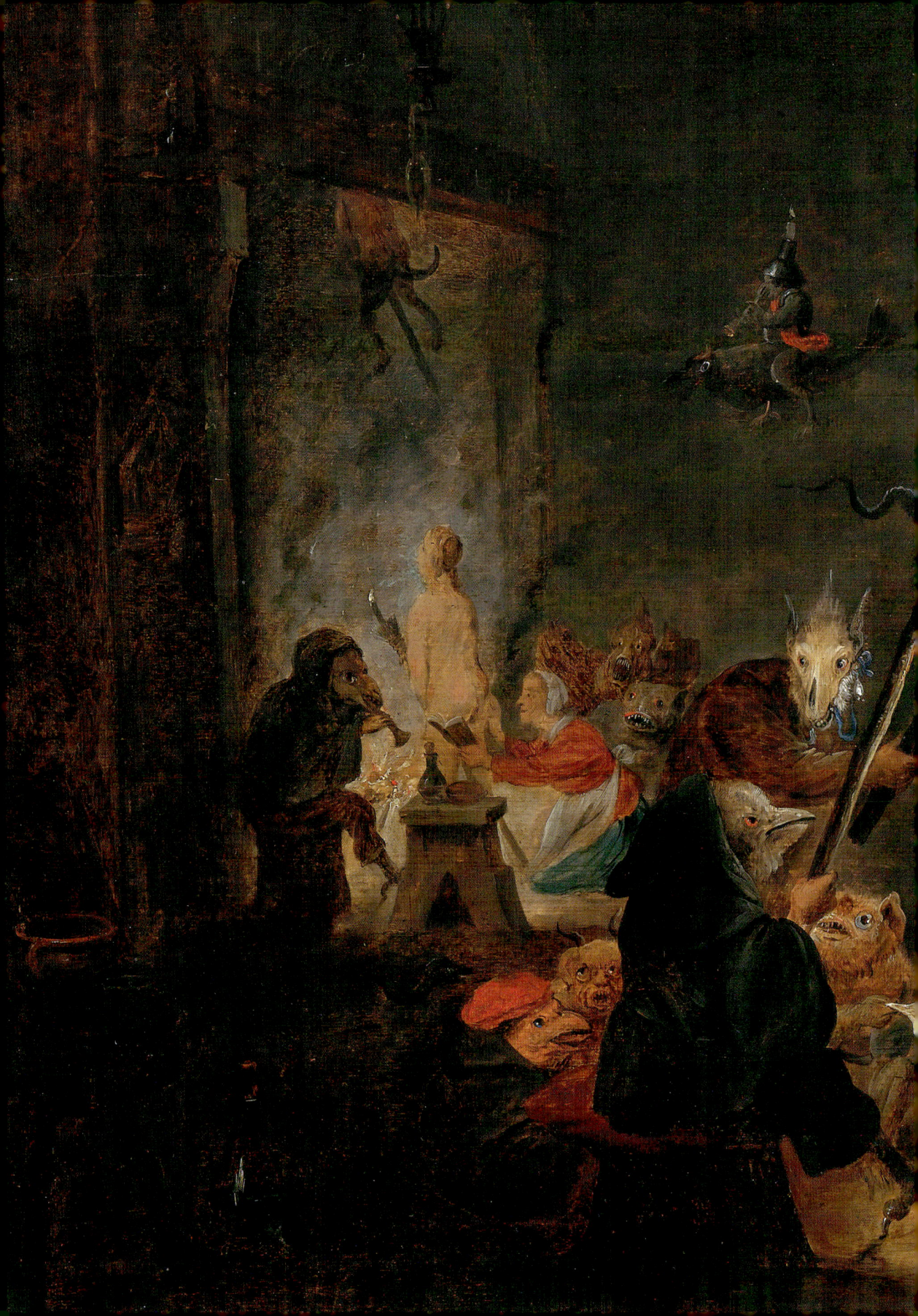

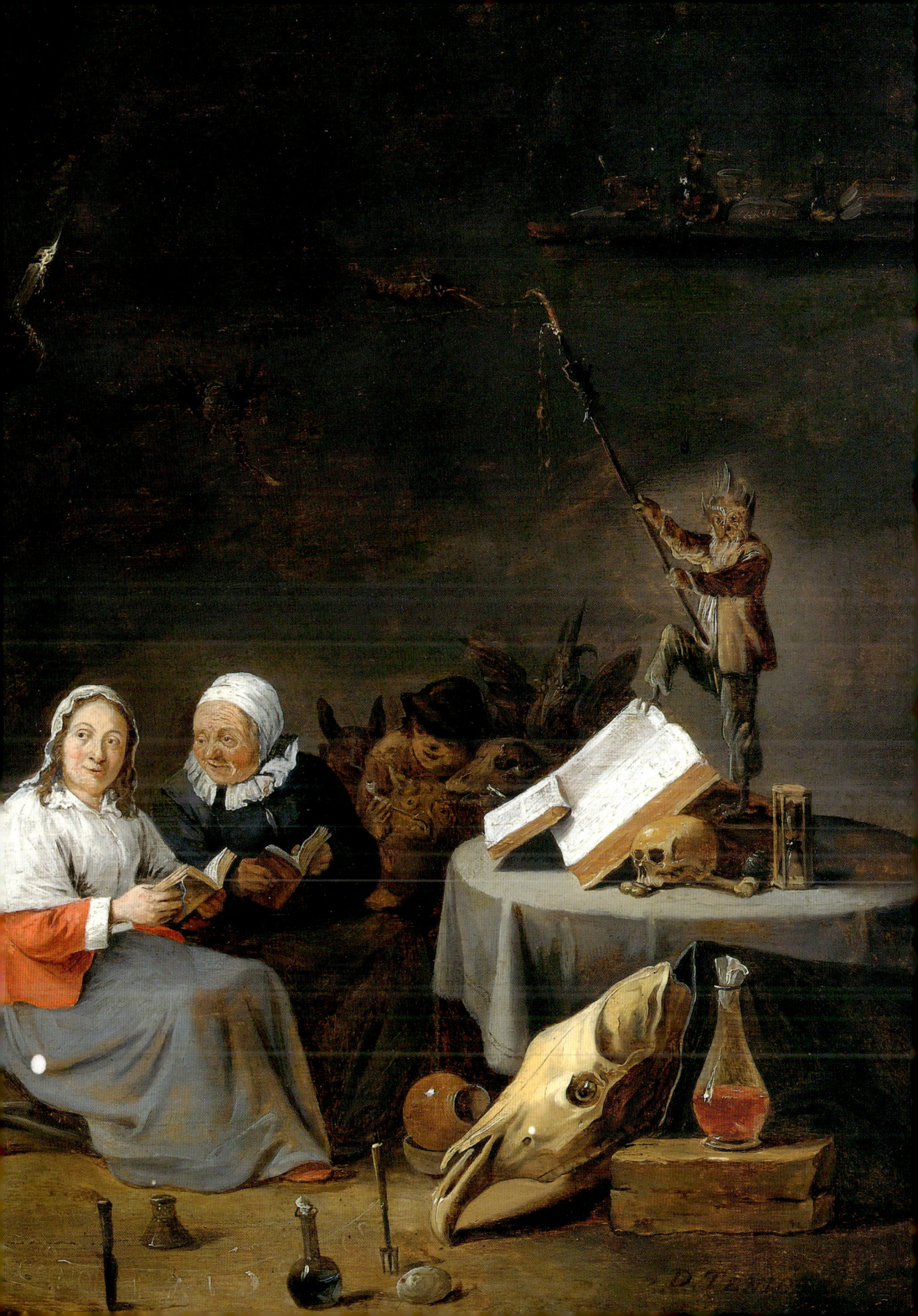

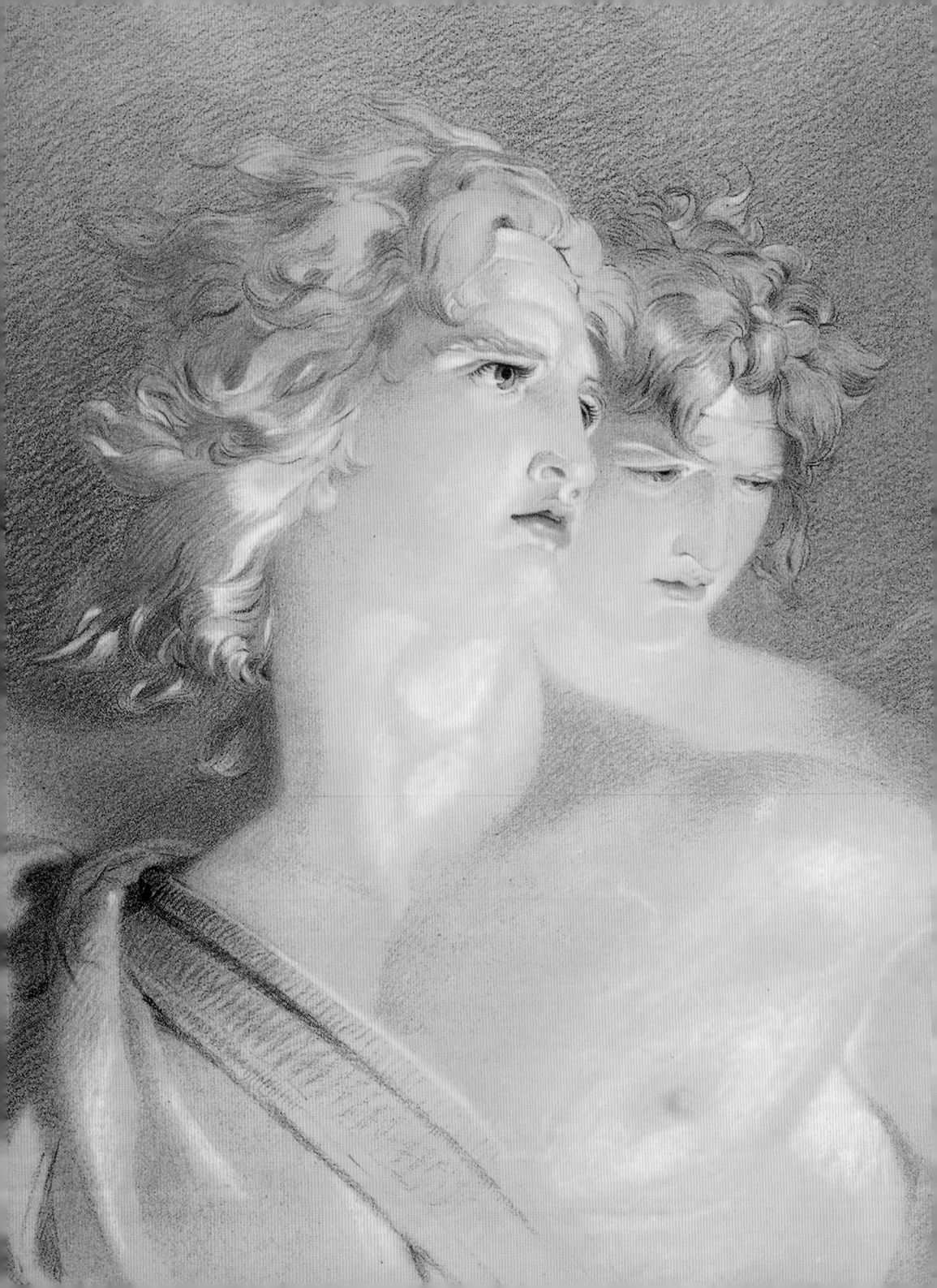

CHAPTER FOUR

Better to Reign in Hell

Demonology in an Age of Reason, c. 1650–1800

I might dare flatter myself by nothing that the scholars of the mysteries
of the Divine Science called Occultism will consider this book one
of the most precious treasures of the universe.

—Anonymous, *The Grand Grimoire; or, the Red Dragon* (c. 1702)

Wherever God erects a house of prayer,
The Devil always builds a chapel there:
And 'twill be found, upon a examination,
The latter has the largest congregation.

—Daniel Defoe, *The True-Born Englishman* (1701)

ON ENLIGHTENMENT DEMONOLOGY

riting in 1818, as the dwindling fumes of the Age of Reason dissipated following the convulsions of revolution which marked the eighteenth century, and the French lawyer Jules Garinet reflected on an unusual trial that occurred in the town of Amiens some fourteen years earlier. Garinet notes in his *History of Magic in France* that a gentleman had been apprehended in Amiens because he was in possession of a collection of diabolical grimoires, including one so powerful that "it was enough to touch it to summon the devil." Here in Picardy, a region already associated with heretical Huguenots, this otherwise nameless man was brought before the magistrates to answer for owning this infernal library. Such a hearing differed from trials during the sixteenth and seventeenth centuries, however, for the magus called to account for his acts was charged not with necromancy, but with duplicity; accused not of being a man capable of compelling demons, but rather a trader in tricks, illusions, hoaxes.

His judges saw him not as a conjurer, but rather a con artist, and there was no sin in consorting with nonexistent demons, but rather the crime of tricking the credulous into believing in them. This difference in arraignment has to do with who was bringing the charges against this faux wizard, for he was not accused by ecclesiastical inquisition, nor by civil authority claiming the divine right of kings, but rather he was in the presence of representatives of the revolutionary republic. Since the storming of the Bastille in 1789 and the Jacobin declaration of a new Year Zero, the French Republic saw itself as the international vanguard

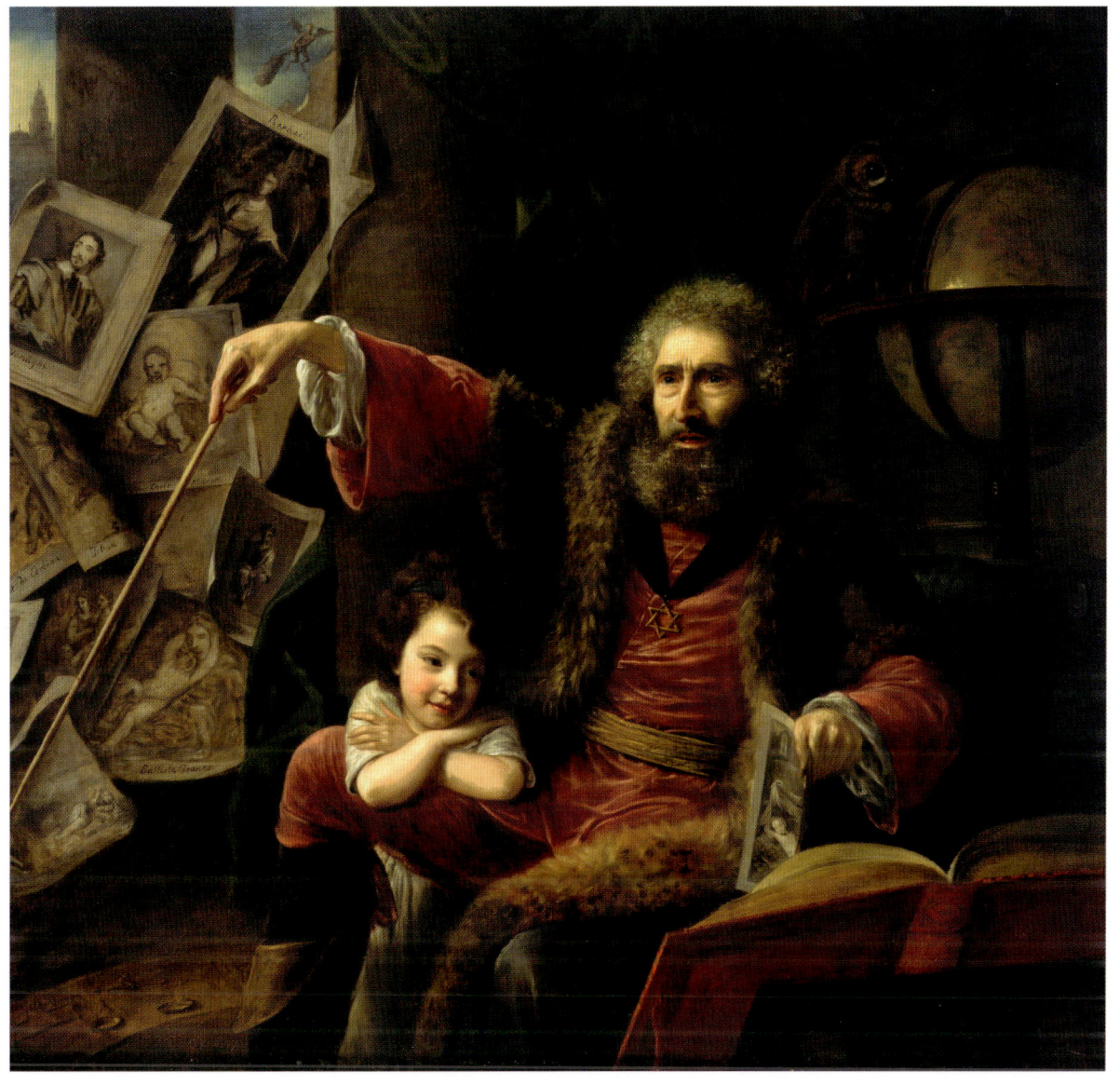

By 1775, the figure of the magus was ripe for mockery, as in the Irish painter
Nathaniel Hone the Elder's The Conjuror, held at the National Gallery of Ire-
land in Dublin. Understood at the time to be a satire on the self-importance
of painter Sir Joshua Reynolds, and the other members of the Royal Academy
(which included Hone), The Conjuror depicts the painter as a pretentious,
doddering, and foolish old man. Surrounded by the accoutrement of conjuration, from the wise owl over his shoulder to the magic wand that he brandishes,
and the Star of David around his neck, Hone mocks Reynolds as a painterly
trickster, an artistic confidence man. Yet by making the work of art synonymous
with that of magic, Hone's painting betrays traces of that archaic sense of the
numinous even in the midst of Enlightenment.

of reason, waging a cleansing war against all superstition and tradition. In an act of puckish iconoclasm, Garinet records how the public minister took the man's infernal grimoire and opened it, so "as the powers of hell were in no hurry to speak, the sorcerer exclaimed that the government commissioner had to be a more skillful magician than he, to silence the devil."

Owen Davies writes in *Grimoires: A History of Magic Books* that this bit of judicial theater "could be seen as representative of the process of popular enlightenment and dechristianization some associated with the Republic." In the republic, there was no room for faithful delusions, for religious illusions, for pious mistakes. No purpose in the personal God of scripture, or His great Adversary. In the republic, there was no room for demons. Yet exorcism is not so easily done, and revolutions have a way of consuming themselves and turning back toward irrationalities. The same year that this magistrate humbled the fake wizard of Amiens, in what would have been Year XIII of the new order in the month of Frimaire, and a little more than a hundred miles south in the restored Cathédral Notre-Dame de Paris, Napoleon Bonaparte would seize his crown from the pope's outstretched hands and declare himself to be the emperor.

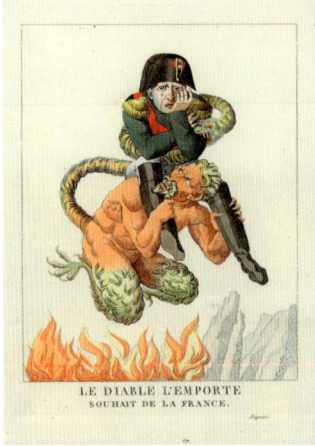
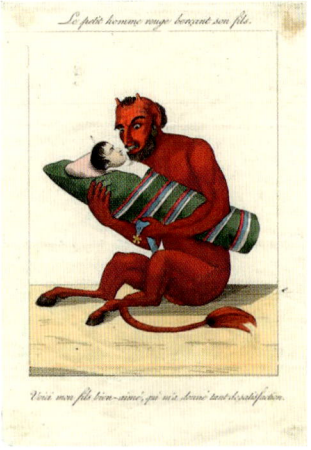

LE DIABLE L'EMPORTE
SOUHAIT DE LA FRANCE.

As with any issue of periodization, the Enlightenment is difficult to delineate. From 1648, when the Peace of Westphalia ended the apocalyptic sectarian Thirty Years' War until roughly the French Revolution of 1789, the age was intellectually defined by something that could be called the Enlightenment. Similar to how the concept of the Renaissance uneasily relates to the actual events of the sixteenth and seventeenth centuries, so too does the Enlightenment reduce and simplify the complexities and contradictions of the eighteenth century. Popularly understood as an Age of Reason, when the scientific revolution was mirrored by political revolutions in America and France, when doctrinaire superstition was rejected in favor of liberty, equality, and fraternity, the Enlightenment was also paradoxically a period of acute popular demonology, with Davies writing that this was a century wherein affordable print meant that for "a fraction of the price the wealth of practical occult knowledge contained in the manuscripts so treasured by … magicians became available to all."

Ironically the revolutionary optimism of democratization also meant the wide availability of works that in the Renaissance were associated with elite conjurors, mages, and necromancers. Now your average laborer could just as easily read about demonic incantation during this supposedly logical age. The Enlightenment did provide a skeptical vocabulary concerning the supernatural, including demonology, which was far more nuanced and richer than that which existed before. Expanding upon the skeptical sentiments of Scot and Weyer from the previous century, Enlightenment philosophes vociferously attacked the superstitions of demonology, so that during what Davies has described as an "age of roving occult adventurers, notorious across Europe in their own lifetimes, men who earnestly explored magic and at the same time exploited the credulity of others" was also dominated by an elite coterie who were increasingly content to expel all angels, fallen or otherwise.

As with the Renaissance, and arguably all periods propelled by the inextricable process of the dialectic, the Enlightenment was marked by deep contradictions as regarding this subject, though different contradictions than those that went before. What ultimately differentiated the skepticism of the Enlightenment was that, unlike a Weyer or Scot, the radical philosophes of the eighteenth century had the option of not just rejecting individual supernatural claims, but indeed the very doctrine of supernaturalism (and thus demons along with it). Yet the history of the period shows, perhaps exemplified by Napoleon's consciously theological coronation, that secularism has a way of simply sublimating beliefs that are hard to dispel, least of all within the individual heart of the one doing the dispelling. The Prussian philosopher Immanuel Kant, whose name is practically synonymous with "Enlightenment" (though he provided trenchant critique of pure reason) wrote that the fundamental imperative of this new age was that humanity must "Dare to know," which inadvertently has its own Faustian gloss to it.

Popular demonology and official skepticism; the widespread democratization of magic; and the enshrinement of an ideology of state-sanctioned rationality in France and the United States—all of these defined the eighteenth century. The Enlightenment was the age of revolution, reason, science, progress, and optimism; it was also one of Black Masses and occultists claiming esoteric knowledge; of secret societies like the Freemasons and the Rosicrucians. Often-times enthusiasts on either side of this divide dabbled in both, so that a claim to occult knowledge and democratic enthusiasms weren't seen as inconsistent. "One of the paradoxes of the Enlightenment," writes John V. Fleming in *The Dark Side of the Enlightenment: Wizards, Alchemists, and Spiritual Seekers in the Age of Reason*, "a paradox long observed and variously explained, is the fascination of many of the enlightened with the *occult*."

Broadsheets, newspapers, and pamphlets were printed with the latest accounts of America's Continental Congress preparing to declare independence from Great Britain in 1776 or of the storming of the Bastille; the same printing presses and booksellers that sold Thomas Paine's *Common Sense* or Denis Diderot's *Encyclopédie* also produced grimoires with names like *The Grand Albert, The Petit Albert, The Grimoire of Pope Honorius, The Grimoire of Pope Leo, The Sixth and Seventh Book of Moses*, and of course the most influential of all, *The Grand Grimoire*, also known as the *Dragon Rouge*, or the "Red Dragon."

It's that last volume which, according to Davies, was most likely in the possession of the conjurer of Amiens. Like all such books, *Dragon Rouge*'s provenance is uncertain, its author (or authors) completely unknown (though attributed to the pseudonym of an Antonio Venitiana del Rabina), but that it was one of the most popular volumes of magic written in the eighteenth century, and certainly the one with the most infernal of reputations, isn't to be doubted. Davies notes that the earliest widespread printing of *Dragon Rouge* is from 1750, but that based on references and quotations from earlier dated texts a first edition of the work can probably be traced back to 1702 (with some material plagiarized from even earlier sources). Noting that *Dragon Rouge* was "the first explicitly diabolic mass-market grimoire," Davies explains how the popular 1750 edition was a prime example of a French tradition known as *Bibliothèque bleue*, cheap mass-produced pamphlets, chapbooks, and other print ephemera designed for widespread consumption. Just as important as the relative availability of *Dragon Rouge* was how it presented the purpose of conjuration. Where works by occultists like Trithemius and Agrippa emphasized that necromancy was done through God, *Dragon Rouge* was unabashedly satanic and wicked. It was as if all of the cultural fever nightmares about malignant sorcerers in the mold of Faust had finally manifested in an actual book that could be held and read—and help you conjure the Prince of Lies while you were at it.

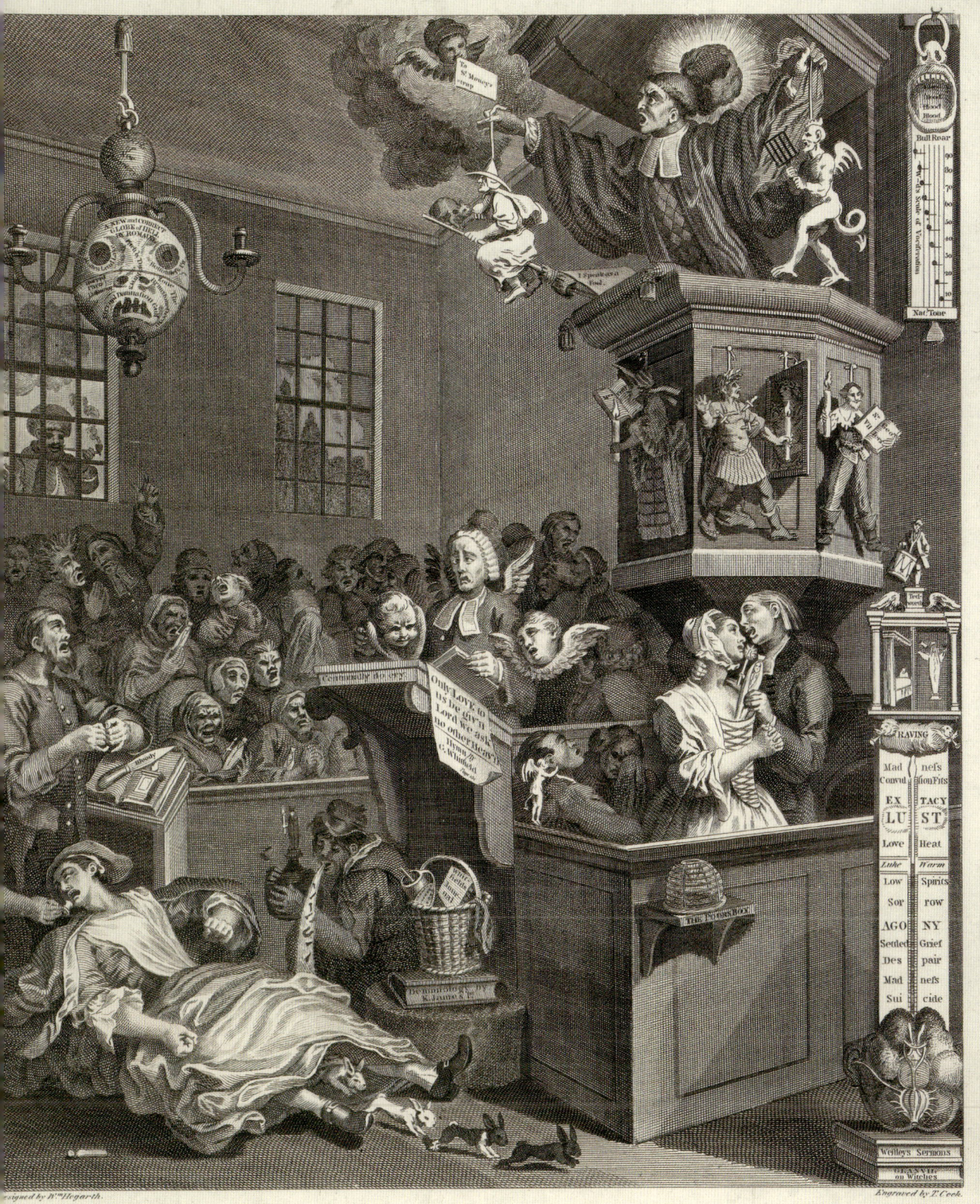

CREDULITY, SUPERSTITION and FANATICISM.

A MEDLEY.

Believe not every Spirit, but try the spirits whether they are of God: because many false Prophets are gone out into the World.

Published by G.G.& J.Robinsons Pater-noster Row October 1st 1796.

1 John Ch. 4 V 1.

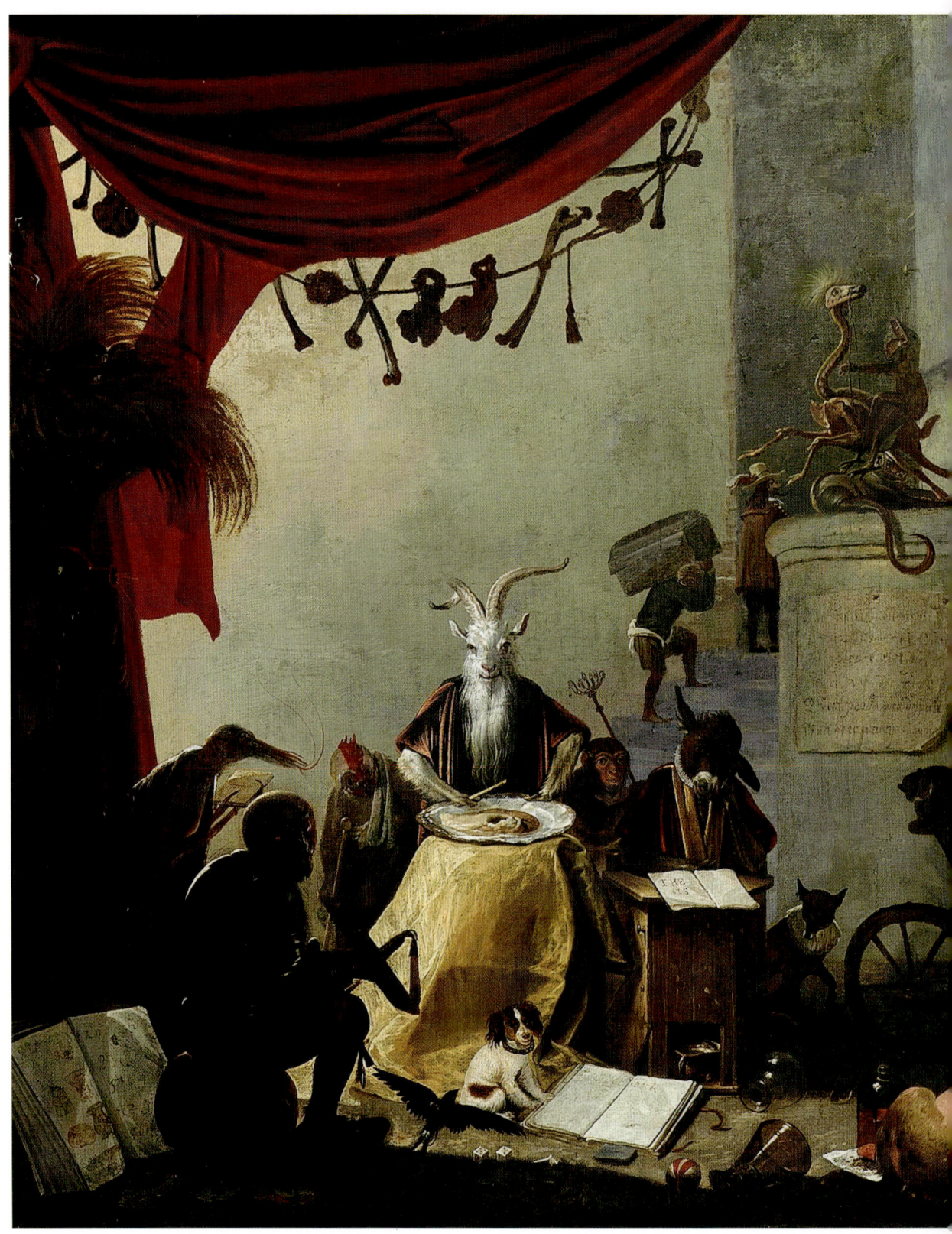

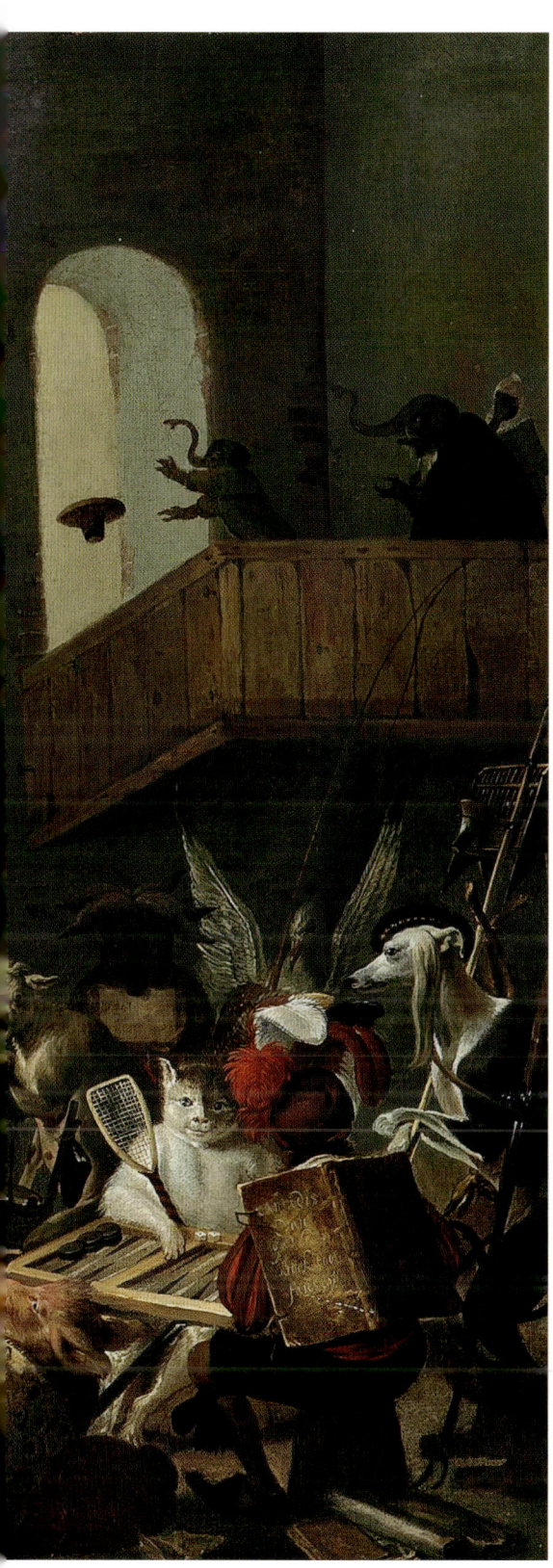

More specific than a vehicle for invoking Satan, *Dragon Rouge* provides instruction for conjuring a particular and novel demon by the fantastic name of Lucifuge Rofocale. For any aspiring initiate into a pact with the Devil, *Dragon Rouge* has an exact script to be followed, which mentions several personages in the demonic hierarchy:

Emperor LUCIFER, master of all the rebel spirits, I beg you to favor me in the call that I am making to your grand minister LUCIFUGE ROFOCALE, desiring to make a pact with him; I beg you also, prince Beelzebub, to protect me in my undertaking. O count Astarot! Be favorable to me, and make it so that this night the grand LUCIFUGE appears to me in human form, and without any bad odor, and that he accords to me, by the pact that I am going to present to him, all the riches I need.

As with the innovation of the name Mephistopheles in the sixteenth century, so Rofocale seems to be unique to *Dragon Rouge*, and is all the more disquieting for it. Effectively hell's prime minister, Lucifuge Rofocale draws from some of the studied skepticism of Mephistopheles, but something about his name also foreshadows the archetype of the urbane, sophisticated, cosmopolitan, elegant, and entirely malignant personification of evil as seen in fictional characters as varied as Bram Stoker's Dracula and Thomas Harris's Hannibal Lecter.

Despite the relative dearth of description applied to Rofocale, his sophisticated-sounding patronym is still possibly a reflection of the role that the Black Mass increasingly had in anticlerical displays of codified religious blasphemy, and the role that educated and powerful men played in secret societies like the English Hell-Fire Clubs and the (non-satanic) Bavarian Illuminati, Freemasons, and Rosicrusians. "Do not disturb me further," Rofocale says in a script reproduced in *Dragon Rouge*, "Tell me immediately what you want." The demon as an impatient and busy man of the world. Clandestine nocturnal gatherings that were once associated with the marginalized—with the impoverished, ethnic minorities, and women accused of witchcraft were now associated with Parliamentarians and barristers, aristocrats and clergy. Lucifuge Rofocale reflects the growing urbanity of the Luciferian imperative, where what's genuine sentiment and what's ironic satire can be hard to disentangle.

Presumably for many readers of *Dragon Rouge* the content was deadly serious. Central to *Dragon Rouge* is this personage of Rofocale, his first name roughly translating from bastard Latin into "flee from the light," and his vaguely Francophone surname simply pronounced as his first name in reverse. Far from simple gimmick, such inversions speak to the purpose of occult conjuration—to undo what's been done, to disorder the orderly, to turn the world upside-down. *Dragon Rouge*'s ethos was precisely this variety of antinomianism, to mire the world in chaos, contradiction, disjuncture, and disarray. Where earlier grimoires promised the mage the ability to use demons for their own purpose, Dragon Rouge had the added intent of theurgy being deployed to specifically revolutionary aims; not just to enact spells and incantation for paltry individual gain, but indeed with the implications that divinity itself might be challenged.

Any revolution, of course, necessitates the establishment of a new system of organization once the previous has been cast aside, and *Dragon Rouge* is no different, taking part in the venerable tradition of intricately describing the various offices and bureaucracies of hell (and often drawing specifically from past works). According to the author, hell is overseen by an infernal Trinity composed of those usual suspects of the fallen angel's rebel leader Lucifer, and then the "Lord of the Flies" Beelzebub governing as prince and Astaroth as grand duke. Beneath these three are six lesser demons, including the intermediary prime minister Rofocale, who are organized along martial lines.

Satanachia is the commander, or chief general, of the demonic horde; the commandant Agaliarept; the lieutenant-general Fleurety; brigadier-major Sargatanas, and the inspector-general Nebiros. As in most demonic bestiaries, *Dragon Rouge* describes its central personages as a horrific mélange of the animalistic and the human. Fleurety has the body of a leopard, while Nebiros (whose name may be associated with Cerberus) is commonly depicted as a three-headed dog. Chief among them is Rofocale, rendered in lurid red ink on the frontispiece of an early nineteenth-century edition of *Dragon Rouge*— a cloven-hoofed demon with the sleek body of an automaton wearing an emotionless, mask-like face and topped with a three-horned hat that evokes nothing so much as the mottled cap of a jester.

Under each of the six lesser demons is an entire horde of unnamed specters, soldiers in the infernal army. "Although there are millions of spirits that are all inferior to those above," the author writes, "it would be useless to describe them because they are employed by the superior ones. To work in their place all of these inferior spirits are employed as if they were workers of slaves." Such divisions aren't unusual in a grimoire, of course; classification and categorization into hierarchies was already the obsession of demonology for a millennium by the time the *Dragon Rouge* was printed. Nor necessarily is the specifically militaristic nature of the metaphor surprising, similar allegorizing also existed in earlier texts. Yet it is worth considering the new resonance of all of these generals, commanders, and lieutenants, and the unnamed millions of "slaves" forced to march underneath their banner.

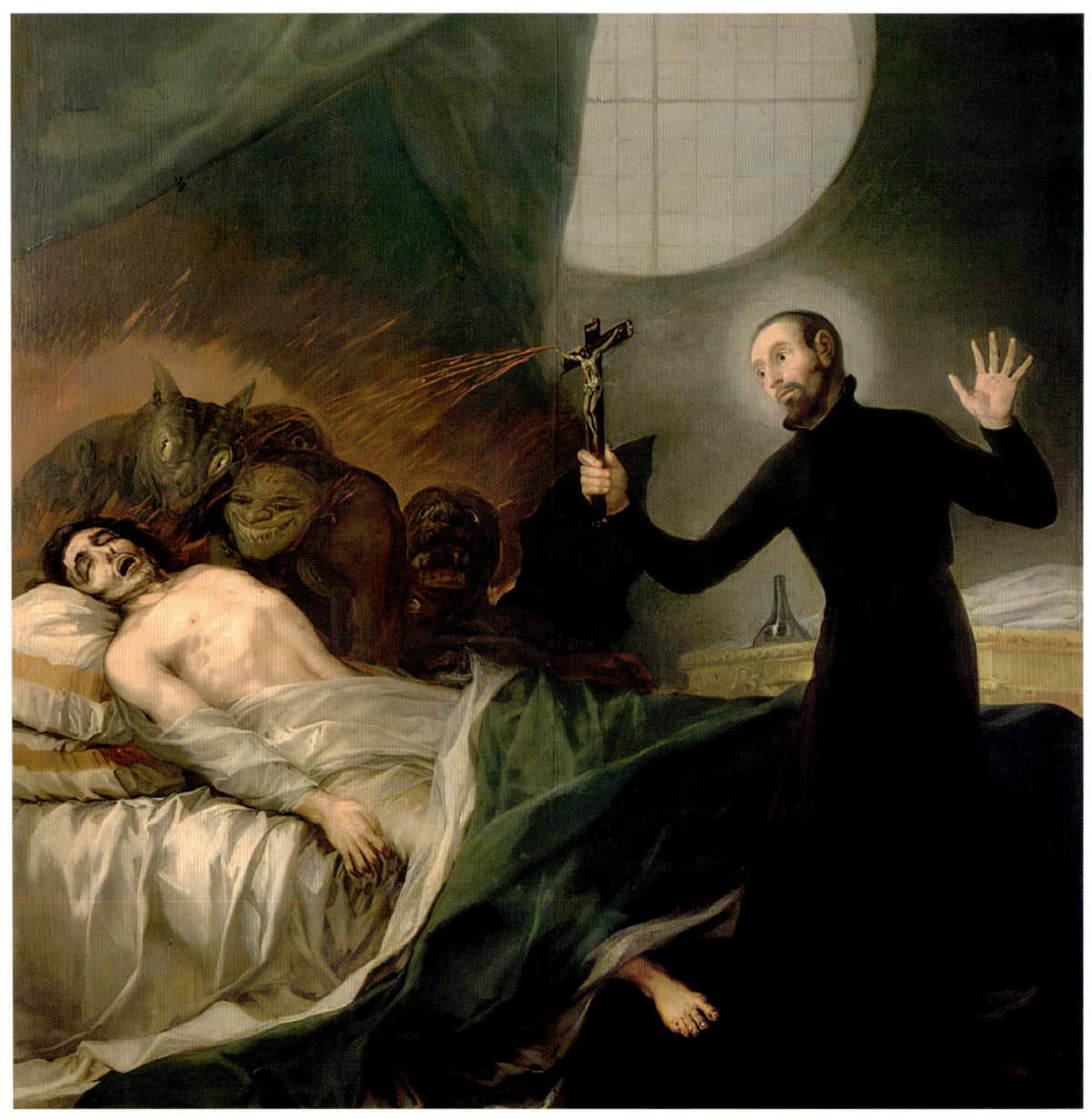

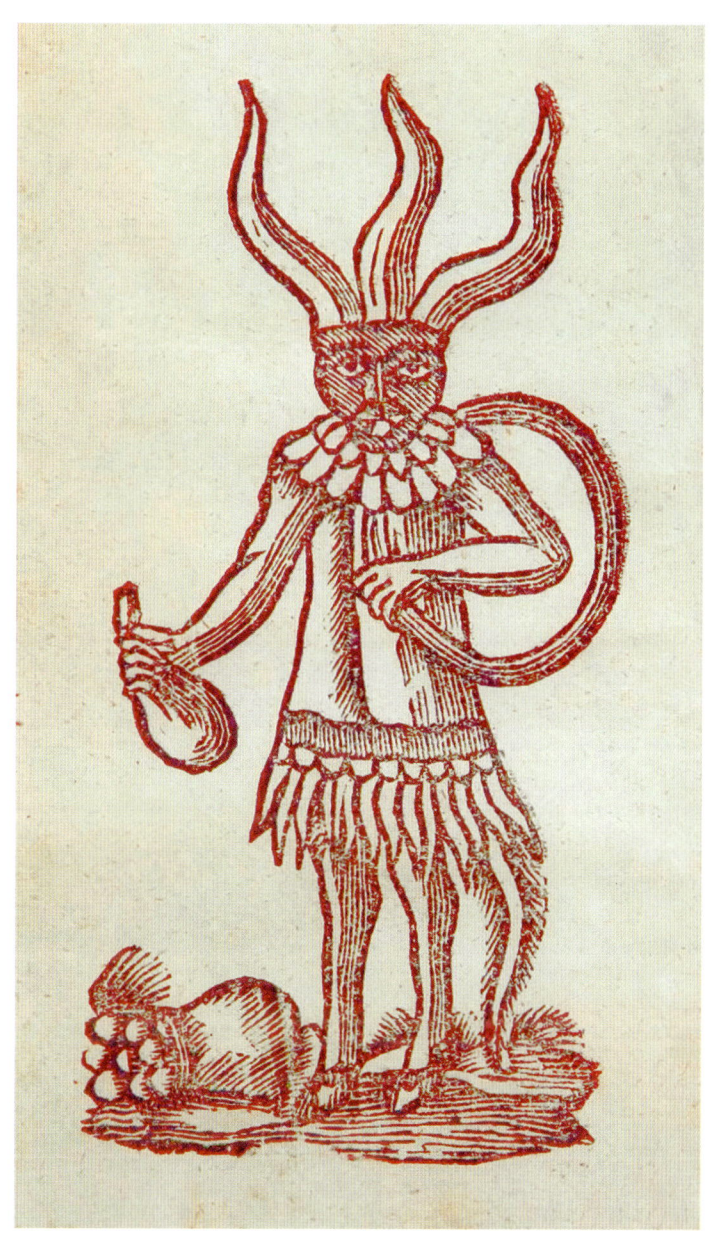

Lucifuge Rofocale from the frontispiece of an 1821 edition of Dragon Rouge.

191

If hell was a kingdom in Dante's imagination, then by the seventeenth and eighteenth centuries it was a nation-state, a republic. And these hellish officers command not a coterie of medieval aristocrats feudally indentured to a king, but rather they're organized into a modern, scientific, regimented, force evoking the New Model Army of Oliver Cromwell's Interregnum, or of the massive professional forces that decimated Europe during the Thirty Years' War. If part of what all of these texts do—the grimoires and the theological tracts, the popular pamphlets and the epic poetry—is to imagine that the sacred realms (of which the infernal must necessarily be included) reflect a transcendent version of our own experience, then by the eighteenth century hell could be imagined as a bureaucracy, just as the nation-state as a political unit began to define itself through that method of organization. Describing the military arm of these new bureaucracies, Tim Blanning notes in *The Pursuit of Glory: The Five Revolutions that Made Modern Europe: 1648–1815* that "armies were now better disciplined and better provisioned . . . [as] one state after another moved to establish control over their armed forces." Just as it is above, so it is here; as it is here, so it is below.

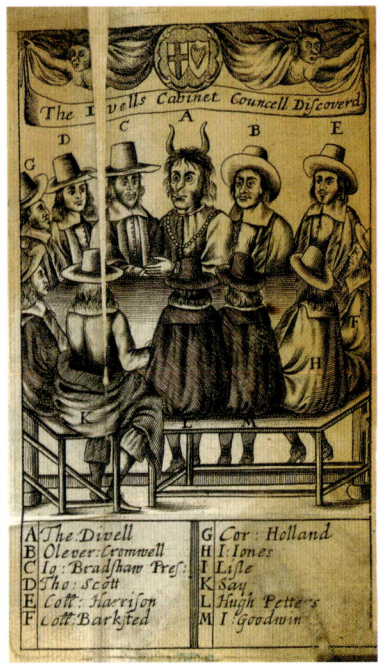

For all that seems archaic about *Dragon Rouge*—its spells, incantations, and formula, its litany of demons and its commitment to magic—an argument could be formulated that the grimoire is a consummate Enlightenment work. Morning star of the Enlightenment, the English scientist and philosopher Francis Bacon argued in his 1620 *Novum Organum*, penned during the waning days of the Renaissance, that "Human knowledge and human power meet in one," and in many ways that's a helpful encapsulation of the age's ethos. From scientific discovery, perhaps motivated by curiosity, comes the power to change the world. Bacon had in mind the way in which pure science could influence technology, but in many ways such an axiom just as easily applies to the ethos of practical magic, and certainly few books see knowledge and power as more synonymous than *Dragon Rouge*.

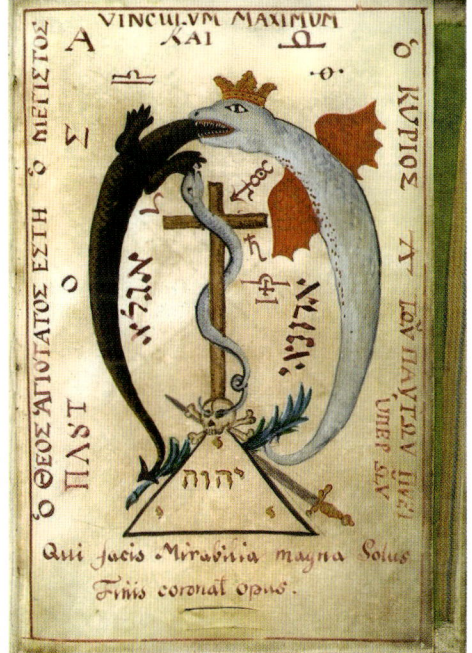

Page from a German grimoire manuscript held at the Wellcome Library in London dated 1717 (though there are convincing reasons to believe that it should actually be dated later) entitled The Key of Hell with White and Black Magic Proven by Metatron. *Claiming authorship from the mysterious Talmudic and kabbalistic angel Metatron, which was the name by which the patriarch Enoch was known after he ascended to heaven, this image is a panoply of magical symbols that were commonly used by eighteenth-century occultists, including an amended ouroboros, a cross altered into a rod of Asclepius, and a Hebrew rendering of the Tetragrammaton, the unpronounceable name of God. Wellcome notes that the volume is "also known as the Black Book, and is the textbook of the Black School at Wittenburg . . . a place in Germany where one went to learn the black arts," ironically the city where Luther's Reformation began.*

Such ideological commitments aren't the only thing that makes the grimoire very much a book for its epoch, for it could be argued that the combination of knowledge and power always results in rebellion, and there is unequivocally a sense of the zestful Luciferian in *Dragon Rouge*. Its attitude is radical; its commitments revolutionary; its proliferation democratic. When the English bibliographer Thomas Frognall Dibdin was on his 1818 grand tour of the continent, he was sold a copy of *Dragon Rouge* by a French bookseller who enthused how popular the title still was. "See, Sir, is not this curious? . . . buy it and read it—it will amuse you—and it costs only five sous."

THE AGE OF LUCIFER

On the brisk winter day in 1649 that King Charles I ascended a Whitehall scaffold to meet his executioner, the poet and pamphleteer John Milton was already crafting sophisticated justifications for this audacious and unprecedented regicide. The defeated Royalists who saw their monarch felled in the English Revolution produced hagiography about Charles, recounting how on the morning of his death he requested an extra shirt so that the spectators wouldn't mistake his chill for fear, how his gentleman Thomas Herbert described the execution as the "saddest sight England ever saw," how before death the monarch exclaimed that he "would go from a corruptible crown to an incorruptible crown." Milton would have none of it, boldly stating in his pamphlet *The Tenure of Kings and Magistrates*—printed only two weeks after Charles's blood splashed on the sawdust of Whitehall—that "How much more justly then may they fling off tyranny, or tyrants; who being once depos'd can be no more the private men, as subject to the reach of Justice and arraignment as any other transgressors."

More than a century before the French would give Louis XVI a haircut by guillotine, the English had done something unthinkable—they'd toppled and killed a king who was supposed to be God's anointed on earth. The war in heaven made manifest in our profane world. For the Parliamentarians who fought against Charles, many of whom were doctrinaire Calvinist Puritans, theirs was a struggle against tyranny and popery, yet there was discomfort among some in the implications of the execution. This was the first time in modern history that a king hadn't been killed by some other aristocratic, or by a foreign equal, but rather by the people themselves, and consequently it's hard not to see some of Milton's enthusiasms for the regicide in the consummate brilliance of his character Lucifer in the epic poem *Paradise Lost*. Completed in 1667, some seven years after the Restoration of Charles's son to the throne, after Milton had narrowly escaped his own capital punishment for his role in the civil war, and *Paradise Lost*'s charismatic central character, despite being the fallen angel who led his demon hordes in rebellion against the Lord, can be interpreted as (perhaps unconsciously) a justification for the poet's own Luciferian inclinations. As the poet William Blake so memorably put it in his 1804 *Milton*, his subject was "of the Devil's party without knowing it."

With stunning erudition, incomparable rhetoric, and a sense of inspiration that itself seemed either divine or diabolical, Milton drew from an array of inspirations so as to "justify the ways of God to man." All of the assorted detritus of theological reasoning about the demonic, from canonical scripture like Revelation to apocryphal works such as the Book of Enoch, provided the narrative scaffolding for Paradise Lost, which elaborated on the story of the rebel angels' fall from heaven with more detail and interiority than had ever been (or would be) rendered. At the time of Charles's execution, Milton was already a respected (if heterodox) polemicist and poet, a committed republican and a Protestant partisan (albeit one with a more unconventional theology than his compatriots may have known). If prior demonology was eccentric, then Milton made it brilliant; if apocryphal scripture was odd, then the pamphleteer endowed it with genius; if the panoply of satanic lore was dross, then the poet made it glitter as gold, and in the process may have dramatized the very temptation that Lucifer offered. Few poets have ever rendered the expulsion from paradise with such incandescent beauty:

Him the Almighty Power

Hurled headlong flaming from th' ethereal sky

With hideous ruin and combustion down

To bottomless perdition, there to dwell

In adamantine chains and penal fire,

Who durst defy th' Omnipotent to arms.

NEXT SPREAD
William Blake's 1795 watercolor Satan Exulting Over Eve, *held at Los Angeles's Getty Museum, was a precursor to the series of illustrations which the artist would later make for* Paradise Lost. *No artist has depicted the work of Milton more than Blake did, and in his own poetry, he set out to liberate the latent Luciferian energies which he thought were implicit in his predecessor. Despite Blake imagining Lucifer after his transformation into Satan, the Great Adversary, who propels himself forward with monstrous dragon wings, his fallen angel is still beautiful.*

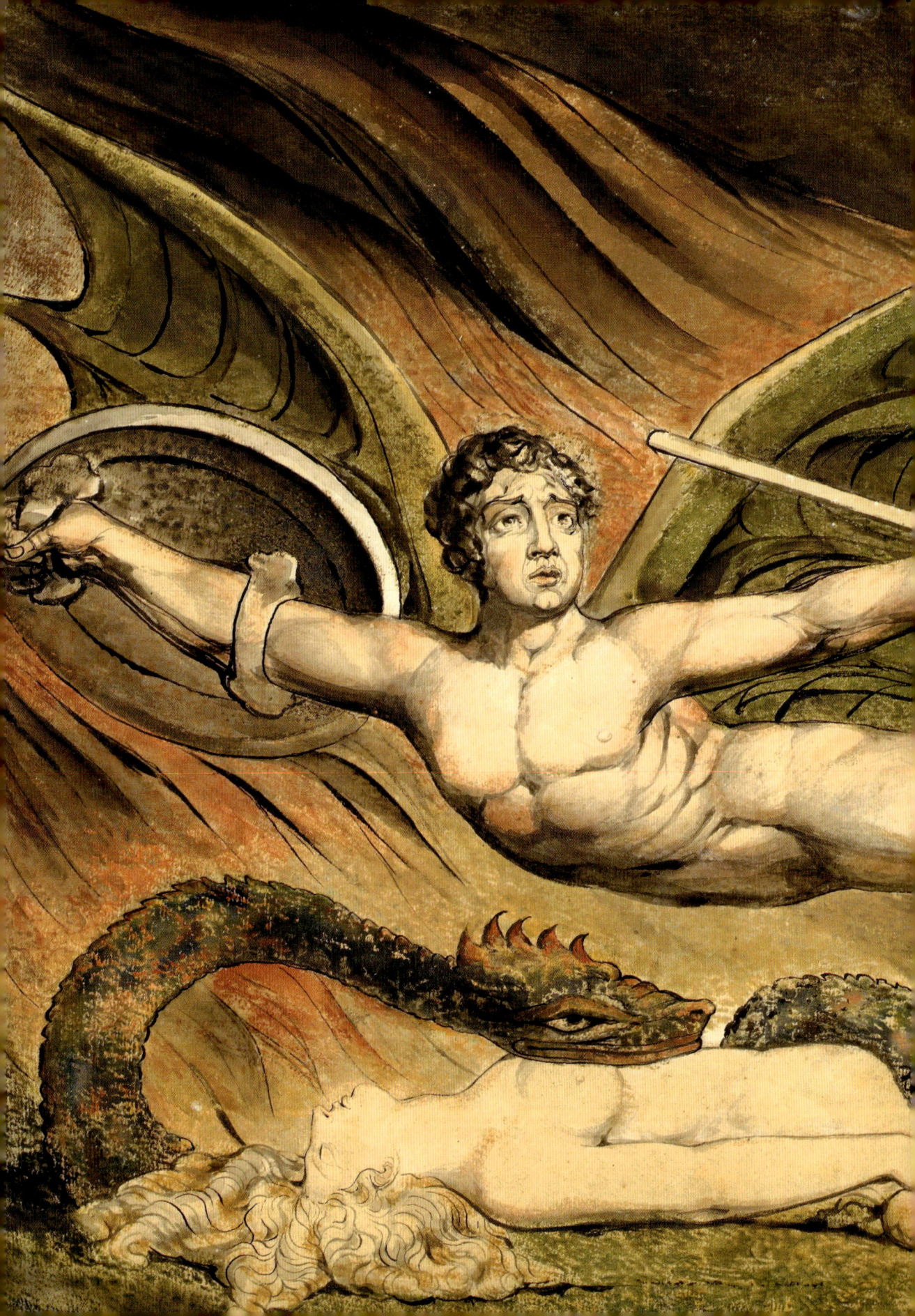

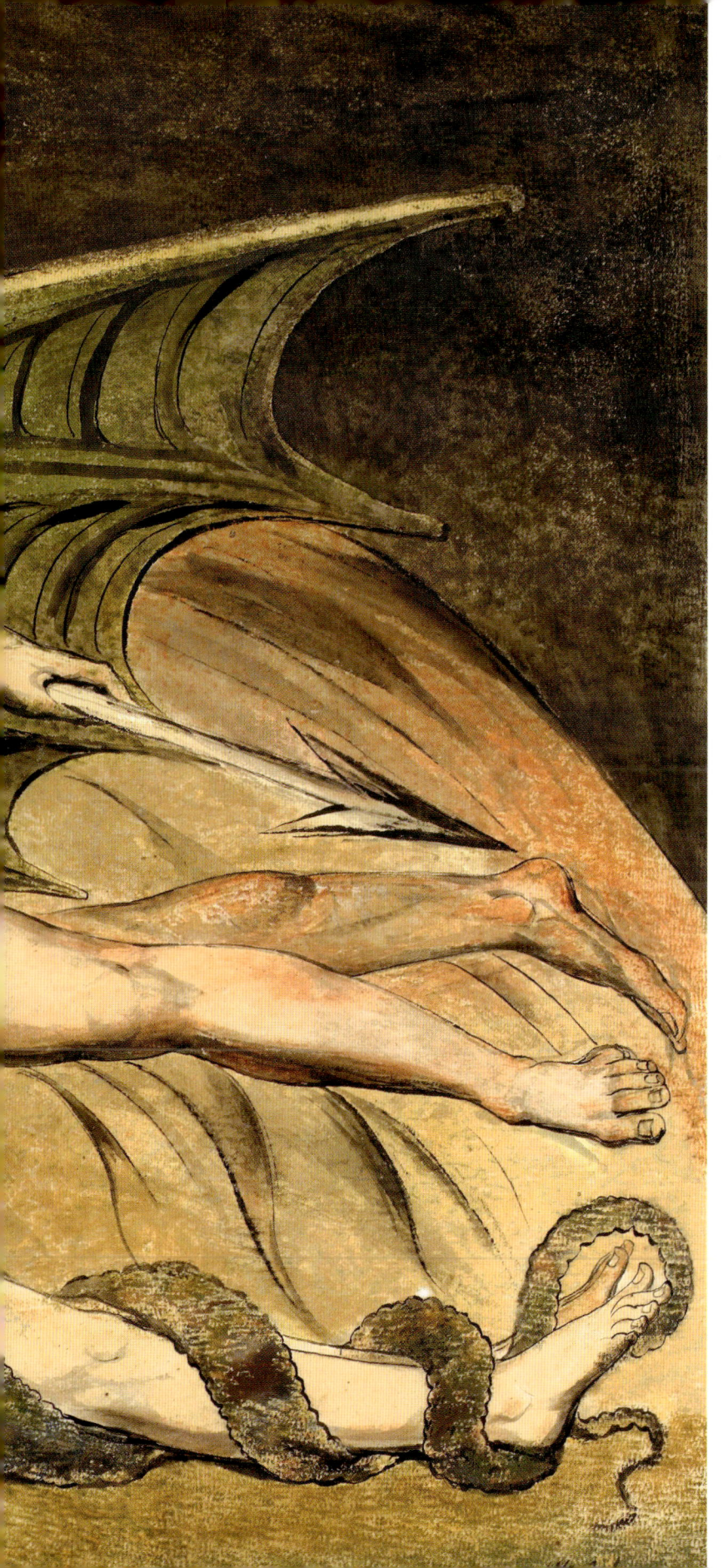

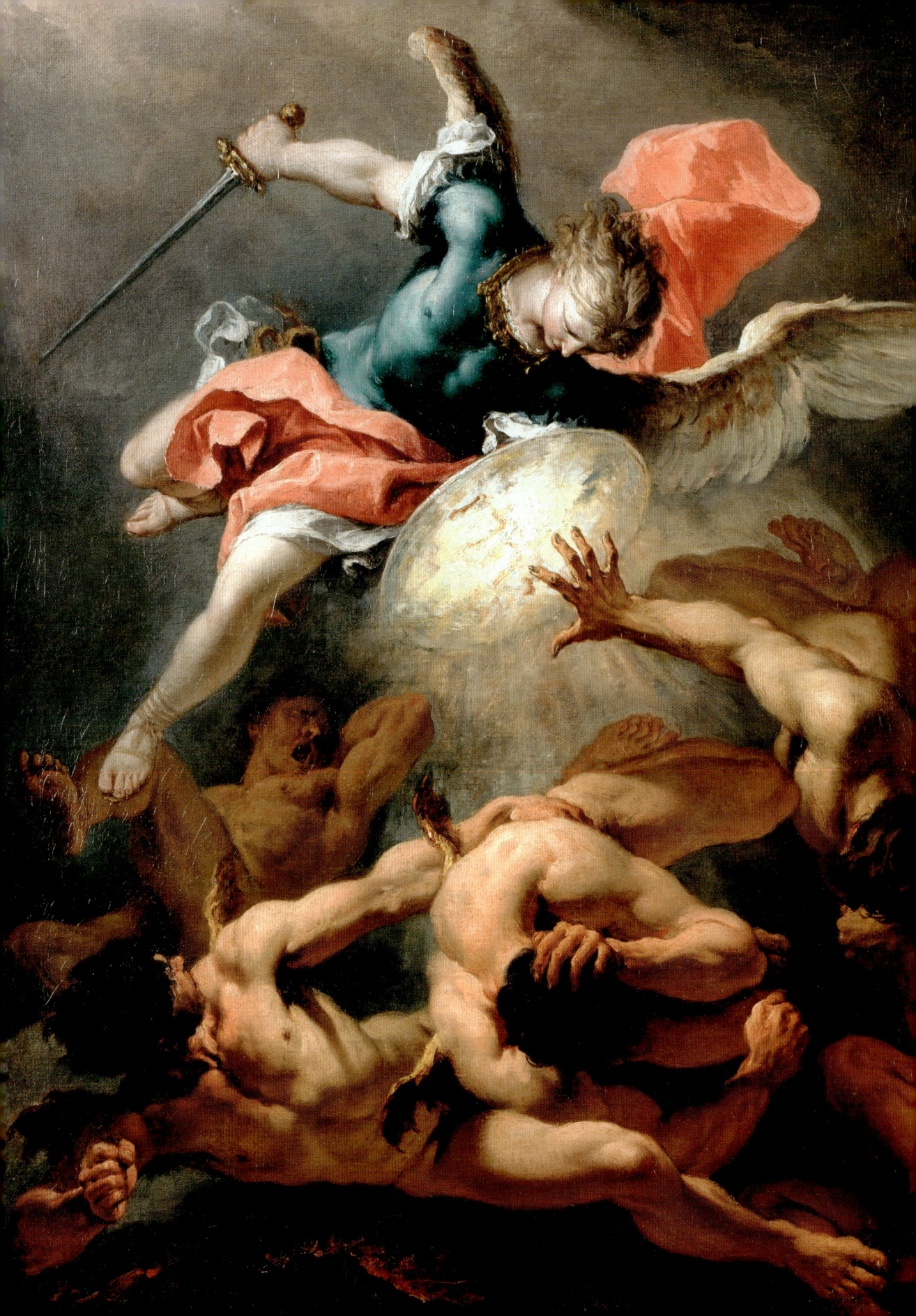

Recondite Puritan that he was, Milton's allegiances are supposedly with God (on paper), but it's hard not to see a bit of Blake's accusal concerning allegiances in the earlier poet's rhetoric, with Lucifer's defeat striking a distinctly romantic note. Deep within the bowels of the fallen earth would Lucifer—transformed by his rebellion into Satan—convene his "Pandemonium," his Parliament of All Demons, where he and his minions would strategize on how to corrupt newly created humanity. "The mind is its own place," Milton writes, "and in itself/Can make a heav'n of hell, a hell of heav'n," as the fallen angels build their republic in this realm of bitumen and sulfur.

From such a tremendous cornucopia of reading—classical sources, scripture both canonical and not, the writings of the Church Fathers, theological tracts, philosophical disputation, and no small amount of his own reasoning— Milton would derive the greatest literary text to ever consider demonology. "Milton," write Thomas N. Corns and Gordon Campbell in *John Milton: Life, Work, and Thought*, "is flawed, self-contradictory, self-serving, arrogant, passionate, ruthless, ambitious, and cunning," bearing no small similarity to his most celebrated artistic creation. Lucifer—that other aspiring regicide. Corns and Campbell write that Milton is "among the most accomplished writers of the Caroline period, the most eloquent polemicist of the mid-century, and the author of the finest and most influential narrative poem in English." Historically only Shakespeare has been more esteemed than Milton, yet the former has nothing among his listed works that matches the theological nuance and complexity of *Paradise Lost*. While scripture and folklore flatten the demons into broad symbols, mere ciphers for human attributes, Milton imbues his fallen angels (and in particular Lucifer) with a fully realized psychological intensity, and in the process, he invigorated the chief fallen angel with a very particular personality that would be astoundingly influential during an Age of Revolution, perhaps more appropriately called the Age of Lucifer.

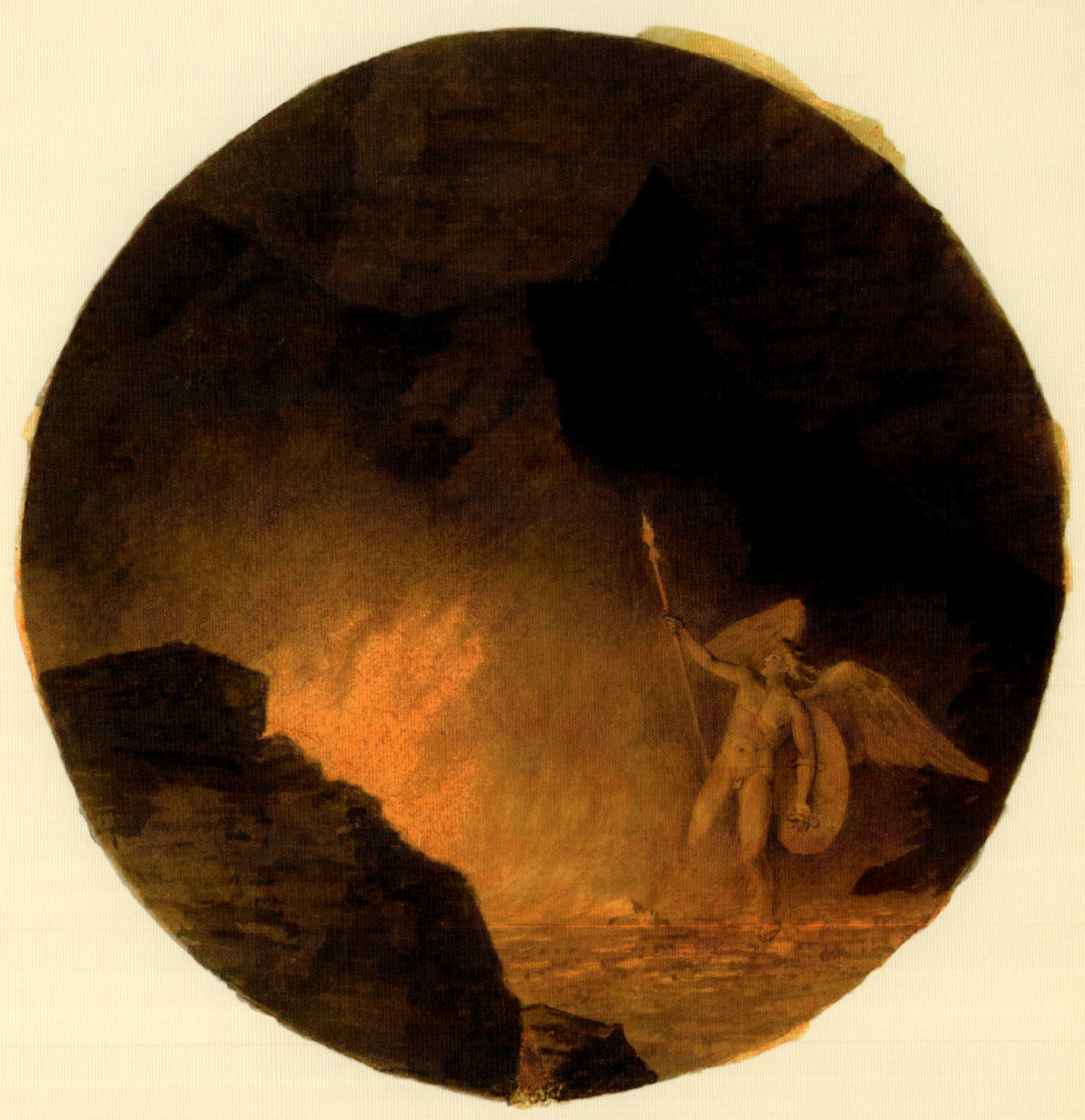

Among the earliest English paintings to depict Lucifer as a sort of Olympian hero, John Robert Cozen's Satan Summoning His Legions *places his beautiful winged demon in a strikingly sublime hell. Housed in the Tate Britain, Cozen's piece was painted in the auspicious year of 1776, when the American colonies declared their independence in an act both criticized and celebrated as Luciferian. Milton was the favorite poet of the young Thomas Jefferson, who in his commonplace book (a compendium of quotations that a writer would preserve for their own edification), a third of the selected excerpts are from the first two books of the twelve book* Paradise Lost—*sections that deal entirely with the fallen angels.*

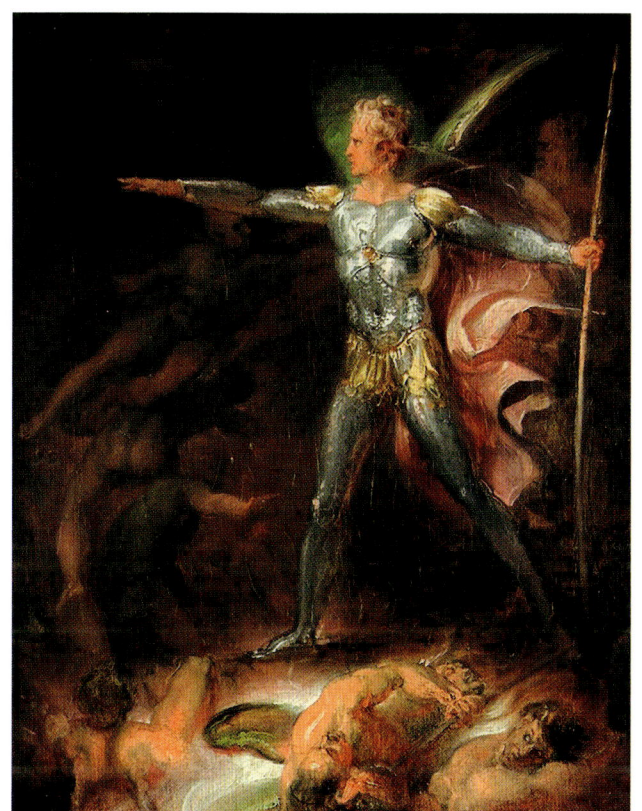

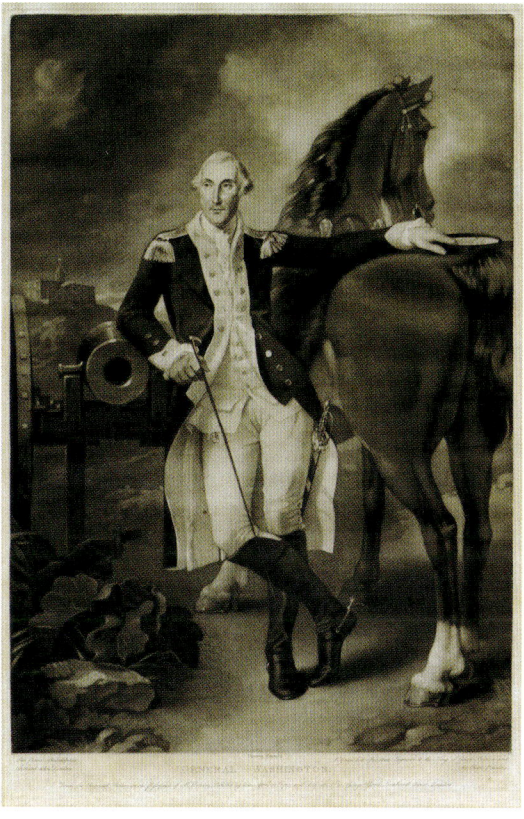

On the left, English painter Thomas Stothard opts to depict Lucifer in his full, heroic, resplendent glory in his 1790 Satan Summoning His Legions, *housed at the Cantor Arts Center at Stanford University in Palo Alto, California. Nothing in the figure's appearance, countenance, or stance would indicate that this is Satan; indeed the martial breastplate and the blond curls gesture toward the fact that we're in the presence of a fully heroic figure. On the right, in a more relaxed pose, though with a strikingly similar build, physique, and profile, is his* General George Washington, *painted in 1785 and now displayed at the Dallas Museum of Art. Conversant with the radical politics of the time, and a friend of Blake's, Stothard embodied the revolutionary aims of a Luciferian age.*

Dramatizing the aftermath of the war in heaven, expanding the few verses of Revelation and Enoch that allude to the Fall into the twelve books of the narrative poem, *Paradise Lost* begins in medias res after the expulsion of the rebel angels but before the "infernal serpent; he it was, whose guile,/Stirred up with envy and revenge, deceived/The mother of mankind." When the epic begins, the demons survey their new status and their current locale of "No light, but rather darkness visible," a vast inchoate "Regions of sorrow, doleful shades, where peace/And rest can never dwell," and still decide that it is "Better to reign in Hell, than serve in Heaven." Perhaps the most famous line in a work full of them, that Luciferian injunction, as duplicitous and dangerous as Milton the poet may think that it is, summarizes the jaundiced and rebellious perspective of this age, whereby heaven itself could be assaulted in the construction of man's own utopia. There is something heroic about Milton's Lucifer, a figure for whom critics from the seventeenth century onward have long noted always receives the best lines in *Paradise Lost*; a captivating revolutionary who challenges the authoritarianism of the Lord in favor of an antinomian liberty.

Paradise Lost is concerned with rebellion and authority, providence and free will, order and chaos, creation and destruction. To reduce it to an epic about demonology is to preclude much of what makes the poem among the most remarkable in the English language, yet the vocabulary of demonology is invaluable to properly understanding *Paradise Lost*. Indeed, part of what makes the work so remarkable is that Milton draws so heavily on the traditions of demonic poetics to render his characters, often with a sense of narrative urgency and explorations of character that simply couldn't exist in the scriptural and apocryphal source materials. Milton populates Pandemonium with familiar fallen beings—Beelzebub, Belial, Mammon, Mulciber, and Moloch are all mentioned in *Paradise Lost*; while familiar concepts like Sin, Chaos, and Death are endowed with their own demonic energies.

Book I of the poem sees the recently defeated demons convening in conference to argue over their options, with each one of the named demons playing different roles in Lucifer's disputation. Beelzebub is closest in eloquence to his master, and appropriately enough the second-in-command over this new realm. "With Atlantean shoulders fit to bear/The weight of mightiest monarchs; his look/

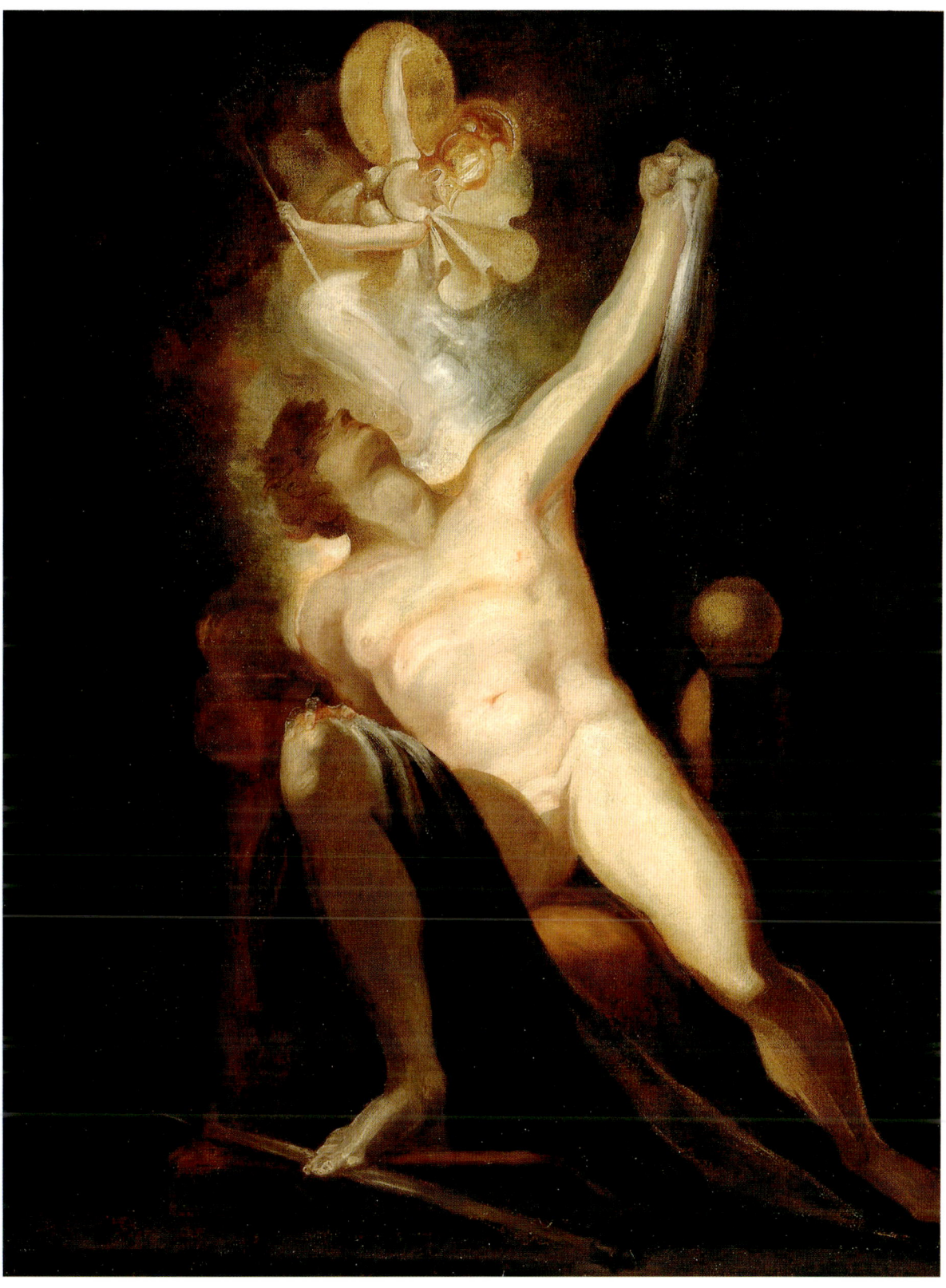

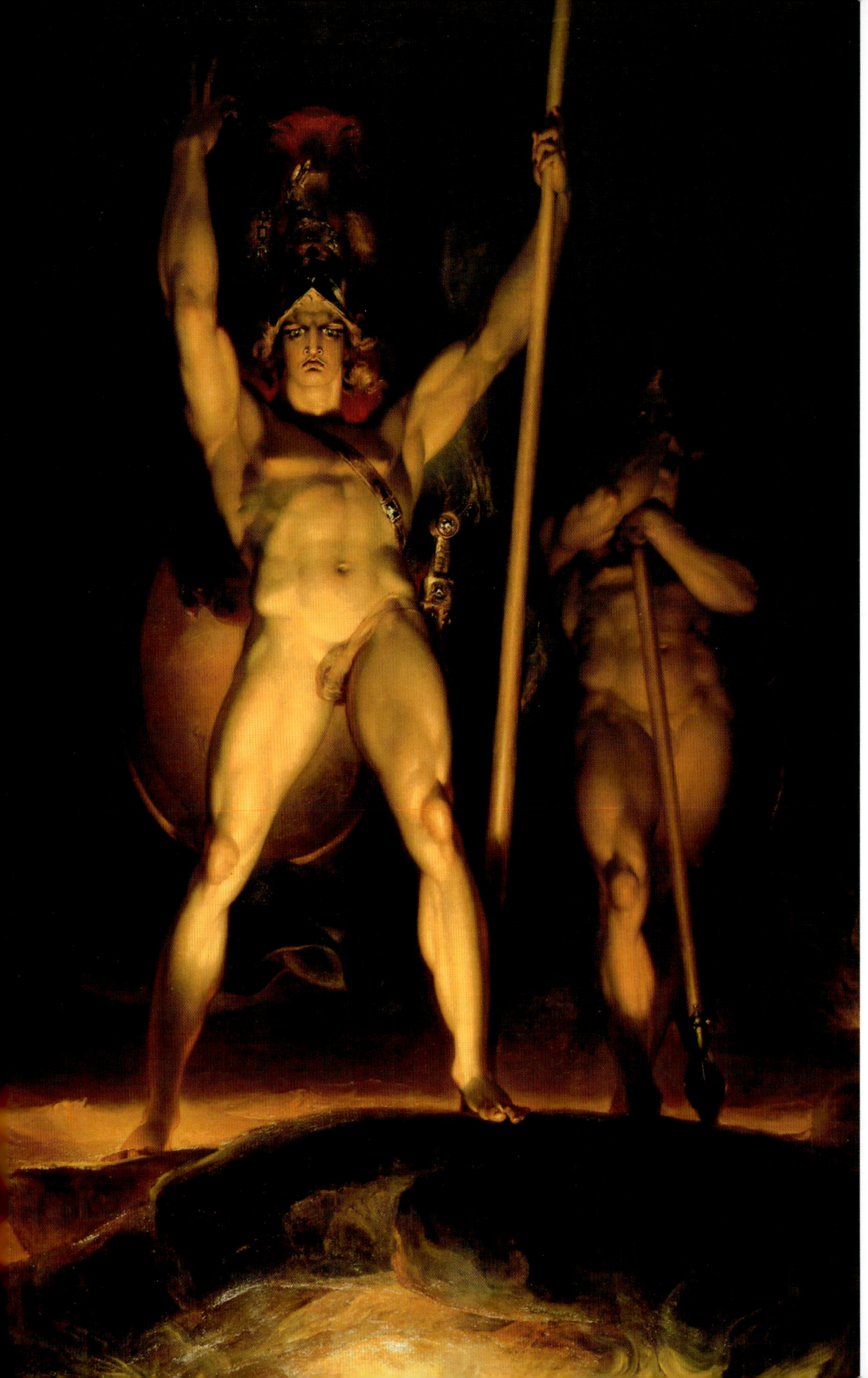

Drew audience and attention still as night/Or summer's noontide air, while thus he spake." Forever loyal to Lucifer, Beelzebub is a steadfast adviser and confident to the rebel leader, and though his dignity be twisted, as a trusted adviser he holds his master's desires close to his own cankered breast. "For so the popular vote/Inclines, here to continue, and build up here/A growing empire," Beelzebub declares, a dream of a hellish sovereignty committed to its own imperialism of sin. By contrast, Belial argues for a more circumspect, or perhaps cowardly, approach toward their enemies in heaven. "A fairer person lost not Heav'n;/he seemed/For dignity composed and high exploit;/But all was false and hollow." Milton writes that Belial's "thoughts were low;/To vice industrious, but to nobler deeds/Timorous and slothful."

Mammon, Mulciber, and Moloch all serve logistical roles in the government and economy of hell, even while they disagree with their leader on the proper course of action to take. Mulciber, for example, operates as the chief architect of hell, and the demon who designed Pandemonium, with Milton drawing the character from Greek mythology; while Moloch, the bull-headed god of the ancient Philistines and Carthaginians, advocates for total war against heaven, burnishing his reputation as the demon to whom children were burnt in sacrifice. Mammon, by contrast, is more cowardly than rageful. True to his role as the demonic incarnation of avarice, he initially rejects the calls to a new war, seeing military incursion as a risk to the accumulation of wealth. "Mammon, the least erected Spirit that fell/From Heav'n," as Milton describes him, "for ev'n in Heav'n his looks and thoughts/Were always downward bent, admiring more/The riches of Heav'n's pavement, trodden gold, /Than aught divine or holy else enjoyed/In vision beatific." Milton's respect is clear, for though Lucifer waged war against the Lord, there's a dignity afforded to Satan that's denied to baser and cruder demons like greedy Mammon.

No character in *Paradise Lost* can match the full intensity of the greatest of demons, however. Not Beelzebub, or Belial, not Mulciber, Mammon, or Moloch. None of the archangels as rendered by Milton are as three-dimensional—Michael, Gabriel, and Raphael all fall far short of him. Adam and Eve are flat when compared to the Serpent, and the abstractions of Sin, Death, and Chaos seem more allegory than personality when measured against Lucifer. Christ appears as a sanctimonious prig and God a boring authoritarian when placed in contrast to the greatest character of English literature, for against all of them, Milton's Lucifer is a triumph who rewrites the age itself. Never has such pathos been imbued unto a loser, never has such nobility been imparted to the rebel. "Alone the dreadful voyage; till at last/Satan, whom now transcendent glory raised/Above his fellows, with monarchal pride/Conscious of highest worth."

Milton was, after all, a revolutionary, and one who advocated for the death of a king. Not only that, but the partisan of what would ultimately be a failed revolution, writing *Paradise Lost* in the seventh year of the reign of his adversary's son, imagining that "Incensed with indignation Satan stood/Unterrified, and like a comet burned." Blake's contention regarding Milton is, despite the latter's Christianity, hard not to find convincing.

Lucifer is at the center of any critique of *Paradise Lost* over the years, though the correct way to interpret him is ever variable. Arguably the demon of Milton's imagination is the progenitor of much of what would come to be called the "left hand path" of theurgy in the Romantic era; that is occultism that embraced the potentiality of black magic. Much of that perspective potentially derives from Blake. His view, ascendant from the late eighteenth century and into the twentieth, held that there was something fundamentally infernal about Milton's perspective, that at its core it acted unconsciously as an encomium for Lucifer. Contrary to Blake's romantic imagining of Satan as noble revolutionary and Milton as a writer unknowingly extolling his virtues, the Christian apologist, fantasy writer, and scholar C.S. Lewis saw the poem as presenting a fairly conventional theodicy, soteriology, and demonology. In his 1941 *A Preface to Paradise Lost*, Lewis admits that the nature of Milton's "magnificent poetical achievement which engages the attention and excites the admiration of the reader" is such that for many, Lucifer will be an "an object of admiration and sympathy."

Yet he wholly correctly notes that the interpretation which holds that Lucifer is in someway the tragic hero of the poem largely originates with Blake's contention, and that in fact "Milton could not have shared ... [that] admiration." Rather Lewis argues that Milton couldn't help but make Satan the most interesting character—since Satan is always the most interesting character to fallen and depraved humans (which is all of us)—but that in and of itself doesn't prove any authorial admiration for the figure. To the contrary, it demonstrates what's so insidious about Lucifer. Critic Stanley Fish squared the circle between the positions of Blake and Lewis in his landmark 1967 study *Surprised by Sin: The Reader in Paradise Lost*, in which he argued that the poem itself enacts the psychological experience of the fall by using beautiful rhetoric to effectively trick the reader into sympathizing with Satan. Milton thus demonstrates to his audience just how captivating and powerful original sin is. "*Paradise Lost* is a poem about how its readers came to be the way they are," argues Fish, so that its method "is to provoke in its readers wayward responses ... [so that] the reader is brought to a better understanding of his sinful nature and is encouraged to participate in his own reformation."

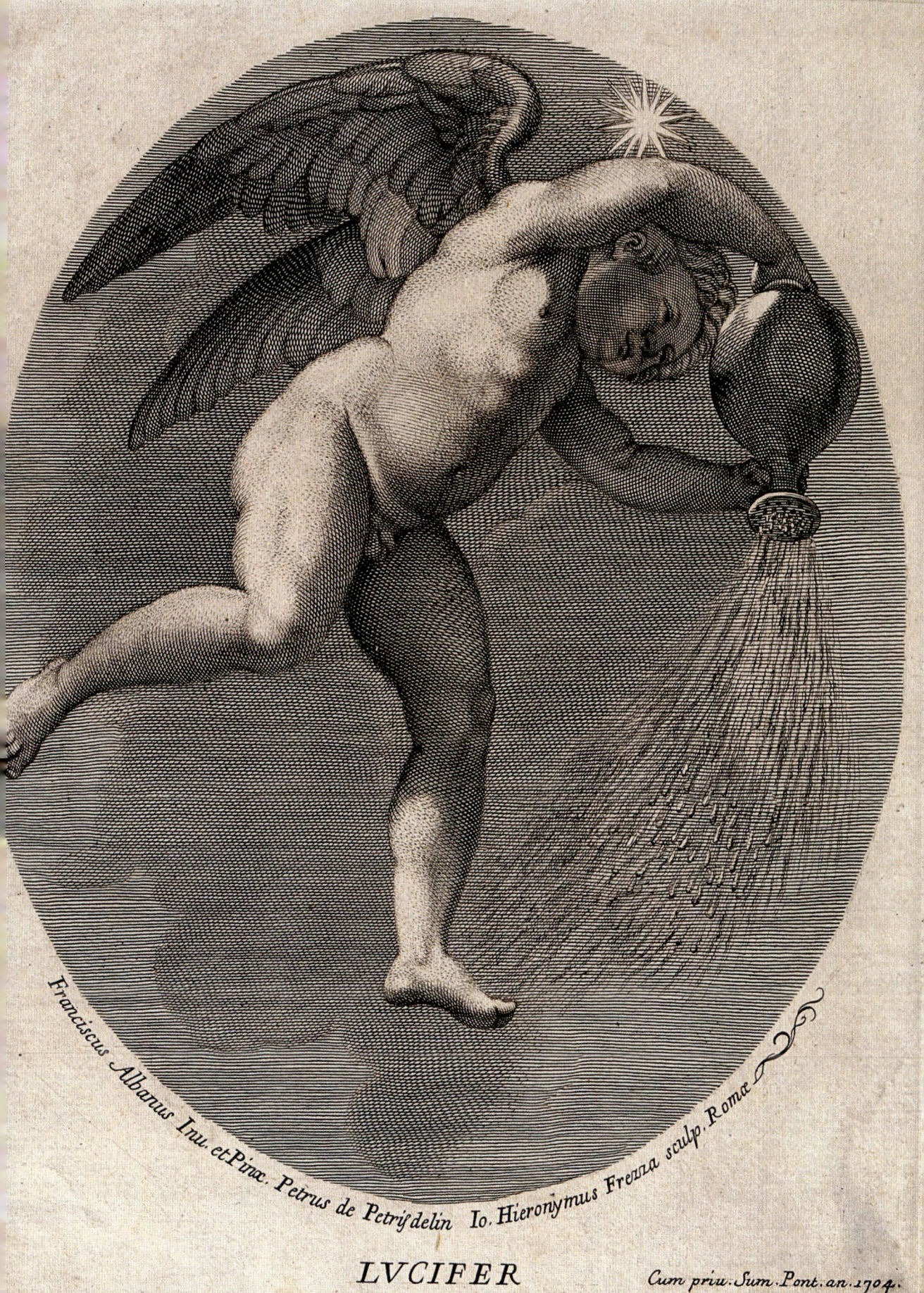

Franciscus Albanus Inu. et Pinx. Petrus de Petris delin Io. Hieronymus Frezza sculp. Romæ

LVCIFER

Cum priu. Sum. Pont. an. 1704.

All of this is crucial in understanding how the Enlightenment could be seen as an Age of Lucifer, for regardless of one's interpretive allegiances concerning *Paradise Lost*, its most fascinating character is still arguably a sui generis creation. Milton doesn't shy away from the bestial in his portrayal of Satan, particularly in the later books of the poem, and yet his fallen angel unmistakably has a heroic countenance. As a reader, whether you're of the Devil's party or not, it still must be admitted that Milton's Lucifer has a bravery in his rebellion, a dignity in his obstinance, a gloriousness in his failure. Unprecedented, for in showing what makes Lucifer so evocative, wherever our sympathies may lay, *Paradise Lost* provides a unifying figure for sedition transformed from a vice into a virtue. The decapitation of Charles I eighteen years before Milton finished his poem speaks to the ways in which the previously unthinkable—the regicide of God's anointed—had been made palatable and necessary in this dawning era. What was once heresy, was now piety; what was once blasphemy, was now faith; what was once treason, was now patriotism. Examine Blake's 1808 illustrations for *Paradise Lost*, drafted at the opposite end of the Enlightenment from the composition of the poem on which the drawings were based. His print *Satan Arousing the Rebel Angels*, depicting the moment in Book I when Lucifer convinces his entourage as to the necessity of an assault on Eden, shows not a serpentine beast, but rather a hard-bodied, toned, beautiful man in a contrapposto stance with arms held aloft and an Apollonian cascade of blond locks. There is more of Prometheus than Satan in this Lucifer.

How aware Milton was of such heroism is a question for biographers and psychologists; the reality is that *Paradise Lost*'s Lucifer would be incomprehensible to readers in previous centuries, and that he's arguably the animus of an era in which tradition was thrown asunder and the archaic orders were toppled in favor of a brave new world. He is the exemplar of two centuries of revolution, when monarchs weren't just replaced, but the throne abolished, where the system wasn't tweaked, but smashed. For good and ill, Lucifer is thus the spirit we see in the machinations of Oliver Cromwell's government, he is the angel behind Thomas Jefferson and George Washington, and the muse of Robespierre. He was at Putney in 1649, in Philadelphia during 1776, and Paris in 1789; he strode past the scaffold at Whitehall, the surrender at Yorktown, and the eighth arrondissement during the Reign of Terror. Such an appraisal is offered in the spirit of a studied neutrality, venturing neither celebration nor condemnation, only that if the purpose of revolution was to "Turn the World Upside Down," as one broadsheet ballad printed during the English Civil War had it, then Lucifer was clearly of this era, the first in which popular rebellion need not be counted as impious. Lucifer as avatar of Enlightenment is implied in his very name, the Morning Star, the Light Bearer, whom Milton said was "from Heav'n/(So call him, brighter once amidst the host/Of angels, than that star the stars among)/Fell with his flaming legions through the deep/Into this place."

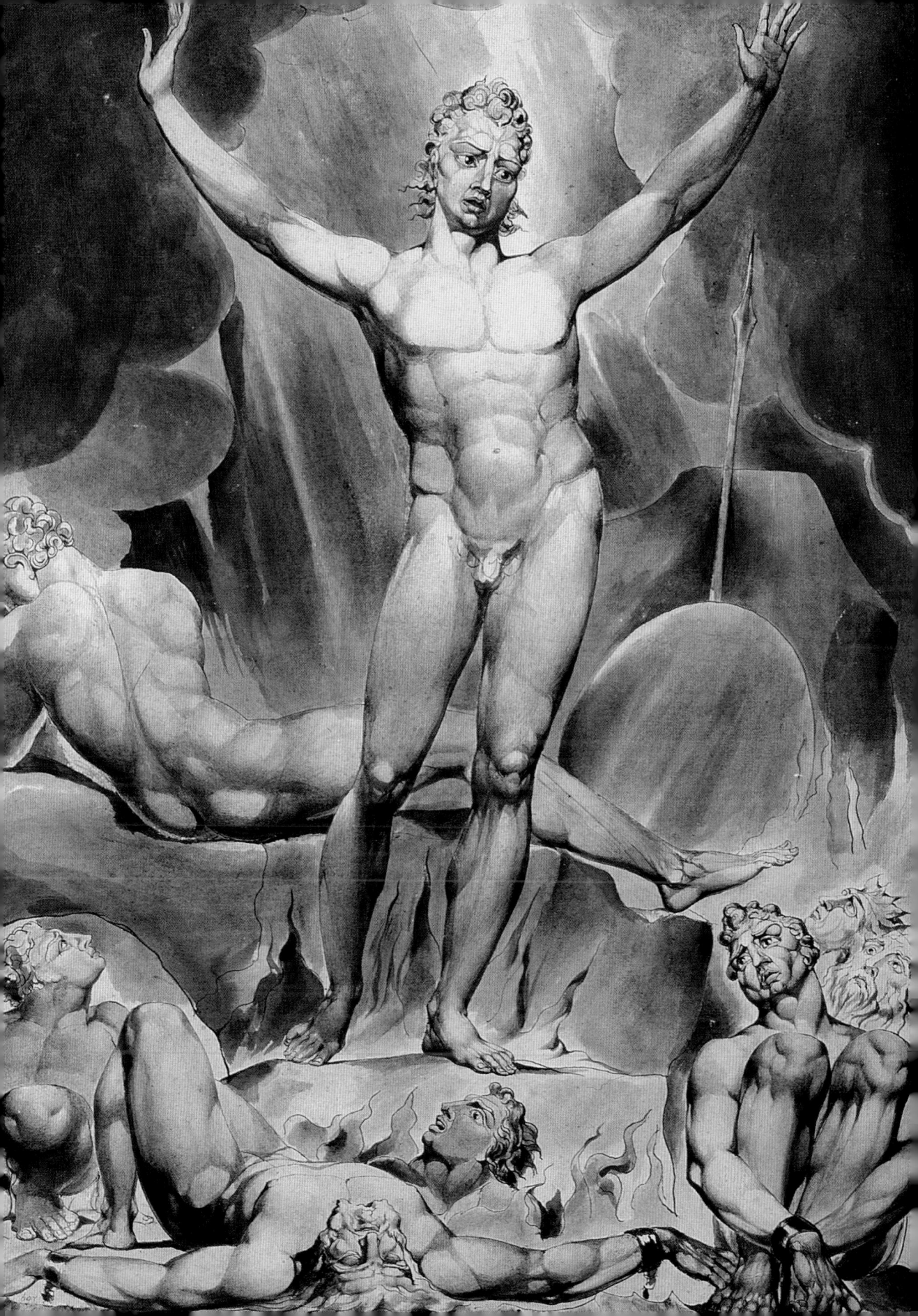

JOHN MILTON'S DEMONS

John Milton lived as a disgraced man by the time he had finished composing and had published his epic poem *Paradise Lost* in 1667. A scholar and poet of uncommon erudition, Milton was a political radical who'd written in favor of free speech and regicide, and had served in the administration of Lord Protector Oliver Cromwell in the years of Interregnum after Britain had concluded her civil wars. With the Restoration of Charles II, son of the executed king whose death Milton had defended, the writer lived in danger of his life, only spared from punishment through the intercession of his friend and well-connected fellow poet Andrew Marvell. Milton's political life had long been concerned with questions of rebellion, of subversion against an unjust king, and of the powerful cacophony of voices that exist in disunion; themes congruent with *Paradise Lost*, where the rebel angel Lucifer thunders that it is "Better to reign in Hell than serve in Heaven."

After Lucifer's expulsion from heaven, he and his generals are forced to regroup in hell, where they establish their own infernal commonwealth. Perhaps the last of the true Renaissance men, Milton was conversant in dozens of languages and was credibly read in the entirety of European culture to that time. *Paradise Lost* reflects his learning and his respect for knowledge, with Lucifer's claim that the "mind is its own place, and in itself can make a heaven of hell, a hell of heaven," a creed that can be interpreted ambiguously, one more bit of evidence in the scholarly debate as to where Milton's true sympathies lay, and which has raged for more than three centuries. In Lucifer's diabolical republic there are a host of fellow demons who act as generals and lieutenants in the new order that they are constructing, a Parliament of All Demons or "Pandemonium." Drawing from the tradition that interpreted ancient deities as being demons in disguise, Milton used his philological expertise to collect a compendium of demons, an irresistible subject for illustrators since the seventeenth century.

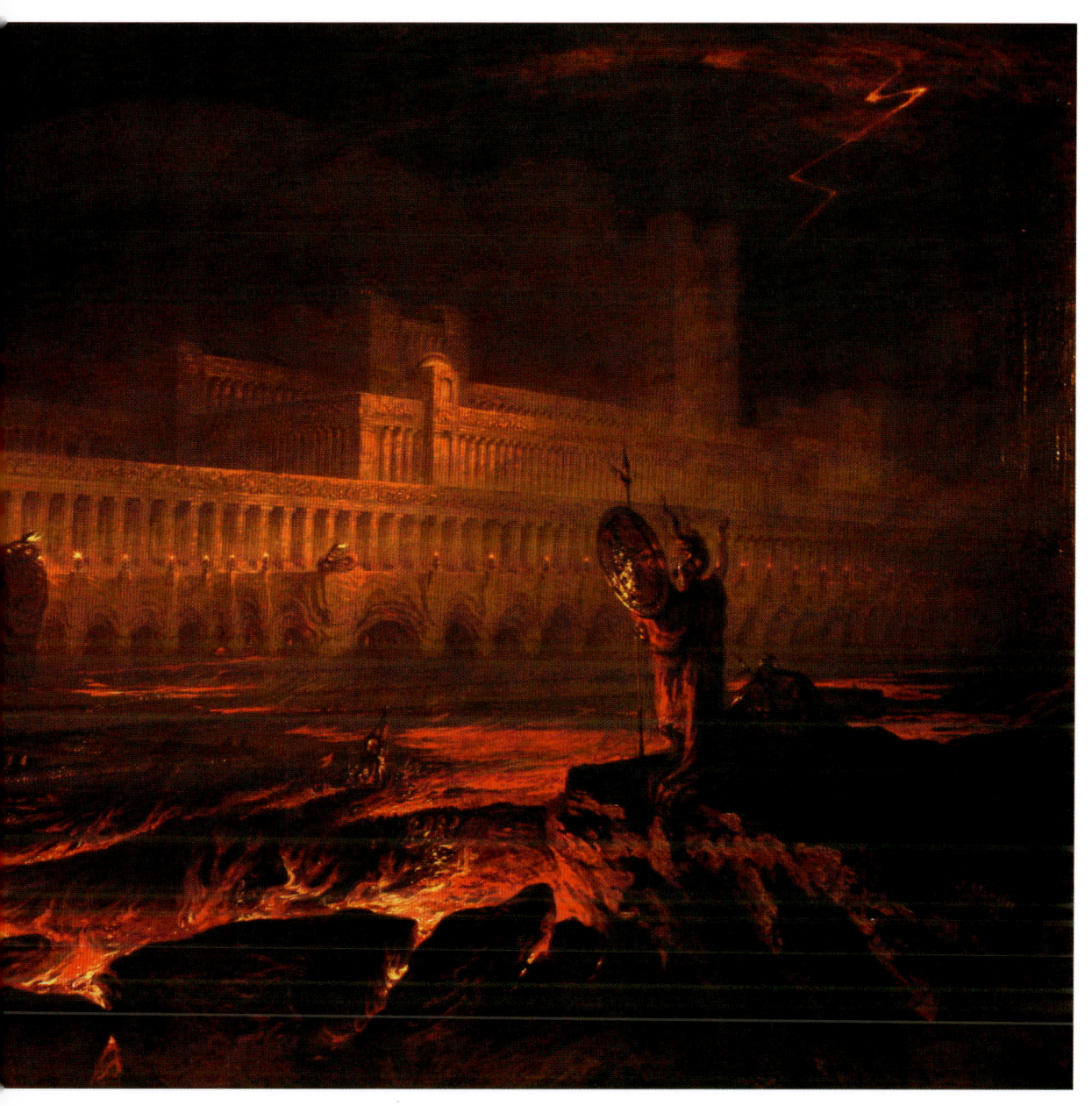

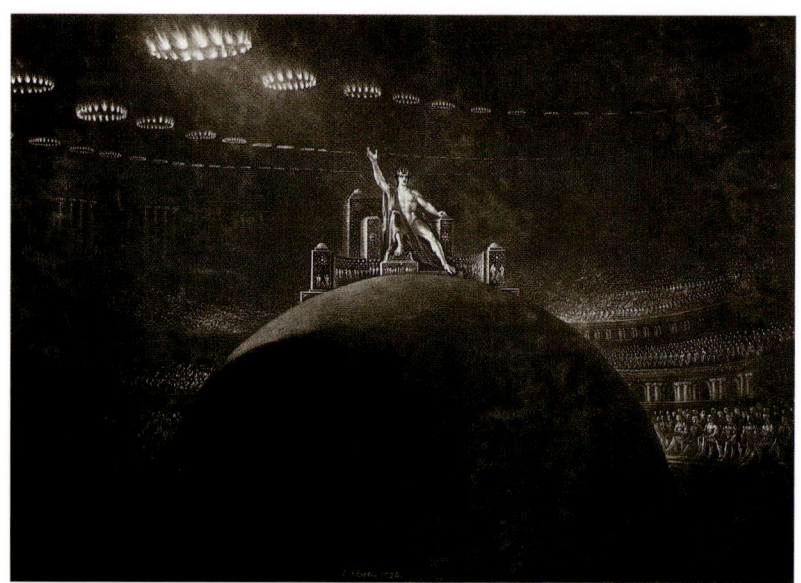

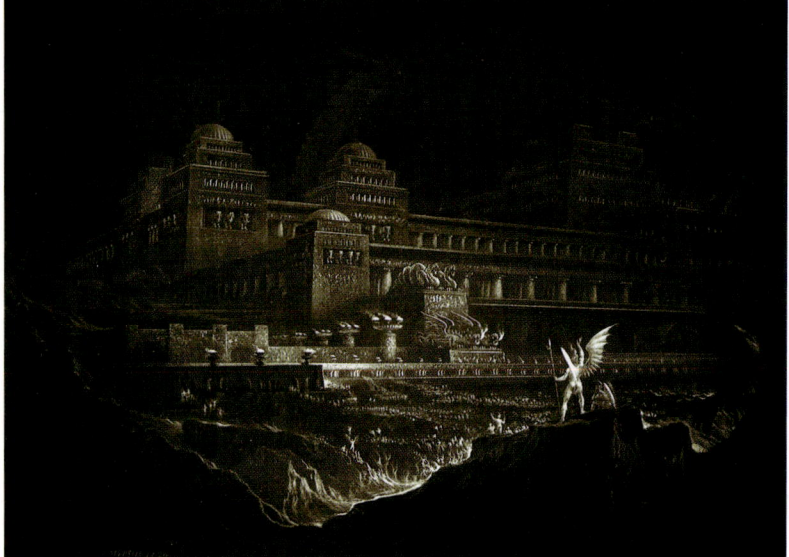

Martin had imagined Pandemonium earlier, in his engraving Satan Presiding at the Infernal Council, *done as part of a series of commissioned mezzotint made between 1823 and 1827. This rendering conveys the full enormity and scope of Pandemonium, with Lucifer sitting on a throne that appears to be situated on a massive sphere, an indication of his designs upon the newly created earth, while throngs of demons fill the seats of the amphitheater beyond.*

Martin's Pandemonium in the earlier series of engravings looks more Babylonian than gothic, with a winged Satan addressing his legions. "Built like a Temple, where Pilasters round/Were set, and Doric pillars overlaid/With Golden Architrave; nor did there want/Cornice or Freeze, with bossy Sculptures grav'n,/The Roof was fretted Gold. Not Babilon,/Nor great Alcairo such magnificence/Equal'd in all thir glories, to inshrine/Belus or Serapis thir God, or seat/Thir Kings, when Ægypt with Assyria strove/In wealth and luxurie."

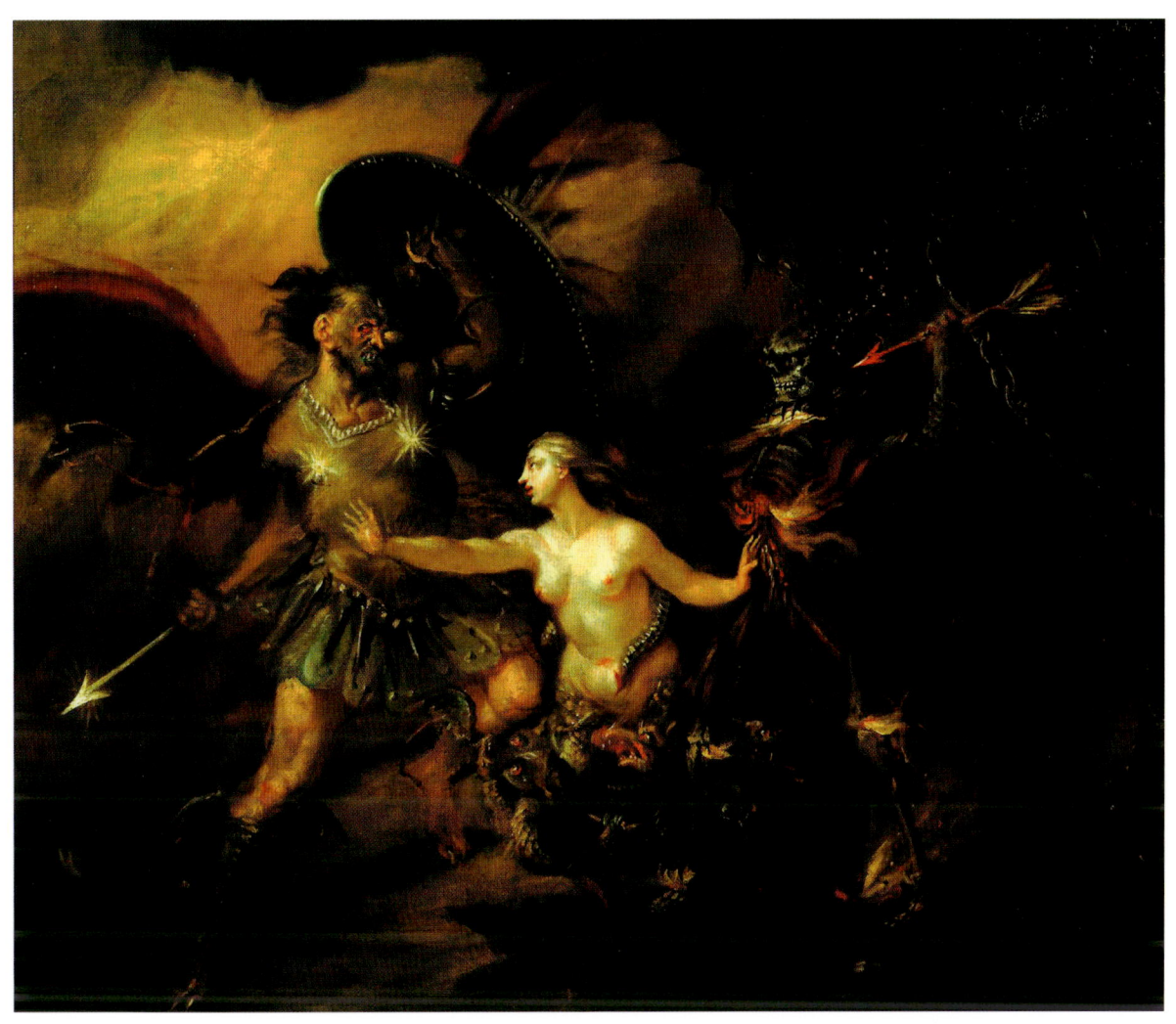

Hogarth dramatizes a scene from Book II of Paradise Lost *in his painting* Satan, Sin and Death *held at the Tate Britain in London. In addition to inventing his own novel cosmologies and theologies, Milton also deployed an idiosyncratic sense of the mythopoeic, writing that Sin was the actual daughter of Satan, and Death is the result of an incestuous union between father and daughter, while Chaos was an indeterminate, eternal, liminal zone between hell and earth answerable to neither God nor the Devil. Such a mythology explains Death as the result of an unnatural coupling between the chief demon and the Sin which he propagates; on the left is Lucifer and his daughter/lover, the former confronting his son Death, who appears as a dark, flaming skeleton. "The other Shape," writes Milton, "If shape it might be called that shape had none/Distinguishable in member, joint, or limb;/ Or substance might be called that shadow seemed,/For each seemed either— back it stood as Night,/Fierce as ten Furies, terrible as Hell,/And shook a dreadful dart: what seemed his head/The likeness of a kingly crown had on."*

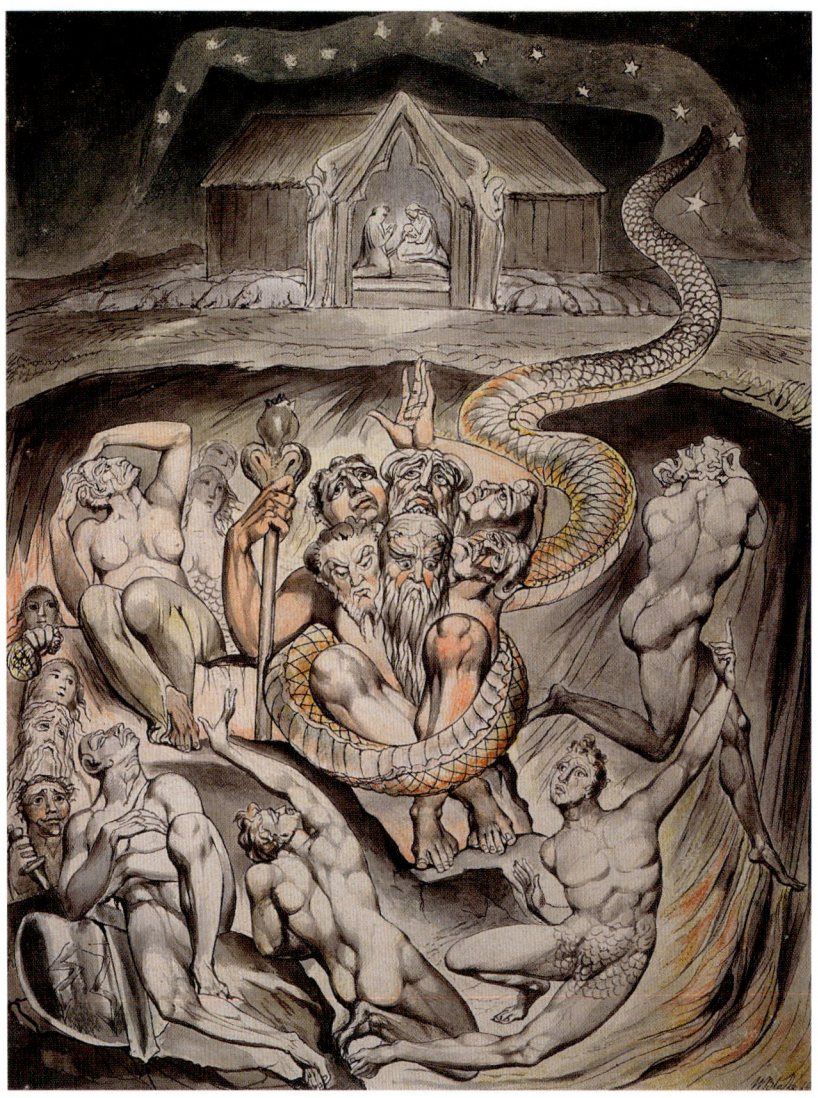

Milton's juvenilia, the 1629 poem "On the Morning of Christ's Nativity," was the subject of this 1809 watercolor by Blake entitled The Old Dragon, *now housed at the Whitworth Art Gallery in Manchester, United Kingdom. As per the title, "On the Morning of Christ's Nativity" recounts the events of the nativity (the Holy Family in the manger is depicted at the top) while also enumerating the various demons that masqueraded as pagan gods and were expelled from power upon the Messiah's birth. "And then at last our bliss," writes Milton in the scene that Blake has illustrated, "Full and perfect is,/But now begins;/far from this happy day/Th'old Dragon under ground/In straiter limits bound,/Not half so far casts his usurped sway,/And wrath to see his Kingdom fail,/Swindges the scaly Horrour of his foulded tail." Several of those demons are rendered in the bottom part of the painting, with many of those beings making appearances in* Paradise Lost *as well. According to independent researcher David McIrvine, who makes an argument about the identities of these figures, going from left to right the outer ring of demons includes Bellus who is looking upward at the goddess Ashtaroth, a serpentine creature (perhaps Leviathan), the Phoenician sea-god Dagon (on lower right with scaley crotch), and the Mesopotamian shepherd-god Thammuz. Of the multiheaded beast in the center, from left to right starting with the central figure; there is the Egyptian syncretic god Serapis, Beelzebub, the Carthaginian god Baal Hammon, Mammon, Asmodeus, and the Syrian god Rimmon.*

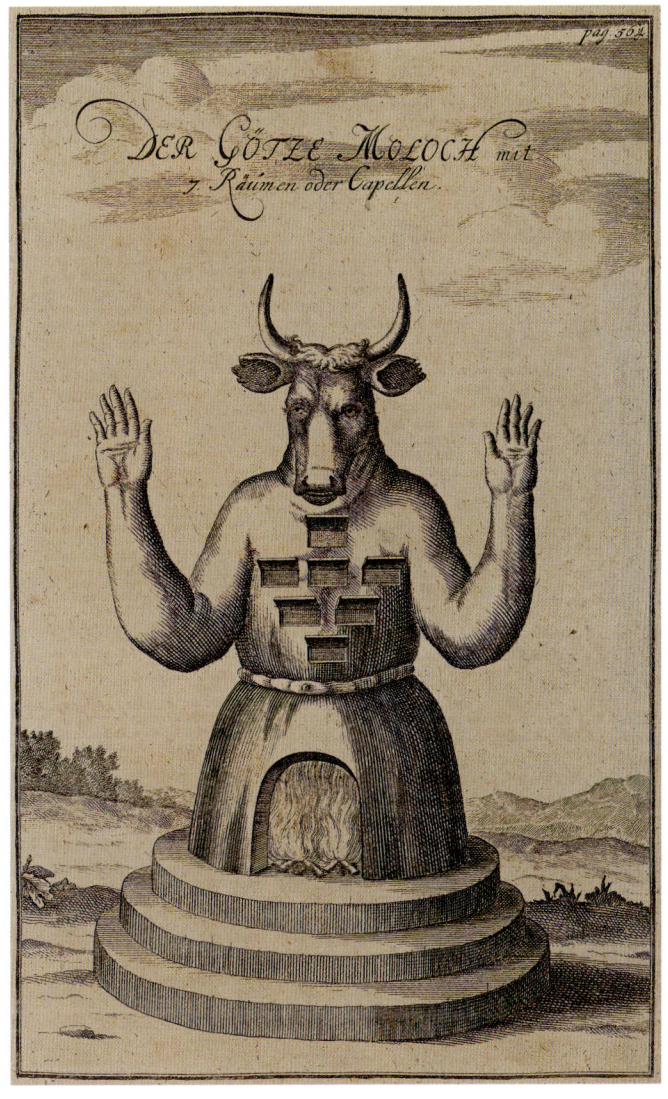

The ancient Carthaginian god Moloch had long figured in both Jewish and Christian accounts as a fearsome demon to whom children were sacrificed. The twelfth-century Talmudic commentator Rashi described how the Carthaginians and Phoenicians would build a statue of the bull-headed Moloch "made of brass; and they heated him from his lower parts; and his hands being stretched out, and made hot, they put the child between his hands, and it was burnt; when it vehemently cried out; but the priests beat a drum, that the father might not hear the voice of his son, and his heart might not be moved." This illustration from Johann Lund's posthumously published Die Alten Jüdischen Heiligthümer *(1711) reflects the tradition which held that statues of Moloch had multiple internal sections in which animals, and children, would be held for immolation. The horror of pagan sacrifice for a demonic deity is emphatically stated by Milton as he describes Moloch as "horrid King besmear'd with blood/Of human sacrifice, and parents tears."*

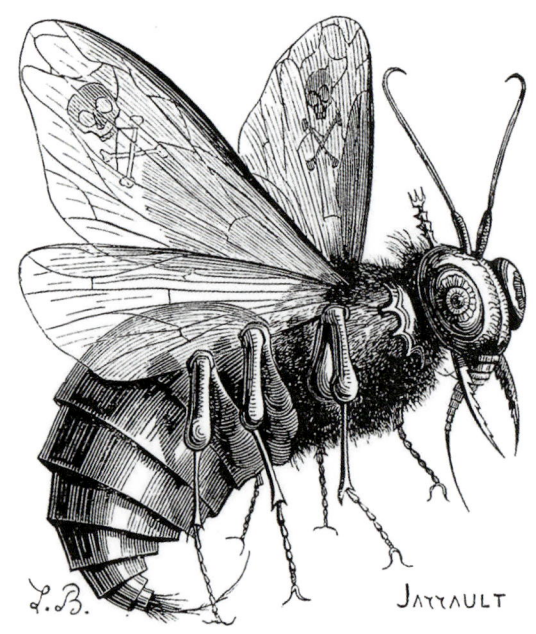

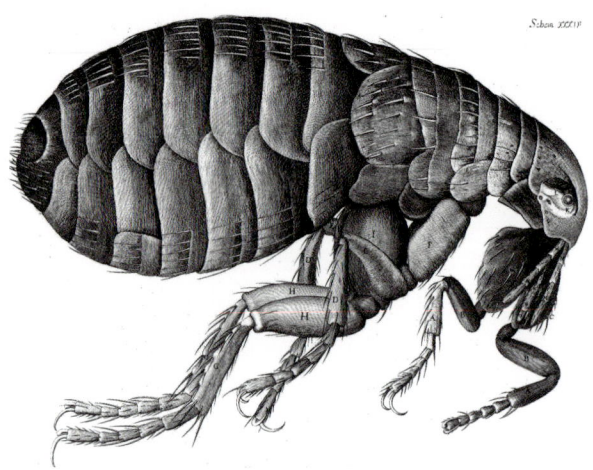

In Paradise Lost, *Beelzebub, whose name from Hebrew translated as "Lord of the Flies," is Lucifer's trusted second lieutenant, confident enough to criticize the assembled in Pandemonium that he must "advise if this be worth/Attempting, or to sit in darkness here/Hatching vain empires." Milton doesn't depict Beelzebub as the demon often is shown, as a grotesque, insect-like monstrosity, which Louis Le Breton does in his illustration for Collin de Plancy's* Dictionnaire Infernal *(1863). Observe the similarities to this magnified illustration of a flea from the Dutch scientist Antonie van Leeuwenhoek's pioneering work with a microscope, where in 1674 he for the first time supplied scientific detail on "this minute and despised creature," as the "demons" of science provided as much wonder and horror of those in theology.*

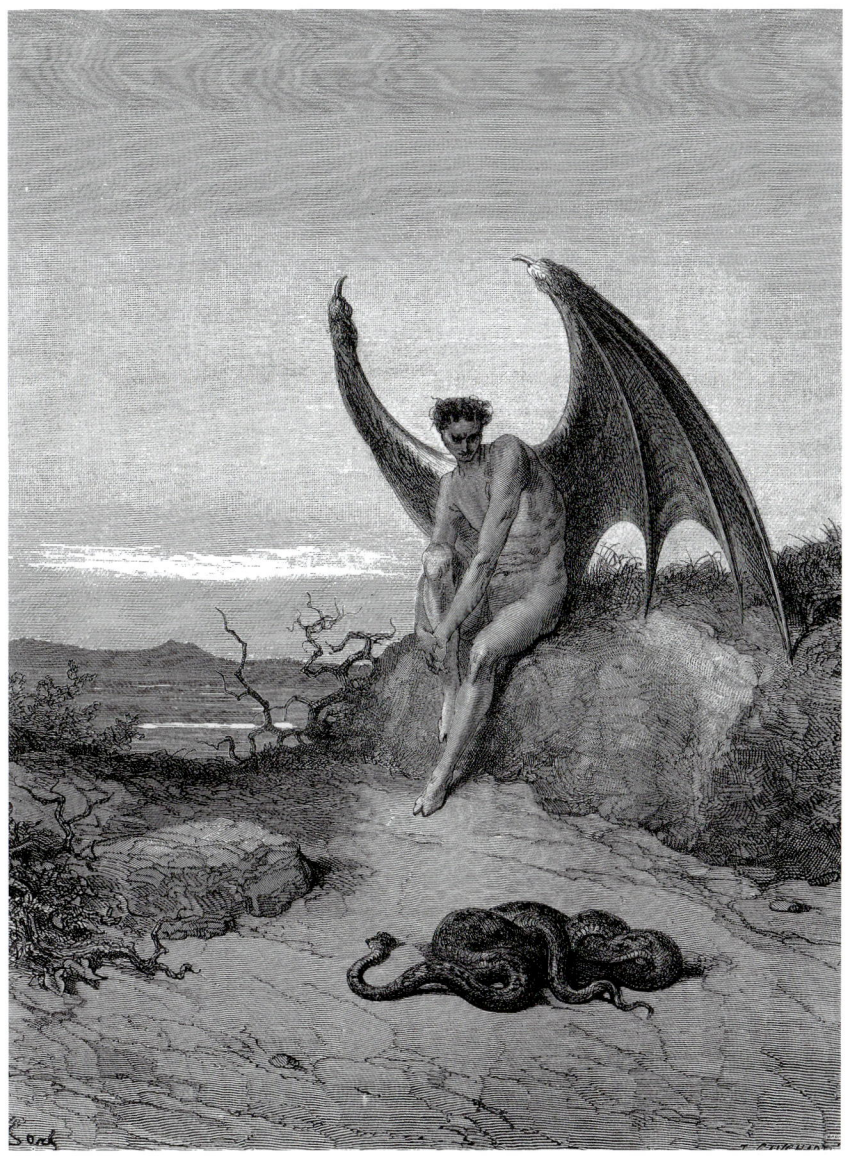

French engraver Gustave Doré was one of the most arresting illustrators of Milton's vision, supplying plates for editions of Paradise Lost *such as this one from 1866. Doré's depiction of the scene from Book IX of the poem whereby Lucifer held "His midnight search, where soonest he might finde/The serpent: him fast sleeping soon he found" owes much to the Romantic tradition of seeing the rebel angel's tale as fundamentally tragic, and the character himself as heroic. In Doré's imagination it's only the grotesque bat wings that mar the otherwise beautiful Lucifer, posing the eternal question of where Milton's dramatic sympathies lay.*

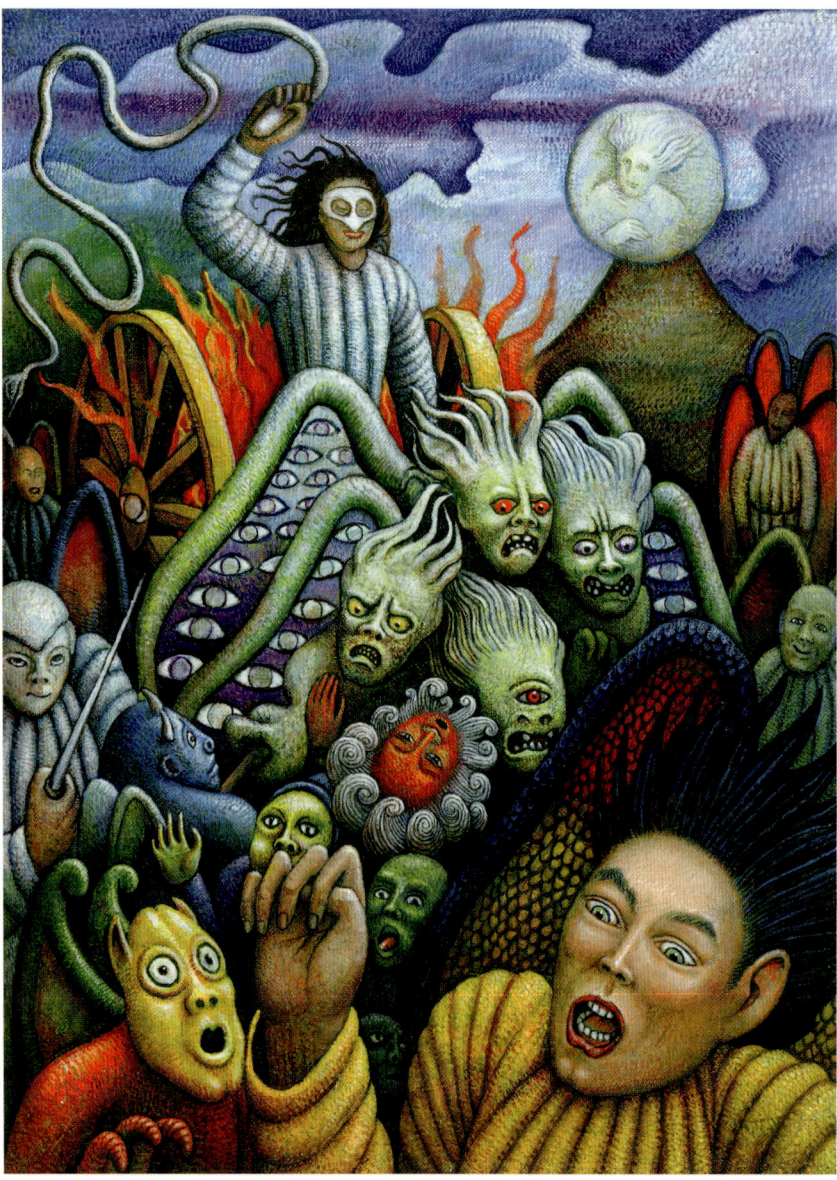

Contemporary artist Terrance Lindall reimagined Paradise Lost for the twentieth century in a series of 1983 illustrations. An illustrator for publishers like Marvel Comics, some of Lindall's Miltonic images appeared originally in the genre magazine Heavy Metal, which focuses on science fiction, steampunk, fantasy, and dark erotica. Several of Lindall's illustrations, which owe much to visionary and outsider art, were featured in a 2008 exhibit for the quadricentennial of Milton's birth held at the Williamsburg Art and Historical Center in Brooklyn, New York. The illustrations above respectively depict the war in heaven, Lucifer's fall, and a fallen angel transformed into a demon, the kiln within his belly possibly indicating that this is Moloch.

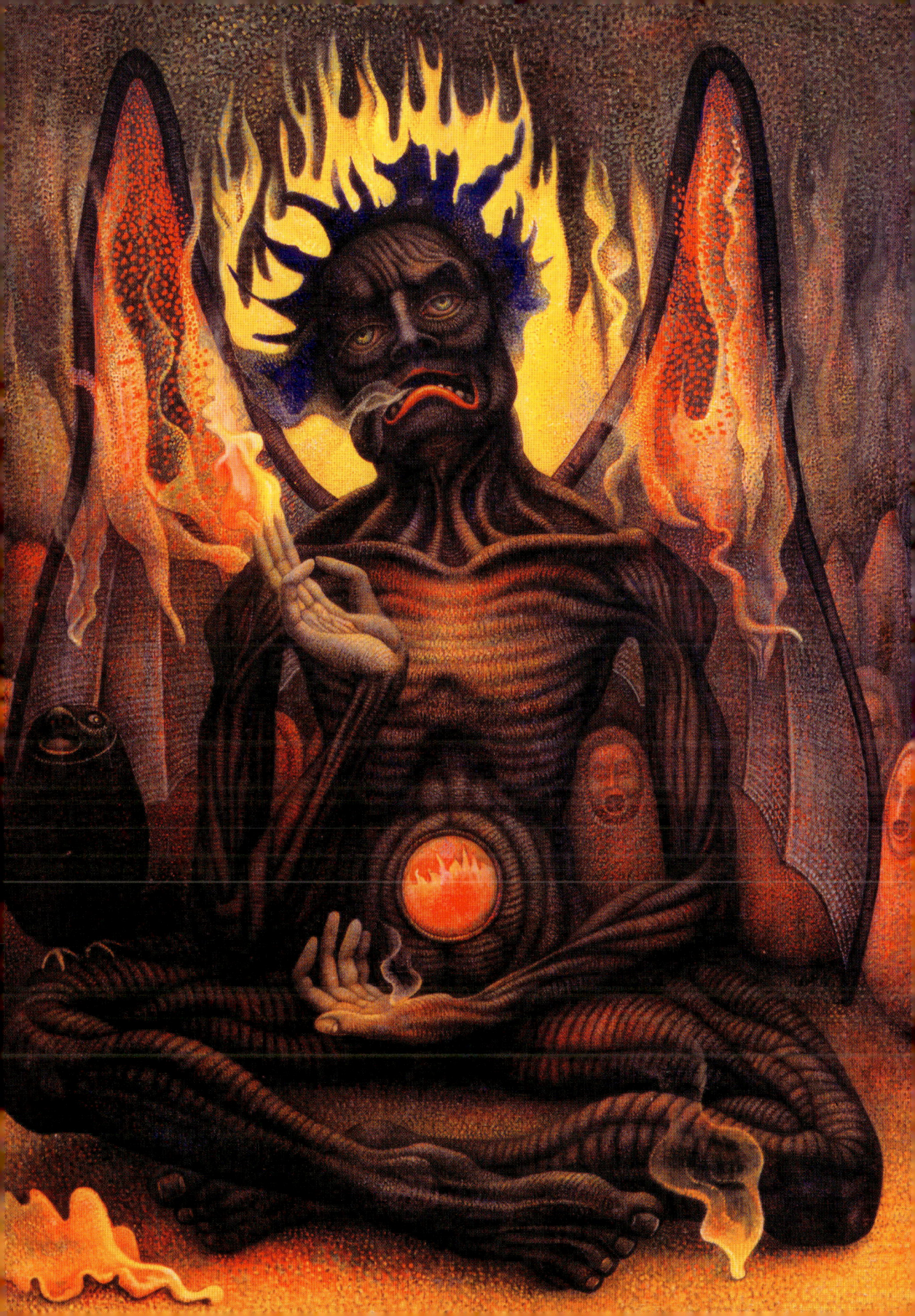

NOLI ME TANGERE

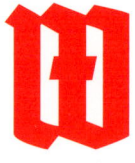hen the lushly colored and grotesquely illustrated *A Rare Summary of the Entire Magical Art by the Most Famous Masters of this Art* was produced in 1775, Wolfgang Amadeus Mozart had finished his Sonata in C, Captain James Cook had completed his circumnavigation of the globe, the chemist Joseph Priestley had presented on the discovery of oxygen before the Royal Society, Dr. Samuel Johnson had published an account of his travels through Scotland, and in Massachusetts the first shots of the American Revolution had erupted at Lexington and Concord. If those other events signaled the victories of Enlightenment in the arts, exploration, science, literature, and politics, then the anonymous German author of this strange manuscript had different concerns. *A Rare Summary*, the original of which is held by the Wellcome Library in London, combines kabbalistic, Rosicrucian, and hermetic symbolism in its intricate depictions of thirty-one monstrous denizens of hell.

Produced during an era of cheap print, *A Rare Summary* instead revels in its physicality; the manuscript is marked with ornamental illustrations in dark blues, organic greens, and lurid reds, the book's frontispiece announcing "Noli me Tangere"—"Touch me not"—the same declaration that the resurrected Christ made to Mary Magdalene upon their encounter in the garden on the first Easter Sunday. By putting the words of Christ into the "mouth" of the book, the author associates the volume with things unseen, language unspoken, realms invisible. There is a sense (in this age of Enlightenment where the tendency is to reduce even the soul to the mechanical) that this book is meant to endow an inert volume with vitality, with consciousness. If Christ's injunction was about the innate danger in experiencing the divine unprepared, then *A Rare Summary*'s frontispiece has an opposite but equivalent warning about the diabolical, for the volume declares itself as a book capable of mustering forth hidden and evil things.

What's contained therein is a listing of the demonic hierarchy between four kings (Lucifer, Satan, Leviathan, and Belial), eight dukes (Astaroth, Magoth, Asmodai, Belzebub, Oriens, Baimon, Aritton, and Amaimon), and twelve subjects (Morech, Nabhi, Tirama, Nudaton, Zagrion, Carufur, Rigalon, Zugula, Ramaison, Kilik, Sumuran, and Aloggiell). Drawing largely from the much earlier *Book of Abramelin*, the volume includes not just illustrations of the demonic hierarchy, but also instructions on how to perform various conjurations, particularly through the use of an inscribed "magic circle" in which the mage must stand while having various alchemical symbols painted on their body and on the ground. What's most arresting in *A Rare Summary* are the horrific, bizarre, and disturbing images. Possibly derived from a personal visual vocabulary of the author, perhaps culled from the unconscious realm of nightmares, the images are often violent and sexual to a degree that's shocking even today, while prefiguring the avant-garde art of the twentieth century, from dadaism to surrealism. The result is a consummately irrational book written in the midst of a supposed Age of Reason.

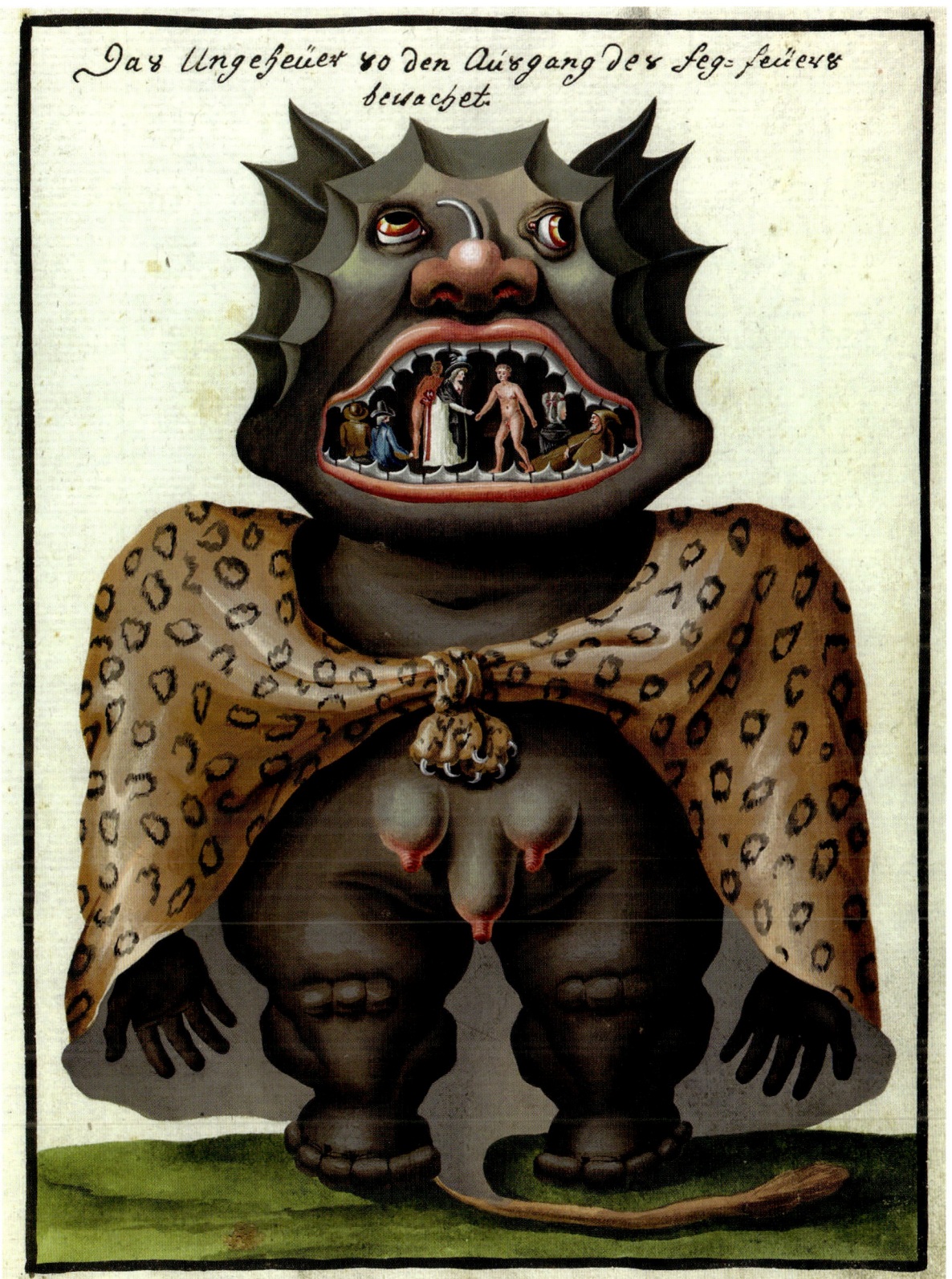

Das Ungeheuer so den Ausgang des seg-feuers
bewachet.

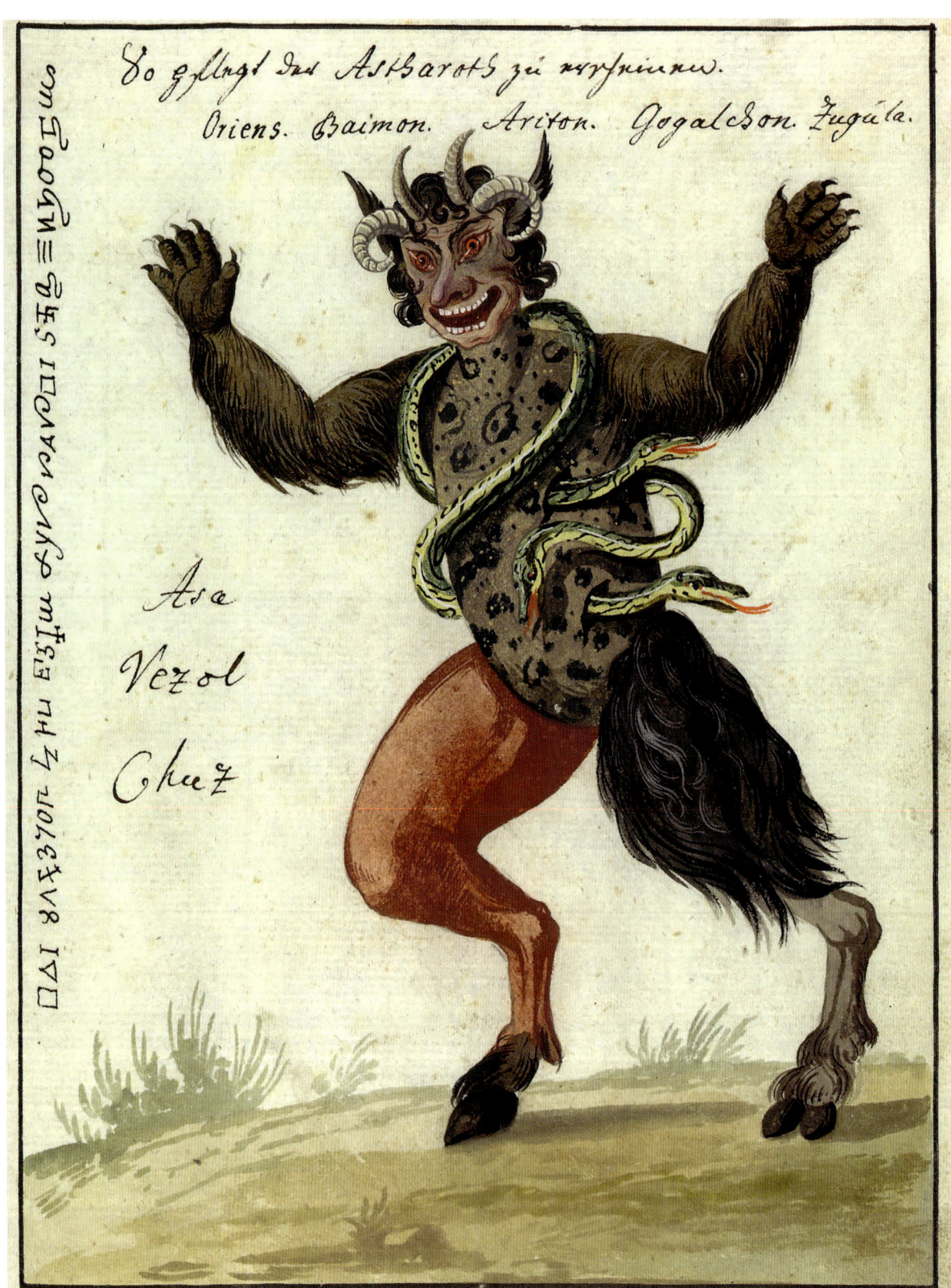

So gfellagt das Astbaroth zu verspünnu.

Oriens. Baimon.   Ariton. Gogaledon. Zugula.

Asa

Vezol

Chez

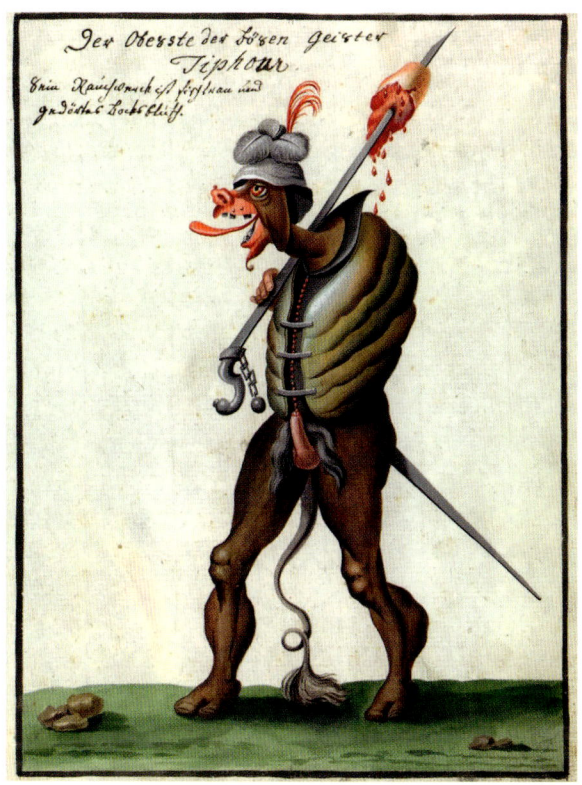

Der Oberste der bösen Geister
Tiphour

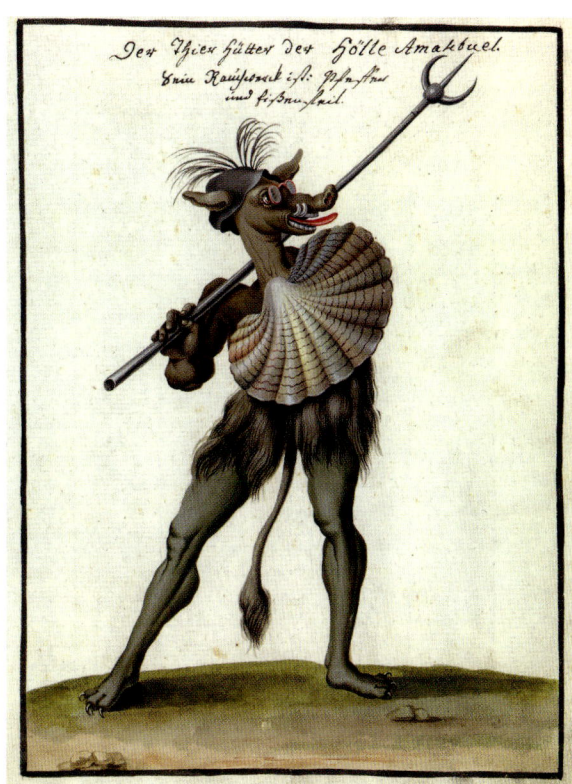

Der Thier hüter der Hölle Amaubuel.

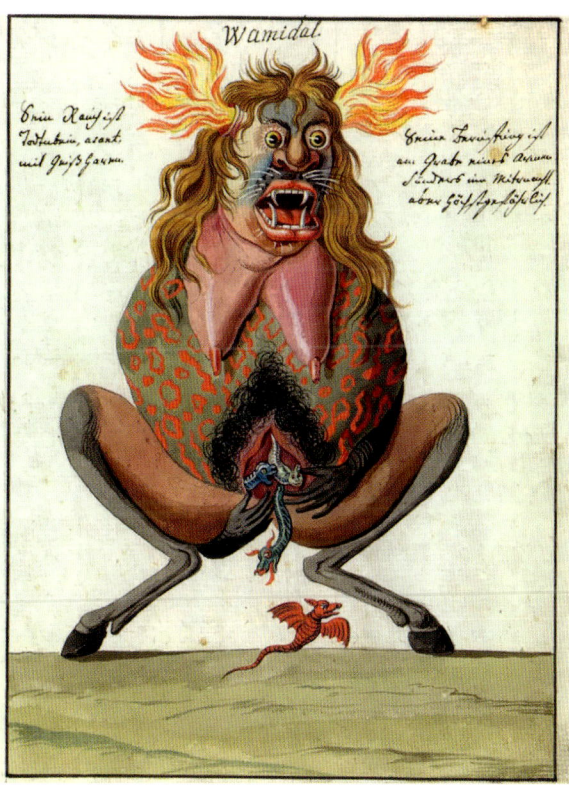

Wamidal

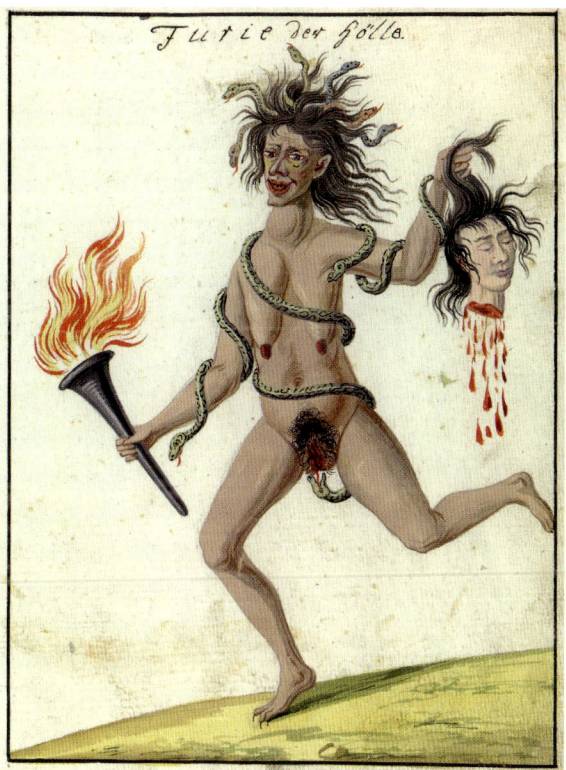

Furie der Hölle.

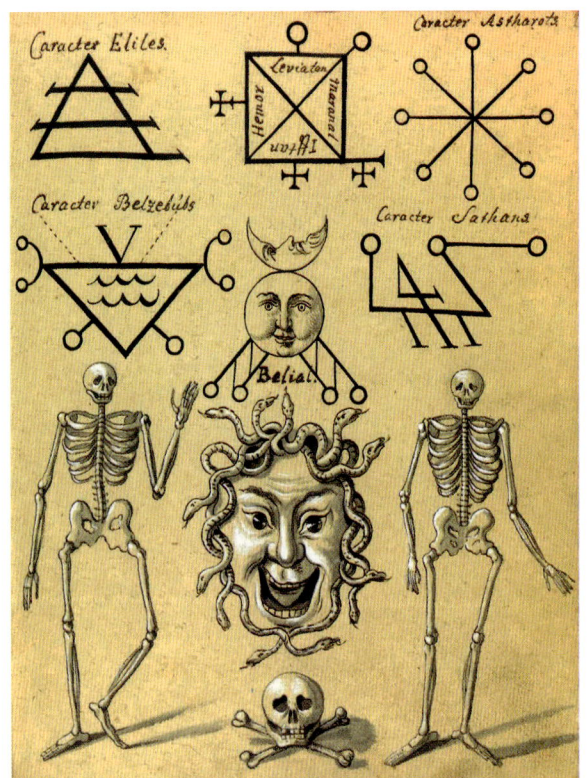

Caracter Eliles.

Caracter Astharoth.

Leviatan
Hemor   Maranai
Satan

Caracter Belzebuts.

Caracter Sathans.

Belial.

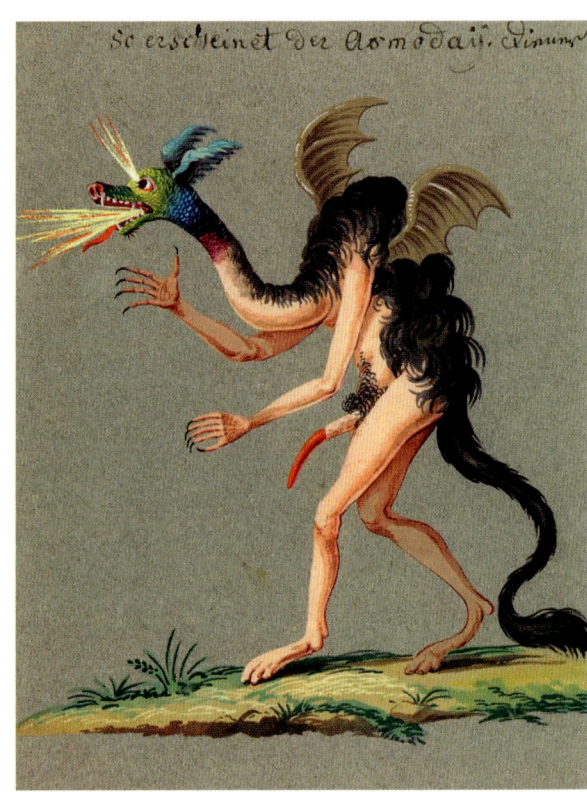

So erscheinet der Asmodaii. Dinum.

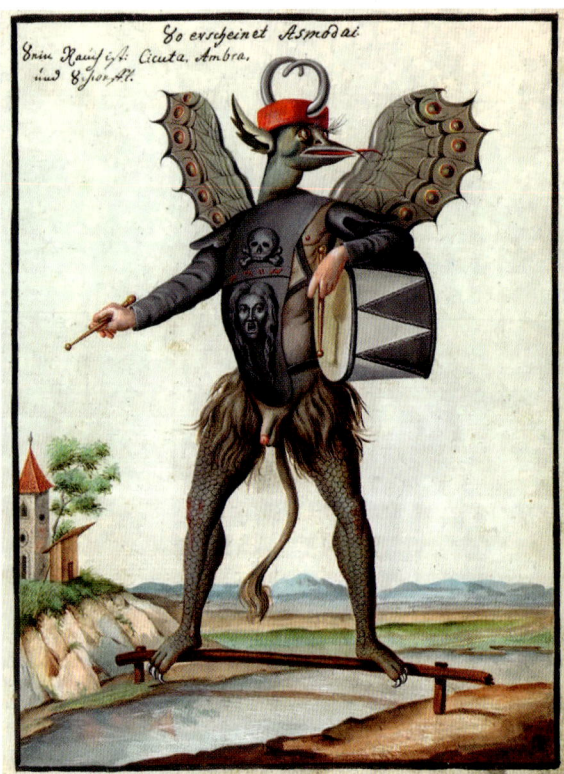

So erscheinet Asmodai.
Sein Rauch ist: Cicuta. Ambra.
und 8.per Al.

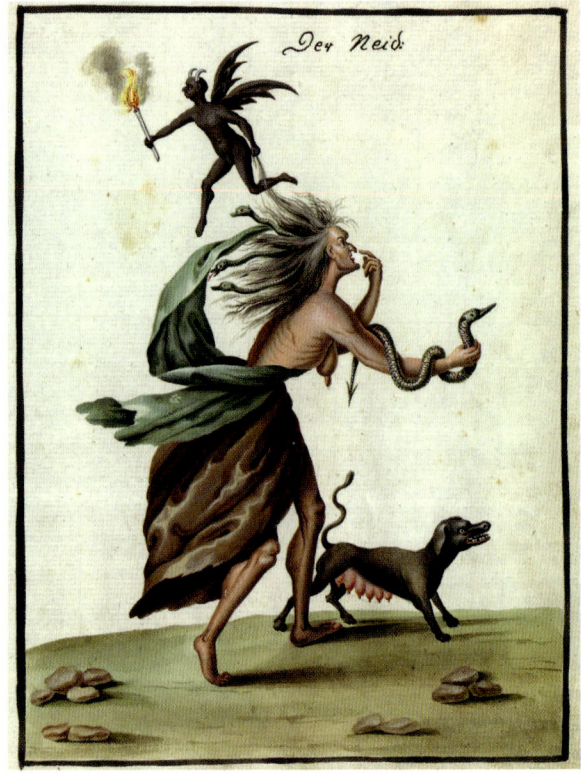

Der Neid.

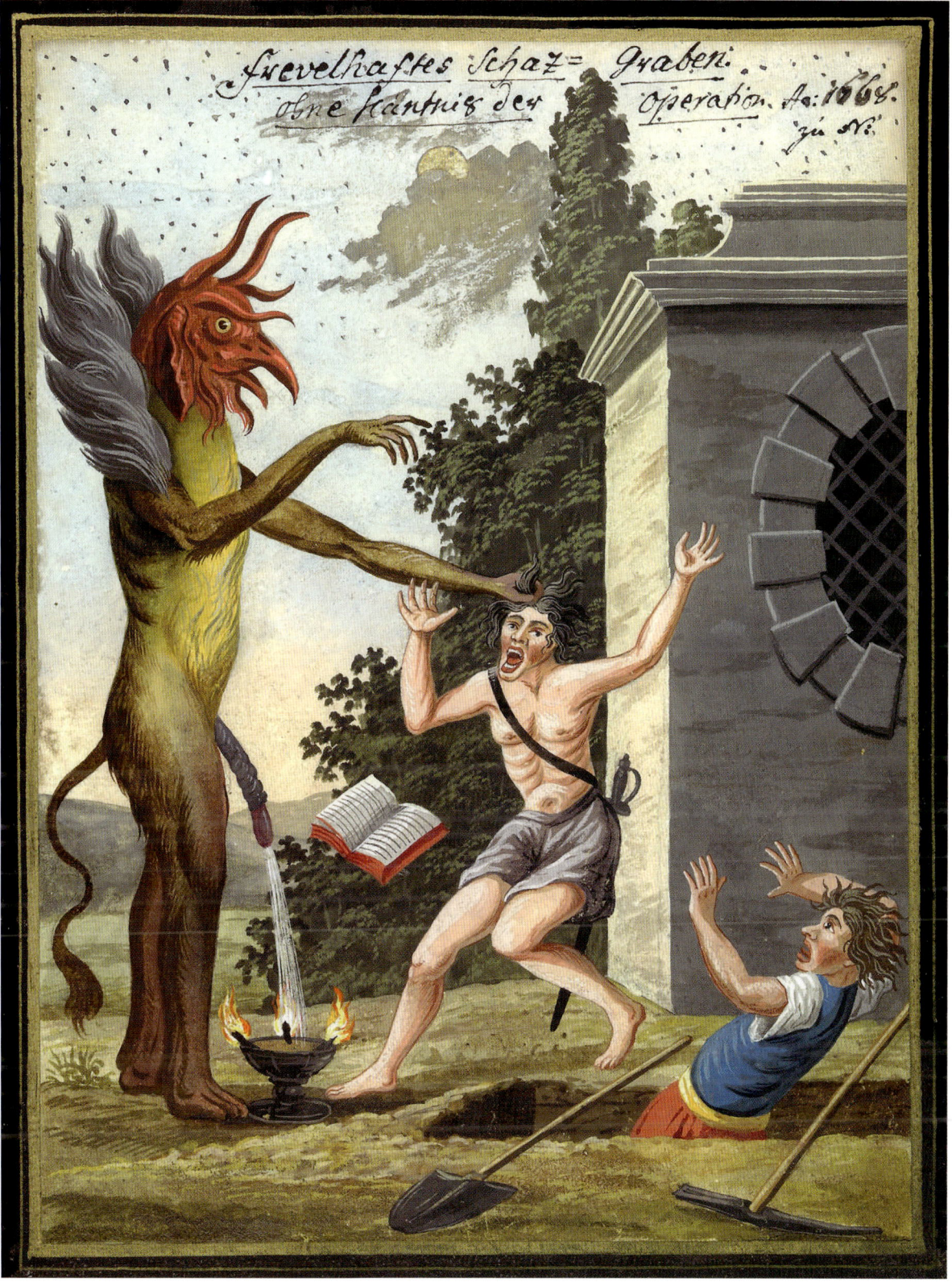

THE MASKED DEMON

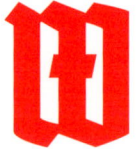hen the satirist, raconteur, and Enlightenment *philosophe* François-Marie Arouet, better known by his nom de plume Voltaire, was about to either merge with eternity or become vermiculated for the conqueror worms (your perspective on which depending on metaphysical inclinations), some unlucky Roman Catholic priest was tasked with administering the sacrament of extreme unction to the dying freethinker. As is the liturgy for those whom are receiving the last rites, the priest would have asked Voltaire, "Do you renounce Satan, and all his works?" Anecdotal legend has it that the learned and famed *philosophe* waggishly responded that "I see no reason to start making enemies right now," and then promptly died.

Impious though Voltaire's deathbed joke may have been, it should be read as more ironic than satanic, for the celebrated advocate of the Enlightenment's own religious beliefs (though they would have included a rejection of orthodoxy) were firmly deistic, holding to a belief in an abstract, impersonal, and rational Creator. In keeping with the anticlerical nature of his intellectual project, and that of the wider Enlightenment, Voltaire repudiated belief in the demonic as only so much medieval superstition, though pure atheism was too radical to countenance. More revolutionary thinkers anticipated a complete and total rejection of the divine, however, even while Voltaire held that atheism should never be discussed in front of the servants, lest they got it in their skulls that you might deserve to have a knife drawn across your sleeping throat. May of 1778 was when Voltaire went forward into that final slumber. Fourteen months later and in that same city the Bastille would be stormed.

Much historiographical debate has surrounded the individual intellectual possibility of atheism in early modernity. While the propensity to doubt is obviously a universal aspect of humanity's emotional inheritance, the specific conditions that match the philosophical designation of atheism would seem to be a relatively recent development. If we think of atheism as referring not just to doubt about the particulars concerning the divine, but the wholesale rejection of even the possibility, then it would seem that such a theological position was only in its very nascent beginnings during the eighteenth century. Writing about the Renaissance, the French historiographer Lucien Febvre argues in *The Problem of Unbelief in the Sixteenth Century: The Religion of Rabelais* that atheism as contemporary people mean it was impossible in the past, and that though the word existed back into antiquity (indeed Christians were counterintuitively accused by pagans as being atheists), it's more properly understood in that context as "a kind of obscenity meant to cause a shudder in the audience of the faithful."

Febvre's argument wasn't that personal doubts concerning the numinous couldn't exist, or that individuals couldn't deny scripture and faith (indeed belonging to one sect over the other demonstrates selective and targeted denials), but rather that the vocabulary of the transcendent so permeated premodern culture that even skepticism was marked by religion. "Every period mentally constructs its own universe," Febvre wrote, "It constructs it not only out of all the materials at its disposal, all the facts (true or false) that it has inherited or acquired, but out of its own gifts, its particular cleverness, its qualities, its talents, and its interests." Understood as such, the Renaissance authors whom Febvre considers couldn't be atheists in the sense that the word is defined today, yet by the Enlightenment there was an emergent discourse of skepticism, materialism, and anticlericalism that would combine into the full-throated atheism of the nineteenth century.

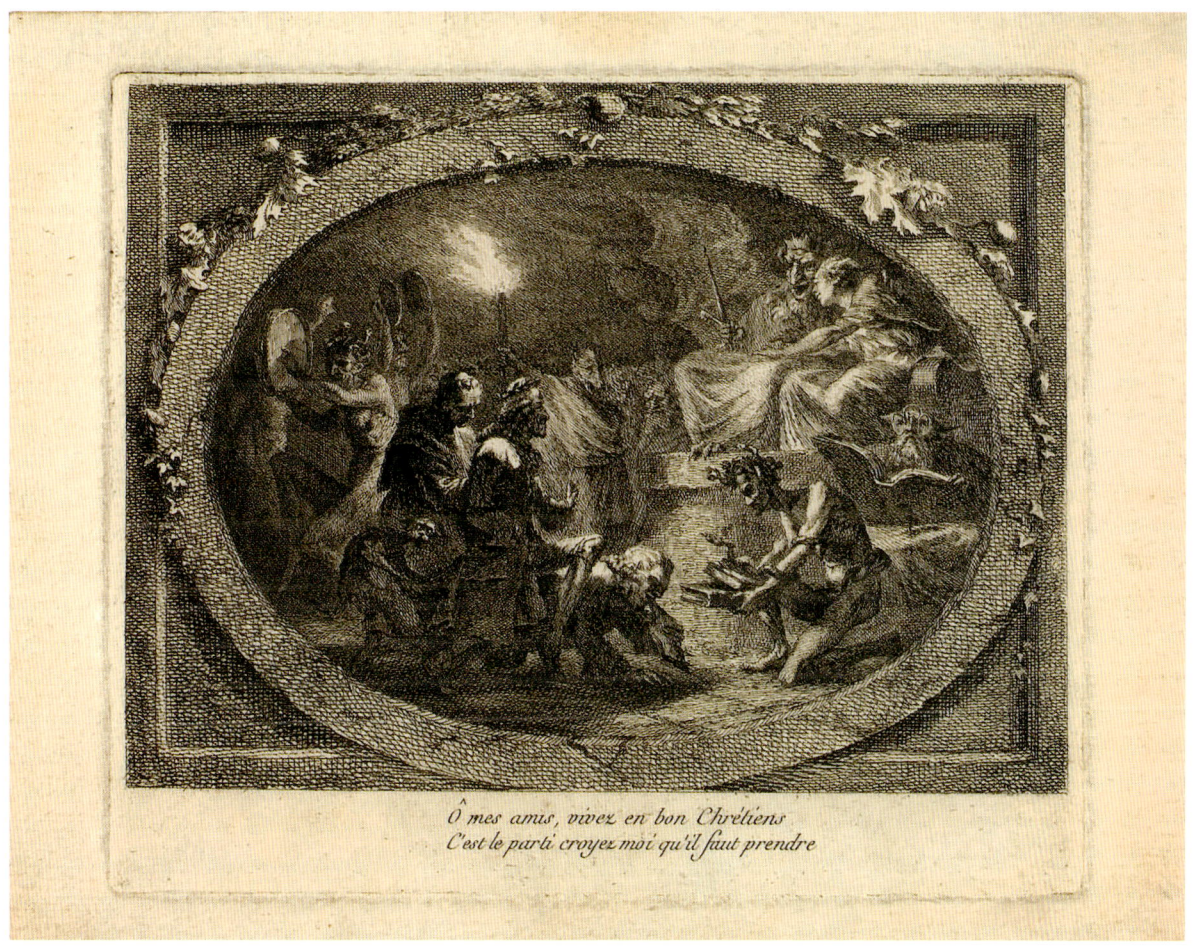

Ô mes amis, vivez en bon Chrétiens
C'est le parti croyez moi qu'il faut prendre

Theodor K. Rabb writes in *The Last Days of the Renaissance and the March to Modernity* that "There is no question that this unprecedented turning away from a reliance, *in the public sphere*, on the all-pervasive power of the supernatural meant that the new era that was coming into being was unlike any that had ever come before." Demonology would be the first aspect of the divine order to be challenged, and the result was arguably the emergence of a vociferous secularism throughout the Age of Reason and into the modern day. Jeffrey Burton Russell explains in *Mephistopheles: The Devil in the Modern World* that "By the 1660s and 1670s the notion that demons might be nothing more than symbols of human evil began to spread," though what could be argued is that the exorcism of demons necessarily meant the elimination of the angels, too. The reasons for this shift are legion, from the increased methodological skepticism of the scientific revolution to the disenchantments of the later Reformation, but arguably the horror of the witch craze may have convinced the majority of Europeans that traditional faith was infected with a deep malignancy. Suddenly the concept of "conjuration" was replaced with that of "hoax," so that "Over the next few decades legislation would gradually appear elsewhere in Europe reflecting this fundamental shift from magicians as diabolic criminals to magicians as frauds."

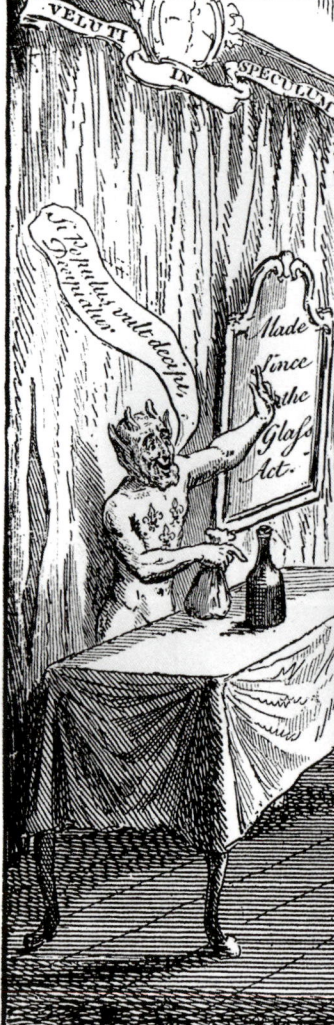

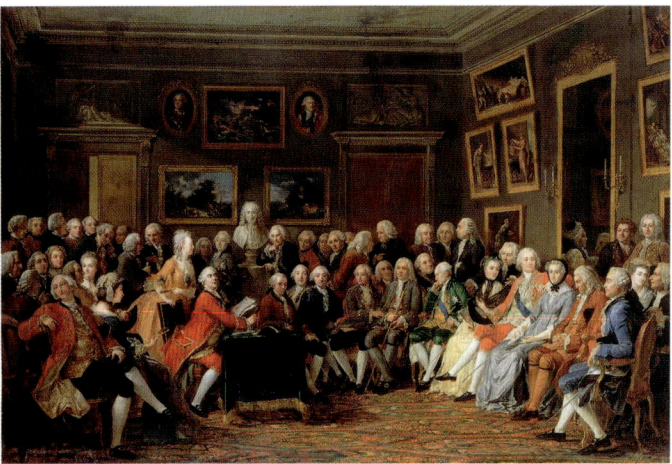

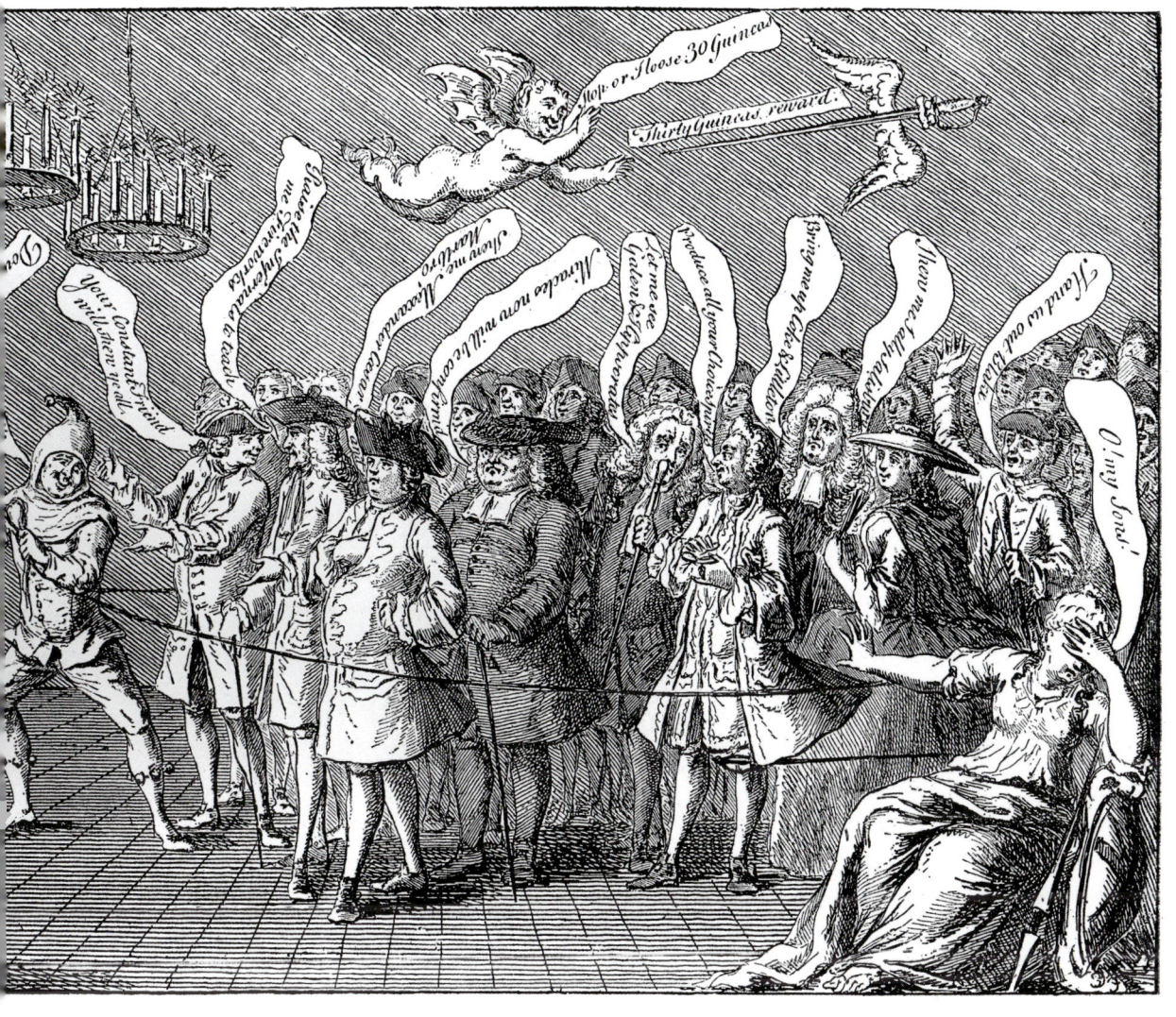

An anonymous 1749 satirical print entitled The Magician, or Bottle Cungerer, English Credulity; or, Ye're all Bottled, *held by the British Museum. The Bottle Conjuror, whose true identity is unknown, was an illusionist supposedly capable of shrinking himself down and disappearing into a wine bottle, with a contemporary advertisement claiming that this "bottle is placed on a table in the middle of the stage, and he (without any equivocation) goes into it in sight of all the spectators, and sings in it; during his stay in the bottle any person may handle it, and see plainly that it does not exceed a common tavern bottle." When the performer neglected to appear on his appointed night, the spectators in the Haymarket theater rioted and nearly destroyed the venue, and the credulity of the audience willing to shell out money for this hoax was the subject of derision among the printers of broadsheets. Regardless of who the Bottle Conjuror was, what's notable is that the magic act (even though not performed) wasn't regarded as supernatural, despite the appearance of the magician in this print appearing nothing so much like a horned demon.*

The eclipse of belief in demons as an organizing explanation for any manner of phenomenon, from psychological aberration to natural disasters, didn't mean the disappearance of the belief. During the Enlightenment many people, if not most, still held to some sort of literal belief in the diabolical, as indeed many still do today. What had changed, however, was that such supernatural beliefs were an all-pervading, all-encompassing paradigm that defined the very parameters of knowledge. "Over the course of the long eighteenth century, the devil disappeared from accounts of religious fanaticism—to be replaced by the clinical language of mental or physical weakness," Susan Justur writes in *Doomsayers: Anglo-American Prophecy in the Age of Revolution*, "The process by which all supernatural presences came to be exiled from the human world as phenomenological realities or explanatory mechanisms was, we now know, a long and circuitous one that had no clear endpoint." Such is the process that the early twentieth-century German political scientist and economist Max Weber called "disenchantment," but which could also be called "dechristianization," or more simply "secularism." Complex, contradictory, and sometimes self-defeating concepts, where the exact nature of alteration can be hard to identify, though *that* culture was altered was undeniable.

That such shifts were rapidly occurring is obvious since so many people were unhappy with them. The Church of England theologian and minister John Wesley is a representative example. He was the founder of Methodism and leader of the pietistic series of eighteenth-century revivals that convulsed the Anglophone world in both Britain and colonial America (often known as the Great Awakening), which has a complicated relationship to the Enlightenment itself, and he was disturbed by the new Enlightenment. Wesley bemoaned that "the infidels have hooted witchcraft out of the world; and the complacent Christians, in large numbers, have joined them in the cry." What's notable isn't that Wesley believed in witchcraft and demons, but that such belief was no longer de facto, indeed that it was becoming the minority position.

Contrast Wesley with Voltaire, whose lives roughly coincided through the length of most of the eighteenth century. As concerns the witch trials, Voltaire defines them in his 1764 *Philosophical Dictionary* as "legal murders committed by fanaticism, stupidity and superstition." Epistemologically and morally, Voltaire's perspective is obviously the correct one, but in comprehending the transition from one era to the next, it behooves us to examine how traces of the residual past continue to endure, albeit under changed form. Twentieth-century French historian and philosopher Michel Foucault speaks of ages being organized along the lines of *epistemes*, grand narratives that a historical period measures and defines itself by. As one episteme alters into another, certain discourses become emergent and some become residual, but nothing is ever totally eclipsed, so that as the Enlightenment reigns ascendent, we might come to see the ways that demons simply put on new masks.

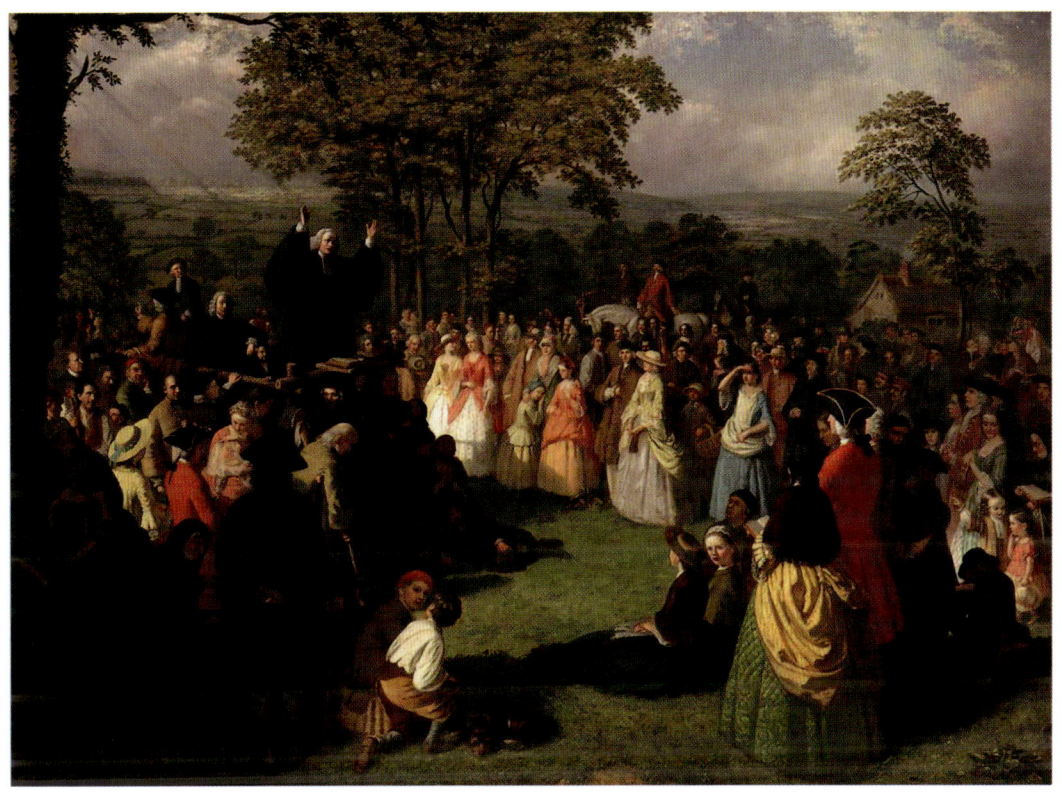

English artist (and veterinarian) Thomas Walley depicts the events of more than a century before in his 1863 painting George Whitefield Preaching in Bolton, June 1750, *housed at the Bolton Museum and Art Gallery in Manchester, United Kingdom. Whitefield was an enthusiastic preacher in the Anglophone world, training in his native England before become a celebrity in the American colonies, where he traveled a circuit from Massachusetts to Georgia. An adherent and exponent of Wesley's Methodism (despite being a priest in the Church of England), Whitefield advocated for an emotional, exuberant, pietistic form of Calvinism. For these Protestants, a belief in demons and exorcism wasn't archaic or Catholic; Wesley himself had been involved in several demonic encounters. Wesley recorded one such exorcism in his diary, dated to September 1739, when he described a tormented woman for whom "the enemy began to tear her, so that she screamed out, as in the pangs of death: but this time was short; for within a quarter of an hour she was full of the 'peace that passeth all understanding.'"*

A more nuanced view of the Enlightenment interprets these centuries as not simply involving the elimination of the sacred, but rather its mutation. Much of what was configured as "secular" was often just sublimated religious sentiments, attitudes, rituals, and ideologies, as Napoleon's self-coronation demonstrates. Justur says that the argument which holds that the Enlightenment signified the disenchantment of the world is a fantasy, "in which the desire of scientific and philosophical thinkers to strip the world of its magical qualities was never matched by their ability to banish witches, demons, ghosts, and other spiritual phenomena from the literary and imaginative landscape." Representative is the career of the Italian magician Giuseppe Balsamo, who fashioned himself as Count Alessandro Cagliostro when he toured the courts of Europe's capitals, lecturing on magic and kabbalah, while conjuring specters, performing tricks, and most popularly leading seances in which great personages held forth from the afterlife. Today Cagliostro is uniformly regarded as a con artist, but for the aristocrats who were willing to pay him for spiritual edification, entertainment, or both, he was a living conduit to a numinous realm that the Enlightenment claimed to have dispelled. Telling that the most popular spirit Cagliostro called forth was none other than the recently departed Voltaire. As Fleming notes, the "sacred and secular were so thoroughly intertwined that even the most thorough 'cleansing' of religious ritual necessarily left a vast body of civic ritual untouched."

If anything, the proliferation of secret societies and the enthusiasm for profane rituals like the Black Mass are indicative of one part of this mutation, whereby with tongues only partially in cheek it could be claimed that a certain satanic energy found itself displaced into civil society. "Philosophy has been a masked ball in which a religious image of humankind is renewed in the guise of humanist ideas of progress and enlightenment," writes contemporary philosopher John Gray in *Straw Dogs: Thoughts on Humans and Other Animals*, but

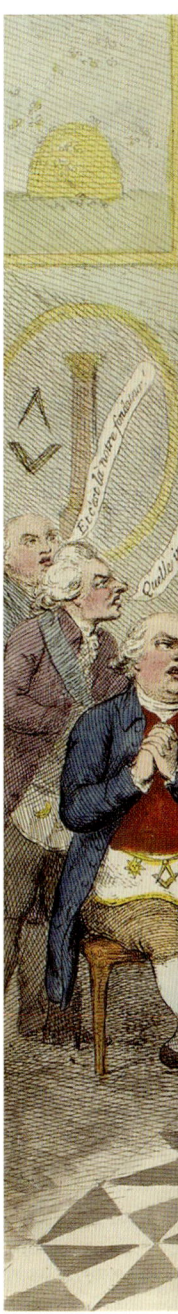

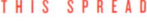

THIS SPREAD

Count Cagliostro, standing at right in black with apron, in a cartoon by British caricaturist James Gillray, at a Masonic meeting in London in 1786. Few groups were as associated (often nefariously) with Enlightenment rationality like the Freemasons, a secret society of dedicated political and religious freethinkers who were often blamed for social upheaval (and erroneously accused of devil worship). Despite their commitment to Enlightenment values of rationality, iconoclasm, and deism, the rituals of Masonry still evidenced traces of an obviously religious past.

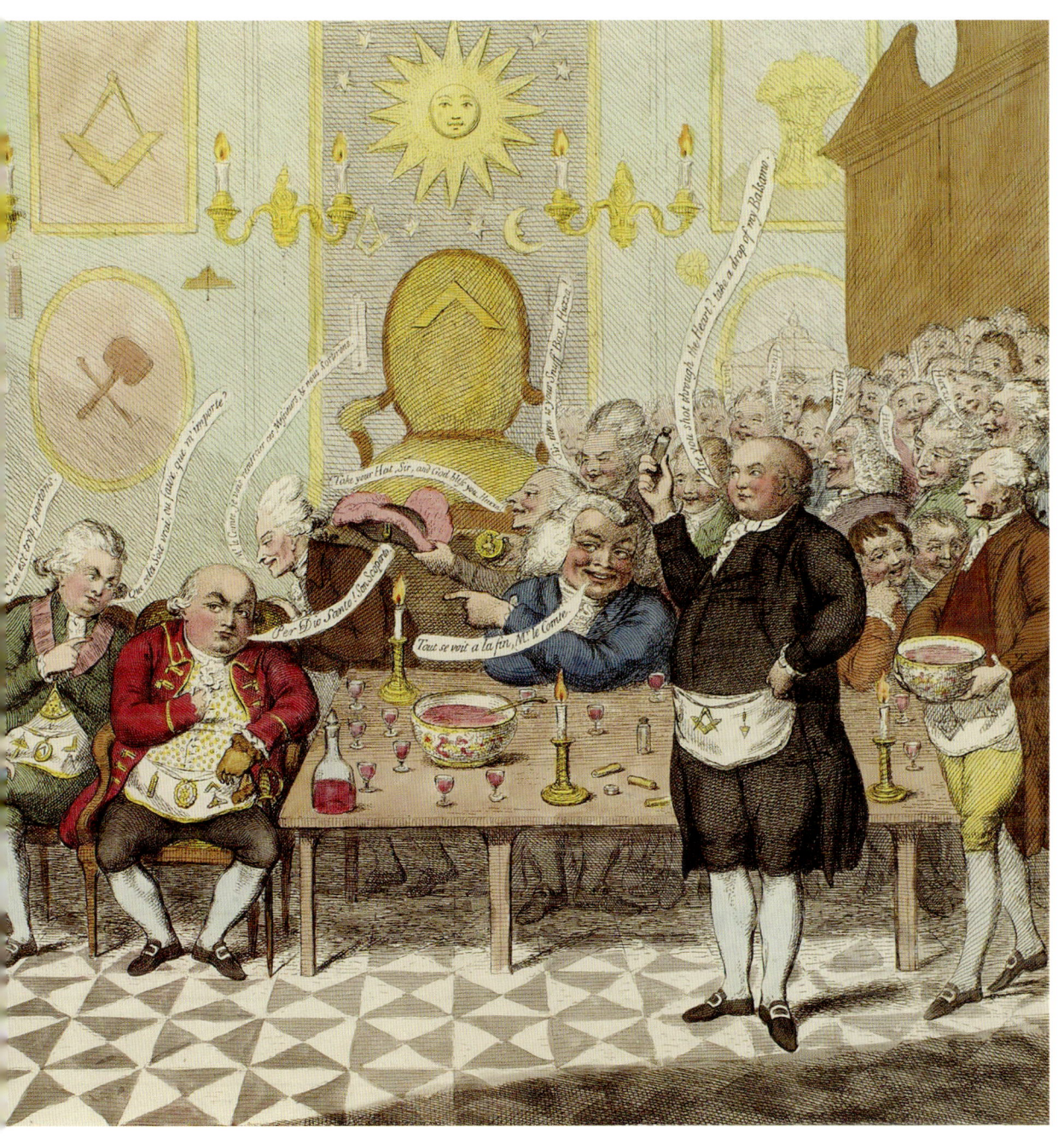

"their core belief in progress is a superstition . . . Outside of science, progress is simply a myth." Which is to say as admirable a goal as elimination of superstition might be, it's a quixotic one. The demonic can never truly be eradicated. Enlightenment demonology is not a contradiction, then. Understood in this way, the elimination of belief in demons engendered a type of atheism, but that "atheism" also engendered a new type of diabology.

It would be erroneous to think that atheism "caused" Satanism, nor should anyone fall into the silly evangelical fallacy that takes them as synonymous, but demonology did undergo startling shifts during the eighteenth century, whereby a type of popularized diabology was engaged (whether jocular or not). This is most clear in the aforementioned Hell-Fire Clubs, gatherings of powerful men (mostly in Great Britain) who pantomimed Catholic ritual and playacted a type of ritual Satanism. Basically fraternities for aristocrats and the socially well-connected, Hell-Fire Clubs featured debauchery from drinking to orgies, such that, as Evelyn Lord wrote in *The Hell-Fire Clubs: Sex, Satanism, and Secret Societies*, eighteenth-century England was "abuzz with rumors of highborn Devil-worshippers who mocked the established Church and religion, and allegedly supped with Satan."

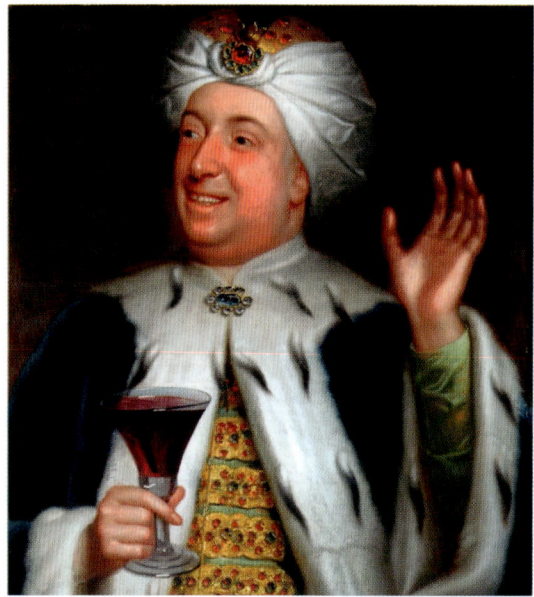

ABOVE

Portrait of Sir Francis Dashwood, eleventh Baron Le Despencer and founder of the most notorious Hell-Fire Club, painted around 1750 by the Dutch painter Adrien Carpentiers and displayed at the former's country house estate and ancestral home of West Wycombe Park. Bedecked in faux-Ottoman garb, Dashwood's persona was carefully cultivated to project irreverency and impiety, despite his powerful political positions, such as being chancellor of the exchequer from 1762 until 1763 during the reign of King George III. Such fashionable Orientalism was also common in demonology, where an attribution of apocryphal writing to a mystic East was a powerful appeal to ethos.

The earliest recorded instance of such a group goes back to 1718, but the most famous manifestations were the periodic gatherings held by Sir Francis Dashwood starting in 1749, which continue to occur over the next two decades. Rumors of Satanism should be viewed cautiously, as it's far more likely that Dashwood and men like him were interested in tweaking the pieties of bourgeoisie society, while also reveling in their own privilege and immunity from threat of censure or opprobrium. Yet the sacrilegious element of the Hell-Fire Clubs can't be discounted either, with Dashwood's group referring to themselves as the "Friars of Saint Francis," and the great satirist William Hogarth depicting their leader as a penitent mendicant praying to a miniature nude woman rather than a crucifix. Such blasphemy speaks to the tolerance of the Enlightenment, but the perverse desire of the participants to engage sacrilege also evidences the enduring presence of religion, for without faith, what would the point of such mockery be?

Associated with Dashwood, Hogarth, the gothic writer Horace Walpole, and even Benjamin Franklin (among others), the members of the most famous Hell-Fire Club convened at the ruins of Medmenham Abbey in Buckinghamshire, to eat, drink, fuck prostitutes, and libel religion, what Jonathan Swift described as a "brace of monsters, blasphemers, and Bacchanalians." Possibly some of these activities included the performance of a Black Mass, a type of inverted and diabolical version of the Catholic (and Anglican) Lord's supper, which had long

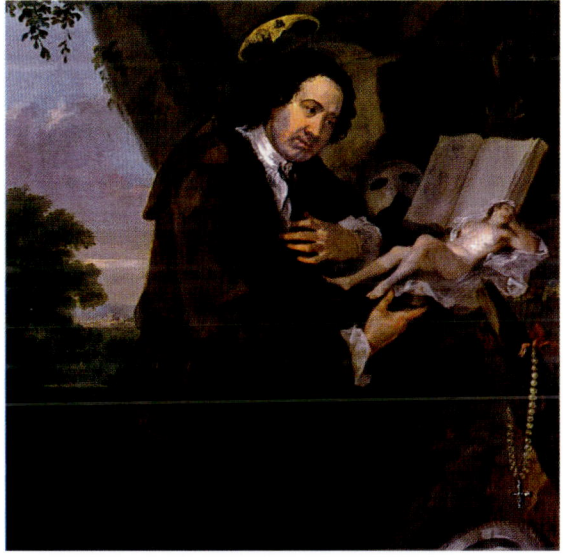

A privately owned Hogarth portrait from 1764 of Dashwood as if he were Saint Francis of Assisi, wearing the cowl of a monk and praying before a miniature nude woman and a copy of the erotic novel Elegantiae Latini Sermonis, *while the powerful Earl of Sandwich, a fellow Hell-Fire Club member, is hidden within the lunar halo above the aristocrat's head. Whether or not the Hell-Fire Clubs are to be taken seriously, as satire, or as some combination, is an issue for debate.*

been rumored to exist but were probably only first widely held in the eighteenth century, only to become a popular activity among bohemians of the nineteenth. The Enlightenment was the "Age of Experience, and the Hell-Fire clubs in all their disguises were out to grab experience by the neck, shake it and see what fell out," writes Lord. "By day the club members might be courtiers, Members of Parliament and respectable members of the community. By night they broke social rules to experience forbidden pleasure."

We must be careful not to be attracted to too lurid an interpretation of the phenomenon; after all, powerful men getting away with impropriety and abuse is disgracefully threaded throughout history, and is scarcely in need of the demonic as means of explanation. The Hell-Fire Clubs do, however, literalize much of this behavior, and their rejection of morality signals a perhaps darker inclination than mere hypocrisy does (which at least pays lip service to the existence of the good). Much legend surrounds these groups, such as their worship of a demon that arrived in the form of a large, horned cat, yet the reality was more prosaic (albeit shameful)— an elevation of abuse, rape, and murder (as by the Irish aristocrat Henry Barry, a

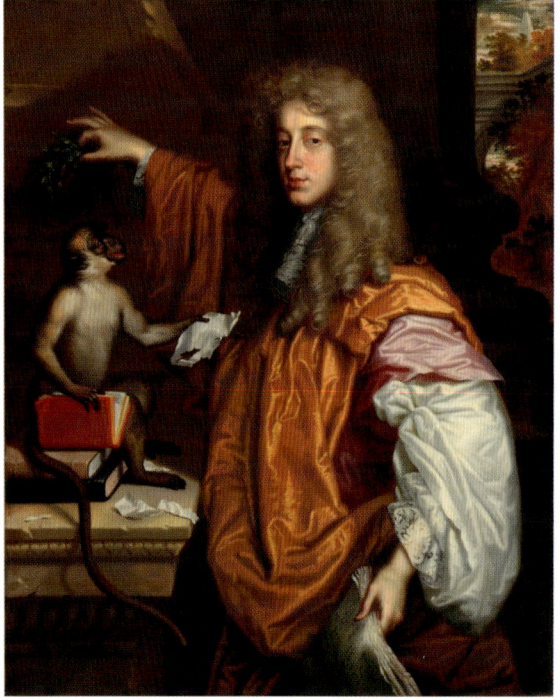

member of a Dublin Hell-Fire Club who burnt his servant to death for fun in 1738, and would see his conviction overturned by pardon). Dashwood and company thus established a kind of pandemonium on earth, and in doing so they pushed the Enlightenment fetishizing of reason, liberty, and individualism to its ultimate logical conclusion, in the process midwifing a type of nihilistic Satanism.

None of this is to suggest that the Hell-Fire Clubs somehow innovated the wealthy and powerful getting away with transgressions—of course not. Nor is it to imply that impiety leads to criminality—if anything the copious records from the witch trials should prove that more than enough evil has been done in the name of genuine faith. What the Hell-Fire Clubs and all of their demonic accoutrement evidence, however, are the ways that an ill-defined, inchoate, antinomian amorality was able to justify certain actions with an ambiguously satirical sense of the demonic, in a manner that would not just have been scandalous in earlier eras, but impossible. The praxis of the criminally privileged may not have been substantially different before the eighteenth century, but the theory was new. Deists, freethinkers, and milquetoast atheists may have argued that the nonexistence or radical redefinition of God had no moral implications, but at least at the level of rhetoric the congregants of Medmenham understood differently. During the Restoration period of the 1660s the radical poet John Wilmot, Second Earl of Rochester, who in ethos was very much a forerunner of the Hell-Fire Clubs, wrote:

For hell and foul fiend that rules
God's everlasting jails
(Devised by rogues, dreaded by fools),
Are senseless stories, idle tales,
Dreams, whimsey, and no more.

Shockingly atheistic for the seventeenth century, and far beyond the dogmas of even the most committed freethinkers in the eighteenth, but also honest. No God, no reward; no demons, no repercussions; any action—sanctioned and unpunished if not caught by your fellow man. As the playwright Molière wrote in his 1664 comedy *Tartuffe*, "Sin in silence is no sin at all." And in a world devoid of angels and demons, the sinner is always alone and it's always silent. Such abolition of perdition didn't actually eliminate demons, however. Nor did it disestablish hell. Telling that, despite their supposed rejection of the supernatural, the members of Dashwood's unsacred order signaled their membership with an unusual self-applied title—"Devils." After hell has been emptied it's ourselves who must become the demons.

If one were looking to find a chief demon in this new fraternity you only need look into the wicked black eyes of Donatien Alphonse François. Chief theorist of self-consuming Enlightenment, of its potential to degenerate into pure nihilism, he is far better known by his title as the Marquis de Sade. In his only confirmed portrait made during his lifetime, a lithograph rendered by

Charles-Amédée-Philippe van Loo in 1760 when his subject was only nineteen years old, de Sade, in a tightly pulled powdered black wig, appears slender and handsome, with a Gallic profile and an aquiline nose, but despite his youthful beauty some of his cold cruelty is seemingly prefigured. Few individuals have more fully had an adjective associated with them than the libertine writer, for whom "sadistic" connotates not just an action, but a total ideology of personal domination, selfish control, abject brutality, and intemperate pleasure. Such concerns were explored by the notorious aristocrat in his philosophical and pornographic writings such as 1785's *The 120 Days of Sodom*, 1791's *Justine*, and 1799's *Juliette*.

Across these works, and in others, de Sade unrepentantly depicted and celebrated all manner of transgressions, including torture, murder, rape, pederasty, incest, cannibalism, necrophilia, and so on. "It is moreover proven that it is horror, foulness—something ghastly—that we want when we are hard," writes de Sade in *120 Days of Sodom*, "and where better to find this than in a corrupt object? Certainly, if it is filth that gives pleasure in the lubricious act, then the greater the filth, the deeper the pleasure . . . ugliness is the extraordinary thing, and all ardent imaginations doubles prefer the extraordinary thing in lubricity to the simple thing." Steadfastly rejecting faith in progress and egalitarianism, as well as revolutionary values like equality and fraternity, de Sade has a complicated relationship with the Enlightenment, though as Geoffrey Ashe asks in his pulp classic *The Secret History of the Hell-Fire Clubs: From Rabelais and John Dee to Anton LaVey and Timothy Leary*, "Is there any connection between liberty and libertinism? Do you, or can you, promote human freedom and fulfillment in general through the personal freedom that sheds morality?"

Frequent prisoner at the Bastille, where he was punished for assault (among other crimes), de Sade rejected virtually all of the emancipatory efforts of the Enlightenment and the subsequent French Revolution, even while he held to a radical type of liberty, justified by our godless universe. Where philosophes like Voltaire and Diderot held to a gauzy faith in a deistic creator, and even revolutionaries as varied as Robespierre and Danton sought to dechristianize France with a religion of their own invention, respectively a Cult of Reason and a Cult of the Supreme Being. De Sade, on the other hand, in an intellectual strategy that would foreshadow Friedrich Nietzsche in the coming century, fully embraced the ethical implications of a totally meaningless existence, and subsequently concluded that the only imperative was to pursue his own pleasure, regardless of how it might violate others. Summarizing the central conundrum of theodicy, his narrator in *Justine* says, "I believe that if evil exists here below, then either it was willed by God or it was beyond His powers to prevent it. Now I cannot bring myself to fear a God who is either spiteful or weak. I defy Him without fear and care not a fig for his thunderbolts."

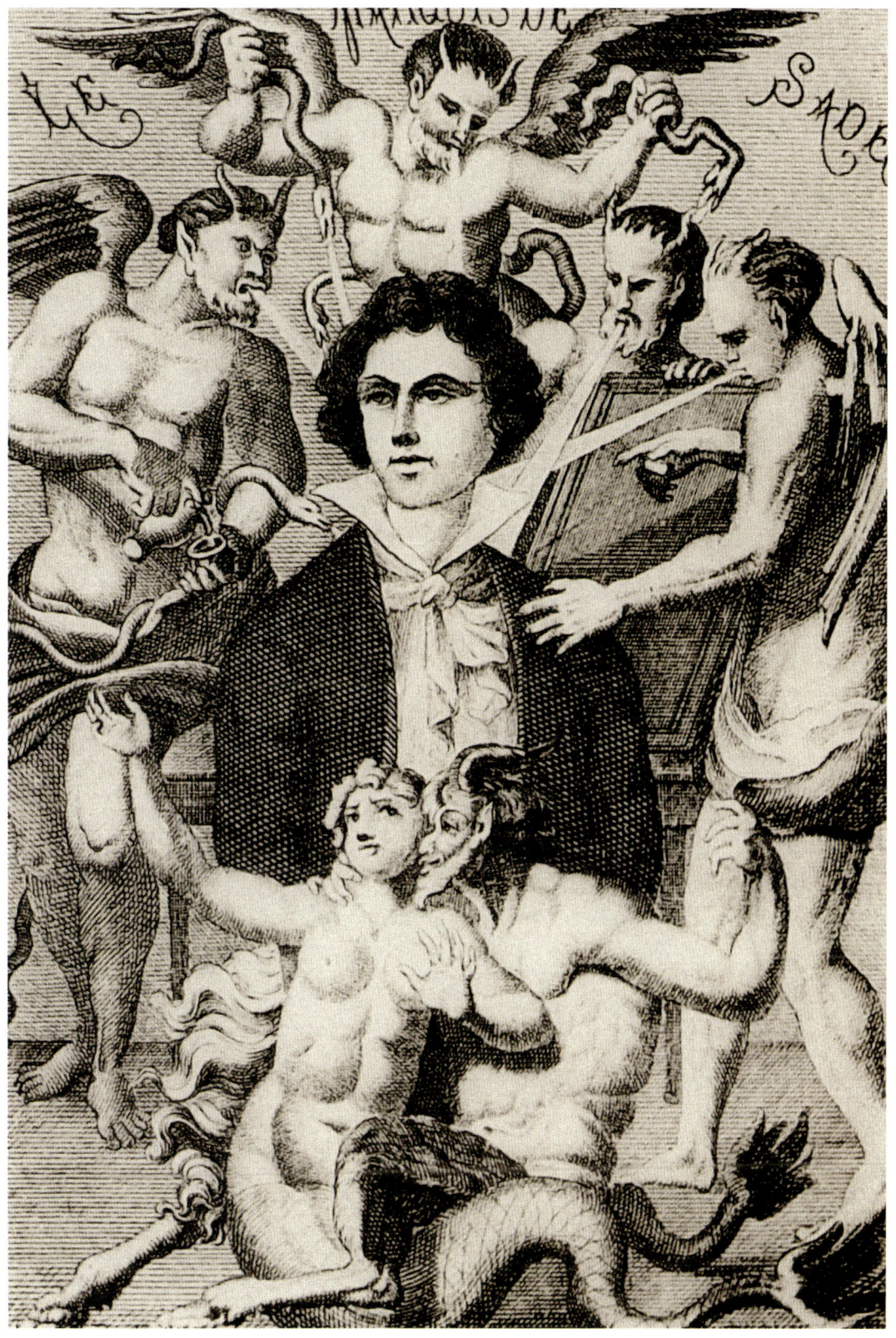

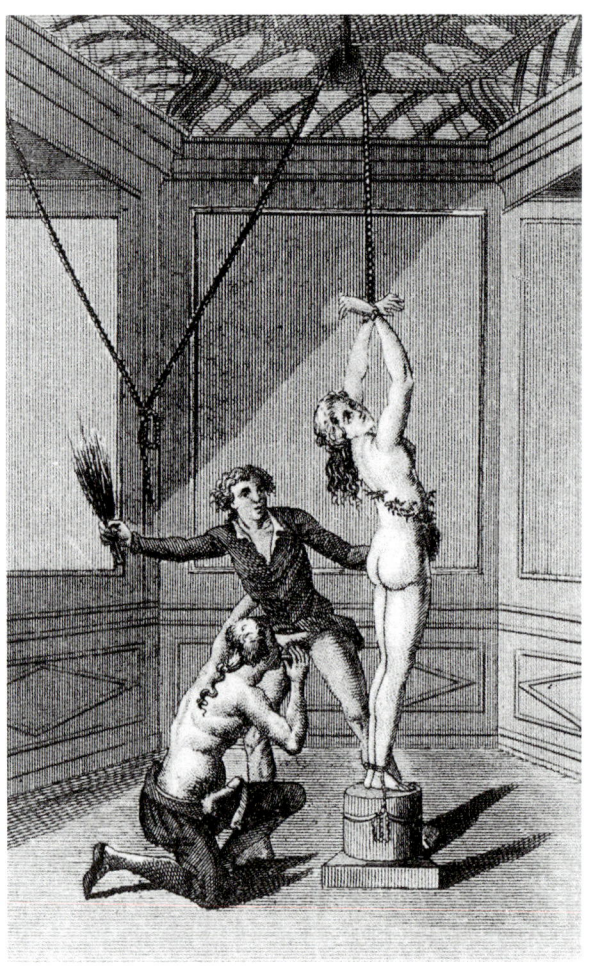
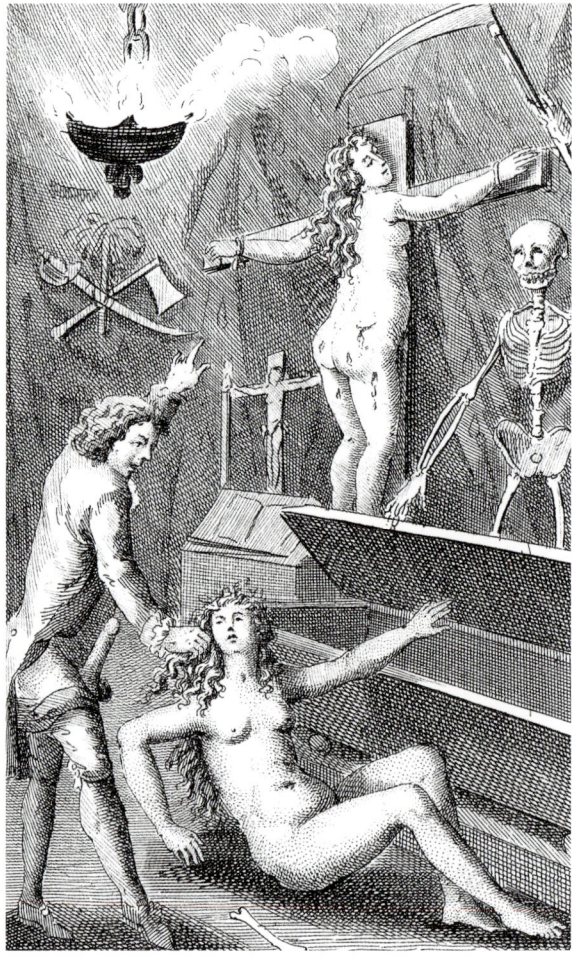

Need it be said that de Sade has stated a Luciferian imperative here, conflating a declaration of war against God with a declaration of war against the *idea* of God, between which there is little difference, and wherein he has already affirmed victory? One might note a metaphysical difference, of course, that Lucifer as lord of demons has an exceedingly different status than a mere human denying the existence of said demons. To claim that this metaphysical difference affectively matters is to miss the point, however. It's to perform a category mistake, for the metaphysics is always secondary to rhetoric, and as involves demonic poetics the ultimate conclusion remains the same whether we speak of Lucifer or de Sade. There can be no real denial of the transcendent, whether sacred or damnable. All that is altered is our syntax. "More powerful than this villainous God, a being still in possession of his power, forever able to brave this author, the *Devil* by his seductions incessantly leads in leading astray the flock that the Eternal reserved unto himself," writes de Sade in his 1795 *Philosophy in the Bedroom*. "Nothing can vanquish the hold this demon's energy has upon us." De Sade has ultimately abolished the demonic not to defeat it, but to declare himself the new Lucifer. Satan is dead—long live Satan!

De Sade "emerges as a thorn in the side of the Enlightenment," writes critic Roger Shattuck in *Forbidden Knowledge: From Prometheus to Pornography*, "a man who carried revolutionary libertinism to patently undemocratic extremes of argument, narrative imagination, and personal behavior." For what's significant is that the ideology of Lucifer and de Sade are identical, whatever the respective "realness" of either of them. This is an ideology of *mechanization*, a reduction of the person into base commodity, to be treated as mere product consumed for the pleasure of those who wield power. In *Philosophy in the Bedroom* one character ask another, "How do you view the object that serves your pleasure?" to which the answer is "As absolutely null." Just as Lucifer's fall is precipitated by his refusal to acknowledge the gloriousness of God's individual human creation, so too does de Sade deny what is singular and sacred in each person, preferring rather to reduce everyone into a vagina to be fucked, a mouth to be penetrated, an anus to be buggered. Such dehumanization is at odds with the Enlightenment's stated political goals, the very antithesis of the understanding of natural human rights, but de Sade also pushes the logic of disenchantment and personal liberty to its very breaking point, demonstrating the fundamental contradictions that defined the entire project.

The reduction of the human to the mechanical, a replacement of the soul with mere friction, may reach its apogee with de Sade, but it marks the Enlightenment and serves as dialectical antithesis to the age's noble aims. Such materialization may seem to be necessary for the process of disenchantment, but paradoxically, far from eliminating the demonic, it enshrines it anew, now with no sacred counterbalance. In that regard, perhaps the most salient demon of the era wasn't Lucifer, but rather a horrific fiction offered forth as a sober and staid scientific thought experiment by the French mathematician Pierre-Simon Laplace in 1814. Pushing the mechanical determinism of the Newtonian physics that defined the new science of the Enlightenment to its extreme, Laplace imagined the existence of an "intellect which at a certain moment would know all forces that set nature in motion, and all positions of all items of which nature is composed," claiming that "if this intellect were also vast enough to submit these data to analyses . . . [then] for such an intellect nothing would be uncertain and the future just like the past would be present before its eyes." Thus, all agency, all free choice, all independence, all freedom is eliminated in favor of a dispassionate calculation. This being's originator didn't call it such, but later writers succinctly referred to it as "Laplace's demon."

The operative metaphor of the Enlightenment—the machine. By the early nineteenth century, animals, humans, the universe, and indeed God Himself had been rendered mechanical; gone were the enchantments of the soul to be replaced with the cold rigor of the clockmaker. In its omniscience and omnipotence Laplace's thought-experiment nearly describes God, perhaps more exactly the Lord of predestination worshiped by the Calvinists, which makes his demonic title all the more telling. With the disestablishment of the sacred, it become more difficult to tell who is an angel or a demon, though what's unassailable is that the new Prince of this World is some sort of machine, and that the terrible logic of efficiency and reduction, of positivism, parsimony, and profit increasingly marked the Enlightenment as it came to a close. In the unfeeling mind of Laplace's demon, we see the cold individualism of modernity and our dark enduring night of imprisoning solipsism. That this was an era defined not just by democratic enthusiasm, but also by the millions of human beings transported on the Atlantic Middle Passage from freedom in Africa to slavery in America, as well as the beginnings of exploitative colonialism and its handmaiden capitalism, is to speak of the ever present demonic and de Sade's honest reckoning with that. Lucifer may not exist, but his way of thinking very much does.

THIS SPREAD

Even two decades before the end of the eighteenth century, dissatisfaction with some of the stated virtues of the Enlightenment could be seen in the nascent Romantic movement, such as in Fuseli's 1781 painting The Nightmare, *held at the Detroit Institute of Arts. Popular as it was scandalous, due to its disturbing imagery and its charged eroticism, the title of Fuseli's painting marks it with a deep ambivalence, as the viewer must ask how real the demonic incubus upon the sleeping woman's chest actually is. Maybe more importantly, the presumed content of the woman's nightmare testifies to the endurability of the satanic imperative, where all of the rectilinearity of logic, the exactitude of reason, and the parsimony of science can't fully disentangle our world from hidden, sacred, and indeed demonic realms.*

NEXT SPREAD

"Millions of spiritual creatures walk the earth/Unseen, both when we wake, and when we sleep," writes Milton in Paradise Lost. *In this engraving from the British artist John Martin, Satan is one of these creatures, appearing to a slumbering Eve to tempt her in a dream. Milton was firmly a man of the Reformation and Renaissance, his radical vision was influential in the Enlightenment, but in many ways, his Luciferian perspective would find its most devoted readers among the Romantics of the nineteenth century.*

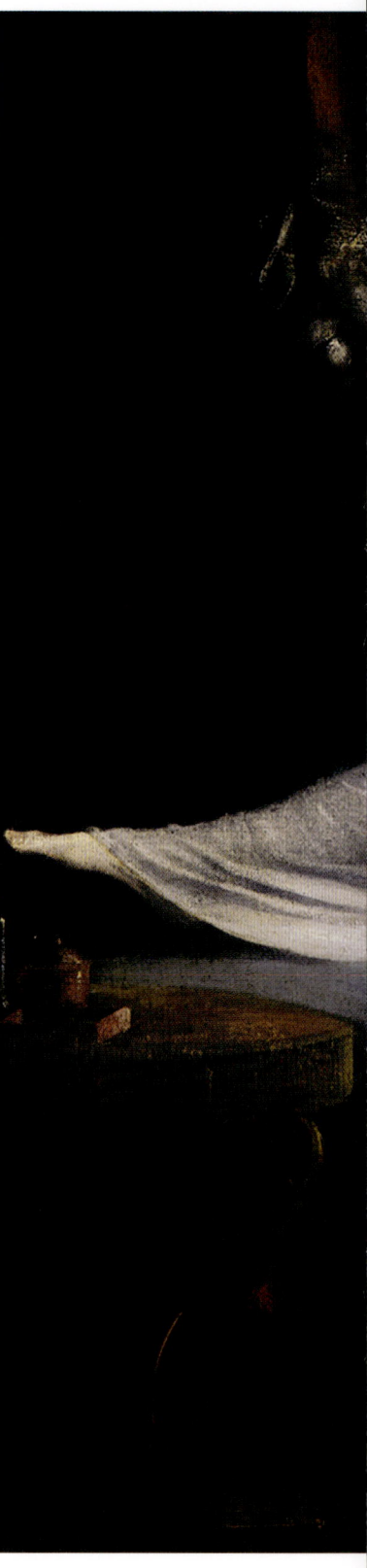

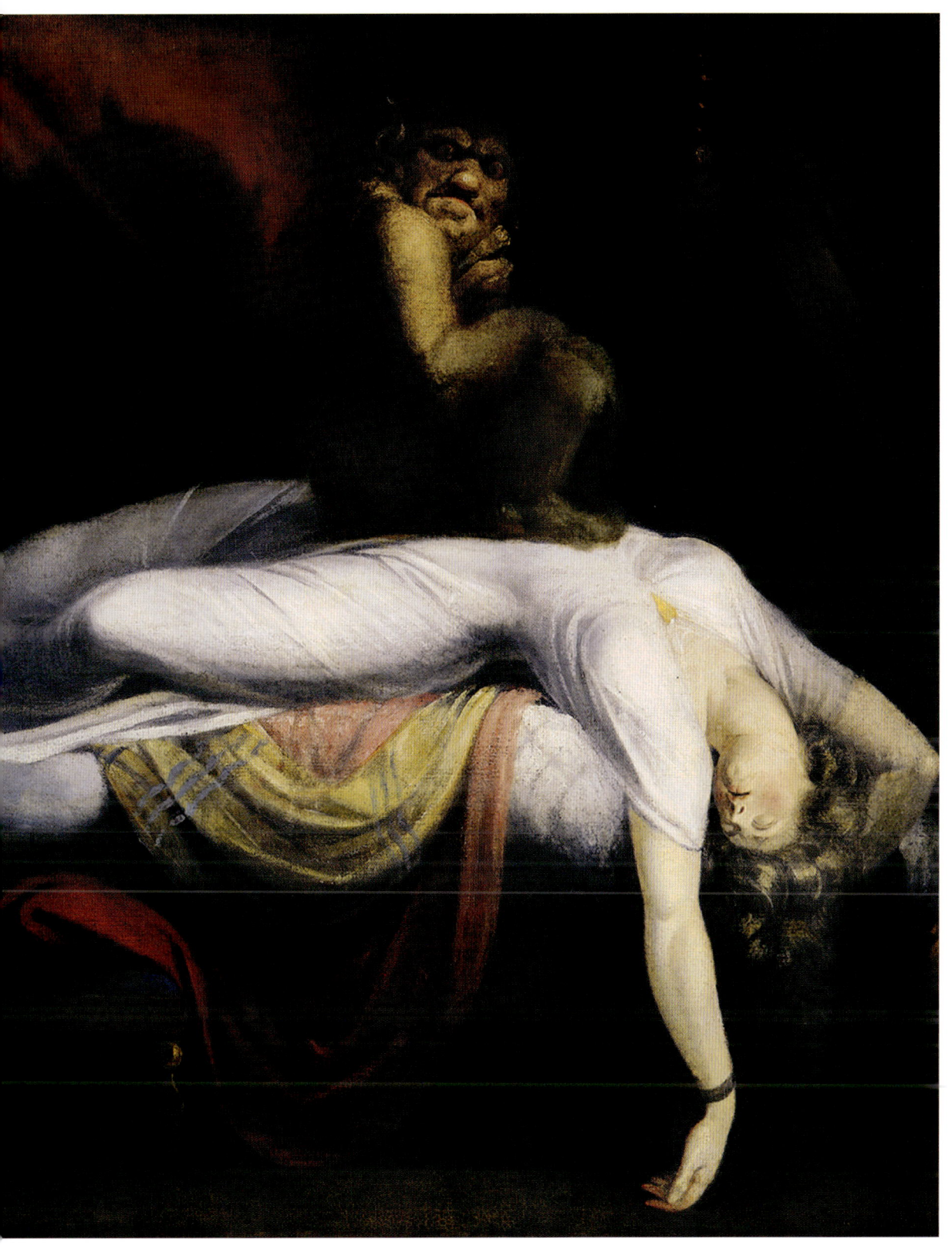

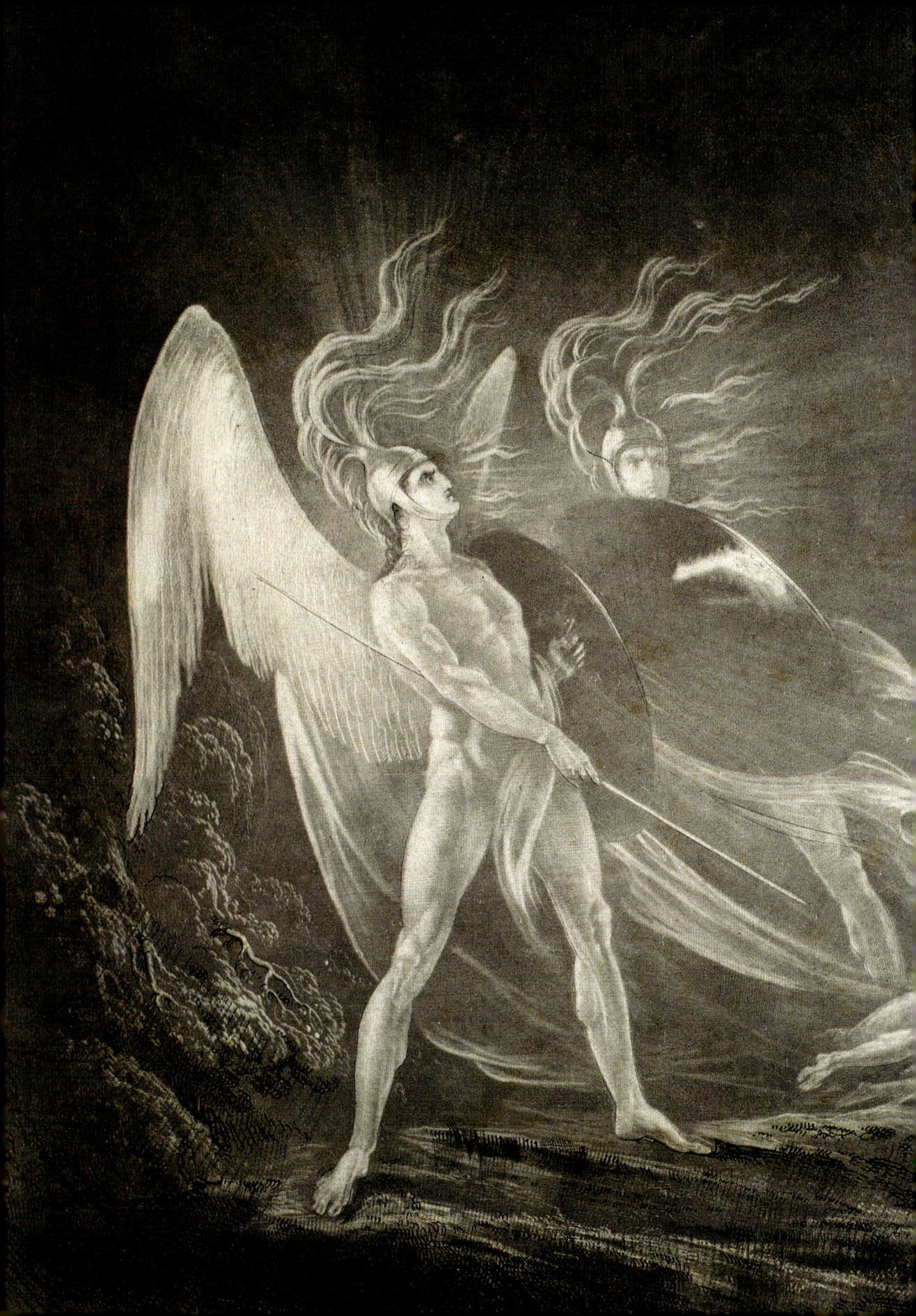

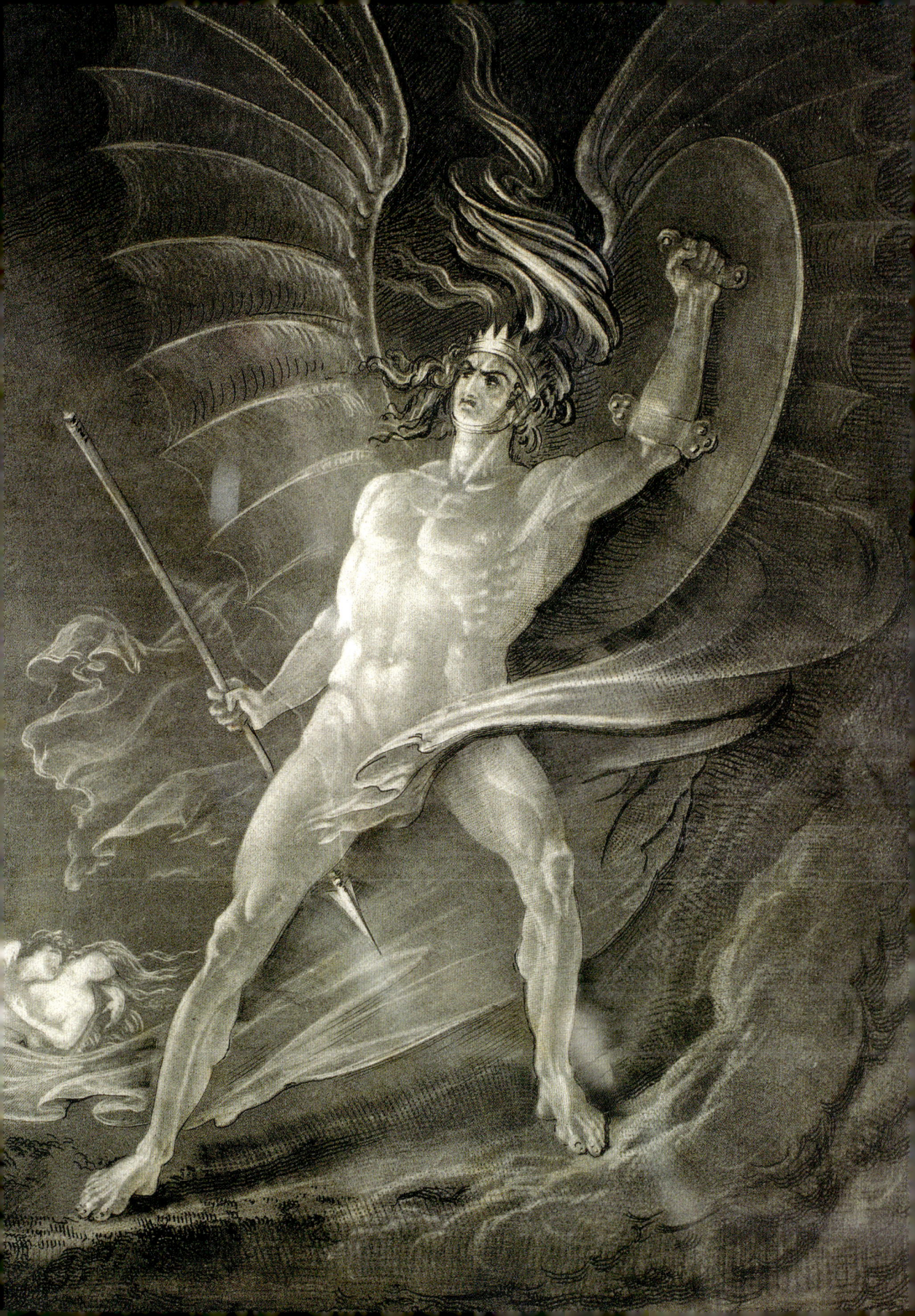

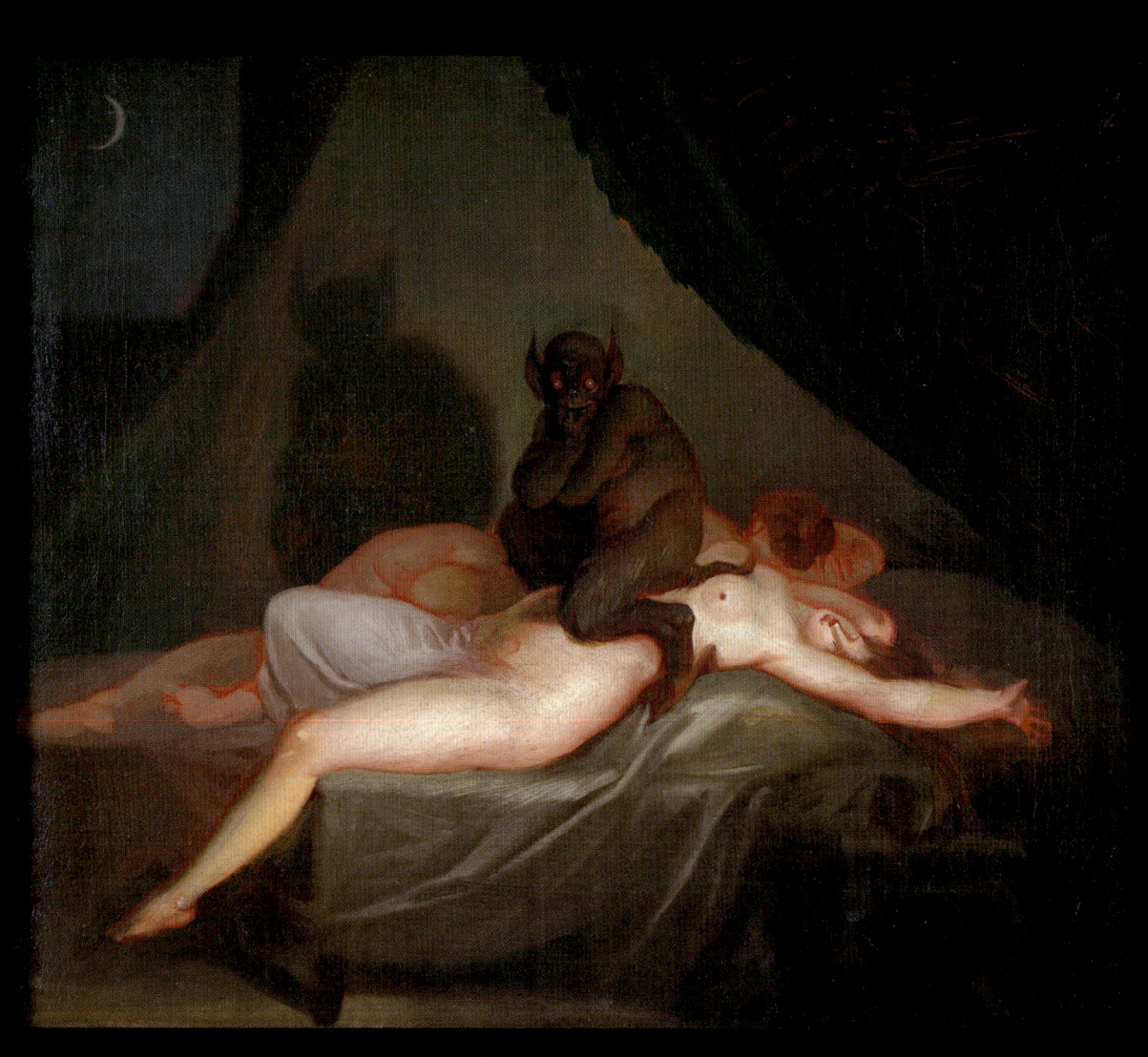

CHAPTER FIVE

The Greatest Trick Ever Pulled

Demonology in the Nineteenth Century, c. 1800–1900

Thus, a fatal law drives the demons downward when they wish
and believe themselves to be ascending.

—Éliphas Lévi, *Transcendental Magic: Its Doctrine and Ritual* (1856)

Upon my life, the tracks have vanished,
We've lost our way, what shall we do?
It must be a demon's leading us
This way and that around the fields.

—Alexander Pushkin, "Demons" (1823)

ON ROMANTIC
AND VICTORIAN DEMONOLOGY

There, in the infernal dictionary, between the entry for a seventeenth-century Anglican theologian named Assheton and one for the Levantine goddess Astarte, is the demon Astaroth. As depicted by the nineteenth-century French artist Louis Le Breton in the 1863 edition of his fellow countrymen Jacques Auguste Simon Collin de Plancy's *Dictionnaire Infernal*, Astaroth is a skinny man with reptilian claws punctuating long hands and feet, hobbled over on the back of a lupine demon, framed by a massive pair of bat wings, a serpentine tail behind him. Astaroth has a thin, Gaelic face, which Collin de Plancy describes as that of "a very ugly angel," his bushy hair kept under the crown of "a very powerful grand-duke." Breton illustrates Astaroth as having an effete, equine visage, dismissive and uncaring eyes, with a slight sneer of cool command. Excluding the chiropteran wings and the hideous demon upon which Astaroth rides, his calculated, intelligent face could be that of one of the French aristocratic armchair intellectuals who dined with the philosophes of the Enlightenment Paris of Collin de Plancy's youth.

Perhaps this connection is intentional, for the seventeenth-century Dominican inquisitor Sébastien Michaelis, who classified the demons he encountered as an exorcist at the infamous monastery of Loudon (which resembled nothing so much as Rabelais's orgiastic Thelema), associated Astaroth with the new rationalist philosophies that were just being born in France. Michaelis's Astaroth was a kind of hellish René Descartes, who drew the nuns and priests of Loudon astray with the pernicious promises of Epicureanism so that they could "Do what thou wilt," and perhaps for Collin de Plancy, born almost two centuries later and living through the convulsions of revolution, the thin, reptilian demon with the aristocratic forbearance still represented some of the dangers of the new learning, for Astaroth "willingly answers the questions he is asked about the most secret things, and … it is easy to have him talk about creation."

Astaroth is a convenient symbol for the oddity of the entire project of Collin de Plancy's *Dictionnaire Infernal*, for the demon is both representative of rationalism and superstition, systematization and the occult, the Enlightenment and the Romantic. The *Dictionnaire Infernal* was first published in 1818 by a dutiful student of the new rationalism, to catalogue the "aberrations and germs or causes of errors," and as released in subsequent editions over the course of Collin de Plancy's life, the secular folklorist found himself gravitating toward orthodox belief by first going though demonology itself—though as Russell has pointed out in *Mephistopheles: The Devil in the Modern World*, Romantic "poseurs who feigned Satanism for esthetic effect cannot be considered real Satanists." By the final edition, the author of the reference's preface could authoritatively claim that Collin de Plancy had "reconfigured his labors, recognizing that superstitious, foolish beliefs, occult sects and practices . . . have come only from deserters of the faith." Perhaps Collin de Plancy had been led astray by Astaroth himself in his 1818 *Dictionnaire Infernal*, motivated as he was by a "proud and unprincipled philosophy," but the publishers of this latest edition wanted to assure the reader that these errors had been eliminated, Collin de Plancy's catalogue of demons now fully congruent with Catholic theology.

The Dictionnaire infernal, which still has yet to be fully translated into English, is a landmark occult work, one of the great texts of Solomonic wisdom in its painstaking, learned, and very weird classification of the demonic hierarchies. Like its creator, *The Dictionnaire Infernal* lay between two eras. It was reminiscent of grimoires, such as Johann Weyer's sixteenth-century *Pseudomonarchia Daemonum*, or the seventeenth-century compilation the *Lesser Key of Solomon*, as well as recalling the systematized compendiums of knowledge from the Enlightenment, such as Denis Diderot's encyclopedia. As such, the weighty five-hundred-page tome is a kind of liminal gloaming book, an in-between shadow volume that collects information on which the author himself always seems to oscillate in degrees of certainty, hung as he is between faith and doubt, belief and skepticism. In part this is born out of ambiguity in classifying the book, for what could be more modern than a dictionary, and yet what could be more antique than the knowledge that is contained within this particular dictionary?

With tongue only slightly in cheek, one could argue that the utopian, completest desire of dictionaries and encyclopedias is our contemporary world's last vestige of that grand Enlightenment hope to categorize, classify, organize, and analyze. When all other values of reason and truth seem to be dying, Diderot's dream lives on in the massive tower of Wikipedia, the last grandchild of the Enlightenment. Despite ancient and medieval precedent across several different languages, the dictionary and especially the encyclopedia were creatures of the early modern era. One can think of historical precursors, after all, Aristophanes of Byzantium compiled a type of dictionary called the *Lexeis* two centuries before Christ. And yet in systematic, technical, and scientific ardor, the modern dictionary is very much of the eighteenth and nineteenth centuries, the provenance of Dr. Johnson or the prophetically bearded James Murray, who in the Bodleian's scriptorium assembled the testament to humanity that is the *Oxford English Dictionary*. Dictionaries are of course ever-growing, ever-expanding, ever-breathing, and ever-living things; as the literary critic Ilan Stavans wrote, "No lexicon is able to grasp the universe entire."

Murray and Dr. Johnson were as Ortelius with his maps, Diderot with his *Encyclopedia*, or Darwin with his collection of moths—for all of them, it was in collection and measurement that there could be positivist knowledge. The dictionary was sober, rational, and practical. Etymology is like dissection, that other Enlightenment innovation, and the dictionary is the dissection theater of the pathologists who compile our word-hoards. Stavans, writing in his 2005 *Dictionary Days* as if he were Dr. Johnson, explains that dictionaries react to "speech copious without order, and energetick without rules," where there is "perplexity to be disentangled, and confusion to be regulated." For Johnson, the dictionary serves to tame vocabulary, for its approach to language is one "reduced to method." Davies agrees, writing that dictionaries are marked by "the desire for knowledge and the enduring impulse to restrict and control it." By this criterion Collin de Plancy's dictionary seems an oddity, more magic book or grimoire than a product of the Enlightenment, for if dictionaries are things assembled by learned academic dons in Oxford scriptoriums, than dark necromancers and wizards write grimoires.

Except Davies wasn't writing about dictionaries, rather he was giving exact definition to the grimoire. Which makes Collin de Plancy's dictionary, whether the rationalist early volumes or the more fideistic later versions, less anomalous than first assumed. A dictionary may be of the Enlightenment, but it is also, appropriately enough, is a type of grimoire. Davies writes that a grimoire is not just "defined by the writing it contains, but the act of writing can itself be magic, and certain words can have active properties independent of the holy or magical texts in which they are written"—a description that is uncannily evocative of the dictionary. If asked to envision a magic book, many people would describe some leather-bound, thick tome, with vellum pages filled to the edge with spidery calligraphy and strange, inscrutable kabbalistic diagrams interposed throughout. A grimoire can conjure a demon; a dictionary simply defines a word. Collin de Plancy's *Dictionnaire Infernal* seemingly does both, for it is somehow simultaneously in the rational tradition of a Dr. Johnson or a Wright, but also part of the long history of demonology, in a line of darkness-shrouded men like Weyer.

There is a completest affinity between both the dictionary and the grimoire. Davies explains that "Grimoires exist because of the desire to create a physical record of magical knowledge, reflecting concerns regarding the uncontrollable and corruptible nature of . . . sacred information." While it's true that the grand experiment of the Enlightenment supposedly wished to illuminate the secret contours of once-forbidden knowledge, to shine the light of rationality upon the shadows of superstition and to make learning accessible to the breadth of humanity, the desire to assemble all possible information is one which the grimoire and the dictionary share. Davies writes that "The list of demons and their powers would become a staple" of grimoires, but listing things is not just a staple of dictionaries, it's their very essence.

And this yearning toward completion, totality, and the all-encompassing is not just a superficial similarity, for in their obsessions with words and language the grimoire and the dictionary share the common faith that believes that mere verbal pronouncements have the ability to rewrite the base of reality itself. Both are partisans of a Platonist philosophy, which sees a type of word-magic as being able to enact transformations in real life. For the rationalist lexicographer, this means that the definitional and organizational logic of rhetoric can affect our lives; for the wizard this means that the gematrial essence and magic of words can conjure alteration, but the ultimate thinking is spookily similar—the uttering of mere words, words, words properly organized can change the world for better and for worse. And with that being the case, best to have a dictionary (or grimoire) at hand to know how to handle any demons that you might accidentally generate.

This connection between the Enlightenment dictionary and the medieval grimoire was of course made literal by Collin de Plancy. He was born in 1793, only six years after the crowning (or most condemnatory) event of the Enlightenment—the French Revolution. Perhaps in reaction to that affair, the demonologist added the aristocratic "de Plancy" to his otherwise plebian name. Indeed it was not just a plebian name, but a positively republican one, for Collin de Plancy's maternal uncle was none other than George Danton, the radical president of the Committee of Public Safety who, like so many of his fellow Jacobins, ultimately found his severed head looking up at the guillotine blade one morning in the month of Germaine. As with his uncle, Collin de Plancy was originally a partisan of liberty, equality, and fraternity, an enthused reader of Voltaire and a zealous rationalist and skeptic; and like his uncle, he would ultimately see himself reconciled to that church he had rejected, with a detour through the darker corners of demonology.

In his original plans for his infernal dictionary, Colin de Plancy understood his purpose as being the revealing of clerical superstition, the *Dictionnaire Infernal* designed to hold up Catholic belief in literal demons as the most base of irrationality. But as the Romantic era was one in which the pendulum was swinging, Collin de Plancy rather infernally went around the other direction, eventually convincing himself of the reality of those very demons whom he wished to disprove existed. Collin de Plancy, as many other men of faux-aristocratic pretensions in the decades after the Revolution, came to reject the goddess of rationality once enshrined by the Jacobins upon the altar of Notre-Dame in favor of older gods (and not always the Christian one).

He is at a halfway point between the rectilinear logic of men like Voltaire and Diderot, and those chthonic poets of a generation hence, Symbolists and Decadents like Rimbaud, Baudelaire, and Verlaine who drunkenly stomped through the rainy streets of Paris clutching their flowers of hell. And Collin de Plancy did not just convince himself that demons were real, but indeed he developed a wish to control them through language, a desire as fervent as that of his former compatriot's Enlightenment rationality in categorizing and defining words and ideas in dictionaries and encyclopedias. The demonologist was a man hung between logic and faith, rationality and belief, halfway between the salon and the Hell-Fire Club, an in-between man, a man of dusk, who hears the screams of such horrific

Le Dictionnaire infernal

1863 EDITION, ILLUSTRATIONS BY LOUIS LE BRETON

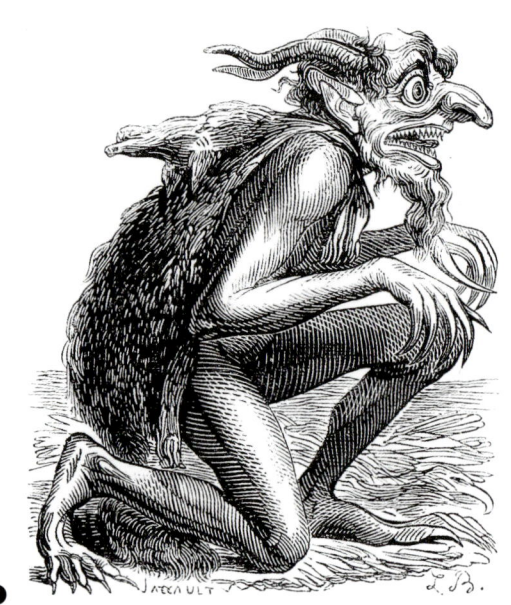

❶

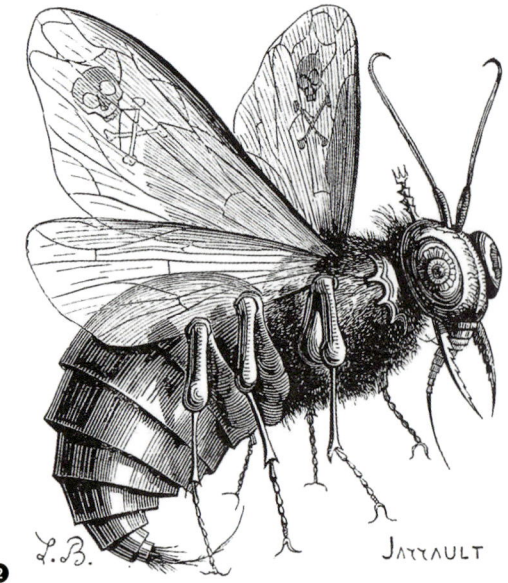

❷

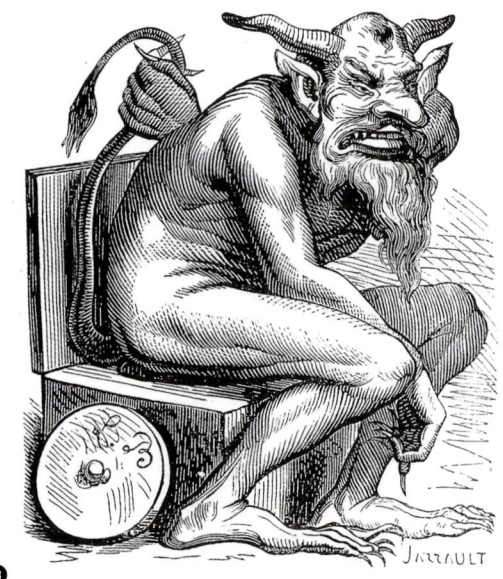

❸

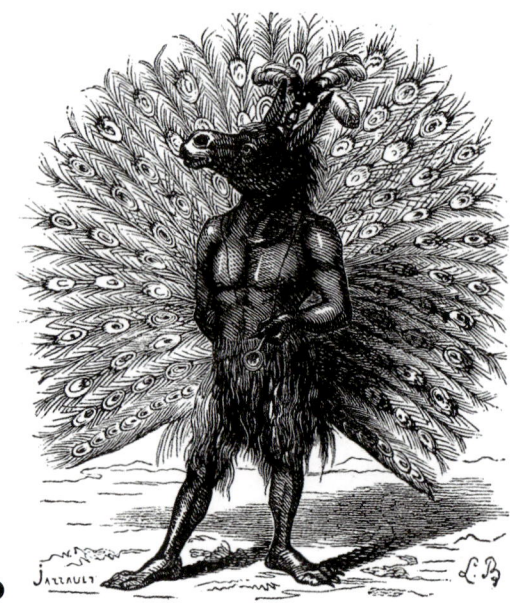

❹

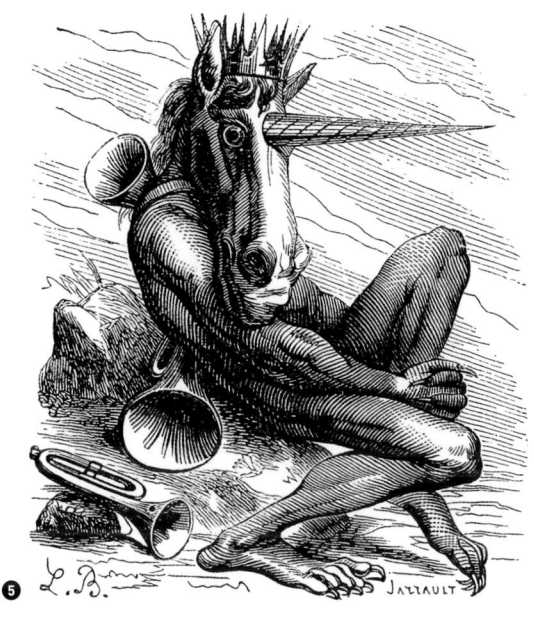

⑤

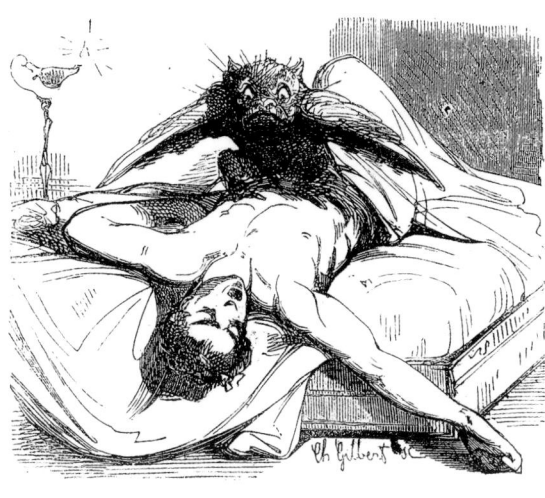

⑥

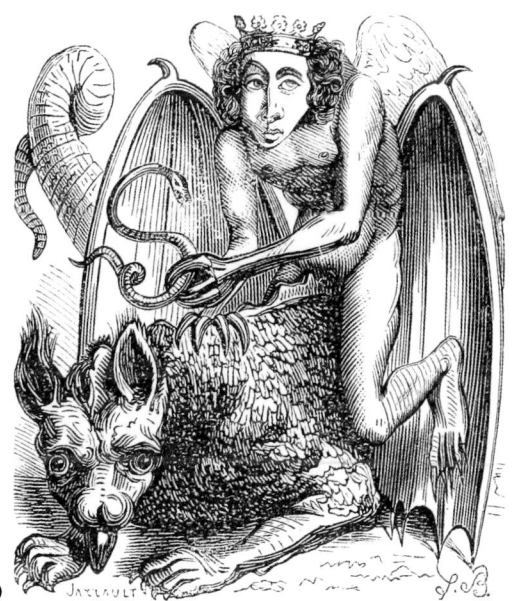

⑦

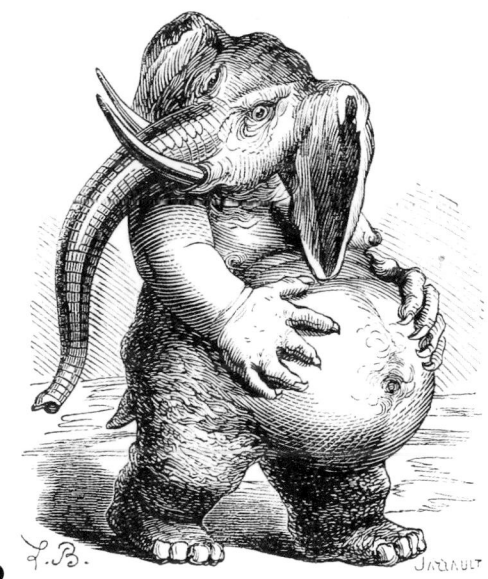

⑧

圖 253

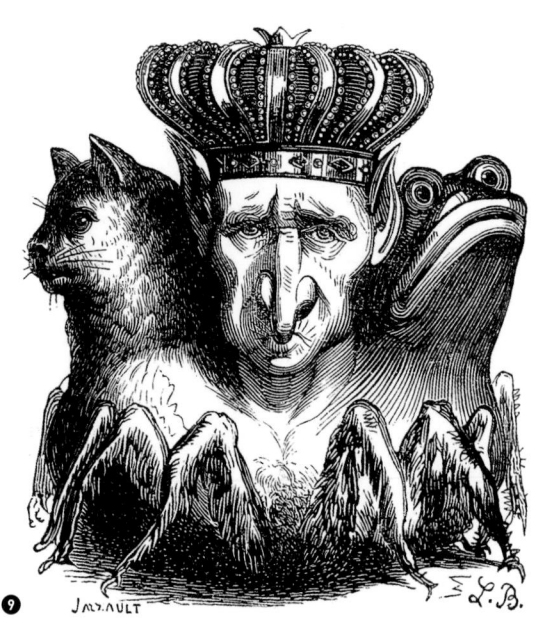

⑨

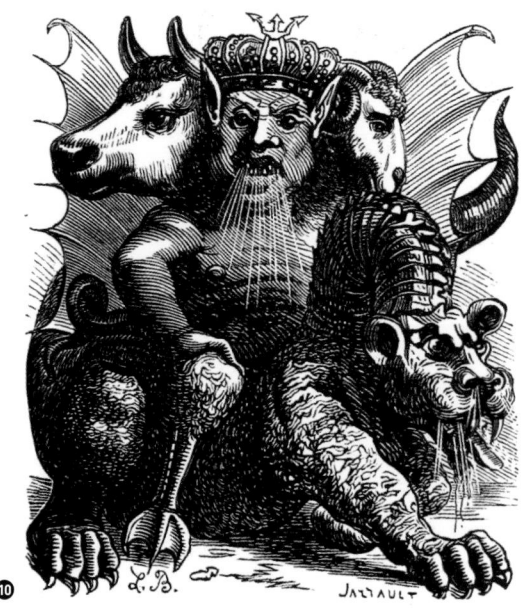

⑩

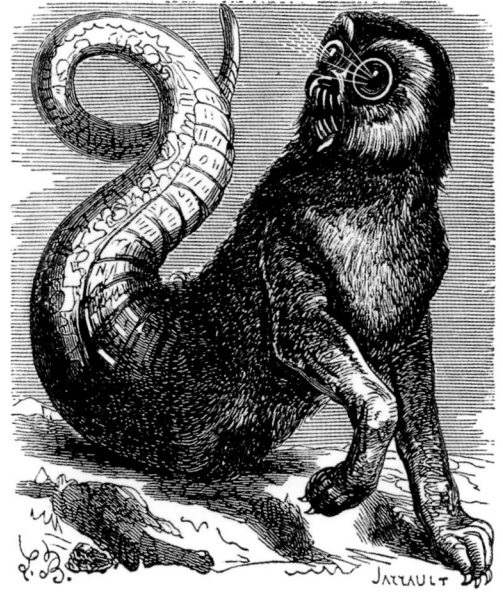

⑪

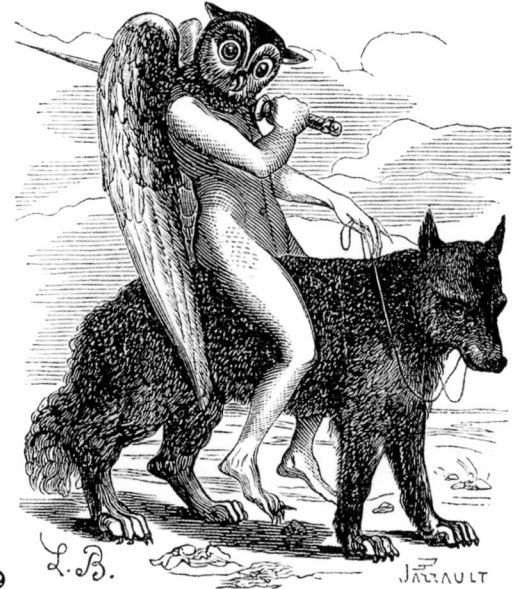

⑫

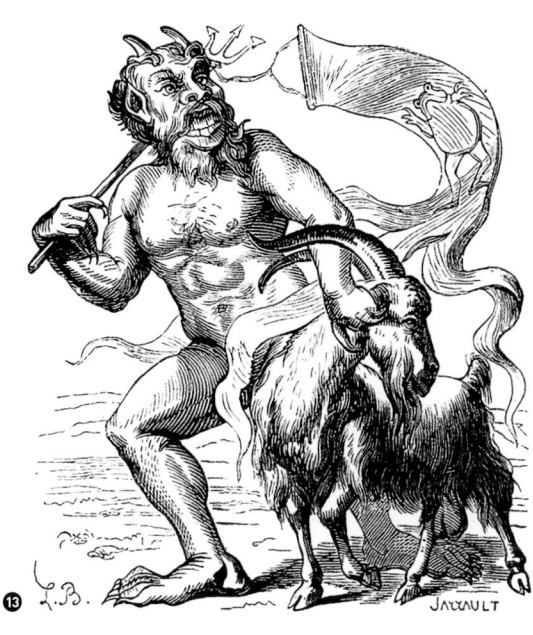

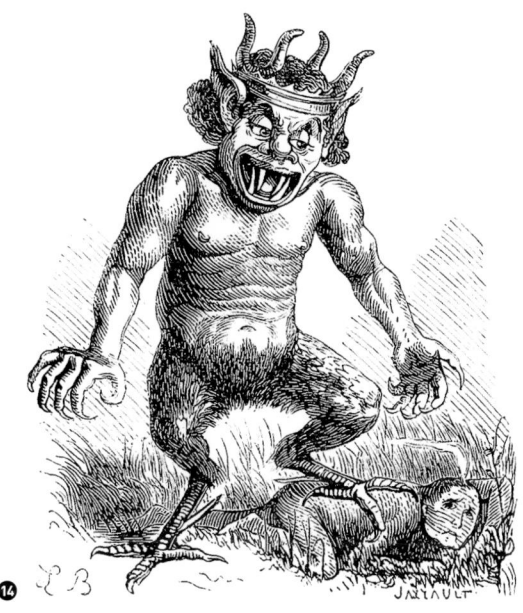

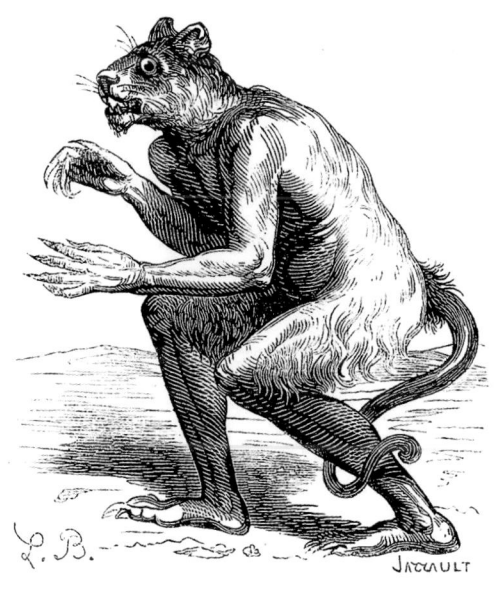

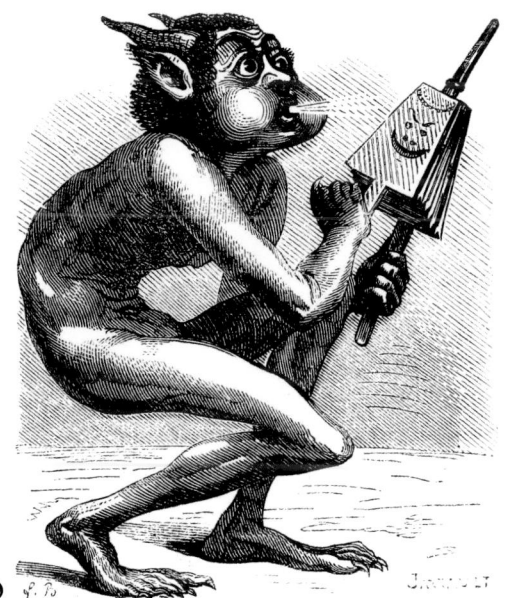

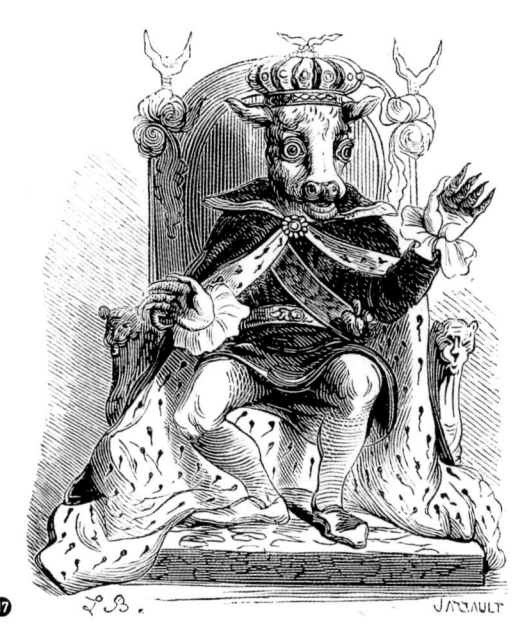

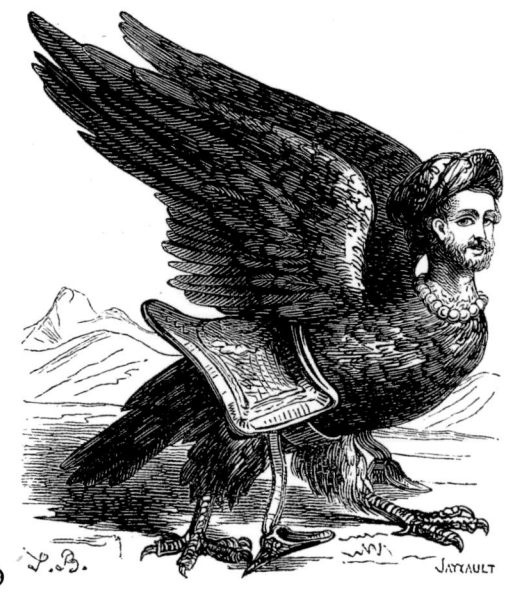

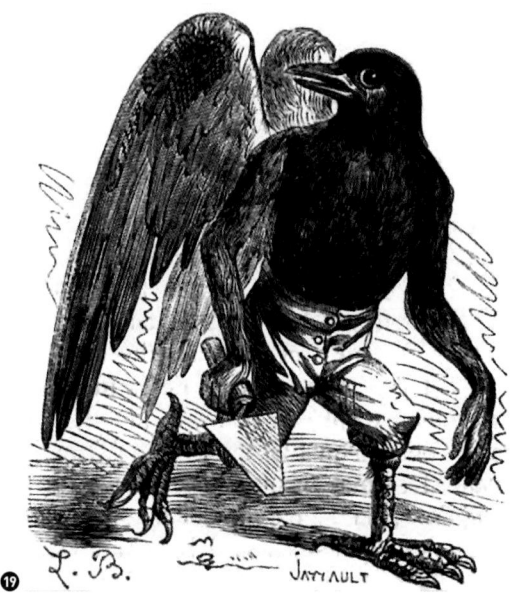

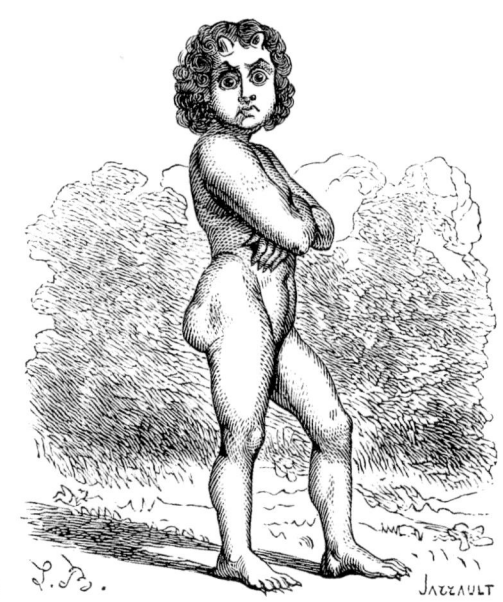

❶ *Eurynome is minor figure drawn from Greek mythology, where he is a daemon of Hades, charged with eating the flesh of the dead. The second-century Greek geographer Pausanias, in the only ancient passage referencing Eurynome, writes that he is "of a color between blue and lake, like that of meat flies; he is showing his teeth and is seated, and under him is spread a vulture's skin."* **❷** *True to his name, Belzebuth is the Lord of the Flies.* **❸** *Belphegor, who finds his origins as an ancient Moabite god, was historically associated with the sin of sloth.* **❹** *Adrammelech, an ancient Semitic god referenced in the biblical Book of Kings, here imagined by Colin de Plancey and Le Breton as an ass-headed peacock god. Tradition has perhaps drawn on ancient pagan traditions which slurred Christianity as being the worship of a donkey-god (with early satirical representations of the crucifixion depicting just that), and then combing Adrammelech with the malevolent peacock deity worshiped in the Kurdish faith of the Yazidis.* **❺** *Unicorn-headed Amdusias, a demon who finds his first mention in the Goetian corpus.* **❻** *Associated with the night-terror of the incubus, the demon Ephialtes lent his name to the naming of a paralyzing anxiety disorder in the eighteenth century. Here, Le Breton clearly draws from Fuseli's example to convey the stultifying helplessness of experiencing a nightmare.* **❼** *Astaroth, often referenced as part of an Unholy Trinity of hell alongside Lucifer and Beelzebub, and whose name is most likely derived from the Canaanite goddess Astarte.* **❽** *The biblical monster of Behemoth, whom Le Breton imagines as looking similar to the Hindu god Ganesh.*

❾ *Bael, a prince of Hell, and a disturbing combination of the human, feline, and amphibian, all made ambulatory by a skittering of fur-covered spider legs.* **❿** *Colin de Plancey and Le Breton envisioned Asmodeus as an anatomical panoply of bestial parts, the fearsome chimera drawing from a bull, ram, bat, serpent, and other creatures.* **⓫** *The Egyptian god Amon reimagined as a serpentine-canine-owl demon.* **⓬** *A demon from the* Ars Goetia *known as Andras, here sporting an owl head evocative of Minerva.* **⓭** *Azazel appears with a satyr-like physiognomy, a stylistic conflation of the Hebraic and the Hellenic.* **⓮** *This potbellied demon named Deumus derives from Durga of Hinduism, a reflection of the growing orientalist fascinations in the century that the dictionary was compiled.* **⓯** *Flaurous, another demon from Goetian tradition, here crouching with the countenance of a panther.* **⓰** *Xaphan, the pyromaniacal associate of Satan who tried to burn down heaven, here clutching a bellows to further spread conflagration.* **⓱** *The bovine qualities of Moloch are apparent in this illustration of the fearsome child-eater, who wears the regalia of European aristocracy.* **⓲** *The demon Garuda, a birdlike creature that appears in Vedic faiths including Hinduism, Buddhism, and Jainism, is depicted wearing a turban as Le Breton's indication of his eastern origins.* **⓳** *First mentioned in Johann Weirs'* Pseudomonarchia daemonum, *and identified as the Great President of Hell in the* Lesser Key of Solomon, *Marphas is illustrated by Le Breton as an appropriately gothic raven.* **⓴** *Lucifer himself, not as a fearsome monster, but as the haughty and prideful child that he is.*

monsters while writing in the sober pen of the classifying naturalist. Collin de Plancy was a one-man demonic Académie Française, measuring, defining, and organizing demons from Abigor to Zaebos in an abecedarium of hellish wonder.

All together Collin de Plancy provided entries (across 582 pages) of sixty-five different demons, including favorites from the pages of Dante, Milton, and others, including Asmodeus, Azazel, Bael, Behemoth, Belphegor, Belzebuth, Mammon, and Moloch alongside their sulfury compatriots. The most interesting edition of the text would be the one released in 1863, illustrated with creepy exactitude by Le Breton, who is otherwise known for his bevy of nautical-themed works. The *Dictionnaire Infernal* has the staidness of a reference work, but the brilliance of Le Breton's engravings, which recall the pictures of his contemporary Gustave Doré, is such that many of us have seen those images repeated over and over in a variety of infernal books. Collin de Plancy's greatest contribution is perhaps the demonic list, which provided such inspiration to his artistic colleague.

It's both edifying and frightening to consider the magnificence of some of these illustrations. For example, among the more minor demons there is "Adramelech, great chancellor of the underworld, intendant of the wardrobe of the sovereign of the demons, president of the high council of the devils" who "showed himself under the form of a mule, and sometimes even that of a peacock," appearing in Le Breton's illustration in full Yazidi glory as an ass-headed version of that ancient pagan god Melek Taus. Or Alastor, described by Collin de Plancy as a "severe demon, a supreme executor of the sentences of the infernal monarch." Breton's depiction shows a deformed, serpentine, horned man who would almost seem like the jovial sort of devil one could envision as the mascot of a New Jersey hockey team, or a southern university, if it wasn't for the bestial gleam in his wild eye and his terrifying sneer. Or Amduscias, in "the form of a unicorn" for whom "The trees bow to his voice," who "commands twenty-nine legions." A few pages later and there is Amon, a horrific hell-beast with globular pitch-black eyes, a "great and powerful marquis of the infernal empire" who appears as a "wolf, with a serpent's tail . . . [whose] head resembles that of an owl, and its beak shows very sharp canine teeth."

As if Le Breton's picture wasn't terrifying enough, Collin de Plancy reminds us that this nightmare creature "knows the past and the future, and reconciles whenever he wants," helpfully adding that "his friends are quarrelsome." That particular demon commands forty legions. Or there is Ephialtes, a pug-faced, bird-winged, wild-eyed little gremlin perched atop the chest of a man like Fuseli's *Nightmare*, for whom Collin de Plancy supplies only a one-sentence description, explaining that he derives from the "Greek name of the nightmare . . . a kind of incubus that stifles sleep." And there is Eurynome, who has "long teeth, a frightful body full of wounds, and a fox skin for clothing." Le Breton depicts Eurynome as a caprine, saw-toothed, double-horned creature on bended knee, frowning at some unseen victim, "showing his great teeth like a starving wolf." And then there is Belphegor, who is associated with the deadly sin of sloth and depicted as leaning forward with pinched brow and strained eyes, clutching his own tail to the side while perched atop a primitive toilet, trying to take a shit.

But Collin de Plancy's concern in the *Dictionnaire Infernal* wasn't just the defecation of minor demons, but indeed providing instruction on both the history and the practical utility of the more exulted among Satan's minions as well. There is Asmodeus, whom the Talmud claimed was born of a succubus who slept with King David, but whom Collin de Plancy argued was "the ancient serpent who seduced Eve." Associated with lust, Asmodeus is presented as a fearsome three-headed monstrosity (with only one of those heads being that of a man), and yet King Solomon (whom the occult tradition claims had a special knowledge of controlling demons) "loaded him with irons and forced him to help build the temple of Jerusalem." Or reflect upon that "heavy and stupid demon" Behemoth. Calling to mind his appearance in the Book of Job, Collin de Plancy writes that some "commentators pretend that it is the whale, and others that it is the elephant," with Breton choosing to depict Behemoth as a bipedal version of the later, clutching his hairy engorged belly like some sort of malevolent version of Ganesh.

Then there is Bael, "the first king of hell," who has "three heads, one of which has the shape of a toad, the other that of a man, and the third of a cat," to which Le Breton has helpfully added a number of fur-covered arachnid legs as well. The Phoenician god Ba'al, from whom Collin de Plancy's Bael derives his name, was associated with all manner of idolatries and blasphemies, and also is the inspiration for that other lieutenant of hell, Belzebuth (or Belzebub, or Beelzebuth), the trusted advisor of Lucifer whose name appears in the records of exorcists from Loudon, France, to Salem, Massachusetts. Literally translated the name is "Lord of the Flies," and Le Breton decided to depict this demon as a startlingly biologically accurate insect, with long pinching mandibles and weirdly human eyes, a skull and crossbones as a finishing touch on his papery thin and veiny wings. If anything, the strange verisimilitude of the insect-like creature makes his image all the more terrifying, his segmented thorax and his spindly arms reminding one of that Enlightenment monstrosity, the flea magnified by Antonie van Leeuwenhoek's microscope a century and a half before Collin de Plancy, which demonstrated that the nightmares of reason and of superstition are not always as divergent as we might think.

And therein lay the similarity between the two genres, the Enlightenment positivist book of natural causes and the magical book of supernatural ones: They are both committed to explanation. As Dr. Johnson argued previously, they required things to be "reduced to method." Collin de Plancy's uneasy place between his rationalist youth and his occult maturity may not be as uneasy as might be assumed, for magic is not the opposite of logic. Magic should not be conflated with mysticism, for the later points to truths beyond language, but the former is as invested in the connection between words and things as reason is. Both magic and reason have as motivating faiths a belief in the inherent explicability of reality: that there is a given order to the world and that human minds can comprehend and control this order. Whether that order is supernatural or natural is incidental, that there is structure to the system is what is important.

Collin de Plancy's dictionary may be a grimoire, or his grimoire may be a dictionary, but fundamentally the distinction between them is less stark than might be supposed. The mystic has shuffled off all earthly language, but the magician is a type of philologist of the sacred, desperately holding on to the presumption that letter and phoneme and syllable and word can mingle together into a comprehensible sentence. Stavans writes that "Dictionaries are like mirrors: they are a reflection of the people who produced and consumed them." If this is true, then the *Dictionnaire Infernal* is not just a reflection of Collin de Plancy, who dwelled among shadows yet desired to illuminate, but it is also a reflection of our own modern world of which the author of that text was an early member. Dictionaries, like grimoires, exist to make explicable our inexplicable reality.

What Collin de Plancy's dictionary demonstrates is the close affinity between the scientist's rationalistic and encyclopedic categorizations, and the occultist's related desire to bring order to disorder. A dictionary, with its words listed like demons, its concern with proper order and grammar (lest our spells don't work) is simply a modern, secular grimoire. The genre establishes how permeable the membrane is that separates our gleaming present from our shadowy past. The *Dictionnaire Infernal*, far from being an archaic remnant, reminds us that our culture is fairly archaic anyhow, or rather more accurately, that distinctions between antiquity and modernity ultimately mean little. If there is any wisdom to be gleamed from the dictionary, it's in the observation that Collin de Plancy's hell is organized as military bureaucracy, demons commanding hellish legions. Like most demonologists, Collin de Plancy places his specters in hierarchies, arrangements of hegemonic pyramids with Lucifer at the top. Whether hell is real or not, Collin de Plancy embodies a more fundamental truth: Demons may or may not have power, but power is always demonic. For we always have been, and always shall be, a demon-haunted world. But, with apologies to C.S. Lewis, what grimoires prove is not that demons exist, but that they can be tamed. If there is any consolation to be found, it's that controlling our demons is possible only if we're able to name them, whether they are of the supernatural or the rationalist variety—and, in either case, a dictionary is what we shall need.

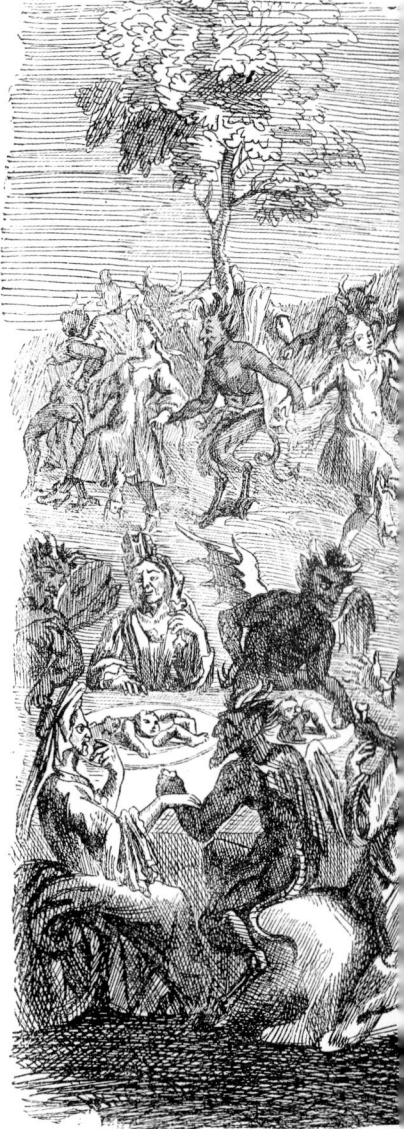

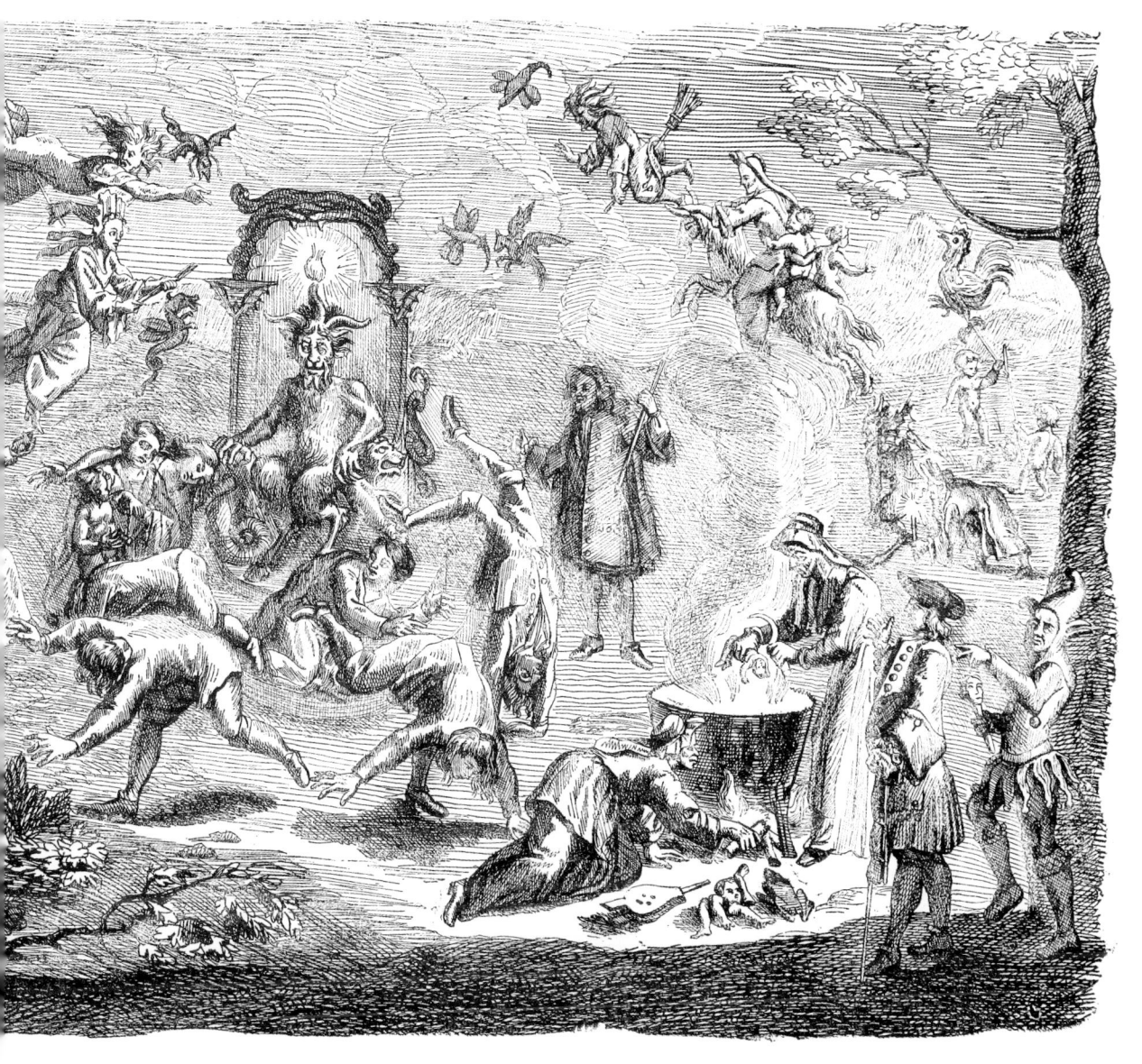

Front piece detail from the 1863 edition showing a witches' Sabbath.

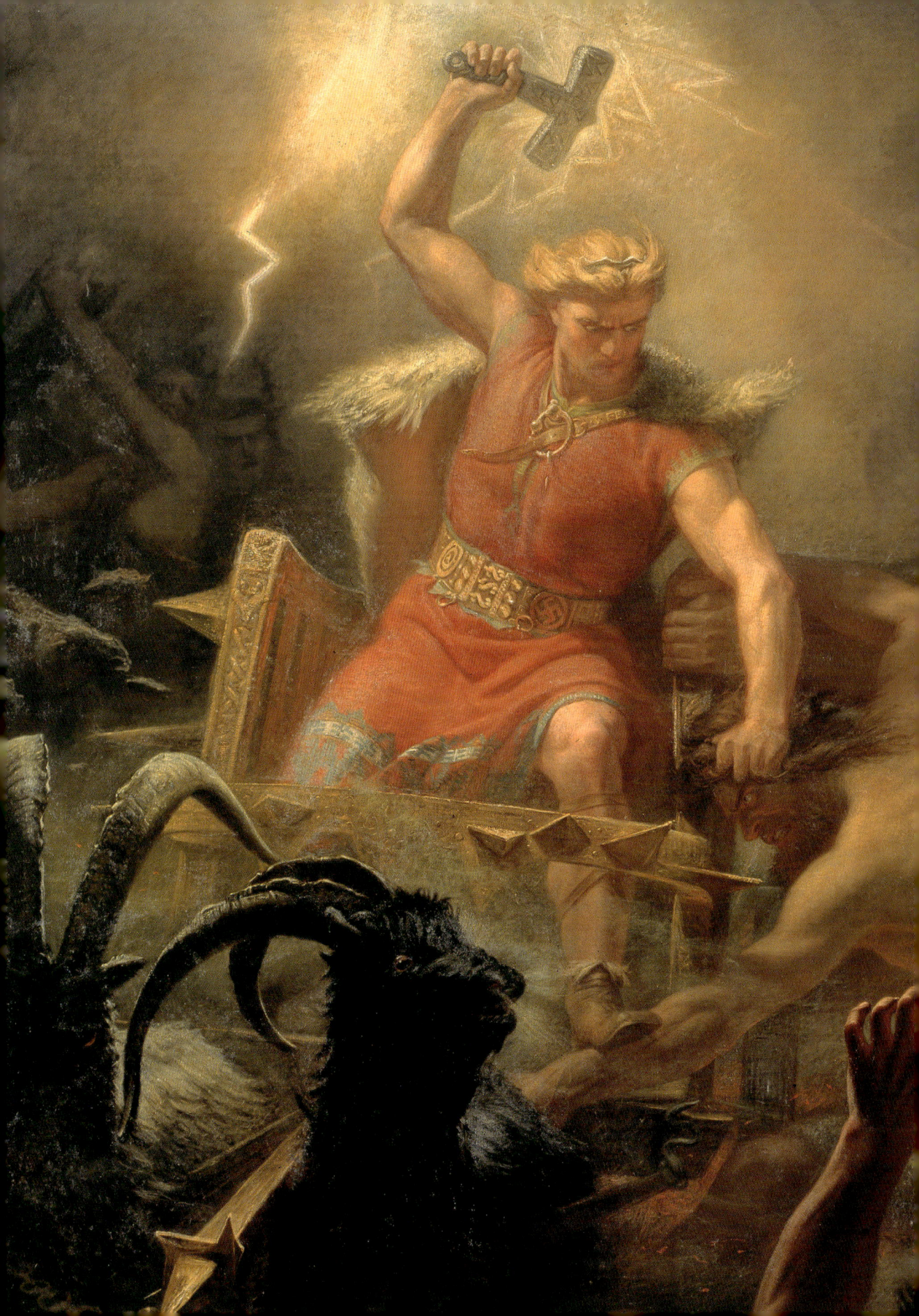

THE AGE OF BAPHOMET

t's not the sharp, twisted, and rough horns, the uncannily human wisp of a beard, or the bleating that sounds like screaming—no, it's none of those things that give goats their unmistakable glint of the demonic—it's the eyes. They have the intelligence of a dog, or even of a primate, but none of the warmth, and with their black slits framed by yellow they appear as if cold, reptile eyes have been placed into mammalian skulls. Goats aren't the only animal associated with the demonic of course; dogs, cats, and bats all have their role as familiars, and other domestic animals are similarly associated, from the bull head of Moloch to the equine countenance of Orobas and the raven beak of Caim, not to mention the demonic attributions of more exotic animals from lions to cephalopods. But the conflation of the caprine with the demonic is so seemingly universal, and so constant from time immemorial, that it's hard not to suspect something of archetypal accuracy in the connection. For an animal inhuman, there's still something unnervingly familiar in the way that they look at us, those eyes that seem to almost have consciousness behind them, albeit a mind that's distant, alien, foreign, other, unfeeling.

Goat-headed deities and demons are replete throughout the history of religious iconography, from cave paintings to the Romantic masterpieces of Goya, yet in 1856 a particularly iconic and totemistic example of the form was introduced in a volume entitled *Dogma and Ritual of High Magic*. Structured in twenty-two chapters that are meant to mimic the number of cards in a tarot deck (long a favored tool in occult circles), the book argued that the natural science that Enlightenment thinkers believed had superseded supernatural ways of understanding was fallacious; that rather a perennial esotericism existed across the philosophies and religions of the world, and that a type of high magic could be distilled from these traditions and understood as a coherent metaphysic. Seeing the tarot as a convenient means of explaining this high magic, the author enumerates how the various cards of the deck connect to occult subjects, with the fifteenth card—the Devil—responsible for much of the notoriety of *Dogma and Ritual of High Magic*.

There the author included his own illustration of a humanoid figure whose head was that of a feral, bestial, monstrous goat. His shaggy face makes the shape of a triangle, the beard tapering to a point, while two curved horns jut out above his ears, a pentagram inscribed on his forehead literalizing the implied shape of his countenance. In a stance of benediction, the two first fingers of the creature's right hand are held aloft as if conferring a priestly blessing, with his left hand in the same position, but pointing toward the ground. A type of kilt or toga covers his legs, with two cloven-hoofed feet crossed beneath, and a raven-black set of angel wings jut out from his human torso, a

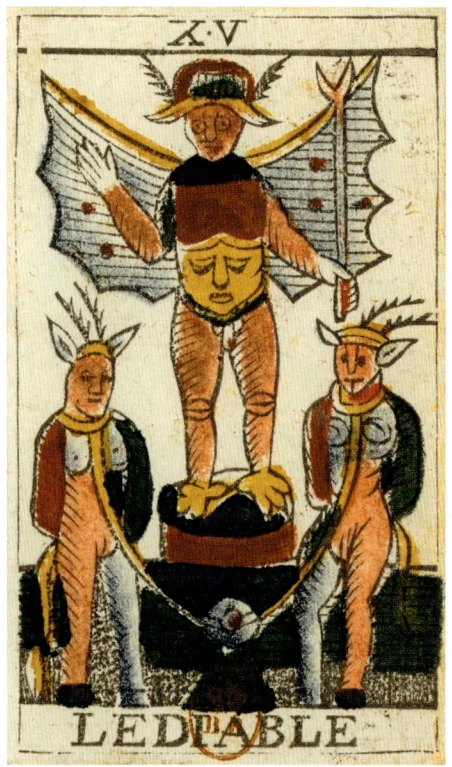

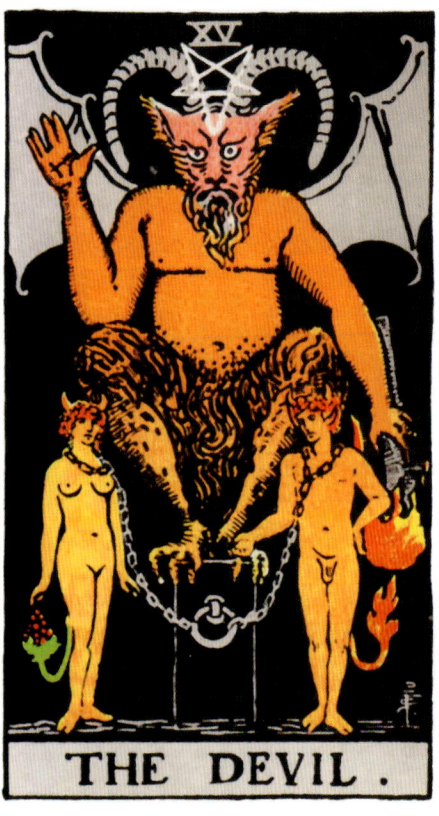

pair of womanly breasts on the being's chest confusing the gender of the beast. And of course, those eyes—staring out at the reader from underneath arched, human eyebrows. As the author's gloss reads, the "beast's head expresses the horror of the sinner, whose materially acting, solely responsible part has to bear the punishment exclusively; because the soul is insensitive according to its nature and can only suffer when it materializes." Clearly evocative of the traditional horned god—Satan. Yet this drawing was labeled as the demon "Baphomet," and it was contributed by the most prominent occultist of the nineteenth century—Éliphas Lévi.

The first thing you must know about Éliphas Lévi is that his real name was Alphonse Louis Constant, for that alteration tells you something of his priorities. Said Hebraization of his name was Lévi's attempt at a bit of Orientalist verisimilitude, such an affectation born from his attraction toward all of the ancient occult learning that he associated with the Near East. Lévi wished to be seen as a hermeticist privy to the secret of the Egyptians and Chaldeans, the Jews and the Greeks, and he constructed his identity as surely as he constructed the most formidable body of occult writings during the nineteenth century. Davies writes that "Over and over again when reading through the voluminous and often turgid library of occult expositions produced during the second half of the nineteenth century, one finds one name recurring over and over again"—that of the polymathic dilettante who would become the most popular writer and speaker on occultism during the age, and who would have a formidable influence on magic through the modern era.

TOP

Its use possibly traceable to the medieval heresy of Catharism, the tarot has been a means of encoding potentially heretical doctrines for centuries, and was particularly popular in Renaissance Italy. By the nineteenth century, it was frequently used as a tool of divination, with the fifteenth card in the deck a picture of the Devil (other cards show a magician, an emperor, death, and even a female pope, among others). This particular card is from the fifteenth-century Tarot of Marseilles.

BOTTOM

Card XV of the Rider-Waite Tarot, designed by occultist A.E. Waite in 1909 and illustrated by Pamela Colman Smith. (The "Rider" is the name of the company that manufactured these cards.) Waite was an associate of Lévi, and he drew directly from Baphomet in his vision for the card.

OPPOSITE PAGE

Baphomet as illustrated by Éliphas Lévi in Dogma and Ritual of High Magic, *published in two volumes, one in 1854 and one in 1856.*

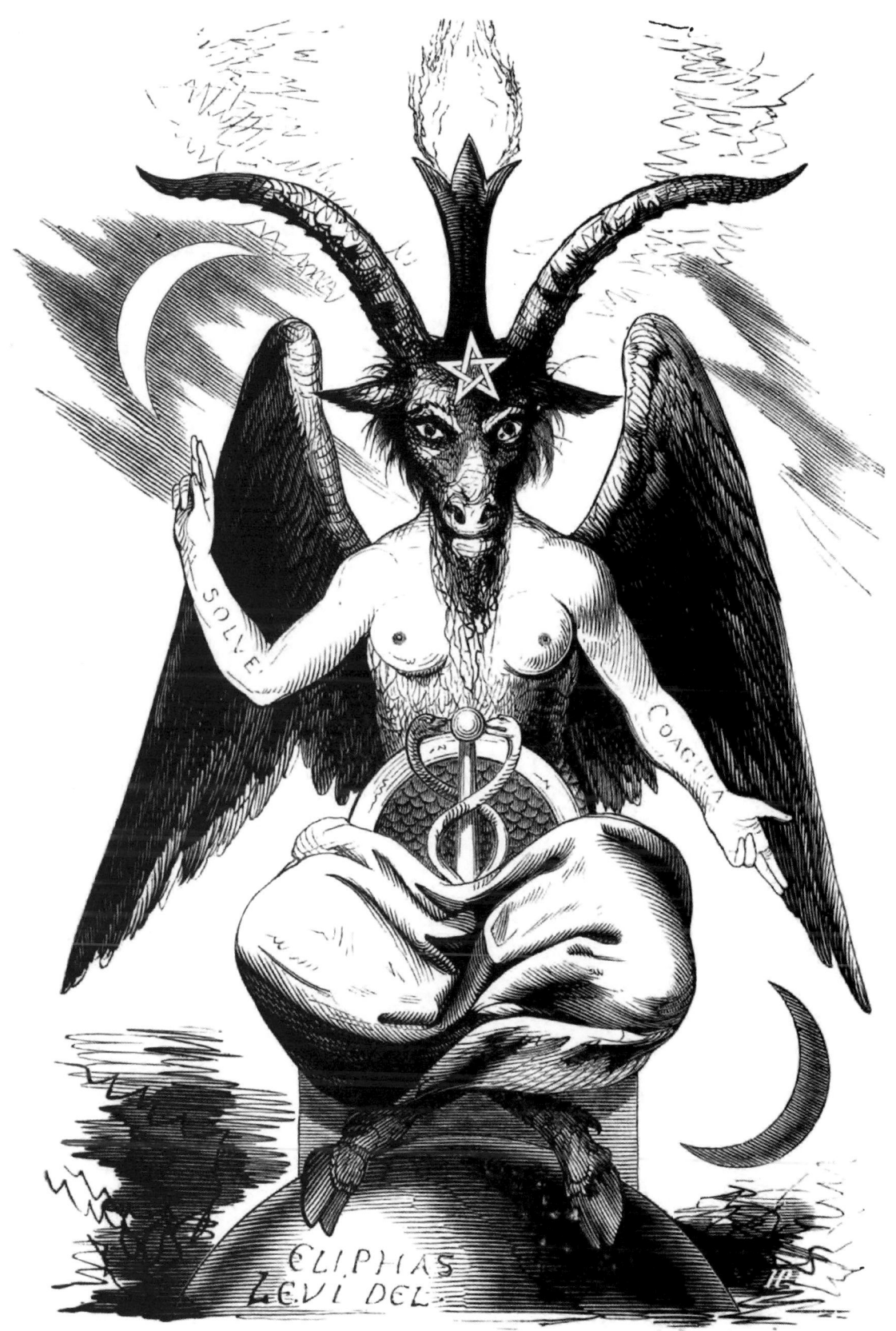

SOLVE

COAGULA

ELIPHAS
LEVI DEL

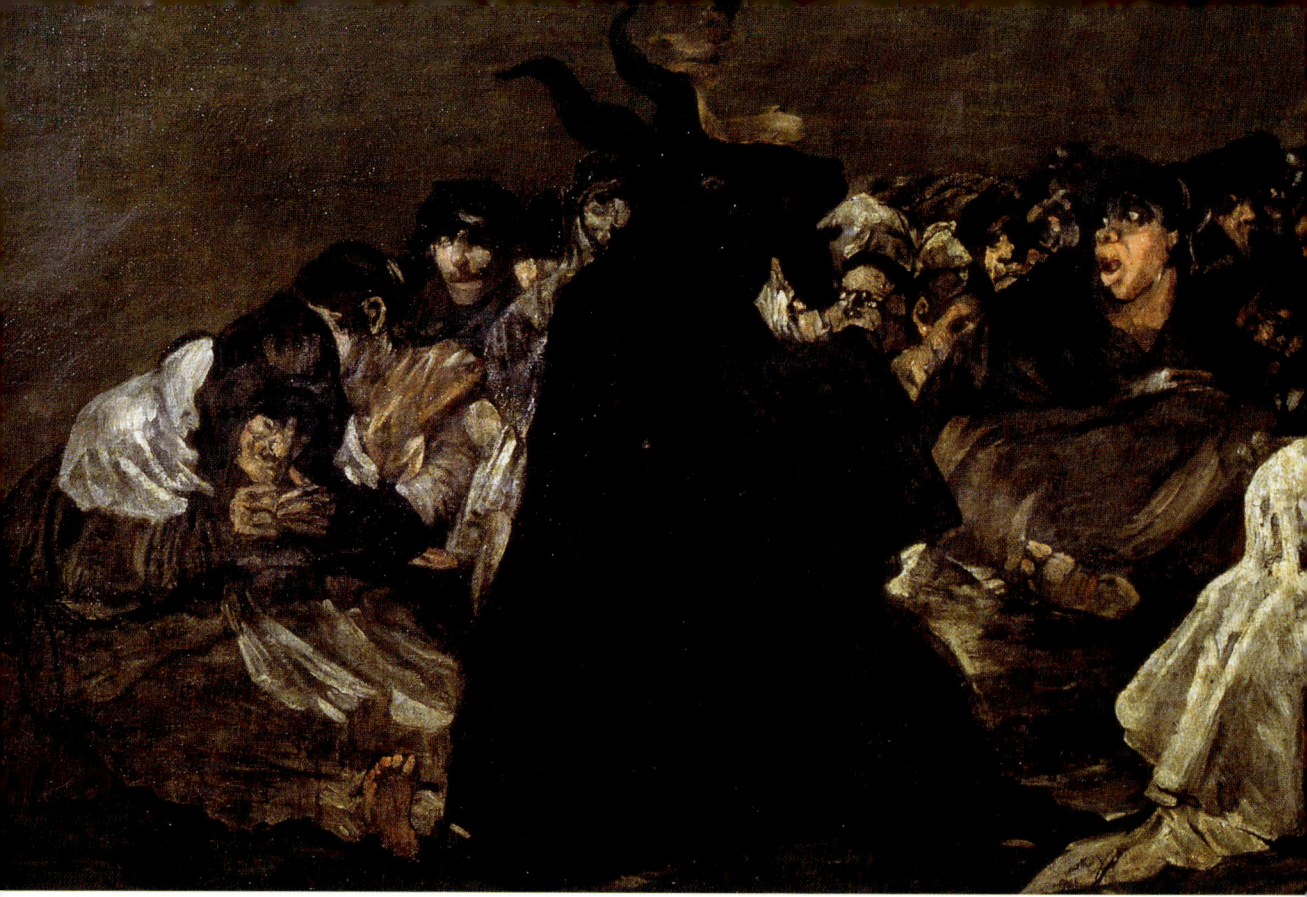

Born to a Parisian shoemaker, Lévi trained to take priestly orders before leaving seminary at the age of twenty-six, claiming that he would not prostrate himself "before the altar of a cold and egotistical cult." Despite rejecting the papacy, Lévi ironically never rejected Catholicism, seeing himself as always a faithful, albeit unconventional, member of the Church. That speaks to his rejection of Black Magic, for he saw conjuration as a grievous sin, yet contributed one of the most iconic symbols of demonology in the form of his illustration from *Dogma and Ritual of High Magic*. Baphomet's blank eyes have been recycled on heavy metal album covers and in the iconography of the twentieth-century Church of Satan, he has become veritably synonymous with the Devil. Certainly understandable, but Baphomet is more complicated than that; he represents the syncretic enthusiasms of nineteenth-century demonology, and the ways in which the Enlightenment understanding of diabology had turned inward again and returned to older perspectives, while preserving the satanic as a figure of rebellion. During the Romantic era, "Theology and metaphysics were superseded by estheticism and symbolism," writes Russell, so that many occultists came to believe that the rebel "angels' first fall had been esthetic, a love of beauty so intense that they desire to grasp and possess it for themselves." Thus Baphomet isn't merely a revolutionary—he is an aesthete, a bohemian, an *artist* who draws upon the raw materials of humanity's collective culture to distill something that is both profoundly ancient and radically new—he is the god of the Romantics.

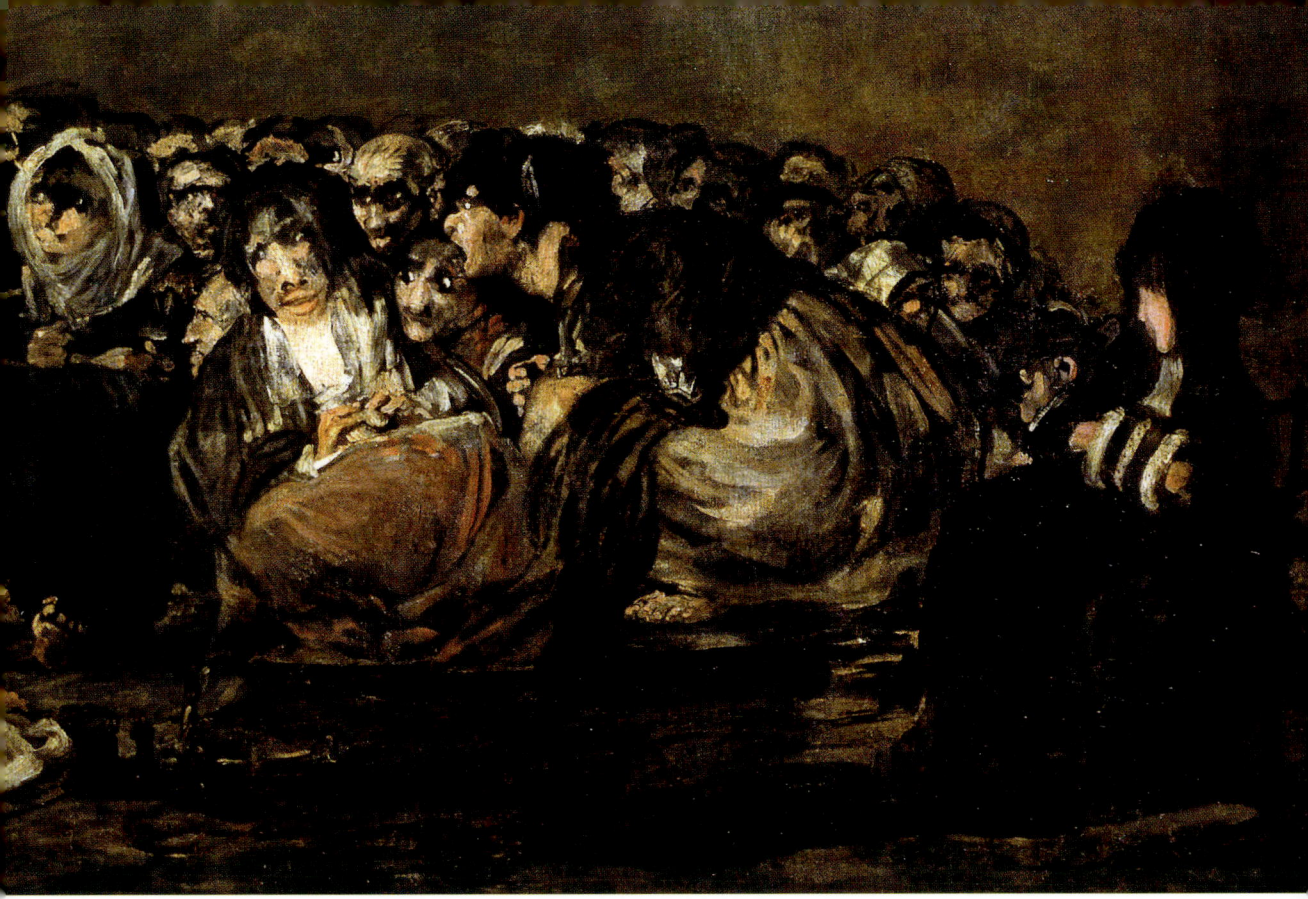

Lévi identifies Baphomet with the great horned god of the ancient, saying that this "phantom of all terrors," this "terrible emperor of night," stalks through history. His figure is the "Ahriman of the Persians, the Typhon of the Egyptians, the Python of the Greeks, the old serpent of the Hebrews, the fantastic monster, the nightmare ... the great beast of the Middle Ages, and—worse than all these— the Baphomet of the Templars." The author didn't invent this name in *Dogma and Ritual of High Magic*, though he certainly popularized it, even if its etymology goes back some nine centuries before. Associated with the sect of medieval crusaders and financiers known as the Knights Templar, the horned creature was supposedly a demon whom they adopted the worship of while fighting in the Levant. Based on the prosody of the word, "Baphomet" is most likely a corruption of the name "Muhammad," though descriptions of the deity certainly

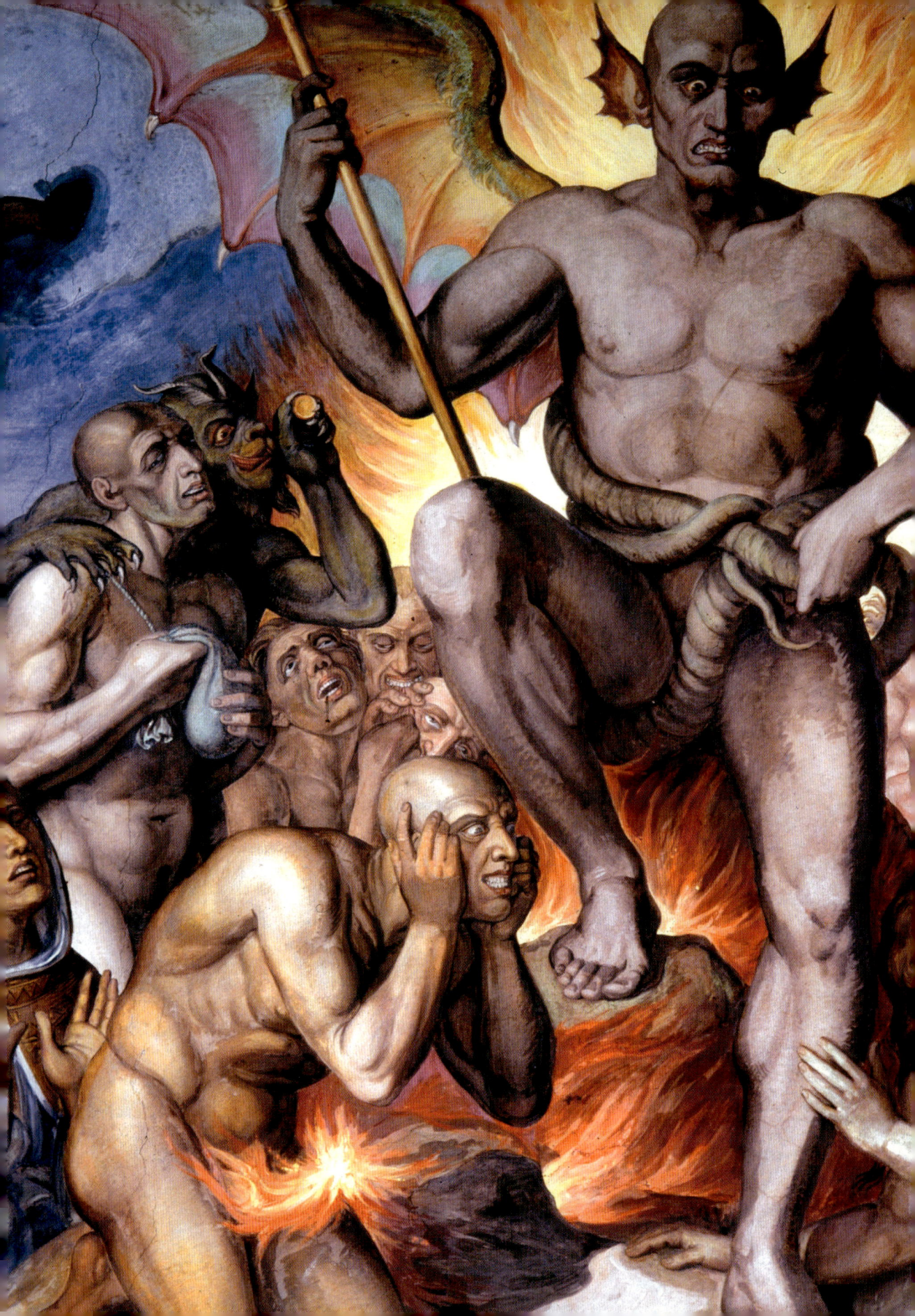

bear no similarity to that of the Prophet. Earliest usage of the name goes back to the eleventh century, when crusaders used the term in reference to Islamic worship, and by the fourteenth century it had been entered into inquisitorial records when the Templars were tried on order of King Philip IV of France for a variety of (dubious) charges that included sodomy, heresy, and blasphemy.

According to court documents from the Roman Inquisition, as quoted by Jules Michelet in his 1860 *History of France*, the Templars were accused of having supplicated themselves before idols, "some of which had three faces, others but one; sometimes, it was a human skull . . . That in their assemblies, and especially in their grand chapters, they worshipped the idol as a god, as their savior . . . that it bestowed on the order all its wealth, made the trees flower, and the plants of the earth to sprout forth." Accusations such as these were almost certainly spurious, even while there is convincing reason to believe that the Templars may have engaged in some unusual rituals as part of their individual initiations. Most historians argue that such elaborate tales were slanders invented by those prosecuting the Templars, such as Philip IV, who had a vested political and economic interest in attacking the wealthy and powerful order. Nor does it need to be said that devotion toward an invented Baphomet bears any similarity to genuine Islamic worship, the bastardized figure just one aspect of the fanciful libels that medieval Catholics invented about Muslims. Despite the inaccuracy of such claims, this fantastical narrative regarding the Templars—an order defined by secret knowledge, cryptic rituals, and the mastery of Oriental magic—became prevalent during the Enlightenment, especially as it was claimed that groups like the Freemasons, Illuminati, and Rosicrucians could anachronistically be traced back to medieval forebears. More incendiary, of course, was anything with the taint of the demonic around the mysterious figure of Baphomet, but as Michael Haag jokes in *The Templars: The History and the Myth*, "Heresy and Satanism make good copy."

Before Lévi would appropriate the name for his own purposes, other occultists had begun to claim that Baphomet was a deity with a long genealogy independent of the Islamophobic machinations of medieval Catholic inquisitors, and that the "demon" was an entity who was valorized by any number of ancient groups, through a continuity of worship over the centuries. Eighteenth-century German scholar Christoph Friedrich Nicolai claimed that the being was a demiurge vaunted by the gnostics, while the French lexicographer Émile Littré traced an etymology based on an imaginative reading of the kabbalah. *Dogma and Ritual of High Magic* has incorporated within itself those understandings, while Lévi also innovates a number of his own fictions about Baphomet's identity.

A gloaming era, the Romantics of the nineteenth century couldn't quite decide whether their rejection of the Enlightenment's values meant a turning back toward more archaic understandings, or if something totally novel was struggling to be born. The Austrian neoclassical painter Joseph Anton Koch's frescoes at Rome's Cassa Massimo in 1825 show the influence of Renaissance art, as well as the visual language of Romantics like Blake.

Drawing upon caprine imagery that he associated with the ancient Egyptian Goat of Mendes, Lévi conflated Baphomet with a number of different beings, while arguing that it's a historical fallacy to understand the deity as being the Christian Devil. For the author, honoring Baphomet was not an exercise in Satanism, for the goat-headed beast wasn't malignant, but rather misunderstood. "[T]he adorers of this sign do not consider, as do we, that it is a representation of the devil," writes Lévi, "for them it is that of the god Pan, the god of our modern schools of philosophy, the god of the Alexandrian theurgic school and of our own mystical Neoplatonists . . . the god of Spinoza and Plato, the god of the primitive Gnostic schools." Without any historical evidence, and in an argument that prefigures Murray in the following century, Lévi maintained that the creature—symbol of a higher god worshiped by the spiritual elites—represented a continuity of tradition that went back to the horned deity of the ancients, a figure to be honored at secret Sabbaths held over the millennia, and that Baphomet was the "Christ . . . of the dissident priesthood."

As with the Renaissance, the nineteenth century was an age of syncretic enthusiasms, with scholars claiming to see threads of influence connecting any number of disparate figures, systems, beliefs, and traditions into a harmonious whole, occluded though knowledge of that synthesis may have been among the wider public. Baphomet is an exemplar of that tendency toward syncretism, the creative firmament of the Romantics and post-Romantics who devised their own religions from the detritus of that which has come before. In 1804, Blake infamously claimed that "I must Create a System, or be enslav'd by another Man," and such a profound metaphysical declaration of independence—simultaneously rejecting medieval faith and Enlightenment reason—was in many ways the central axiom of Romanticism, and of the occultism that marked the nineteenth century. "The depersonalization of Satan, his reduction to a symbol, and the unmooring of the symbol from Bible and tradition meant that the idea of the Devil could float free of its traditional meanings," writes Russell. To construct one's own religion, one's own "System," is an audacious exercise in ersatz ex nihilo self-creation, and if anyone could be said to have done so it was Lévi.

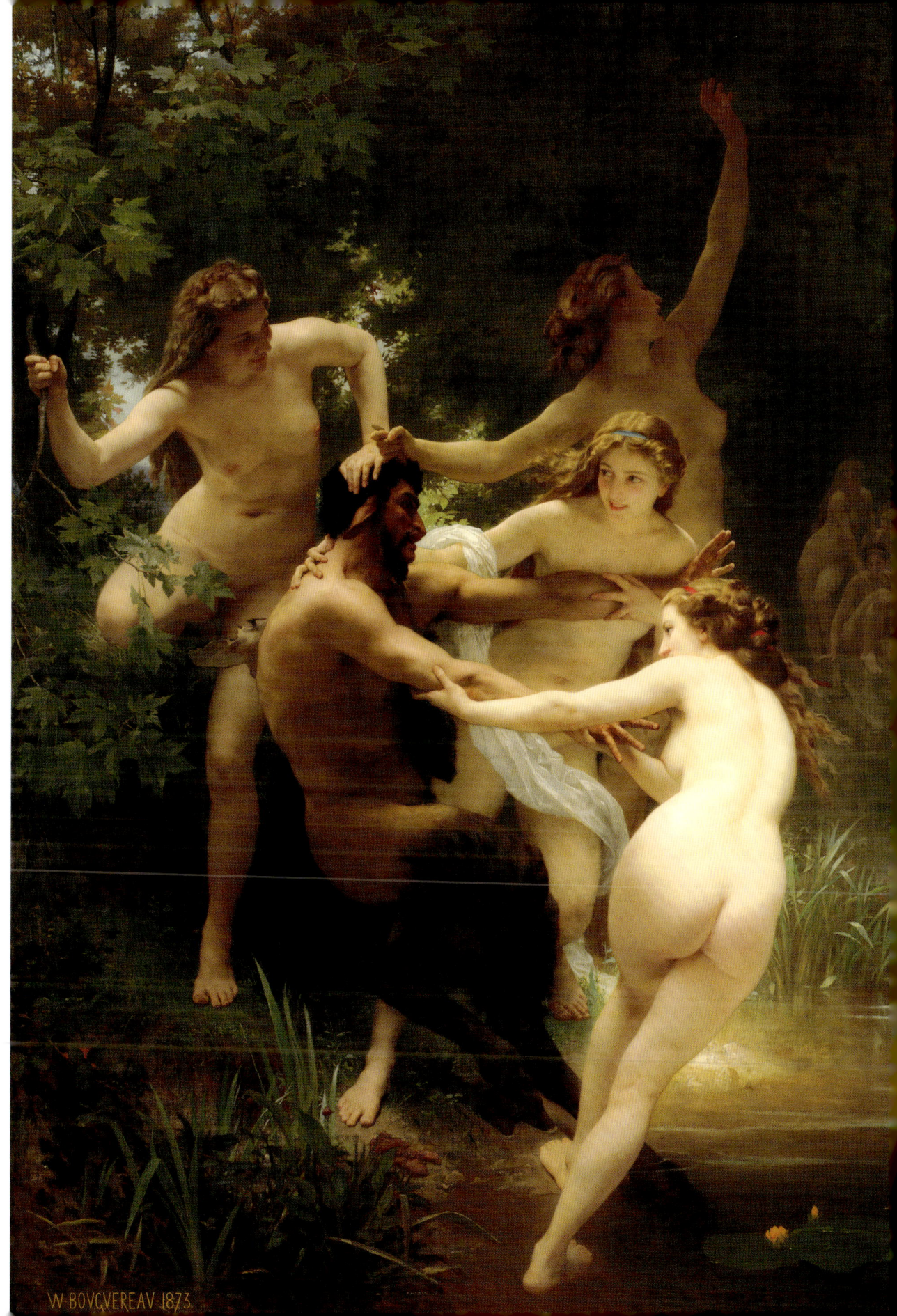

W·BOVGVEREAV·1873

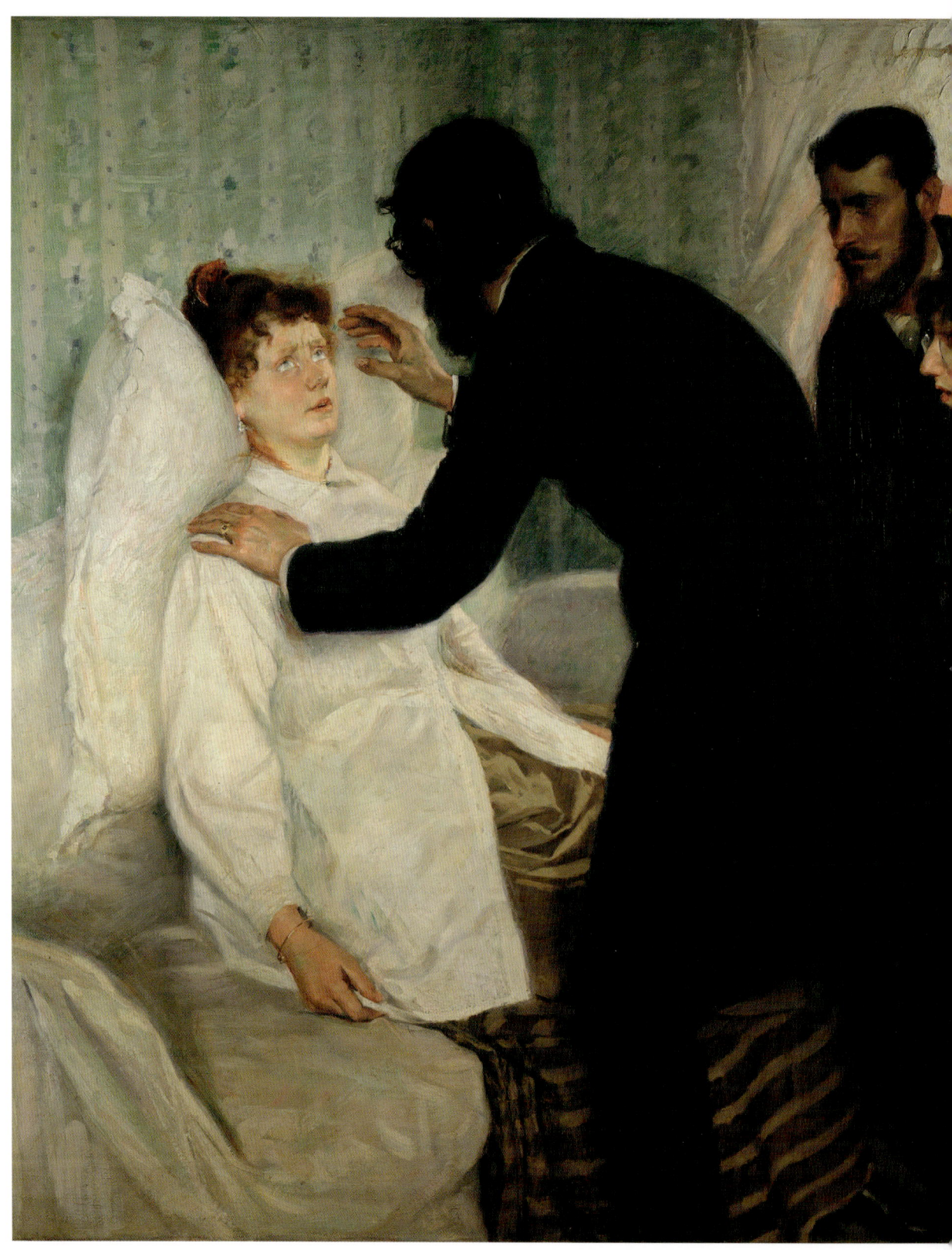

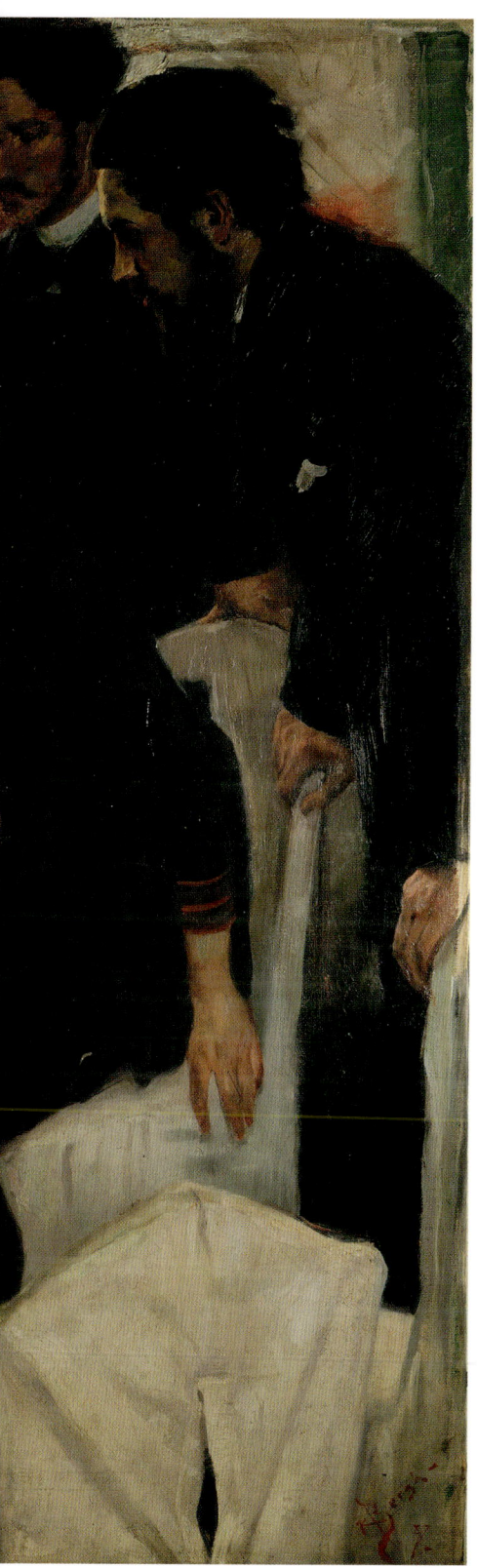

Davies writes that "During the early nineteenth century new pseudo-sciences such as mesmerism renewed intellectual interest in universal hidden forces . . . that truly galvanized public interest in the occult and provided a magnetic focal point for the swirl of disparate esoteric groups and ideas circulating in educated society." Various occult movements proliferated across Europe and America during the nineteenth century, from the occult Symbolist writers (who were strongly indebted to Lévi), the American syncretic religion of Spiritualism, which grew out of the Second Great Awakening and became popular around the time of the Civil War, and the baroque complexities of Russian writer Helena Blavatsky's Theosophy, as well as the darker currents of the Decadent writers (and their embrace of the actual Black Mass as a liturgical anti-sacrament). Baphomet is variously used or ignored by individual thinkers and writers across these movements, and yet his spirit marks the boldness and proliferation of such spiritual inventions that occurred during this century.

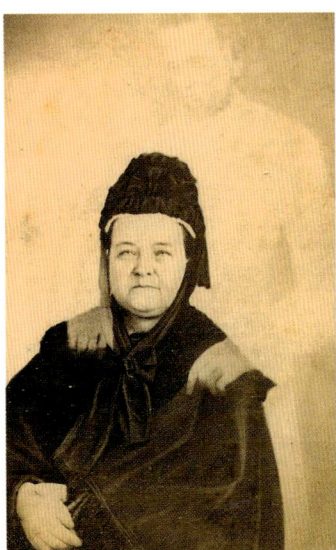
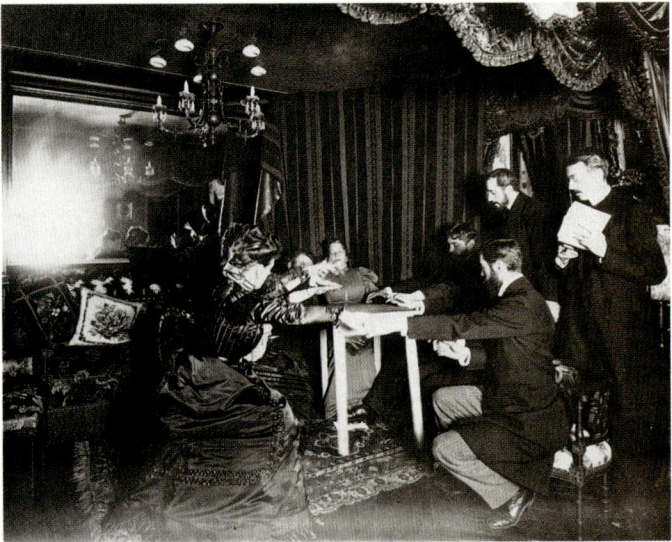
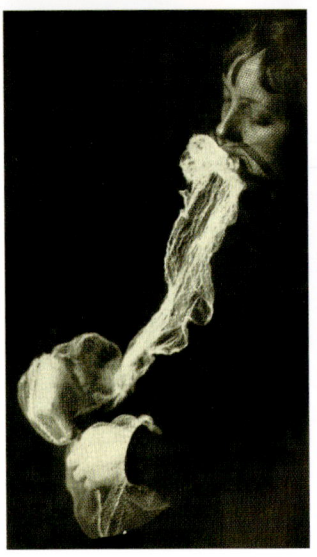
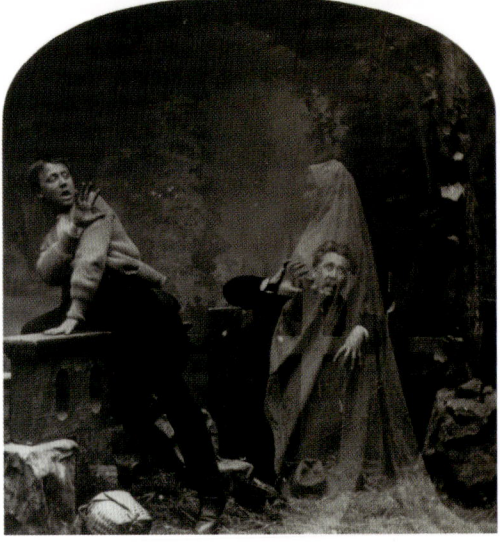

Spiritualists were innovative in term of using modern technology like photography to (depending on your perspective) either provide visual evidence of the spirit realm or to huckster gullible believers. Top to bottom, left to right, a photograph of First Lady Mary Todd Lincoln taken in 1869 by the medium William H. Mumler, with her husband, President Abraham Lincoln, a ghostly presence over her shoulder; a séance held in 1898 Paris with the Italian medium Eusapia Palladino, and featuring an "orb" specter; the medium Stanislawa Popielska producing ectoplasm, a type of spectral life force, as photographed by the German parapsychologist Albert von Schrenck-Notzing in 1913; and an almost comically hoaxed photograph taken through double exposure by the Melander and Brothers company in 1889. While the vast majority of "spirit photographs" seem amateurish, self-evident forgeries today, the most proficient (particularly those featuring ectoplasm) are still disquieting. Deception or authenticity weren't the only explanations for the provenance of spirit photographs, of course, with the 1866 Second Plenary Council of Baltimore, a gathering of American Catholic bishops, concluding that "There is little reason to doubt that some of the phenomena of spiritism are the work of Satan."

In the United States, the fervent evangelical revivals of the Second Great Awakening that burnt across the frontier during the first few decades of the nineteenth century resulted in the emergence of new sects, including the Seventh Day Adventists, the Jehovah's Witnesses, and the Mormons, with one of the most unusual groups being the loose affiliation of vaguely Christian gatherings known as Spiritualism. Combining a belief in the occult with Yankee Protestantism, and promoting the holding of seances, the uses of divination, and the manipulation of strange symbols, the Spiritualists emerged in upstate New York in 1848 when a trio of young girls known as the Fox Sisters claimed that they had made contact with spirits in another world, though the series of knocks, pops, and bangs that the specters used to communicate turned out to be an elaborate hoax concocted by the siblings. Despite that, Spiritualist adherents held a hope that the occult could supplement traditional religious faith, and that it could be placed on a scientific footing for explaining esoteric phenomena. Spiritualist speakers like the medium and proto-feminist Cora L.V. Scott and Paschal Beverly Randolph, a free Black man who introduced Rosicrucianism to America, lectured throughout the United States, holding forth on topics like the European occultists Emanuel Swedenborg and the scientist Franz Mesmer, an early researcher on hypnosis.

While some Spiritualists were con artists and grifters, the movement itself could be shockingly enlightened, advocating for radical positions concerning abolition and suffrage. "The standard-bearers of the American occult took a different path," from their European antecedents, writes Mitch Horowitz in *Occult America: White House Séances, Ouija Circles, Masons, and the Secret History of our Nation*. "They sought to remake mystical ideas as tools of public good and self-help." At its core, however, what defined Spiritualism was the same thing that distinguished European esotericism: a belief that the profane world was a dim reflection of a transcendent and sacred one, and that as it is here so it is above, as it is here, so as it is below. Matter can only be understood in terms of the spirit, so that as Scott said, "when the physical scientist declares that he has discovered the process of creation, he omits the one power of creation that alone is capable of solving the mystery." Conventional ministers rejected as either hoax or demonic manifestation the spirit visitations and the communication with the dead that Spiritualism championed, but Spiritualists themselves also had something to say about demonology, partially drawing from continental occultists like Lévi.

Writing in *Ghosts of Futures Past: Spiritualism and the Cultural Politics of Nineteenth-Century America*, Molly McGarry observes that "Spiritualists understood witchcraft as a sister belief, a past manifestation of otherworldly power, born of an American culture more likely to persecute messengers than to attend to sacred signs." Spiritualists may have believed that the individual beings who were interpreted as demons in previous centuries were real, but they also thought that they had been misnamed. Writing not of the Spiritualists, but of their European occult contemporaries, Russell notes that their "admiration for Satan was not Satanism, however—not the worship of evil—for they made the Devil the symbol of what they regarded as good." Satan had less of a role in American Spiritualism, but in the same way that Lévi and his associates rehabilitated the idea of Satan—redefining something like Baphomet as a symbol of good—so too did the Spiritualists reconfigure phenomenon like demonic possession as actually being a medium's connection with specters from the afterlife.

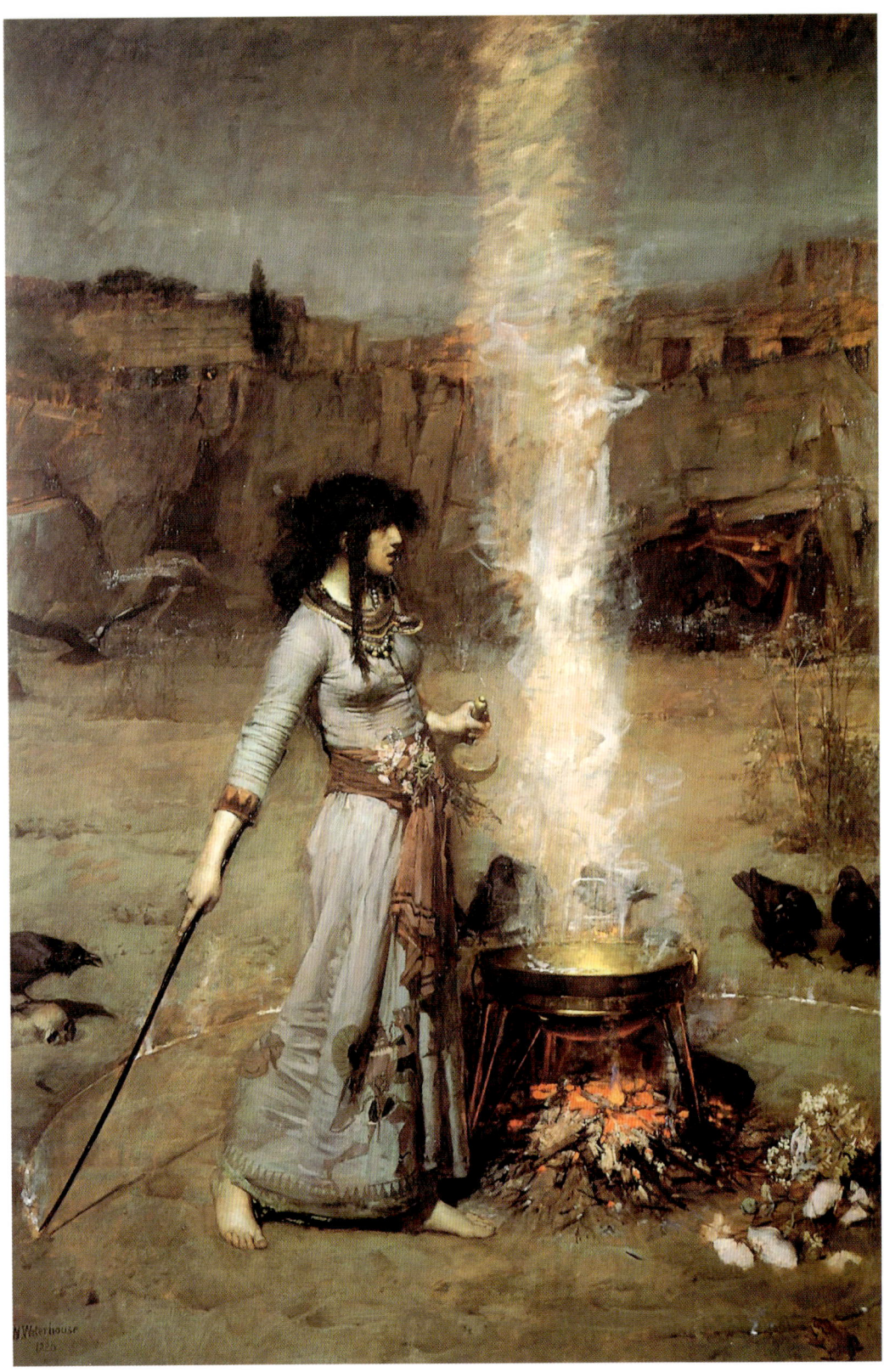

Perhaps even more enduring than American Spiritualism was the Theosophy of Madame Blavatsky, which unlike the former generated a fully realized demonology that perhaps evidenced some of the inversions of Lévi's goat-headed beast. An exemplary example of the Victorian predilection toward perennialism, which held that all religions were fundamentally composed of the same mystical core, Theosophists believed that a group of Tibetan masters, who had achieved both supernatural powers and unnaturally long life spans, were in possession of secrets that were disseminated through the person of Blavatsky. A Russian émigré to New York who was conversant with all of the leading occult luminaries of the age, Blavatsky promulgated her philosophy in 1877's *Isis Unveiled* and 1888's *The Secret Doctrine*. In that later volume, Blavatsky writes that "what is contained in this work is to be found scattered throughout thousands of volumes embodying the scriptures of the great Asiatic and early European religions, hidden under glyph and symbol, and hitherto left unnoticed because of this veil."

Blavatsky's demonology was complex, combining Vedic Hindu and Buddhist traditions with gnosticism, kabbalah, and Western esotericism. Russell explains that in a principle deriving from dualistic Manicheanism, Blavatsky saw Satan as "the shadow side of Jehovah, the darkness without which the Light could not shine so clearly. Lucifer is a necessary part of creation . . . the Logos, and so is assimilated to Christ." According to Theosophical tradition, angels were either self-created, self-existent, or something called "Fire-angels." The first of these types remained loyal to God during the war in heaven, but as Russell writes the "Fire-angels rebelled and made humankind with knowledge and therefore true freedom." Following that Promethean imperative (with precursors in Blake, Milton, and the gnostics), Blavatsky valorized Lucifer as the liberator of humanity who took arms against the demiurge that rules our reality, while worshiping him as "Satan, the serpent of Genesis, the real creator and benefactor, the Father of Spiritual Mankind." Across the corpus of her writings, Blavatsky mentions Baphomet by name a grand total of five times (though she was certainly familiar with Lévi's writings). Yet there is much of Baphomet in Blavatsky; not necessarily Lévi's invented dogma itself, but that same spirit of invention that the figure embodies, that alchemical transfiguration of disparate arcana into new doctrines, new deities from a dark realm of the hidden mind.

OPPOSITE PAGE

It would be simplistic to reduce nineteenth-century European occultism, American Spiritualism, and burgeoning neo-paganism into one another, especially since the first frequently claimed connection to Christianity, and the second was explicitly—if idiosyncratically—Protestant. Yet all three broad movements evidenced an increasing reevaluation of an idealized ancient paganism, and of the women who were persecuted in previous centuries as being witches. English painter John William Waterhouse's pre-Raphaelite composition The Magic Circle, *held by the Tate Britain, is indicative of the changing perspective concerning witches as a new romanticization that helped to encourage the proliferation of Wicca and other neo-pagan faiths in the twentieth century.*

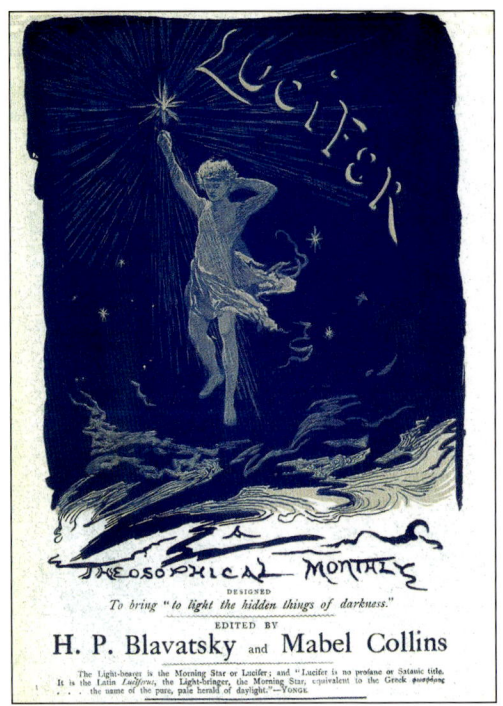

Baphomet is the avatar of this anarchic, creative potential—the veritable spirit of this age. Insomuch as iconoclasm toward traditional pieties is blasphemous, then Baphomet is a Lord of Blasphemy (despite Lévi's unconvincing protestations of orthodoxy). Audacity marks creation and creativity, as any individual's claim toward taking part in such a divine prerogative must by necessity be at least a bit heretical. A smidge of the Luciferian is thus about Baphomet, though the pure creation that he represents treats rebellion only as a means unto an end. Baphomet is all the more powerful for being a demon so obviously not just conjured, but instead created by a man—a symbol of humanity's ability to play the role of deity for themselves, and thus perhaps the most heretical idea possible. For the partisans of Romantic and Victorian occultism, this was no mere Baconian empiricism, the taming of nature through science and technology, but rather the ability to rewrite the code of transcendence itself, to make the individual partner in the very constitution of reality. In a word, they achieved the rediscovery of magic. The Age of Reason had eliminated the pre-modern denunciation against heresy, but rather than purge the earth of all manner of superstitions, the Enlightenment had ironically allowed for their unfettered freedom, so that in the firmament of the age, Baphomet could produce a multitude of children, endlessly regenerative.

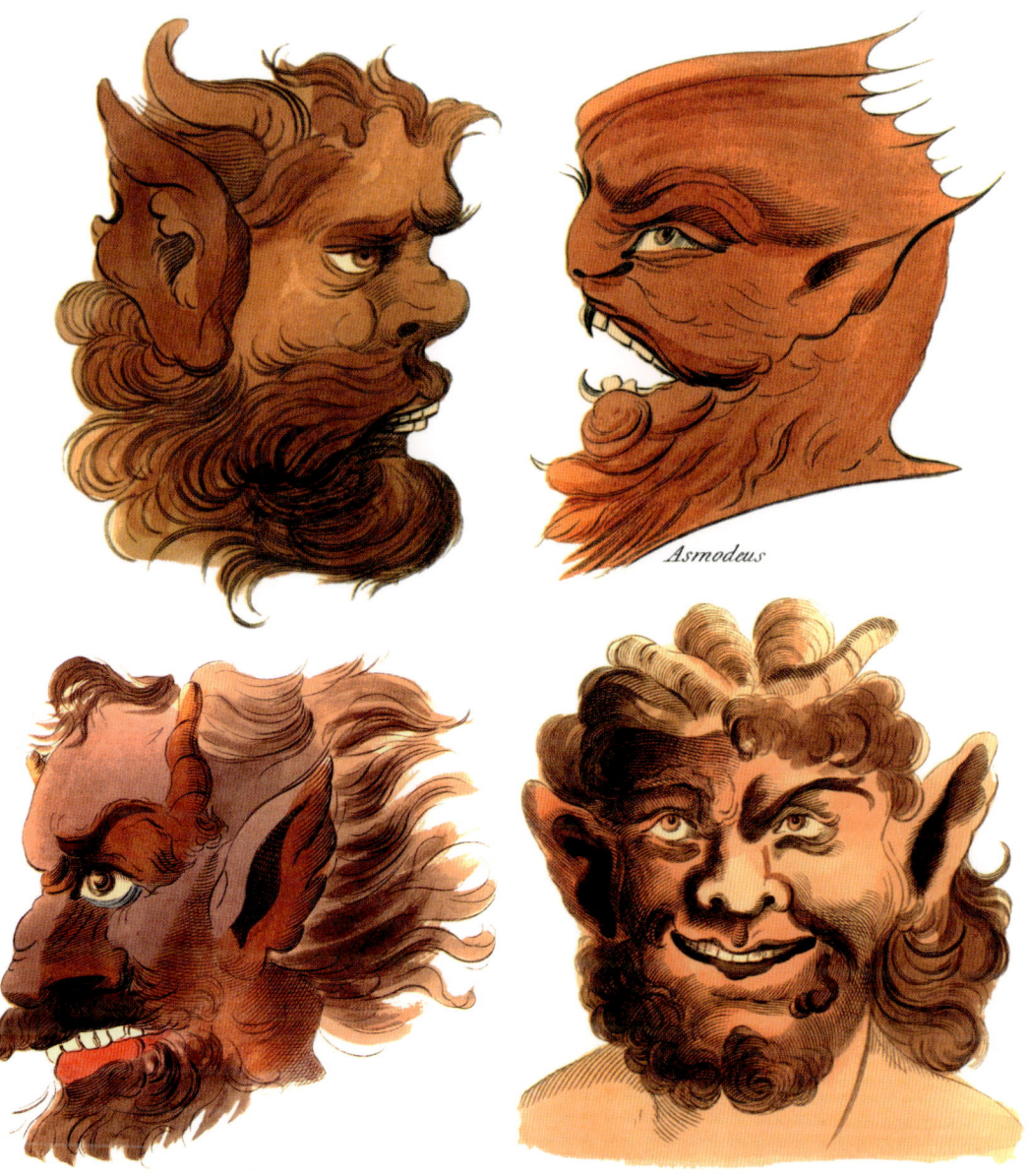

Asmodeus

Page from the English occultist Francis Barrett's 1801 grimoire The Magus, or Celestial Intelligencer, *held in the Vail Collection at the libraries of the Massachusetts Institute of Technology. Showing various demons as envisioned by Barrett, what might first strike viewers of the illustrations is precisely how* human *the beings appear. Malevolent, possibly; feral, perhaps; ugly, undoubtedly. Yet when Barrett goes to draw those supreme paragons of fallenness that are the rebel angels, the most convenient picture that he can supply is that of his fellow man. This speaks to the ways in which his coming century would, depending on your interpretation, abolish the idea of demonology in favor of a naturalistic secularism, or make it so all-encompassing that humanism itself must be understood through the figure of the devil.*

DAMNED BY THE FLESH

"During his sleep his inflamed imagination had presented him with none but the most voluptuous objects," wrote Matthew Lewis of his titular character Ambrosio in the 1796 gothic potboiler *The Monk*. "Matilda stood before him in his dreams, and his eyes again dwelt upon her naked breast. She repeated her protestations of eternal love, threw her arms round his neck, and loaded him with kisses: He returned them; He clasped her passionately to his bosom, and … the vision was dissolved." So much implied in that occluding ellipsis. *The Monk*'s narrative is convoluted; in the previous scene Ambrosio originally was led to believe that Matilda was a novice fellow Capuchin named Rosario, only to have her feminine identity revealed to him, and to then finally have that identity even further complicated when it's discovered that the woman to whom the monk has given into his lusts is actually a demon. As with much gothic literature during this time period (though certainly not all), Lewis's novel isn't particularly good. Lurid, exploitative, prurient, *The Monk* traded in salaciousness and deviant sexuality in the dross of anti-Catholic polemic, attracting English Protestant readers with erotic stories about occult practices in dark medieval monasteries hidden away in the darkest corners of Spain. Lewis was nineteen when he penned *The Monk*, and it's obvious.

Despite its clear aesthetic deficiencies, *The Monk* and similar novels have much to tell us about demonology in the Romantic period, especially the intersections of sexuality and the diabolical. Eroticism has always been latent in any discussion of demonology, as the ancient example of Lilith demonstrates. Yet by the nineteenth century, especially as new heights of prudery were encouraged during the Victorian era, stories about demons became a new way to explore repressed attractions and forbidden lusts under the guise of the theological and mythological. During the first half of the nineteenth century, erotic lithographs depicting consensual sex between women and an assortment of prodigiously phallused demons were sold as pornography, one master of the form being Eugène Lepoittevin in *The Erotic Devils*, his 1832 compendium of pictures showing hellish beings gleefully fucking a variety of otherwise decorous, upstanding, and respectable ladies.

Better known for his staid maritime and landscaping scenes, in *The Erotic Devils* Poittevin turned toward fine-line drawing of demons performing cunnilingus, engaging in anal sex, dispensing golden showers, and otherwise taking turns fucking joyful, willing partners. Other artists, like Achille Devéria, produced similar pictures for sale. Robert Stewart, the compiler of the images for Delta of Venus, an archive of vintage pornography, says that the form is "gleefully obscene … they capture the mischievousness of lust." The genre, though it is certainly graphic, doesn't use the demonic as a means to represent evil per se, but it certainly encourages an association of sexuality with impishness and the Dionysian. There are precursors to such representations; medieval theatergoers often used devils as jocular figures more than as fearsome ones, and such associations are rife in antiquity, whereby satyrs are more sexy than satanic. By the 1840s the invention of the daguerreotype and then later photography encouraged more realistic pornography, but for a brief period the demonic was a convenient idiom for women and men to explore the diversity of sexual pleasure during an otherwise repressed century.

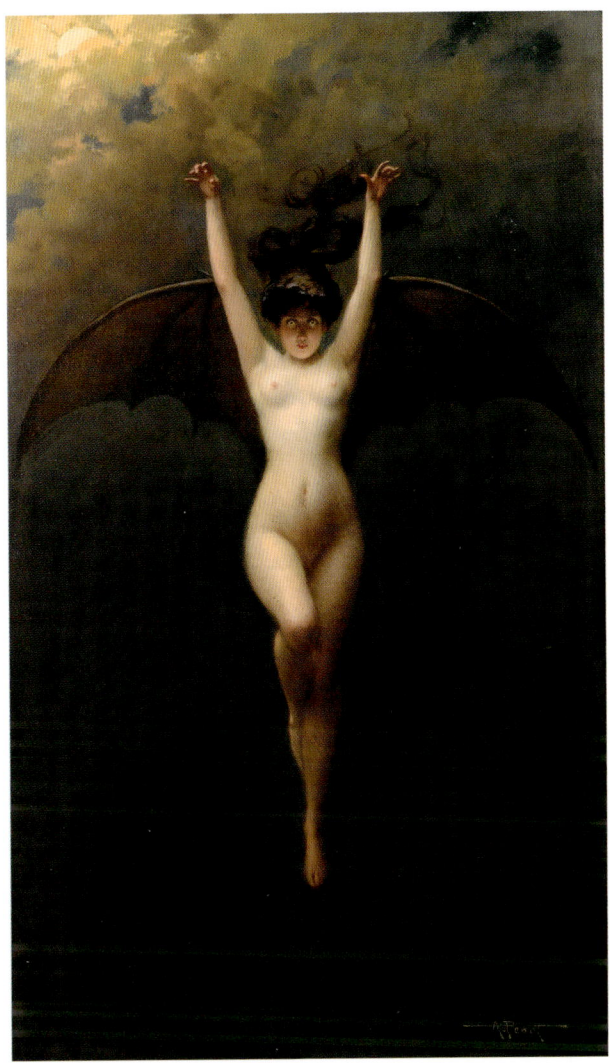

ABOVE

The erotic intent in French painter Albert Joseph Pénot's c. 1890 work The Bat-Woman, *held in a private collection, is obvious. Evoking the figure of the succubus, most prominent of whom is Lilith, Pénot's classically beautiful nude woman both celebrates as well as warns viewers about the relationship between sexuality and the demonic.*

NEXT SPREADS

Most celebrated as an illustrator of landscape and maritime scenes, the French lithographer and painter Eugène Lepoittevin was popular in his own lifetime for the erotic images he produced, particular those of a demonic bent. Here the demons are a bit less scurrilous, though still wicked, from his 1832 collection *Les Diables de Lithographies*, where other sinful appetites are indulged.

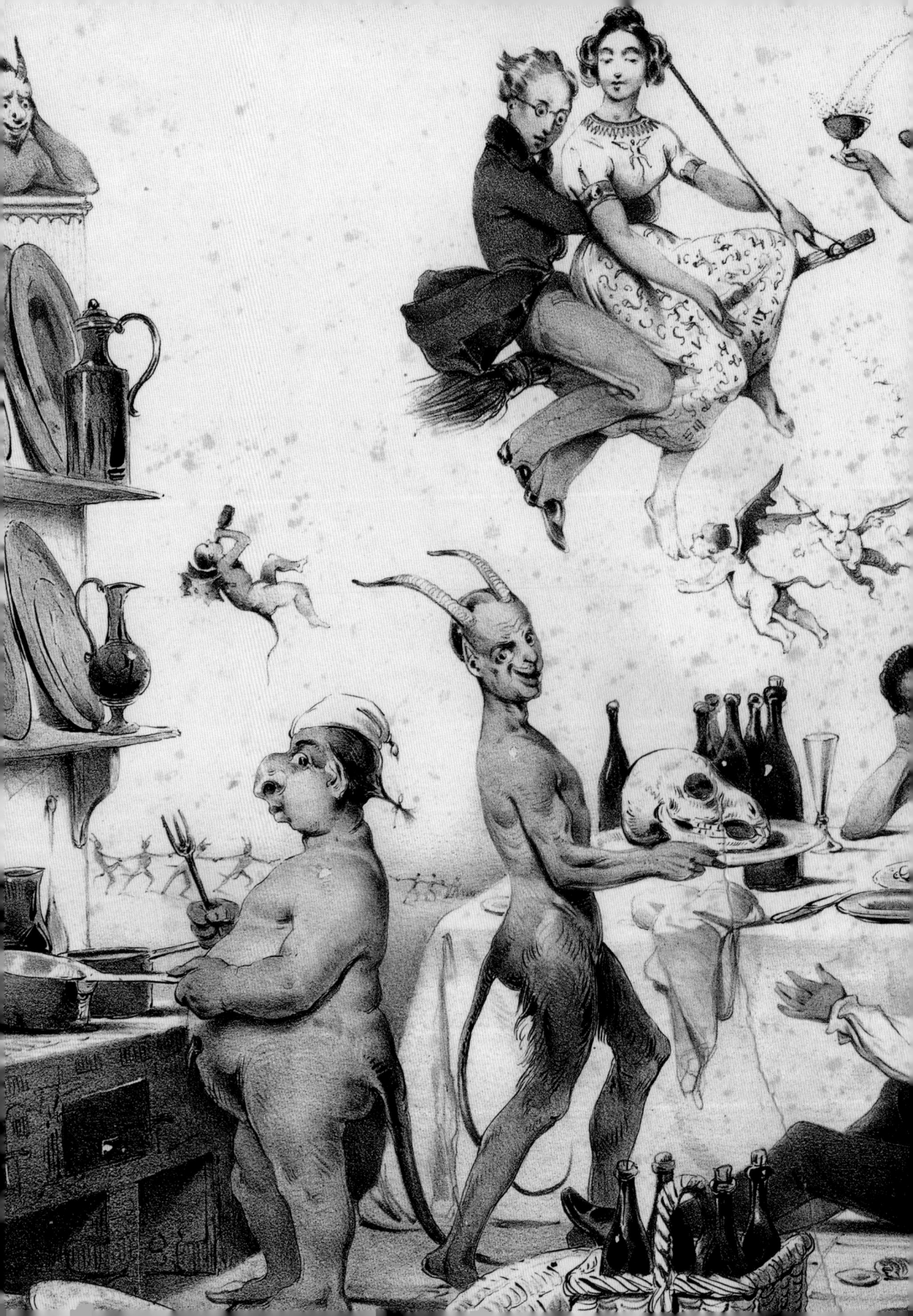

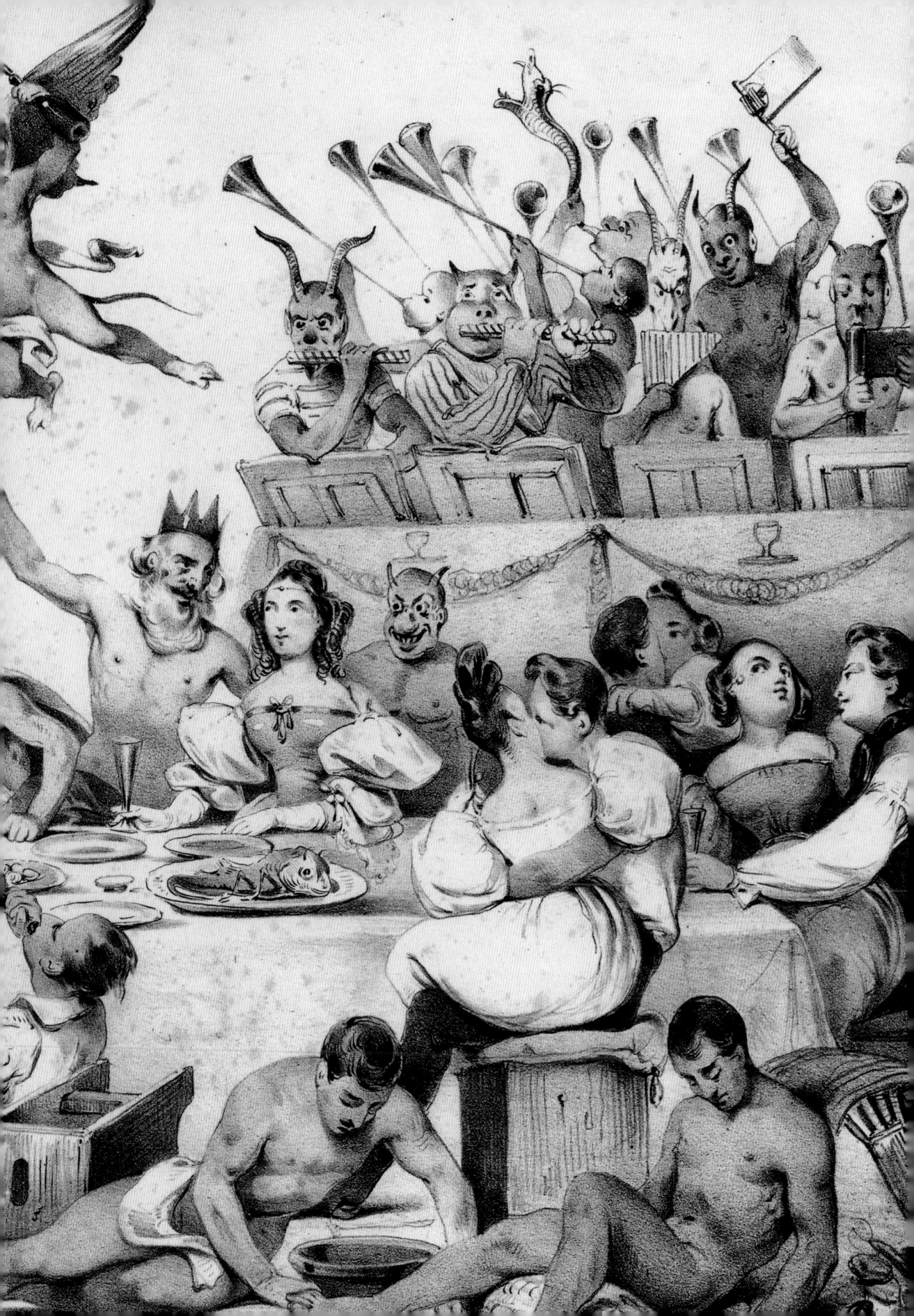

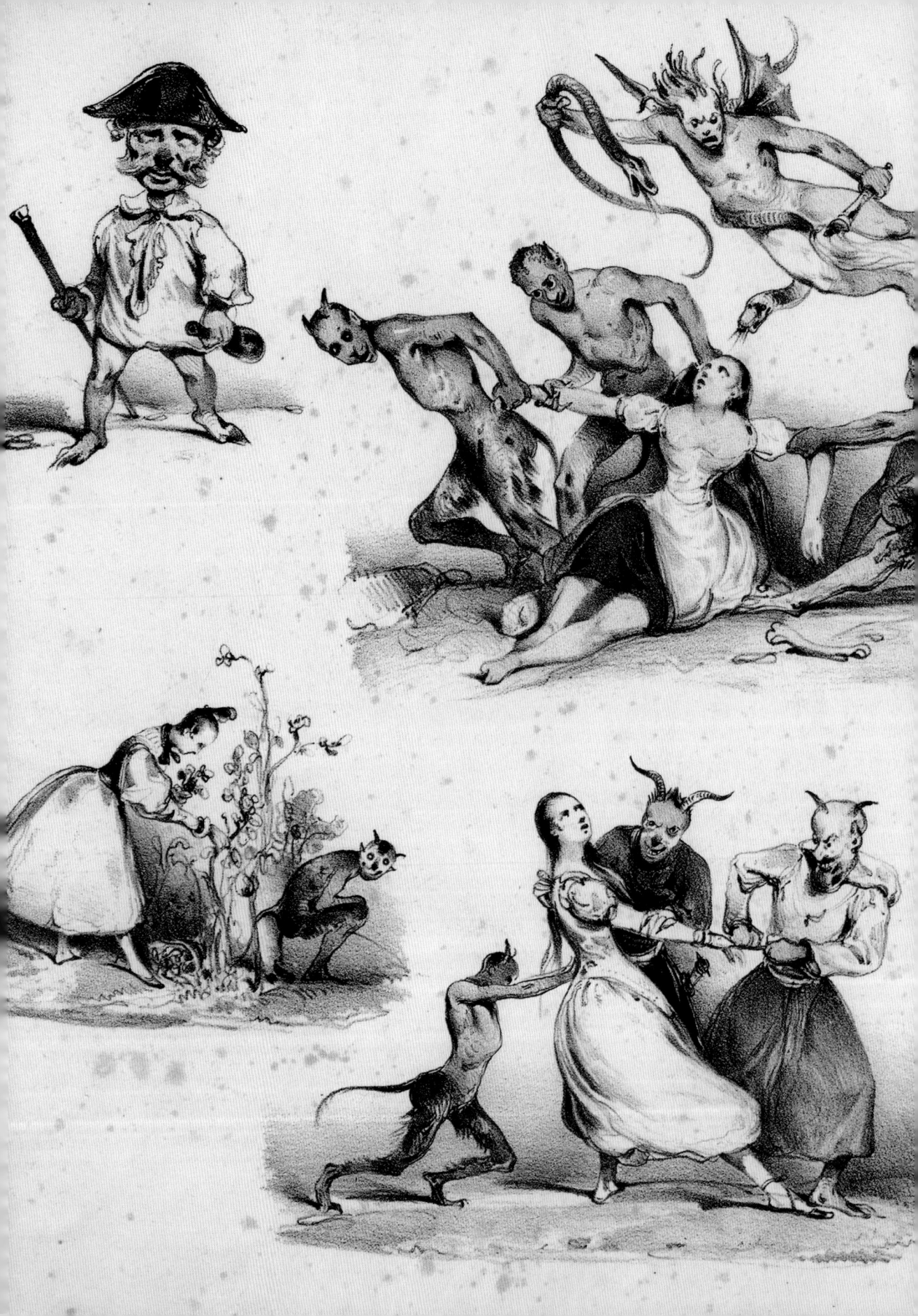

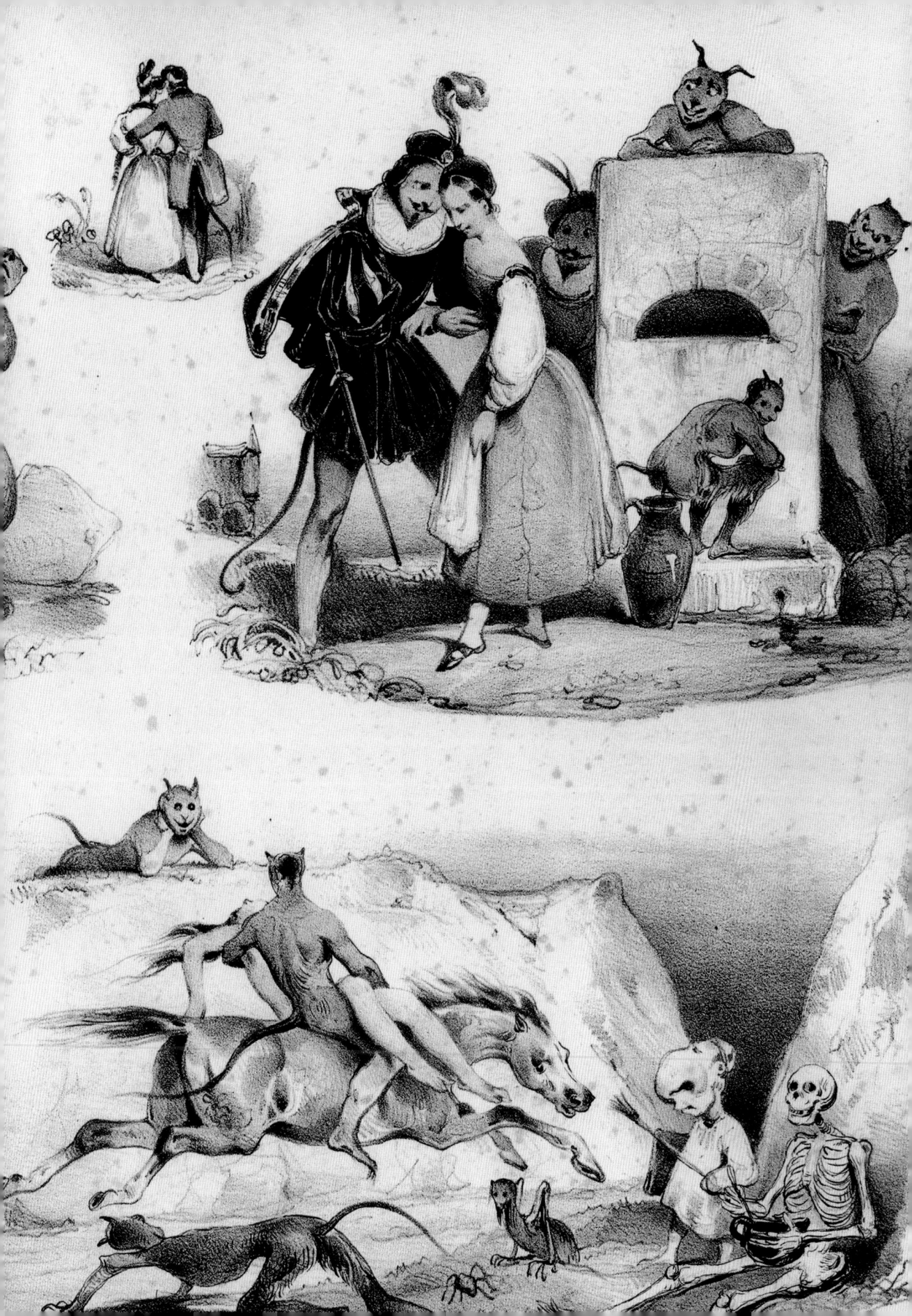

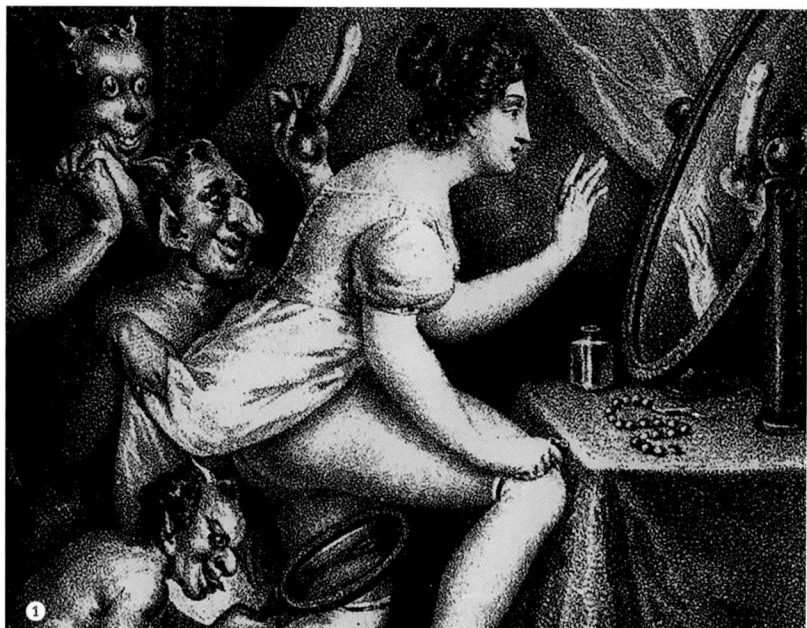

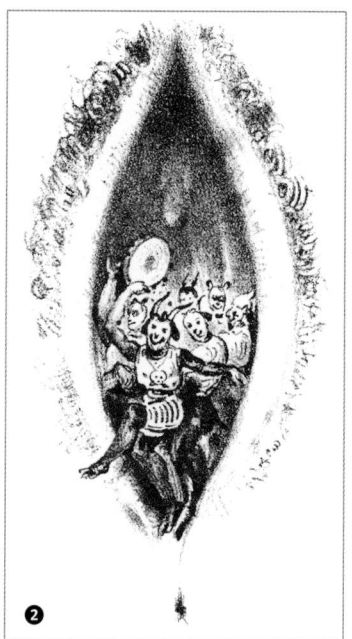

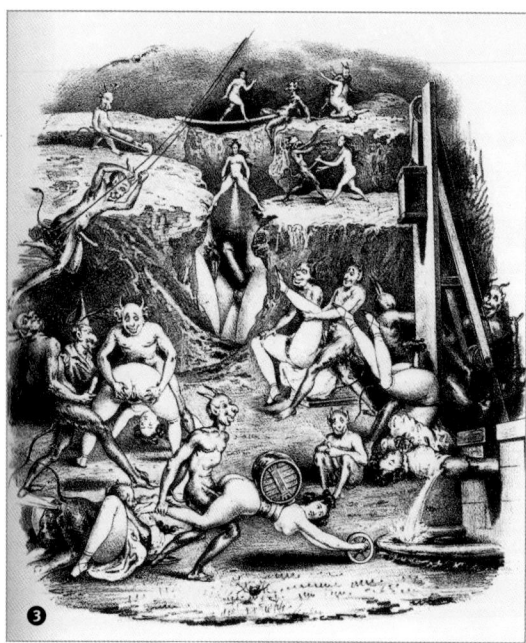

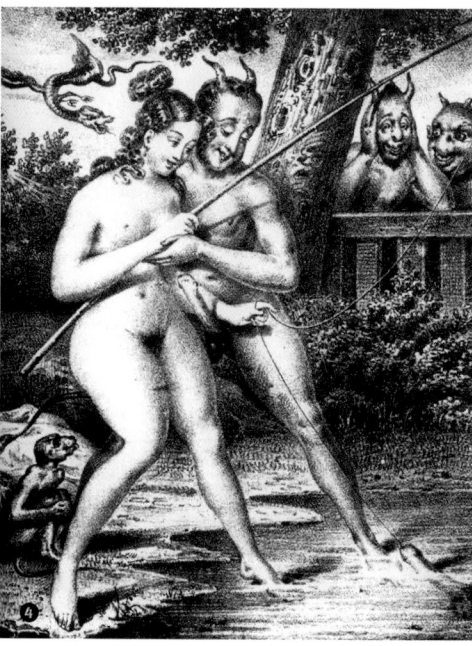

❶ *A gaggle of grotesque demons attends a woman in her toilet in this drawing from* The Erotic Devils, *one brandishing a dildo, another using a mirror to glimpse upskirt.* ❷ *A parade of demons emerges from a woman's vagina. Whether or not the image is a misogynist slur, a Dionysian celebration of women's genitalia, a strange joke, or something else entirely, is ambiguous.* ❸ *A Boschian orgy from* The Erotic Devils, *with women copulating in an assortment of positions with an assortment of comically ugly devils.* ❹ *Shades of a parodic Genesis, as a nude woman (with a serpent whispering in her ear) and a demonic paramour spend time "fishing" for phalli in a garden, while two voyeuristic compatriots watch from behind a fence.*

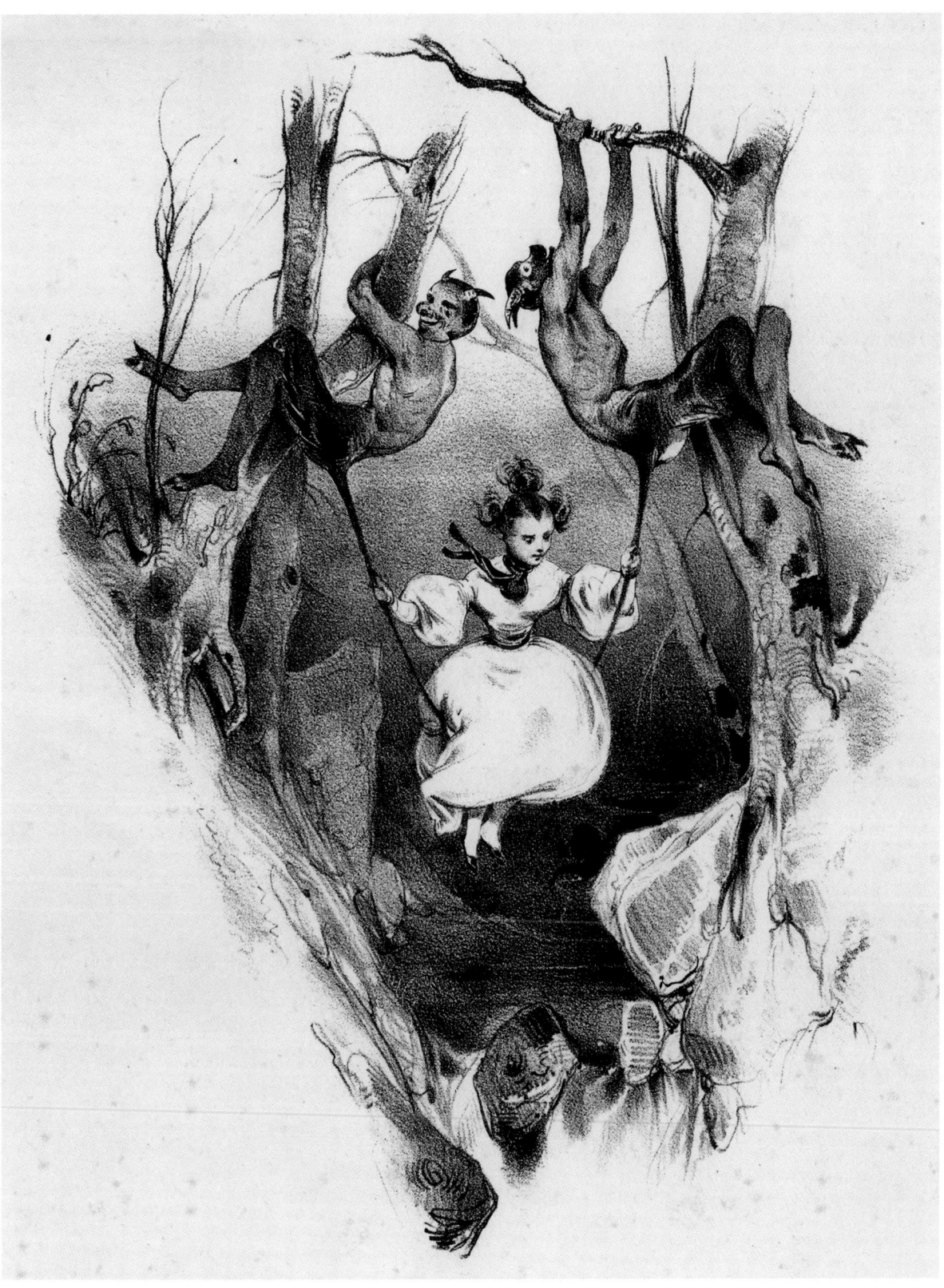

表 287

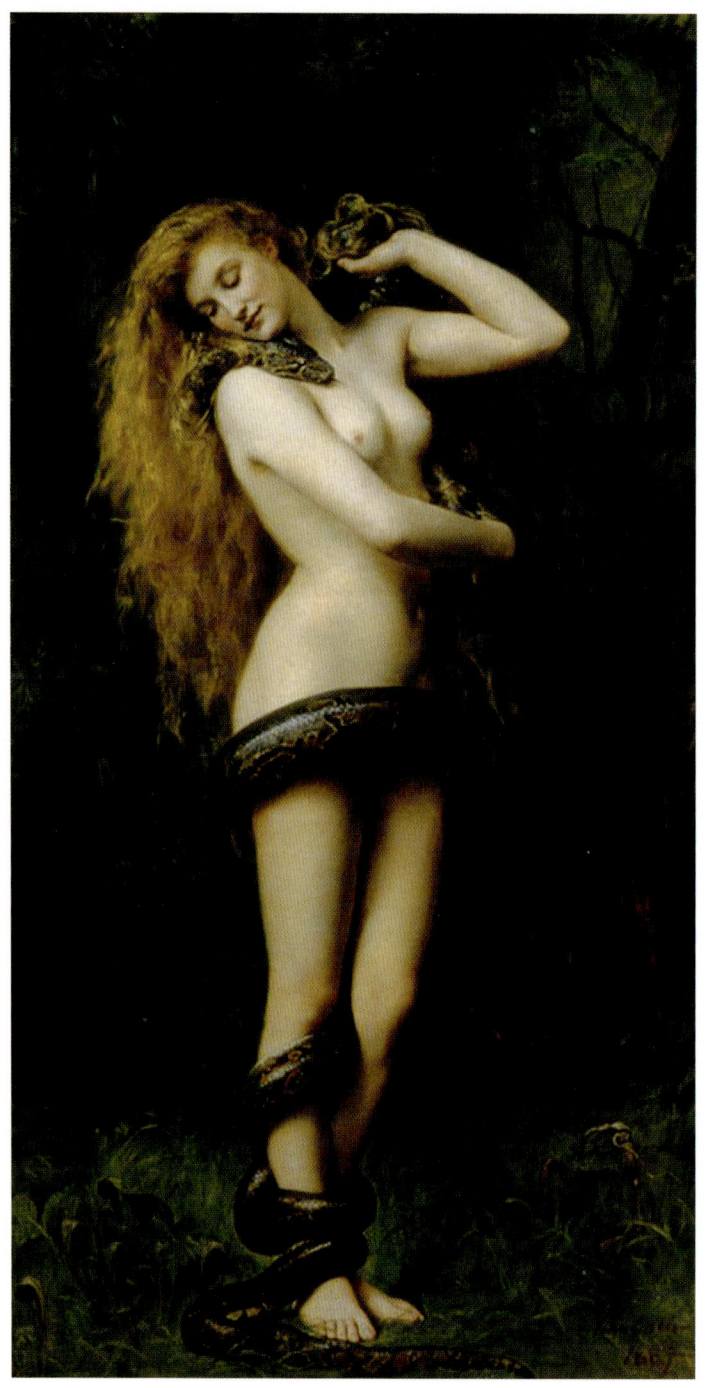

In the pre-Raphaelite English painter John Collier's 1889 composition Lilith, *held the Atkinson Art Gallery in Southport, England, the bird feet and claws are gone in favor of a traditional female nude, the only indication of the demonic is the serpent slithering up her body.*

PARISHIONERS AT A BLACK MASS

S pitting, urinating, defecating on a crucifix—bedecking an altar screen with a pentagram rendered in human effluence—piercing the surface of a consecrated host until blood oozes out— fucking upon the altar where the sacrament is performed—sacrificing a human on that same altar. These are the lurid and horrific connotations of the phrase "Black Mass," a diabolical inversion of the Catholic rite, and a mocking of the miracle of transubstantiation that accompanies the presentation of the Eucharist before the faithful. Related to the trope of the witches' Sabbath, the Black Mass was supposedly an opportunity for demon worshipers to both prostrate themselves before Satan, while sullying the holiness of Catholic ritual. Participants in the supposed Black Mass were often educated and powerful clerics, as opposed to the marginalized women who were accused of having attended the witches' Sabbath, but what unites both events is that "evil is master and is worshiped," as Richard Cavendish writes in *The Black Arts: A Concise History of Witchcraft, Demonology, Astrology, and Other Mystical Practices Throughout the Ages*.

Fear of the Black Mass has long existed before its reality. Medieval Catholics demonized Judaism with the blood libel, attributing to Jews any number of heinous (and nonexistent) crimes, from the sacrifice of Christian children to collect blood for the baking of Passover matzah, to the claim that they would abscond from churches with transubstantiated communion wafers, which would then be pierced and crucified until they actually bled, in imitation of the original deicide at the crucifixion. Even earlier than the slanders of such bigoted fantasies—which were often the inspiration for anti-Semitic violence—and ironically Christians themselves were accused of similar nocturnal rituals by their pagan critics in the earliest centuries of the first millennium. Christians supposedly gathered in catacombs, as many learned pagans said, to engage in orgies and to practice furtive cannibalism. Such libels may have been deliberate misunderstandings of the ritual Eucharist, but they also demonstrate the convenient propagandistic function of demonology. As Norman Cohn writes in *Europe's Inner Demons: The Demonization of Christians in Medieval Christendom*, the point of such slanders, whether directed at Christians or Jews, was to make their target seem "absolutely anti-human, and those who indulged in them were put outside the bounds of humanity," a mechanism that "could sometimes be used to legitimate persecutions."

It must also be said that such allegations made little sense since they assumed the validity of theological beliefs that those indicted didn't share. The violation of a communion host, for example, presumes that the person doing the violating believes the Eucharist to be sacred, which of course medieval Jews wouldn't have. A Black Mass only makes sense as a concept if you already believe in the Mass. Which is to say that there were charges over the years, leveled at those implicated in magic and witchcraft, which indicate that ritual desecration of liturgical objects may have occasionally been part of some ceremonies by wayward members of the Church, though scholars have disagreed on the reality of the ceremony in pre-modern times. Historian Jules Michelet gave a sympathetic (and largely unsubstantiated) account in his 1862 study *Satanism and Witchcraft*, asking his readers to:

Imagine the scene—a wide heath, often in the neighborhood of an old Celtic dolmen, at the edge of a wood. The picture is twofold—on one side the heath brightly lighted up, and the crowds of people feasting; on the other, toward the wood, the choir of this church whose vault is open to heaven … Midway between the two, resinous fires burn with yellow tongues of flames and ruddy embers, making a vague, fantastic veil of smoke. In the background the Sorceress set up her Satan, a great wooden Satan, black and shaggy. In virtue of his horns … he might have passed for Bacchus; but his virile attributes unmistakably proclaimed him Pan and Priapus … While some beheld only an incarnate terror, others were moved by the haughty melancholy that seemed to enfold the Exile of Eternity.

Despite Michelet's exceedingly elaborate speculations, the Black Mass as an actual verifiable phenomenon can't be established as occurring with any regularity until his own century. It's perhaps prefigured in the blasphemous orgies of the Hell-Fire Clubs, where the almost entirely Protestant membership had no problem pantomiming Catholic ritual, but the genuine Black Mass that involved inversions of the Latin missal, molestation of liturgical objects, and sometimes the participation of clergy, was an innovation of anti-clericalism in largely Catholic countries.

Often associated with the literary and artistic circle known as the Decadent movement, the Black Mass became both an opportunity for theatrics and for blasphemy—an aesthetic performance as much as a mockery and inversion of the sacred rites. French novelist Joris-Karl Huysmans's fictionalized a Black Mass in his notorious 1891 book *The Damned*, which had his thinly veiled roman à clef Durtal attending such a ritual after he and his lover Madame Chantelouve discover that a sect of Satanists have been meeting in Paris since the Middle Ages. Huysmans describes a nocturnal meeting of the worshipers in a former Ursuline convent—the Satanic priest delivering a twisted version of the liturgy, the desecration of the host by the frenzied congregants, and then:

The women fell to the carpet and writhed. One of them seemed to be worked by a spring. She threw herself prone and waved her legs in the air. Another, suddenly struck by a hideous strabismus, clucked, then becoming tongue-tied stood with her mouth open, the tongue turned back, the tip cleaving to the palate. Another, inflated, livid, her pupils dilated, lolled her head back over her shoulders, then jerked it brusquely erect and belabored herself, tearing her breast with her nails. Another, sprawling on her back, undid her skirts, drew forth a rag, enormous, meteorized; then her face twisted into a horrible grimace, and her tongue, which she could not control, stuck out, bitten at the edges, harrowed by red teeth, from a bloody mouth.

The scene is almost Boschian in its excess, the Black Mass prefiguring a taste of hell on earth. Clearly evidencing a thinly veiled fear of women's sexuality, it perhaps shouldn't be surprising that Huysmans's Decadent sensibilities turned back toward the Church, with the writer living the last years of his life as a religious oblate. He'd claimed that the grotesque scene in *The Damned* was based on his own experiences, but there has been skepticism in that regard.

Still, as a source he cited his confidant, the defrocked Catholic priest Joseph-Antoine Boullan, who was notorious for being a student of Satan and feuding with other Parisian occultists. Partners with a former nun named Adele Chevalier, she and Boullan supposedly sexually consummated their performance of the Black Mass upon the altar, and frequently engaged in orgiastic intercourse with a variety of demons. Decades after Boullan had been laicized by the Church, and after he'd served jail time for defrauding credulous followers, it was revealed that in 1862 he and Chevalier had a child whom they sacrificed as part of a satanic ritual, the theater of the Black Mass pushed to an authoritarian, cruel, and evil conclusion. After Durant leaves the Black Mass in *The Damned*, Chantelouve turned to him and asks, "Did you expect to meet saints here?"

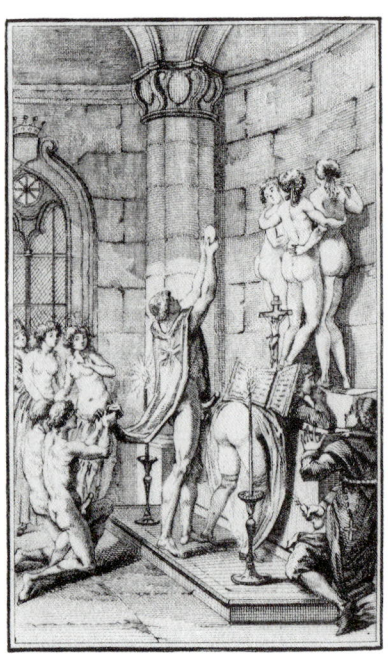 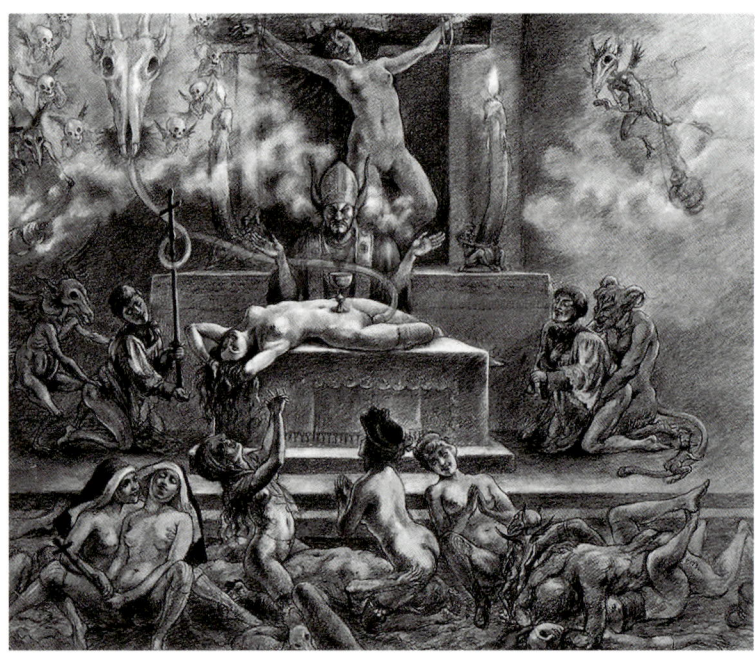

ABOVE LEFT

A 1797 engraving of an orgiastic Black Mass from the Marquise de Sade's Justine, or the Misfortunes of Virtue. *Note the erect priest offering the wafer before three women standing on the altar, a pantomime of the Christian Trinity, but also in their stance a reference to the Three Graces of classical art.*

ABOVE RIGHT

A rather elaborate drawing by the Belgian engraver Félicien Rops entitled Black Mass, and showing just that. Associated with both the Symbolist and Decadent movements, Rops developed a reputation as a preeminent illustrator of occult and diabolic themes.

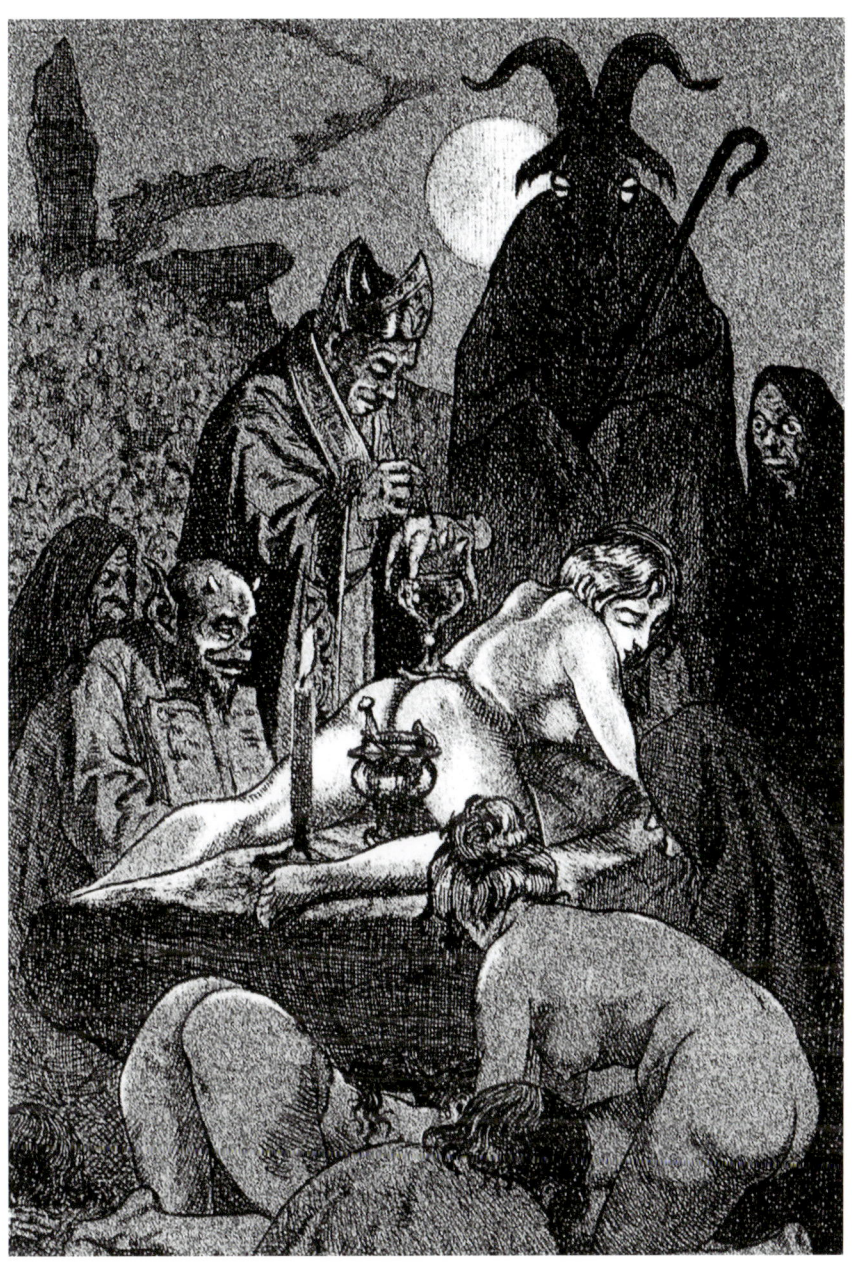

An illustration by the French illustrator Martin van Maële, known for his erotic themes, of a Black Mass as described by historian Jules Michelet, and included in the 1911 edition of his study Satanism and Witchcraft. Largely sympathetic to the Black Mass as a locus for resistance against authoritarian religion, Michelet's claims for the widespread practice of the ritual is largely unsubstantiated, though there are some examples, such as those performed by the seventeenth-century defrocked priest Étienne Guibourg on behalf of Madame de Montespan, the mistress of Louis XIV.

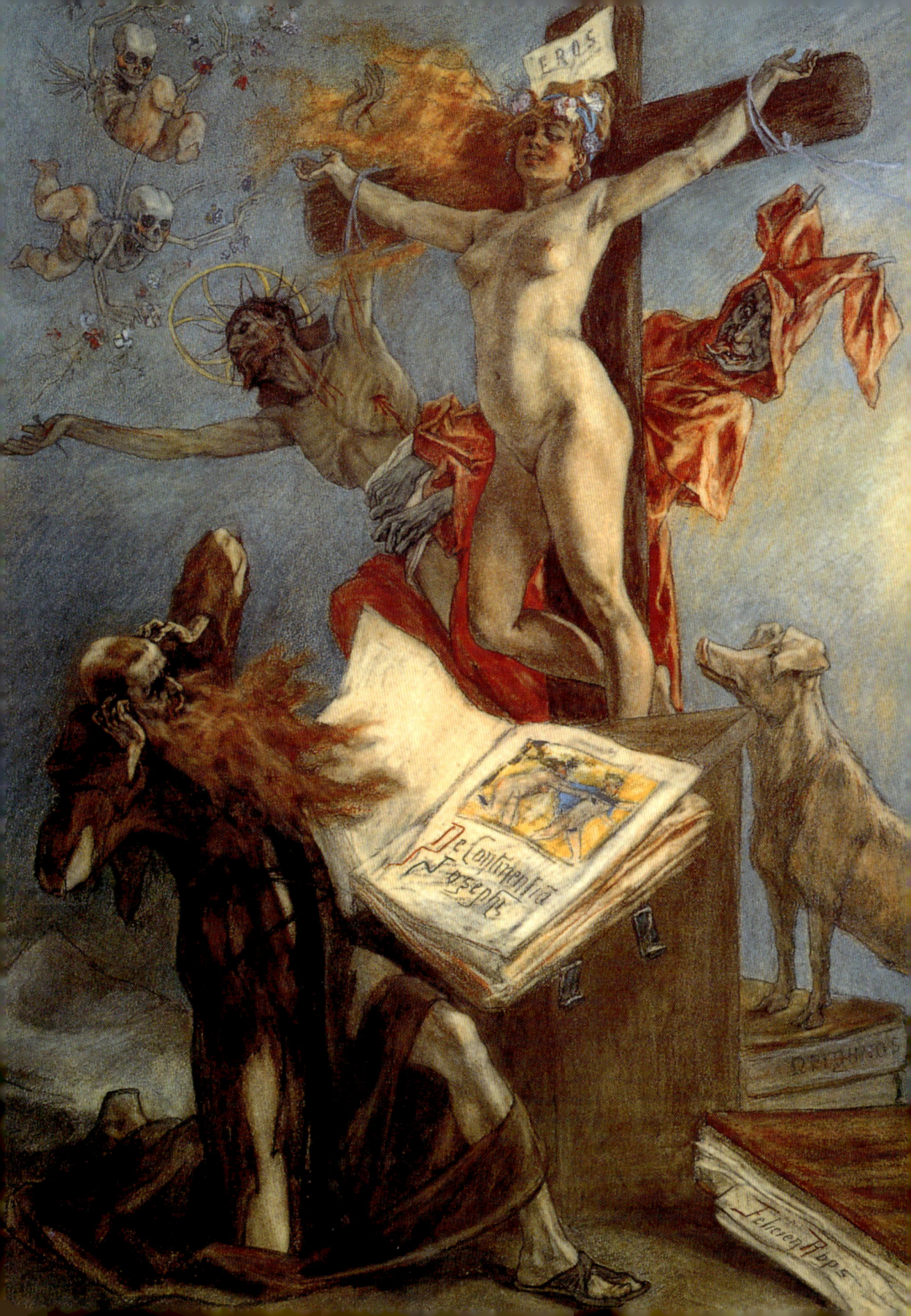

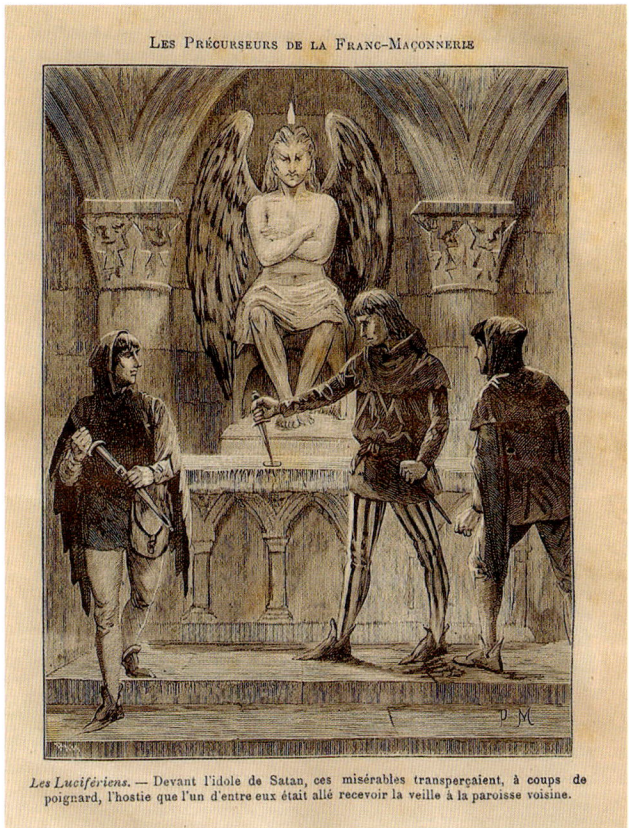

LES PRÉCURSEURS DE LA FRANC-MAÇONNERIE

Les Lucifériens. — Devant l'idole de Satan, ces misérables transperçaient, à coups de poignard, l'hostie que l'un d'entre eux était allé recevoir la veille à la paroisse voisine.

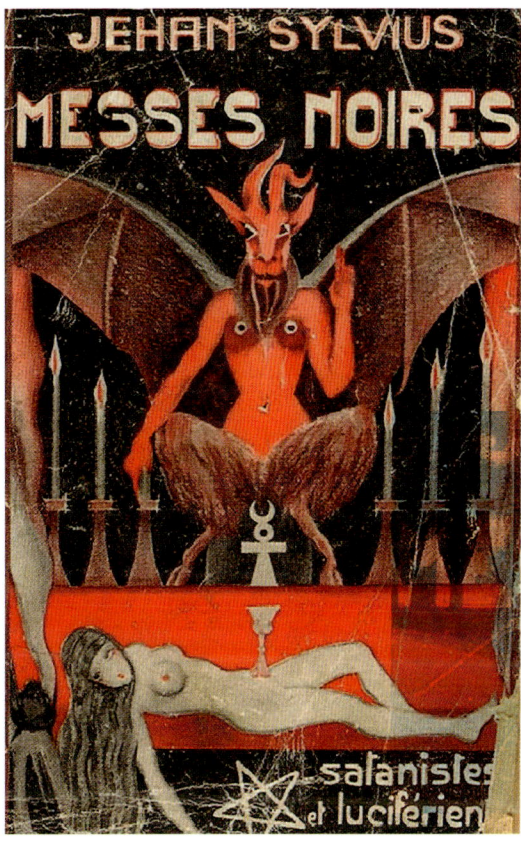

JEHAN SYLVIUS
MESSES NOIRES

satanistes et luciférien

Félicien Rops brings a particularly blasphemous caste of mind to his 1878 watercolor The Temptation of St. Anthony, *held by the Royal Library of Belgium in Brussels. In this rendering, Satan has expelled Christ from the cross in favor of a lithe, nude woman intended to sway the monk from his vocation. Rops's series the Satanic Ones traded in sexuality, violence, and impiety in a manner that was shocking to Catholic French audiences, with Huysmans writing that the artist "has painted demonic rapture as others have painted mystical yearnings."*

An illustration by Pierre Méjanel showing ritual host desecration, wherein the piercing of the transubstantiated wafer is meant to literally reenact the deicide. This drawing was included in Léo Taxil's book 1886 The Mysteries of Freemasonry, *and it should be said that such practices as described therein don't actually have a corollary in Masonic ritual. Also note that the devilish idol before whom they make their sacrifice has more of the Apollonian than the Dionysian about him.*

Cover to a 1926 printing of the surrealist cult writer Jehan Sylvius's Black Masses, *demonstrating the enduring appeal of Lévi's Baphomet, while accomplished in a vaguely art nouveau style.*

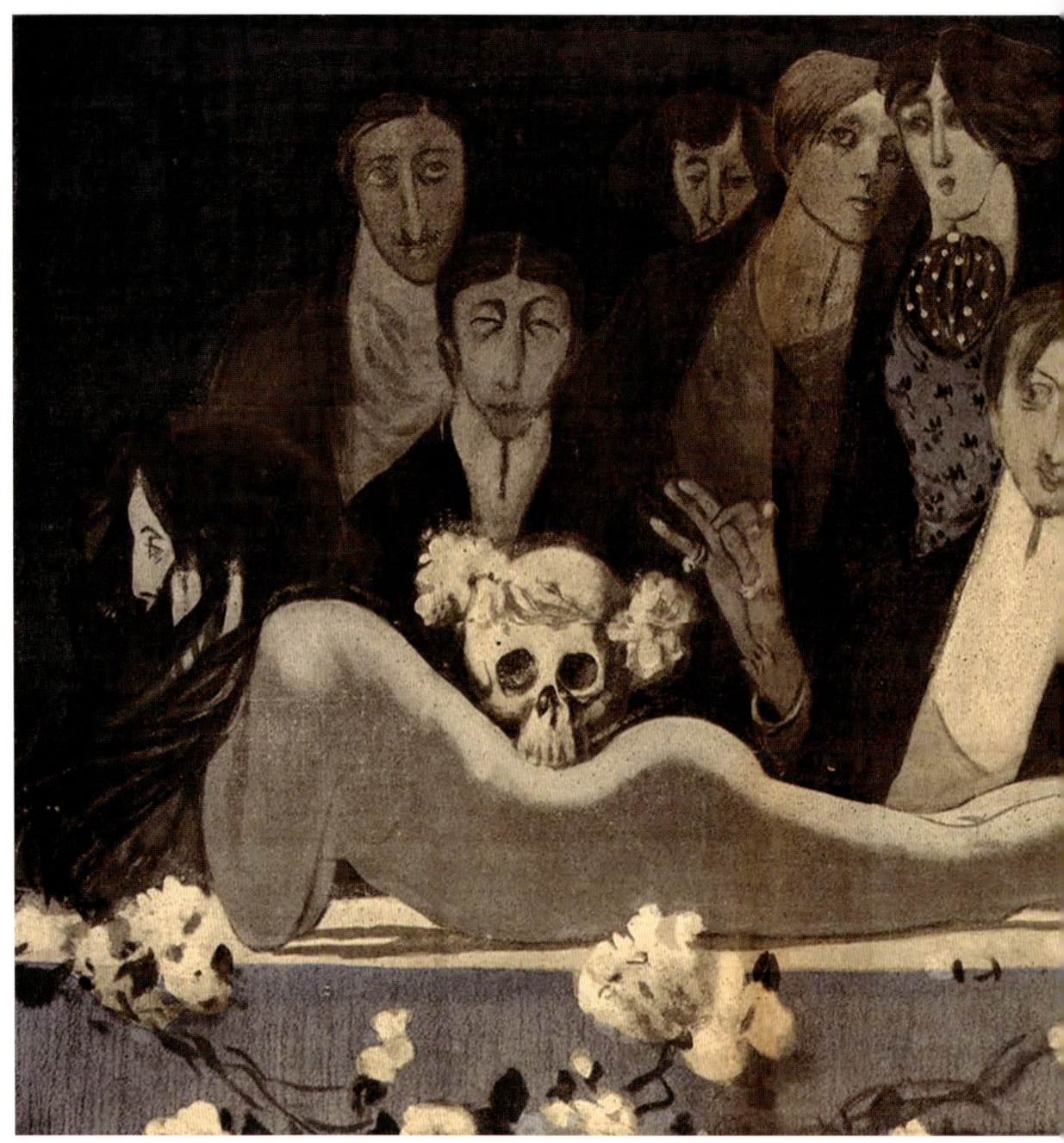

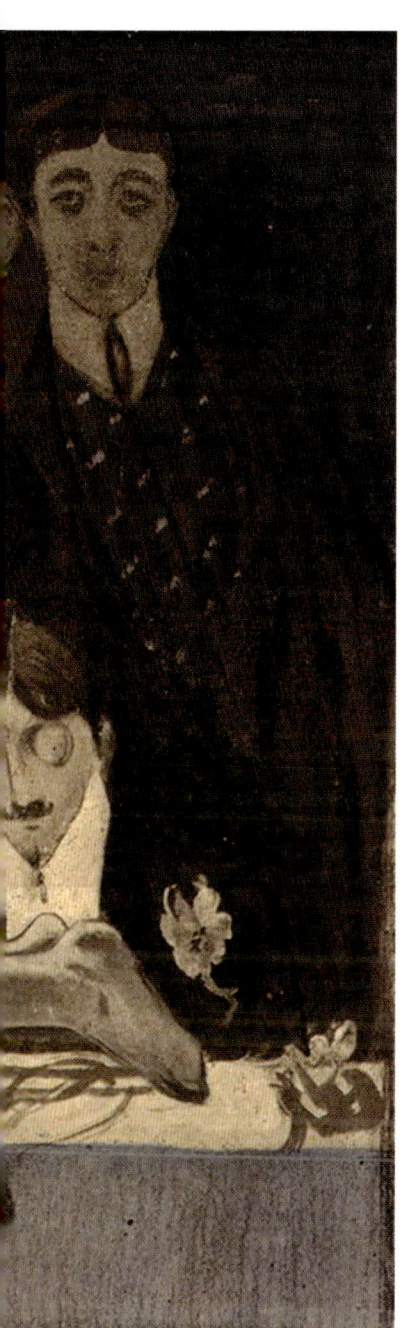

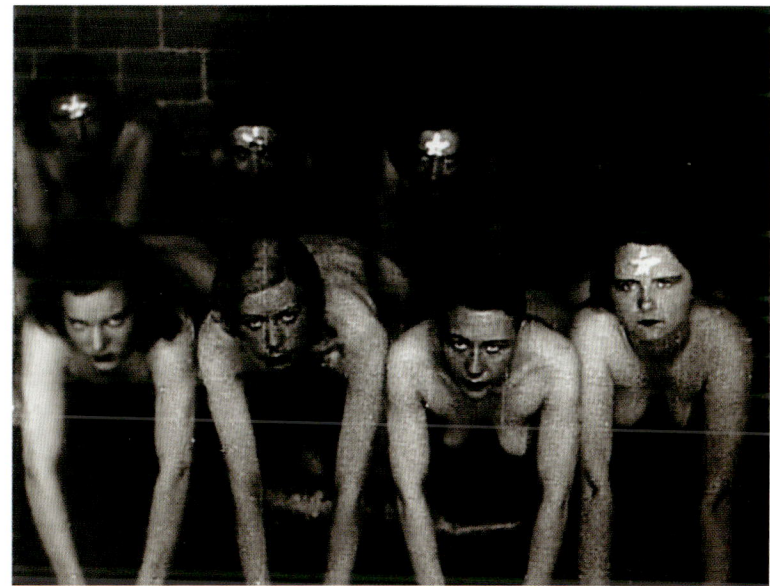

ABOVE

Stills from the anonymously directed 1928 French pornographic film Black Mass. *Running at only six minutes, the movie is clearly inspired by Huysmans account in* The Damned, *with actual sex acts performed before "priests" representing Lucifer and Astarte. In such an enactment, the question can be considered as to what the difference is between a dramatization of a Black Mass, and an "actual" Black Mass (with there being an argument that the film has clearly recorded the later).*

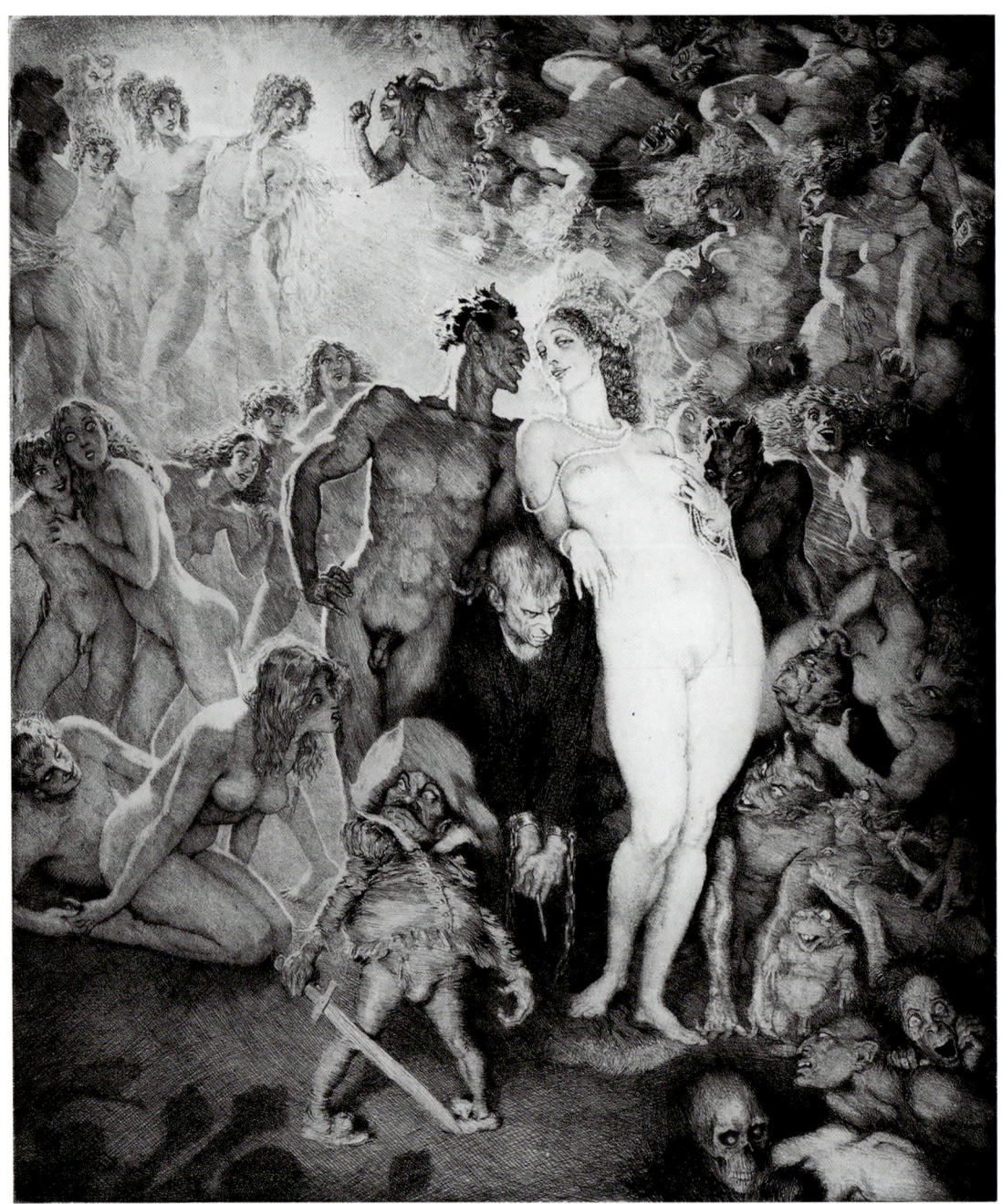

Australian illustrator Norman Lindsay indulges a frank eroticism in his 1930 evocation of a Black Mass entitled Self-Portrait *(he's the stooped figure in the middle). Attracted to pagan and occult themes, Lindsay was maligned as anti-Christian (a designation which didn't bother him), and a celebration of the demonic nature of sexuality was a common theme of his.*

WAILING FOR A DEMON LOVER

Percy Bysshe Shelley, at the age of nineteen, was called to account by the dons of Oxford for having sent to every bishop and college head at the university a pamphlet with the incendiary title of *The Necessity of Atheism*. Raised by a stolid member of Parliament who represented West Sussex, the poet had been sent to the University of Oxford with the expectation that he would ascend to positions of respectability and responsibility as befitting a young man of his class, and yet under the influence of his radical friend, the appropriately named Thomas Jefferson Hogg (a cowriter of the pamphlet), Shelley would embrace revolutionary commitments in both politics and religion. Calling upon the iconoclastic zeitgeist of the age as it transitioned from the Enlightenment into the Romantic, Shelley would emphatically declare, "There is no God!," to which the sober and serious academics of Oxford responded by ensuring that the poet would never receive a degree from the university.

Shelley, however, maintained that his was a consistent atheism, for as the respectable Anglican clergy had long since expelled Satan from their theology as surely as they would expel a student from their university, so too did the poet understand that if there is no Devil there can scarcely be any God. "There may be observed in polite society a great deal of coquetting about the Devil, especially among divines," writes Shelley in his posthumously published and undated essay "On the Devil, and Devils." Discovered and printed by his wife Mary Shelley (herself the author of the Promethean and Miltonic Frankenstein), the essay was perhaps too scandalous to release while the author was still alive, and so it awaited an audience until after the poet would drown in the Bay of Naples, immolated in a pyre on the beach underneath the shadow of smoldering Vesuvius. Shelley writes that the modernizing clergy qualify hell as "metaphorical of the torments of an evil conscience and by no means capable of being topographically ascertained. No one likes to mention the torments of the everlasting fire and poisonous gnawing of the worm that liveth forever and ever." His implication is clear—Shelley may be an atheist, but unlike his religious critics he's at least an atheist who takes God and the Devil seriously. And, to emphasize that his rejection was more against pious conventionality than the transcendent, Shelley writes that the "hypothesis of a pervading Spirit co-eternal with the universe remains unshaken."

If mainstream Enlightenment figures (however one defines any of those terms) rejected demonology as superstition, while simultaneously holding onto the husk of a milquetoast deism, then the Romantics embraced the more radical atheistic currents of the previous century, as they also countenanced an occultism, which if it didn't literally believe in devils, was certainly amenable to their symbolic import. "The occult was abandoned by the architects of the Age of Reason, but it was not forgotten," writes Gary Lachman in *The Dedalus Occult Reader: The Garden of Hermetic Dreams*, "and in the years that followed, it became a kind of reservoir of *rejected knowledge*, available to the artists, poets, writers, philosophers and musicians who were dissatisfied with the new, Newtonian dispensation." Proponents of the Romantic movement during the late eighteenth and early nineteenth centuries infamously advocated a host of virtues that were in opposition to the stated values of the Enlightenment; emotion over logic, irrationality over reason, the particular over the universal, the concrete over the abstract. Such subversions opened the door to the demonic, even if when Satan returned, it was more as a convenient symbol than as a person.

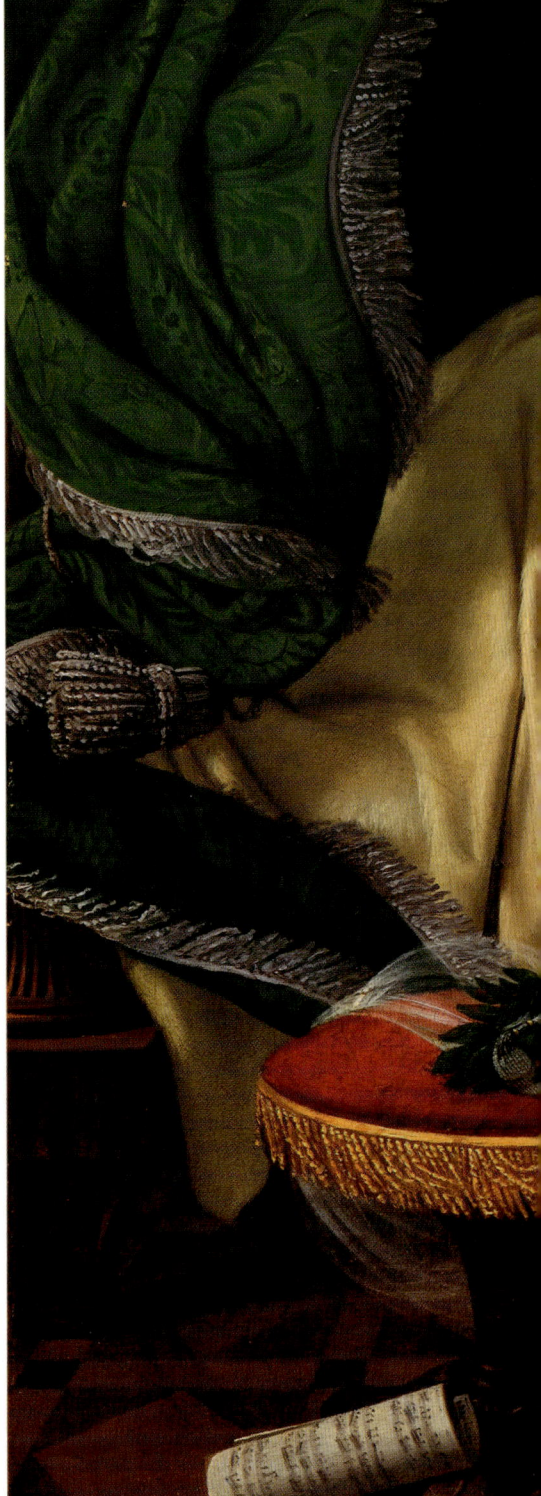

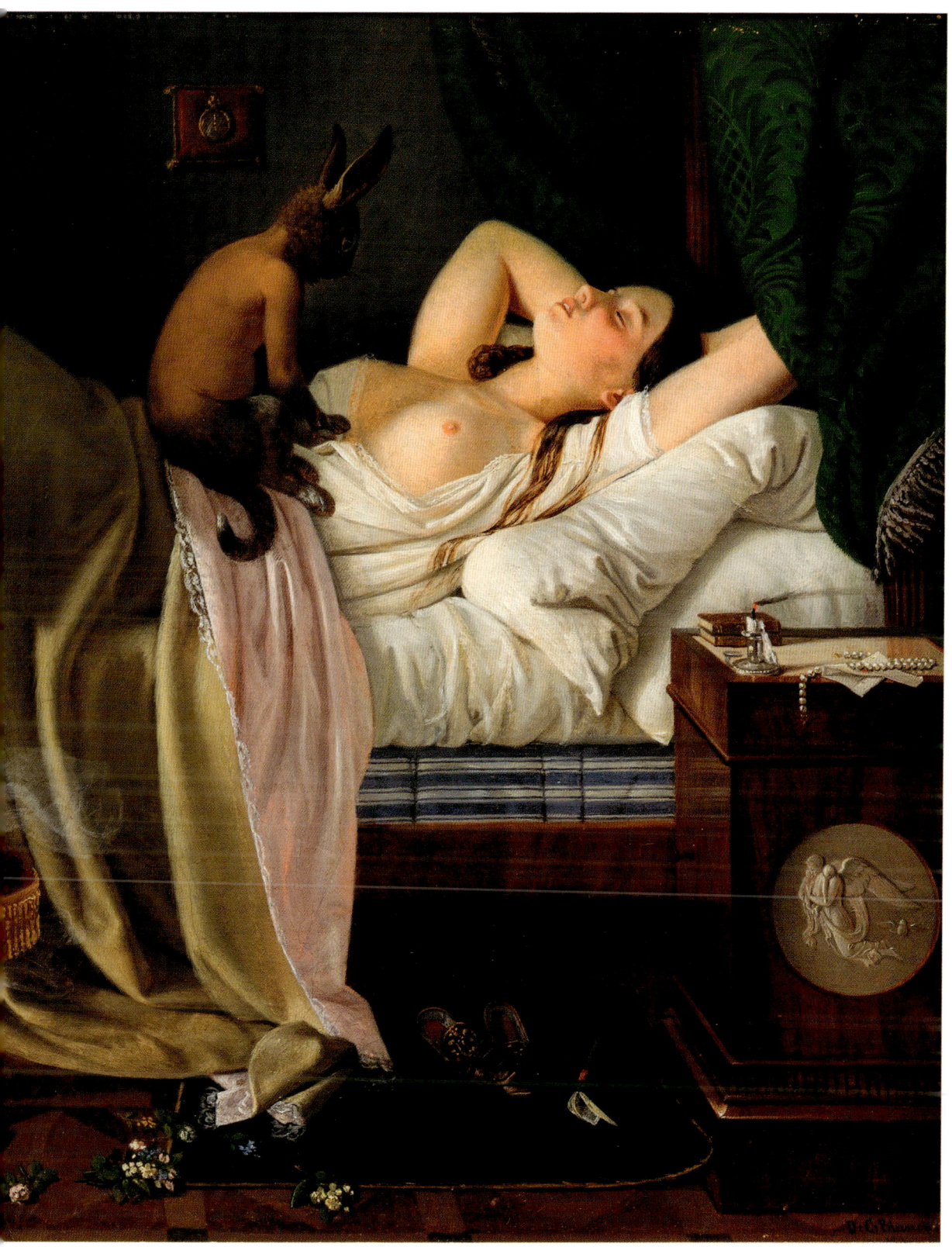

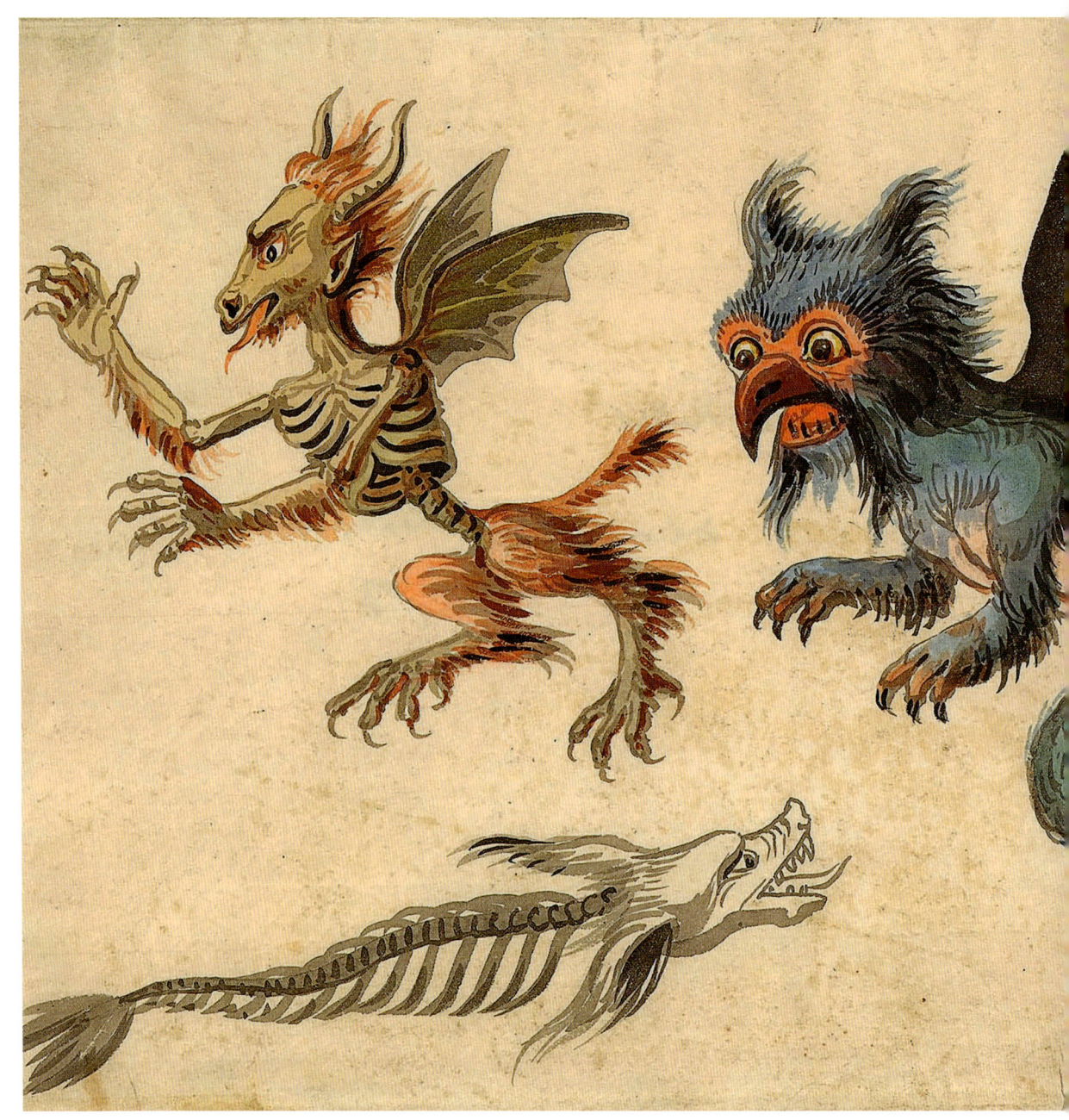

Circa 1850 sketch by the Russian theatrical set designer Andreas Leonhard Roller entitled Three Fantastic Flying Figures *held by the Morgan Library and Museum in New York. Most likely used for set designs at the Russian Imperial Theatres, Roller's drawing is a reminder that Romanticism's exploration of the macabre wasn't just invested in the uncanny, but also frequently with whimsy.*

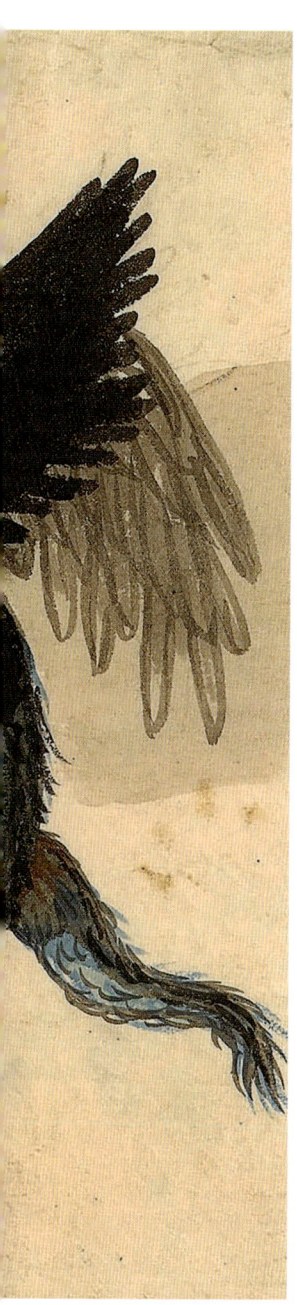

It would be a mistake to see this as a reduction; to the contrary, there is something inflationary in making the demonic an all-purpose signifier that can variously represent rebellion and evil, destruction and creativity, nobility and wickedness—though the artist must carefully deploy such metaphors, lest they be completely drained of meaning. During the Romantic era and into the Victorian, the satanic thus functioned as an artist's mechanism, a weapon within the allegorical arsenal of the *Bohème démoniaque*, of the devilish avant-garde. If in the Renaissance demonology was a subject for the magician, and during the Enlightenment it was material for the anti-clerical, then during the nineteenth century it was primarily fodder for the artist (though perhaps that profession is simply a combination of the other two). Such is the invocation made by Samuel Taylor Coleridge in his 1816 poem "Kubla Khan" wherein he writes of a "woman wailing for her demon lover" or of John Keats in *The Eve of St. Agnes* telling of how the wizard Merlin has "paid his Demon all the monstrous debt." These kinds of references were done less in the service of diabology than that of aesthetics, a creedal sacrament in the Church of Creation that held "Art for art's sake" as the highest possible commandment.

If Baphomet was the lord of Romanticism, than just as Lévi was able to birth such a creature from his own mind, the demon embodied the way in which poets during the period began to think of themselves more like magicians able to craft their own reality rather than as scribes dutifully recording the naturalistic details of God's creation. Critic Meyer H. Abrams explains in his influential study *The Mirror and the Lamp: Romantic Theory and the Critical Tradition* that in discussion of the purpose of art, the metaphor of the "mimetic mirror [is] familiar in older aesthetic theory," but by the nineteenth century such an understanding of poetry merely reflecting an objective world was replaced by the metaphor of the lamp, where the artist sees the world as being "bathed in an emotional light he has himself projected." Suddenly poets are practicing not just prosody, but theurgy; for the Romantic, versifying was conjuration and mere atheism doesn't mean the extinction of the demonic, for artists would now be able to also create ex nihilo. From *Frankenstein* to Shelley's *Prometheus Unbound* and Lord Byron's closet-drama *Caine*, an archetype of poet as genius creator—as magus, wizard, and necromancer— permeates the literature of the period, lending itself to a mad and vibrant diabolism.

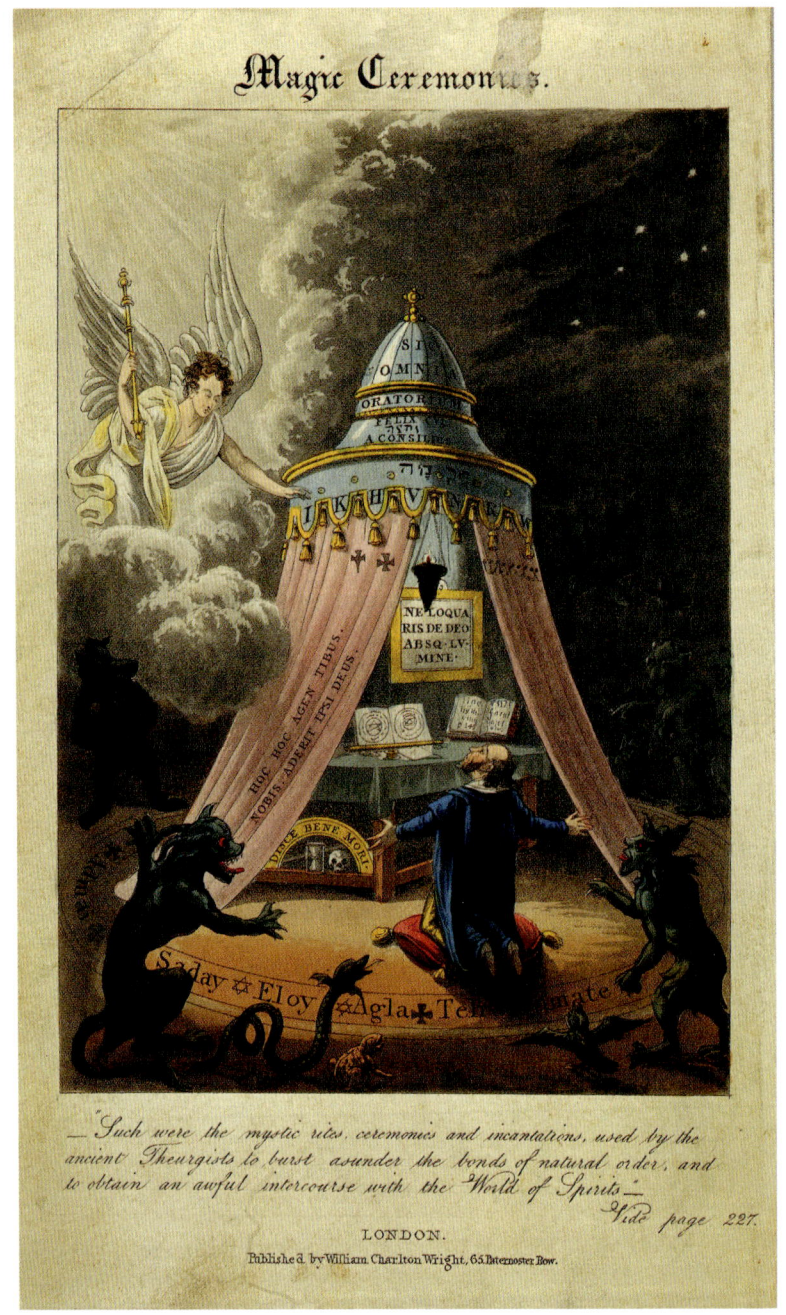

No single literary work exerts quite as much influence across the nineteenth century in this regard as Johann Wolfgang van Goethe's two-part closet drama *Faust*. More than simply a variation on the old legend from the author's native Germany, or an adaptation of Marlowe's play, Goethe's *Faust*—the first part published in 1808 and the second part posthumously in 1832—is the prototypical Romantic masterpiece, casting its shadow across the entire century. "I love those who yearn for the impossible," he writes in the second part of the play, and indeed *Faust* in its ambiguities, complexities, and depths conveys the anarchic potential of this revolutionary moment. Combining the traditional Faust narrative with post-Enlightenment philosophy, Romantic aesthetic theory, and a purposefully relativist theological perspective, Goethe's play is partially a rejection of Enlightenment values, though it doesn't countenance anything as conservative as a return to medieval perspectives. At the center of *Faust* is Mephisto, Goethe's variation on the famed demon, with Russell writing that he "appears both as the opponent of God and as the instrument of the divine will; as the creator of the material world and as God's subject; as the principle of matter against the principle of spirit; as evil against good; as chaos against order; as a stimulus to creativity; and in many other aspects." Fleshed out from the skeleton of allegory, Mephisto is the embodiment of humanity's shadow consciousness, what Faust despairs of when he says, "In me there are two souls, alas, and their/Division tears my life in two."

As with most of the bohemians of the nineteenth century, Goethe's own theology was purposefully confused and confusing; at home with the irrationalities of faith, but far from any sort of traditional piety. Toward the end of his life he delineated an idiosyncratic cosmology concerning final things, which if he had not in mind when he started writing *Faust*, was at least his post hoc synthesis of his beliefs as they'd developed over the course of writing, while making clear that his perspective was not literal. According to Goethe, the Christian Trinity was not eternal, but rather the Son was produced by the Father who collaborated in the creation of the Spirit, with all three existing in a state of perfection. The fourth thing to be created was Lucifer, and the disruption of that divine and harmonious Trinity is what introduced imperfection into reality. From Lucifer derived the angels—both fallen and unfallen—and, as Russell writes, "Impressed by his own creative powers, he concentrated more and more deeply upon himself, gradually losing touch with reality," and out of this solipsism would come the material universe itself, so that our lineage is traceable not to God, but the demiurge of Satan.

The only thing that prevented the total collapse of our world into malignancy was God's graceful infusion of light into the universe, so that from the "tension between selfishness and openness, darkness and light, comes the tension in the world and in humanity between the downward-closing diabolical force and the upward-opening divine force," as Russell explains. No myth is literal, of course; it's the nature of mythopoesis that a contingent narrative is crafted to explain meaning as it needs to be explained to a given audience during a particular time and in a certain space. What's clear from Goethe's myth is that the great Romantic theme of creation was given a theologically ambiguous gloss, so that this vision of reality as generated through the mad and brilliant narcissism of a figure like Lucifer, we have a concurrent picture of the dangerous and ingenious poet, reflecting the world not through a mirror, but illuminating it with his lamp.

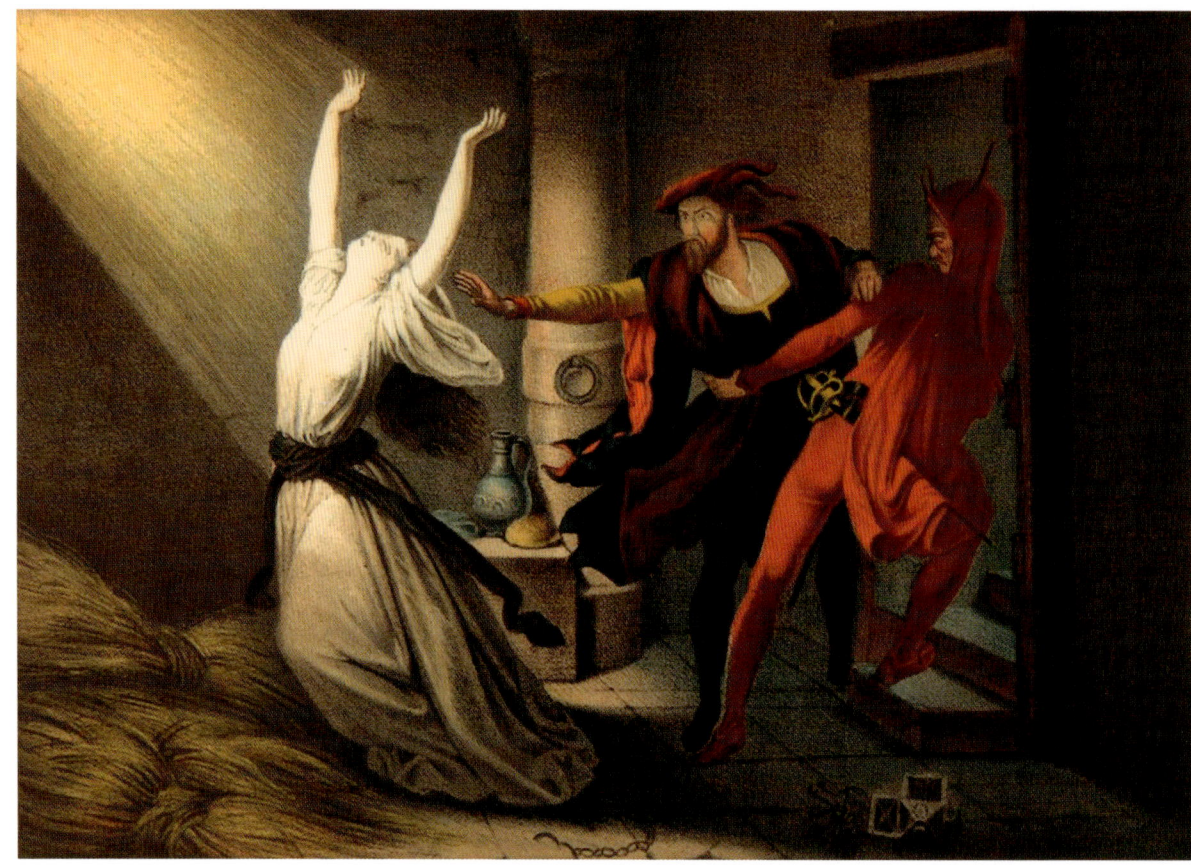

An 1846 lithograph by the German painter Joseph Fay depicting the scene in Goethe's Faust *wherein the wizard attempts to liberate his imprisoned beloved Gretchen (a scene with no corollary in Marlowe). Notice that Fay has depicted Mephisto as wearing the stage costume of a demon, an odd and fascinating recursive commentary, in which a real demon under the guise of being a man wears the costume of a fake demon. Whether conscious or not, such a visual joke lends itself to the themes of illusion and artifice explored both by Goethe, and more generally, by the Faust legend.*

A 1918 art nouveau–style poster designed by Richard Roland Holst for an Amsterdam production of Robert Schumann's oratorio Scenes from Goethe's Faust, *composed between 1844 and 1853.*

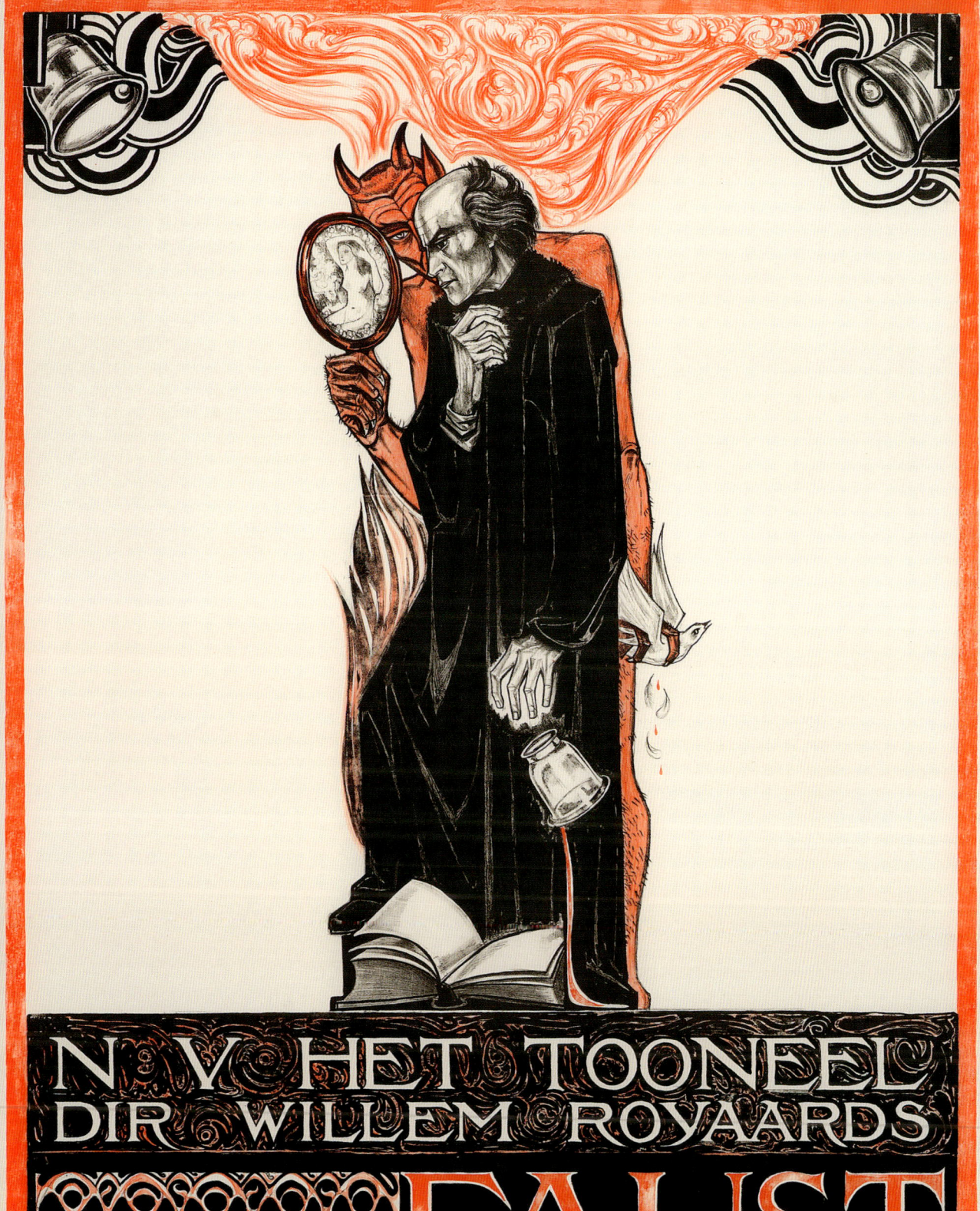

N. V. HET TOONEEL
DIR. WILLEM ROYAARDS

GOETHE'S FAUST

DRUK V. SENEFELDER · R. N ROLAND · HOLST fc. '18

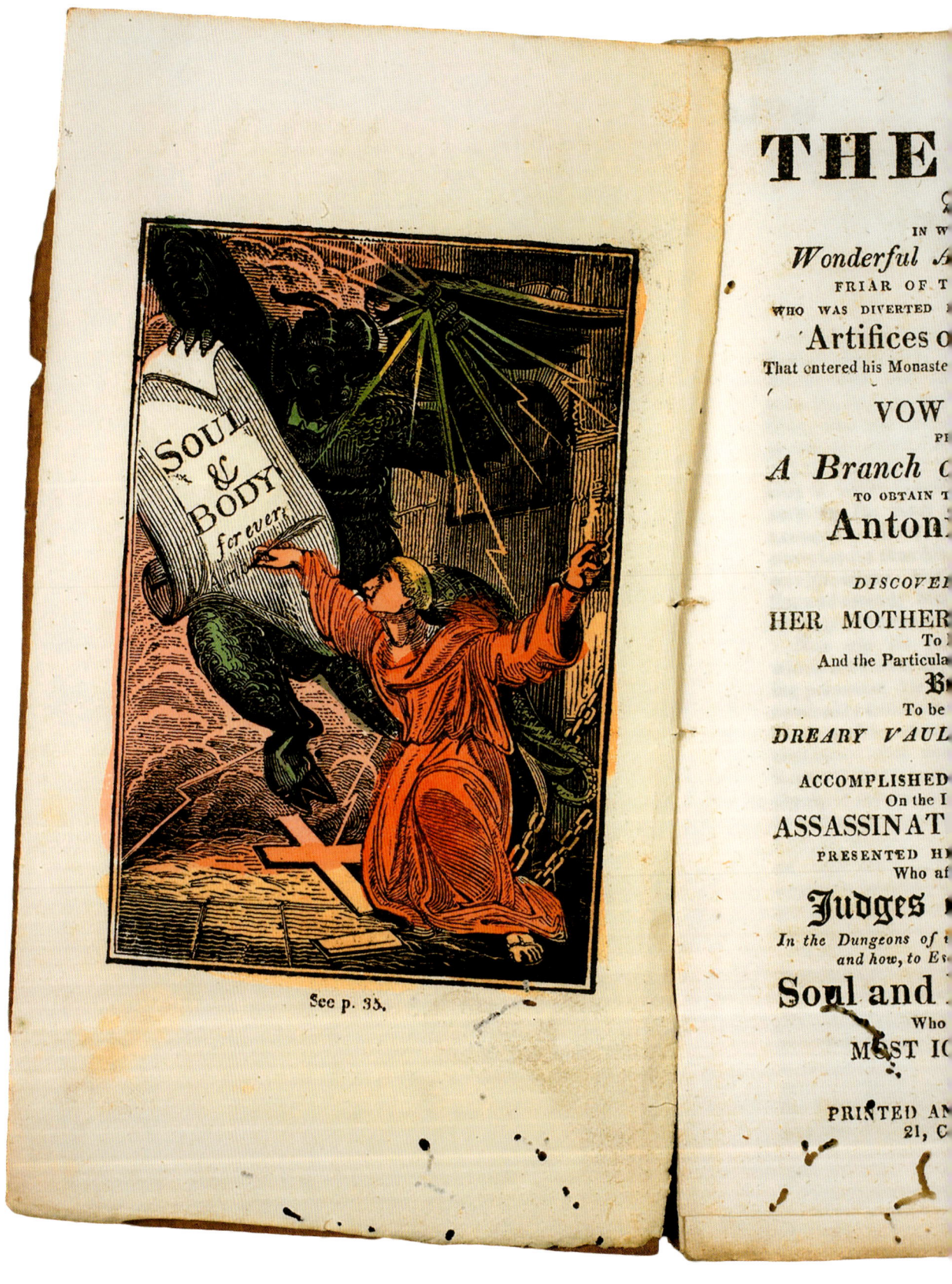

See p. 35.

THE

IN W

Wonderful A

FRIAR OF T

WHO WAS DIVERTED

Artifices o

That entered his Monaste

VOW

P

A Branch o

TO OBTAIN T

Antoni

DISCOVE

HER MOTHER

To

And the Particula

B

To be

DREARY VAUL

ACCOMPLISHED

On the I

ASSASSINAT

PRESENTED H

Who af

Judges

In the Dungeons of

and how, to E

Soul and

Who

MOST IO

PRINTED AN

21, C

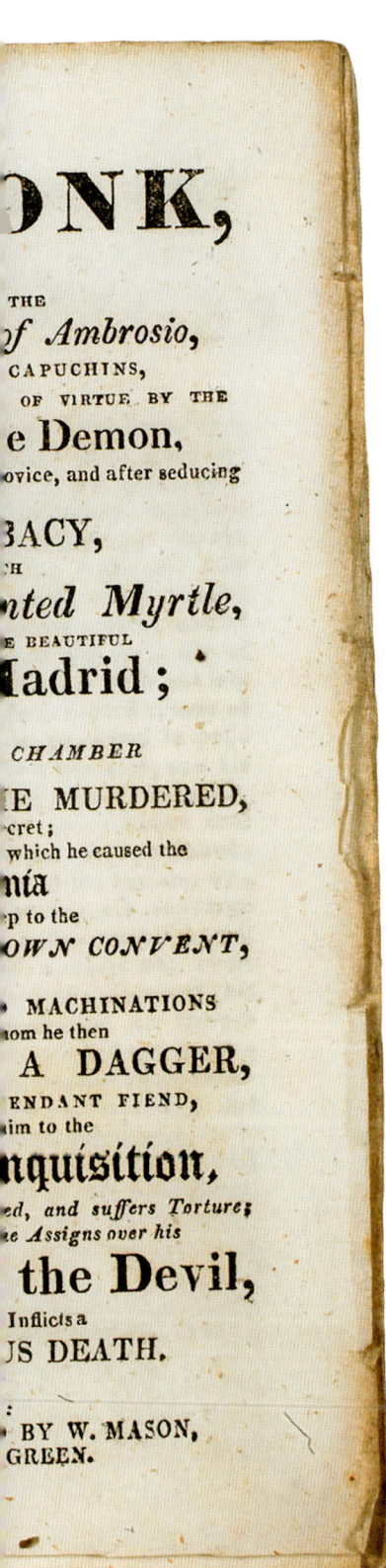

Faust is commonly regarded as a Romantic masterpiece, a canonical work daring in its innovations and brilliant in its executions, but there was a seamier side to Romantic demonic poetics in the form of gothic literature, which pushed the major concerns of the period regarding emotionality to their most lurid extremes. Horace Walpole's 1764 *The Castle of Otranto*, Ann Radcliffe's 1794 *The Mysteries of Udolpho*, Charles Maturin's 1820 *Melmoth the Wanderer*, and in the United States, the immaculate short stories of Edgar Allan Poe, were all exemplars of the mode, trading in a set of shared tropes that often included the supernatural, as well as narrative conceits such as hidden family secrets, exoticized locales, transgressive sexuality, and frequently (especially in English novels) anti-Catholicism. The overall sense of the gothic was of a genre of grotesquerie veritably stewed in the macabre, the morbid, the mysterious, the medieval, the disturbing, and the demonic. Matthew Lewis's 1796 pulp classic *The Monk* is a case in point, telling a faux-medieval tale about the titular character Ambrosio, and his intercourse with the demon Mathilda during the height of the Spanish Inquisition, and the manner in which occult impiety promises terrible powers. "Why shrink you from me?" Matilda asks the monk, "Your suspicions are right, though your terrors are unfounded ... Like you I shuddered at the thoughts ... Like you I had formed a terrible idea of the consequences of raising a daemon ... Judge what must have been my joy at discovering that my terrors were imaginary: I saw the Daemon obedient to my orders."

Gothic writing undeniably had the stench of popularity about it; horror novels written for a mass audience, even while many of its themes were drawn from (and in turn influenced) more serious literature. French Symbolists, members of a literary avant-garde enamored with the supernatural as much as writers of the gothic, mined many of the same tropes, narratives, imagery, and themes, albeit to often much more formally experimental effect. The influence of nineteenth-century occultism more generally and of Lévi more specifically is replete in the history of the period's literary avant-garde, with Symbolists like Charles Baudelaire, Arthur Rimbaud, Paul Verlaine, and Stéphane Mallarmé deeply enmeshed in the imagery of the esoteric. "In many ways, the history of literary occultism is the history of Symbolism," writes Lachman, "the literary search for a 'higher world' begins its paradoxical descent into decadence and the *fin de siècle*." Symbolists shared with their nineteenth-century predecessors a fascination with demonology, and like the Romantics they rejected arid rationalisms, with a Luciferian glee at the contradictions of the age. As Baudelaire infamously noted, "The greatest trick the devil ever pulled was convincing the world that he didn't exist."

In his sensuous, erotic, and transgressive 1857 anthology *The Flowers of Evil*, Baudelaire penned a liturgy for the damned, writing satanic verse that explored the dark latency of demonic imagery. "The Devil is active at my side," writes Baudelaire, "He swims around me like the impalpable air;/I swallow him and feel him burning my lungs,/Filling them with an eternal, guilty desire." Baudelaire gained notoriety as a translator of Poe, having introduced him to a French reading public that (arguably still) appreciated him more than his readership in his native America, the poet's free verse *Flowers of Evil* both gesture toward a Romantic past, but also to a dawning modernity (a word which, incidentally, the poet coined). Arguably the tradition that Baudelaire works in goes back even earlier than Romanticism; the Symbolist obsession with the esoteric relationships between language and reality evocative of the same Neoplatonist concerns of the Renaissance humanists. Lachman writes that "Like the potential for transcendence inherent in language itself—it's ability to speak 'otherwise' and 'change' reality—sophisticated occultism is about the power of words, the efficacy of language and writing." It's a connection that Baudelaire himself makes, writing of how "Hermes Trismegistus/Slowly rocks our enthralled minds,/And the rich metal of our wills/Is vaporized by this learned alchemist." As with the magicians of the sixteenth and seventeenth centuries, Baudelaire's concern is the manipulation of sacred letters to evoke some sort of daemonic control over existence. In the Renaissance they called it magic; in the nineteenth century they just call it art.

Within *The Flowers of Evil*, Baudelaire crafts a litany of praise for Satan, drawing from past Luciferian traditions that attempt to exonerate the demonic as a wellspring for coiled creative energy. Baudelaire writes:

> Prince of the exile, you have been wronged,
>
> Defeated, you rise up ever stronger....
>
> You who, even to lepers and accursed outcasts
>
> Teach through love a longing for Paradise....
>
> You who know in what corners of envious nations
>
> God hoards his precious gems....
>
> You would teach us to console the frail and suffering
>
> By mixing saltpeter and sulfur....
>
> Glory and praise to you, lord Satan, in the highest,
>
> Where once you reigned, and in the depths
>
> Of hell, where you lie defeated and dreaming.
>
> Let my soul one day, in the shadow of the tree of knowledge,
>
> Rest next to you.

With its second-person injunction, the poem is clearly written in the form of a prayer. Addressing himself to Satan, Baudelaire offers up these supplications as encomium, address, and plea. Catholic theology traditionally maintains that there are five different functions of prayer— praise, intercession, supplication, thanksgiving, and spiritual warfare—each mode of address serving a distinct purpose in the life of the worshipper. By that standard, Baudelaire's poem fulfills each one of those rationales for prayer. He engaged praise ("Glory and praise to you, lord Satan"); intercession ("You who know in what corners of envious nations/God hoards his precious gems"); supplication ("Let my soul one day . . . Rest next to you"); thanksgiving ("You who, even to lepers and accursed outcasts/Teach through love a longing for Paradise"); and spiritual warfare ("Where once you reigned," with perhaps a hope that so too shall he again). The poem as prayer embodying every purpose for why one might pray—the only difference is who it's directed toward.

Baudelaire's demonic theology doesn't just invert the normal words for good and evil; he doesn't simply declare God to be the latter and Satan to be the former, which is ultimately an idiosyncratic use of vocabulary more than a genuine subversion. No, *The Flowers of Evil* has about it a genuine Luciferian ethos, so that his demonic theology, which holds that Satan was punished for finding Paradise so perfect that to serve humans is actually an act of impudent idolatry. The position that Satan was effectively exiled for loving God too much has its precursors in both the writings of the Church Father Origen as well as the story of the fallen angel Iblis in the Qur'an, but for Baudelaire there was something arrestingly contemporary about it. For if Baudelaire holds any orthodox opinion, it's that Satan is truly prince of this world, for "It is the Devil who pulls the strings that move us . . . Each day we take another step down into hell,/Deadened to horror, through stinking shadows." And here the poet knowingly addresses his own self-corrupted audience, for "Reader, you recognize this delicate monster,/ Hypocrite reader, my likeness, my brother," spoken just as if he were Mephistopheles whispering in Faust's ear.

Baudelaire championed that chthonic sense of apocalypses' creative possibility, writing in an anti-psalm that the Devil "leads me far from the face of God,/ Panting and broken with weariness, into the midst/Of the deep and deserted plains of ennui," and where he "thrusts into my confused sight/Dirty clothing, open wounds,/And the bloody costume of Destruction." The imagery is unsubtly sexual; all of this thrusting, the vaginal wound, the bloody menstrual costume, but it also invokes the fecundity of Dionysian destruction, where from obliteration is the possibility of new creation, an intertwining of Eros and Thanatos. If philosophers in previous centuries had understood the world as the immutable creation of God, where humanity's sole prerogative was to move around the materials that already existed, then the dawn of modernity in the nineteenth century understood things rather differently, appropriating for our own ends the demonic imperative of self-creation into the realm of science, technology, economics, and faith. These were, after all, the decades of the industrial revolution, when Blake's "dark Satanic mills" belched sulphur into the once bucolic countryside, and where Nathaniel Hawthorne bemoaned the "mechanical demon" that was the train, an era that Karl Marx would describe in *The Communist Manifesto* as being one in which "all that is solid melts into air."

Marx's language is wizardly, his rhetoric one of conjuration. An adamant atheist and materialist himself, in part encouraged by the Darwinian challenge of the Victorian era, Marx couldn't help (as is true of everyone) have a theological inflection to his language. "There is a specter haunting Europe," Marx and Friedrich Engels wrote in the introduction to *The Communist Manifesto*, and such hauntings speak to the endurance of the ghostly, even within our ostensibly secular age. In his 1845 *Theses on Feuerbach*, Marx thundered that "Philosophers have hitherto only interpreted the world in various ways; the point is to change it," a shift in priorities not dissimilar to how poets had begun to see themselves not as describing reality, but creating it. A turning away from the mirror and a turning on of the lamp. This embrace of the creative firmament—that demonic power and energy—marked the politics and philosophy of the nineteenth century, with the anarchist theorist Pierre-Joseph Proudhon gushing, "Come Satan … you have been defamed by priests and kings, that I may kiss you and hold you against my breast." Enthusiasms such as these were politically ecumenical, for a spirit of remaking the world in the revolutionary's own image would come to mark both the radical left and the revanchist right, defining the next century's totalitarianisms of communism and fascism.

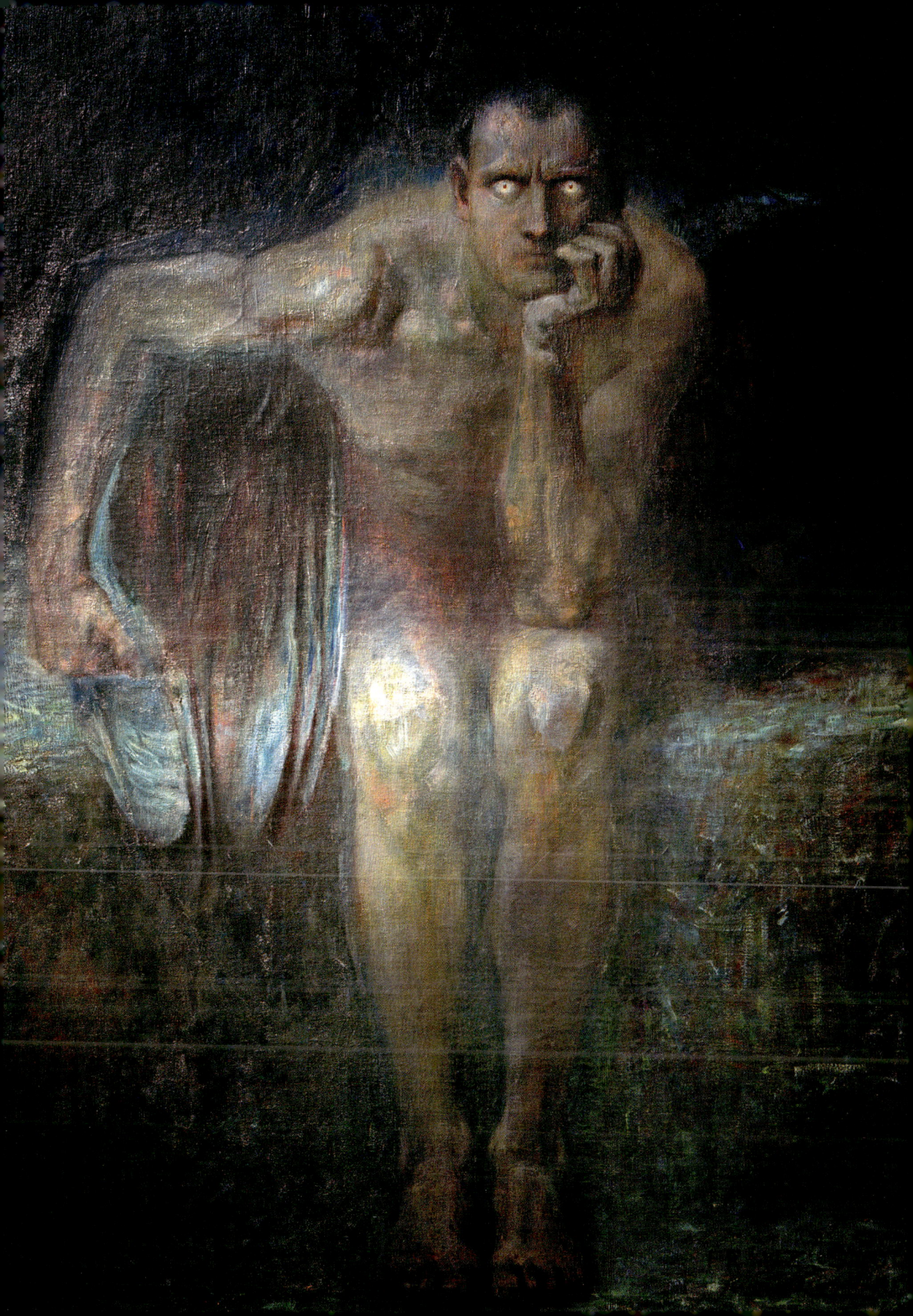

"Now the world laughs, the cruel curtain parts,/And the wedding feast of Light and Darkness is set," writes the German philosopher Friedrich Nietzsche in his 1885 *Thus Spoke Zarathustra*, a mythopoeic rumination on the implications of living after meaning has been drained from reality, after God has departed from this world. Sometimes anachronistically associated with the fascism of the twentieth century (which was encouraged by his anti-Semitic sister), Nietzsche was certainly a nihilist, and along with Fyodor Dostoevsky and de Sade, one of the few figures to take the moral implications of atheism seriously, and not just as a marker of bourgeois elitism. When he declares "God is dead!" that logically means that the Devil has expired as well, but as Russell writes "Nietzsche identified the Devil with Dionysius, who was for him the rich, ambivalent, but generally positive symbol of creativity, chaos, fertility, destruction, sexual license, and courage."

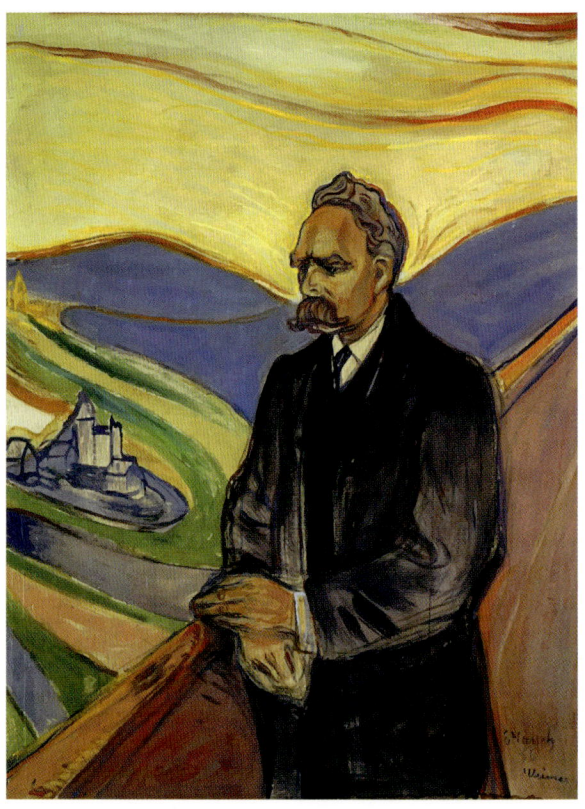

The Devil may be dead, but Nietzsche's terrifying brilliance was able to comprehend that that simply meant humanity could now crown itself as the new Satan. This, then, was to be the ultimate null point from which even the devils flee, a demonological absolute zero—something beyond good and evil. Like a prophet of dark emptiness, a Christ of the abyss, Nietzsche would look into the future, and in his 1888 autobiography *Ecce Homo* he would predict that soon "there will be wars, the likes of which have never been seen on earth before." These new battles would seem more like that original war in heaven than anything ever fought by men before. Suffering from tertiary syphilis, and institutionalized in a Weimar insane asylum, Nietzsche succumbed to pneumonia in 1900, the last year of the nineteenth century. Six months after his death would see the dawn of the twentieth, and with it the Somme and Verdun, Gallipoli and the Marne, Stalingrad and Normandy, Auschwitz and Hiroshima.

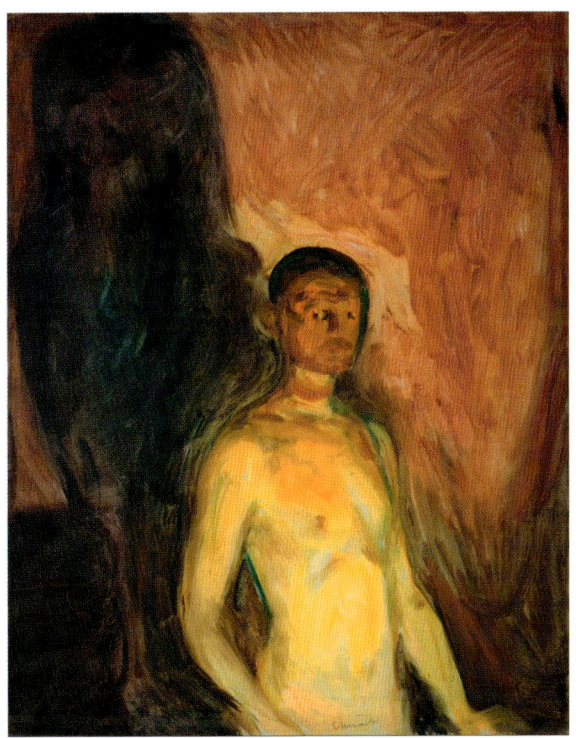

Edvard Munch's 1903 painting Self-Portrait in Hell, *housed in Oslo's Munch Museum, is an appropriately self-reflective introduction for the twentieth century. Satan may be abolished and hell may be ostensibly empty, but the demons are very much on this earth, for now humanity has given itself the power to usher in the literal apocalypse, with no need for God or the Devil.*

If demons have been variously feared as avatars of absolute evil and honored as symbols of high-minded independence, then as the nineteenth century hurtled further into modernity, they increasingly became signifiers used in pop culture and advertising. Demons populated twentieth-century music, film, and low culture forms like comics books. Steve Banes's 2016 compilation (on the left) gathers examples of "Satanic comics" from the golden age of comics in the 1950s; lurid, violent, and disturbing occult-themed works that parents worried were corrupting their children. As David Hadju notes in The Ten-Cent Plague: The Great Comic-Book Scare and How it Changed America, *these were works "Created by outsiders of various sorts, comics gave voice to their makers' fantasies and discontent in the brash vernacular of cartoon drawings . . . and they spoke with special cogency to young people." On the right is an original 1969 cover from the first issue of* Shock *magazine, designed by Bernard Baily, which published horror comics that explored the occult, supernatural, and demonic.*

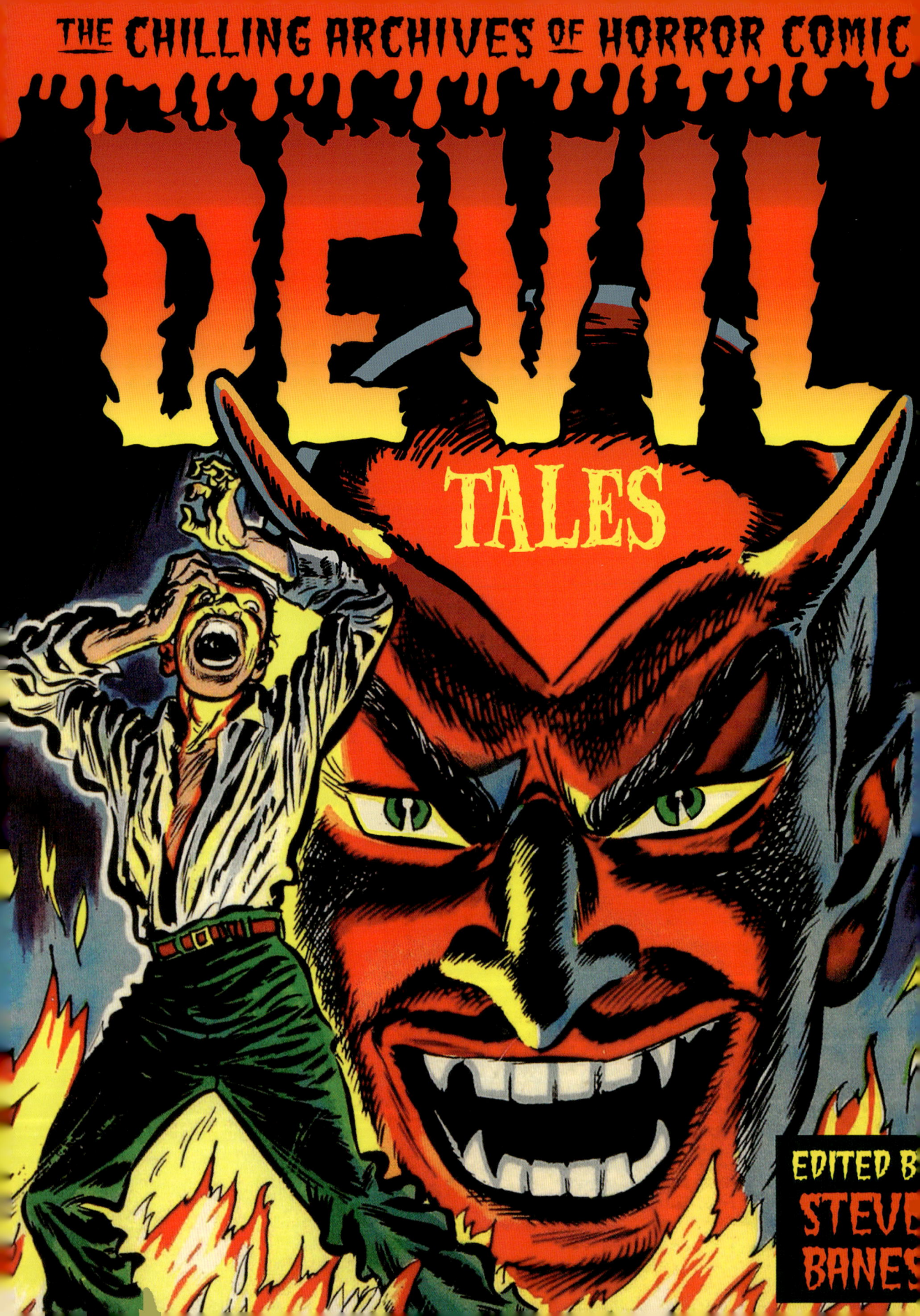

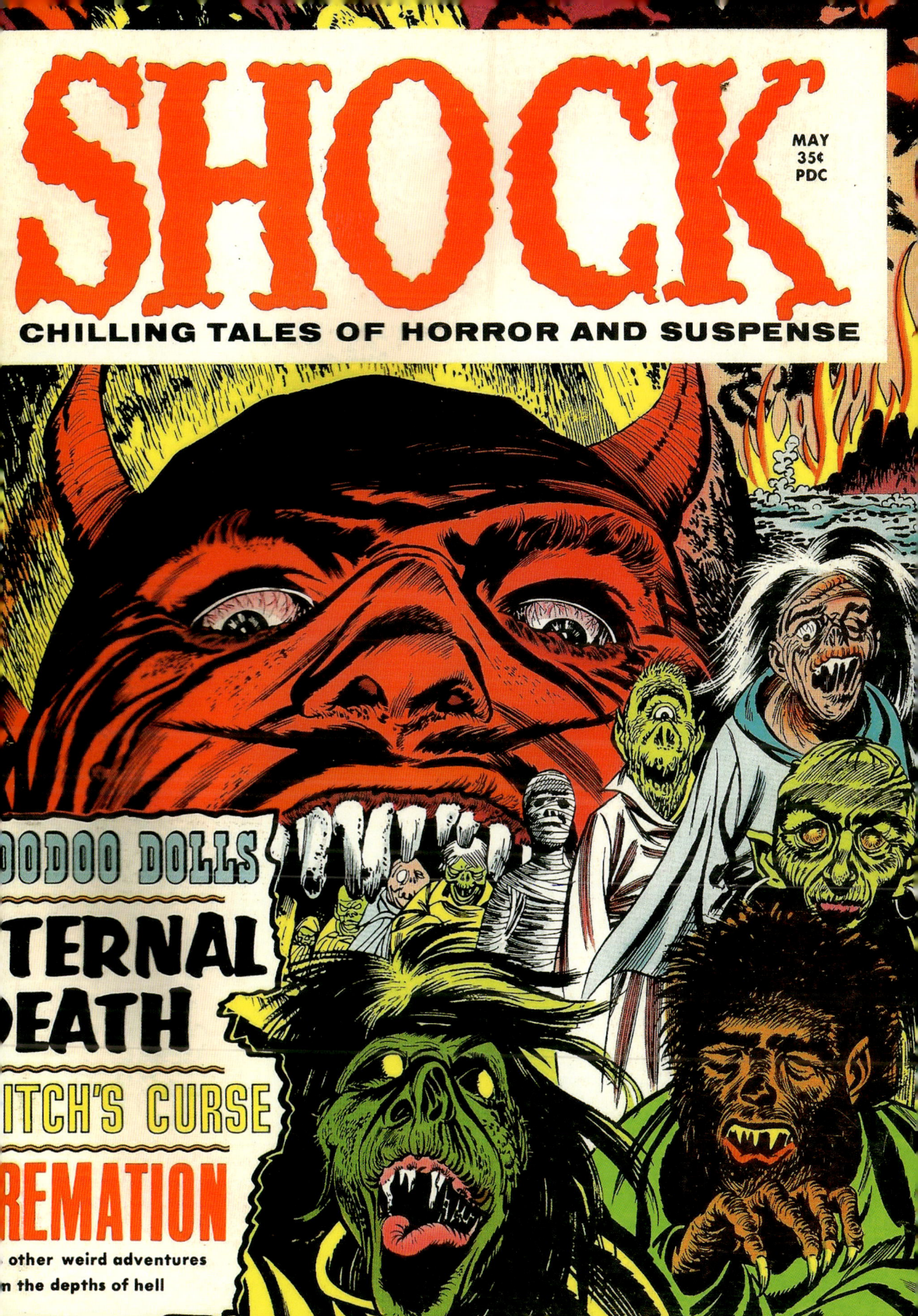

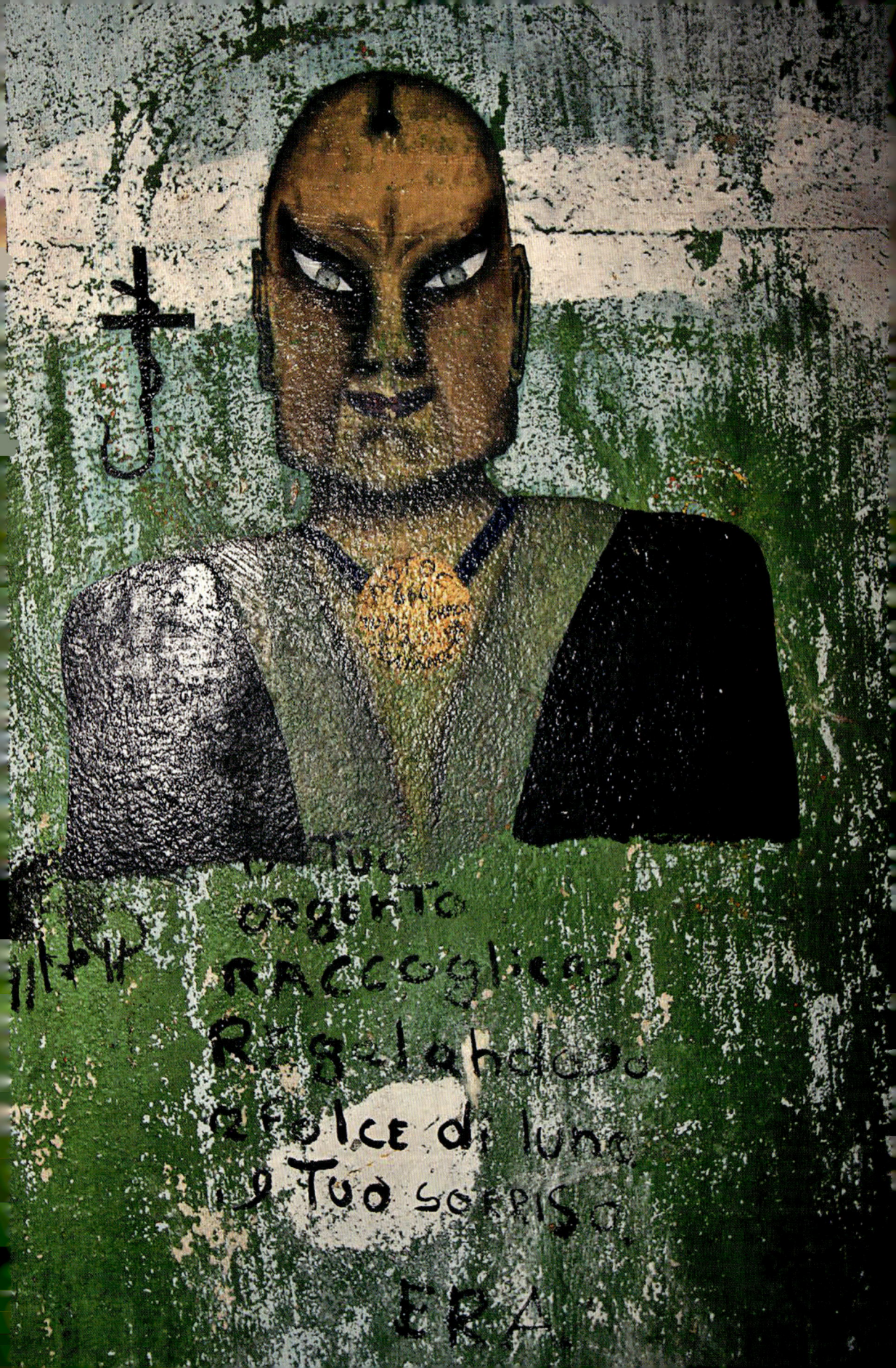

CHAPTER SIX

Do What Thou Wilt

Demonology in the Modern Age, c. 1900–2000

My light! O my father the Devil! It hath made all things one,
being perfect, even as doth the Darkness!

—*Magical Record of the Beast 666: The Diaries of Aleister Crowley,
1914–1920*

Evil is unspectacular and always human,
And shares our bed and eats at our own table.

—W.H. Auden, "Herman Melville" (1939)

ON MODERNIST DEMONOLOGY

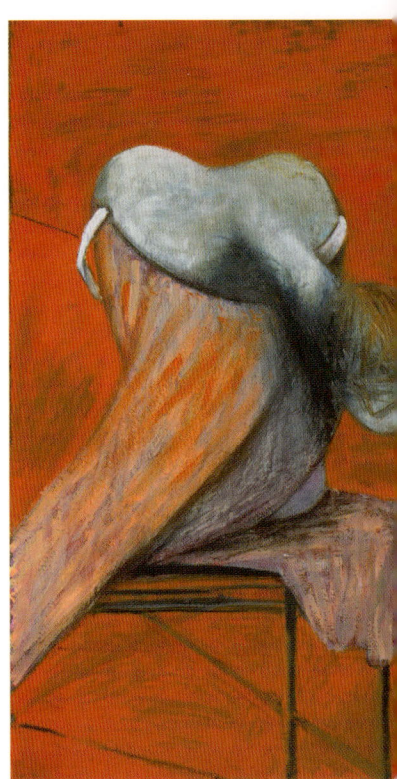

Along the pristine blue of the Tyrrhenian Coast, not far from Palermo, is the small village of Cefalù. Based on its name, which had endured for millennia, it was presumably founded by the Greek colonizers of Sicily in the centuries before Christ, and like all of the island, Cefalù has been buffeted and reshaped by centuries of history. Cefalù has been ruled by Greeks, Carthaginians, Romans, Vandals, and Ostrogoths, Byzantines, Arabs, Normans, the Aragonese, the Spanish, and since Risorgimento, the Italians. In 1920, the village had been part of a unified Italy for only sixty years when a wealthy, middle-aged British graduate of Cambridge—son of a Warwickshire brewer with parents who were congregants in good standing at the local fundamentalist Plymouth Brethren church—purchased a modest villa on a hill overlooking the Mediterranean, a crumbling white-washed building with a red terra-cotta tile roof, almost entirely subsumed by the wild lavender, thyme, rosemary, and oregano plants that blanketed the otherwise arid perch that the house sat on.

Inside of the house, the Englishman bedecked the plain walls with intricate murals—an inverted pentagram rendered in blood-red ink, a yellow cyclops whom he referred to as an "idol," green gibbering goblins, and ash-faced demons. Joined by his lover, a Swiss woman named Leah Hirsig—he fondly called her his "Scarlet Woman"—whom he met while living among bohemian circles in New York City's Greenwich Village. They named their villa Thelema Abbey after the antinomian monastery in François Rabelais's sixteenth-century novel *Gargantua and Pantagruel*, where "Do what thou wilt" was the whole of the law (Sir Francis Dashwood had the same line inscribed above Medmenham Abbey). Here, in this "chamber of nightmares," they would found an academy of occultism where a bevy of acolytes would cycle through, engaging in orgies and psychedelic drug trips, performing conjurations, channeling spirits and demons, and founding a new left-hand faith known as Thelema. He fancied himself the "most wicked man in the world," and by 1923 the new fascist government of Benito Mussolini would agree, serving Aleister Crowley a notice of deportation, leaving Thelema abbey behind to decay into the rugged Sicilian hillside.

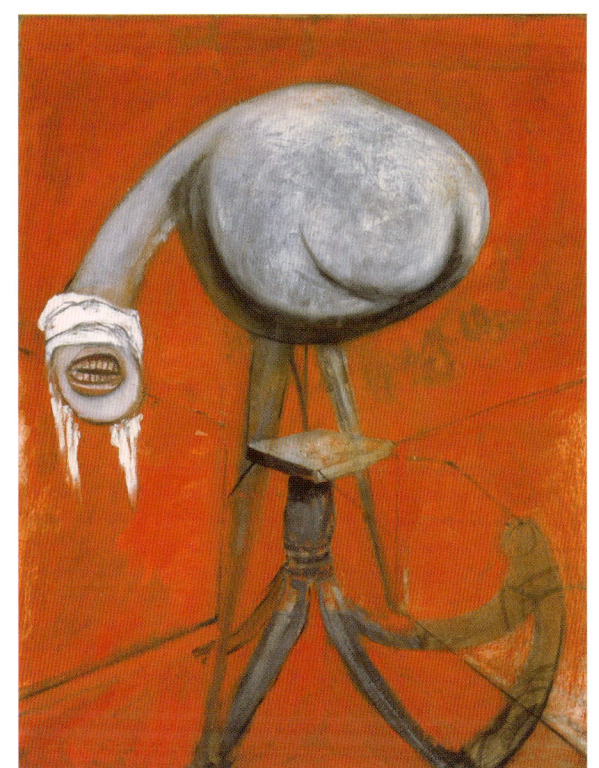 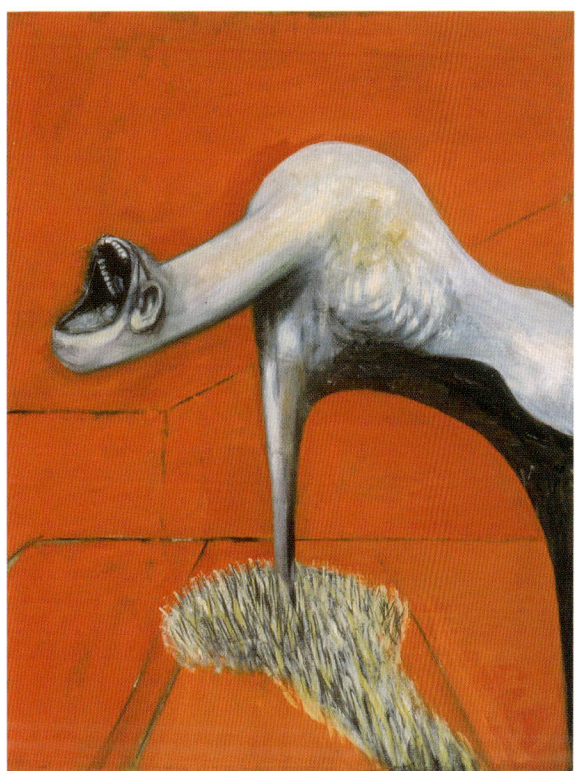

World War II was not yet over when the British painter Francis Bacon com-pleted his triptych Three Studies for Figures at the Base of a Crucifixion. *Held by the Tate Britain today, when Bacon's composition was first exhibited at the Lefevre Gallery of London in 1945, spectators were shocked at the disturbing aesthetic of the painting that would in many ways signal Great Britain's arrival as a mature bastion of artistic modernism. Part of what still unnerves us about Bacon's painting is that the demons, or "figures," of his study are figurative enough to evoke that which we've seen before (for example, they clearly have mouths), while also being so abstracted and alien that viewers feels as if they're in a completely different dimension. The result is less a rejection of tradition than the uncanny feeling that we're seeing something more real than reality. When combined with the indefinite article in the title, there is an upsetting flat-tening of time, the feeling that the crucifixion at which these demons are present may as well be our own.*

A 1921 photograph of Crowley shows the writer and magician at the height of his occult powers; with penetrating gaze he poses for the picture with two slightly open fists pressed against either side of head, eyes wide and a slight grimace on his face. He wears an unusual peaked hat, the hood of the druidical robe he is wearing. Affixed upon his head covering is a triangular magical symbol with an Egyptian Eye of Horus in the middle, golden threads in the shape of a Star of David emanating from the sigil. This is the Crowley of popular imagination, the English gentleman dabbling in demonology, and in the process becoming the most infamous and celebrated of twentieth-century occultists, our era's equivalent of Éliphas Lévi (whom the former claimed to be in a past life, as well as being the reincarnation of Cagliostro, and the wicked Borgia pope Alexander VI). "The popular image endures of Crowley as a vicious Satanist who employed illicit drugs and perverted sex to enliven the weary charade of his blasphemous 'magick,'" writes his biographer Lawrence Sutin in the reconsideration *Do What Thou Wilt: A Life of Aleister Crowley*. Yet as Sutin claims, such reductionism does a disservice to a fascinating figure who is "most emphatically a part of the spiritual history of this century."

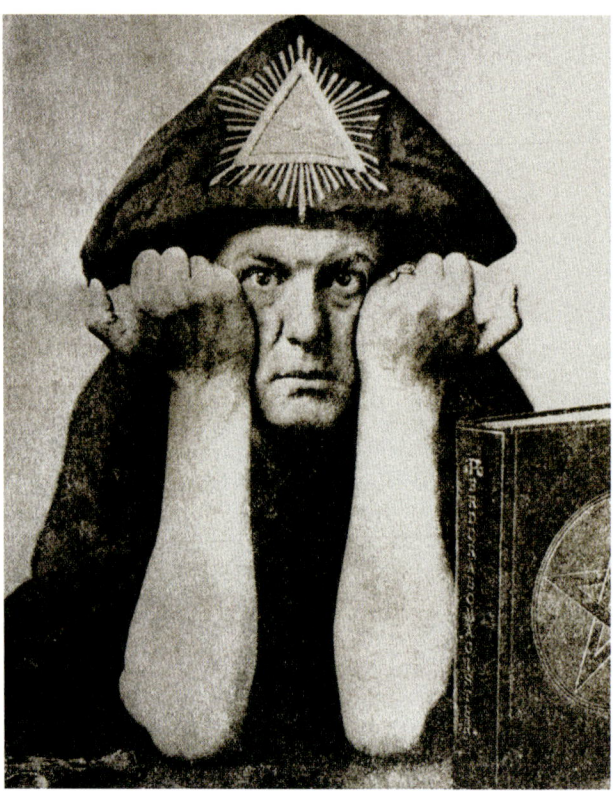

As a figure, Crowley connects the Victorian occultism of Lévi and Blavatsky with modernist aesthetics and philosophical thought; he is the conduit from which nineteenth-century Spiritualism transmutes into all of the accoutrement of contemporary magic, from automatic writing and Ouija boards to the rock music of the Rolling Stones, Led Zeppelin, David Bowie, and Black Sabbath. Marked by deep contradictions, Crowley was both a fearless, openly bisexual proponent of sexual freedom, and at times an advocate for an aristocratic fascism; a bohemian libertine, and possibly an agent of British intelligence (shades of Marlowe); a synthesizer of the Western esoteric tradition that drew upon gnosticism, kabbalah, and hermeticism, and an inveterate plagiarizer; a talented avant-garde modernist poet who was published alongside (and sparred) with William Butler Yeats, and a bit of a hack. Because his intellectual origins are so firmly in the nineteenth century—he was twenty-five in 1900—he was enmeshed in the transatlantic mélange of Spiritualism and Theosophy that marked that era, from ectoplasm to séances, but he was able to funnel such material into a singular vision. Of course demonology would necessarily play a central role in his constructed faith of Thelema (Koine Greek for "will"), dealing as it did with those dark unseen things of our world, and man's ability to try and control them for his own purposes.

"I am alone," Crowley writes in 1904's *The Book of the Law*, the central text of Thelema, and a powerful grimoire in its own right. "There is no God where I am." Perhaps it's more appropriate to say transcribes than "writes," for Crowley maintained that *The Book of the Law* had been imparted to him by a supernatural being named Aiwass while on honeymoon in Egypt with his first wife, Rose Edith, that same year. To claim that one's composition had an astral origin was not unusual among the modernists. Much of the modernism of T.S. Eliot, Ezra Pound, and Yeats finds its primogeniture in a strange species of Victorian occultism—it's a short road from the technique of automatic writing, where a medium empties their mind and channels their unconsciousness (or the spirit realm) for insight, to the stream of consciousness that marks James Joyce and Virginia Woolf. Poet Edward Hirsch gives a representative example about Yeats in *The Demon and the Angel: Searching for the Source of Artistic Inspiration*, when he recounts:

Yeats's young wife Georgie surprised him by attempting automatic writing. He was so excited by the obscure messages, by the disjointed but profound spiritual instructions coming through, that he offered to give up poetry and devote himself entirely to deciphering and systematizing the discoveries. "No," was the answer, "We have come to give you metaphors for poetry."

The Irish poet, unassailably canonical, would claim that much of his poetry was generated by a spirit named Leo Africanus. No mere eccentricity, for the Portuguese poet Fernando Pessoa, famous for writing under the guise of dozens of different complex personalities known as heteronyms, claimed a similar genesis for his verse. Perhaps explicable through the psychoanalytic theories of a Sigmund Freud or a Carl Jung, there wasn't necessarily any stigma attached to such unusual accounts of inspiration. As for Crowley, he claimed that Aiwass was an entity independent from his own consciousness, privy to certain mystical secrets that would form the basis for Thelema, chief among these being three commandments—"Do what thou wilt' shall be the whole of the Law;" "Love is the law, love under will;" and "Every man and every woman is a star." From those axioms were generated certain implications about the power of radical creativity for the exemplary individual, who in the practice of ritual magik (which Crowley spelled with a "k" to differentiate from mere stage illusions) could affect their surroundings.

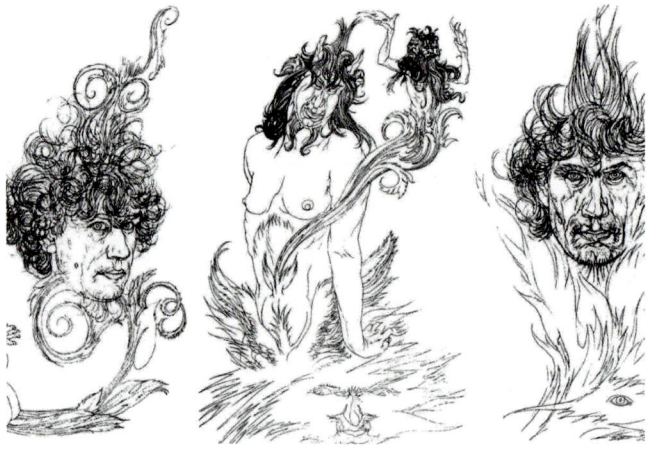

Many of the methods embraced by the modernist avant-garde find their origin in occult practice, with the process of automatic writing being a primary example. In automatic writing, which in effect is similar to stream of consciousness, though it differs in execution, an individual empties their mind of focus and lets their unconscious dictate the course that composition will take. For occultists like Crowley and Yeats, the origins of the resultant words were spirits, specters, or demons. For visual artists there was an equivalent method known as automatism, which was specifically associated with the surrealists. Similar to how writers were meant to strip their awareness away to nothing so that the unthinking mind itself could render unforeseen compositions, artists let their unconscious dictate drawings and paintings. English occultist Austin Osman Spare was one of the great initiates and theoreticians of surrealist automatism, and this 1921 drawing was made through the method. It shows three related Dionysian figures, either drudged up from the unconscious or perhaps from wherever such creatures exist. The original is held by the Viktor Wynd Museum of Curiosities, Fine Art and Un Natural History in London.

"The voice was of deep timbre, musical and expressive, its tones solemn, voluptuous, tender, fierce, or aught else as suited the moods of the message," Crowley recalls of Aiwass in his 1936 memoir *Equinox of the Gods*, this tall, dark man in his thirties wearing either Assyrian or Persian costume, "active and strong, with the face of a savage kind, and eyes veiled lest their gaze should destroy what they saw." *The Book of the Law* has a complex eschatology, making a tripartite division in history (similar to a group of heretical medieval Franciscans known as the Joachimites) between a matriarchal Age of Isis, which was associated with ancient paganism, a patriarchal Age of Osiris associated with the Abrahamic traditions, and a coming libertine and antinomian Age of Horus, in which self-actualization would alter human consciousness, with Crowley declared by Aiwass as the prophet of this new Aeon. And Aiwass himself? Crowley is clear that this being, this "praetor-human," had many different identities, known variously as Lucifer, Baphomet, and Satan. "There is a splendor in my name hidden and glorious," *The Book of Law* states, "as the sun of midnight is ever the son." A diabolical theophany not so different from the beginnings of other revealed religions, but Crowley's new faith was Luciferian through and through, interested in an exultation of the individual above mundane sacrifice, a type of ritualized Nietzscheanism that paradoxically combined both nihilism and a reverence for the numinous.

Like Blavatsky, Crawley drew together an ecumenical assemblage of traditions, from dharmic and Vedic thought in India, to kabbalah and gnosticism, but his most formative influence was the secret society known as the Hermetic Order of the Golden Dawn. Based in London, with lodges in the capital, Edinburgh, and ultimately Paris, the Hermetic Order of the Golden Dawn borrowed the hierarchy of Freemasonry (from which it emerged), combined with much of the philosophy of Rosicrucianism, along with a nineteenth-century orientalist obsession with all things Egyptian that proliferated after the translation of the Rosetta stone. Davies writes that their "magic was obviously not that of the cunning-folk who continued to provide magical solutions for the misfortunes of the general populace of Britain at the time," and indeed the society had an impressive list of (alleged) upper-class members, drawing particularly from artistic types attracted to the performative rituals of the group, including the Irish novelist Bram Stoker, the English novelist Arthur Conan Doyle, the Welsh novelist Arthur Machen, the English radio broadcaster Algernon Blackwood, the Irish poet Yeats, and the Irish actress Sara Allgood (the society believed in the complete equality of the sexes).

NEXT SPREAD

German surrealist Max Ernst's 1937 painting Fireside Angel, *currently held in a private collection, expresses the modern demonic with a distinctly novel horror. Completed for Paris's International Exposition of Surrealism, Ernst's painting was finished shortly after the fascist victory in the Spanish Civil War, and only two years before the beginning of the Second World War, prefiguring a satanic madness about to envelope the globe. That the demon's visage appears not unlike an eagle, which Ernst would have seen emblazoned on Reich buildings and in Nazi pageants before he went into exile from Germany, should not go without comment.*

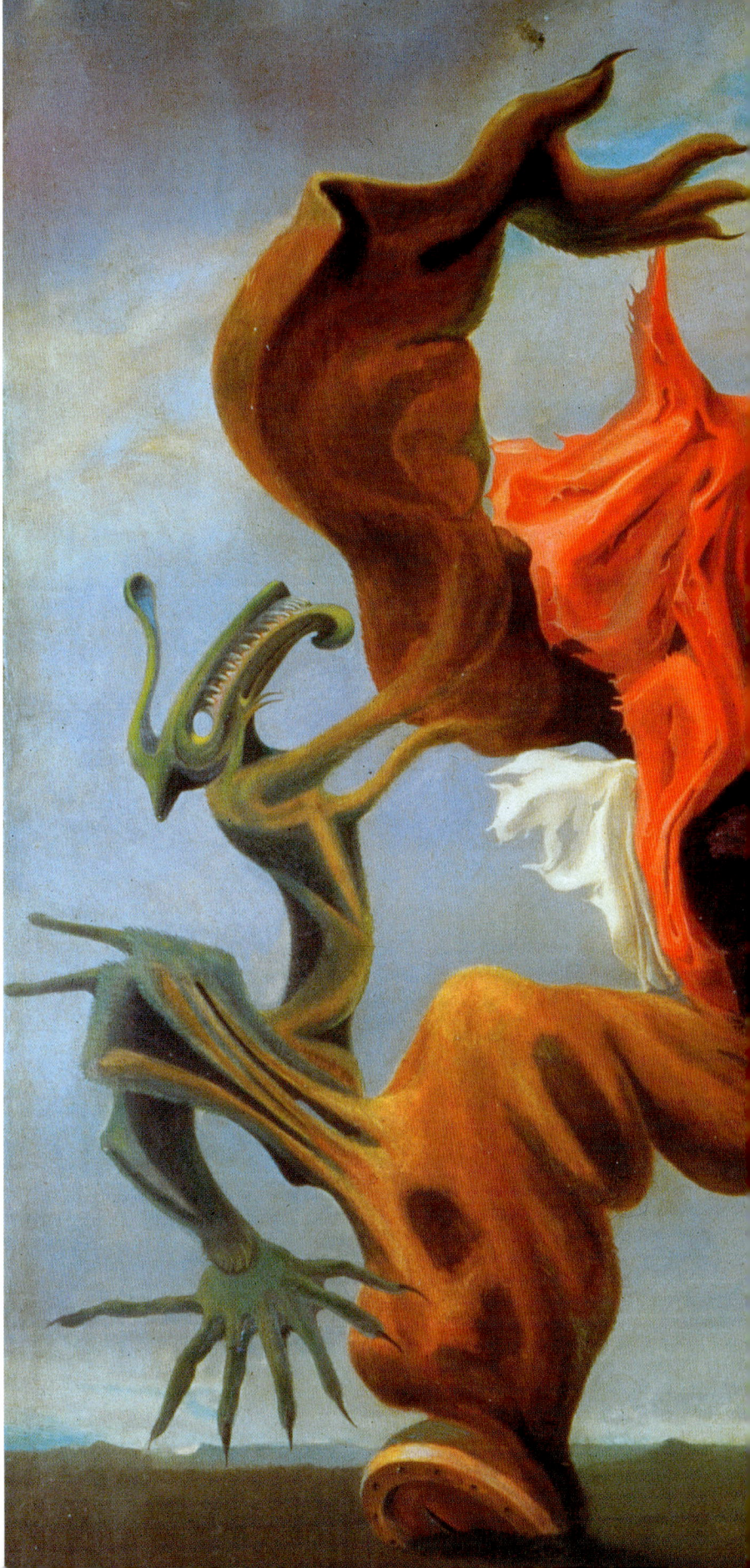

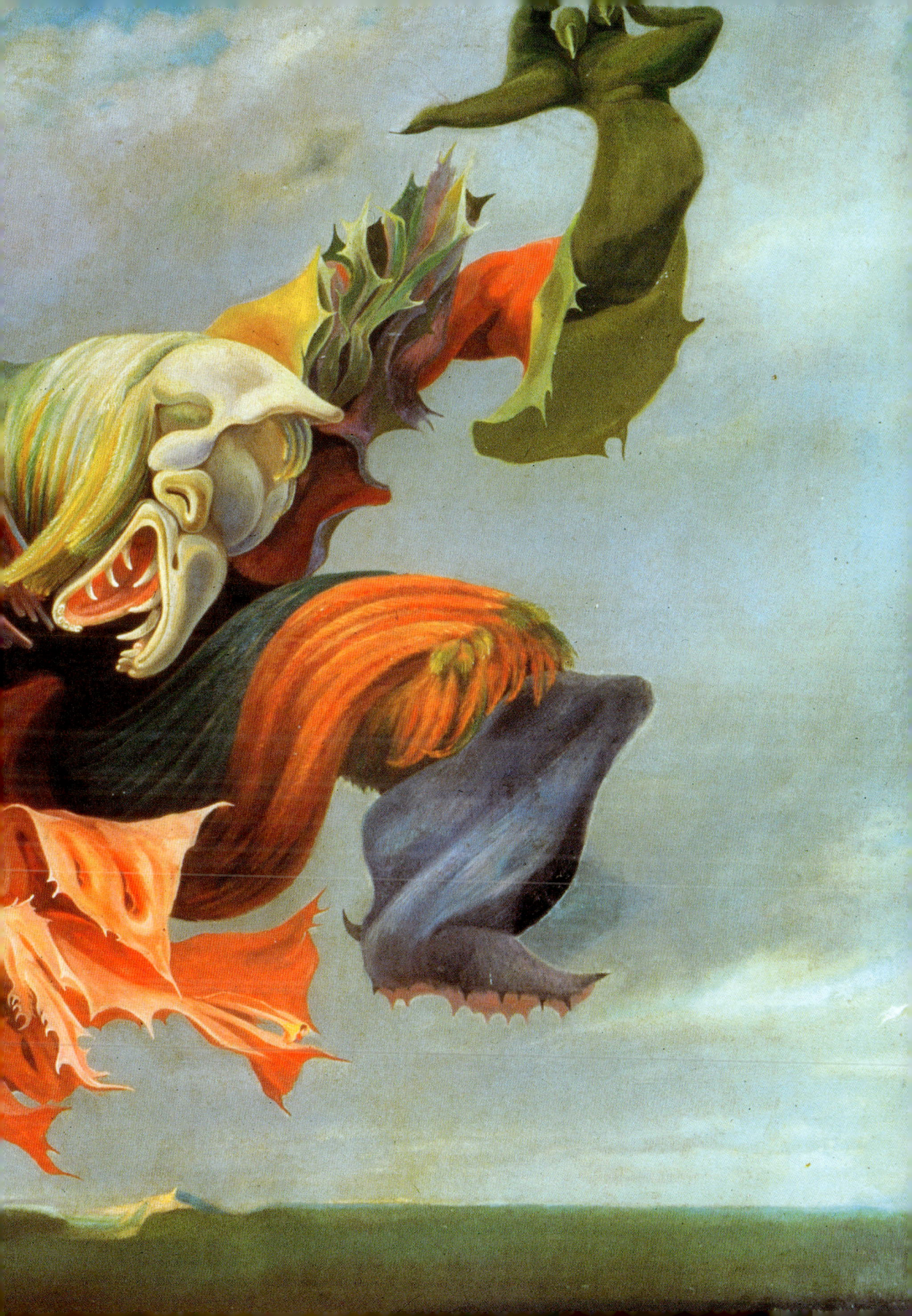

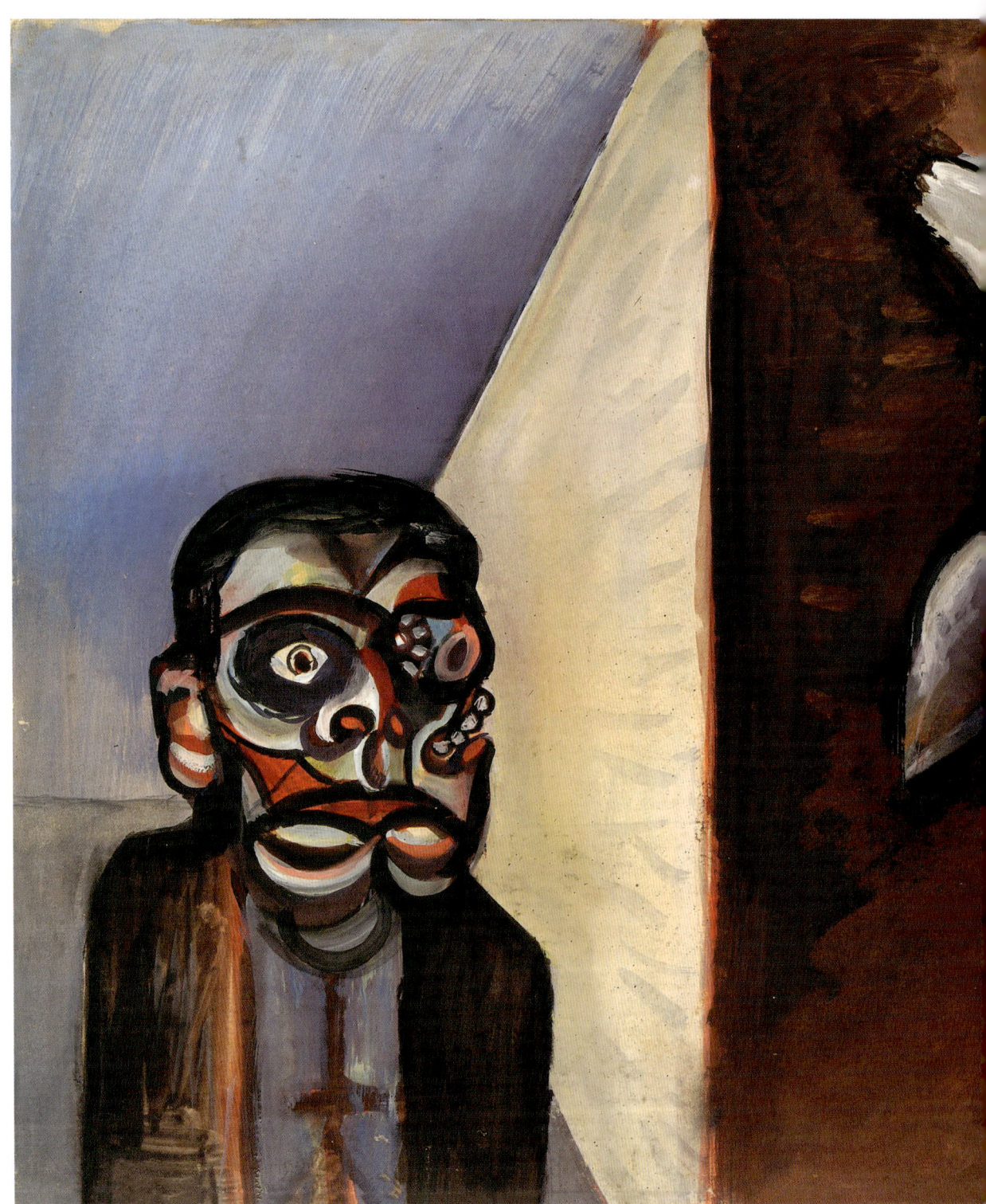

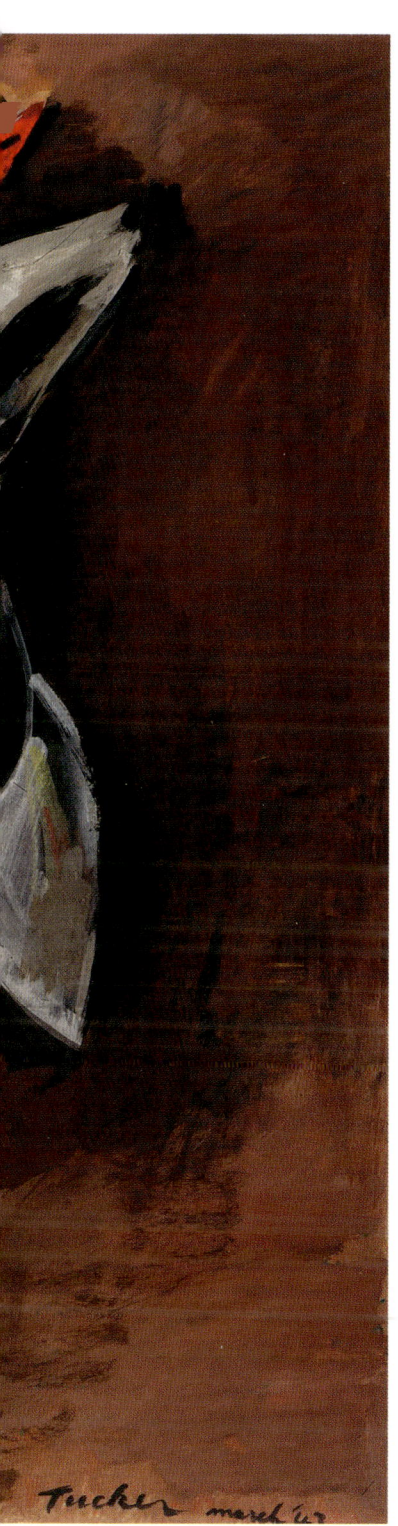

The ceremonies of the group would impress upon young Crowley the importance of theatrical ritual, but his presence within the Hermetic Order of the Golden Dawn directly precipitated its dissolution. Already infamous within English occult circles, schism resulted when one of the order's leaders, Samuel Liddell MacGregor Mathers, initiated Crowley into a higher level of the group against the wishes of most of its members (including Yates). By 1903, a year before the revelation of Thelema, the order was effectively defunct, even while offshoots existed into the following decades. Crowley had received what he needed, however; an education as well as an initiation, which was invaluable as the prolific author quickly developed a wider reputation for not just wickedness (however overblown), but esoteric knowledge as well.

During the remainder of his life, Crowley was exceedingly well-traveled, making his home in Tunis, Mexico, Nepal, Scotland, the United States, Sicily, Algeria, and Germany, but ultimately dying in his native England in 1947. During his life he made himself infamous through his exploits, including founding a successor organization to the Hermetic Order of the Golden Dawn named the Ordo Templi Orientis, climbing the Himalayan peak K2, faking his own death with the help of the poet Pessoa, and infiltrating German-American groups during World War I on behalf of the British government.

He was also motivated by a certain logographia, writing dozens of books, tracts, and pamphlets, often with particularly strange titles, including *777* published in 1909; *Magick Book IV: Liber ABA*, appearing in four volumes between 1911 and 1936; *Liber XV: The Gnostic Mass* in 1913; *The Book of Lies*, that same year; *Moon Child* in 1917; and *The Confessions of Aleister Crowley* in 1929. While much was made of his supposed wickedness, it was in that last volume where Crowley made as emphatic a declaration of belief in the dangers of denying the existence of evil as has been made during the twentieth century: "The pious pretense that evil does not exist only makes it vague, enormous and menacing . . . The way to beat an enemy is to define him clearly, to analyze and measure him," which is an unassailable summation of magic's fundamental position on language. Poetry and incantation—a permeable membrane, for which Crowley has been largely ignored when compared to his poetic contemporaries, almost surely because his occult infamy is far greater than any literary reputation. Yet even if he's not the equal of Yeats, Crowley wasn't without talent, as can be seen in an excerpt from his most popular lyric, "Hymn to Pan:"

I am Pan! Io Pan! Io Pan Pan! Pan!

I am thy mate, I am thy man,

Goat of thy flock, I am gold, I am god,

Flesh to thy bone, flower to thy rod.

With hoofs of steel I race on the rocks

Through solstice stubborn to equinox.

And I rave; and I rape and I rip and I rend

Everlasting, world without end.

Manniken, maiden, maenad, man,

In the might of Pan.

Written in Moscow in 1913 and first published six years later in the journal *The Equinox*, the lyric was respected enough by Pessoa to be translated into Portuguese, and it's the most anthologized of Crowley's poems in non-occult publications. Formally inventive, with the punctuation calling to mind Gertrude Stein, the "Hymn to Pan" also evidences an admirable formal ear, engaging intricate internal rhymes and an alliterative rhythm that is evocative of Ezra Pounds's experimentation with Anglo-Saxon verse.

An occult writer who claimed to be unimpressed with Crowley's legacy was an American fifty-five years his junior born in Chicago, who variously moonlit as a burlesque-show organ grinder, a carnival barker, and a crime scene photographer for the police before going on to declare himself to be the Black Pope of the Church of Satan. Anton Szandor LaVey (born Howard Stanton Levey) was interested in promulgating teaching a tad less ethereal and a bit more visceral than did his forerunner, seeing in the ritual of Satanism an opportunity to promulgate his own profoundly individualistic philosophy filched from Nietzsche, acerbic *Baltimore Sun* columnist H.L. Mencken, and Ayn Rand, the libertarian cult leader and author of the maximalist and turgid novel *The Fountainhead*. By contrast to his other inspirations, the Black Pope supposedly considered Crowley a "druggy poseur whose greatest achievements were as a poet and a mountain climber," and the so-called wicked initiates into the Law of the Prophet of the Aeon of Horus as being "rather innocuous," according to Blanche Barton, his third wife and the Magistri Templi Rex of his church, in *The Secret Life of a Satanist: The Authorized Biography of Anton Szandor LaVey*. If the Ordo Templi Orientis was a secret society dedicated to an elitist, old-world sense of the aristocratic scholar parsing ancient grimoires for secret knowledge, than the Church of Satan was something different, equal parts geek show, tent revival, and Vegas spectacle.

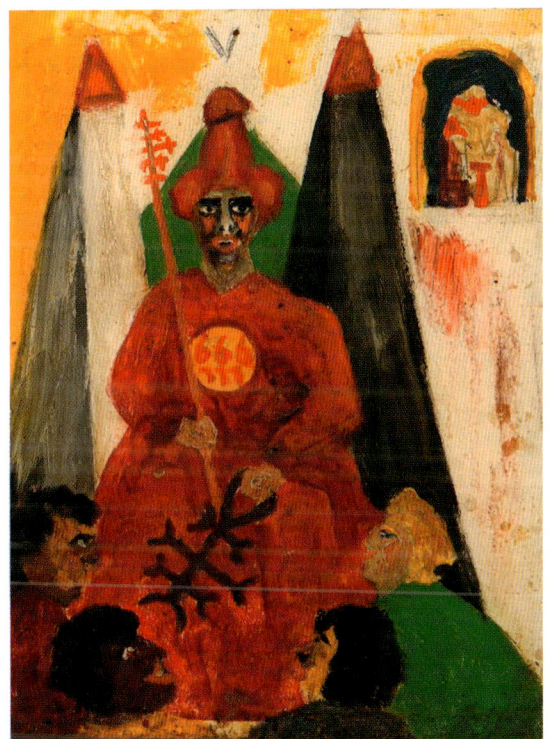

Gary Lachman writes in *Aleister Crowley: Magick, Rock and Roll, and the Wickedest Man* in the World that though his subject "did practically everything he could to disgust and infuriate the British society he loathed with an often tedious obstinacy, he also always wanted its acceptance," going so far as to frequently wear a Highlands costume and fashioning himself as Lord Boleskin, "and to be taken for what he never quite was: an English gentleman." By contrast, LaVey was fully of the national spirt in his own country, where despite the satanic pretensions of his dark faith, his teachings that were equal parts about self-invention and selfishness were perfectly attuned to the hyper-capitalist ethos of the United States. If LeVay rejected Crowley as a fake he at least shared a similar understanding of the importance of showmanship, and as an American he knew that more than saints and heretics what his countrymen thrilled to was a new type of person—*the celebrity.*

Throughout the early 1960s, LaVey's Victorian townhouse in the Richmond district of San Francisco, which he painted a dark black, was known for the lectures he'd give on subjects like hypnosis and chaos magic, as well as for the debauched parties that he threw. In *Satan in America: The Devil We Know*, W. Scott Poole describes the founder of the Church of Satan as a "kind of dark hippie who promised self-transcendence through fulfilling personal desire rather than universal love and peace." By 1966, LeVay was already an eccentric celebrity in the counterculture of San Francisco—no small doing—when on Walpurgisnacht of that year he ritualistically shaved his head and declared it Year One Ano Satanas (his new theatrical appearance may have been inspired by a magician character played by Borscht Belt comedian Don Rickles in an episode of the steampunk show *The Wild, Wild West*, which aired only a month before). There's not necessarily a contradiction between the pretensions of LeVay's systematized Satanism and his commandeering of pop culture; if anything it speaks to his mastery of that American tradition of hobbling together the detritus of old traditions, often with tongue firmly in cheek, so as to generate something completely new, albeit perhaps with a bit of the stench of bullshit about it.

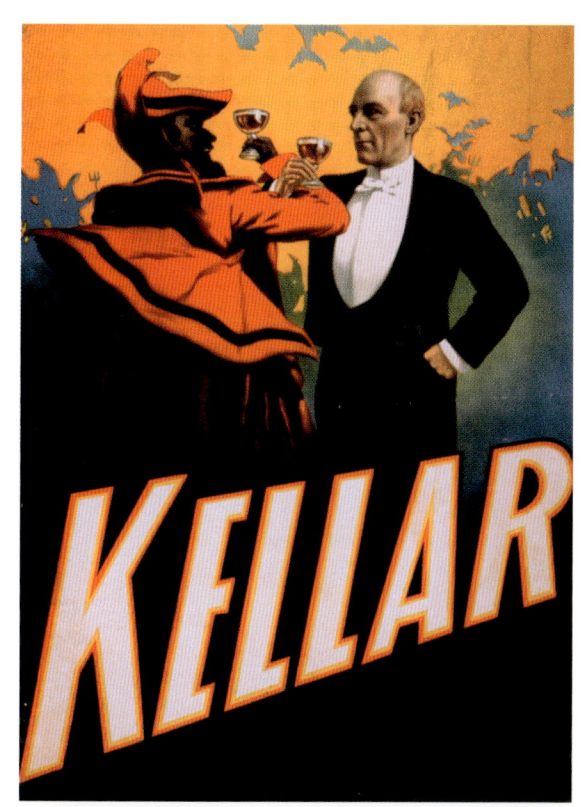

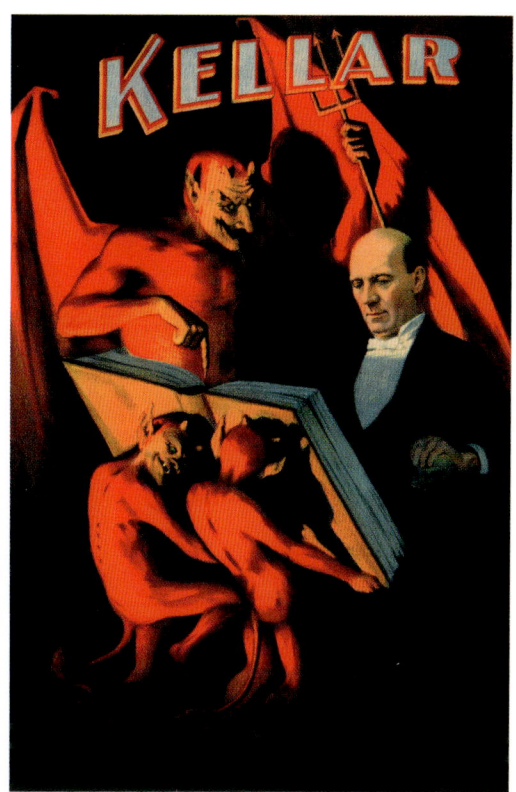

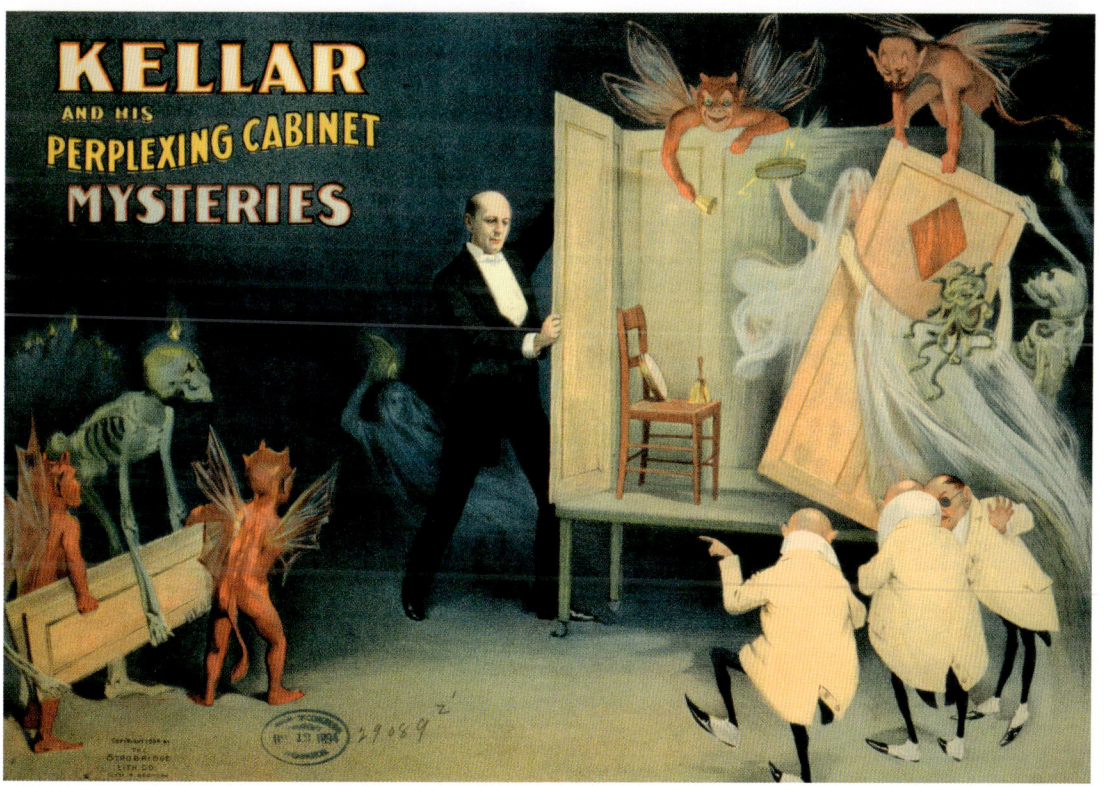

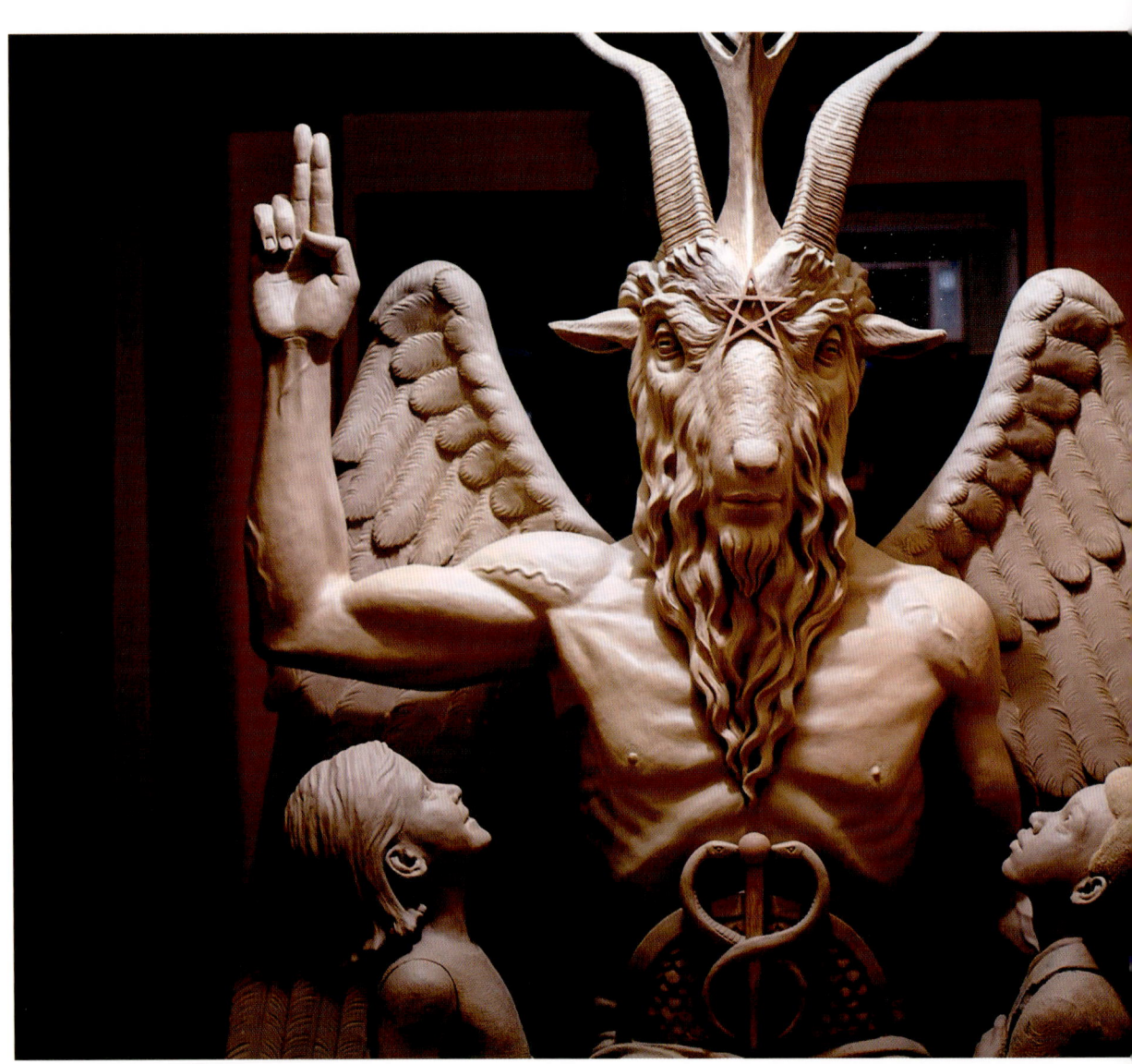

Despite his shaved pate and his devilish goatee, the vampiric uniform of the black cape and the almost comical felt devil horns he wore, LeVay was firmly of the lineage of the tent revival preacher, the medicine show huckster, the confidence man, the circus ringmaster. For a brief period, there was something of "an odd form of chic" about the church, as Russell writes, with LeVay attracting prominent members, from actress Jayne Mansfield to performer Sammy Davis Jr. In this regard LeVay was a San Francisco original, fitting into the potent stew of countercultures that marked the city during the 1960s, from the relatively benign hippies of Haight Ashbury to the wholly more maligned Peoples Temple of the Pentecostal preacher Jim Jones, with David Talbot writing in *Season of the Witch: Enchantment, Terror, and the City of Love*, that despite the Black Pope effectively being "just a carny showman at heart," the church he founded "reflected the dark side" of San Francisco. The sixties counterculture was less singular than might be presumed, however, as the mélange of movements that descended upon the city during the Aquarian age resembled nothing so much as the heady group of sects that marked the Second Great Awakening of a century before.

Self-invention, and the duping of credulous folk who are perhaps in on the joke anyhow, is the national hobby, as exemplified by figures like P.T. Barnum and Mark Twain (two of the dozens to whom the first edition of LeVay's *Satanic Bible* would be dedicated), and if the Black Pope had a disdain for Crowley, perhaps it was because the latter was so *British* while the former was consummately *American*. And indeed from the 1960s until his death in 1997 (from a pulmonary edema while ironically being treated in a Catholic hospital) LeVay was the theatrical face of American Satanism. Because of the innate hokiness of much of LeVay's schtick—the B-movie appearance, the exploitative witches' Sabbaths held in the Black House, the carny show accoutrement—it can be easy to forget that the Church of Satan was singular in its existence: the first organized religion ostensibly devoted to the worship of the Devil.

THIS SPREAD

An eight-foot-tall (2.4 m) statue of Baphomet, a bronze version of which was unveiled in 2015 at the Detroit branch of the Satanic Temple (a separate organization from LeVay's Church). Originally intended for the grounds of the Oklahoma State Capitol, the statue was designed as part of a first amendment challenge in opposition to the display of a granite copy of the Ten Commandments. Rejecting the reactionary social Darwinism that defines much of the Church of Satan's theology, the Satanic Temple has emerged in recent years as a champion of religious freedom and the separation of church and state. Note the hilarity of the young children learning at Baphomet's feet.

From the founding of the church, LeVay offered satanic rituals, including marriages, funerals, and baptisms (indeed his daughter was the first to be baptized in the faith, at the age of three). This was something unprecedented in the history of Western religion—for all that there can be discussion of past and supposed Satanists, from the Kurdish Yazidis, to the Templars and the Hell-Fire Clubs, those claims are often at best a misinterpretation and at worst slander. But with the Church of Satan, LeVay arguably did inaugurate a type of Anno Satanis One. Certain caveats must be made, however: LeVay himself made clear that he didn't believe in a literal Satan, and that he himself was a steadfast materialist who rejected the existence of the supernatural, even while schismatic groups from his hierarchy are theistic. Davies explains how, for the Church of Satan, the Devil is rather a "symbol of revolt against Christian hypocrisy and societal authority. Satanism is about the worship of the self, of the identity and potency of the individual."

Furthermore, though LeVay did believe in "magic," he emphasized that panpsychic things were of the natural world, but often simply not yet explained by science. The lower sort of magic included phenomenon like hypnosis and illusions, whereas the more sophisticated sort of magic involved theatrical and blasphemous rituals meant to iconoclastically question received wisdom. "White magic is supposedly utilized only for good or unselfish purposes," writes LeVay in 1969's *The Satanic Bible*, "and black magic, we are told, is used only for selfish or 'evil' reasons. Satanism draws no such dividing line. Magic is magic, be it used to help or hinder. The Satanist, being the magician, should have the ability to decide what is just, and then apply the powers of magic to attain his goals." To that end, LeVay emphasized that his Satanism wasn't just nontheistic, but of the "Left Hand Path," that is, it embraced a variety of magic often interpreted as malignant.

More interesting than the metaphysics of the church was its ethics, for within LeVay's Satanism there was a conscious rejection of anything that could be interpreted as the Golden Rule. The bulk of the church's theology is outlined in *The Satanic Bible*, a book rushed into print by the romance publisher Avon to try and capitalize on the popularity of *Rosemary's Baby*, with Davies writing that the volume "consisted of the corpus of mimeographs they had already produced, bulked out with a mish-mash of other texts, including a plagiarized extract from an obscure social Darwinist political tract published in 1896, and an adapted version of Crowley's version of the 'Enochian Keys' of John Dee." Demonology, by its nature, has historically been a discipline of synthesis more than that of analysis, and in this regard LeVay was little different from Blavatsky or Lévi. Even more obviously appropriated than the sections of *The Satanic Bible* that found their origins in [[the work of]] past occultists were the "Nine Satanic Statements" in LeVay's prologue, a type of infernal Decalogue, where among other principles he implores that "Satan represents indulgence, instead of abstinence!," "Satan represents kindness to those who deserve it, instead of love wasted on ingrates!," and "Satan represents vengeance, instead of turning the other cheek!" Most humorously, LeVay writes that "Satan has been the best friend the church has ever had, as he has kept it in business all these years!"

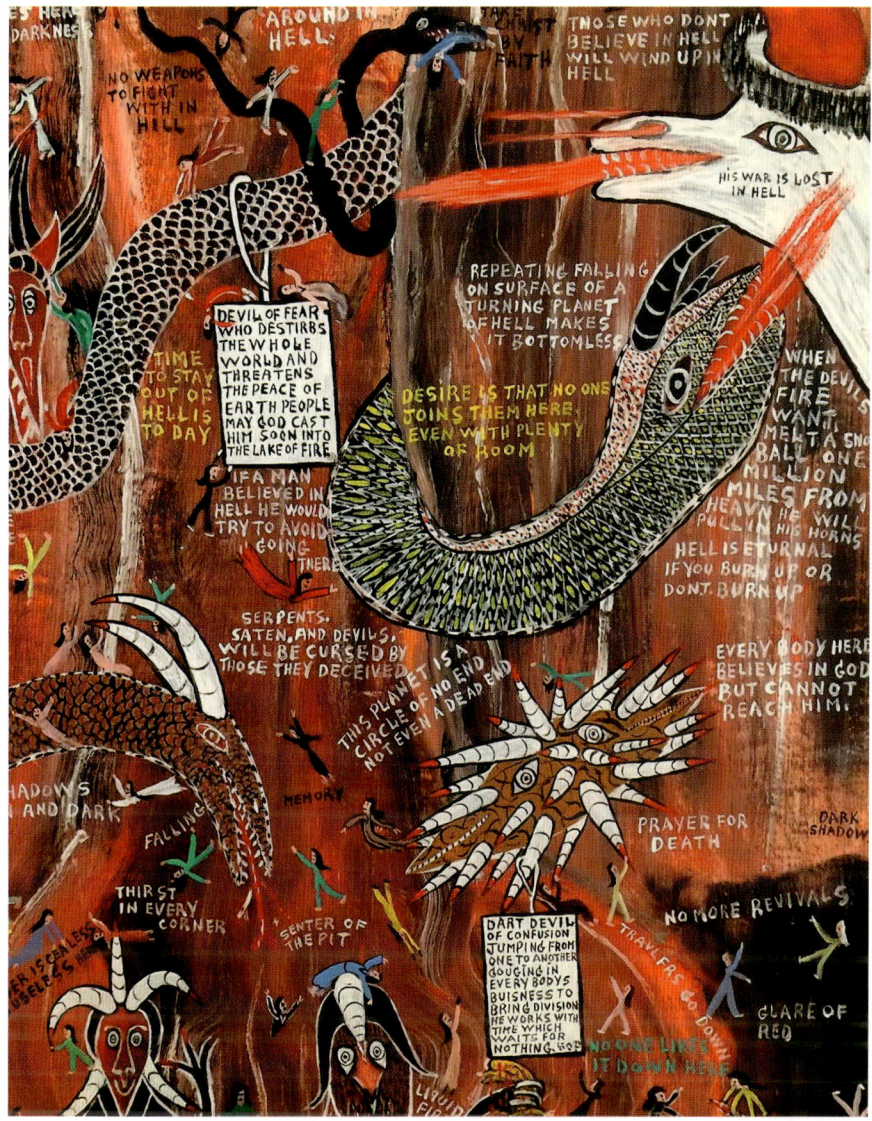

Detail from American outsider artist Howard Finster's 1980 Vision of the Great Gulf on Planet Earth *depicting his visions of Hell, with the original held by the Smithsonian American Art Museum in Washington, D.C. A self-trained painter and Baptist preacher, the Georgian used his visionary art to promulgate his own deeply supernatural Christian beliefs, where demons are very much real and to be feared. As he inscribed on the back of the painting, "To leave out teaching of hell from the Bible is like taking down red lights in a congested street in your city. The more you hide hell from the world the more go there" (sic). Popular in the 1980s, particularly among rock groups like R.E.M. and the Talking Heads, for whom he designed album covers, Finster's work evokes what critic Greil Marcus calls "that old, weird America" of geek shows and tent revivals, as well as some of the aesthetic of LeVay's performances.*

Talbot notes that many of the sentiments in *The Satanic Bible* were at odd with the emancipatory politics of much of the sixties, quoting the Black Pope as having been dismissive of the hippie culture of his adopted city, claiming that it was a "mire of ignorance, stupidity, and egalitarianism." Reactionary politics with a counterculture patina also defined an entirely less benign manifestation of California several hundred miles to the south in the person of Charles Manson. It's notable that when Manson Family associate Tex Watson came to murder the pregnant actress Sharon Tate, he declared, "I am the devil; I'm here to do the devil's work." In prose that reads as a pantomime of Nietzsche as filtered through the King James version of the Bible, LeVay thunders in *The Satanic Bible* that:

In this arid wilderness of steel and stone I raise up my voice that you may hear. To the East and to the West I beckon. To the North and to the South I show a sign proclaiming: Death to the weakling, wealth to the strong! Open your eyes that you may see, Oh men of mildewed minds, and listen to me ye bewildered millions! For I stand forth to challenge the wisdom of the world; to interrogate the "laws" of man and of "God!"

Such doctrines—the ruthless selfishness, the valorization of pure egocentricity, the elevation of narcissism—appear nothing so much as the supply-side dogmas of extreme libertarianism, and indeed in 1970 LeVay told a reporter for the *Los Angeles Times* that "My religion is just Ayn Rand's philosophy with ceremony and ritual added."

If anything marks LeVay's Satanism, it's a steadfast rejection of the Romantic's Luciferian revolutionary, for the Devil of his California diabolism is positively elitist, reactionary, and conservative. A thesis that LeVay might not take issue with, for in a tabloid article later compiled in the 2010 anthology *Letters from the Devil: The Lost Writings of Anton Szandor LaVey*, he claimed that "To sum up our political doctrine, Satanism IS Americanism in its purest form." Strip away the hypocritical Christianity, and American values of rapacious consumption and bellicose imperialism aren't necessarily all that different from the capitalist peons of *The Satanic Bible*. "Actually, in view of the vast numbers of religious leaders defending and expounding the extreme liberal philosophy of the hippie or drug culture," LeVay writes in that same column, "conservative organizations will (and already do) find Satanism far more compatible with their doctrines than they now think it to be."

Like many bullshit artists, LeVay's thinking expresses a blunt honesty, and there's a wisdom in seeing how his doctrines concerning selfishness, consumption, and authority are, in many ways, already the status quo. "A Satanist knows there is nothing wrong with being greedy, as it only means that he wants more than he already has," wrote LeVay in *The Satanic Bible*. With a similar obsession concerning strength, power, vitality, success, and wealth, a Californian contemporary of LeVay's wrote that "Any system that penalizes success and accomplishment is wrong. Any system that discourages work, discourages productivity, discourages economic progress, is wrong." That sentiment, expressed by the author of the autobiography *Ronald Reagan: An American Life*, is arguably as far from the ethics of Christ's beatitudes as anything ever uttered by LeVay, proving that the god of this world was always closer to the faith of the Black Pope than he perhaps feared.

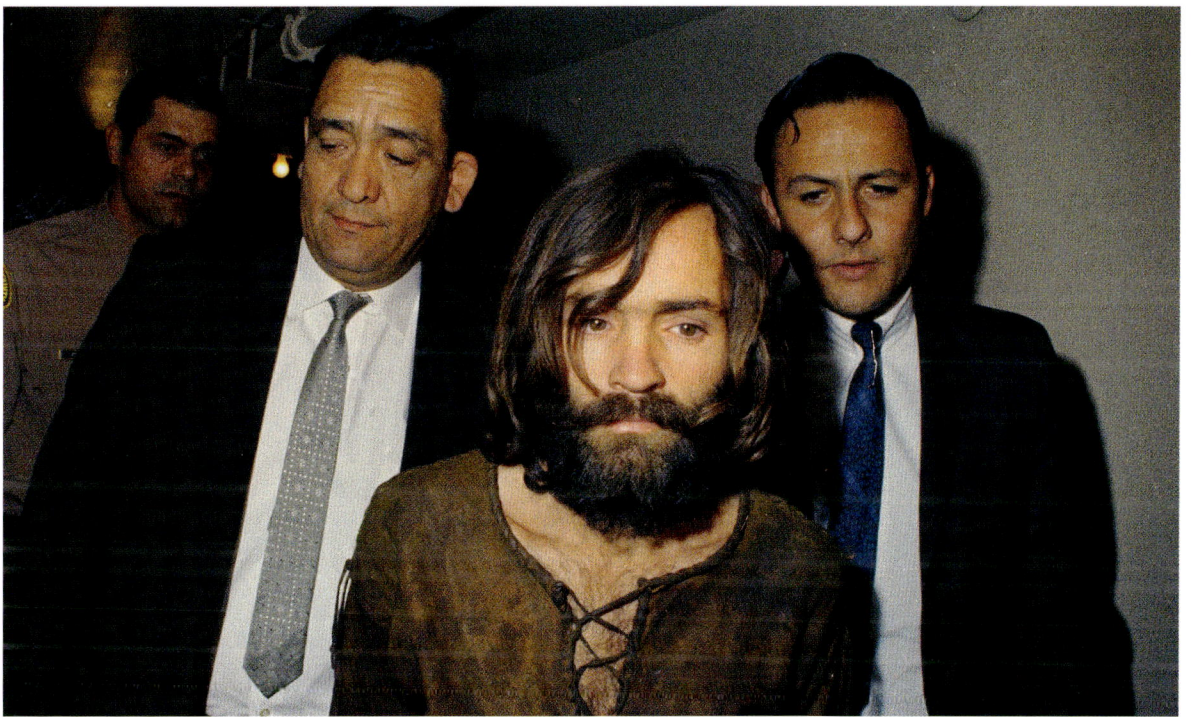

ABOVE

LeVay wasn't the only participant in the 1960's California counterculture whose politics eschewed to the right, though he was wholly more benign than Charles Manson, pictured here after his 1969 arrest in the conspiracy to murder, among others, actress Sharon Tate. Incidentally, LeVay claimed to have been an adviser to Tate's husband, director Roman Polanski, when the later was filming Rosemary's Baby *a year before, with the Satanist maintaining that the eyes and hands of Satan pictured in the film were his. With a bohemian appearance and almost messianic forbearance, Manson looks the part of a malignant anti-Christ. "Nobody," he responded to a journalist who asked who he was some twenty years after the murders. "I'm nobody. I'm a tramp, a bum, a hobo. I'm a boxcar and a jug of wine. And a straight razor if you get too close to me."*

The Gipper wasn't name-checked in the copiously long dedication of *The Satanic Bible*, but he was seemingly the only person who wasn't. In the first two editions of the book, LeVay name-checks the quack Austrian psychoanalyst Wilhelm Reich, the Russian Orthodox mystic and counselor to the Romanovs' Grigori Rasputin, the German filmmaker Fritz Lang, the American comedian W.C. Fields, British novelists George Orwell and H.G. Wells, and (among several others) a thin, avian-profiled, blue-blooded New England WASP with an underslung jaw who was the primogeniture of the genre of weird fiction, and the inventor of the most famed grimoire of the twentieth century, which was no less terrifying for being completely fictitious. His name was H.P. Lovecraft and he promulgated what was arguably the most terrifying literary vision of the twentieth century.

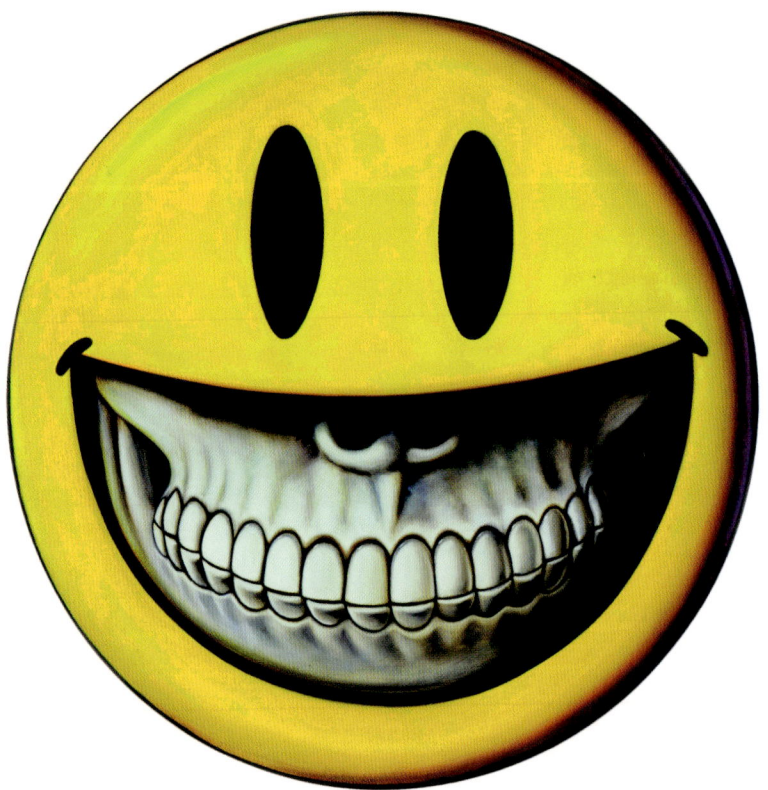

ABOVE

Contemporary American artist, sculptor, and culture jammer Ron English explores the deep malevolence hidden within otherwise plucky and optimistic commercial culture, as in his ironic revision of the iconic "Smiley Face" ideogram, the latter of which is most often associated with advertiser Harvey Ross Ball's designs from the early seventies. English's smiley face, recalling both advertising and the inanity of the emoticon, defamiliarizes the simple symbol to remind us that a human skull is hidden beneath. Such a work gestures toward the memento mori tradition of the Renaissance, but it also serves as a helpful metaphor for the malignancy hidden beneath our politics and our reality. Few things would seem more cheery than a grinning smiley face, but as with the optimistic bromides of a Ronald Reagan gushing about America as a "shining city on a hill," a wholly darker reality is hidden within. In a metaphysical sense, it's a potent reminder that underneath the reality of appearances there is a cold, unfeeling, inert core, written about by authors like H.P. Lovecraft. Whenever you see a smile, remember that you're looking at a skull covered with taut meat.

Born in Providence, Rhode Island, in 1890, Lovecraft was privy to all of the racial and religious bigotries of his social class (and then some); a man of reactionary politics and bleak sentiment. Not much is worth recommendation in Lovecraft's personality, regardless of the brilliance of his prose, though perhaps it takes a malignant soul to pen such diseased stories. Long dismissed as a mere hack scribbler for pulp magazines, there has been a rediscovery of his work by scholars over the past generation, and horror writer Stephen King described the aesthetic import of weird fiction in his introduction to the French novelist Michelle Houellebecq's study *H.P. Lovecraft: Against the World, Against Life*, arguing that the "fiction of horror and the supernatural, utters a resounding NO to the world as it is and reality as the world insists it must be." Perhaps even to slant King's claim a bit, and part of what makes Lovecraft's fiction so terrifying is that it provides an accurate picture of the world as it is (at least in philosophical inclination, if not the details).

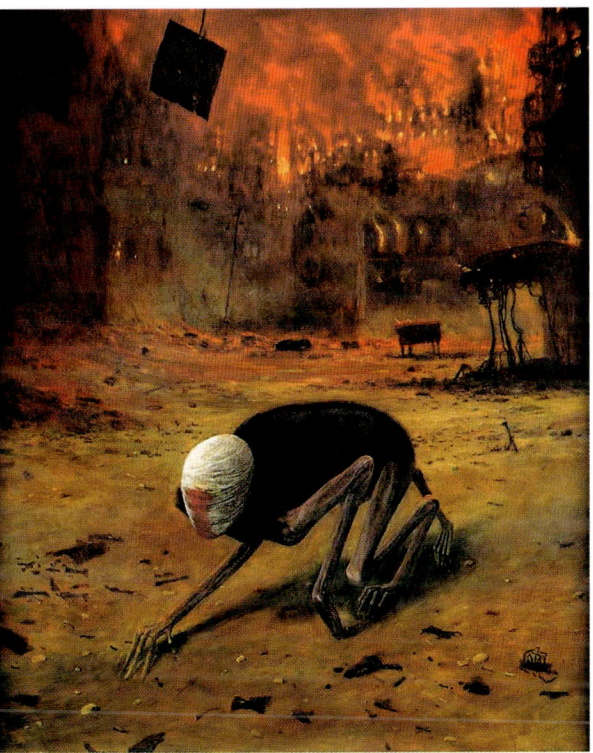

ABOVE

Polish artist Zdzislaw Bekiński is sometimes categorized as a "dystopian neo-surrealist," and while his abundantly disturbing compositions clearly owe something to the surrealists of the first half of the twentieth century, his paintings also come from a singularly terrifying vision. In this piece from 1970 held by the Historical Museum in Sanok, Poland, officially untitled but often called Crawling Death, *an insectoid creature skitters across a decimated, postapocalyptic urban landscape. It appears as if swaddling is around the human-shaped head of the animal, with blood staining the face (have the eyes or nose been removed?). So alien is the scene, and so uncanny, that though Bekiński claimed his work was uninterpretable, it's hard not to see a bit of Lovecraft's vision concerning the pure meaningless terror that percolates just beneath our experience.*

In novellas such as *At the Mountains of Madness* and *The Shadow Over Innsmouth*, both published in 1931, and in the short stories "The Rats in the Walls" and "The Call of Cthulhu," which were respectively published in 1924 and 1928, and the multitude of stories by multiple authors that would make up the intricately constructed mythology known as the Cthulhu Mythos, a unique perspective was promulgated. Lovecraft wrote some of the most disturbing American prose since Poe, not just for its narrative elements, but also because of his cold and unsparing metaphysic of meaninglessness. Writing at the confluence of horror, gothic, and science fiction, Lovecraft's "weird fiction," with its submerged ancient cities and cephalopod Elder Gods, its antique volumes by mad Arabs and its libraries of occult books sequestered in sleepy New England towns, was as complete an expression of nihilism as was written in the twentieth century. Lovecraft's imagined grimoire, known as *The Necronomicon*, envisioned a reality overseen by powerful Elder Gods, hidden from the view of us, their insignificant lessers. Arguably the literary corollary to Nietzsche, but with somehow a more pessimistic perspective than even that philosopher, Lovecraft drained Enlightenment materialism of any of its residual Christian affect, which had long since transformed into a moribund bourgeoise ethics. He examined God's tomb with an unjaundiced but watery eye, providing an expression of pure bluntness regarding the score.

"Life is a hideous thing," Lovecraft wrote in "Facts Concerning Arthur Jermyn and His Family" first published in *The Wolverine* in 1920, "and from the background behind what we know of it peer daemonical hints of truth that make it sometimes a thousandfold more hideous. Science, already oppressive with its shocking revelations, will perhaps be the ultimate exterminator of our human species—if separate species we be—for its reserve of unguessed horrors could never be borne by mortal brains if loosed upon the world." Divorced from the sense of wonder that animated the Enlightenment's Scientific Revolution, Lovecraft sees the entire litany of discoveries that have unseated humanity from our pride of place as a testament to the ultimate meaninglessness of our unfeeling

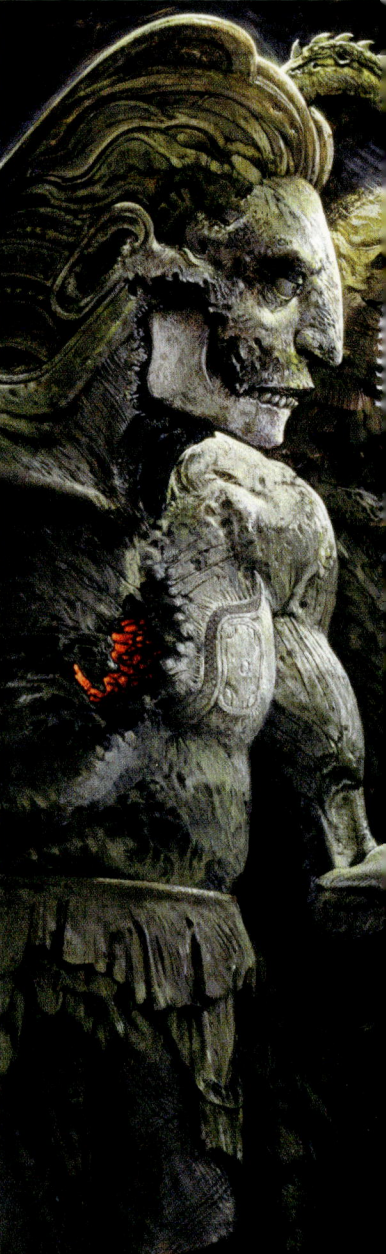

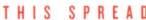

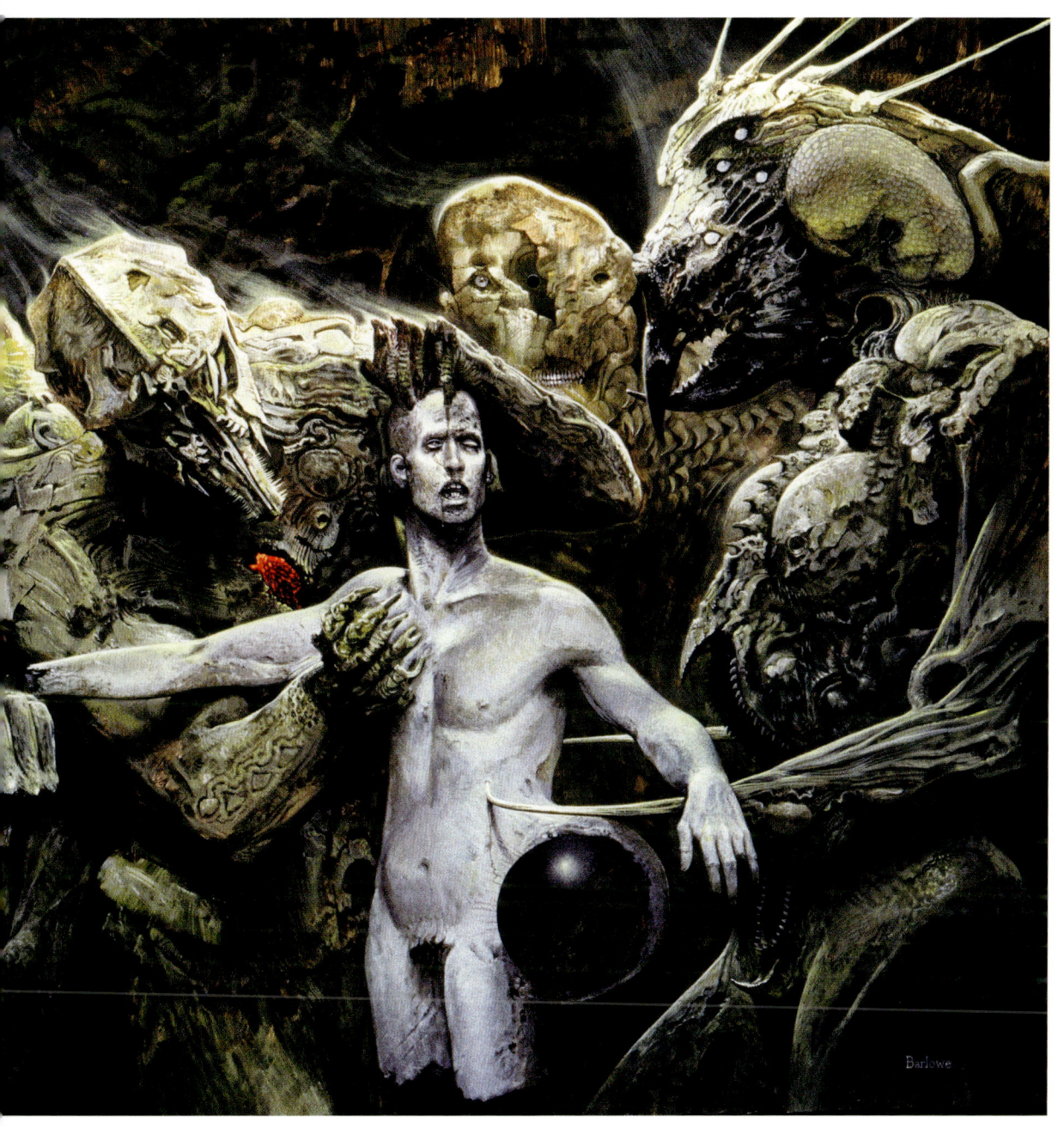

universe, and a quarter of a century before Hiroshima he understands how that same sense of discovery can ultimately condemn us to oblivion—not that it matters much in the scheme of things.

Writing in his most celebrated tale, "The Call of Cthulhu," Lovecraft gave his most infamous pronouncement in regard to the enormity of a universe that, rather than lacking in demons, becomes almost equivalent with the very concept of them: "The most merciful thing in the world, I think, is the inability of the human mind to correlate all its contents." Across his corpus, Lovecraft illustrated how a world drained of the supernatural doesn't necessarily lose its demons, for devils made of mere atoms can be just as hellish as anything dreamt of by Dante. Like Dante, and Milton, Lovecraft was adept at building fictional universes, and the resultant narrative world that he created has certain touchstones for his readers: the white-steepled environs of Arkham, Massachusetts (based on his native Providence), the faculty steeped in esoteric knowledge at Miskatonic University, and the mysterious grimoire in its library entitled *The Necronomicon*, which Davies describes as "the most enduring and influential fictional grimoire."

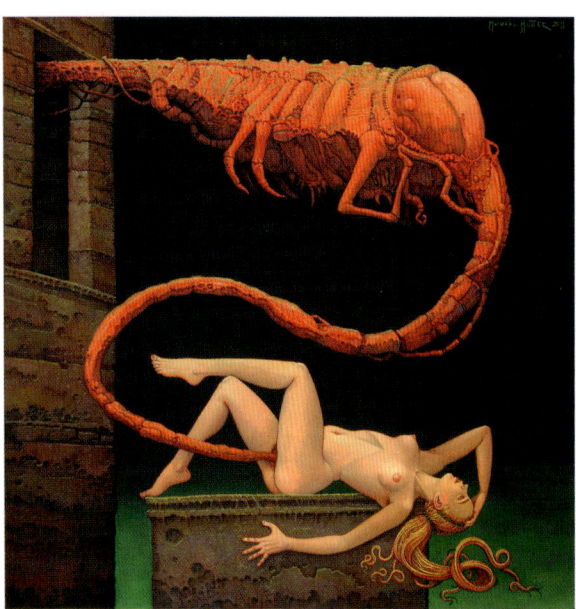 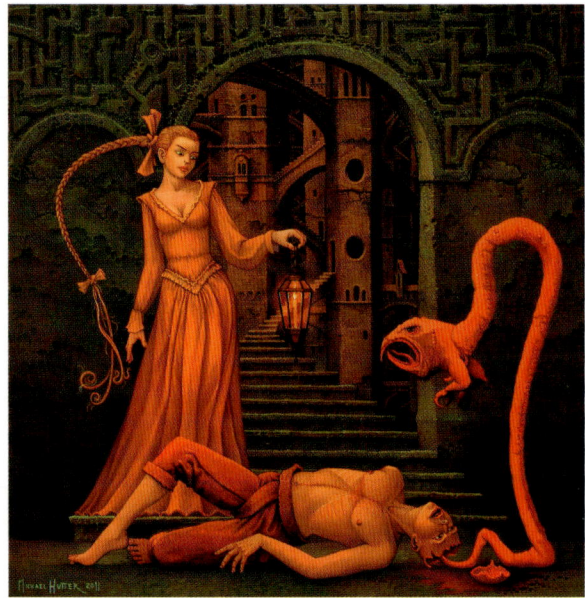

First appearing in his 1924 story "The Hound," *The Necronomicon* purports to have been authored by Abdul Alhazred, an, eighth-century Mad Arab, its contents possibly concerned with the worship of what Lovecraft called the Elder Gods. Lovecraft flushed out the reception history of the book in several stories; there are Greek, Latin, and English translations of the work (the last one rendered by John Dee), and it appears at certain important historical junctures, from the Roman Inquisition of the thirteenth century to Salem in the seventeenth century. So compelling is Lovecraft's invented history that many readers assumed the book to actually exist, and several subsequent works have been published that claim to be the "real" grimoire, despite the concept being an invention of the Rhode Island author. Quoted fragments of the fictitious book appear throughout Lovecraft's writing, but as Davies makes clear, there are still "appetizingly few references to the *Necronomicon*, and so the exact nature of its contents is never clear to the reader. Was it a source of mystical secrets, a demonological disquisition, or a book of practical magic?" Therein lay the power and terror of the *Necronomicon*, for the most sublime possible category of existence is nonexistence—a true null point, a genuine literary absolute zero—so that the imagined volume unspools reality by virtue of its very nothingness. *The Necronomicon* is thus the perfect modernist, or perhaps post-modernist, grimoire—an imagined work whose transcendent power can only be approached through the *via negativa*, which can only be read obliquely by a mind predisposed to see reality as it actually is, at a slant.

Abdul Alhazred was a worshipper of one of the Old Ones, in this case the entity known as Yog-Sothoth. In Lovecraft's stories, ancient cults, guilds, and societies have knowledge of these gargantuan creatures, who though not omnipotent might as well be when compared to the insignificance of humanity. These demons that Lovecraft has invented, the denizens of the "new artificial myths" that he constructed, are the aforementioned Elder Gods, most famous of whom is the ancient, unspeakable horror of the deep sea known as Cthulhu. "It seemed to be a sort of monster," Lovecraft says of Cthulhu in its first appearance, and continued … or a symbol representing a monster, of a form which only a diseased fancy could conceive. If I say that my somewhat extravagant imagination yielded simultaneous pictures of an octopus, a dragon and a human caricature, I shall not be unfaithful to the spirit of the thing. A pulpy, tentacled head surmounted a grotesque and scaly body with rudimentary wings; but it was the *general outline* of the whole thing which made it shockingly frightful.

Cthulhu is joined by other Elder Gods of Lovecraft's invention, as well as the contributions of later writers who have added to the Cthulhu mythos; there is the malevolent assemblage of cosmic spheres known as Yog-Sothoth, the primordial chaos deity Azathoth, who lives in the coldest and blackest environs of the distant universe, and the goat-headed Shub-Niggurath. All of the Elder Gods are beings beyond traditional time and space; they are immeasurably ancient, to the point of appearing eternal, and they are so much greater than us in dimension and intellect that we appear to them less than as flies do to us. Cthulhu, and its partners, are truly beyond good and evil in a manner that Nietzsche didn't even quit anticipate, but they are not supernatural in origin. Houellebecq asks and answers his own rhetorical question—"What is Great Cthulhu? An arrangement of electrons, like us."

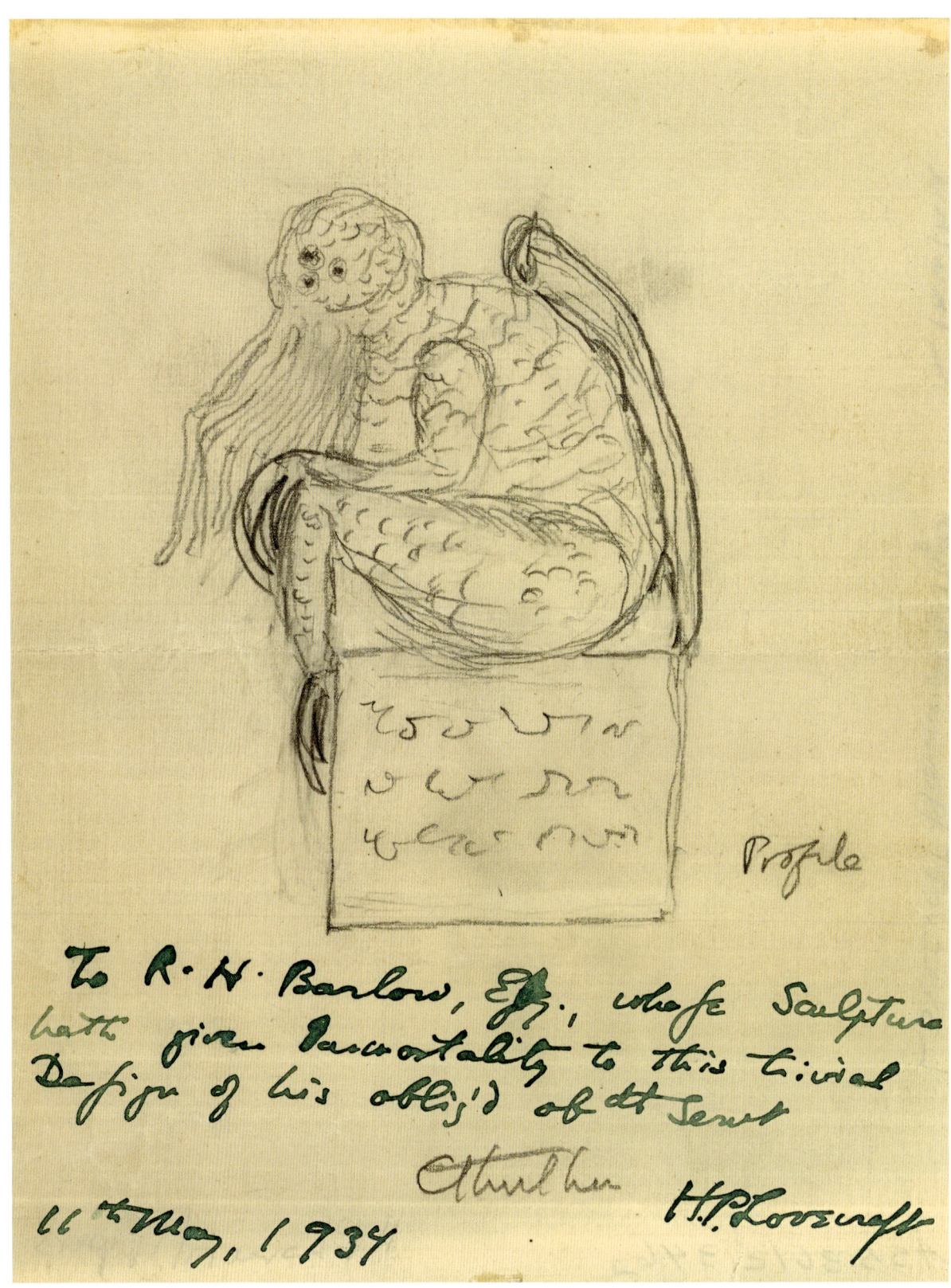

Profile

To R. H. Barlow, Esq., whose Sculpture
hath given Immortality to this trivial
Design of his oblig'd ob.dt Serv.t
Cthulhu
H. P. Lovecraft
16th May, 1934

Herein lies what's so startling about Lovecraft's demonology—mere secularism does nothing to dispel it, for his is a thoroughly materialist cosmology. Contemporary weird fiction author Thomas Ligotti, who is strongly influenced by Lovecraft, explains in *The Conspiracy Against the Human Race* that "Philosophically, Lovecraft was a dyed-in-the wool scientific materialist. Nevertheless, he is a felicitous example of someone who knew ravishments that in another context would qualify as 'spiritual' or 'religious.'" Within his corpus there is still a sense of transcendence, a sense of the numinous, but there steadfastly is no salvation, redemption, or most of all meaning. The author termed his position as "cosmicism," his sense that all which modern science had discovered—evolution through natural selection, the trend toward entropy, the gargantuan spaces and silence of the universe—demonstrated the sheer terrifying indifference of reality toward us. Disenchantment does nothing to quell the howls of demons—it actually makes them infinitely worse. Poole explains that Lovecraft "rejected the category of the demonic just as he rejected the category of the divine. But in doing so he shaped the cosmos itself as a kind of devil, at least to human beings."

As a result, the Lovecraft corpus, regardless of the person who was responsible for creating it, is one of the most potent of meditations on the demonological in the twentieth century, even if its author wouldn't think of it as such. "Few beings have ever been so impregnated, pierced to the core, by the conviction of the absolute futility of human aspiration," writes Houellebecq. According to Lovecraft, Houellebecq explains, the "universe is nothing but a furtive arrangement of elementary particles. A figure in transition toward chaos. That is what will finally prevail." That's what makes Lovecraft's perspective so chilling—it's fundamentally demonological not just in spite of its materialism, but in large part because of it. His is a secular demonology, a scientific occultism. Disbelief in demons gives us no respite, for when the supernatural is abolished, the faces of devils can still assemble out of inert matter itself, the atoms willing themselves to think, and to dominate.

THE AGE OF MOLOCH

3 n 1914, only a few months before the Austro-Hungarian archduke Franz Ferdinand would be assassinated by a Serbian nationalist in Sarajevo, and on a movie soundstage in Turin, not far from where the Fiat and Alfa Romeo automobile factories would soon be commandeered for the production of arms and munitions, the director Giovanni Pastrone had constructed a massive golden idol to the demon Moloch. Nothing had ever been shot that was quite as ambitious as Pastrone's silent film *Cabiria*; the movie single-handedly inaugurated the epic as a cinematic genre, and its sheer grandiosity necessitated technical innovations such as the tracking shot, whereby the action could be followed by a camera as if the viewer were actually a participant in the scene, techniques that would be commandeered by contemporaneous directors like the American D.W. Griffith. Such innovations were commensurate with the over two-hour-long *Cabiria*, where audiences observed the eruption of Mount Etna, saw a Roman armada that was invading Syracuse destroyed by a heat ray that was built by the scientist Archimedes, espied the Carthaginian general Hannibal command his legion of fearsome (actual) elephants over the snowy Alps, and infamously witnessed the near-sacrifice of the title character to the Phoenician deity who thirsted for the blood of children.

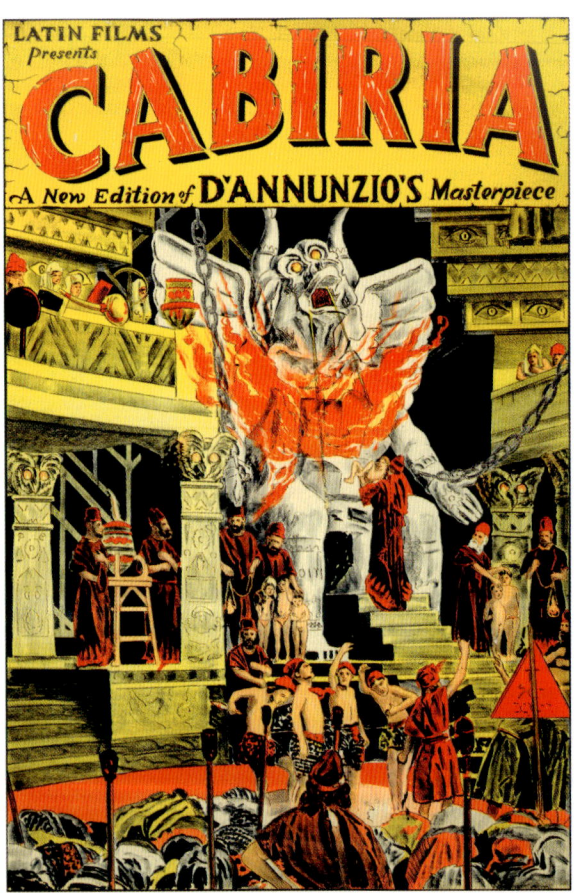

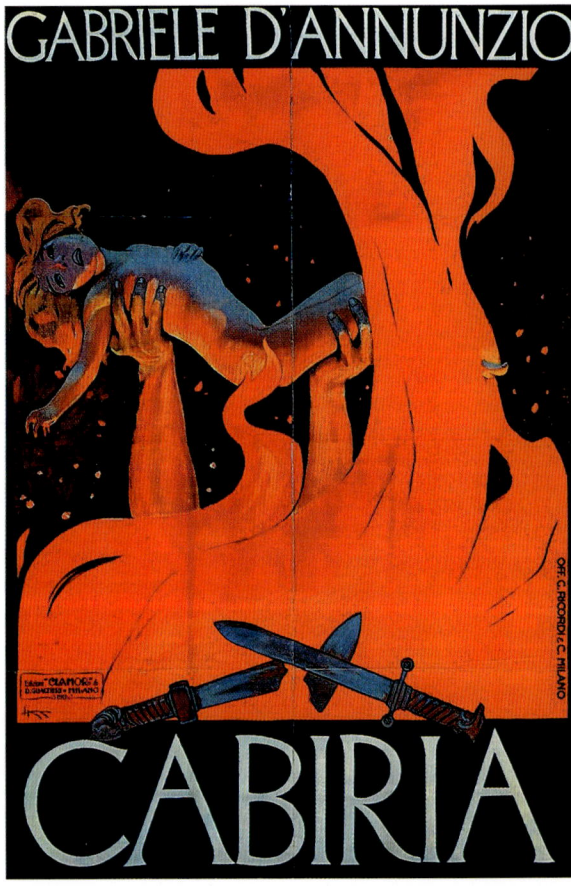

Released in April 1914, Europe would be convulsed in apocalyptic war only two months later, far more horrific than the Second Punic War as imagined by Pastrone. The sclerotic aristocracy of Germany and Great Britain, Austria-Hungary and France, Italy, and Russia would soon consume itself in a fearsome mechanized warfare that had never before been seen on this earth. This wasn't the frigid nobility of Hannibal's assault across the Po Valley, but rather the anonymity of industrialized warfare, the "ecstasy of mad fumbling" spoken of by the British poet and war casualty Wilfred Owen as he invokes the terror of fitting a mask during a mustard gas attack, the madness of slow and brutal trench warfare, the rapidity of Gatling guns on the front lines, the ghosts of the dead who "In all my dreams before my helpless sight . . . plunges at me, guttering, choking, drowning." In Owen's "Dulce et Decorum Est" there is no need to invent hell, for the poet merely needs to describe what he's seen.

In the spring before Europe would sacrifice itself to the guns of August, and audiences had thrilled to the horror of young Cabiria, the beautiful daughter of a Sicilian gentleman farmer, kidnapped by Phoenician pirates only to ultimately find herself marked for immolation within the bronze belly of Moloch's statue, along with a hundred other unfortunate children. Based on traditional descriptions of the idol by the classical author Livy, Pastrone's Moloch is a massive, golden-winged beast, bull-headed with three glowing eyes, his body covered in stylized occult symbols, and his gaping mouth fit for the devouring of the sacrificed, his belly a fiery kiln where the condemned are burnt alive. Cabiria is saved by a trio of Roman spies, but the children of other mothers wouldn't be as fortunate in the years that followed the film's release—half-a-million men would be killed during the four months of the Gallipoli campaign in 1915; 519,000 dead at the Marne in 1914; almost 700,000 dead at Verdun in 1916; an astounding 1,113,000 dead at the Somme in 1916; over 2 million during the Brusilov Offensive of that same year. On a single day of the Great War—August 22, 1914—27,000 young men would be killed during the Battle of the Frontiers; no doubt some of them only a few months before had watched *Cabiria* with tense faces and gripped knees, wondering how this child would ever escape the fires of Moloch?

Cabiria's screenwriter, responsible for all of the movie's intertitles, was Gabrielle D'Annunzio, an infamous Abruzzese modernist poet, novelist, and libertine. On Christmas Day in 1915 he addressed a Roman audience after the Italian Parliament had voted to enter the war: "The slaughter begins, the destruction begins," the poet enthused. "All these people, who yesterday thronged in the streets and square, loudly demanding war, are full of veins, full of blood; and that blood begins to flow." With convictions that wouldn't have been foreign to the Carthaginians of his film, D'Annunzio shouted, "We have no other value but that of our blood to be shed." For D'Annunzio, and intellectuals in his stead such as those affiliated with the modernist artistic and literary movement known as futurism, there was dignity, valor, and nobility not just in war, but in violence specifically. Sacrificial bloodletting was a good unto itself, for as the poet F.T. Marinetti, who despite being a thorough modernist was a protégé of the classical dandy D'Annunzio, would gush in *The Founding and Manifesto of Futurism*, published in 1909, "We will glorify war—the world's only hygiene." World War I was a battle fought on behalf of a decaying conservative order, but the means by which it was fought were resolutely modern in their terrifying efficacy, and from that historical inflection point, figures like D'Annunzio and Marinetti saw a new world quivering to be born.

"We affirm that the world's magnificence has been enriched by a new beauty: the beauty of speed," writes Marinetti in his manifesto. "A racing hood is adorned with great pipes, like serpents of explosive breath—a roaring car that seems to run on grapeshot is more beautiful than *The Victory of Samothrace*." The futurists, true to their self-designation, violently rejected the past, rather seeing beauty in mechanization and industrialization. Marinetti's claim, with its evocation of the gleaming chrome and steel of the automobile, was an appropriate sentiment for Turin, that industrial powerhouse of the Italian car industry. In a nation so beholden to the past, the Parthenon of Rome and the Florentine Duomo of the Renaissance, Turin represented a radical break with tradition, a modern roaring city of technology and industry. During the twentieth century there were many Turins, such as Bremen and Hamburg, Glasgow and Manchester, Detroit and Pittsburgh. If the futurist credo in honor of engineering calls forth an Alfa Romeo racing car, than it also evokes the ingenious mechanisms of a Maschinengewehr 08 machine gun, or a Renault FT tank. Marinetti, no doubt, would have no problem with that comparison. For that matter, not only does the valorization of mechanization conjure cars, guns, and tanks, but mighty Moloch himself, for even within Livy (who almost certainly made such a claim up) it's specified that the idol is a contraption of gears and pistons, a machine with a blazing furnace in its belly that burns as hot as the Bessemer Converter of a steel mill.

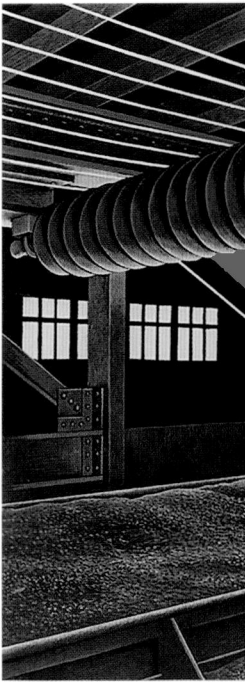

Because the twentieth century saw not just death on an unprecedented scale, but death which was made impersonal, managerial, and industrialized, the modern era is clearly the realm of that Canaanite Lord Moloch. The equation that marks the alienated bureaucratic ethics of the twentieth century saw death camps that appeared as factories, but also factories that were as death camps, as the dominant occult faith of these decades was an omnipresent industrialized capitalism, where humans were instrumentally reduced into mere marks in a ledger commandeered within a system ruled by that which Moloch most hungered for—profit. In making the claim that different epochs have their own guardian demons, if you will, care should be taken that such arguments are not put forth in any kind of spirit of crude literalism. Nor could it be denied that any age could certainly have its share of other candidates. When considering the twentieth century, there are other demons who arguably mark these alienated years just as well. Mulciber, hell's chief engineer, would seem to embody the technocratic positivism of the modern age exceedingly well; Mammon, with his unyielding avarice, is perhaps even more appropriate as a symbol of our age.

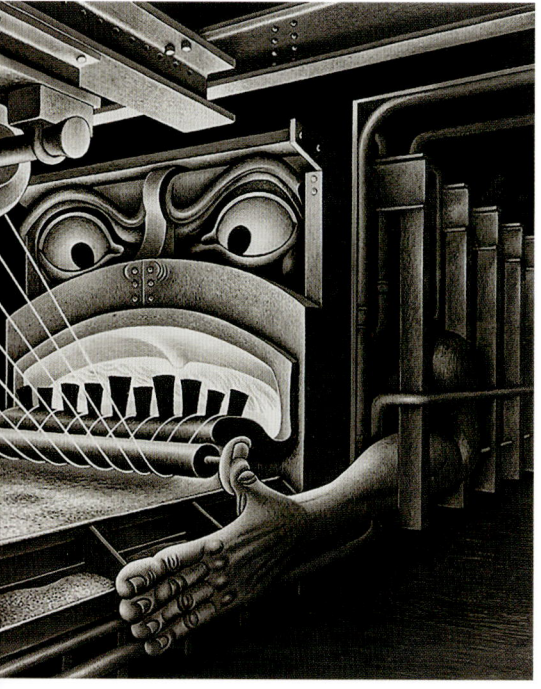

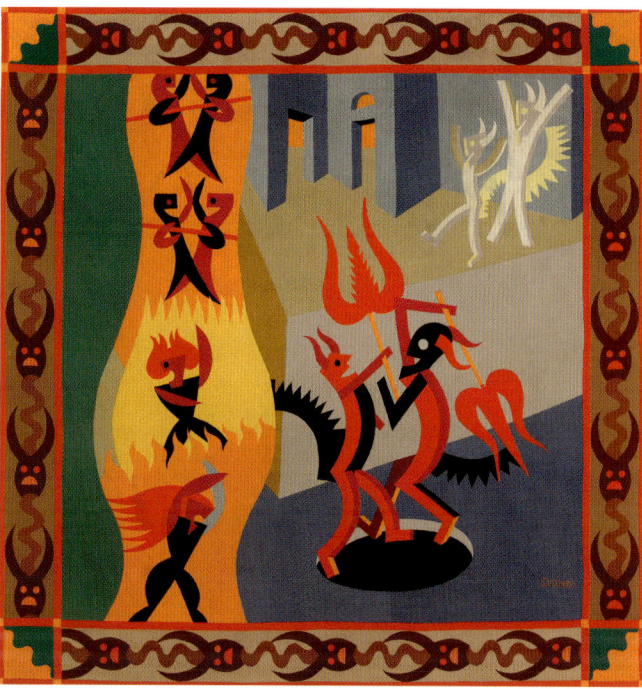

ABOVE LEFT

Russian-American commercial illustrator Boris Artzybasheff imagines a consciousness similar to that of Moloch as occupying a steel mill in his satirical 1945 drawing Wire Hell Fire.

ABOVE RIGHT

Despite the futurist rejection of traditional culture, particularly that of their native Italy, artist Fortunato Depero drew from Dante's The Divine Comedy *in the design of his performance space Cabaret del Diavolo. Structuring the space around the* Inferno *section of that epic, his 1922–23 tapestry* Little Black and White Devils, the Dance of Devils, *held by New York's Guggenheim Museum, provides an irreverent gloss on the poem.*

That's the demon that best personifies the contemporary moment according to Eugene McCarraher in *The Enchantments of Mammon: How Capitalism Became the Religion of Modernity*. Questioning the theoretical model, which argues that the long shift to modernity, beginning in the sixteenth century, was accompanied by a process of religious "disenchantment," McCarraher rather claims that ours is still a reality intimately enmeshed in the dogmas of a revealed religion. It's just that that faith happens to be capitalism. The supposed hyper-rationalism of this economic system may seem to make capitalism an odd candidate for being a religion, for as McCarraher writes "nothing seems more thoroughly secular than the modern business corporation, the Leviathan of the twenty-first century and the preeminent institution of our gilded age," though readers will note that the author cannily uses the name of one of God's monsters to describe such an organization. McCarraher argues that capitalism is not just a religion, but the dominant one of modernity, and a particularly toxic faith at that.

He explains that the cultural patronage role once played by the Church has been supplanted by the corporation, that the sale of commodities is a replacement for the veneration of relics, that corporate logos are "neoliberal totems of enchantment," that the individual self becomes the ultimate subject of worship, and that salvation is replaced with profit (and lest one think that the difference with the latter is that it's "real," question how much numbers on a computer screen actually exist). "Far from being an agent of 'disenchantment,' " McCarraher writes, "capitalism . . . has been a regime of enchantment, repression, displacement, and renaming of our intrinsic and inveterate longing for divinity." Central to this argument is the understanding that nothing is ever truly not theological—that secularity is a defined abstraction more than a reality—and that it's ultimately an impossibility for something to be devoid of the transcendent, the numinous, the divine, or the sacred. He explains that this religion's . . . animating spirit is money. Its theology, philosophy, and cosmology have been otherwise known as "economics." Its sacramentals consist of fetishized commodities and technologies—the material culture of production and consumption. Its moral and liturgical codes are contained in management theory and business journalism. Its clerisy is a corporate intelligentsia of economists, executives, managers, and business writers, a stratum akin to Aztec priests, medieval scholastics, and Chinese mandarins. Its iconography consists of advertising, public relations, marketing, and product design. Its beatific vision of eschatological destiny is the global imperium of capital, a heavenly city of business with incessantly expanding production, trade, and consumption.

McCarraher is convincing in his claim that multinational capitalism is an all pervading faith, with a metaphysics and ethics that orders our lives more than the medieval Church even did for the faithful of those centuries. What must be emphasized, however, is that not all theologies are equal, and in the "Mammonism" of capitalism, McCarraher sees what he calls a "misenchantment." Hence the appropriate election of Mammon as the name of this corrupt deity, this false idol promising salvation to be purchased through cash or credit. The invisible hand of the market that strangles the throats of the majority of people, which strangles the throat of the world's environment, is attached to Mammon's arm.

Why couldn't the contention also be made that ours is an era of Moloch? I would argue that Mammon isn't a god of this fallen world, but that he is a lesser demon who answers to a more all-consuming deity. For Moloch is to whom all systems that reduce humans to the utilitarian and to the instrumental must answer. Mammon is a capitalist—as is Moloch. But Moloch is also a fascist, a totalitarian. He is such because on some level Mammon's reasonings are understandable— to amass more wealth and more profit. But the rationale of Moloch is of no rationale, he is where meaning goes to be annihilated. There is no utility in the heated cavern of his empty chest, only pure nothingness. Insomuch as it's accurate to say that fascism is the stage of late capitalism wherein all of the contradictions of

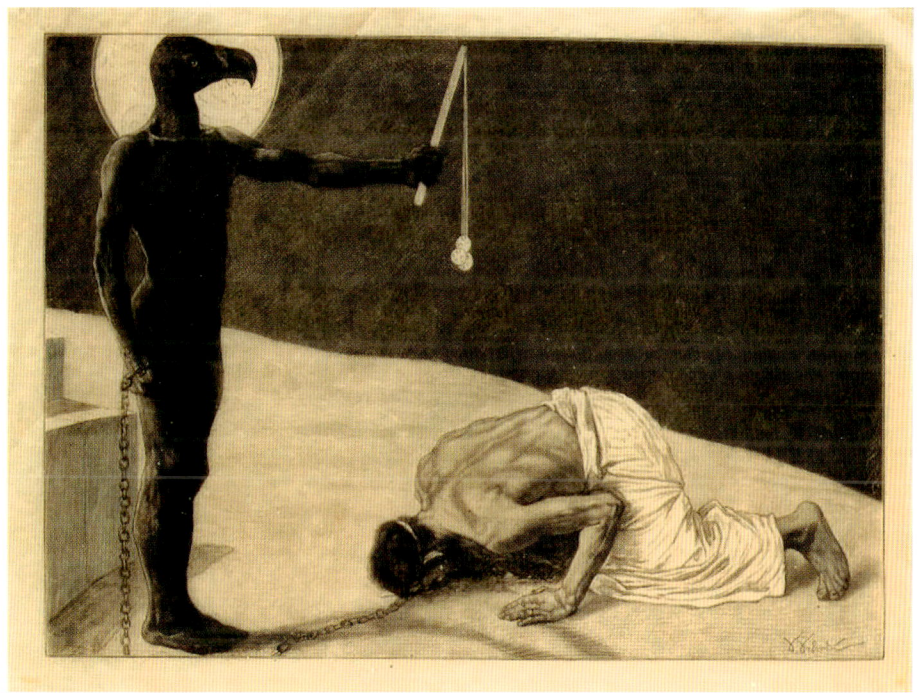

that system desperately try to reconcile themselves, then Mammon and Moloch are fundamentally the same entities. Yet the later rages with an altogether more irrational, more absurd, more nihilistic appetite, a consumptive logic that is ultimately self-defeating. Such is the mantra of senseless greed without purpose. Indeed as the irrational reality of fewer and fewer people consuming more and more at the expense of the many pushes us toward ecological apocalypse, Mammon's mask will fall off and reveal Moloch beneath. For if Mammon is the lord of the factory, than Moloch is the god who oversees the concentration camp and gulag. Mammon greedily commands more and more accumulation of wealth, but Moloch's shriek is the same as D'Annunzio's: "We have no other value but that of our blood to be shed."

The bronze roar of Moloch has been heard throughout twentieth-century cultural and literary history, recorded by some of our most adept demonologists who work under the guise of being artists and writers. A visual similarity exists between Moloch—a being depicted as a structure that is literally a mechanical forge and kiln—and for the sites of industry that make capitalism possible. Thomas Bell's underread 1941 proletarian novel *Out of This Furnace* catalogs the tribulations of Carpatho-Rusyn and Slovak immigrants working in the steel mills of Homestead, Pennsylvania, where descriptions of the mill cast a distinctly Molochian color. "The blast furnaces at Rankin flared intermittently through the rain, like half-smother fires; on the Homestead side a Bessemer converter vomited yellow flames toward the low-hanging clouds and caste a sheen on the river . . . The valley of steel was stirring out of its Sabbath lull." The language of consumption is clear, the almost organic steel mill is capable of vomiting out its flames in a valley that reads less like Pennsylvania and more like Gehenna.

Nebraska author Tillie Olsen, daughter of Russian-Jewish immigrants, described a similarly hellish aspect of industry in her also underread novel *Yonnondio: From the Thirties*, written in that decade albeit published in 1974. *Yonnondio*'s narrative concerns the Holbrook family of Wyoming, where the father works backbreaking, dangerous hours in a local coal mine. His daughter Mazie describes her father's vocation descending literally into the ground, Olsen writing (in dialect) that:

A phrase trembled into her mind, "Bowels of earth."
She shuddered. It was mysterious and terrible to her:
"Bowels of earth." It means the mine. Bowels is the stummy.
Earth is a stummy and mebbe she ets the men that come down.
Men and daddy goin' in like the day and comin out black.
Earth black and pop's face and hands black, and he spits
from his mouth black. Night comes and it is black.
Coal is black—it makes a fire.

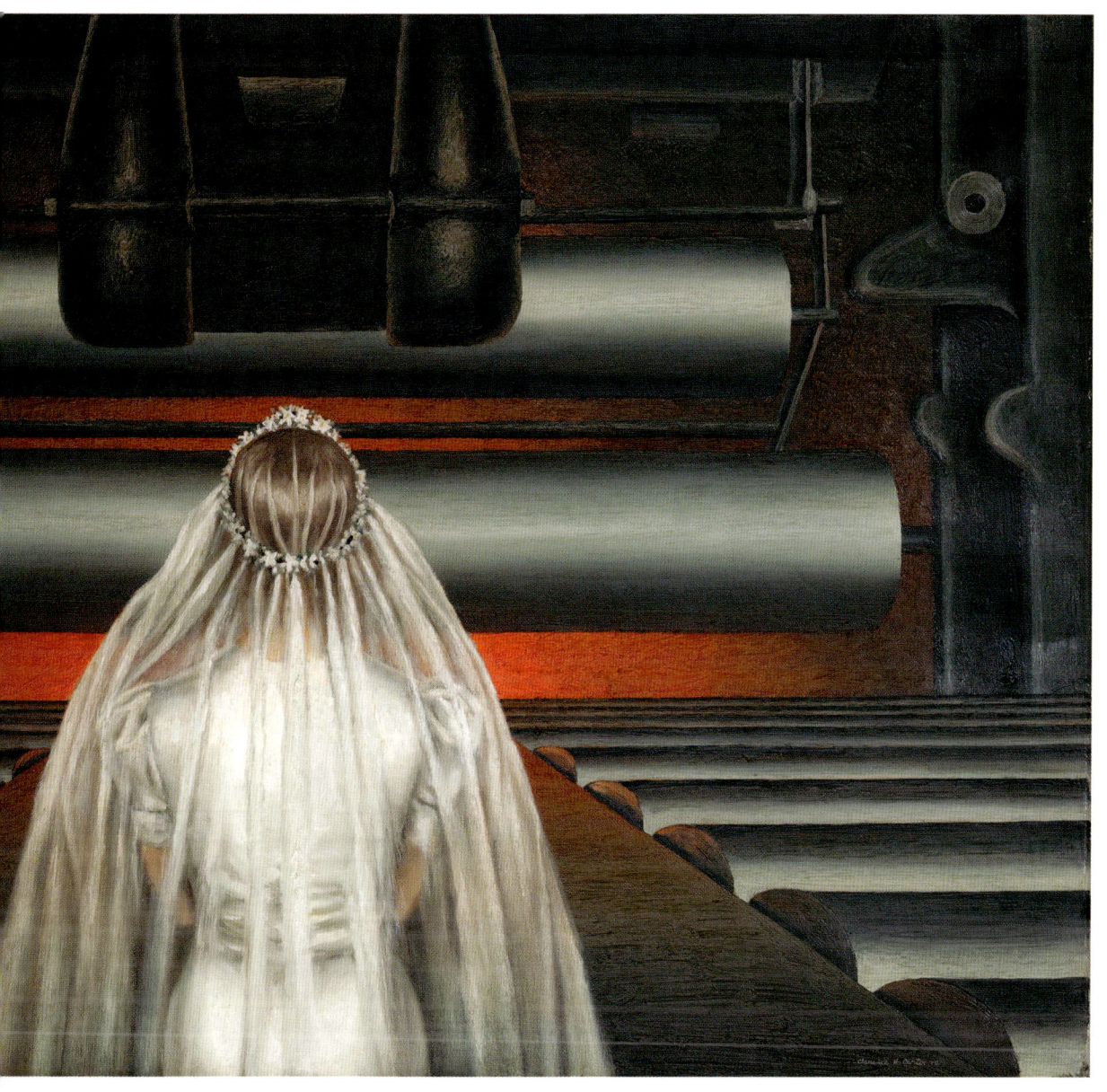

ABOVE

American painter Clarence Holbrook Carter's War Bride, held by the Carnegie Museum of Art in Pittsburgh, Pennsylvania, was finished in 1940—a year before the United States's entry into World War II. The arresting sleekness of the composition belies just how disturbing its theme is, the young bride walking down an "aisle" toward her husband, the machinery of a steel mill. A harbinger of all of those war brides to be widowed over the next four years, there is also an unmistakable sense of ritual sacrifice, the virgin brought before the Moloch-like forge of industry to give her life for the state.

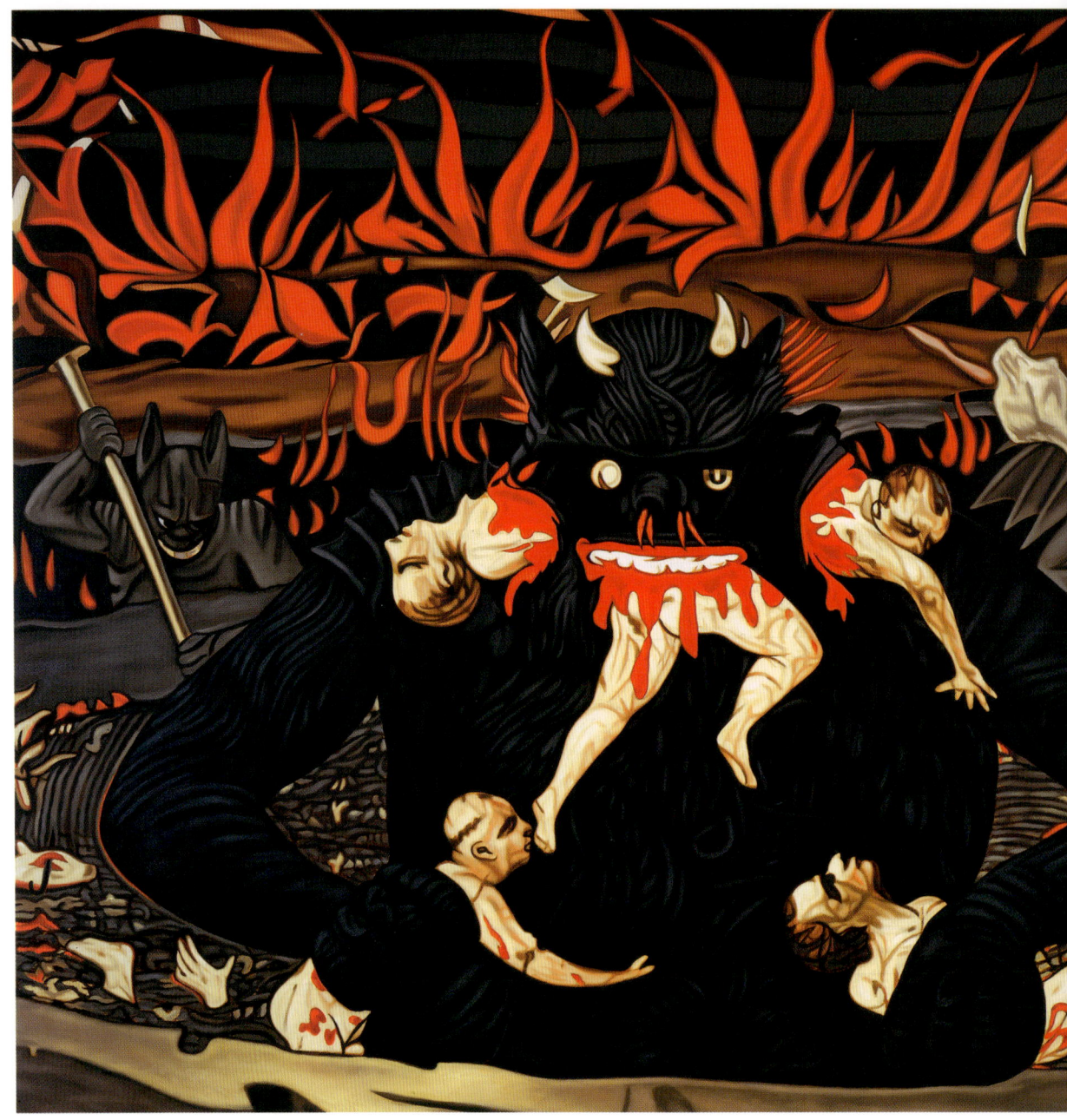

A depiction of Lucifer rather than Moloch, American artist Richard Phillips's 2007 Hell owes much to the visual idiom of the Middle Ages (particularly the Italian artist Fra Angelico), and literary sources such as Dante. Despite the faux-medievalism, there is something arrestingly modern about Hell (perhaps the wild-eyed spirit of devouring by which the Devil so enjoys himself), with Phillips intending the piece to be a protest against the ongoing Iraq War. Phillips' image recalls not just war, but the din of the assembly-line factory as well, with hell depicted as a forge for torture.

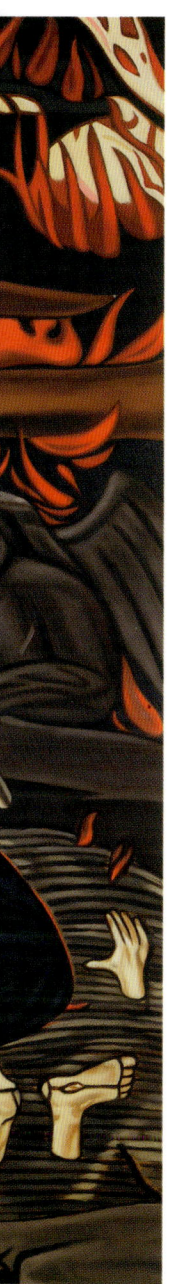

The imagery of the earth swallowing Jim Holbrook as surely as Moloch swallowing an infant, the cancerous blackness emerging from his mouth, and the flames produced by the chthonic god that is the coal mine—all of it is unmistakably demonic. Such horrors are made even more literal in Upton Sinclair's 1906 working-class muckraking novel *The Jungle*, which chronicled the degradation of the immigrant laborers in Chicago's meatpacking industry, where his story about unsafe conditions and contaminated beef led to a spate of regulatory governmental reforms. In Sinclair's description of this exploitative system, the factory system is as if an incarnated demon, with the associations of butchery, consumption, and blood, is transforming Chicago into perdition. "It was a monster devouring with a thousand mouths, trampling with a thousand hoofs," Sinclair writes of the meatpacking plant, "it was the spirt of Capitalism made flesh."

Capitalism isn't defined only by factories, of course; it's also the machinations of the bureaucratic state in conjunction with big business; what at its most extreme Mussolini called *corporativismo fascista*. Moloch resides not just in the mill, but also the office; not just in the mine, but in the market. No contemporary "demonologist" understood the nature of that system better from a literary standpoint than the Czech Jew Franz Kafka, who put forward a reflection of the world every bit as bleak as that offered by Lovecraft, albeit more subtle (and funnier as well). One of the few authors to be elevated to the level of an adjective, the word "Kafkaesque" denotes absurdity, irrationality, arbitrariness, and faceless oppression. Kafka's reality wasn't the emotive irrationalism of the ecstatic Romantic, but rather the anxious, paranoid irrationalism of the individual assaulted by state and corporate powers that are as ineffable, omniscient, and omnipresent as the gods of old. Steeped in the old-world conventions of kabbalah and the dark humor of the Yiddish theater, Kafka was a prophet of the coming totalitarianism of the twentieth century in his short stories and novellas like *The Trial*, written in 1915, and *The Castle*, written in 1922 (both were published posthumously after the author died of tuberculosis in 1924).

Neither of those novellas depicts anything that could be traditionally understood as a demon, but in Kafka's portrayal of a solitary individual whose life is an unwilling, arbitrary sacrifice to a massive, barely comprehensible order, there is a whiff of the smoke from Moloch's belly. In *The Trial*, his roman à clef Joseph K. is arrested, charged, and tried by his unnamed but powerful government, all while never being told the nature of the crime of which he is accused. "Where was the judge he had never seen?" asks Kafka, "Where was the High Court he had never reached?" For the protagonist of *The Trial*, the state has become as God (and the Devil) once were—remote, invisible, all-powerful beings who control the individual. *The Castle* explores similar themes, when the character K. (again, notice the autobiographical name) arrives at an unnamed village that is controlled by anonymous bureaucratic managers who reside in an impenetrable fortress at the center of the town.

K. must justify his presence in the town to those managers, and he is forced to interact with them through the alienating, pointless, and dispiriting filling out of forms, the ultimate meaningless liturgy of the modern age's great faith, the castle a Tower of Babel embodying the unseen apophatic state. In *Salmagundi Magazine*, biblical scholar Robert Alter describes Kafka's vision as a "balancing act on the razor's edge, peering into the abyss of nihilism and leaning back against the framework of authoritative religion." With shades of Nietzsche's warning about what comes to those of us who stare into the abyss, there is no cauldron blacker than the furnace in Moloch's chest, whose fire burns but gives off no light, the exemplary metaphor for those systems that grind down men like Joseph K. Filling out paperwork is no marginal activity, for both the corporate and bureaucratic state use paperwork to facilitate their actions, whether benign or criminal. Kafka was able to comprehend how unfeeling rational bureaucracy metastasizes into dystopia. Critic George Steiner notes in his introduction to *The Trial* that a "concrete fulfillment of augury, of detailed clairvoyance, attaches to his seeming fantastications... The spiritual possibility exists that Franz Kafka experienced his prophetic powers as some visitation of guilt." Three of Kafka's sisters and his lover would all perish in Hitler's concentration camps.

The road to Auschwitz was paved with millions of IBM punch cards and forms filled out by middling intermediaries in Berlin government offices. One of the things that marked Moloch's reign during the twentieth century was this seemingly dispassionate nature of mass murder, the way in which genocide was unfeelingly promulgated by a state Leviathan larger than any of the multitude of evil men who composed its organs. Think of the horror of the assault on Guernica, the Basque town that in 1937 was pummeled by the German Luftwaffe and the Italian Aviazione Legionaria at the invitation of the Falangist dictator Francisco Franco, as Spain was in the midst of civil war. Such a campaign was organized by military apparatchiks in Madrid, Berlin, and Rome, and carried out by men in airplanes who never saw the faces of the innocents whom they killed, as surely as the faces of the sacrificed were hidden within the bronze belly of Moloch. Thousands of Franco's own countrymen died in incendiary explosions, as both Mussolini and Hitler were able to demonstrate the brutal efficacy of their air force; children sacrificed in the immolating fires of technology, murdered by and on behalf of monstrous, flying mechanical creatures.

The Spanish painter Pablo Picasso's massive composition *Guernica*, made for the 1937 Paris International Exhibition in the months after the attack, is the ultimate artistic statement about those horrors. Picasso's chromatically muted, gray-and-black, cubist mural harkens back to medieval altarpieces with their frantic invocations of hell; the artist presents an abstracted tableaux of the horror of the assault as it happens. On the far right a figure screams in agony; another holds a candle outside of her window to see what carnage has been wrought from above, a person drags themselves through the street, perhaps wounded, while another one lays dead on the ground. A gored horse brays in the background while gray flames burn throughout. In the upper-left-hand portion of the painting are three essential figures—a woman screaming while cradling a dead infant, a light bulb sending out squibs of dread gray luminescence, and impassively surveying all of the action, a massive bull.

A painting as rich in allegorical significance as any produced during the Middle Ages or the Renaissance, *Guernica* still alludes easy interpretation beyond its unambiguous anti-war and anti-fascist message, but as regards the meaning of any particular figure, there is an ambiguity. Christian symbolism is replete throughout the composition; the dead soldier in the street has a wounded palm, perhaps in imitation of the stigmata, and the grieving mother combines both the nativity and the pietà into a stunningly tragic synthesis. The bull, in particular, has generated much discussion. Critics, such as Picasso's friend the poet Federico García Lorca, see the bull as representing the stoic suffering of the Spanish people, with that creature having particular and obvious cultural resonance, while others, such as the art historian Jerome Seckler, have claimed it was representative of Franco's cruelty. Another clear connotation is toward the mystical beast of the Minotaur, a creature that Picasso identified with and was obsessed with because of its potent sexual virality. For what it's worth, Picasso wrote in a letter to his Paris art dealer in 1947 that "this bull is a bull. . . . If you give a meaning to certain things in my paintings it may be very true, but it is not my idea to give this meaning." Worth considering that rather than a Minotaur, *Guernica* provides a glimpse of Moloch, the flames of war sacrificing God's children in the streets of the city below, a keening mother grasping her immolated baby.

Moloch is not just alluded to, but rather directly engaged with, in the greatest poetic expression of American alienation written in the middle of the twentieth century. "Moloch the incomprehensible prison!" thundered out poet Allen Ginsberg's voice at a reading in San Francisco's Six Gallery in 1955, "Moloch the crossbone soulless jailhouse and Congress of/sorrows! Moloch whose buildings are judgement! Moloch the vast stone of war! Moloch the/stunned government!" In lugubrious, unspooling, blank verse, Ginsberg's epic poem *Howl* denounced the American military-industrial complex across 112 serpentine lines. Oft-associated with the Beat movement that included his friends Jack Kerouac and William S. Burroughs, Ginsberg's verse is indicative of a postwar American avant-garde that both denounced the demons of modernity while embracing a new spiritual vocabulary to speak of good and evil. Written a decade after the United States had incinerated Hiroshima and Nagasaki, and composed in a world where an uneasy détente between America and the Soviet Union could dissolve into a mushroom cloud at any instant, *Howl* unabashedly accessed a Jewish prophetic urgency to denounce the latent, demonic violence that defined modernity. Structured in three distinct sections (with a "footnote" at the conclusion, which functions as a coda), all of Part II of *Howl* is given over to the anatomization of Moloch.

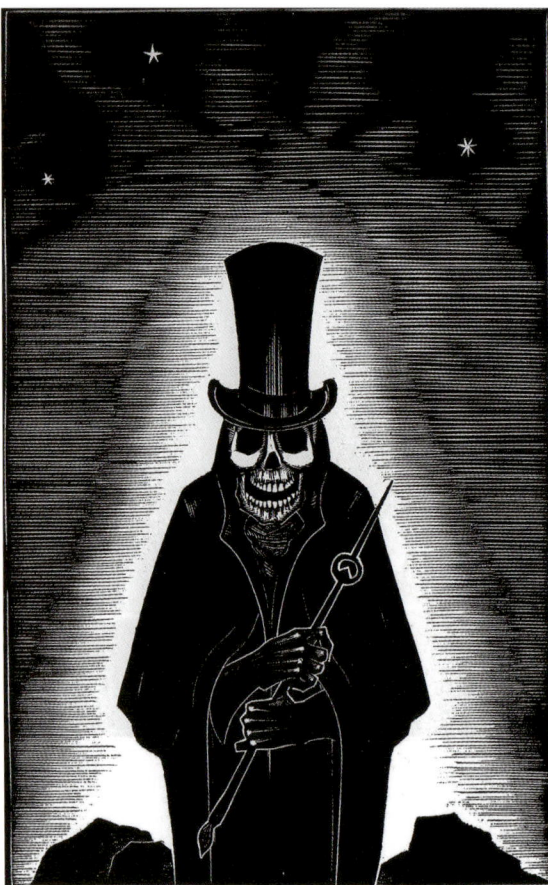
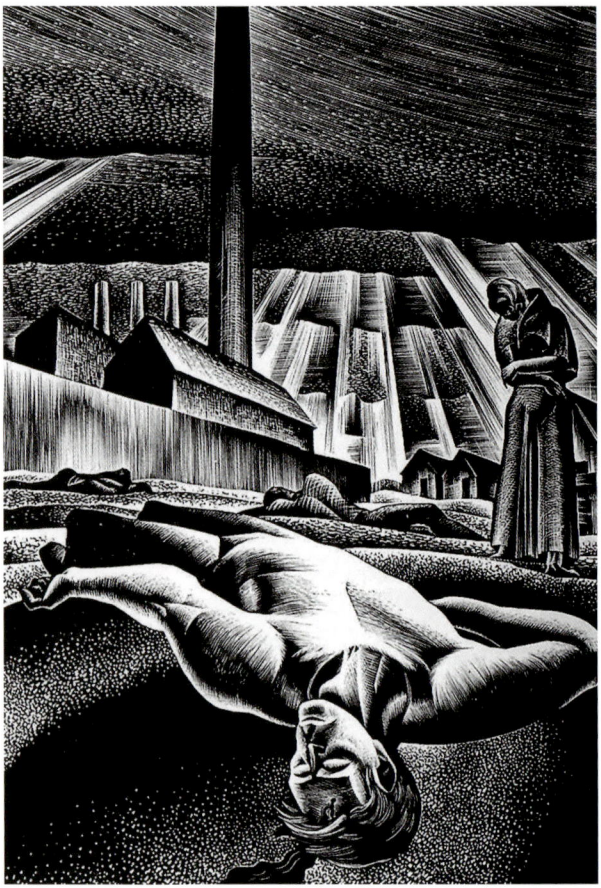

Allen Ginsberg would admit in an introduction to an illustrated edition of his collected poems published in 1996 that he was strongly influenced by the engraver Lynd Ward's 1932 "wordless novel" Wild Pilgrimage. *Precursor to the mature comics form known as the graphic novel, the largely forgotten visionary Ward drew from German expressivist art and the tradition of mezzotint to produce visionary books composed entirely of wordless woodcut images.* Wild Pilgrimage *is a strongly proletarian text, reflecting Ward's socialist sympathies, providing depictions of faceless, dehumanizing industry that clearly influenced the second section of* Howl. *In the image on the left, note the Grim Reaper wearing the top hat of the capitalist.*

Hirsch argues that *Howl* is a "poem that is a faithful, almost helpless witness, a prophet of its own demonic American spirit." True to the injunction of prophecy being a mode meant to hold a people accountable for their sins, *Howl* correctly condemns the triumphant American state and the corporations that it exults for a pervasive emptiness that kills both at home and abroad. Ginsberg writes against "Moloch whose mind is pure machinery! Moloch whose blood is running money! Moloch whose/fingers are ten armies! Moloch whose breast is a cannibal dynamo! Moloch whose ear is a/smoking tomb!" The poet's lines, supposedly written to match how long he'd be able to sustain a continuous line of verse before losing breath, add to the incantatory aspect of *Howl*; the anaphoric repetition of "Moloch" at the start of each line is of the theurgic tradition that emphasizes the necessity of properly naming those demons whom we wish to expel. Ginsberg writes:

Moloch whose eyes are a thousand blind windows!
Moloch whose skyscrapers stand in the long streets
like endless Jehovahs! Moloch whose factories
dream and croak in the fog! Moloch whose smoke-
stacks and antennae crown the cities!

Moloch whose love is endless oil and stone!
Moloch whose soul is electricity and banks!
Moloch whose poverty is the specter of genius!
Moloch whose fate is a cloud of sexless hydrogen!
Moloch whose name is the Mind!

In terms of rhythm the poem owes everything to the blank verse and listing poems of Ginsberg's great antecedent Walt Whitman, but the imagery is borrowed from European surrealists, modernists who demand that the only accurate reflection of reality is one that fully plumbs the insanity that defines the experience of modern life. In Ginsberg's portrait of a demon, Moloch is composed of steel and concrete, his blood is oil, he consumes women and men and excretes profit. In *Howl*, Moloch is an incarnation of pure rapacious consumption that is nihilistic and without meaning.

What Ginsberg ultimately expresses in *Howl*, but which more importantly defines the Age of Moloch for all of us, is how an intractable network of connection has made us all culpable in global evils, how a malevolent economics that forces us to trade within a demonic system has sutured us all into the great, bestial, monstrous body of a creature named Moloch. Nobody can opt out of this culpability; the tin, tungsten, aluminum, and tantalum in the computer on which these words were written has funded insurgencies in the Democratic Republic of the Congo, the coffee that the author drinks as he writes comes from beans farmed by exploited workers in Costa Rica, the clothes that he wears as he composes these words were sewn by children in sweatshops in Vietnam. Poole writes that "We embrace the sensationalism of individual violence rather than face the more imposing horror of established, systematic, institutional violence that perhaps resides at the very heart of our social order." Easier for us to get a prurient thrill at grotesque stories about the Manson Family, the Zodiac Killer, or the Night Stalker rather than considering the wide prevalence of evil for which we're all culpable.

While it is true that there are countercultural options to try to avoid Moloch's all-encompassing grasp, they are normally only possible for those who have already gained a high degree of privilege. For the rest of us, that which marks post-modernity and late capitalism is how we've all been enlisted into a collaborationist army where the responsibility for travesty rests on our shoulders in a manner that was impossible before the ascendancy of international capitalism—it's the democratization of atrocity where sin is equally distributed to all. The twentieth century is marked by a certain unfeeling technocracy, the culmination of positivism, privatization, and puritanism (where each of those reflect humanity's increasing alienation respectively from aesthetics, the commons, and divinity), whereby the individual is paradoxically idolatrized as the ultimate unit while also being ground underneath the heal of massive, impersonal systems. The ultimate irony of the twentieth century is that all of the nightmares of the religious imagination—the existence of hell and the finality of apocalypse—were made possible by technocratic expertise in both the concentration camp and the nuclear blast. Ours is an apocalypse whereby we all live in Moloch's belly, and we're forever pulling more and more people into the forge with us.

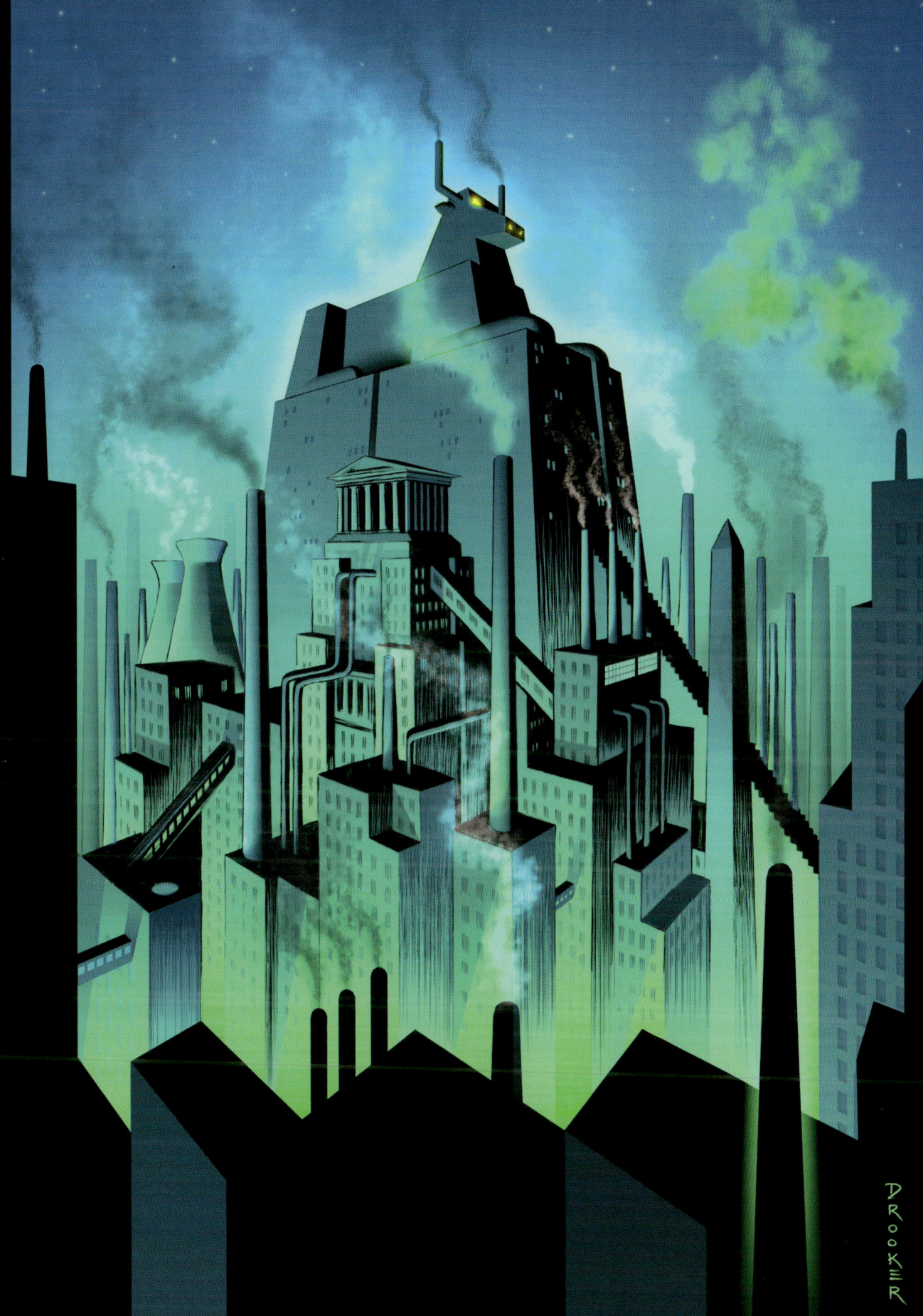

SATANIC PANIC AND PARANOIA

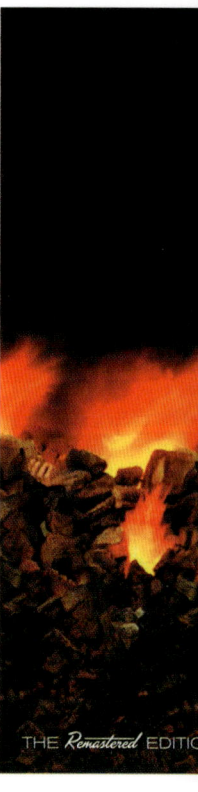

THE *Remastered* EDITIO

I n 1983, a Los Angeles woman who suffered from both paranoid schizophrenia and chronic alcoholism accused her estranged husband and her son's preschool teacher of having sodomized her young son. Child abuse is of course horrifically common, but the allegations that Judy Johnson leveled against the teachers of the McMartin Preschool included details that strained credulity—that children were taken into a network of subterranean tunnels beneath the school where they were conscripted into Satanic rituals, that they witnessed human sacrifice, and most bizarrely that they saw actual witches flying. The Canadian psychologist Lawrence Pazder, who coined the phrase "Satanic Ritual Abuse" in his book *Michelle Remembers* published three years before, was enlisted as an expert by the LAPD. Several arrests were made, despite lack of evidence, and what followed was the longest and most expensive trial in American history, though it resulted in no convictions. Critics noted how police psychologists asked purposefully leading questions to young children, and in the years that followed, the accused were exonerated, while many of the victims admitted that they'd been encouraged to level such accusations by the authorities.

The McMartin Preschool case was the most notorious instance of a spate of accusations against teachers and caretakers that occurred throughout the decade; not just that children had been raped, but that they had been abused in the context of ritualized satanic activity. By the end of the 1980s, some twelve thousand allegations had been made across the United States, with Poole writing that this was a "moment in American cultural life when the devil occupied a place in public discourse not held at any time or place in America since the New England settlements of the seventeenth century." Pazder's *Michelle Remembers* was arguably the instigator of the phenomenon, a bizarre book in which he claims that through hypnosis he had recovered repressed memories from his patient Michelle Smith, who was suffering from a dissociative identity disorder, where she was now able to recall being victimized by her mother and a cabal of satanists throughout her youth (Pazder and Smith later married). Despite *Michelle Remembers* being the sort of book that should welcome copious skepticism—among other claims, Pazder says that there is a millennia-long spate of millions of Satanists in respectable positions engaged in ritual abuse and human sacrifice, and that actual supernatural events occurred because of these ceremonies—the author would be consulted by police departments and prosecutors throughout the decade.

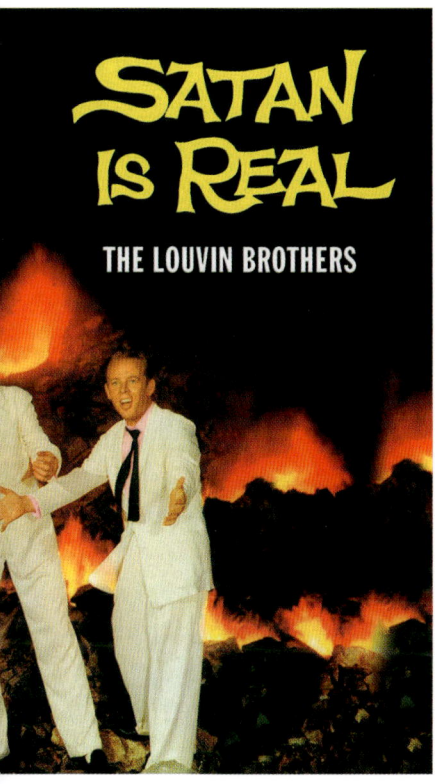

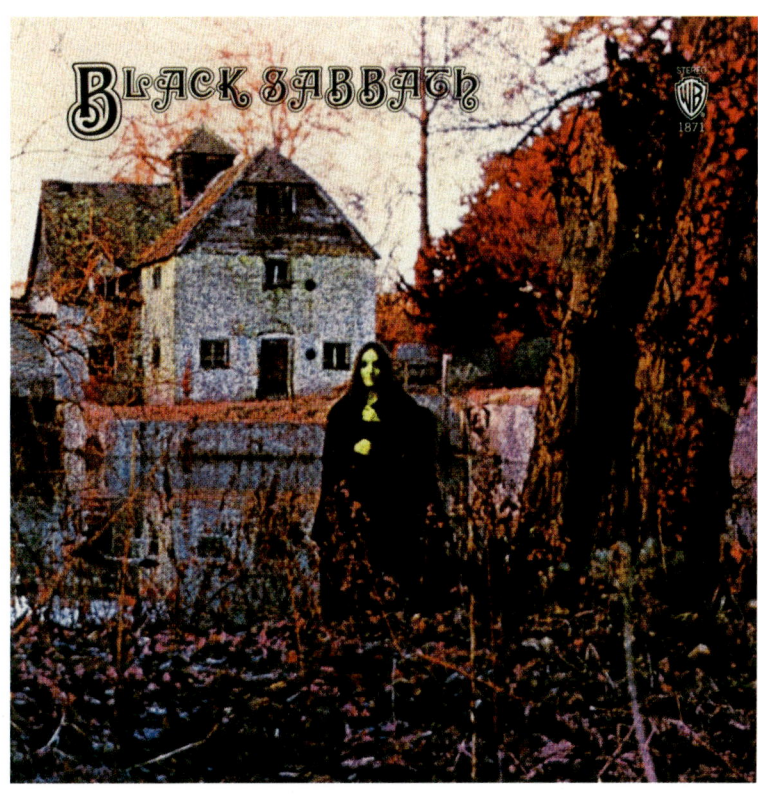

LEFT

The 1959 country gospel masterpiece by the Louvin Brothers *Satan Is Real* is many things—earnest, faithful, and more than a bit corny. One thing which it isn't, is ironic. "Satan Is real, working in spirit/You can see him and hear him in this world every day," sang the brothers on the title track, "Satan is real, working with power/ He can tempt you and lead you astray." Predating the satanic panic by two decades, *Satan Is Real* evidences that for American evangelical Christians, demons are neither metaphor nor symbol, but rather very much a literal manifestation of evil in the world.

RIGHT

British metal band Black Sabbath's debut self-titled 1970 album was not the first rock album to engage with occult and gothic themes, but they quickly became synonymous with the dark arts in music. "What is this that stands before me?" crooned vocalist Ozzy Osbourne in the title track, "Figure in black which points at me." From their name to the use of satanic symbols including pentagrams and inverted crosses, the musicians of Black Sabbath played with demonic imagery, including mentioning Aleister Crowley in song lyrics. Bassist Geezer Butler remarked in the liner notes to a 1998 live reunion album that "I'd been raised a Catholic so I totally believed in the Devil." For conservative Christian critics of the band, Black Sabbath was accused of engaging in subliminal messaging to try and sway their adolescent fans to demon worship, even though their imagery was in reality largely schtick.

America's satanic panic unified several disparate groups, such as law enforcement, psychologists, tabloid reporters, dubiously credentialed experts on cults, and evangelical Christians. Though factions and individuals disagreed on the nature of the satanic threat, all involved agreed that there was a conspiratorial network of millions of women and men in covens throughout the United States dedicated to the ritual abuse of children. "The 'satanic panic' drew on a vast collection of historical images," writes Poole, "and many Americans used the imagery of Satanism to express their anxieties about the nature of evil." As Poole emphasizes, such fears were obviously not without precedent; the satanic ritual abuse paranoia of the eighties recalled the antisemitic blood libel of the Middle Ages, and the witch persecutions of the early modern period, albeit this latest manifestation of paranoia was in an ostensibly modern, secular, and scientific society. Nor was it limited to the most disturbing of allegations, as "experts" on Satanism identified rock music, role-playing games, the goth subculture, comic books, and movies as part of a coordinated conspiracy by demon worshipers to influence the youth of America. Ironically and tragically, many legitimate experts on child abuse have noted how the prurient nature of the satanic ritual abuse phenomenon deflected attention from actual occurrences of widespread child sexual abuse, such as that which was disturbingly frequent in the Catholic Church.

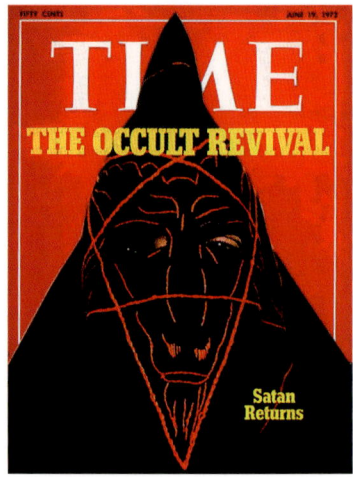

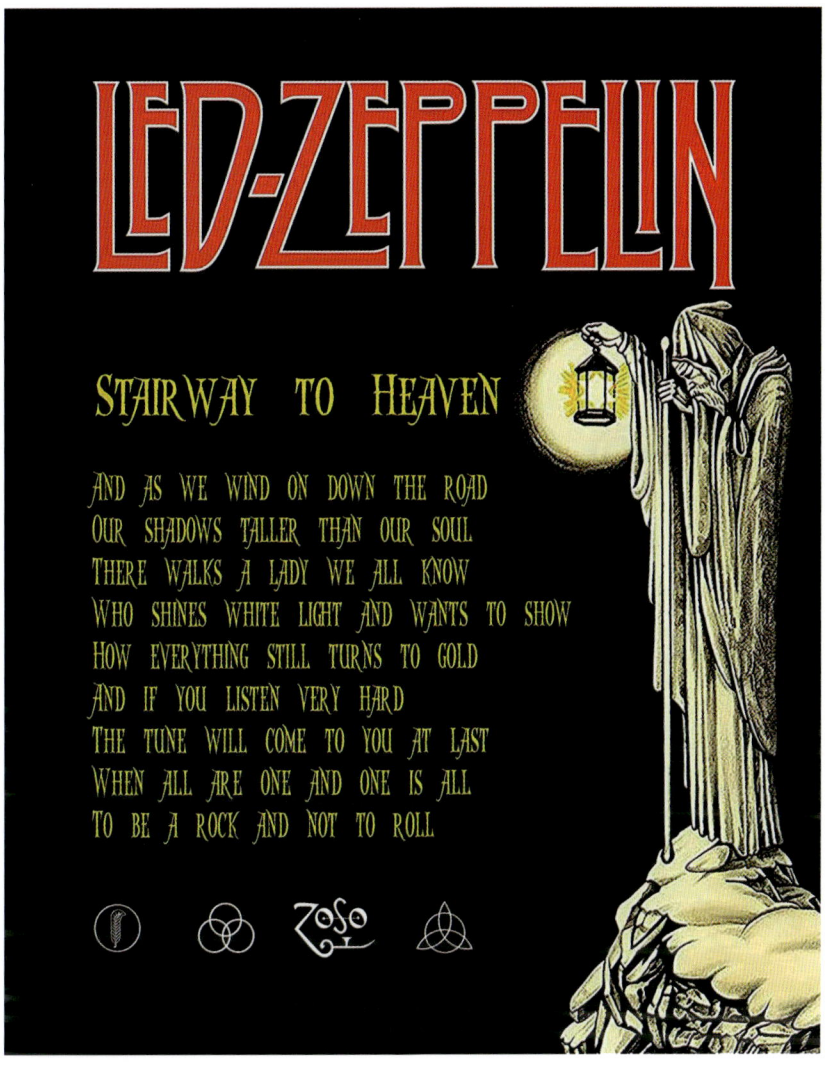

LED-ZEPPELIN

STAIRWAY TO HEAVEN

AND AS WE WIND ON DOWN THE ROAD
OUR SHADOWS TALLER THAN OUR SOUL
THERE WALKS A LADY WE ALL KNOW
WHO SHINES WHITE LIGHT AND WANTS TO SHOW
HOW EVERYTHING STILL TURNS TO GOLD
AND IF YOU LISTEN VERY HARD
THE TUNE WILL COME TO YOU AT LAST
WHEN ALL ARE ONE AND ONE IS ALL
TO BE A ROCK AND NOT TO ROLL

British rock group Led Zeppelin combined American blues music, the writings of J.R.R. Tolkien, and a general interest in mythic themes to produce some of the most beloved popular music of the 1970s. Their most famous track is their more than eight-minute long 1971 song "Stairway to Heaven," off of their album Led Zeppelin IV *(more popularly known as* Zoso *after runic symbols on the cover), a high-volume number built around enigmatic lyrics that builds toward a tremendous crescendo. Naturally fascinated with the occult, Led Zeppelin cofounder Jimmy Page bought Aleister Crowley's Boleskine House on the shoals of Scotland's Loch Ness in 1971, where he supposedly wrote some of the lyrics to "Stairway to Heaven." Those lyrics became an issue of controversy during the satanic panic, when the evangelical television network Cornerstone claimed that the band had encoded demonic concepts in the song through something called "backmasking," whereby a track played backwards revealed subliminal messages. According to some, if the lyric where Robert Plant sings "If there's a bustle in your hedgerow, don't be alarmed now" is played backwards, it reveals the (more comprehensible) message of "Here's to my sweet Satan/The one whose little path would make me sad whose power is Satan,/He'll give you, he'll give 666/There was a little tool shed where he made us suffer, sad Satan."*

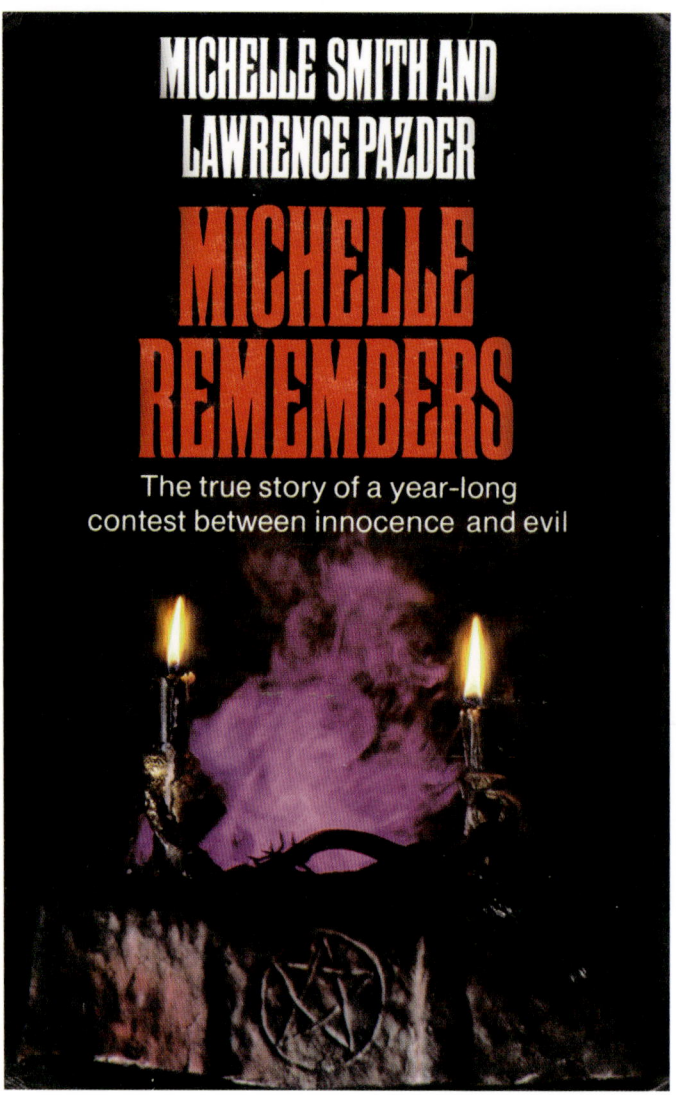

ABOVE LEFT

While fear of a literal Devil has existed since America's colonial period, the publication of psychiatrist Lawrence Pazder's 1980 Michelle Remembers signaled the beginnings of a modern satanic panic, whereby millions of Americans believed that there were covens of otherwise respectable women and men worshiping the Devil and abusing children as part of a widespread occult religion. Pazder claimed that through hypnosis, his patient Michelle Smith (whom he later married) had been forced into grotesque satanic rituals as a small child. Belief in the existence of satanic ritual abuse, as Pazder called it, wasn't uncommon among evangelical Christians, conservative Catholics, tabloid news reporters, law enforcement, and even some mental health professionals during the height of the panic. Unsurprisingly, virtually none of Pazder's or Smith's claims could be substantiated, and most were directly disproven.

DEMONS OF POP CULTURE
AND POSTMODERNISM

hen director William Friedkin's adaptation of William Peter Blatty's horror paperback *The Exorcist* was released in 1973, Warner Brothers was so sure that its box office returns would be minimal that it was initially screened in only twenty-four theaters around the country. At the time of this writing, *The Exorcist* is the ninth-highest-grossing film of all time, with the franchise of multiple sequels and reissues garnering a collective 1.8 billion dollars when adjusted for inflation, by far the most popular horror movie ever made. Blatty's novel was supposedly inspired by an actual case of demonic possession in Cottage City, Maryland, which the author learned about while he was an undergraduate at Georgetown University in 1949. Both the novel and the film adaptation of *The Exorcist* detail the tortures of twelve-year-old Regan, daughter of a famous actress living in Washington, D.C., while filming a movie at Georgetown, who inadvertently invites the demon Pazuzu into possessing her after playing with a Ouija board. As Regan's behavior becomes increasingly erratic, and psychiatrists are at a loss to rationally explain what's tormenting her, two Roman Catholic priests are invited to administer the rite of exorcism, for as the film's tagline promises, "Somewhere between science and superstition, there is another world. The world of darkness."

The Exorcist was a bona fide cultural phenomenon; denounced by evangelical Christians who thought it was demonic, and by Catholics who worried that the film presented the Church as superstitious and medieval, the movie was so visceral that "Only days after the film's nationwide release, reports began to filter in of bizarre physical and psychological reactions that American audiences were having in response to the disturbing images on the screen," as Poole writes. Though the most popular of movies about demonic themes, it was Roman Polanski's *Rosemary's Baby* that inaugurated the cinematic trend in 1968, an unnerving psychological study of a New York woman who fears that she's been tricked into carrying Satan's progeny. The infernal trinity is rounded out by the Richard Donner-directed 1976 film *The Omen*, wherein the United States's ambassador to Great Britain discovers that his wife and he have been unwittingly conscripted into the adoption of the Antichrist. Russell argues that the popularity of these movies "encouraged an interest that had its origins in the repression of the sense of radical evil, in fear of the bomb and societal violence, in cultural despair, and in the need to fill the void left by the absence of traditional religion by something resembling religion."

Friedkin's movie, despite some official opprobrium from the Church, was estimably traditional, if not conservative, in its metaphysics. To wit, *The Exorcist* claims that there is such a thing as objective, absolute evil; that that evil is caused by a fallen angel named Satan, and that demons are his servants and emissaries; that these beings are capable of possessing human beings, and that the only recourse in that circumstance is the intercession of the Roman Catholic Church. Demonology in popular culture didn't always take such orthodox forms, however, as the postmodern devil is ever mercurial. Some of the most venerable themes in demonology would be secularized in contemporary urban legends, including that of the vampiric Black-Eyed Kids, the stories of extraterrestrial abduction promulgated by the so-called Greys, and the internet meme tales about the Slenderman. Even when we're done with demons, they're not always done with us, whatever names we choose to call them by.

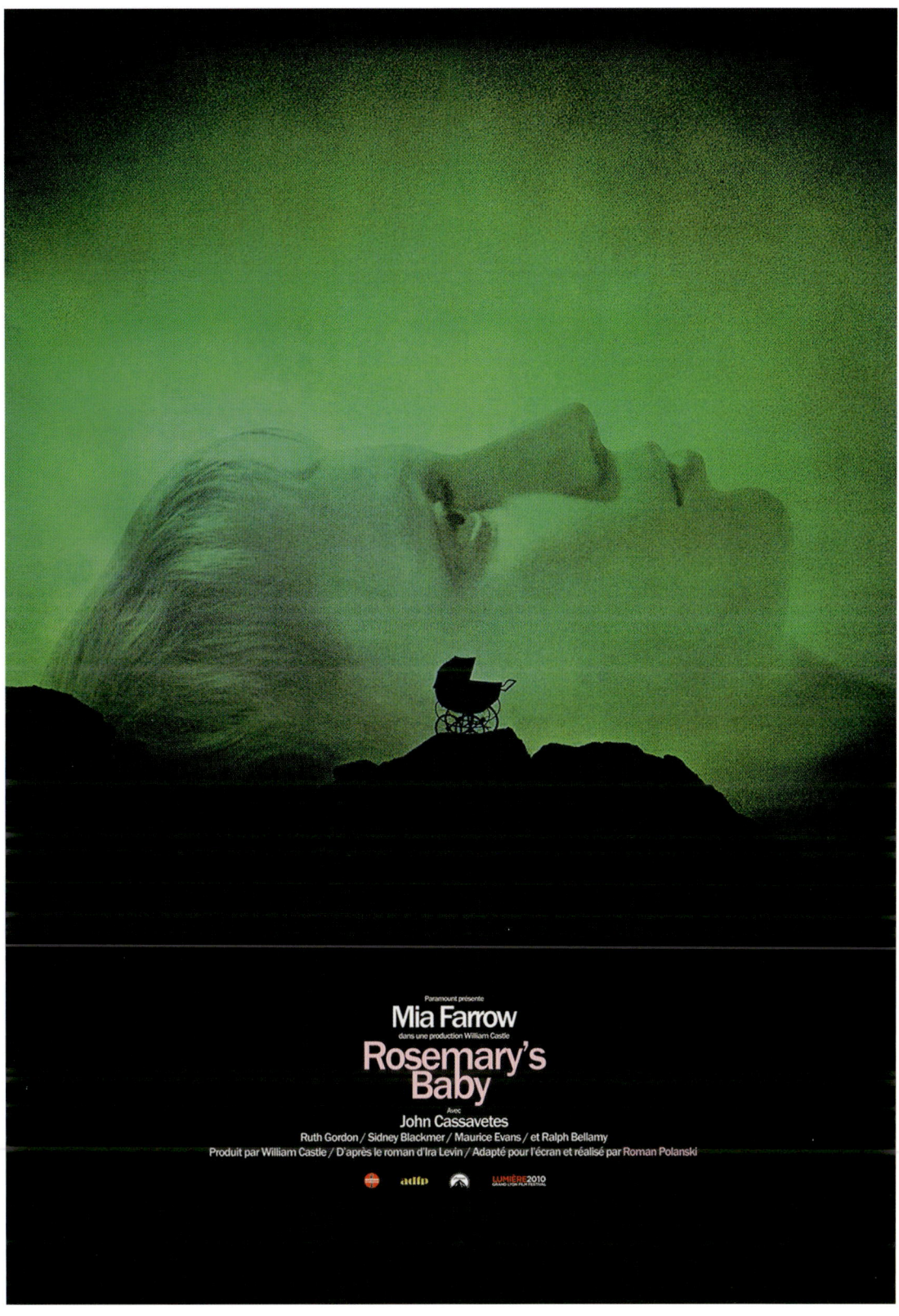

Paramount présente
Mia Farrow
dans une production William Castle
Rosemary's Baby
Avec
John Cassavetes
Ruth Gordon / Sidney Blackmer / Maurice Evans / et Ralph Bellamy
Produit par William Castle / D'après le roman d'Ira Levin / Adapté pour l'écran et réalisé par Roman Polanski

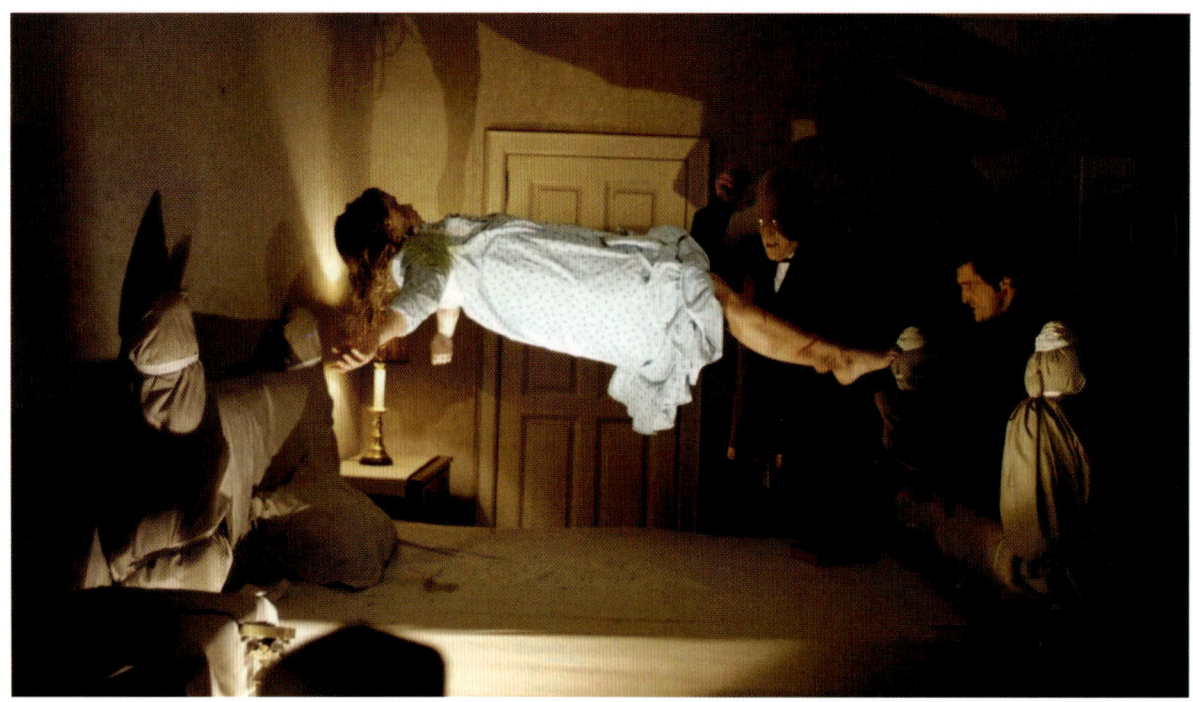

There is no ambiguity that Regan's possession is real; it isn't a hoax, psychosis, or personality disorder. As The Exorcist *makes abundantly clear in its intense scenes of demon possession, this supernatural phenomenon is actually happening "Especially important is the warning to avoid conversations with the demon," Fr. Merrick tells Fr. Damian. "We may ask what is relevant but anything beyond that is dangerous. He is a liar. The demon is a liar. He will lie to confuse us. But he will also mix lies with the truth to attack us. The attack is psychological . . . and powerful. So don't listen to him. Remember that—do not listen."*

If the theology of The Exorcist *was explicitly Catholic, then director Richard Donner's 1976 apocalyptic movie* The Omen *hews to a distinctively evangelical Protestant understanding, even if the movie itself was intended for a secular audience and the director and screenwriter were Jewish. In its story about U.S. diplomat Robert Thorne (played with typical steely resolve by Gregory Peck) and his wife Katherine discovering that their son was perhaps switched with the infant Antichrist after birth,* The Omen *presupposes what's technically referred to as a pre-millennial dispensationalist eschatology. That's to say that the theology of the film has it that the Antichrist will literally reign on earth before the millennium of the end times. As conservative evangelical Christians became an increasingly potent political force in the last decades of the twentieth century, this sort of apocalyptic worldview (and all that's problematic about it) became more mainstream.* The Omen *Polish one-sheet designed by artist Andrzej Klimowski, 1977.*

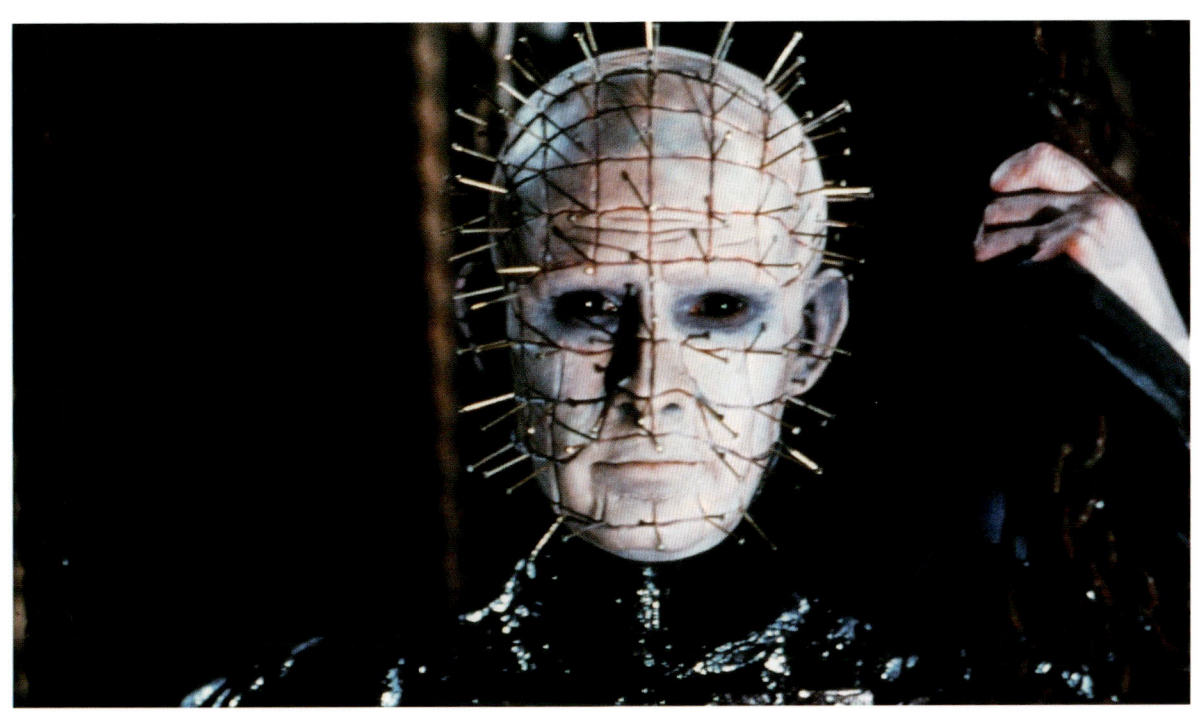

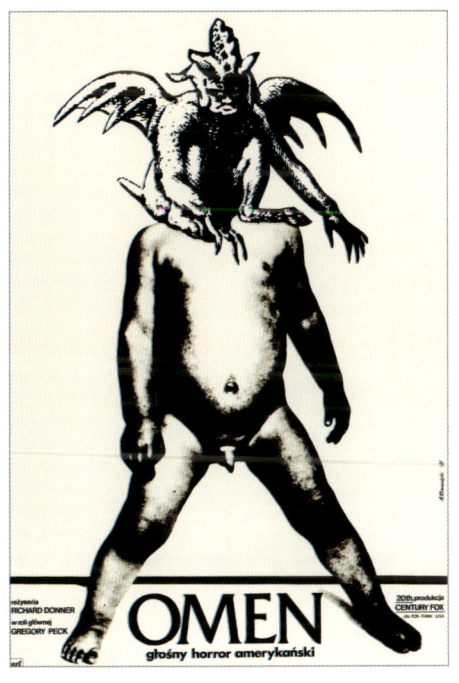

British screenwriter and director Clive Barker's 1987 horror film Hellraiser invented a novel visual idiom to explore the demonic, drawing from both sadomasochistic and totalitarian imagery, as well as that of the circus freak show. The demons of Hellraiser are technically beings known as Cenobites, formerly human Lovecraftian entities from another dimension who exist both beyond good and evil, as well as pleasure and pain. Summoned into our reality by the mechanism of a cursed puzzle box, the Cenobites take a strange, disinterested pleasure in the physical and spiritual torture of mere humans. The character of Lead Cenobite, more colloquially known as "Pinhead," quickly become an audience favorite, and appears in an astounding ten movies in the franchise.

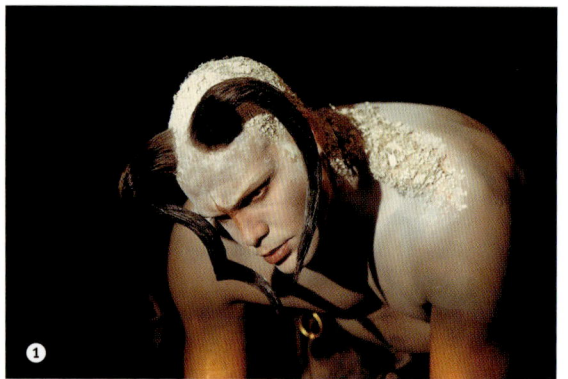

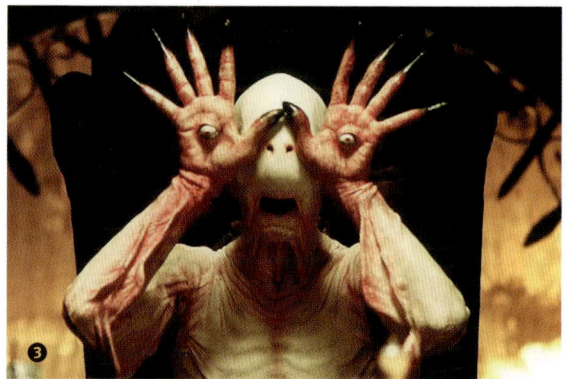

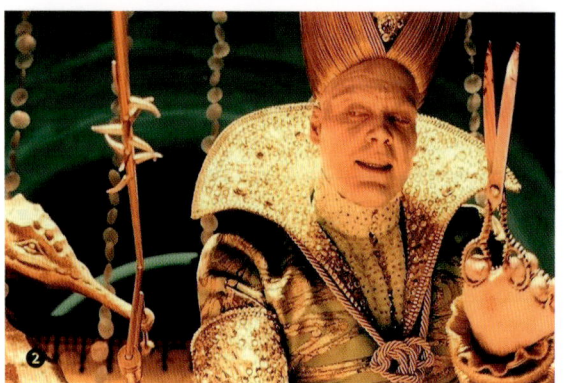

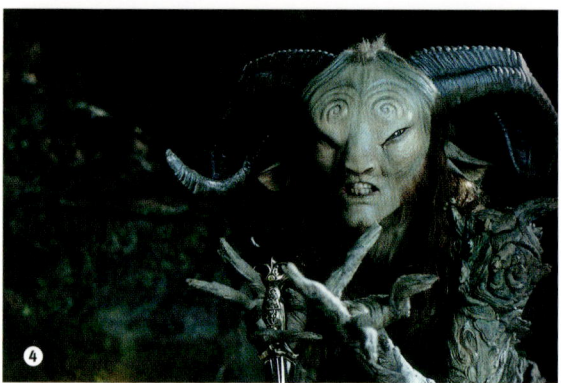

❶ Indian director Tarsem Singh's critically under-valued 2000 horror film The Cell imagines that it's possible to use sophisticated technology to enter the subconsciousness of another human being. Serial killer Carl Rudolph Stargher, as played with oily intensity by Vincent D'Onofrio, has been appre-hended. His final victim, however, is still missing, and she will be killed by a mechanism which causes a glass cube to fill with water at a predetermined time, unless psychologist Catherine Deane, performed by Jennifer Lopez in a surprising turn, can enter his mind and find where his victim is hidden. The Cell's perspective is not dissimilar to Milton's contention regarding the mind being its own place, and Deane discovers that Stargher's subconscious is a hell filled with its own demons, the kernel of innocence that the serial killer could have been as a child tortured by the psychological monsters of his adulthood. In this image, Stargher appears as a horned demon, yet he is a manifestation more of the id than of a literal hell. **❷** Singh began his cinematic career directing music videos for, among others, R.E.M.. That sense of mor-dant excess thrums through the imagistic splendor of The Cell, which is as much visual art as it is a film. In this scene, we see "King Stragher," the manifestation of all of the serial killer's wicked desires for brutal omnipotence over his fellow humans. **❸** Mexican director Guillermo del Toro's 2006 magical realist

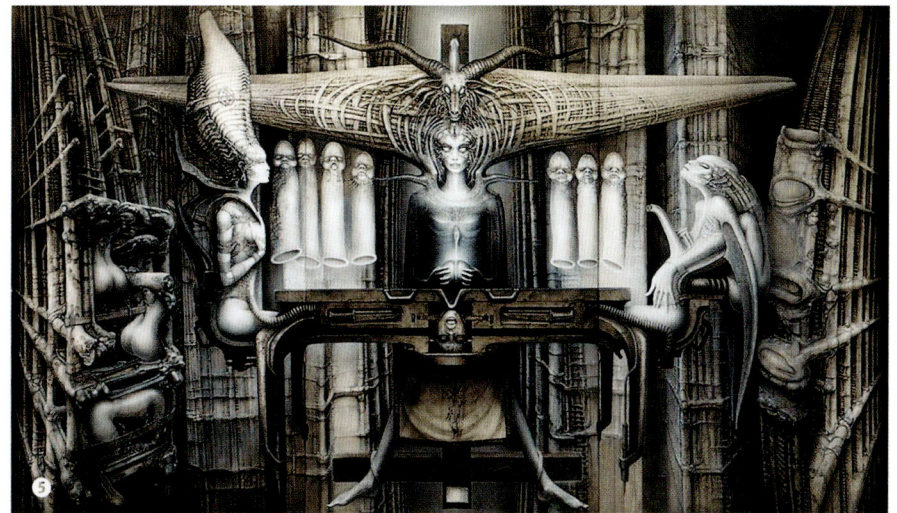

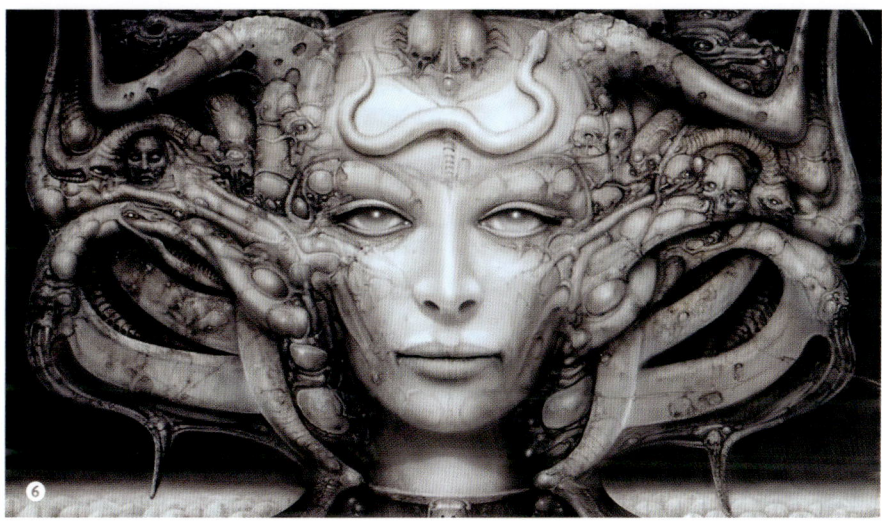

fable Pan's Labyrinth *deployed exceedingly creative costuming, special effects, and cinematography to tell a deeply disturbing narrative about good and evil in the aftermath of the Spanish Civil War. Borrowing from the idiom of the fairy tale, young Ofelia creates an intricate dream world to contrast with the reality of her cruel abuse at the hands of her Falangist stepfather. Celebrated physical actor Doug Jones memorably played the Pale Man, a freakish creature who is all waddle and loose skin, with his eyes in the palms of his hand, and who is motivated by an insatiable appetite for children.* ❹ *Doug Jones also plays the Faun in the film, presumably the Pan referenced in the title, though he is not called as such in*

the movie. True to the ethical ambiguity of satyrs in Greco-Roman mythology, the Faun's own moral status is ambivalent, though he certainly has more than a bit of the demonic (and daemonic) about him. ❺ *Few designers helped craft the artistic vocabulary of industrial horror, cyberpunk, and the postmodern gothic more than the Swiss artist H.R. Giger. Sought after for album covers and for film work, Giger imagined reality as a cold, metallic, unfeeling nightmare realm that was equally sleek and grotesque. The top picture is 1974's* The Spell II, *while the lower is a detail from* No. 250 Li I, *also painted in 1974. The title of the latter is a reference to his lover, the actress Li Tobler, as well as possibly to the succubus Lilith.*

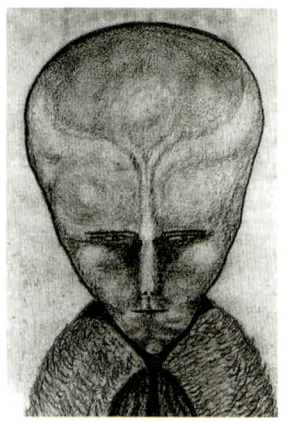

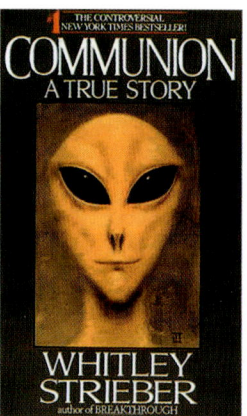

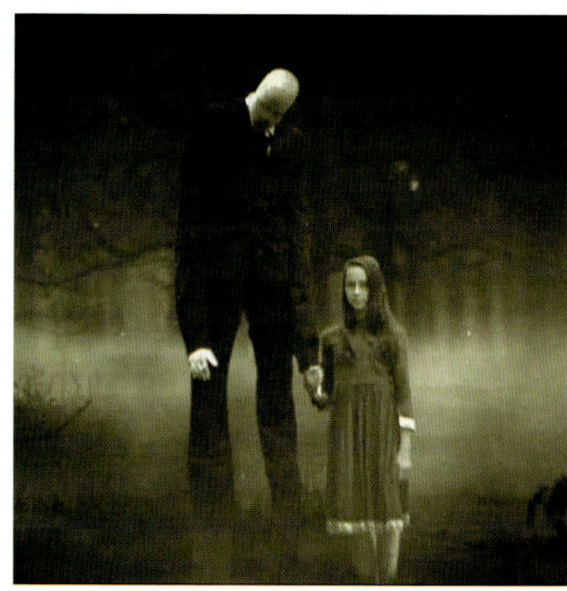

Much of the medieval narrative of demonic posses-sion—the nocturnal visitations, the sexual violation, the appearance of frightening and otherworldly beings—has been secularized into accounts of alien abduction. Other than the explanatory mechanism of the origin of their respective entities, accounts of demons and aliens are startlingly similar. The most common physiognomy for aliens in the contemporary world are the so-called Greys; short, sleek, hairless androgynous creatures with massive heads and huge almond-shaped black eyes. Much of the popularity of that genus of extraterrestri-als can be attributed to the narrative in science fiction author Whitley Strieber's supposedly nonfiction 1987 book Communion, *which in a manner not dissimilar to* Michelle Remembers, *has the author recovering repressed experiences, in this case his abduction and molestation by aliens. Ted Seth Jacobs' cover art for the book has become iconic; by comparison, examine Aleis-ter Crowley's 1917 drawing of Lam, an otherworldly, demonic entity whom he supposedly encountered.*

Conceived of by Eric Knudsen on the internet forum Something Awful, *the demonic Slenderman is an unset-tling example of the fictional interceding into actual life. An example of the internet genre of "creepypasta," a variety of constructed folkloric urban legend that web denizens invent to unsettle one another, Knudson's Slen-derman is a mysterious creature similar to the bogey-man or the Pied Piper, who lures children away to their doom. Knudsen included in his original 2009 post two Photoshopped pictures of Slenderman lurking behind children, with one photograph captioned, "Notable for being taken the day which fourteen children van-ished and for what is referred to as 'The Slender Man.' . . . Actual photograph confiscated as evidence." Slen-derman became a popular meme, his story collabo-ratively shaped by thousands of online writers until he effectively became "real." The image is from a 2017 HBO documentary entitled* Beware the Slenderman, *produced after the 2014 near-fatal stabbing of a twelve-year-old Wisconsin girl by two of her classmates, the perpetrators claiming that Slenderman had ordered them to commit murder.*

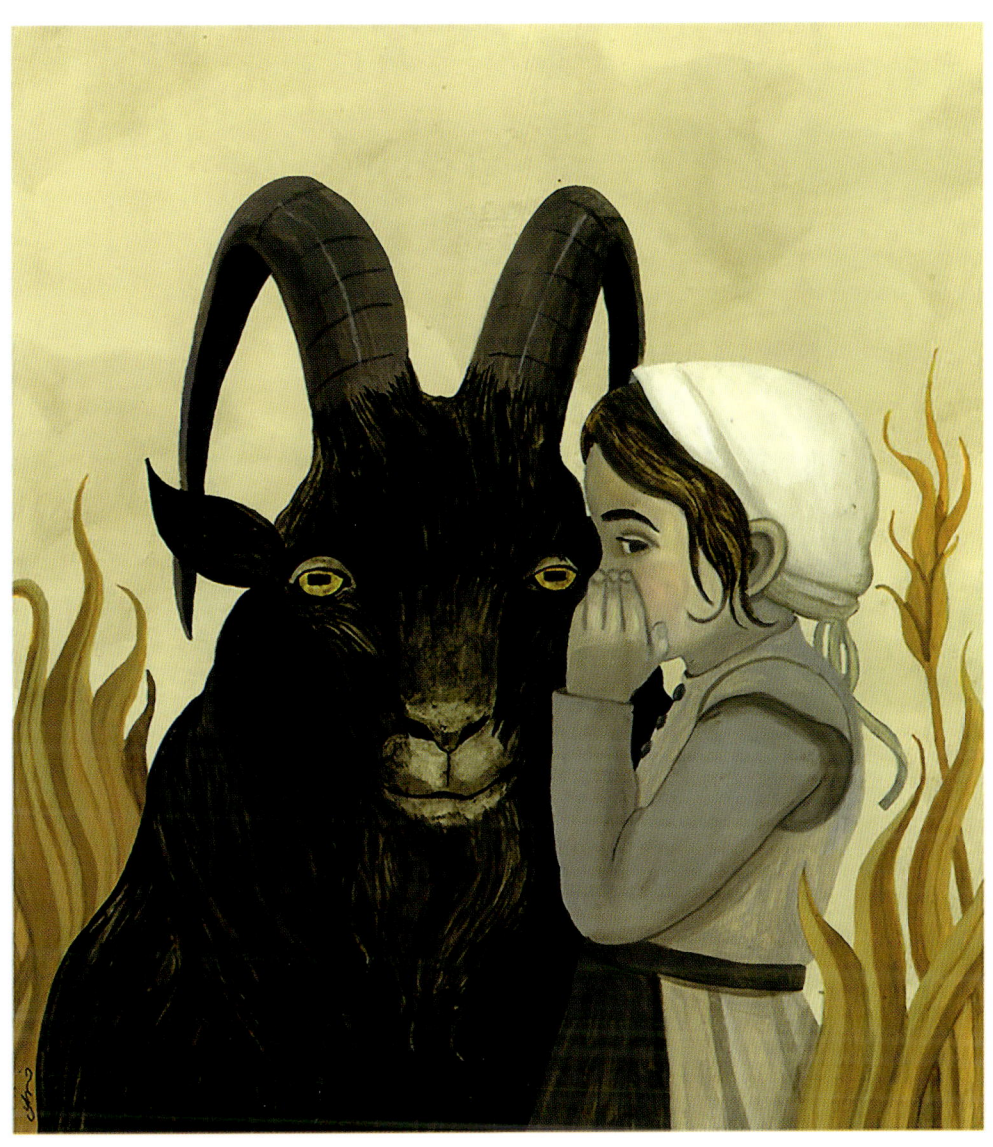

American artist Jorge Mascarenhas's painting The Goat Whisperer *is evocative of the 2015 folk horror film* The Witch: A New England Folktale *by American director Robert Eggers. Reminiscent of films like Robin Hardy's 1973 classic* The Wicker Man, *Eggers's film tells the tale of a family of seventeenth-century Massachusetts Puritans banished into the wilderness, where supernatural events seem to focus on the ominous farm goat Black Phillip. Terrifying in its execution,* The Witch *proves that sometimes our most familiar imaginings of the demonic are still imbued with a charged horror.*

OF FINAL THINGS:
THE EVER-PRESENT PROBLEM OF EVIL

saac Bashevis Singer's short story "The Last Demon," published in the 1964 anthology *Short Friday and Other Stories*, was written in his Upper West Side apartment, some seven thousand miles from the Warsaw in which he first made his name as an exemplary Yiddish stylist, penning in a language spoken by a people the vast majority of whom had just been murdered by the Nazis. Drawing from Jewish folklore and kabbalah, magical realism and surrealism, Singer's voice was distinctively his own, a contemporary author of parables that are deceptively simple, but often contain far darker truths. Though written in the idiom of the seventeenth-century shtetl, Singer's work is intimately concerned with evil in the modern world. "I, a demon, bear witness that no more demons are left," speaks the narrator of Singer's story. A solitary entity, the demon wanders the emptied Polish settlement of Tishevitz, "a godforsaken village." The demon discovers that the mikvah, the ritual bath, is empty; that the streets are deserted, that there is nobody left to tempt. "The community was slaughtered, the holy books burned, the cemetery desecrated," he laments. "There is no further need for demons."

Like any contemporary work of mature literature that seriously engages with the ethical dimension, Singer's story is haunted by the Holocaust. As an event the Holocaust acts as a rupture in our traditional theodicies, with both God and the Devil somehow dying within ovens constructed by man. "Why demons, when man himself is a demon? Why persuade to evil someone who is already convinced?" asks the narrator of Singer's story. Certainly there had been evils before, but the regimented, mechanized, rationalized, industrialized, efficient wholesale murder of millions of children, women, and men stands as a moral singularity in human history, a veritable null point that forces philosophers and theologians to not just question God (for as Fyodor Dostoevsky had noted a century before, the death of a single innocent child invalidates the Lord), but to question myths of progress, goodness, and humanity itself. Theodicy concerns itself with the question of how an omnipotent and omnibenevolent God can possibly allow evil in the world, but the Holocaust amended that traditional problem with new concerns. As the philosopher Theodor Adorno wrote in his 1951 essay "Cultural Criticism and Society":

Auschwitz irrefutably demonstrated the failure of culture. That it could happen in the midst of all the traditions of philosophy, art, and the enlightening sciences, says more than merely that these, the Spirit, was not capable of seizing and changing human beings . . . Whoever pleads for the preservation of a radically culpable and shabby culture turns into its accomplice, while those who renounce culture altogether immediately promote the barbarism, which culture reveals itself to be.

That it was the land of Beethoven and Goethe, supposedly the most cosmopolitan in the world, which committed its most evil atrocity, was not lost on Adorno. It's the paradox that the poet Paul Celan writes of in his 1945 lyric "Death Fugue," wherein a camp commander "writes in the German-born nightfall/the gold of your hair Margarete/he writes it and steps out of doors and the stars are aglitter he whistles his hounds out/he whistles his Jews off has them spade out a grave in the ground/he orders us play up for the dance." In the camps humans didn't just die, but so did a collective belief in humanity.

What then of evil in the twentieth century? And when men have taken on the mantle of the satanic so completely, is there an obscenity in speaking of something as now seemingly insignificant as demons, mere metaphors, symbols, stories, folktales? A central paradox of the Holocaust, which is already an aporia in our traditional ways of understanding, is that it simultaneously demands a response from orthodox faith as to how God could allow such evil to flourish, while also conclusively demonstrating that objective, absolute evil—cold, unfeeling, pointless, rapacious, and cruel—existed. If medieval myths of God's goodness, of God's existence, were challenged by Auschwitz, than so too were Enlightenment and Romantic myths about humanity's goodness, about the possibility of civilization itself. As journalist Lance Morrow notes in *Evil: An Investigation*, "Auschwitz disabuses us of illusions about the depths to which even an advanced civilization may sink . . . It humbles the moral and cultural pretensions of civilizations that have been heir to the Enlightenment," which is why the twentieth century's most trenchant thinkers and writers—Christian and Jewish, religious and secular—have taken evil seriously, especially because the faces of the demons themselves are now so completely human, so completely banal.

Not just Auschwitz, of course, but the whole horrific narrative of the twentieth century. There are those who with Panglossian panache and Pollyannish optimism argue that the past century was not as hellish as might appear. Linguist Steven Pinker sunnily claims that ours is "an unusually peaceful time," in his

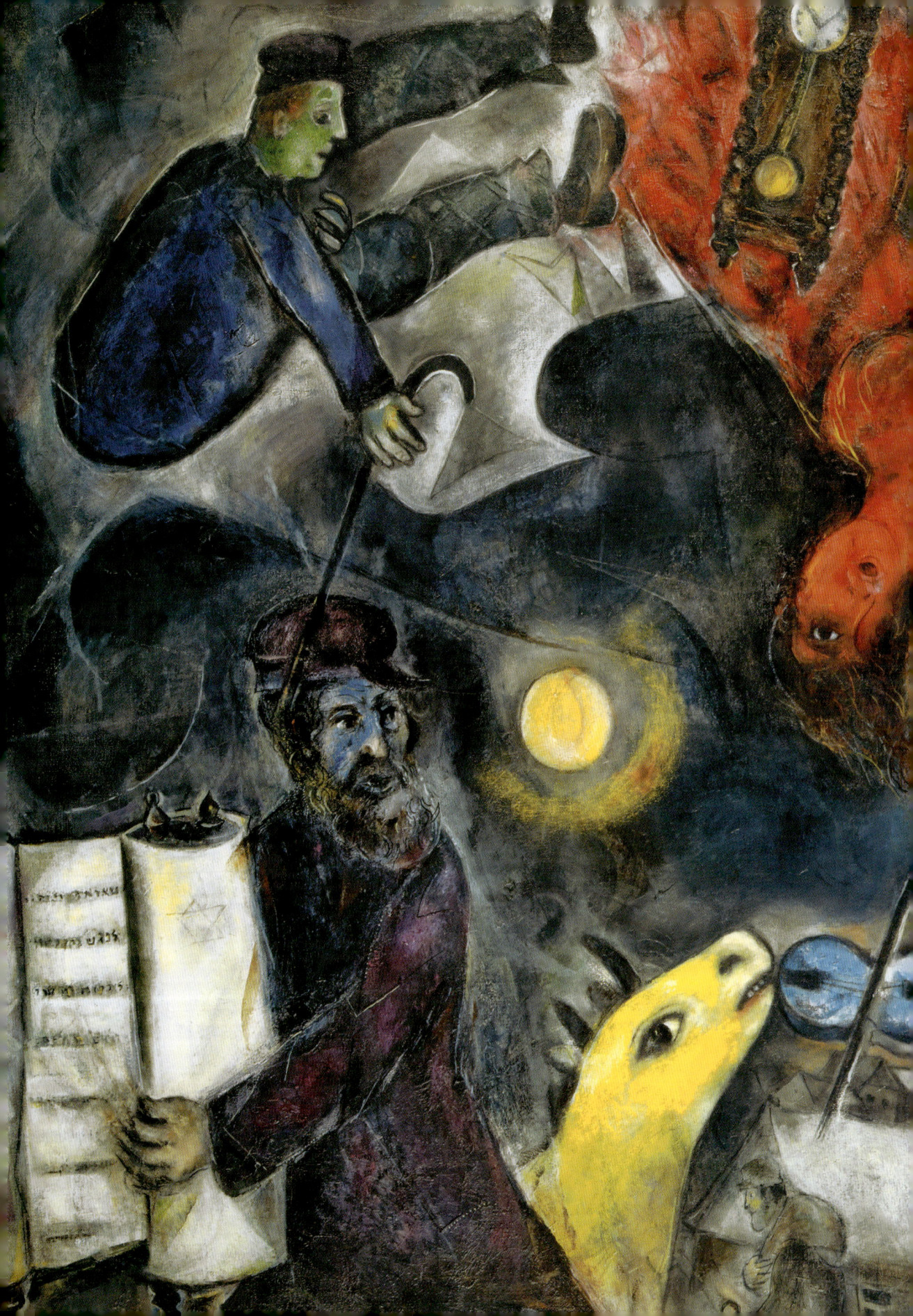

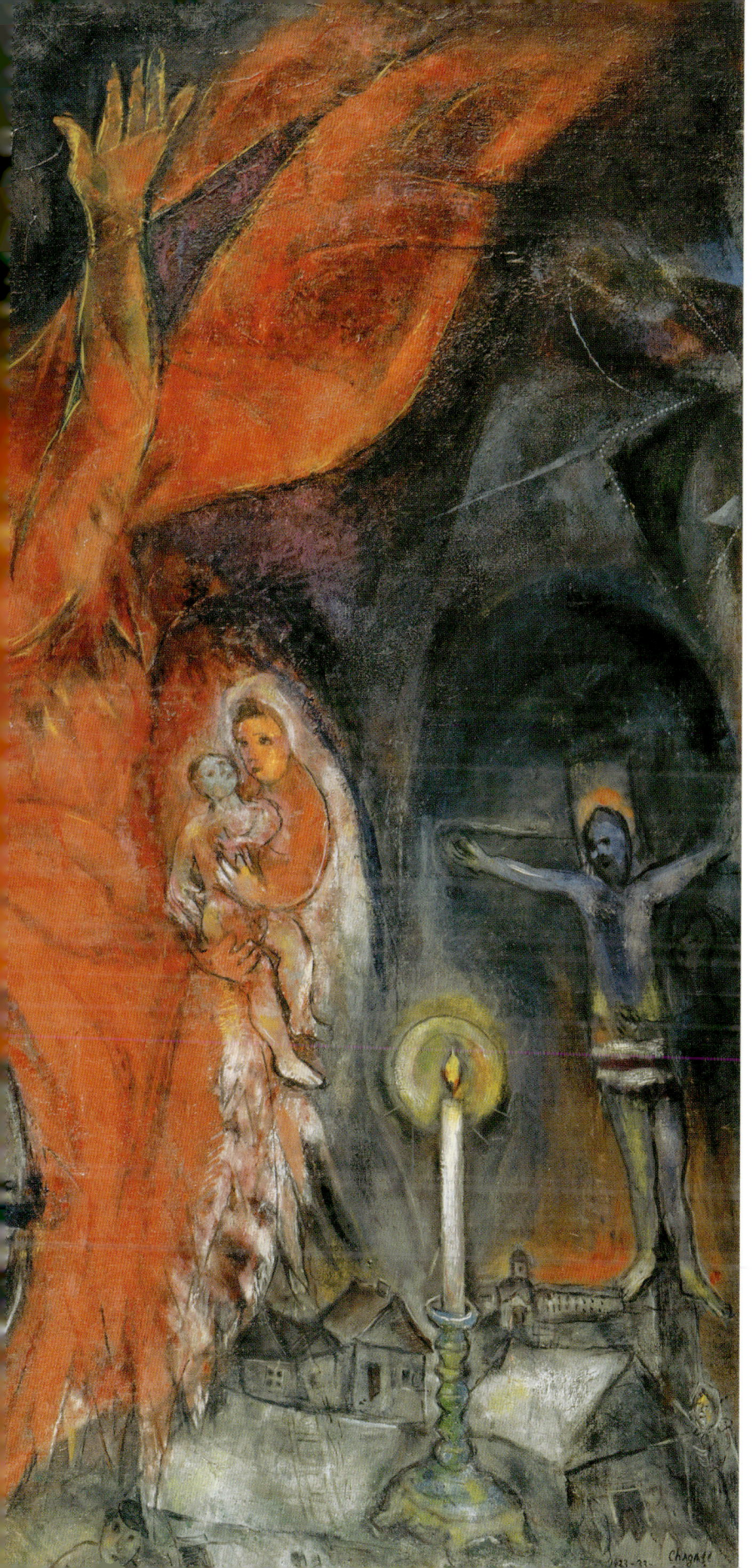

controversial study *The Better Angels of Our Nature: Why Violence Has Declined*, enthusing that the contemporary era is "an age of empathy." Jonathan Glover provides a more sobering score in *Humanity: A Moral History of the Twentieth Century*, noting that "large-scale cruelty and killing is only too familiar: the mutual slaughter of the First World War, the terror-famine of the Ukraine, the Gulag, Auschwitz, Dresden, the Burma Railway, Hiroshima, Vietnam, . . . Cambodia, Rwanda, the collapse of Yugoslavia." Pinker's approach to contemporary demonology is to deny that any problem needs to be explained, while Glover enumerates precisely what the problem is—when evil has come into such sharp focus, what rationality can be used to explain it, what vocabulary can be used to describe it? The twentieth century has only made the issue of theodicy more pressing. There are, as contradictory as they may be, multiple serious approaches to the issue of evil that were prominent in the twentieth century.

Walking through the rubble of east London in 1941, the Luftwaffe laying waste to the British capital during the horror of the Blitzkrieg, literary scholar C.S. Lewis would have been intimately aware of evil's tangible existence. During that dark season Lewis was invited by the BBC to produce a series of radio broadcasts that explained the fundamentals of orthodox Christianity to a lay audience, and the result was *Mere Christianity* (published a decade later), one of the most popular works of apologetics to be written in the modern era. Lewis's approach to the question of evil, and by proxy demonology, was estimably traditional, conservative, and conventional, but the nature of brilliant apologetics is to make the orthodox radical again. His approach to evil was Augustinian through-and-through, claiming that metaphysically the "powers which enable evil to carry on are powers given it by goodness," as he writes in *Mere Christianity*. Philosophically the Augustinian position, holding as it does to the radical monotheism of God's being, is as respectable to the status quo as it is often disappointing to those who see in evil something radically other, yet Lewis's poetic powers don't skirt an accurate description of the experience of evil. Lewis writes that "evil is a parasite, not an original thing," and there's something crucial in the wisdom which holds that wickedness is fundamentally about negation, about nothing.

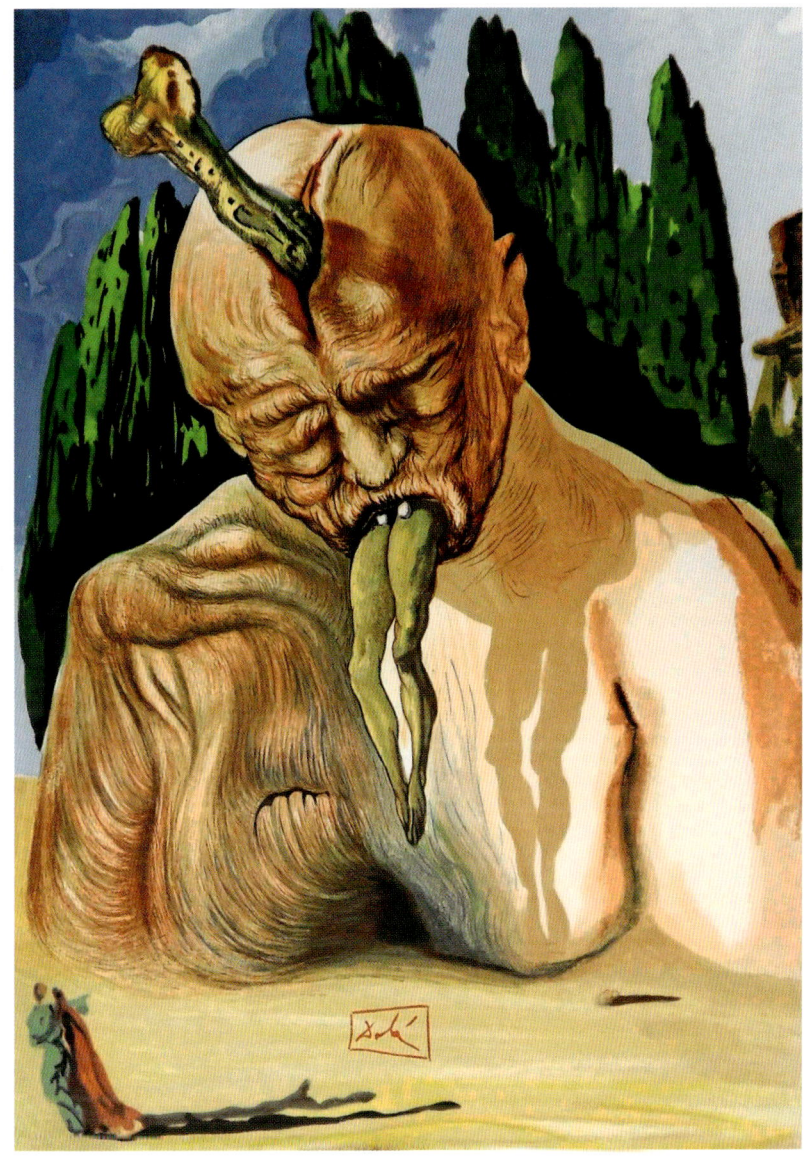

*Salvador Dali's mature works evidence a rediscovery of his youthful Cathol-
icism, as the surrealist increasingly engaged religious themes. In the lead-up
to the seven-hundredth anniversary of Dante's birth, the Italian government
charged the Spaniard with the fashioning of a hundred paintings in honor of
the event. A Devil Logician, painted around 1960, is Dali's depiction of Lucifer; the legs of one of the traitors tortured in the ninth circle of hell appearing
nothing so much like the tongue of the fallen angel. Particularly interesting
is the title for this painting of a decaying, deformed, decomposing Satan. By
implicating logic itself, Dali condemns the rectilinear positivism of the contemporary age, the unfeeling technocracy whose ultimate conclusion was the
concentration camp and the nuclear blast.*

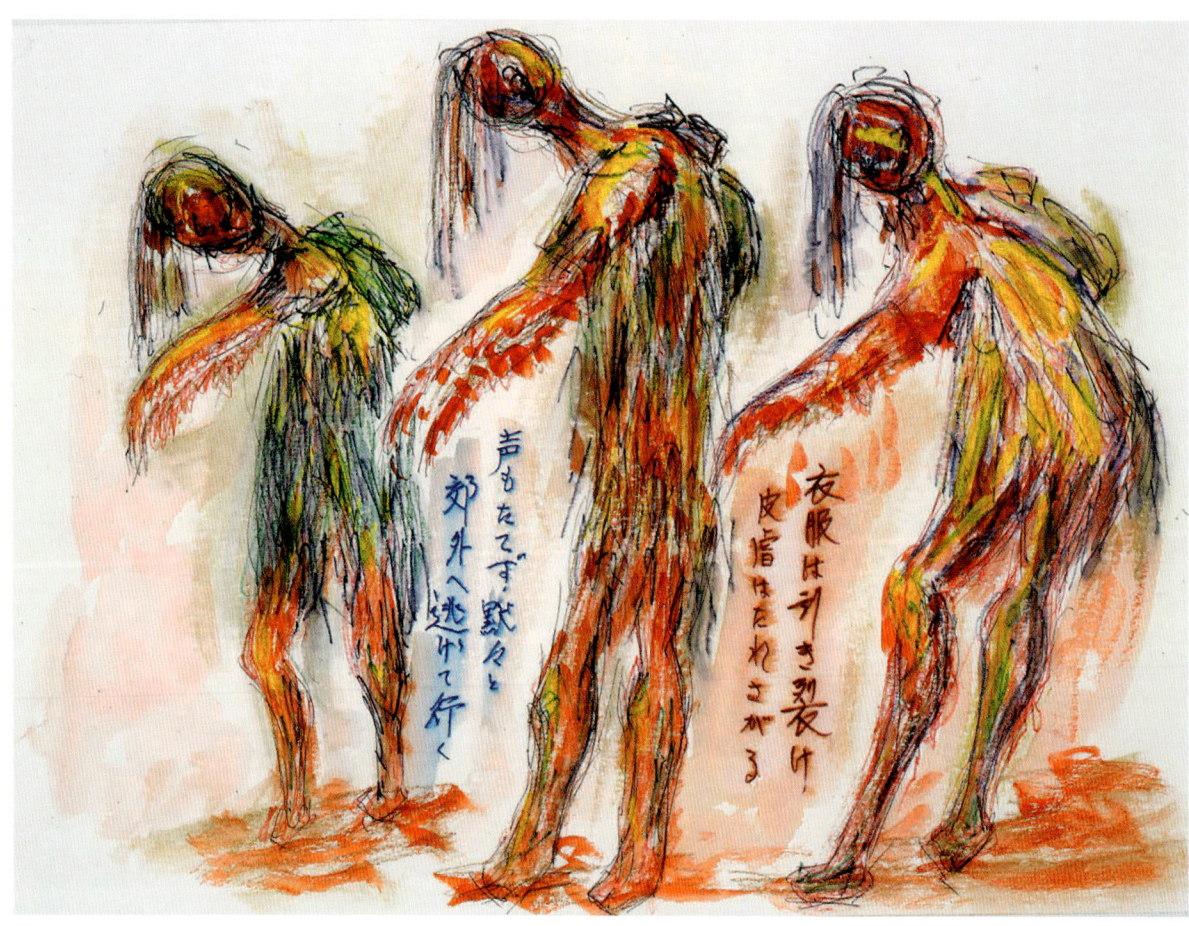

声もたてず 黙々と 郊外へ逃げて行く

衣服は引き裂け 皮膚はたれさがる

ABOVE

In anticipation of marking the thirtieth anniversary of the bombing of Hiroshima, the Japanese Broadcasting Corporation began collecting, among other effects, survivor testimonials that included artwork made by those who lived through the nuclear attacks. Of arguably limited military importance, the incineration of a largely civilian population marks the horrific conclusion to history's most horrific conflagration. The invention of atomic weapons is indicative both of humanity's capability for brilliance, and our insatiable appetite for destruction. Artist Kichisuke Yoshimura, whose painting is held at the Hiroshima Peace Memorial Museum, recalls that "On the riverbank I saw figures that seemed to be from another world. Ghost-like, their hair falling over their faces, their clothes ripped to shreds, their skin hanging. A cluster of these injured persons was moving wordlessly toward the outskirts." A cruel irony of modernity is that while scientific thinking expelled belief in hell, apocalypse, and demons, modern technology willed those very concepts into existence.

As much an imaginative writer as a theologian, Lewis's 1942 novel *The Screwtape Letters* provides some of the most poetic and emotionally satisfying explanations of evil from the past century, regardless of one's personal faith. An epistolary novel, *The Screwtape Letters* records the correspondence between the titular senior demon and his nephew Wormwood, as the former tutors his charge in how to tempt a man into damnation. Though his theology was thoroughly traditional, Lewis's depiction of contemporary evil was often startlingly modern. Screwtape, in a line that evokes the train cars bringing humans from Prague, and Warsaw, and Berlin to Auschwitz, Dachau, and Bergen-Belsen, tells his nephew, "We want cattle who can finally become food," a chilling evocation of the rapacious consumptions of evil. This hunger is about filling a void that can never be satiated, the consumptive illogic of modernity pushed to its more disturbing extreme. Russell argues that Lewis's "most original contribution was the suggestion that demons are motivated by both fear and hunger . . . they roam the world seeking human souls to devour in a terrified effort to fill the famished void . . . But no amount of eating can mitigate their infinite emptiness," so that the ultimate conclusion of modern, nihilistic utilitarianism, as it runs through the sweatshop, the gulag, the concentration camp, the nuclear blast, and climate change, is apocalypse itself.

Writing in a 1961 preface to a new edition of *The Screwtape Letters*, Lewis said:

The greatest evil is not now done in those sordid "dens of crime" that Dickens loved to paint. It is not done even in concentration camps and labour camps. In those we see its final result. But it is conceived and ordered (moved, seconded, carried, and minuted) in clean, carpeted, warmed, and well-lighted offices, by quiet men with white collars and cut fingernails and smooth-shaven cheeks who do not need to raise their voice. Hence, naturally enough, my symbol for Hell is something like the bureaucracy of a police state or the offices of a thoroughly nasty business concern.

Tellingly Lewis notes that his is "the Managerial Age." Such a demonology merges the study of devils with anthropology (in the theological sense of that latter word), for in the rejection of all of the symbology that we associate with the satanic—the horns, the forked tongue and tail, the cloven hoofs—there is not a rejection of the idea of the demon itself per se. To the contrary, when the grinning hellmouth becomes the sparkling smile of the tyrant, when the cloven hoofs the bluchers of the managerial bureaucrat, the horns the neatly parted hair of the politician or businessman, there is a deadly serious understanding of what precisely is at stake when it comes to evil. Notably this awareness that evil can often be smiling, that the truest demon appears not as such, doesn't require the Christianity of a Lewis, but marks any sober analysis of evil in the contemporary context.

Lewis's preface prefigures some of the same conclusions of the philosopher Hannah Arendt in her infamous account *Eichmann in Jerusalem: An Account on the Banality of Evil*, published in 1964. A secular Jewish existentialist, Arendt herself was a refugee from Hitler's Germany when the *New Yorker* commissioned her in 1963 to report on the war crimes trial of Adolph Eichmann then occurring in Jerusalem. One of the architects of the Nazi "Final Solution" of the Holocaust, Eichmann had been responsible for the deportation of eighty thousand Moravian Jews into the ghettos of Poland (who were later liquidated), he was present at the 1942 Wannsee Conference wherein the details of the Holocaust were planned with exacting detail by Nazi high command, he subsequently oversaw the large-scale deportation of Jews to Treblinka, Belzec, and Sobibor, and he personally oversaw the extermination of Hungary's Jews, making him directly responsible for the deaths of 564,000 children, women, and men. All of this Eichmann perpetrated with a lifting of a pen, with the filing of paper.

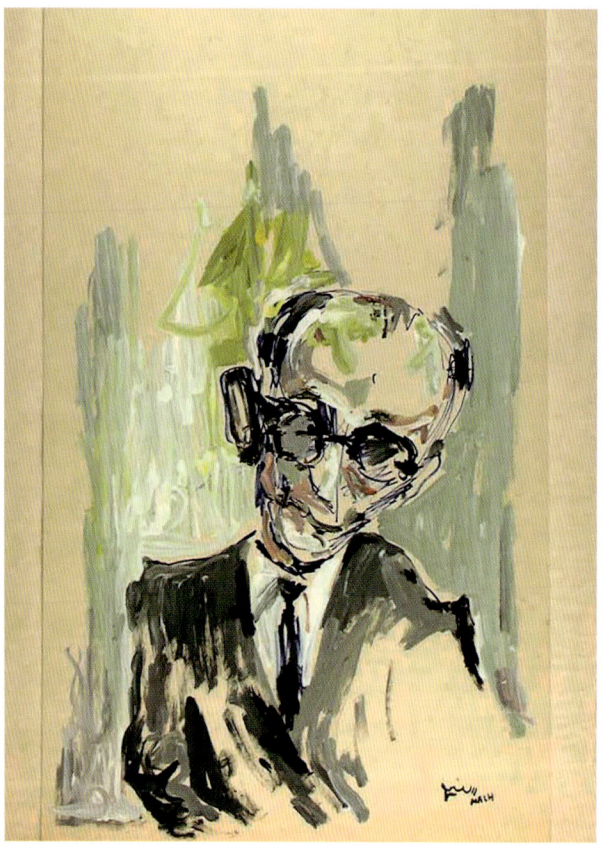

Israeli artist Jona Mach's 1961 composition Adolf Otto Eichmann, *held by the Yad Vashem Art Museum in Jerusalem, depicts the defendant while on trial, seated within a bulletproof glass box, an attempt to shackle the devil. The sheer ordinariness of Eichmann is a demonstration of Hanna Arendt's contention about the banality of evil.*

Eichmann evaded capture after the war (even while he was detained for a period by the Allies, who were unaware of his true identity), and had lived for the following decades under an assumed identity in Buenos Aires, Argentina, until he was apprehended by Israeli Mossad agents in 1960 and sent back to Jerusalem. During the war, Eichmann had been instrumental in preparing the logistics for the forced expulsion of Jews in Nazi-occupied Europe, and had dispassionately switched to the details of genocide when it was decided that the Reich would exterminate Jews in the camps. A man devoid of any particular intelligence, creativity, attractiveness, or anything else that would make him exemplary, Eichmann was directly implicated in the murder of six million people. When Arendt saw Eichmann in Jerusalem, ensconced within a glass cube to protect him from would-be assassins during the proceedings, she noted that he looked as remarkable as a "dry cleaner." Photographs show an unassuming, balding, skinny, bespectacled man in an ill-fitting suit; a completely uninteresting and average person for whom there appears to be nothing of the demonic.

"The trouble with Eichmann," Arendt noted, "was precisely that so many were like him, and that the many were neither perverted nor sadistic, that they were, and still are, terribly and terrifyingly normal." Indeed the Israeli team of psychologists that examined Eichmann to see if he was fit to stand trial concluded that he showed no signs of mental illness or of a personality disorder, so that even those potential justifications for his actions would be inadequate. Commenting on his average (or even below average) intelligence, his reversion to cliché, his mealymouthed defenses about following orders, and his pathetic need to belong to something that he saw as bigger than himself, Arendt coined the phrase "banality of evil" to describe the managerial bureaucrat who personally oversaw the murder of more than half a million people (and was of course implicated in the deaths of more than eleven million more). Morrow explains that "Arendt's phrase seeks to orient us to a new configuration of evil as . . . banal as Adolf Eichmann's bureaucratic routinization of death: production quotas, train schedules, paperwork."

Long criticized by those who felt that she had minimized the Nazis' crimes, Arendt's simple and salient point about the prosaicness of evil still remains integral. To observe the banality of evil isn't to abolish the concept—to the contrary—it's to acknowledge that evil exists everywhere, and that the most seemingly average of people are capable of it. In a letter to the scholar of kabbalah Gershom Scholem, Arendt wrote that "Today I think that evil in every instance is only extreme, never radical: it has no depth, and therefore has nothing demonic about it. Evil can lay waste the entire world, like a fungus, growing rampant on the surface." Though Lewis was a believer and Arendt was an atheist, both concurred on the strange and dangerous normalcy of evil, the way in which modernity had unmasked demons not as incomprehensible monsters, but perhaps as our friends and neighbors. There are other approaches to the question of evil that emerged in the aftermath of Auschwitz, including a variety of radical theological ones (associated with figures such as Gabriel Vahanian, William Hamilton, and Thomas J.J. Altizer), which took very seriously some of the earliest injunctions about the nature of evil (and perhaps the origin of demons), and that acknowledged the bifurcated nature of divinity itself, the darkness and the light that exists within that entity, that being, that symbol that we've elected to call God.

Rabbi Richard Rubenstein was one of the central proponents of exploring how we talk about God in relation to the horrors of the twentieth century, writing in his 1966 *After Auschwitz: Radical Theology and Contemporary Judaism* that he felt "compelled to say that we live in the time of the 'death of God.' This is more a statement about man and his culture than about God . . . When I say we live in the time of the death of God, I mean that the thread uniting God and man, heaven and earth, has been broken." Notably the idea of good and evil remain, for what does Auschwitz, what does Hiroshima, what does Verdun, and Dresden, and My Lai, and Abu Ghraib demonstrate other than the existence of visceral, objective, tangible, obvious, and real evil? Far from pointing to some rarefied abstraction existing beyond good and evil, they've proven in the most comprehensible manner possible—in our souls—that evil exists, even while both God and his angels, Satan and his demons, seem more poetry than reality. That a Christian like Lewis, an atheist like Arendt, and a nonconformist Jew like Rubenstein could, in part, point to similar conclusions affirms that we're beyond theology, we're beyond mere poetics. There is something of the wicked behind the veil, and the language that we use to describe it, the names we give the demons, is contingent and relative. Our words fail us, but that something is there—something often quite close to us—can't be ignored.

To ask if demons are real or not is the wrong question; it's like trying to make an equation out of the relationship of truth and beauty, or to attempt and locate the human soul in the pineal gland. Like all sacred and fallen things, demons point to some reality beyond us, they are more than simply real in the way that other things are. But despite their abstraction, despite their ephemeralness, traces of them are easily apparent if you're looking. When SS-*Obergruppenführer* Reinhard Heydrich called a group of Nazi functionaries to the Berlin suburb of Wannsee in January 1942, the group met in a mansion built in the style of a Renaissance Italian country house that overlooked a pristine lake. There Heydrich spoke to a group that included SS-*Gruppenführer* and head of the SS Race and Settlement Office Otto Hoffman, SS-*Gruppenführer* and Gestapo Chief Heinrich Müller, and SS-*Oberführer* Karl Eberhard Schöngarth, along with a dozen other participants (Eichmann took the minutes). A buffet was set up, cognac and brandy were served. Cigars were distributed. Participants remembered it as a convivial affair. And in a ninety-minute presentation, Heydrich explained the precise and exact manner in which the Reich would murder the remainder of Europe's Jews. At the conclusion of the war, Eichmann told a friend that "I will leap into my grave laughing because the feeling that I have five million human beings on my conscience is for me a source of extraordinary satisfaction." So, you ask—are there demons?

NEXT SPREAD

Written, produced, and animated in 1973 in a Czechoslovakia then suffering under Soviet invasion, the Polish-Jewish illustrator Roland Topor's Fantastic Planet *is an encapsulation of demonic themes throughout the twentieth century, albeit in sublimated form. A science-fiction allegory,* Fantastic Planet *tells the story of humans on an alien world who live according to the machinations of the gargantuan Traags, who are effectively elder gods. While there is nothing supernatural in* Fantastic Planet, *the perennial demonic themes of domination and subjugation still endure, even in interstellar space. This strange being of Topor's is perhaps as absurd as it is disturbing, a pithy enough description of the jaundiced twentieth century as well.*

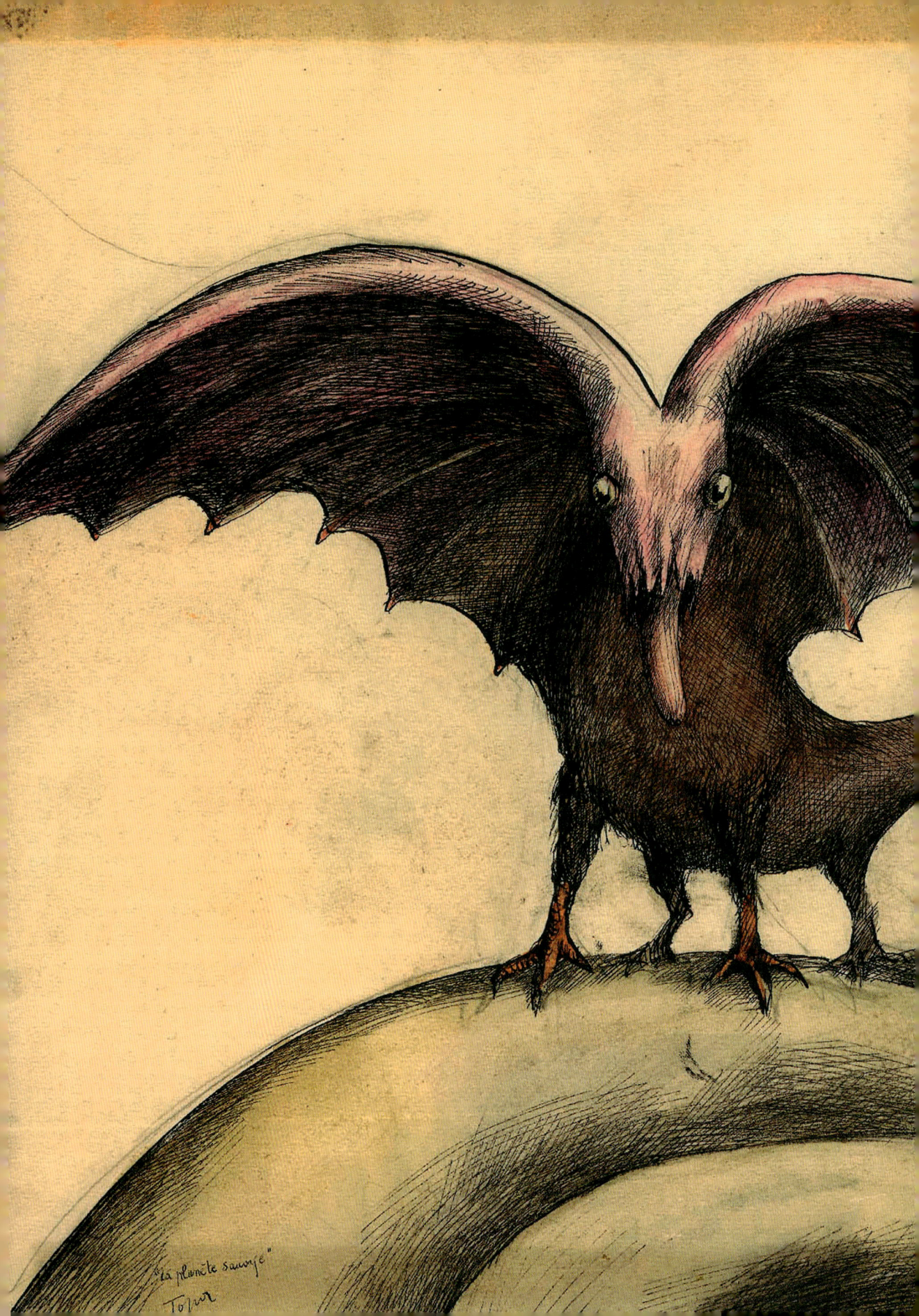

"La planète sauvage"
Topor

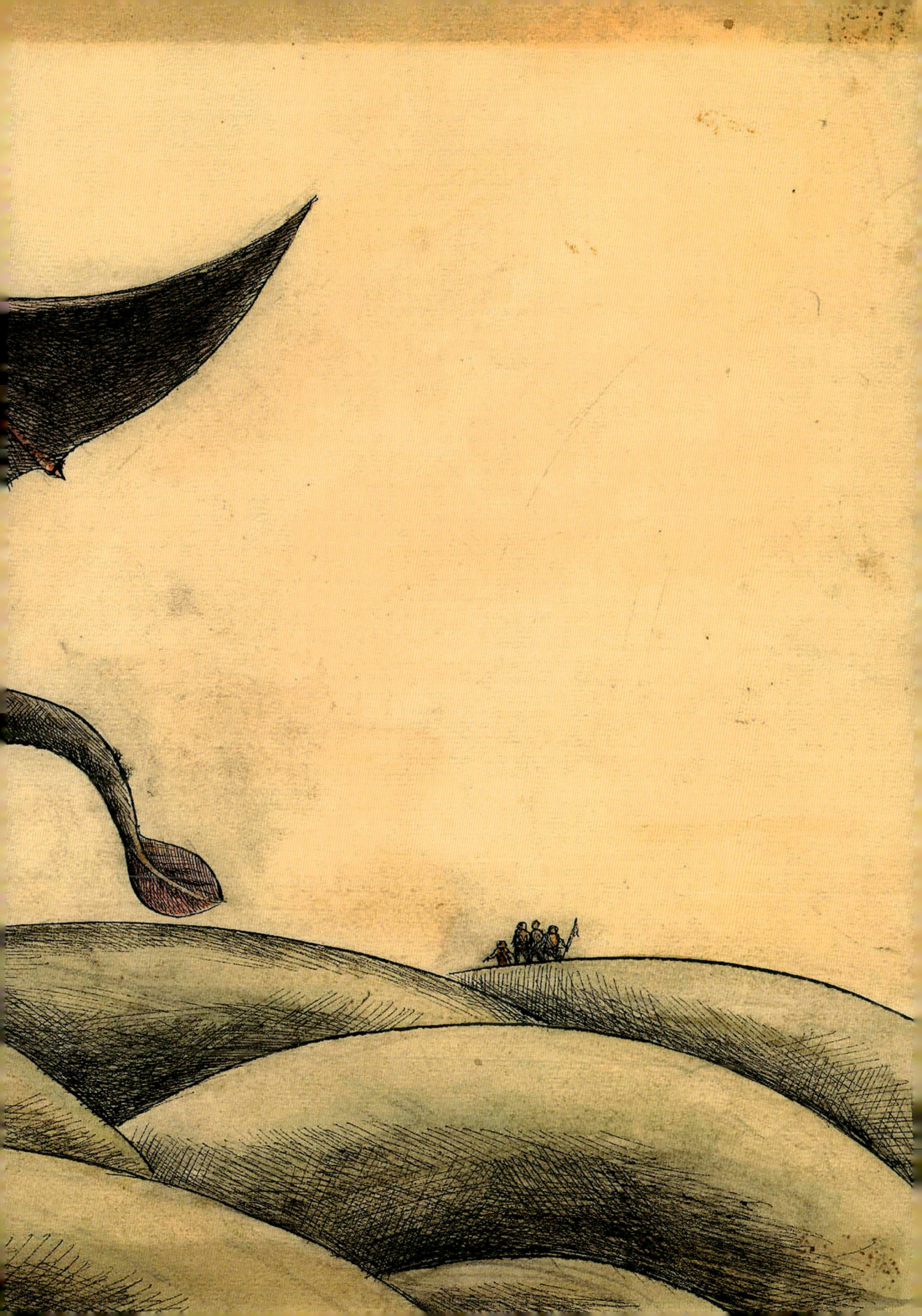

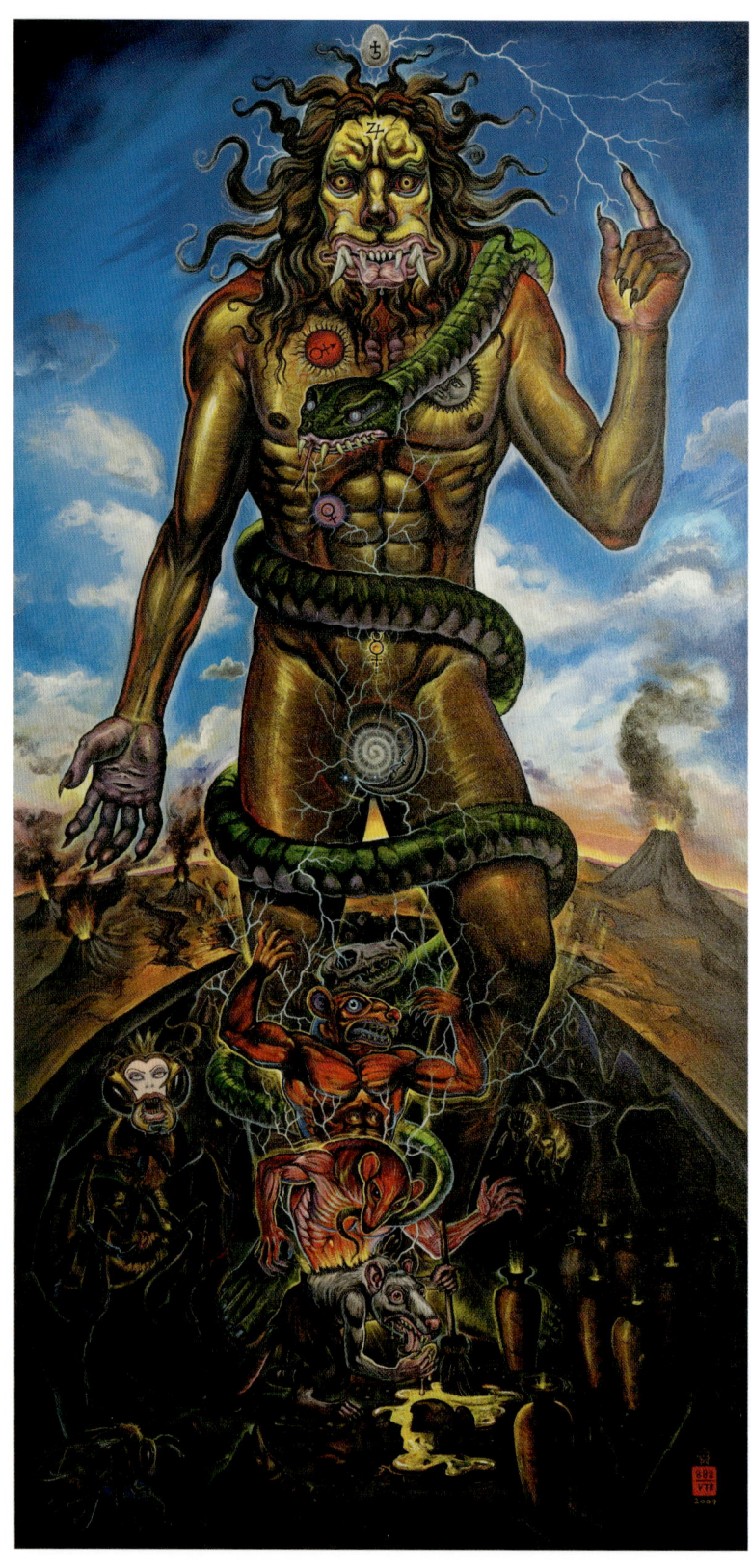

CONCLUSION

What of Demonology Today?

On a sunny December day in 2016, a twenty-eight-year-old struggling actor with a history of drug and alcohol abuse drove the little under four hundred miles from his home in the Piedmont of North Carolina to the bucolic Washington, D.C., neighborhood of Chevy Chase, where he fired three shots from an AR-15 into a popular hipster pizzeria. Storming into the establishment, which he and a growing contingent of online conspiracy theorists believed was the nexus of an underground ring that involved some of the United States's most powerful politicians, the man hoped to uncover the dungeons where he had been told girls and boys were being horrifically abused by a coven of Satan worshipers. In the back of the pizzeria, all that he found was an office; a computer that the manager worked on, and filing cabinets with employee information. After his arrest, he told a reporter for the *New York Times* that "the intel on this wasn't a hundred percent."

CNN anchor Chris Cuomo referred to the assailant as "either mentally ill or really stupid;" four years later and a *Washington Post* column by Max Boot, which was about the rise in similar online conspiracy theories, was entitled "Welcome to the United States of 'Idiocracy.'" Cuomo and Boot aren't wrong, believing that an utterly prosaic restaurant—the same sort that in any number of American towns families gather after work or school or the game—houses a satanic coven is stupid and silly and puerile. Fantasists who trade in such urban legends are easy to mock; men and women who in a desperate search for meaning in a society where so little is granted have chosen to fall for such obviously ridiculous stories. Those who knowingly spread such disinformation, for economic incentive or political power, deserve nothing but our scorn and opprobrium. But while the fantasy that compelled a North Carolina man to drive to a Washington, D.C., pizzeria in the hopes of freeing children in bondage is silly, stupid, and puerile, it's also incredibly dangerous. The demonization of whole segments of society has only increased over the past decades, and if the history of demonology has taught us anything, it's how deep the precipice might be. Whatever motivated that man with the AR-15 into potentially shooting up a restaurant, he seemed to be spurred by a genuine belief that what he was doing was good. There's a crucial observation here—when it comes to being haunted by demons, it's a perilously thin line between thinking you're fighting them and actually being possessed by them.

As I was finishing *Pandemonium*, the fruits of such satanic paranoia manifested in a violent assault on the U.S. Capitol itself, wherein (among several divergent contingents), those who shared in the pizzeria assailant's delusion hoped to execute lawmakers upon impromptu scaffolds, an echo of America's darkest past. Such paranoia resulted in the closest that the United States has ever come to a coup, perpetrated by men and women who believed that they were combatting demons, and who (to my eyes), paradoxically proliferated their own profound evil instead. "America has been in love with the dark at almost every stage of its history, eager to view its enemies as satanic," writes W. Scott Poole in *Satan in America: The Devil We Know*. "A country such as the United States, deeply infused with a religious sense of its identity and mission, easily slipped into the tendency of rendering its enemies, foreign and domestic, as diabolical...." As I wrote captions for the final chapter, distracted by images on television playing out only a few miles from where I live—marauding crowds storming through the Capitol, smearing feces on its walls and looking for representatives and senators to lynch—I couldn't help but think that I was witnessing evil.

At least one motivating argument of *Pandemonium* has been that there is a certain theological lexicon—words like "wicked," "sinful," "evil," and "demonic"—which have a spiritual, ethical, political, and intellectual utility. I firmly believe that when we abandon such a vocabulary, whatever our own personal theologies may be, we lose the ability to properly designate certain things that need to be understood honestly and with clear eyes. "A gulf has opened up in our culture between the visibility of evil and the intellectual resources available for coping with it," writes critic Andrew Delbanco in *The Death of Satan: How Americans Have Lost Their Sense of Evil*. "The repertoire of evil has never been richer," he claims, "Yet never have our responses been so weak. We have no language for connecting our inner lives with the horrors that pass before our eyes in the outer world." I largely agree with Delbanco, wishing that more would bluntly identify the litany of horrors that have become so commonplace—the imprisoning of migrant children in cages, the obscene gulf between the rich and the rest, the plague that at the time of this writing has killed a half-million of my countrymen, and the apocalyptic threat of climate change—as precisely what they are. Demonic.

When Delbanco says that we have no language for the demonic, surely he means those like himself—educated, secular, urban. Plenty of people in this country have the word "satanic" in their lexicon, and they tend to direct it toward people like Delbanco (and myself). Which is the cruel reality of the lexicon of evil; an argument can be made toward its epistemological and ethical utility, but an honest accounting of history demonstrates that those words themselves are frequently used to further evil by those who think that they're acting with the best

PREVIOUS SPREAD
Drawing from both classical iconography and Western esotericism, American painter Christopher Ulrich's pop surrealism presents intimations of a distinctly postmodern apocalypse, where epistemological relativism and the digital revolution conspire together to bring about the demise of truth itself. His Aeon, painted at the turn of this century, presents an image as if from Revelation, but as distinctly filtered through the madness and horror of our own time.

NEXT SPREAD
Hieronymus Bosch's triptych The Garden of Earthly Delights, *painted between 1490 and 1510. At the top of the right panel, a fiery cityscape, collapsed and burning skyscrapers, twisted steel I-beams and crumbling concrete, the haze of nuclear fallout across the skyline of a once-mighty and modern metropolis. In the flames emerging from collapsed buildings we see Manhattan on fire, we see London burnt to the ground, a harbinger of the apocalypse, once the realm of myth and poetry now literalized by technology.*

of intentions. *Pandemonium* is certainly filled with examples of what the logical conclusion of demonization is, whether it's in the pogroms instigated by those who believed in the blood libel, the auto-da-fé of the Reformation witch hunts, or the gas chambers of the Holocaust. "Charles Baudelaire was wrong. The devil's greatest trick is not to convince us that he does not exist," writes Poole. "It is, instead, to convince us that he lives in our enemies; that he surrounds us, and that he must be destroyed, no matter the cost, no matter the collateral damage." An uncomfortable fact of history is that where people see demons, they will soon burn people as demons—the ultimate ironic victory of Satan, perhaps.

That I can't help but see a whiff of the demonic in the actions of those who would piously intone that it is they who are fighting what is satanic can't help but be a bit ironic. *"I'm not the demon! You're the demon!"* Certainly, there are important lessons to keep in mind about hubris and humility in this regard. Thus we have a contradiction, and a fearsome one at that—how do we preserve a vocabulary that properly identifies evil without becoming perpetrators of it ourselves? A judicious accounting of the historical record will show this to not be a particularly new problem; it will also show that there has yet to be a solution. If we completely abandon those words that properly convey the enormity of everything from the Holocaust to nuclear war—words like "evil," "satanic," and "demonic"—we risk falling into a latitudinarian relativism, a wishy-washy capitulation to wickedness that refuses to properly grapple with the boot on our necks. At the same time, if we're zealous and indiscriminate in the application of those words, we risk becoming exactly what we're claiming to be fighting against. How to chart a course between the Scylla and Charybdis of relativism and absolutism has always been the central enigma of such ethical engagement.

"Evil," you see, is very real, whatever we call it. Being able to properly name the demons that bedevil us has always been the central concern of any legitimate demonology. "Evil as I see it is indeed metaphysical," writes critic Terry Eagleton in *On Evil*, "in the sense that it takes up an attitude toward being as such, not just toward this or that bit of it. Fundamentally, it wants to annihilate the lot of it." If true evil is the desire to obliterate existence, to "annihilate the lot of it," then our world, perched between ecological collapse and the ever-present reality of potential nuclear armageddon, can't quite afford to abandon the concept of evil at this particular juncture. Jeffrey Burton Russell argues in *Mephistopheles: The Devil in the Modern World* that the demonic "has been defined as the spirit that seeks to negate and destroy," and we'd be foolish to pretend that such a force isn't real, regardless of how we parse its ontological particulars. Yet one particular point on which we must steadfastly be careful and precise about isn't *whether or not we should* apply such a word as "demonic," but *how we should* apply it. Since this neologism of demonic poetics is concerned with language as much as it is with metaphysics, maybe the solution is less one of theology than of grammar. Of "demons" and the "demonic"—when it comes to applying those words to our fellow humans, let us eschew the former even while begrudgingly admitting that the latter is sometimes appropriate. When confronting evil in this epoch of apocalypse, so much may ultimately depend on being able to tell the difference between a noun and an adjective.

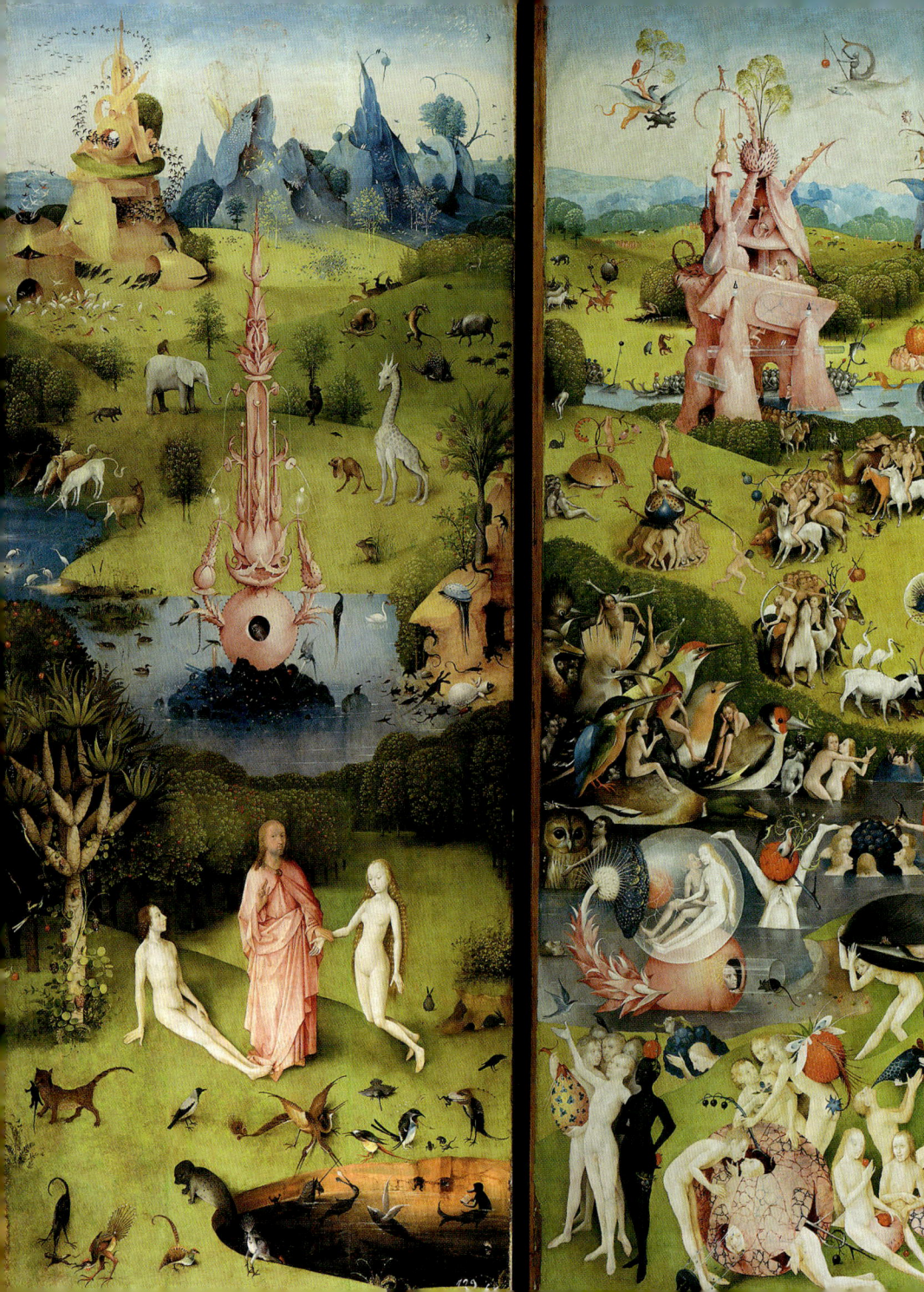

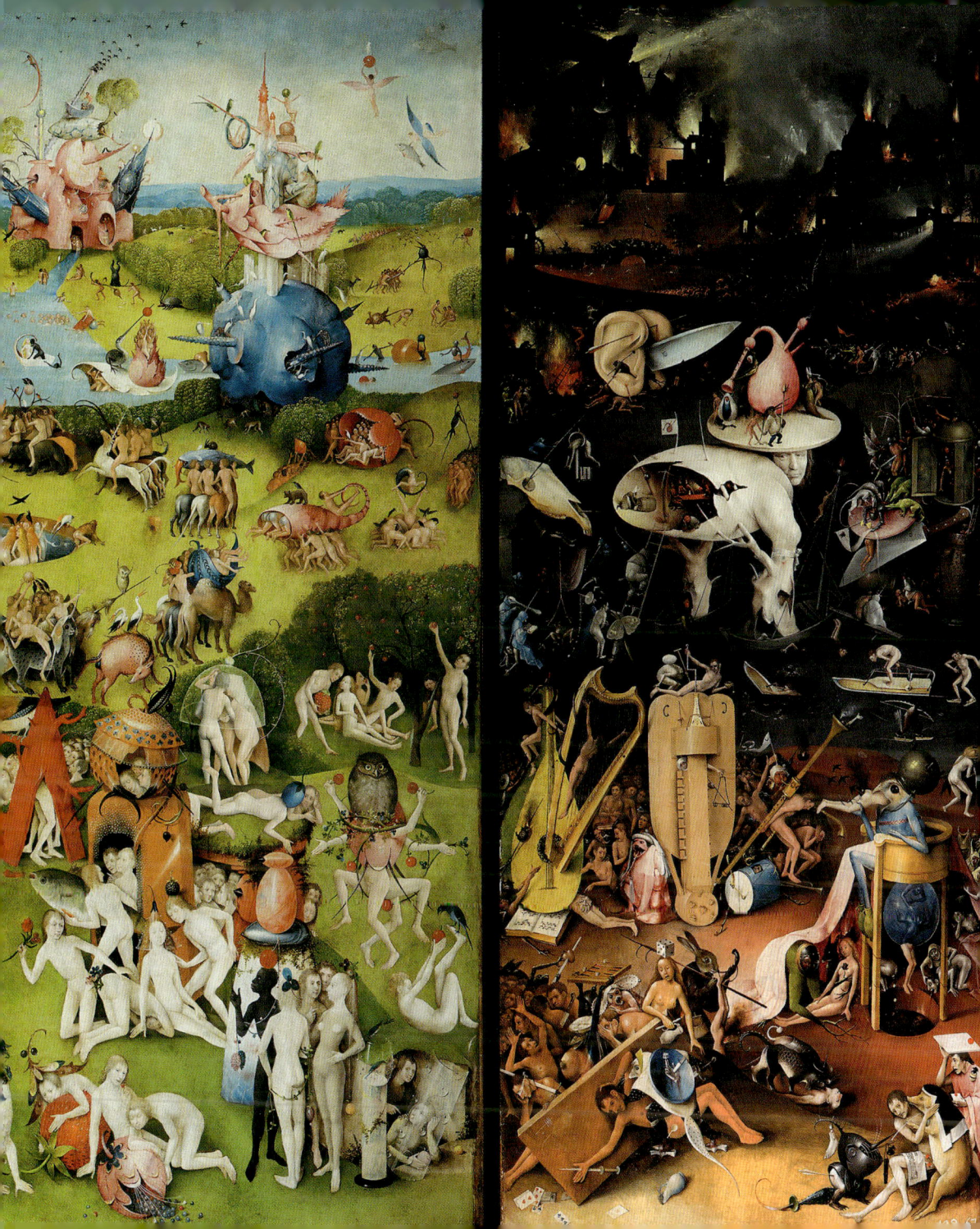

BIOGRAPHY

Ed Simon is an author of several books and a staff-writer for the literary site The Millions. Simon has a PhD in English, and is an expert on the literature and religion of the Renaissance and Reformation. His work has appeared in *The Atlantic*, *The Paris Review Daily*, *The Washington Post*, and *The New York Times*, among dozens of others. He is most recently the author of *Printed in Utopia: The Renaissance's Radicalism* and *An Alternative History of Pittsburgh*.

ACKNOWLEDGEMENTS

Thanks are owed to my editor Rodolphe Lachat, as well as to my literary agent Akin Akinwumi, both of whom had the vision to help see this project come to fruition. Acknowledgment must also be made to the numerous literary critics, historians, theologians, and philosophers whose primary scholarship made *Pandemonium* possible. Finally, I must acknowledge the love and support of my wife and son, the most important things in my life.

CREDITS

Pandemonium

Text: Ed Simon
Cernunnos logo design: Mark Ryden
Book design: Benjamin Brard

Front cover : *A Rare Summary of the Entire Magical Art by the Most Famous Masters of this Art*, 1775
Back cover: *Le Dictionnaire infernal*, by Louis Breton, 1863

Library of Congress Control Number: 2021933722

ISBN: 978-1-4197-5638-2
eISBN: 978-1-64700-389-0

Printed and bound in China
10 9 8 7

Abrams books are available at special discounts when purchased in quantity for premiums and promotions as well as fundraising or educational use. Special editions can also be created to specification. For details, contact specialsales@abramsbooks.com or the address below.

Abrams® is a registered trademark of Harry N. Abrams, Inc.

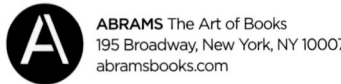

ABRAMS The Art of Books
195 Broadway, New York, NY 10007
abramsbooks.com

ABRAMS is represented in the UK and Europe by Abrams & Chronicle Books,
1 West Smithfield, London EC1A 9JU and Média Participations,
57 rue Gaston Tessier, 75166 Paris, France.
abramsandchronicle.co.uk and media-participations.com
info@abramsandchronicle.co.uk

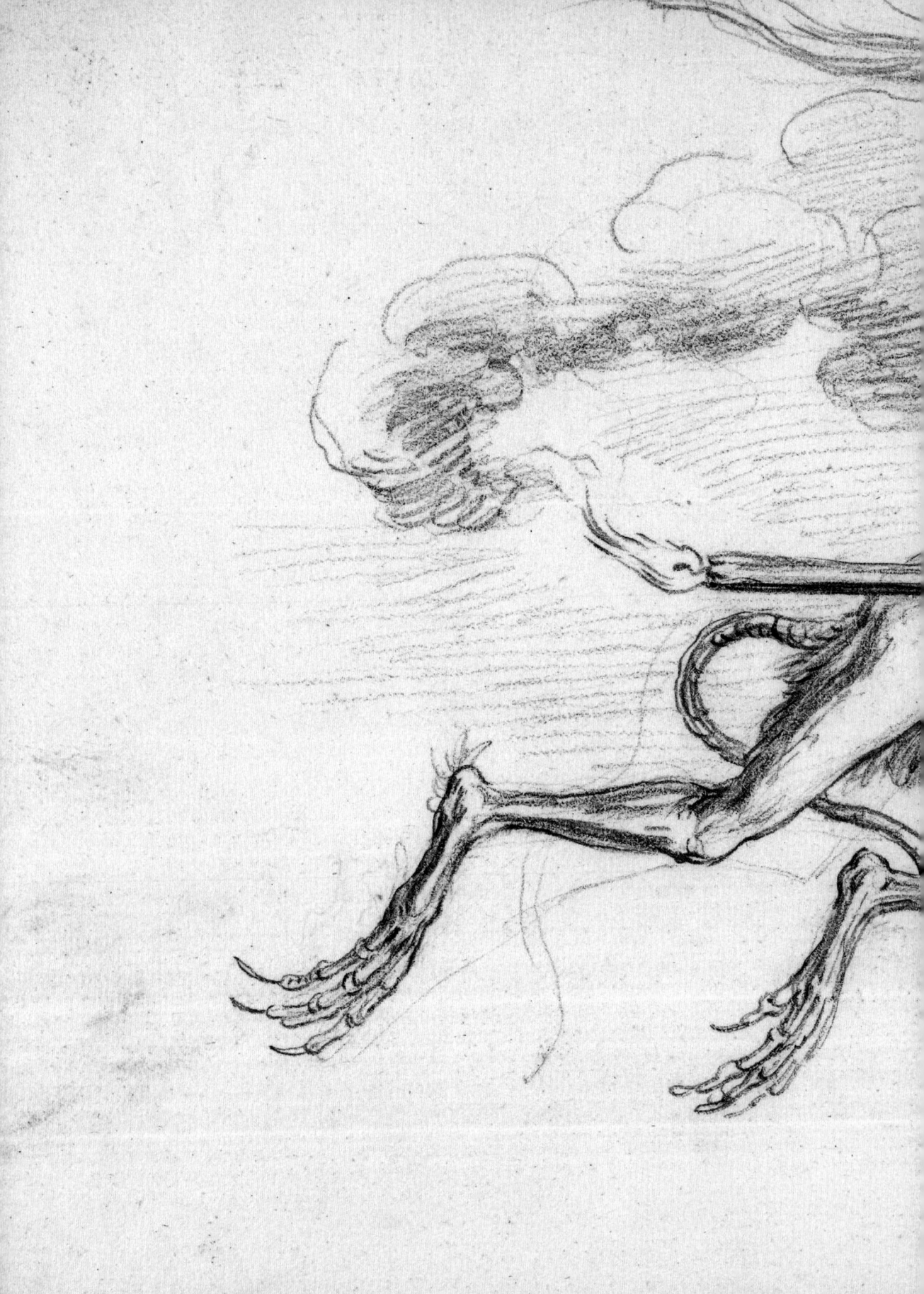